CW00470675

1982

From One Extreme to Another

Eddie McKenzie

Rock & Roll Is Dead Publishing

ISBN 9798730220171

Cover portrait by Matthew Simpson.

ONE MORE OF THEM
ONE LESS OF US

This, primarily, is a book about music.

However, it is also a book about the *events* of 1982, and how these two appeared to become increasingly estranged, of how after a few years of musicians being *one of us*, they pulled away to become *one of them*. Whilst the previous few years had witnessed social commentary in the charts, through the anger of punk, the despair of new wave, the isolation of post-punk, the anti-racism of Two-Tone, and the call to arms of roots reggae, chart acts in 1982 tended to avoid singing about the world. Instead, they retreated into fantasy, into what would become known as *aspiration*, returning to songs of love and desire instead of songs of hope and hate. It was a year of escapism, and by escaping the reality of Britain the artists were able to re-invent themselves as success stories.

Ask any handful of people what the ultimate year for popular music was and you will receive a separate handful of conflicting responses. Some will express to you that 1965, with The Beatles, The Rolling Stones, Bob Dylan, and The Kinks at their peak was the climax, others will claim that things never improved after the *summer of love* in 1967. Jon Savage penned a tome clarifying why 1966 was the highlight of popular culture, David Hepworth wrote an alternative one arguing it was 1971. Old punks in London will claim that nothing came close to the exhilaration of 1976, whilst other old punks outside the capital will say that 1977, with the *Silver Jubilee* and all that entailed, was even better. Thatcher's Southern children will ruminate about the *second summer of love* in the late 1980's, with all-night raves around the orbital, whilst the Northern branch of the identical generation will converse in reverence of Madchester, Spike Island, and 1990. Another generation will eulogise 1995 and the Britpop wars, whilst their younger brothers and sisters long for 1991, with The Strokes, The Libertines, and other skinny-legged guitar bands. Comedian James Acaster even wrote a book to explain why 2016 was the best year for music ever. Some people, astonishingly, may even say that today is about as good as it is ever has been or is going to get.

A vast amount of these individuals will love a year that just so happens to coincide with the period when they were between fifteen and twenty years old. There is a quotation from Hepworth at the commencement of his book, in which he states *"at this point you may raise a sceptical eyebrow and say that… the music of the year in which you turned twenty-one, or eighteen or sixteen or whenever you felt most alive, still speaks to you in a way that no other year does. That's natural. That's just growing up. We all have precious memories of one soft infested summer when we were young. For us too the soundtrack thereof will always be rock's annus mirabilis"*.

In that case, given my age, I should be arguing that the paramount year for music is somewhere flanked by the commercial morality of Live Aid in 1985 and the baggy zenith of The Stone Roses in 1990. And yet, the little loved year of 1982 is the one I elect to hold in high regard. Finding others who embrace 1982 with the same comparable affection as myself is a challenging. What exactly was there to love in that year? The Falklands War and a thousand dead? Thatcherism and the dream of privatisation? High unemployment whilst Duran Duran supped champagne on a luxury yacht? The Cold War and a fear of nuclear annihilation? Renèe, Renato, and the Goombay Dance Band? 1982 can never escape from the shadow of Thatcherism, the conflict in the Falkland Islands, the aftermath of the *royal wedding of the century*, the beginnings of large shoulders and red braces, the decline of *real* musicians and the rise of the machines. 1982 is hard to defend, difficult to love, being forever tied to a vile decade defined by the twin towers of greed and poverty, a decade where music seemed to become increasingly inauthentic, and visuals became more important than sound.

And yet, I make my attempt, triggered by my son asking "*Dad, what was the best year for music?*". Without thinking I answered "*1982*", to which his natural next question was "*Why?*" I sat down to write a paragraph for him to explain my rash decision... and it kept on growing. Of course, 1982 is probably not the best year ever (there's a strong argument for 1979): I could have chosen any year and made a strong argument, but I made my bed, so I'd better lie in it.

Many of the musical releases and historical events in 1982 turned out to be dead ends, however there are also some recurring characters, and in reading you will be required to keep a note of several *plots* and recrudescent themes at the same time. People also turn up in unexpected places. How exactly did French and Saunders keep the Teardrop Explodes from imploding in Australia? Why was Simon Cowell providing the bail money for a paedophile? Why were so many people rude to Michael Jackson? The answers all lie within…

Below is a link to a playlist on Spotify to accompany this book:

https://sptfy.com/1982FromOneExtremeToAnotherBook

JANUARY

The clock had just struck midnight at the end of New Year's Day when a telephone call was received by the London headquarters of *The Guardian* newspaper. At the other end of the line, a voice swiftly and efficiently claimed to be a member of the Welsh Army of Workers, a collection of Cambrian nationalists with vague links to the Official IRA, and gave the location of two bombs which had been planted in England. The Free Wales Army, as they were formally known, had not been in discernible action since the late-1960's, but what was left of the Friday midnight shift at the broadsheet decided to alert the police anyway.

Within thirty minutes, houses in the vicinity of the headquarters of Severn Trent Water Authority in Birmingham were evacuated, in advance of a bomb exploding on the roof of an outhouse. An hour later a second bomb was discovered and defused outside the main complex of the International Development Corporation in Stratford.

The explosive devices were in response to STWA arrogating millions of gallons of water from the Welsh hills to meet the needs of the Midlands, by means of compulsory purchase orders with no payment or compensation made to locals affected, as well as the IDC's plan to develop part of the Snowdonia National Park.

Barely thirty-six hours into the year, and 1982 had started explosively.

3rd – 9th January 1982
#1 single: The Human League: Don't You Want Me
#1 album: The Human League: Dare

The first new music chart of the year, on Sunday 3rd January, arrived like the unwelcome hangover of 1981, with the piquant tang of an age where the country was divided between an office party of conga lines and the hokey-cokey, galvanized by an efflorescent patriotism in the aftermath of Charles & Diana's wedding the preceding July, or else the disconsolation of rising unemployment, racism and burning street riots during the same searing summer month. If you read the tabloids or believed the official government line, then the country was renewed, with the dark days, strikes, hardships, and power-cuts of the 1970's eradicated.

The residue of 1981's party was conspicuous in light entertainment, in the songs your granny and little sister could sing simultaneously, with Abba (*One Of Us*), Cliff Richard (*Daddy's Home*), The Tweets (*The Birdie Song*), Brown Sauce[1] (*I Wanna Be A Winner*), Ken Dodd (*Hold My Hand*) & Barry Manilow (*The Old Songs*) still loitering around the top forty, as well as on Saturday night television, where Larry Grayson's[2] pantomime homosexual camp posturing and *polari* as host of 1970's favourite *The Generation Game* came to an denouement with a compilation episode. Grayson had resolved to end his tenure as anchor of the show whilst still at the top, attracting up to twenty-five million viewers each week. He anticipated being offered a new Saturday evening show, but when no proposition was forthcoming from the BBC, Grayson went into an involuntary semi-retirement. Instead, the BBC offered the host slot for *The Generation Game* to Liverpudlian comedian Jimmy Tarbuck, and when he chose to pass, cancelled it indefinitely.

The changing of the guard at the BBC continued the following evening when Peter Davidson took over as the fifth Doctor in the popular sci-fi series *Dr Who*.[3] Davidson's modus operandi was modelled on an Edwardian cricketer, clearly influenced by the *mien* of the movie *Chariots of Fire* and the televisual adaptation of *Brideshead Revisited*, both substantial successes the previous year. Davidson proved to be popular in the role, despite following on from the inimitable Tom Baker, starring in sixty-nine episodes between the start of 1982 and spring 1984, when he handed the role over to Colin Baker, however the real glory days of the show appeared to be over.

℧ ℧ ℧

The party atmosphere was only a fraction of 1981's chart story, as former left-field artists increasingly stole into the top forty with songs which knowingly sounded like the

---

[1] Brown Sauce was an act consisting of Keith Chegwin, Maggie Philbin, and Noel Edmonds, all presenters of the children's Saturday morning television show Multi-Coloured Swap Shop. The song was provided by Scottish songwriter B.A. Robertson.

[2] Grayson had spent thirty years working as a drag artist, building up a camp comedy act with a series of entendre-filled imaginary characters such as Slack Alice and Pop-it-in Pete. His agent was Michael Grade, who persuaded his uncle Lew to commission a television series starring Grayson in the early 1970's. Grayson started his tenure as host of the Generation Game in 1978, taking over from the seemingly irreplaceable Bruce Forsyth.

[3] My doctor was Tom Baker, though much to the disgust of many of my friends I later developed a fondness for David Tennent.

most commercial pop but were frequently the consequence of innate intellectual deliberations and decisions. It was one of these acts who started 1982 at the top of both the album and single charts, with their third long player *Dare*, and a fourth single from it, a duet entitled *Don't You Want Me*.

In any traditional pop career, the Human League would not even have still existed in 1982, with founder members Martyn Ware and Ian Craig Marsh having abandoned ship

just over a year previously following an increasingly fractious relationship with singer Phil Oakey. After initially beseeching Marsh to stay with the band in the toilets at a Siouxsie & the Banshees concert, the relationship got "*as acrimonious as you can get without physical violence*".[4] As part of the severance Oakey retained the name of the band, but also the financial obligations and commitments, whilst Ware and March were granted 1% royalties on the next album. It was an arrangement which satisfied neither party, as the remaining members, non-musician Oakey and Philip Adrian Wright, whose role it was to contribute slides and visuals for the band, were unlikely to be able to produce anything worth taking 1% from, whilst the *commitments* included a British and European tour due to commence in two weeks. In an act that teeters on the line between perspicacity and irrationality, Oakey went straight out in his native Sheffield on a Wednesday night and enlisted two schoolgirls, Susan Ann Sulley and Joanne Catherall, after observing them dance in the Crazy Daisy Nightclub. The two had no experience, but such was Oakey's belief in their allure he made them permanent members of the band at the conclusion of the tour, and the Human League set about releasing a sequence of classic singles which took them to the top of the charts within a year.

First up was *Boys & Girls*, a track left over from the Human League Mk 1, which was recorded by John Leckie and rush-released in February 1981 by Virgin Records to hopefully make back some of the money invested. The track did not feature the freshly recruited girls, however they did appear on the cover of the single, and it reached number forty-eight, providing them with their biggest (near) hit to date as well as going a long way towards Virgin agreeing to finance the next single. Within a month, they were back in the studio recording *The Sound of The Crowd*, written by Oakey and new recruit Ian Burden, a former member of Sheffield rivals Graph, which signalled the inception of a rewarding working relationship with producer Martin Rushent. The producer took an instant aversion to the track, insisting they scrap it and start again, this time with him in charge. One month further on and the song was released in a cover highlighting the band's new colour-concept marketing trick, where *Red* stood for dance music and *Blue* was pop music, "*for Abba fans*", and commenced a languid passage up to number twelve in the charts. The idea of an electronic Abba was at the front of Oakey's mind throughout this time, with Rushent later claiming "*the only master plan that existed was how the band should look.*" The Human League were now on a roll and in July 1981 they reached the top three with the double A-side of *Love Action* and *Hard Times*, written by Oakey and another new member, former Rezillos guitarist Jo Callis[5], and then in quick succession by *Open Your Heart*, chart topping album *Dare*

---

[4] At one point Oakey was spotted chasing Ware down a street in hometown Sheffield, hurling obscenities at him, as well as glass milk bottles from the doorsteps.

[5] Callis had written most of the Rezillos material, including their fantastic hit "*Top of the Pops*". He then formed a band called Shake, who my older brother saw live at Grangemouth Town Hall in early 1980 after winning tickets in the local paper.

(which critic Paul Morley described at the time as *"the first Human League greatest hits collection"*) and single *Don't You Want Me*.

Two factors can be identified when attempting to ascertain reasons for this upturn in fortunes for the band: producer Martin Rushent and the introduction of the two female singers.

Rushent had started his career as an engineer on Shirley Bassey[6] records in the 1960's, before coercing UA to sign the Stranglers and producing their first two albums. Becoming an in-demand punk producer, he worked with the Buzzcocks, Generation X, & 999, before growing weary of recording guitar bands. Setting up his own studio, Rushent became engrossed in the potential and impact of new technologies on recording, purchasing himself a Linn LM-1 drum machine, a Roland MC-8 Microcomposer, and Jupiter 8 and Fairlight synthesisers. These were all only a couple of years old, and at the time unproven instruments in the realm of pop music but would go on to develop into the prevailing creative tools characterizing the sound of the decade. The worldwide success of Rushent and the Human League went a long way to ensuring the types of sounds created by the machines became endorsed by the industry and public. But were they even instruments? Certainly, there was animosity to drum machines, sequencers, and synthesizers amongst the *muso-rock* fraternity, the regions where guitars ruled, and it was this enmity that led to allegations that this was not *real music*, that it somehow seemed deficient of soul, that the people creating the music were not *real musicians*, were bankrupt of musical ability, and the music was therefore lacking in any *real merit*. That many of the new British acts who embraced synthesizers, such as Soft Cell and Japan, also cavorted with *traditional* sexual provinces infuriated the older, more *traditional* musicians. The panoptic opinion in the music industry was that acts had to pay their dues, to earn the right to success through thousands of hours of practice, and after the *offence* of the uncultivated punk musicians, synthesizers were a further slap in the face. Queen had even made a proud point of claiming *"No synthesizers were used in the production of this record"* on their first handful of albums[7]. However, as John Lennon said in a Rolling Stone interview in 1970: *"I'm an artist, give me a tuba, I'll bring you something"*; it did not matter how you created music if it was good. What the Human League created in 1981 was indeed great music: music, sounding equally fantastic loud in clubs or blasting from a hand-held transistor radio, music that could be danced to, music that spoke to universal human emotions such as love, heartbreak, happiness, and *the things that dreams are made of*. So what if it was not based upon a blues scale? Maybe it was time to move on from that cliché?

It was this advancing of music that Rushent was most responsive to when he spent a small fortune on new equipment. His first problem after purchase was to determine where the parameters of the equipment were, and so commenced work on a series of recordings with Pete Shelley, frontman of The Buzzcocks. These were meant to be demo recordings for a solo album, and no doubt would eventually have been re-recorded with guitars and real drums, however Rushent and Shelley loved them so much that they were released as they were under the name *Homosapien*[8]. Whilst soliciting the recordings round record companies, they came to the attention of Simon

---

[6] Rushent claimed he learned everything he knew about creating uncluttered space within music from these Bassey recordings.

[7] This changed once Freddie Mercury brought influences in from the gay clubs he regularly visited.

[8] I advise you to track this album down... it is quite simply superb and was denied the exposure it deserved when the BBC banned it for "explicit homosexual *references*". Such were the times we lived in.

Draper[9] at Virgin, who was looking for someone to help the Human League bring their new songs to a more burnished and commercial state.

The recording took time, principally because the band and producer had to learn how to painstakingly programme the sequencers, but also because the inexperience of Sulley and Catherall meant their vocals took two full days to record for each track, coupled with them having to return to school every few days to complete their A-Levels. Rushent explained "*The girls… were very young, very inexperienced, and while both of them would mature into really good singers, back then they could barely sing their way out of a paper bag. They did add a certain unique charm to the whole album. Had we used professional singers it wouldn't have been the same.*" The girls, however, were a considerable selling-point for the band, adding a soupçon of provincial piquancy (to the extent they were offered a separate deal by Virgin Records in 1982); to the average adolescent girl, Sulley and Catherall's back-story, vocal limitations, and look made them seem less like quintessentially aloof pop stars, and more like a friend or older sister. Complementing and contrasting their approachability was Phil Oakey, with an asymmetrical haircut inspired by Veronica Lake, make-up inspired by the New Romantic movement, and unisex clothes inspired by an aspiration to alarm. This look had assisted the band the previous year when Oakey had to visit the girls' parents and persuade them to be permitted to go on tour with the act: Sulley's father was not altogether convinced Oakey was even a man and reckoned his daughter would be safe with someone who manifestly could not be attracted to women.

For the typical muso observer of *Top of the Pops* in 1981, Oakey was a conundrum. To the older generation he manifested the impression of being observably homosexual, yet there also appeared to be a carnal chemistry between him and the two girls. There was the redolence of sexual reconstruction in the air in 1982, and the previous generation were hesitant to accommodate it. Oakey was one of a whole chart-full of idiosyncratic men and women, people who fashioned their own anomalous distinct personas without of the assistance of stylists and marketing. These men and women had taken their prompt from the punk movement's insistence on DIY ingenuity, inventiveness, and individualism, but had moved the ethos on, appending other influences along the way. Now they were embracing the pop charts and bringing their singular vision to the music.

As *Don't You Want Me* was occupying the top of the charts, EMI decided to cash-in on some old Human League material by releasing a stereo version of their first single *Being Boiled*[10]. Entering the first chart of the year at number fifty-three, this was not your orthodox chart fodder. *Being Boiled* was the first song written by the act once Oakey had joined, being captured on a domestic tape recorder in an abandoned factory for a grand total of £2.50 before being released as a single in 1978. For many, such as founder member of Depeche Mode Vince Clarke, this song, and the rudimentary quality of it, was the synthesiser *year zero* moment, much more than punk had been: it declared anybody could generate glorious music. Lyrically, the track was a critique of silk production, with "*Little people like your offspring boiled alive for some god's stocking*" being about as detached from the office party of 1981 as you could conceivably get, however Oakey later admitted "*I thought I was interested in Buddhism but then I got the book and realised it was Hinduism*". However, to EMI the subject of

---

[9] Draper was the first cousin of Richard Branson and helped set up Virgin Records. Draper oversaw the music side, Branson the business side.

[10] I remember sitting out the back garden one clear freezing Sunday evening in January 1982 with my neighbour, listening to the charts on my transistor radio and looking at the skyful of stars. Wondering at the universe before us I ventured some thoughts on the insignificance of existence. "*Shut up*" he told me, "*'Being Boiled' is on*".

the lyrics was of no consequence: The Human League were the hottest musical property in the country, and they retained the rights to some tracks. There was money to be made, just as Decca had realised the previous year when Adam & The Ants had hit the top of the charts, with their own re-release of *Young Parisians*. *Being Boiled* began galloping up the charts, eventually reaching number six by the end of January. Virgin, The Human League's current label, suddenly realised they had their own version of *Being Boiled* wrapped up inside a previous E.P. entitled *Holiday '80*, and promptly re-released this, reaching number forty-six simultaneously.

After seven hit singles and a chart-topping album within an eleven-month period, the public anticipated The Human League's continued presence in the top forty in 1982, however there was to be no more new material for practically twelve months. In recent years, a band taking a year off is accepted practice, however in 1982 bands were expected to release an album a year, along with subsequent singles. It is not that the band stopped working during this time, but instead began to spend more time in the United States, where *Don't You Want Me* was beginning a long ascent up the Billboard Hot 100. At one point the band appeared on the television show *Solid Gold*, which caused a bit of a problem. *"We wouldn't allow them to have their dancers on with us,"* explained Sulley, *"That wasn't our thing at all; it was way too… showbiz. I can remember leaving the set with the guy from the record company shouting at us 'You'll never, ever work in this country again!'"* Two weeks later *Don't You Want Me* went to number one.

ʊ ʊ ʊ

The revolution in how music was being generated which The Human League had played such a significant part continued throughout the year, and on into the decade. Computerisation in music became the norm in the industry; within ten years there was scarcely a track in the charts not created on machines, and within twenty everything was recorded digitally. The digital revolution was taking over the planet, and in the first week of the year the Commodore 64 was released, going on to become the largest selling home computer of all time, retailing at an implausible (for the time) cost of $595, and boasting an impressive 64kb of RAM.[11] The C64 was initially a business computer with augmented 8-bit graphics to allow spreadsheets and pie charts to be displayed, however once neophyte programmers realised it was perfect for coding, it became the gamers platform of choice. Games were produced in cassette format, which took seemingly endless minutes to load, however it was not long until programmers developed a way to play music whilst this was happening. The whole process was abetted by the Sound Interface Device, or SID chip, which was responsible for all the music and sounds. The SID chip[12] was acutely limited, being able to play only three notes at a time, obliging programmers to be ingenious when sound-tracking games. The chip also had a glitch which allowed a virtual fourth channel to be used as a simple sampler, and this was taken advantage of to include vocals into games.

Three months after the Commodore, a financially viable British competitor, the Sinclair ZX Spectrum was released, retailing at £125 and with 16K of memory. Following on

---

[11] To give you an idea, the computer I am using right now which is a bottom of the range HP, has 50,000 times the power.

[12] The inventor of this chip was musician Bob Yannes, who then used the technology to form the company Ensoniq, specializing in producing synthesizers and samplers, many of which were later used by the likes of Daft Punk and Beck.

from the ZX80[13] and ZX81, Clive Sinclair's computer went on to sell over five million copies worldwide and was something of a game-changer. For a multitude of future professional coders in the United Kingdom, the colour ZX Spectrum was their introduction to computers, and had been designed in Cambridge and manufactured in Dundee... even if the parts were sourced from elsewhere in the world. The Spectrum was staggeringly unreliable, with a return rate of 30% and a rumour that returned computers were commonly repackaged and sent out to another customer. Despite this, within a year 66% of computers in British homes were built by Sinclair.

British Prime Minister Margaret Thatcher was initially circumspect in espousing the advanced technology, and it was up to those in the cabinet encircling her to encourage the I.T. agenda, accentuating the fear of being left behind Japan and the United States. Secretary of State for Education and Science Sir Keith Joseph's request to inject money into the sector was met with a forceful "*NO*" from Thatcher, regarding the idea as "*socialism...a waste of money*". A mixture of incessant badgering by the cabinet, paired with the private sector failing to rise to the challenge, soon changed her mind and 1982 was declared *Information Technology Year*, and a few days later Thatcher argued on BBC4's *The World This Week* that "*technology gives the opportunities for new products.*" The government initiated a deal to put a computer into every school which was rolled out across the nation during the year. The preferred computer was the BBC Model B, which was beyond the budget of most households, but did have the advantage of a weekly training program broadcast by the corporation. The BBC had initially asked Clive Sinclair to construct the machines, however the entrepreneur had vetoed adjustments to his machine which would have made his computer more commodious for the required purpose, and lost the contract to Acorn Computers, who struggled to meet the demand in the first year of production. There were still substantial shortfalls in the computer when the first episode of *The Computer Programme* aired on the BBC in January 1982, presented by Chris Serle, a former member of consumer programme *That's Life!* The viewing figures approached seven million and reached far beyond young males, the previous stereotype of computer users.

Computers in the early 1980's were principally sold to households as a solution to their problems, promising to balance your accounts and organise your diary; in reality, the ones affordable to the public only had the power for children and teenagers to play basic games. Not that this was why parents purchased them: most were blackmailed by advertising into being anxious their children would be left behind in the technological capital necessary to succeed in the future.

As primitive as these machines were, they were instrumental in allowing the public to own a computer and were considerable contributors towards the acceptance of "advanced" technology in the home. Over time, bands like The Human League did not seem so futuristic anymore but were situated in the *here* and *now* instead. What the Human League did, however, was help exemplify the sound of the 1980's: synthesizers and electronic music were the future.

ʊ ʊ ʊ

There are many brilliant myths of revelry and carnage involving Ozzy Osbourne, and a considerable proportion of them occurred in 1982. The *Diary of a Madman* tour had started at the end of October 1981, just one month after the one-hundred-and-fifty date year-long *Blizzard of Ozz* tour had finished. Ozzy simply did not know how to do anything else but play live, however a life of travelling, lack of sleep, and prodigious

---

[13] I was gifted a ZX80 by a friend of the family, with its unbelievable 1KB of memory. My friends had the ZX Spectrum, and I was insanely jealous. I really, really wanted to play *The Hobbit*.

amounts of drink and drugs eventually took their toll on his health, and after a date in Ravensburg, West Germany, the rest of the European tour had been cancelled. His manager Sharon Arden flew Ozzy to England and booked him into a mental health clinic, where it became apparent he was suffering from the effects of his first marriage breaking down as well as considerable substance abuse. By the end of December, Ozzy was deemed ready to go back on the road again for the first leg of his American tour.

After a show in San Diego on Monday 4th January, the band booked into the Grant Hotel in the downtown area of the city, where a party was organized in Ozzy's suite. One of the groupies in attendance pestered him to sing a song she had written, which he agreed to do if she provided a lap dance. Just as she got started, Arden erupted into the room screaming *"What the fuck is going on? Get that whore out of my sight!"* As well as acting as his manager, Sharon had had been conducting a not-so-secret affair with Ozzy for over a year, and the pressure was beginning to have a negative effect.

"For fuck's sake, Sharon, I was just having some fun!" Ozzy slurred, causing Sharon to storm from the room. This was all the trigger Ozzy needed, letting out a primal scream and hauling the mattress from his bed towards the window. With the help of guitarist Randy Rhoads he threw it from the balcony into the swimming pool, followed by a chair, and then the entire contents of the room. Bass player Rudy Sarzo retired to his room, got changed out of his stage clothes, and packed his suitcase in anticipation of them being evicted from the hotel.

ʊ ʊ ʊ

It is worth noting there was not a single new entry into the first top forty of 1982, as the industry closed between Christmas and New Year. There were, however, a couple of noteworthy new songs outside the top forty, the first of which was *Drowning in Berlin* by The Mobiles[14].

For a band originating from Eastbourne, the song was plethoric with pretence, from the ambiguously disquieting adolescent lyrics of the scanty verses, and the *Cabaret* thud of the chorus, right through the crapulent fairground of the middle eight with *"Are they*

alone in Berlin" articulated unnecessarily in German. The band were still playing local pubs in Bexhill-on-Sea when the call came for *Top of the Pops* and must have believed themselves to be a new ice-cool Siouxsie & the Banshees but were instead much closer to the pre-teen *weltschmerz* of Toyah Wilcox.

One place they were right on the mark was in the citing of Berlin. This was a time when Britain's infatuation with the United States was on the ebb, and Europe, particularly the Western Europe which faced the Cold War front of the Warsaw Pact, was in fashion. It was still close enough to the Second World War for Europe to exhibit the cicatrix of conflict, however they were also living in a reconstructed continent, one lionised by Kraftwerk with their *Trans-Europe Express*, by Ultravox a year previously with their own slab of high artifice *Vienna*, and even by Simple Minds in *I Travel*. The idea of traversing the continent on

---

[14] My brother bought this seven-inch single, and a few years later gave me his entire collection. I loved it at the time. I like to think my fascination with Cold War Berlin started here.

an overnight train to a still-divided Berlin seemed incredibly utopian to young people[15], and bands at the start of the 1980's tapped into this, inspired by David Bowie's lionising of the city.

Of course, *Drowning in Berlin* had no substantive significance, was simply an aloof sheath stretched thin over a constructed juvenile frame. It did, however, enter the charts at number forty-eight before beginning a slow rise over the next few weeks to peak at number nine. The Mobiles struggled to repeat the success, with follow-up single "Amour Amour" stalling at number forty-five in March, and they were soon back to the day jobs.

ʊ ʊ ʊ

Rudy Sarzo was astonished to find himself wake up on Tuesday 5th January in the same San Diego hotel after Ozzy Osbourne had trashed his own room. In mid-afternoon the bass player located Ozzy and Sharon sitting downstairs in the lounge enjoying a cocktail as if nothing had occurred. Sharon, beckoning him over and insisting he join them before going for a late lunch, signalled to the waitress for another round.

"*Sorry, ma'am, but I've been asked by the manager not to serve anymore alcohol to Mr Osbourne*" the waitress apologised.

"*Are you calling my husband a drunk?*" demanded Sharon as she lifted her husband's drooling head from the table where he had passed out, "*That's it! Nobody calls my husband a drunk and gets away with it! We're checking out of this shit-hole immediately.*"

The band, crew and luggage were hastily assembled and pressured onto the tour bus, as Sharon visited the toilet and urinated into a pint glass. She approached the waitress and said in her sweetest voice "*Did I forget to give you a tip?*" before throwing the yellow liquid at her and yelling "*Here's your tip, you cunt!*"

Sharon then sprinted onto the bus and screamed "*Go! Go! Go!*"

ʊ ʊ ʊ

Record companies have consistently lacked awareness of what songs are destined be successful. Certainly, in 1982 singles and albums were released without much in the way of a fanfare, and once in the shops press agents would try their best to whip up enthusiasm amongst radio stations and the public. The result was singles very rarely entering the chart at a high position, often taking a convoluted route to success. One such example finally broke into the charts on the at the humble position of number sixty-seven after having been on sale at least a couple of weeks and was performed by a band who were on the brink of being forgotten.

---

[15] ...and what do you know? In 1989 at the age of nineteen I found myself drawn to West Berlin. Of course, I lived the dream and caught a continental over-night train to get there. As we crossed the transport corridors through East Germany the conductor put his head into the sleeper cabin we were sharing with some Irish guys and made an announcement in German. My mate who had studied the language in school insisted he had said "*Two hours to Berlin*". Imagine our surprise when two minutes later we rolled into Zoobahnhof. As we scrambled out of our beds and crammed everything back into our rucksacks the train pulled out, and we watched in despair as the track crossed the Berlin Wall. The conductor passed again, and with a shrug announced in English "*Next stop, Moscow.*"

The Stranglers enjoyed a run of punk-inspired hits between 1977 and 1979 but had not troubled the top thirty for over three years when they released *Golden Brown*[16]. Taken from *La Folie,* an album released in November 1981 containing one previous flop single, *Golden Brown* appeared a radical deviation for a band which had been as disreputable as The Sex Pistols in the high days of punk. Written in 3/4 time, with an extra bar of 4/4 every fourth time round, and utilizing a harpsichord, the track provided another aural parlance for pop music. The music had been written by keyboard player Dave Greenfield who had been tinkering with it for quite a while, trying to reconcile it with the end of numerous other songs, however the lyrics were by vocalist Hugh Cornwall, and their subject matter have been a matter of contention ever since. People

heard what they wanted to hear: on one level it was a simple song about a girl, but on another more axiomatic level it was a song about the heroin trade, venerating the "*golden brown texture*" which "*lays me down with my mind she runs*", as the trade; "*through the ages she's heading West*". Cornwell himself admits it is the latter, claiming heroin "*really is the most dangerous and wonderful drug*". The song mimicked the warm miasma of a narcotic hit, with Cornwall's intonation detached, later entangled in his own revelry whilst echoing the guitar solo in deep reverb. A video featuring the band and accentuated a North

African location helped to sell the *hookah mood*, as the song joined Lou Reed's *Perfect Day* and the La's *There She Goes* in a list of impeccable pop songs celebrating the rush of narcotic stupor.

The record company detested the song, did not see the potential in it, and complained it was un-danceable, however the band insisted. Entering the chart at such a low position, it looked as if the record company were correct, and no doubt the band would have been finished if Jimmy Young at BBC Radio 2 had not unexpectedly made the song his "Record of the Week", propelling it up to number twenty-five. From there it rose to number two, only being kept off the top by a new entry of The Jam's *Town Called Malice*. As the single perched at number two, bass player Jean-Jacques Burnel divulged to the press the candid subject matter, and overnight the radio play evaporated. The success of the single granted a career injection to The Stranglers which lasted decades afterwards, and at one point during the year, the company Sunbeam gave away a free copy of the single with every one of their GRII Double Sandwich Maker. America viewed the song differently, and with it not being comfortably classifiable was never released as a single across the Atlantic.

What was striking about *Golden Brown*, other than the fact it is simply meritorious and was what Hugh Cornwell said was "*so different from everything else that it sound*[ed] *dangerous*", is that it was part of a progression of prodigious hit singles over 1981 and 1982 which were utterly *nonpareil*: nothing sounded like them previously, and nothing has sounded like them subsequently. From *Ghost Town* by The Specials six months before, through *Golden Brown*, to *Come On Eileen* by Dexy's Midnight Runners six months later, there ran a corrugation of creativity unfettered by record company interference, inventiveness that was fresh from the minds of self-made individuals and bands who constructed the music they visualised, rather than replicating the music they heard on the radio. There was no-one from marketing telling them they needed to sound fashionable, or if there was, they were being comprehensively ignored. This may prove to have been the last great age of musical mavericks, non-conformists, and

---

[16] Paul Leishman lived along the street from me. He had a hamster called *Golden Brown* and played this single to it every night.

eccentrics, of people who were not petrified of being unconventional, of standing out, even of ridicule. The thing these people had in common was they had come through the punk experience and had tapped into the *"be creative"* aspect of the movement rather than the *"loud and angry"* sound cliché. The following year, record companies began to clamp down on this individuality, to gain some authority over the musicians, and the next strain of pop stars coming through were not veterans of the punk wars, but instead enthusiastic Thatcherites.

ʊ ʊ ʊ

Despite the promise of technology, machines still let humans down, and on Saturday 9th January, Mark Thatcher, son of the British Prime Minister, along with co-driver Anne-Charlotte Verney and mechanic Jackie Garnier, were forced to stop in the Sahara Desert to repair a defective steering arm in their Peugeot 504.

At the age of twenty-nine Thatcher already had a succession of failed business ventures behind him and returning from one of these in Hong Kong resolved to indulge his enthusiasm for motor sports by entering the 10,000-kilometre Paris-Dakar rally without any experience of this type of driving, admitting later that he *"did absolutely no preparation"*.

Thatcher and his crew had been traversing the Sahara as part of a convoy during the race, and when they were forced to stop the other cars took note of their position before continuing onwards towards the end of the day. The break for maintenance meant that Thatcher became isolated from the rest of the pack, and once underway again the car became lost. As darkness descended, they were also dealing with the problem of a shattered rear axle casing, so the threesome decided to stop until morning. There were close to salt mine and could see trucks about a mile away in the distance, but the first rule of safety in the rally was that you did not abandon your vehicle in the desert.

The trio set up camp and awaited help.

ʊ ʊ ʊ

One song on the first chart of 1982 had been kicking around for years, and its time had finally come. *The Model* by Kraftwerk had already spent eleven weeks in the top seventy-five without pestering the all-important top forty, however its pedigree extended back much further than that. Originally included on the album *The Man-Machine* in 1978, the song had only ever been released as a single in the band's native West Germany when it was included as a B-side to their most recent British single, *Computer Love*.

Kraftwerk had been formed in 1969 in Dusseldorf by students Florian Schneider and Ralf Hutter, initially functioning with a fluctuating line-up whilst releasing three undistinguished Krautrock[17] albums using traditional instruments such as guitars and drums. By the fourth album, 1973's *Ralf und Florian*, the band were cognizant with drum machines and the use of a vocoder, and within a year the conventional instruments had been abandoned in favour of freshly acquired synthesisers. The music migrated from free-form jams towards a more disciplined electronic pop music. They broke through with the album and single *Autobahn*[18], which reached the top ten in both the United Kingdom and United States. Not long after this, the band more-or-less gave

---

[17] Do not ever call a German band Krautrock... they hate it!

[18] The original album version was twenty-three minutes long! The single was shortened to just over three minutes.

up touring, opting to work in reclusion at their own Kling Klang Studios, producing what are now revered as classic electronic albums such as 1977's *Trans-Europe Express* and the following years' *The Man-Machine*. As well as being electronic classics, these albums eventually had a substantial and significant impact on early hip-hop in New York, where their prolonged instrumentals were used as back-beats for the new art form of rapping. Kraftwerk, meanwhile, locked themselves away and spent three years concentrating on two tasks: recording new album, *Computer World*, released in 1981, and re-configuring their studio so that it could be made portable, allowing them to take their electronics on tour in the same year.

Back in 1977, Kraftwerk were principally considered to be not much more than a cursory curiosity whose world of electronic music and robots were a transient vagary. At that time, very few people could see what the future held for music; most assumed that rock and roll would endure with guitars and blues scales, and there would be no

room for this ostensibly detached music sung in a German accent. What they could not grasp is that there was as much acumen and emotion in Kraftwerk's nine-minute *Neon Lights* as there was in any three minutes of a Stax or Motown track, it was just that the understanding of what constituted a human soul was shifting. In an ever-shrinking world, in the globalisation of industry and humanity, people were discovering that the easier it was to communicate and travel, the more detached they were becoming. We could talk to anyone on Earth but found what we had to say to them, or what they had to say to us,

was not especially worth saying. Parts of the planet which had at one time appeared enigmatic and mysterious to us, were becoming routine through the mass media and over-exposure on the screen. Less and less astounded us, mesmerised us, and the real journey now seemed to be one towards internal introspection, and our evolving inner fascination would increasingly be sound-tracked by electronic music.

What was remarkable about Kraftwerk was that they seemed to come from nowhere, with no perceptible precedents. David Laurie said of their sound "*There is zero rock and roll. There is precisely no Beatles DNA here. There's no DNA at all, in fact; only machine code*". It is an astonishing claim to make, but Kraftwerk have conceivably become more influential than any other musical artist since the Second World War. There is nothing in the charts nowadays owing a sonic debt to The Beatles, yet almost everything has a technological lineage to the work made by an act isolated in Dusseldorf in the mid to late 1970's.

By 1981 the future had caught up with Kraftwerk and they sounded very much *of the time*. Numerous acts, from the Human League to Fad Gadget, had taken up the synthesizer as their agent of delivery, and paved the way for Kraftwerk to finally achieve the long overdue acknowledgement as pioneers. *Computer Love* hung around the lower ends of the top seventy-five for months before radio stations started to play the other side, a mid-paced pop song called *The Model*. The song concerned a man looking back at an old flame who has since gone on to become a successful fashion model, yearning to encounter her once more. Kraftwerk, however, were contra to veneration of the individual, sending robotic versions of themselves out on tour, and even asserting "*in Germany in the thirties we had a system of superstardom with Mr Adolf from Austria and so there is no interest for* [us] *in the cult of personality*".

The Model was a progressive sounding song that suspired for yesterday, almost as if the lyrics were struggling against the accelerating march of history demonstrated in the music accompanying them. The song was also a preeminent *pop* track full of hooks, and was recognised by many as such, as it began to climb the chart, finally reaching the top spot for a week.

Just as Kraftwerk attained their commercial peak, they seemed to lose the inclination to move forward. Five years were spent labouring on the follow-up album by which time music, particularly in the form of electro and hip-hip, had caught up. The Germans struggled with the fact that the next album *Electric Café* was not technologically cutting-edge enough for a band of their reputation as innovators, and this may be the reason they never released another long player of new music, instead preferring to tour the world absorbing the post-rave sycophancy of the nostalgia market.

With the success of *The* Model, the appreciation of Kraftwerk's back catalogue promptly multiplied, as both *The Man Machine* and *Trans-Europe Express* entered the album charts, and a re-issued *Showroom Dummies* peaked at number twenty-five in the singles chart. Kraftwerk would not be the only act in 1982 who had been working towards success for the preceding few years, only to disengage from pushing forward.

10th – 16th January 1982

#1 single: Bucks Fizz: The Land of Make Believe
#1 album: The Human League: Dare

People would have been wise to stay indoors and tune to their radios on Sunday 10th January as Britain was plunged into a mercilessly bitter night, with a record -27.2 °C recorded at Braemar in Aberdeenshire. This followed what had been an abnormally frosty few weeks with the coldest December on record, as air was drawn down from the Arctic by a series of mid-latitude cyclones, and some areas of England were completely cut off with several feet of snow. Over the next week the polar air kept on coming, expanding onto North America and culminating on what became known as *Cold Sunday*, the 17th January, where a record-breaking -52 °C was recorded in Minnesota.

If the public had tuned in, they would have expected to hear the new top forty singles chart announced during a two-hour countdown on BBC Radio 1. Veteran Tony Blackburn had been presenting the show since 1979 but was now considered at thirty-eight to be too old, not *1980's* enough, and this Sunday a new host took over. Curiously, this new host was even older; forty-two-year-old Tommy Vance, another dependable of broadcasting, and regular anchor of Radio 1's *Friday Rock Show*. His

authoritative articulation and far-reaching musical awareness would grace the chart rundown for the next couple of years until thirty-eight-year-old Simon Bates returned.

Anyone listening to the chart rundown would have heard Buck's Fizz, having spent the previous week at number two, replacing the Human League at the top with their new single *The Land of Make Believe*.

Bucks Fizz had been brought together by songwriter and producer Andy Hill in early 1981 to perform a song in the British heats for the Eurovision Song Contest, and comprised Mike Nolan, Bobby G, Cheryl Baker, and Jay Aston. Nolan had performed in a 1970's boy-band called Brooks[19] alongside future pop star Limahl, Bobby G was a

---

[19] Brooks were put together by future Shakin' Stevens manager, Freya Miller.

twice-divorced plumber, Baker had sung with previous Eurovision entrants Co-Co[20], and Aston[21] had been employed as a dancer. Together they performed a song written by Hill entitled *Making Your Mind Up* whilst providing a gimmick by removing the girls' skirts at a lyrically pertinent moment, and in May 1981 won the Eurovision Song Contest, subsequently reaching the top of the charts. This was followed with the diminishing returns of three further singles, the last of which failed to even breach the top seventy-five. Success seemed to be all over for the act when Hill recruited Peter Sinfield to help him compose *The Land of Make Believe*. Sinfield had been a former member of prog-rock giants King Crimson, and had produced the first Roxy Music album, so it seems idiosyncratic that he should turn up and write something as *mainstream* as a Buck's Fizz single. Sinfield has subsequently attempted to assert the lyrics of the song were an attack on Thatcherism and her policies, however closer scrutiny makes it difficult to countenance this claim, and one suspects it this was an effort to cover-up writing such palpable fluff.

The track however, and this is where we may part company in our opinions, can be claimed to be a superlative pop song… just not one that has any modicum of tenability. There is something about Bucks Fizz, unthreatening clean-cut singers being regarded as manikins for a backroom songwriting / production team, that has prevailed, from the Monkees to the Bay City Rollers. By the end of the 1980's this arrangement had become the norm in the British music industry, and into the next century became the respected and conventional method and route to success by generations of kids. Previously these acts were full of people in their twenties who had been knocking on the door of success for years beforehand, *paying their dues*, whereas in the future they would be propelled to instantaneous stardom after just a couple of auditions, usually at an age where they had not yet learned from experience.

Bucks Fizz were at their commercial apex in early 1982, receiving "Best Group" at the Daily Mirror Rock & Pop awards, being nominated in the same category at the Brits, however they never managed to obtain credibility, and even the Labour Party released a badge which proclaimed "*The Tories have a worse record than Buck's Fizz*".

ʊ ʊ ʊ

On Tuesday 12th January it became evident no-one had seen Mark Thatcher or his party for three days during the Sahara stretch of the Paris – Dakar rally, and so he was declared missing. His mother, Margaret Thatcher promptly got on the telephone to the British ambassador in Algeria and petitioned him to make this a priority. The Algerians committed four aircraft, a helicopter, and land forces, while the French had three aircraft flying reconnaissance and the RAF diverted a Hercules to Dakar to assist with the search, which the Prime Minister insisted on paying for personally.

Realising no-one was coming back for them, the missing party rationed their water to last for a fortnight and concentrated instead on keeping out of the sun.

Back in the United Kingdom, his mother told television reporters there was still no news, appearing fatigued and vulnerable, somewhat different from her reputation as *the iron lady*. Her husband, Denis Thatcher was gifted the use of the United Biscuits private jet and flew to North Africa to join the search.

ʊ ʊ ʊ

---

[20] Co-Co came eleventh in 1978 with *The Bad Old Days*.

[21] Aston took part in the Miss England competition in 1978, having already been crowned *Miss Putney*.

For the past two years medical centres in New York, San Francisco, Miami, and Los Angeles had begun noticing an expanding number of young males with PCP (*pneumocyctis carinii pneumonia*), with a disproportionately high number of them gay. Initially, contracting numerous communicable diseases concurrently was thought to be responsible, or else prolonged use of amyl nitrate which was known to be decidedly carcinogenic.

At the end of 1981 doctors ascertained that the first victim in Britain had died of the disease at Brompton Hospital, and at the dawning of 1982 no-one could comprehend what the disease was, how it was acquired, or if there was a cure. By May 1982, over one hundred men in the United States had been killed by what was now being labelled GRID (*Gay Related Immune Deficiency*), and police in San Francisco were wearing gloves and masks when dealing with the gay community.

The medical profession remained perplexed and was desperate to identify anything categorical about the disease. Dr David Auerbach and Dr William Darrow began interviewing the earliest reported cases of the disease and ascertained a disproportionate number of victims reported sexual contact with the one person: Gaetan Dugas[22].

Dugas was a French-Canadian flight attendant who by his own admission averaged 250 sexual partners every year and had done since 1972 when he became active. His vocation took him all over North America, and in most cities he would visit gay clubs and bathhouses, delighting in unprotected sexual activity with multiple partners. Even after being diagnosed with what was initially known as *gay cancer*, Dugas continued his promiscuous behaviour. The doctor administering his chemotherapy in New York encouraged Dugas to abstain, however he once encountered him coming out of a gay bathhouse and stopped. "*What are you doing there?*" he asked. "*In the dark nobody sees my spots*" Dugas replied, referring to the purple Kaposi's Sarcoma lesions on his body. When a total of forty people were diagnosed as having caught the disease from Dugas, he was requested to visit the San Francisco Health Department, where he was advised that the evidence was conclusive: he was infecting people every time he had sex. "*I got it! Let them get it!*" was Dugan's reply, and a rumour started in the Bay area about a blond man with a French accent who would put the lights up in bathhouses after orgies and point to purple lesions on his body saying "*I've got gay cancer! I'm going to die and so are you!*"

The paucity of explanation from medicine was alarming to the gay community. Andy Warhol's diary entries for 1982 are peppered throughout with mentions of "*the gay cancer*", with much being made of his anxiety of catching it by sharing eating utensils. In the absence of facts, New York playwright Larry Kramer set up the Gay Men's Health Crisis on Tuesday 12th January, a non-profit making organisation dedicated to providing help and support. One of the first volunteers, Rodger McFarlane, offered to run a hotline using his home telephone number. On the first day, he received one-hundred-and-twenty-five phone calls and realised exactly how far-reaching but undiagnosed the problem was.

ʊ ʊ ʊ

A pattern had been established over the previous couple of decades which saw the Greater London Council (GLC) being controlled by the opposite party to government, so when Margaret Thatcher and the Conservatives won power in May 1979, a group of young Labour members, led by thirty-four-year-old Ken Livingstone, initiated plans

---

[22] Dugas was labelled *Patient Zero* in the medical community for many years, a myth which has since been dispelled.

for the next council elections in 1981. Producing a magazine entitled *Labour London Briefing*, they raised issues of race and gender disparity, which many in the party felt were a digression from class struggle. Future editions tackled disability, male violence against women, gay rights, and alternatives to the traditional family, whilst a feature on transvestism was denounced in the tabloids, and even Labour leader Michael Foot stated he had not discerned there were so many *perverts* in the party[23].

True to form, in the May 1981 local elections, the GLC was dominated by an Andrew McIntosh and the Labour Party, only for the leader to be deposed by a Livingstone-led leftist coup the following day. The reform of the council agenda was introduced rapidly, with the doors to County Hall thrown open for citizens to hold community meetings, and extravagant entitlements such as chauffeur-driven cars for councillors were phased out. Livingstone adhered to what was ostensibly a Marxist approach to politics, proposing policies and initiatives, sometimes for municipal reasons and sometimes just to exasperate the Conservative councillors.

The right-wing press indulged in an orgy of outrage, christening Livingstone *Red Ken*, and wasting a fortune attempting to dig up dirt, with the Daily Telegraph going into apoplexy because he "*appointed a black man to chair the police committee*". Livingstone and the GLC addressed issues of discrimination at a time when "*not a single reporter or print worker was black, no reporter on any paper was openly gay and no woman held a position more senior than editorship of a woman's page*".

When the first indications were that Labour would win the GLC elections in May 1981, the Conservative-led council commenced selling off all the scheduled council housing to the private sector, thus cutting the supply of economical habitation. At the end of 1981, the government attempted to undo the work of the GLC by demanding cuts to local council budgets, aware that Labour-led regions would suffer most from eroding services. When the GLC introduced fare subsidies for public transport, half a million people switched to buses and the tube, and car usage dropped along with city centre pollution. The government combatted this by informing the transport companies involved that if they accepted the GLC subsidies to cut fares, then central government would cut their own subsidies by an equivalent amount, undoing the work of Livingstone. Then the Conservative-led Bromley Council took the GLC to court, arguing they had a legal obligation to make the London Underground break even financially. The courts ruled in favour of Bromley Council, as did the Law Lords on appeal, and on Tuesday 12th January Livingstone reluctantly agreed to obey the law.

Meanwhile, the press persisted in their campaign against what they dubbed the *Loony Left*, fabricating stories such as the banning of black coffee or blackboards on grounds of racism, many of which passed into folklore as *fact*. What really provoked them, however, was the setting up of a Women's Committee, chaired by Valerie Wise, which they characterized as being full of "*spikey-haired dungaree-wearing lesbians*". Instead, the groups set up by the Women's Committee were more engrossed in pursuing ideas which would later become enshrined in British laws, such as paid maternity leave, subsidised childcare facilities, and equal employment opportunities. *The Sun* and *The News of the World*, however, were more interested in her insistence of being called *chair* instead of *chairman*.

ʊ ʊ ʊ

That Liverpudlian band the Teardrop Explodes even reached 1982 is something of a miracle, given their erratic line-up and precarious mental health. Formed by accident

---

[23] One junior contributor to *Labour London Briefing* was a young Jeremy Corbyn, who spent most of his time exposing *traitors to the cause* within the Labour Party.

in 1979 when Julian Cope started prolonged jam-sessions with friends based around one chord, success happened quickly for the band. The Teardrop Explodes first gig, supported by Echo & the Bunnymen playing *their* first as well, occurred two months after forming. Within another couple of months, they had released their debut single and appeared on Granada Television. Further independent single releases throughout 1980 on Zoo Records, the label run by their managers Bill Drummond and Dave Balfe, were practically guaranteed to be *record of the week* in the music press, and the critical acclaim led to a deal with Mercury by the end of the year.

Then an unforeseen thing happened to The Teardrop Explodes in 1981: they became *bona fide* pop stars. Somehow, this drug-fuelled psychedelic band of eccentrics from the punk scene of Liverpool became genuine pin-ups, with teenage girls screaming at their concerts and singles riding high in the charts. Cope loved it, and at the same time abhorred what he had become, trying his hardest as the year progressed to undermine everything the band stood for. He went weeks without washing either his clothes, his body, or his hair, and still the girls screamed. He made a wilfully more sombre second album, *Wilder*, which failed to sell as well as their debut when released at the end of the year. The latest single from the album stalled outside the top forty, and it looked as if his plans of disruption were starting to work.

Cope was fast receding into an acid shell, insisting on playing a six-week residency under the name *Club Zoo* in an abandoned factory in Liverpool, during which he held court in a tent on the top floor. On another floor cult movies were projected onto the wall, whilst on a third smaller bands were invited to play. Whichever acts were in town would drop-in to join in the festivities. Fried after a year of unyielding acid, Cope was becoming paranoid, and drew an *X* onto his torso in permanent marker to ward off evil spirits, which he would go on to top up throughout the year.

In January 1982 they tried to repeat the whole experience in Dublin, taking over McGonagle's Bar, whilst staying at Bailey's Hotel. Every night, after the gig, they would withdraw to the hotel where a party would begin which would last until the morning. On the second night an eighteen-year-old American student from Trinity College turned up with bags full of acid, which she freely dispensed. She claimed her father was road manager for The Grateful Dead and was insistent the band adopt her. Cope would later claim she was *"the first person I'd met who was intolerably crazy"*, which coming from him was rich.

The teenager insisted Cope try her acid, however he was already tripping on mushrooms and declined. The American wailed until he agreed, but only on the condition she take some as well.

"No way", she said, *"On acid, I could never handle that you're more famous than me"*.

"But you're not famous at all" exclaimed Cope, bewildered.

"Well, don't fuckin' rub it in!" she screeched back.

From that night on, the American inveigled herself into the entourage of the band, following them back to Liverpool where she ensconced herself in Cope's flat, by then sub-let to Echo & the Bunnymen drummer Pete De Freitas. She started receiving weekly parcels of LSD delivered from her father in America to the apartment, using Cope's name on the outside of the envelope, which she then sold to everyone and anyone for twenty pence each.

Her name was Courtney Love.

ʊ ʊ ʊ

When twenty-two-year-old singer with Visage Steve Strange asked pop star Kim Wilde, one year his junior, on a date it seemed like they could become the *hot young couple* of 1982. Driving sixty kilometres from her parents' house on Wednesday 13th January,

Wilde was full of anticipation for the evening, however upon arriving at Langan's Brasserie in London's Mayfair she encountered Strange and a horde of photographers waiting. Strange, having tipped off the press, hauled Wilde to his side and posed cheek-to-cheek whilst flashlights erupted, and questions were hollered. After an intensely public meal, Strange persuaded Wilde to accompany him to the Embassy Club around the corner, where a whole different assemblage of photographers had been summoned. Strange, knowing how to work the press, and also needing to deflect from rumours of his homosexuality which in 1982 would kill any pop star's career dead, had set up the whole night, suckering an unsuspecting Wilde into his spectacle.

Inside the Embassy Club, Lemmy from rock band Motörhead, started to unashamedly flirt with Wilde, infuriating Strange who feared his subterfuge was about to be scuppered. The two faced off and a fight was only averted by Strange's quick gesturing to the door staff. Afterwards, with a theatrical wink, Strange claimed "*I don't know who tipped off the guys from the press. It sure wasn't me*".

ʊ ʊ ʊ

Former Welsh milkman Michael Barrett had been in the music business a long time and was finally seeing the fruits of his labour. Under the name of Shakin' Stevens, Barrett was already thirty-four-years-old in 1982 and would not have been judged too harshly for giving it all up and settling down into a more *regular* career.

Barrett started his musical career in 1969 as the card-carrying Communist frontman of a Welsh rock and roll revival band called The Sunsets. By the end of that year they were supporting The Rolling Stones in London, just a week after the ill-fated Altamont Festival, and within a few more weeks had signed to John Peel's Dandelion label. From there, they were *discovered* a second time by Dave Edmunds who arranged for them to sign to Parlophone Records, and produced a debut album before stealing their arrangement of *I Hear You Knocking* for himself and hitting the top of the charts. The band became the innocent victims of a contractual wrangle between Edmunds and Parlophone, and were thrown off the label before picking up a deal with CBS a year later. After an album on CBS, and another on Polydor, the Sunsets decamped to

Europe where they discovered a more responsive audience for their raucous rock and roll. The rest of the decade was spent touring across Europe and up and down the UK[24] to an audience keen to hear some rough and ready rock and roll, and watching footage of the band from the early to mid-1970's reveals them to be a 1950's-influenced version of music comparable to that which was being created by Doctor Feelgood at the same time. In 1978 Shaky was reluctantly press-ganged into joining the West End musical *Elvis!* on the understanding he would return to the band after the run. Three separate actors took the role of Elvis in the musical, with Tim Whitnall[25] playing young Elvis, Stevens playing middle Elvis, and 1960's star P.J. Proby[26] playing Vegas Elvis. At the end of the run, with a profile considerably higher than before Stevens embarked on a solo career, scoring a few minor hits in 1980 before reaching the top of the charts twice in 1981.

---

[24] The Sunsets played at my local nightclub, the Maniqui, in 1972.

[25] Tim Whitnall later found work as the narrator for *The Teletubbies*.

[26] P.J. Proby is perhaps best remembered for the publicity stunt of splitting his trousers live on stage during a performance. The caper backfired when he was banned from both the BBC and ITV.

Managed and controlled by Freya Miller, Stevens' relationship with the music press was problematic, many of whom felt he had lost a lot of the edge present in the Sunsets and was now an inconsequential prime-time entertainer suitable only for children's television and grannies. The image was not much helped by a choice of songs throughout the 1980's that bordered on saccharine, however, here was a performer who had spent more than a decade paying his dues in a manner that the old musos would appreciate and was a consummate professional when it came to putting on a show.

1982 began where the success of the previous year had left off, with his latest single *Oh Julie*, a Cajun-flavoured slice of rock and roll written by Stevens and driven by the guitar of Mickey Gee, a backing musician for Tom Jones and Joe Cocker. *Oh Julie* entered the chart at number thirteen, rising up to number three, then to the top spot by the end of the month, giving Shaky his third chart topper. It was already turning out to be another remarkable year for him and he was the most successful artist in the middle of a mini-rockabilly revival, for also hitting the charts in January were The Jets and The Stargazers.

The Jets were three brothers, Bob, Ray, and Tony Cotton, who were in the process of having their third (and biggest) hit single with an old Perry Como track, *Love Makes the World Go 'Round*[27]. The single would eventually peak at number twenty-one, and the trio troubled the top seventy-five twice more throughout the year with *The Honeydripper* and *Somebody to Love*. The Jets had toured as support to Shakin' Stevens the previous year, where Freya Miller had placed harsh restrictions upon them: they were not permitted to wear black and white, and were ordered to stay in their dressing room whilst the main act was on stage.

The Stargazers had been formed the previous year and signed to Epic Records by Muff Winwood. *Groove Baby Groove* was to be their most successful hit single, reaching number fifty-six, however the band continued for years afterwards, playing rock and roll revivals up and down the country and priding themselves on their authenticity. They too fell foul to the strict rules for support bands on a Shaky tour when on the September and October 1982 dates they were instructed that "*anyone who laughs at Shaky is off the tour*".

Shaky had quite a turnover of musicians throughout 1982, as he dissociated himself from the musicians he worked with. In the studio, all the music would be arranged and recorded before the singer entered to add his contribution once everyone had left. On tour, Shaky travelled separately and kept to himself in his own dressing room with a crate of Kestrel Lager[28]. That did not stop him coming alive onstage, as 1982 was the year he completed a world tour of the United Kingdom, Australia, New Zealand, South America, and Europe, with a revolving-door policy regarding musicians: guitarist Mickey Gee was replaced by ex-Rockpile Billy Bremner, who was in turn replaced by Mike Festa, *who in turn* was replaced by Les Davidson, Meanwhile, piano player Geraint Watkins was replaced by Pete Wingfield, who was then replaced by Gavin Povey, whilst the brass section from Graham Parker's Rumour joined for some territories.

---

[27] When The Jets appeared on *Top of the Pops* dancing right next to them in the audience was an unknown but very noticeable Boy George.

[28] Kestrel Super Lager was a Scottish & Newcastle 9% brew priced cheaper than every other competitor. My friend, Gordon Corbett and I bought a couple of cans from the off-licence when we were fourteen, then spent a long time in the grounds of Falkirk Old Parish Church pretending to enjoy it and faking drunkenness. We both waited for the other to turn their back so we could pour out a little bit and then pretend we had drunk it.

A couple of months after topping the chart with *Oh Julie*, Stevens released a version of *Shirley*, originally by John Fred and his Playboy Band back in 1959. Despite being a cover version, the lyrics were copyrighted jointly by Red Stick Music and Shaky Music, as manager Miller began insisting on a share of the royalties in exchange for covering a song.

Shirley reached number six, and the hits kept on coming throughout the year: *Give Me Your Heart Tonight* (number eleven), Jackie Wilson's *I'll Be Satisfied* (number ten), and an EP of Christmas songs, including a version of the Elvis Presley classic *Blue Christmas*, which peaked at number two in December, along with a platinum selling album (also called *Give Me Your Heart Tonight*).

ʊ ʊ ʊ

It was the Algerian Frontier Police who discovered Mark Thatcher's missing rally party in the Sahara Desert on Thursday 14th January, fifty kilometres off-route. It was reckoned they were only two days from death, and afterwards mechanic Jackie Garnier laid the blame at Thatcher's feet, indicating consternation that he insisted on navigating by compass only. After a low pass by a military airplane, a rescue helicopter was sent with a Land Rover.

Once ensconced at the Tahat Hotel in Tamanrasset, Algeria, Mark Thatcher started celebrating surviving by running up an eleven-thousand-dinar bill, a third of which was for drinks bought freely for anyone in the proximity. When presented with the bill, Thatcher refused to pay, forcing British diplomats and local police to become involved. Pressure was applied in the pertinent places, and the bill was waived, however Whitehall now turned attention to finding ways to stop Mark Thatcher from selling his story to the British press[29].

ʊ ʊ ʊ

With their fourth album released a couple of months before, The Police embarked on a world tour which would take them through until September 1982 and consolidate their standing as one of the most successful bands on the planet. After a cursory sprint around Britain and mainland Europe over Christmas and New Year, the three-piece opened their North American tour with a date at the Boston Garden on Friday 15th January.

Following the soundcheck, singer and bass player Sting and guitarist Andy Summers deposited their guitars adjacent to some massive industrial-looking boilers. Two hours later, the band returned and collected their instruments to commence their warm-up for the concert. As Summers plugged his cherished Fender into a practice amplifier, no

---

[29] Thatcher had always been a bit of a political embarrassment to the career of his mother, trading upon her name in copious business enterprises. In 1984 he was implicated in an array of record-breaking arms sales to the Saudi royal family, which he denied despite being bought a million-pound house in Belgravia by those entangled in the affair. Complications with tax saw Thatcher move to Switzerland, the United States and then South Africa, where he operated a loan shark company. His immoral comportment reached a nadir in 2004 when he was arrested under suspicion of funding and helping to plan a military coup in Equatorial Guinea in exchange for oil rights. Thatcher was found guilty, given a four-year suspended sentence and a fine in excess of one hundred thousand pounds. He now lives in a house gifted to him in Barbados, is known as Sir Mark Thatcher after inheriting his late father's title and has estimated personal assets of sixty million pounds in offshore accounts.

sound emerged from the speaker. The lead was exchanged first, then the amplifier, leading to the undeniable conclusion that the fault lay with the guitar. Over the next few minutes it became apparent that the enormous boilers were carrying some kind of electrical current and had demagnetized the pick-ups on the guitar. Word was sent out and a local electronics expert arrived to replace the pick-up, however the guitar just did not sound the same as before. Summer had played this guitar for over a decade, and it had been instrumental in achieving the sound which had made The Police a worldwide success.

Everything recorded after this night sounded different.

℧ ℧ ℧

The decision to host the 1982 FIFA World Cup in Spain had been made back in 1966, and life had transformed considerably in the country during the intervening years following the death of fascist dictator General Francisco Franco in 1975, as political parties on all sides acceded a *pact of forgetting* and the country pushed towards democracy. New laxity permitted tourism to flourish at an unprecedented pace, and in May 1982 Spain even became a member of NATO. Britain, however, remained apprehensive of the nation with Lord Carrington's report in January stating "*the central question... is the survival of democracy itself*". Accelerating numbers of Brits had been holidaying in the country, over four million in 1981, but as Lord Carrington pointed out "*about a hundred... are languishing in Spanish jails*".

The draw for the event in Madrid on Saturday 16th January was overseen by Sepp Blatter, a man who as President of FIFA would be banned from working within football for six years in 2015 following corruption and money laundering charges. Any pretence of a legitimate and transparent draw was banished early on when Scotland were drawn in the same group as Argentina. All indications from FIFA back-channels beforehand were that Scotland would be in the same group as Brazil. The draw was adjourned, and after some jiggery-pokery, re-drawn with Scotland and Brazil together. In other parts of the draw one of the cages containing the teams broke down, one of the small balls within which the name of a team was contained broke open, and another had to be coaxed from the chute by official fingers.

℧ ℧ ℧

Things were at a new low for punk pioneers The Damned in January 1982. Drummer Rat Scabies was rumored to be departing the band (again), their last couple of albums had failed to set the chart alight despite pushing the band into new musical territory, they were without a record company or manager, and finances were so drastic that they had resorted to playing one-off live dates just to earn enough money to stay alive. Meeting in a pub in Hammersmith at noon on Saturday 16th January to set off for one of these dates at the Mayflower in Manchester, guitarist Captain Sensible arrived drunk having been up all night mixing recordings for new band Dolly Mixture, and immediately set about verbally derogating Scabies, as well as pulling the seat from under him as he was about to sit down. This type of conduct was commonplace for The Damned, who constantly operated as if they were the Bash Street Kids on a school outing; good natured brutality and boisterous badinage was part of their everyday existence. The hectoring continued in the van, at which point Scabies decided he had had enough and clambered out the door, running off into the street. As a band who existed on the margins of unremitting disintegration, this was no big deal, and they merely rounded up U.K. Subs drummer Steve Roberts and played the gig.

A couple of days later Scabies returned, and the pantomime continued.

17th – 23rd January 1982

#1 single: Bucks Fizz: The Land of Make Believe
#1 album: The Human League: Dare

By the third week of the year, all the singles record companies had been holding back to avoid getting lost during Christmas started to be released, and the charts were full of memorable new entries. The highest of these, at number thirty-one, was a curio entitled *Maid of Orleans* by Liverpool act Orchestral Manoeuvres in the Dark.

OMD, as they had shortened their name to by 1982, were not actually from the city of Liverpool, but originated from the Wirral, across the River Mersey. Their two main members, Andy McLuskey and Paul Humphreys, had been playing together in a succession of bands since the mid-1970's, nonchalantly edging towards becoming a Kraftwerk-influenced electronic pop act. In 1979 they found themselves signed to the newly formed and fabulously fashionable Factory Records, and with a debut single entitled *Electricity* were acclaimed as a new wave of Northern bands, alongside Joy Division and the Teardrop Explodes, with their record sleeves created by soon-to-be-celebrated Mancunian designer, Peter Saville. Moving to Virgin Records subsidiary Din Disc, over two albums and four singles they began their assault on the charts with pop songs about nuclear bombs and hydro-electric plants.

1981 saw them modify their sound with the purchase of a Mellotron, a keyboard more associated with prog-rock bands of the early 1970's than post-punk acts. The key to the Mellotron's *nonpareil* tone was the way it generated sounds: utilising samples recorded on tape, so when you hit a key the sample would be played at the appropriate pitch. OMD employed it to propagate choral sounds for the album, providing the songs with a manifestly perennial ambience that refused to date as technology moved on.

The new sound unlocked a more human facet to OMD's song-writing, and on the resultant album *Architecture & Morality*[30] they seemed to be singing about the connection between people rather than the allure of machines.

Maid of Orleans was the third single from the album, and the record company had been boasting for several months about a track that was "*as catchy as 'Mull of Kintyre' but twice as hip*". Catchy, the track certainly was, however you would never know from the opening thirty-five seconds, which featured a montage of incongruent noises, imbricated and dissonant. People switched off before the song truly started, and radio stations were hesitant to play the track. It was an audacious move by the band, confident that people's patience would be more than rewarded once they arrived at the melody. And what a melody it was! Starting in 6/8 time and feeling like a waltz, we are greeted by a single repeating kick drum to which is added an unfussy bass line punctured by the intermittent fusillade of a snare. Then the hook kicks in, sounding like God's bagpipes escorted by a chorus of seraphs, leading to an understated first verse. "*If Joan of Arc had a heart would she give it as a gift*" sings McLuskey, not entirely deserting the band's proclivity for esoteric lyrics.

---

[30] In October 1982 I stood in Walmart in Rochester, Minnesota with this album and *Combat Rock* by The Clash in my hands, trying to decide which one to buy. I chose this, and it was to be the first long player I ever bought myself.

The *Maid of Orleans* was another name for *Joan of Arc*[31], however the band had already had a top five hit with a track of that title a few months previously, and so the track had to be renamed to avoid confusion. Directly after the first verse we have a duplicate of the hook, but with an electrifying modification of key from *D#* to *C*, allowing McLuskey to raise his pitch an octave for the second verse, after which we have a double repeat of the hook before fading out. And that is it: one instrumental hook and four lines of arcane lyrics, however at the end of the song you are left feeling as if you have experienced something hermetically esoteric, as if there was a conceivable answer to love and life within the four minutes. It was to be OMD's consummate four minutes, one which they did not endeavour to recreate within their career. In keeping with a theme of chart music at the time, the song was unparalleled: nothing had sounded like it previously, and nothing has sounded like it since.

Whilst the song crawled its way up the charts, eventually settling at number four, the band toured their album throughout mainland Europe, before a protracted North American tour. The song became a worldwide smash, reaching number one in several countries, and becoming the biggest selling single of 1982 in Germany, helping the album to shift four million copies. The United States, however, remained ignorant of their appeal for several more years until, helped by inclusion on the soundtrack of a John Hughes teen movie, they broke big in 1986.

Maid of Orleans however was something of a full stop in the story of OMD. Whilst touring, their road crew kept telling them that if they kept on going like this they would be as big as Genesis, with an HGV for each of them and their equipment. Like the Kraftwerk fans they were, McLuskey and Humphreys were horrified at the prospect, and made a calculated retreat from the public eye, re-emerging in 1983 with an album which could only be construed as *commercial suicide*. *Dazzle Ships* contained Cold-War influenced songs created with recordings of the speaking clock, the noise of machines, and the interval signal of the Czech Radio Foreign Service. The first single from the album featured lead vocals by a *Speak & Spell* child's toy. The album foundered and the band lost three million fans, however the years since then have been gracious to *Dazzle Ship* and listening now It is easily seen as their most forward-thinking recording, often acclaimed as a misplaced classic[32].

℧ ℧ ℧

For the serious music aficionado, the New Musical Express was the bible through the 1970's and early 1980's. Often journalists such as Julie Burchill, Tony Parsons, and Charles Shaar Murray experienced a similar status as the artists. To these people, music was more relevant than life or death, and Murray once stated "*This stuff mattered to us, and we thought we were being read by people who also thought it mattered…. We were taking on the music business in defence of the musicians, or taking on the musicians in defence of the audience, or taking on the audience in defence of the art*". By the early 1980's the NME had embraced politics, and no artist worth their salt could be interviewed without being interrogated about the issues of the day. They were expected to be able to discuss with authority Derrida or Brecht and their role in a post-modern society, to elucidate upon Central American revolutionaries and African coups,

---

[31] The song had been written on 30th May 1981, the 550th anniversary of Joan of Arc's death. Even though *Maid of Orleans* was written first. Andy McLuskey threw it away until drummer Malcolm Holmes asked where the waltz song had gone. It remains the highlight of their live show, often requiring the band to pause for minutes at a time to soak up the applause.

[32] Then they spoiled it all by becoming successful again with more pop songs about railways and scientists. Andy McLuskey even wrote some great songs for Atomic Kitten, the big sell out that he is.

and to be experts on Eastern European cinema. For many teenagers their own politics, cultural references, and perspective were formed and informed by an interview in the weekly paper.

By 1982, however, the NME had reached a crisis point. Journalists such as Paul Morley and Ian Penman had fallen under the spell of Roland Barthes and were driven to find new ways of writing about rock and pop. Barthes believed that artistic evolution could only happen by fracturing the traditions using the very form of those conventions, and that eventually the subversion would become the norm, and therefore the new established practice. Barthes also argued that modern myths existed around prosaic objects to make them covetable and to preserve the status quo of the ruling class. These myths were not consciously created, but instead were part of a cultural memory and consensus as to the collected meanings of objects and images. Therefore, Duran Duran sipping champagne with supermodels on a yacht later in the year bought into the idea of affluence, youth, travel, attractiveness, extravagance, and expense; it sold the idea that the lifestyle of the ruling class was both seductive and unobtainable at the same time.

Barthes believed that "*the cultural work done in the past by gods and epic sagas is now done by laundry detergent commercials and comic strip characters*", an idea that has since acquired acceptance, well on the way to becoming the convention itself. Our shared culture has become *Star Wars*, *Room 101* and *Big Brother* from George Orwell's novel *1984*, Michael Jackson, internet memes and *Game of Thrones*, not the past Norse myths, Biblical legends, or epic journeys of Homer.

That little from 1982 ended up surviving in our mutual cultural myths, with possible exceptions of *E.T.* and Simon Le Bon on a yacht, implies almost everything else from the year has been set adrift from society's memory. Anyone who did not live through the year cannot possibly fully understand references to Renée & Renato, Ossie Ardilles, Clive Sinclair, or Martin Fry's gold suit. Musically, the year swayed between the norm-setting, soon to be learned-behaviour of the rock stars of the 1960's and 1970's, and the major pop stars of the 1980's. 1982 was merely a pause for breath between two giant edges of semiotic symbols. The new journalists at the NME chose to write in metaphor, carousing with the structure and expectations of language and journalism, "*employing punctuation like a weapon*". Unfortunately, their new approach was not what the readership wanted, and the circulation fell significantly throughout the year.

On Monday 18th January, the most successful pop star of the previous year was featured on the front cover of the New Musical Express. Adam Ant had never been popular with the cerebral music press, and perhaps protested too much that he did not care, that he was simply a "*song and dance man*". Inside, a four-page interview Paul Morley picked over the past year, particularly the recently concluded spectacular British tour, *The Prince Charming Review*. Against the grain for a reflective music journalist, Morley had loved the show and was going through a conversion to the idea of what he termed *New Pop*. Morley felt music should have "*colour, dance, excitement… intelligence, intrigue* [and] *a love of the little things in life*". Conflicted by the party-line regarding what he was expected to write, and what he felt about the show, Morley searched for acumen in what Adam and the Ants were doing, questioning the frontman about his motivation. In particular, he was curious about Adam's naked ambition, and his statement that the highlight of last year had been meeting the Queen, an odd thing for a former punk to say. "*I'm sick and tired of being told that because I don't drink and don't smoke, that I'm a goody-two-shoes*" seethed Adam, "*Okay, so I'm a goody-two-shoes. So what? I don't like drugs and that is a threat to the rock and roll establishment. Rock and roll has become the establishment.*"

At the back of his mind, Adam took note of the phrase *goody-two-shoes*, storing it away for future use.

Whilst the NME circulation floundered, surging significantly in popularity was a glossy colourful fortnightly magazine intended for a younger readership. *Smash Hits* reigned supreme throughout 1982, selling over half a million copies every fortnight, compared to just under a quarter of a million for the NME and less than seventy-five thousand for Melody Maker[33]. Some competition came in the form of *No.1 Magazine* which sold around a quarter of a million copies each issue, however nothing came close to the new kid in town.

Smash Hits had first been published in November 1978 by former NME journalist Nick Logan as a song-words magazine, resisting his publishers demand to turn it into a John Travolta and Bee Gees-themed magazine called *Disco Fever*. The vibrant shiny pages were ideal for the New Pop of the early 1980's, celebrating the surface without stressing the substance. Paul Morley may have coined the phrase *New Pop* in the NME, but it was *Smash Hits* which ran with the notion, depicting the mostly male pop stars as unthreatening sexualised commodities for a female readership. The *Smash Hits* journalists in 1982 included David Hepworth, Mark Ellen, Dave Rimmer, and future Pet Shop Boys frontman Neil Tennant, all of whom embraced the pop acts with open and irreverent arms[34]. The formula worked throughout the decade, and the more vacuous and superficial the magazine became, the more successful it was. Celebrating capitalism and aspiration, selling a glamorous lifestyle to teens and younger, *Smash Hits* was often viewed as a Thatcherite publication, however like *Top of the Pops* it only ever echoed the public rather than led them. By 1989 the circulation was over a million copies each issue, whilst the serious music press had backed themselves into an *indie* ghetto from which they found it difficult to retreat.

Nick Logan quickly moved on from *Smash Hits*, setting up a new lifestyle magazine in May 1980 aimed at an older readership. Turned down by every publisher in town, he used £3500 of his own money to buy paper from Finland, printed 75,000 copies of *The Face*, and sold 57,000. *The Face* was published monthly and covered music, clothes, and the dancefloor, and was aimed squarely at London *club kids*, or those who wanted to be them. It became the new arbiter of youth coolness, rakish and sleek with a look devised by Neville Brody, a starving designer who applied his Dada and punk graphics to the pages, creating an artefact which was so *of the moment* that it could not help but be a success. This was followed by imitators such as *iD* and *Blitz*, as youth currency moved from words to pictures.

ʊ ʊ ʊ

Given the public's unwillingness to tolerate intractable subjects such as unemployment and nuclear weapons defiling their glistening pop music, it is a miracle that *The Boiler* by the Special AKA and Rhoda Dakar was ever released. Dakar had been the singer with all-female band The Bodysnatchers who had formed in London during summer 1979, inspired by the burgeoning ska revival. They played their first gig in November, supporting future Pogues frontman Shane McGowan and his band, The Nips, and by their third gig were performing at Debbie Harry's birthday party and signing to Two-Tone Records.

---

[33] Mark Ellen: *"I remember looking down into the NME from the Smash Hits office in 1981 and being so relieved I'd switched sides."*

[34] This was my *Smash Hits*: I started buying and reading it in July 1982 after stealing one from a tent-mate at a Boys Brigade camp in Carnoustie. My brother had bought it back in 1979, when it was much more of a *new wave* proposition.

Two-Tone was the creation of Jerry Dammers, keyboard player and brains behind Birmingham act The Specials. This band had prompted something of a mini revolution at the turn of the decade, playing ska with the energy of punk, mixing black and white musicians onstage, and using social commentary and politics as the basis of their lyrics. The band's line-up morphed between 1977 and 1979, during which time they were invited to tour and share management with The Clash, becoming involved with the Rock Against Racism movement. This exposure allowed Dammers to negotiate a deal with Chrysalis Records, not to sign the band but to sign a label instead, which guaranteed funding for fifteen singles a year, of which a minimum of ten had to be released. Two-Tone Records took off at the end 1979, with *Gangsters* by The Special AKA (as they were known at the time), *The Prince* by Madness, *On My Radio* by The Selecter, and *Tears of A Clown* by The Beat all hitting the top ten. The label was influential in providing a new business model for bands, one where they did not need to sign to the majors but could start their own label *and reach the charts!* Throughout 1980 the success continued, with The Bodysnatchers joining the label as well as a summer tour with The Specials and The Go-Go's. Rhoda Dakar and the band continued until 1981 when they split, with most of the others going off to form The Belle Stars.

The Specials peaked in summer 1981, when they hit the top of the charts with the exquisite *Ghost Town*, a track about inner city conflict, the same week riots broke out in the cities of Britain. However, there was also internal conflict within the band and at the pinnacle of their success Terry Hall, Lynval Golding, and Neville Staples, the three frontmen, left to form a new act called The Fun Boy Three. Dakar, who had already sung some backing vocals on the second album, slipped in nicely as a replacement.

The Boiler had been an unrecorded Bodysnatchers track, however it was felt by Dammers to be covering far too an important subject matter to never see the light of

day on vinyl. He suggested The Specials record a version with Dakar, the process of which became an interminable process. The musicians on the recording only faintly resembled the Specials the fans would have recognised, with Dammers on keyboards and drummer John Bradbury the only two remaining members. They were joined by Bodysnatchers bass player Nicky Summers, former touring trumpet player Dick Cuthell, and Swinging Cats guitarist John Shipley.

The track itself is a standard twelve-bar-blues chord progression played with a relaxed ska offbeat. It is the lyrics, however, that deliver the punch of the song. In them, Dakar narrates a spoken word monologue about a girl with low self-esteem who goes on date with a man she has just met. Every verse recounts an event that would appear to be a happy experience, however each final line brings the listener down to earth as she repeatedly refers to herself as an *old boiler*, undeserving of his attention. The song takes an ominous turn when the man endeavours to get her to come back to his house, then gets irate when she refuses. Her low self-esteem sees the narrator relent, only to be dragged into an alley and raped, culminating in sixty seconds of calamitous screaming, accompanying by unhinged drums and a chaotic free-form trumpet.

The six minutes of the song are an astonishingly harrowing and excruciating listen, first with the distress of the narrator's low self-esteem, and then with the torment of the actual rape. There was never a chance the single was going to be a success, however Dammers felt it was more important to make a declaration about the treatment and expectations of women at the time than to worry about profits and chart positions. It was a brave and foolhardy move, and yet the song jumped to number thirty-five with hardly any radio coverage.

In the same week the single was released the BBC documentary series *Police* broadcast their third episode on Monday 19th January, entitled *A Complaint of Rape*. The series was following the Thames Valley Force as they went about their daily business, and this episode featured a woman who claimed to have been raped by three men. She was shown being aggressively questioned by three male police officers regarding the alleged assault, who eventually dismissed the accusation out of hand with the statement "*This is the biggest bollocks I've ever heard*". The detectives were following rape interrogation training instructions coached in every police college up and down the country, a second ordeal and debasement for violated women to endure, of which official statistics showed there had been over a thousand of in the United Kingdom in 1982. That was just the ones who were successful with the prosecution.

There was a public protest regarding the program immediately, and the subsequent bad publicity for the police forced them into forming new rape squads involving female officers. The film was placed under lock and key, never to be shown on television again, and even though the officers involved had all seen the footage before broadcast and thought they had done nothing wrong. The series marked the end of the open relationship television had with the police, and they would never again be allowed unfettered and uncensored access to the law.

ʊ ʊ ʊ

Entering the charts this week were a bunch of Belfast lads by the name of Stiff Little Fingers, originally formed as a rock covers act before being converted by punk early in

1977. Their first single in 1978, *Suspect Device*, was released on their own label and with the patronage of John Peel sold 30,000 copies without bothering the charts. In the late 1970's and early 1980's it was feasible for bands to make a small living from releasing their own singles, selling tens of thousands of copies without coming to the notice of national radio or the charts.

SLF played fast combative punk with killer melodies and lyrics which discoursed *the troubles* in Northern Ireland without taking any side other than a stance of anti-violence. They moved to London in 1979 and got involved with the Rock Against Racism movement whilst releasing a series of celebrated singles and albums, initially on their own label and then later for Chrysalis Records. As the new decade rolled around, SLF continued to breach the lower reaches of the charts without becoming a household name, all the time building up a large and loyal live fan-base. The song-writing style of frontman Jake Burns had evolved, becoming more personal, as well as tackling issues other than Northern Ireland.

Their new single was the lead track from an EP, *£1.10 or less*, the title referring to the maximum price the public should pay for the four songs. The lead song was called *Listen* and was without a doubt the most commercial sounding and refined track the band ever released. It could be called an anthemic ballad, starting with a simple single guitar riff before the whole band enters. Lyrically, it deals with male insecurities and an inability to commit to a supporting partner, hitting hard with a massive sing-along chorus culminating in the line "*Why don't you listen to your heart*". In another perfectly plausible world, the song would have stormed to the top of the charts, however for some reason it stalled at number thirty-one. It was the last time the band bothered the top forty, though various versions would tour successfully for many years afterwards.

ʊ ʊ ʊ

Tourists were scarce in the Falkland Islands, usually restricted to naturalists looking to study the seal population, so when an Argentinian architect turned up in Port Stanley, fifty-four-year-old Governor Rex Hunt was more than happy to show him around. Hunt had been a resident of the islands for under two years but according to the Foreign Office had "*gone native*".

There were no roads on most of the islands, with numerous tiny communities only accessible by sea, so the two wandered around Port Stanley, ending at Government House, after which the architect requested duplicates of the plans. "*And like a fool*" Hunt later stated, "*I gave him the photocopies*".

ʊ ʊ ʊ

Lurking outside the top forty was XTC with another sensational single called *Senses Working Overtime*. XTC had been formed in Swindon ten years previously by songwriters Andy Partridge and Colin Moulding, along with drummer Terry Chambers. After spending years under the influence of the New York Dolls, they adapted briskly to the development of punk, and in 1977 rode its coattails to a deal with Virgin Records, recruiting keyboard player Barry Andrews along the way.

XTC were far too astute and autonomous in their influences and expression to adhere to a punk sound, and their tracks often harked back to classic 1960's pop and garage. Over the course of four albums and ten singles, some of which were *bona fide* hits, they built up a reputation as pop eccentrics, and *Senses Working Overtime* was a comeback single after a year out of the charts. It was the first release from their forthcoming album, which had been produced by Hugh Padgham, an up-and-coming studio engineer who would go on to play a large part in the 1980's, providing bluster to many of the decade's larger artists such as Genesis, The Police, David Bowie and Phil Collins[35].

There is no sign of that bluster on *Senses Working Overtime* though; the song is unveiled gradually, starting with some plucked guitar notes and a sense of foreboding

as the singing joins in. One by one the instruments come in, first the bass, and then a kick drum. Partridge later revealed that he had sat down to wilfully write a hit single, and foremost at the front of his mind was *5-4-3-2-1* by Manfred Mann. He envisioned the verses as being a minor key illustration of medieval woes and worries, with lyrics about assuring the cattle were fed and everyone was sleeping safely. This was combined with some astute touches such as the jingle of plough harnesses, some "*wretched land-people sounds*" for backing vocals, and the noise of crows at the very end of the song. After each verse the track bursts into a bridge that can scarcely accommodate its excitement at the wonder of the world, and it is this sense of awe that the song is meant to be about; an awareness of the beauty of England's landscape, proclaimed in the middle-eight cry of "*England's Glory*". At the end of each bridge we get a reverse Manfred Mann count leading into a major-key earworm chorus, ending with "*Pain and pleasure and the church bells gently chime*".

---

[35] Padgham is credited as creating the "gated" drum sound during the recording of Phil Collins *In the Air Tonight,* a technique which would, for its sins, go on to be synonymous with the blustering sound of the 1980's.

Partridge was going through a phase where he was writing about Britain, and England in particular, celebrating the prosaic and ordinary, in much the same way as a whole series of English bands had done, from The Kinks' kitchen vignettes to Madness' tales of London life, through to Blur's *Modern Life* trilogy in the 1990's.

The melody was contagious and helped the single climb the charts to number ten. It was the biggest hit XTC ever had, and they prepared for the release of their album and a world tour, the latter of which would lead to a critical change in their career.

ʊ ʊ ʊ

Also entering the top seventy-five this week, but crucially not the top forty, were a London based band called Theatre of Hate with a song entitled *Do You Believe in the Westworld?* Theatre of Hate, who were fronted by Kirk Brandon and began life as a prosaic punk band before being swept along with the post-punk ethic, were now creating something much more compelling, with tribal rhythms and brass in evidence on their latest recordings. Brandon was an engaging frontman, who later took Boy George to court to repudiate the assertion that they had been lovers in the early 1980's[36].

Lyrically the song alluded to the Cold War, as many did during the 1980's, with references to Ronald Reagan in the line "*on a wind in walked a cowboy*" and Russia as "*the circus with the bear*". The backdrop for the song was a deserted old west town ("*tombstone*"), with the title of the song referring to the 1970's sci-fi cowboy movie *Westworld*.

Theatre of Hate had been working with Clash guitarist Mick Jones on their new album, of which this was the lead single. Jones was a scintillating songwriter and guitarist in The Clash but has spent a long time since demonstrating how maladroit he is at production, and the Theatre of Hate recordings evidenced this. They were regarded by the industry as a disappointment compared to the blistering live reputation of the band, and furthermore Jones had insisted on playing guitar over the tracks. It speaks volumes that just as their new album was coming out in February 1982, the band chose to release a live album, *He Who Dares Wins*, at the same time.

The single ricocheted around the edges of the top forty, and despite a potentially lucrative *Top of the Pops* appearance and a John Peel session at the start of February,

failed to get any higher than number forty. In the week unemployment rose above a record three million people, the public did not want to be reminded of dismal subjects such as the Cold War, unless it was wrapped up inside a memorable melody.

The spectre of unemployment hung heavy over the decade but never seemed to perturb the Conservative government as much as one would hope. Secretary of State for Energy, and future Chancellor of the Exchequer, Nigel Lawson had previously stated that he considered high unemployment to be a price worth paying to defeat high inflation, whilst current Chancellor Geoffrey Howe proclaimed that the effects of unemployment had to be made "*harsher… for those elements of the labour force that were insufficiently mobile*".

Within the millions of unemployed only a third were woman according to official statistics, however the reality was different given only 60% of women were actively in

---

[36] Brandon took George to court for *malicious falsehood* rather than *libel* because that entitled him to legal aid. Brandon lost the case in 1997 and was forced to pay legal fees.

the workforce. The other 40%, considered *housewives*, were not included in the statistics, whilst those who were employed found themselves out of work on a regular basis, given the services cut first in the face of Thatcherite policies tended to be the part-time jobs traditionally held by women such as cleaners and dinner ladies.

The high levels of unemployment did not decline until 1986, and only then because the government found ways to discount huge swathes of people who had been forced onto training courses and sub-minimum wage jobs by the threat of withdrawn benefits.

℧ ℧ ℧

Seventeen-year-old Des Moines native Mark Neal had his younger brother to thank for bringing home a live bat from Lincoln High School. It only took two weeks for his attempt at domesticating a bat to fail, and he found himself in possession of a dead flying mammal. Unsure what to do with the body, the impressionable Neal was persuaded by friends to wrap it in a bag, tuck it inside his jacket, and smuggle it into the Ozzy Osbourne show at the Veterans Memorial Auditorium on Wednesday 20th January. Surely, if anyone was going to appreciate a dead bat, it was Ozzy who had spent a good part of the last year assailing his audience with 25 lbs of pigs' intestines and calves' liver on a nightly basis.

Halfway through the show, Neal got close enough to the front to propel the dead bat onto the stage. Ozzy saw it land and thinking it was a rubber toy decided to play up to his character by biting the head off. *"Immediately, though, something felt wrong. Very wrong."* Osbourne ruminated in his autobiography, *"For a start, my mouth was instantly full of this warm, gloopy liquid, with the worst aftertaste you could ever imagine"*.

Immediately after the concert, Ozzy was rushed to Broadlawns Medical Centre in Des Moines for rabies injections from *"a syringe the size of a cigar... directly into his stomach"* and was back onstage in Milwaukee two nights later.

℧ ℧ ℧

European Son by Japan had been ignored by the press and public when first released in 1979, but by early 1982 its time had come. Japan were formed in 1974 in London by four working-class school friends, fronted by David Sylvian, specialising in epicene glam, influenced by Roxy Music and David Bowie and looking like *"Hanoi Rocks on their way to court"*. Over the next few years they became immersed in a glam-rock amalgam, eventually signing with the German disco label behind Boney M, Hansa-Ariola in 1977[37]. Their first couple of albums were swiftly released without denting any charts, however the band did manage to pick up an influential manager in the form of Simon Napier-Bell.[38]

In 1979 the band worked with the illustrious Euro-disco producer Giorgio Moroder on a one-off single, *Life in Tokyo*, a dazzling piece of glacial pop with a floor-to-the-floor beat and sing-along chorus. Once again, they failed to chart, but their love of a more electronic sound, one that was principally European, sexually ambiguous, and unreservedly disconnected, was sealed. The band continued to indulge this passion on their third album *Quiet Life*, which broke into the British album charts, peaking just outside the top fifty: not a huge hit, however the album had an immeasurable influence on the New Romantic movement the following year, so much so that the first Duran

---

[37] On the same day as The Cure during an open audition.

[38] Napier-Bell had first made his fortune in the music industry by writing the lyrics for Dusty Springfield's *You Don't Have to Say You Love Me* before looking after the interests of The Yardbirds and Marc Bolan.

Duran album would undoubtedly not have existed in terms of sound or visuals without Japan.

With their third album Japan had satisfied their contractual obligation to Hansa-Ariola and transferred to Virgin Records who were much better positioned to help the band  break in Britain. Over two albums and a handful of singles they slowly insinuated themselves into the charts, and by the end of 1981 their old label Hansa started to look at the treasure they had in their back catalogue. This was a common move by labels in the early 1980's: to release a band from their contract and then exploit them when they subsequently became successful. It happened to Adam & The Ants, it happened to The Human League, it happened to Ultravox, and it was now happening to Japan. This was, of course, only made possible by the fact that the record industry in the early 1980's permitted bands a second act. It was anticipated that bands would mature and improve over several albums, and if their first couple failed it did not mean that the band were creatively finished.

Japan may have influenced the New Romantics, but they ventured to distance themselves from the movement. There was no need for this effort: where the New Romantics were all about effigy and exterior, Japan had profound cerebral and artistic roots. Spandau Ballet never spoke of French composer Erik Satie as an influence or recruited Yellow Magic Orchestra keyboard player Ryuichi Sakamoto to play on their albums. To put it another way, all were influenced by Roxy Music, but whilst New Romantics wanted to be Bryan Ferry, Japan were enamoured by Brian Eno.

European Son had been recorded at the conclusion of 1978 and remixed by Penguin Café Orchestra member Steve Nye. It was originally released as a B-side before Hansa realized how much it chimed with the musical environment at the end of 1981. The song sounded like a track from the breakthrough Ultravox album, *Vienna*, but with Duran Duran's Simon Le Bon singing. That both those acts emerged a year after *European Son* was initially released shows how far ahead of the game Japan were in 1979. The song had been written by Sylvian at the end of an American tour and expressed the alienation of a European in an alien continent, with references to boardwalks and luncheonettes that seemed at odds with the Euro-disco of the soundtrack. Lyrically, the song did not give much away at all, with only sixteen short individual lines, and oblique references to "*Suffragettes in Washington*", however one suspects that was the point, to leave a nebulousness that would echo the isolation of a stranger in a strange land.

Musically, the song was a pale imitation of their own *Life in Tokyo*, but still managed to power along, backed by phased sequencers and Mick Karn's innovative fretless bass.

ʊ ʊ ʊ

If Japan were the sound of the future, there was also a punk revival in 1982 as well. First into the top seventy-five were the Anti-Nowhere League with their cover version of Ralph McTell's *Streets of London*. McTell's original verses compared the commonplace quandaries of people, those who were destitute, desolate, elderly, and ignored, ending with the chorus "*How can you tell me you're lonely and for you the sun don't shine? Let me take you by the hand and lead you through the streets of London, I'll show you something to make you change your mind*". This wretchedness, darkness, and social commentary was an ideal subject matter for a punk make-over… if it had been 1977. This, however, was 1982, and five years were a long time in popular music.

Music had moved on, society had moved on, and the Anti-Nowhere League sounded like uninspired relics.

When punk first arrived in London, creating itself from a combination of disenchanted, disenfranchised youths and older manipulative, *arty* types who had been through the hippy years, it was revolutionary. With hindsight, we can see the musical and political precedents, but at the time it seemed to come out of nowhere and acted as a *year-zero* scorching fire. You were either with them or against them; there was no middle ground. A lot of the early punk, however, is rather unlistenable, the unavoidable consequence of people being inspired to pick up instruments without being able to play them. It was

this enthusiasm and freshness of methodology that was also the most remarkable aspect of punk; you did not need to devote years learning blues scales to create something; all you required was an idea.

People had two different motives for their inclination towards punk. The first was a liberty of creativity, the freedom to push boundaries, not just in music but across the creative industries. The people who were attracted to punk for this reason went on to become some of the most influential movers and shakers in the British arts scene over the next couple of decades. Painter Nicola Tyson noticed "*As the number of fans shot up, punk became more yobbish and less underground, arty and Warholian. The early Sex Pistols fans… were the idols of the arty punks. They were camp and sophisticated, very gay-influenced, and their defiance influenced by the arch flamboyance of Bowie and Roxy Music*". The other reason some people liked punk was for the sound. This set stagnated in the interminable duplication of distorted guitars, sneering vocals, "shock" lyrics, and fast tempos, creating a scene that was exceedingly constricting, one where to deviate from the prototype was forbidden. To develop as an artist could lead to denunciations of *selling out*. For journalist Tony Parsons "*Punk changed when it started to attract non-art-school punks. You started seeing punks with mohawks begging and to me that was an appalling sight. They should have been forming bands or writing fanzines.*" Sex Pistols guitarist Steve Jones summed it up by claiming this wave of acts "*completely lost the plot of what punk was all about… when it changed from the excitement of what you could become to hanging onto a uniform… you're not bringing anything new to it… at that point you might as well be a Teddy Boy*".

The Anti-Nowhere League fell into this second category after being formed in London in 1980. They bribed Rat Scabies in a public toilet to gain a tour support with The Damned, before slipping effortlessly into a scene that encompassed acts such as Discharge and The Exploited. *Streets of London* was their debut single, and featured a track on the other side entitled *So What?* in which frontman Chris Exall spouted a lexicon of objectionable acts he had undertaken, followed by a chorus of "*So what?*" This list contained the customary adolescent targets, but also a few more that time would render as intolerable such as boasting that he "*Fucked a schoolgirl*". As you would expect, the B-side was beloved by the type of people who were still wearing bondage trousers in 1982, and became band's theme tune, later to be covered by Metallica.

The single stalled at number forty-eight, but there were other bands with a similar outlook on music also making waves in the British top seventy-five in January 1982. One of these was Charged GBH, later reduced to GBH (short for Grievous Bodily Harm), who entered the charts with a single called *No Survivors*. Everything that was true of the Anti-Nowhere League was also true of GBH: they were raucous, snarling, and concise. As well as trying to stay true to the sound of 1977 punk, they also took an influence from the metal act Motörhead, particularly in the heads-down velocity of the music. However, where the Anti-Nowhere League were still trying unremittingly to shock mum and dad, GBH had a more political predilection to their lyrics, albeit a rather

naïve one. Their latest single, *No Survivors* was an anti-war song, referencing conscientious objectors during the First World War and the sacrifice in vain of the fallen in French fields.

GBH were part of a movement which went under several names, including *UK82*, *Street Punk*, *UK Hardcore*, and *Real Punk*. This was punk through an apocalyptic Cold War filter, and was influenced by, and in turn also influenced, many American hard-core acts of the decade. Some of the youths involved in the British scene went on to become part of the travelling community and the rave scene, others went onto become involved in right wing politics, whilst many more stayed the same... punks into their sixties. If the bands in the scene are to be applauded for anything it is that they had commitment, as evidenced by how many of them were still making the same music thirty years later.

1982 was the peak of success for the Anti-Nowhere League and GBH, with the former having a further two top seventy-five hits with *I Hate People* and an unbridled parcel of misogyny called *Woman*, as well as a (minor) hit album *We Are... The League*, and the latter hitting the charts with single *Give Me Fire* and the album *City Baby Attacked by Rats*, whilst the bands continued a long career of looking like Kenny Everett's idea of punks.

ʊ ʊ ʊ

A successful Italian newspaper declared in 1922 that "*Italy is a fertile breeding ground for bankruptcies and banking scandals*", and this was certainly to prove to be the case in 1982. Corruption and financial misconduct have invariably seemed a way of life in Italy, to be expected and forgiven. Even in the Vatican there were often monetary irregularities, such as the Franklin National Bank collapse in 1974 when Vice Chairman Michele Sindona[39] used his connections within the Holy See, the American Republican Party, and the Sicilian drug cartels to launder and lose tens of millions of dollars.

A similar scandal had been fermenting the last four years within Italy's second largest private bank, Banco Ambrosiano. In 1981 chairman Roberto Calvi was found guilty of exporting several billion Italian lire, given a four-year suspended sentence, and fined nineteen million dollars. Astonishingly, though perhaps not for Italy, he was permitted to keep his position at the bank.

Over the past decade the unassuming Calvi had been building an impressive inventory of shell companies in Luxembourg, Chile, Lichtenstein, and the Bahamas, using them to illegally transfer money out of Italy. He seduced major companies into lending him money, which was subsequently loaned to other organizations. These financial obligations were used as leverage, and the organizations threatened with the withdrawal of investment unless they laundered money for Banco Ambrosiano.

Calvi could be inordinately persuasive and in November 1981, despite being out of prison on appeal and bail, he convinced office equipment company Olivetti to invest in Banco Ambrosiano. The chief executive of Olivetti was Carlo De Benedetti, who was certain he could turn the ailing fortunes of the bank around and invested fifty million lire for a 2% share. It almost immediately became clear that Calvi was not about to give

---

[39] Sindona was poisoned with cyanide in his coffee whilst in prison in 1986.

up jurisdiction in any way when he refused to approve a request for the accounts of the bank to be examined. When De Benedetti reiterated the demand, he found his family threatened by shadowy figures, and the more he heard about the bank's dealings from outside sources the less enamored with the whole business he became. He raised his concerns with Calvi and was assured by the banker everything was okay, it was all in "*the hands of the black cassocks*": in other words, the Vatican.

De Benedetti finally decided enough was enough and announced his departure from the deal on Friday 22nd January, cutting Banco Ambrosiano loose from what was monetary aegis in the eyes of the financial sector and public. It was an action which would have severe repercussions for Calvi, Banco Ambrosiano, and Italy over the next year.

ʊ ʊ ʊ

As one of the original British punk bands The Clash had started out as a reaction against numerous things, one of which was made manifest in *I'm So Bored with the U.S.A.* from their 1977 debut album. By 1982 though, everything had altered, and they were effusively enamoured by American culture. Whilst Malcolm McLaren would attempt later in the year to capture the eclectic array of culture in New York, The Clash had already journeyed the same path in 1980 with their *Sandinista* album, mixing disco, funk, rock and roll, dub, and punk. Towards the end of 1981 guitarist Mick Jones took over production duties for their next release, and demanded the album be completed at Electric Lady Studios in New York, following disparate sessions in London over the previous few months. New York had become the dominant influence on Jones, and he was keen to fuse fundamentals of hip-hop into the sound. Meanwhile, vocalist Joe Strummer was wandering in the opposite direction, submerging himself in primeval rock and roll and rockabilly, and it was this tautness between old and new which would ultimately prove to be so efficacious on the album.

Despite the two chief songwriters pulling in contrasting directions, the principal problem facing The Clash at the start of 1982 was the heroin addiction of drummer Topper Headon. He had recently been arrested at Heathrow Airport baggage terminal, drawing attention to himself by being the only individual observing his baggage go around the carousel several times, and been fined £500 just before Christmas on the provision that treatment was pursued. In court, the judge had declared "*Unless you seek treatment, you will be the best drummer in the graveyard*". Following a short period in re-hab at The Priory, not least to permit the band to clear up visa issues regarding a forthcoming Japanese tour, Headon flew to New York to continue working on the album, and immediately fell back into his old habits.

The album, initially to be called *Rat Patrol from Fort Bragg*, needed to be complete by Friday 22nd January when the band were due to fly to Japan to start the tour. Upon arriving at the airport in Tokyo the following day Jones and Strummer were astounded to find scenes approximating Beatlemania awaiting them. Their Japanese promoter, Mr Udo[40], met them at the airport, and transported them to their hotel in the city centre. In the reception they enquired about procuring some weed, the *acceptable* drug of choice for most of the band and were informed by Mr Udo that inflexible Japanese drug laws meant there was no prospect of any being found. At this news Jones and

---

[40] Serjuri Udo is something of a legend in Japan. Every touring band went through him, and this ultra-polite middle-aged family man would do whatever it takes to ensure they received whatever they wanted. This included offering Ozzy Osbourne's band the opportunity to have their testicles sanded by Geishas, making sure Mötley Crüe got out of jail, and losing a fortune when Paul McCartney got busted for drugs.

Strummer burst into tears, a sure sign that their practise was a slight bit more than recreational. Mr Udo was humiliated at having let down his guests, a serious transgression in Japan, and commenced crying as well before offering to fly to Thailand and smuggle back the necessary merchandise. The band informed him not to bother. That night, after agitated and desperate phone calls and enquiries, the two were led to a club in Tokyo where it was understood they could purchase drugs. Once inside, the doors were sealed as Jones and Strummer were chaperoned to a miniscule backroom and presented with scarcely enough weed to create one joint. Strummer became furious, bellowing at the Japanese dealers, much to everybody's humiliation. Even Japanese drug dealers believed in dishonour. For the next ten days the band were required to function without drugs for the first time in years.

The following night The Clash played the first of seven successive nights at Shibuya Kohkaido in Japan, asserting they would not play unless the crowd were permitted to stand. This was the first time a Japanese audience had been allowed this freedom, and the local press professed the band *men of principle* for standing their ground.

24th – 30th January 1982

#1 single: Shakin' Stevens: Oh Julie!
#1 album: Barbra Streisand: Love Songs

North of the border, the notoriously grim and gritty city of Glasgow had been undergoing a transformation in the last handful of years. After the clearing of slum housing in the 1960's, the Council had fallen under the spell of Le Corbusier's concrete high-rise future, creating neoteric edifices to solitude and social alienation, before realising the error of their ways and switching to a program of restoration of formerly eschewed tenement buildings. "*Epidemics of stone-cleaning and tree-planting... transformed* [Glasgow's] *former blackness into chequered works of salmon pink, yellow and green,*" Ian Jack found on a visit to the city in 1982, "*Old buildings have been burnished and refitted. Museums, delicatessens and wine bars have opened, and thrive. New theatres occupy churches. There are business centres, sports centres, heritage centres, art centres.*"

Paralleling this renaissance, a new sound had also been stirring. Postcard Records had been started at the end of 1979 by Edwyn Collins and what John Peel described

as a "*horrible, truculent youth*", Alan Horne. Horne was a Glaswegian hustler who ran the label from a wardrobe in a tenement house for two years, signing bands such as Orange Juice (featuring Collins on vocals), Josef K, Aztec Camera, and Australia's Go-Betweens. The Postcard bands were wannabe art students who styled their label, with tongue firmly in cheek, as "*The sound of young Scotland*", an allusion to the Motown slogan. These acts were equally enthralled by the noise of the Velvet Underground and the pop of Motown, creating music that was percipient, sardonically romantic, full of jangly guitars, and most importantly not like anything that had come out of Glasgow before. They were enormously influential on many of the acts from the city for the next decade and beyond, with their anti-macho rock stance.

Orange Juice were the flagship act of the label, and through a succession of critically acclaimed singles had built their reputation enough for them to sign to Polygram in late 1981. The first thing they did was to release a version of Al Green's *L.O.V.E. Love*, a move premeditated to purposefully provoke the post-punk crowd, and a dramatic lurch away from the abrasive sound of the last few years towards a pop-soul direction. Taking their Gretsch guitars the band then set about recording their debut album with former Blockheads producer Adam Kidron smoothing the uneven edges. Collins first choices had been John Fogerty or Alex Chilton, neither of whom were even approached. In January they released another single, *Felicity*, which reached number sixty-three in the charts. Within this single, and the album released immediately in its wake (*You Can't Hide Your Love Forever*) were the seeds of many of the acts of the coming decade, from the self-depreciating lyrics and jangly chiming guitars being a huge influence on the Smiths, to the mixture of horns and guitars being used more triumphantly by the Style Council.

Felicity is a song which gets more thrilled with itself as it goes on, with scratchy guitars and lyrics exclaiming "*This is the sound of happiness*". There is a sagacity in the use of the line "*Take me to the bridge*" in debt to James Brown, just as the band go into the bridge of the song. The album was teeming with such moments, a concoction of innocent dumbness and perceptive allusions, and with a major label behind them and support from people such as John Peel, managed to climb to number twenty-one in the album charts.

The album had initially been recorded the previous summer at Regent's Park Studios in London and bankrolled by Rough Trade who were of the understanding they would be the ones to release it. The title was borrowed from a line in *Hi Dear* by Jonathan Richman and the Modern Lovers, and the recordings reveal a band who had suddenly been given a bit of a budget but did not quite know what to do with it. Horns were brought in, female backing vocalists employed, and future Curiosity Killed the Cat keyboard players called upon, all of which could not camouflage a band playing at the limit of the studiously amateur abilities. There are some cracking songs such as the self-mocking opener *Falling and Laughing* or the ballad *Untitled Melody* whose guitars drew from the third and fourth Velvet Underground albums. There are also tracks which sound good but are missing a killer melody, such as the James Kirk-written *Wan Light* or *Satellite City*, the latter about the disco located above the Glasgow Apollo where Orange Juice were playing early in 1978 when they were first discovered by Alan Horne. However, the roguish, knowing, discerning lyrics shine through, best demonstrated on cynical love song *Consolation Prize* in which Collins declares "*I wore my fringe like Roger McGuinn's*" whilst stating "*A thousand violins will play it for you while you sit and roll your deep blue eyes*". The band loved tempo changes and precarious vocals, with uncluttered meandering guitars emphasising Collins unsure anti-virile stance which is summed up with the repeated line "*I'll never be man enough for you*". Throughout the album there are self-condolatory songs of love, but at the end all is redeemed by final track *In a Nutshell* with its charming chorus of "*Goodness gracious, you're so audacious*" showcasing a band who were not panicked by literacy.

The cover of the album was originally meant to have a group photograph taken by Jill Furmanovsky, however this was scrapped at the last minute when guitarist James Kirk and drummer Steven Daly left[41], and replaced with an image of two dolphins leaping from the water. In a pop music culture partially influenced by Orange Juice's turn away

---

[41] Steven Daly: "*Strange mix of personalities in the group, to be fair. We actually invented 'social distancing'.*"

from punk towards danceable pop, others were barging through the door the band opened, and there was a danger they would be left behind.

One such band cultivating a parallel jangly furrow, albeit in a more *preppy* way, were Haircut 100. The story goes that they were formed when three of the band were dumped by their girlfriends on the same day, however this turned out to be a press agent myth, one that simultaneously let the teenage girls know that the band were single, moderately vulnerable, and requiring mothering. Such press stories did little to help the band be taken seriously by other musicians, a problem stoked by their appearance: all plus-fours and cricket jumpers secured over their shoulders by the sleeves.

Despite seeming to come out of nowhere, the band had been formed in 1977 by singer and guitarist Nick Heyward along with school friend and bass player Les Nemes when they were sixteen years old, developing through several names until they emerged in 1980 as Haircut 100 along with Graham Jones (guitar), Pat Hunt (drums), Phil Smith

(saxophone), and Mark Fox (percussion). Signing to Arista Records, the band reached the top five with their debut single *Favourite Shirts* in the second half of 1981, and by the start of 1982 when Hunt had been replaced by Memphis drummer Blair Cunningham, the band had a contagious new single ready to go.

Love Plus One was one of those tracks that is an irrefutably dazzling pop song, one that you could not help but like, regardless of the marimba riff[42], jangly guitars, and saxophone solo. The words were nonsensical, with two of the lines being nothing more than "*Ay ay ay ay ay ay*", though a story later did the rounds that the song was written about the Falklands War. Given that it was released two months before that conflict kicked off, some people had obviously fallen for a Nick Heyward practical joke.

Everything about the song that should irk you is also what made it so marvellous. Who could help themselves singing "*Ay ay ay ay ay ay*" along with the song? Of course, the ascent of the song to number three in the charts was helped by Heyward's lost-puppy-dog looks, a feature the record company were eager to exploit, insisting he make an appearance in the video wearing nothing but a loincloth.

Musically, the song was accomplished with the band sounding admirably tight throughout and a considered arrangement which allowed the track to build and peak at the perfect times. If ever there was a position advertised for a perfect pop song, *Love Plus One* would be on the shortlist.

ʊ ʊ ʊ

Ozzy Osbourne had just entered the stage from his usual pyramid and clutched the microphone stand with both hands at the Assembly Hall in Champaign, Illinois, on Tuesday 26th January, when he started to feel unwell. As the opening notes of *Over the Mountain* rang out, he sang two words, and then collapsed. The audience assumed it was part of the show, and the cheers raised the roof before Ozzy was pulled offstage by girlfriend Sharon Arden and members of the road crew, assisted by the stage-dwarf John Allan dressed in a monk's outfit. As the band completed the song Ozzy was rushed to Carle Clinic and the rest of the concert cancelled.

---

[42] The Marimba was played by producer Bob Sargent *"who loved to play on the records he produced"* according to Nick Heyward.

In hospital, it became clear the rabies shot he had received a couple of days previously after biting the head off a dead bat had reacted with the quantity of alcohol and drugs in his body, and he was ordered to rest for a few days. The following night's show in St Louis was cancelled, after which the tour continued.

ʊ ʊ ʊ

In the same week Haircut 100's *Love Plus One* first appeared in the top seventy-five, a song by a band called Modern Romance, *Queen of the Rapping Scene (Nothing Ever Goes the Way You Plan)*, also entered the charts. Both bands were mining a pop-funk seam with one eye set assuredly on the charts, and the other on the dancefloor.

Modern Romance had their roots in a new wave act called The Leyton Buzzards and even managed to appear on *Top of the Pops* with their single *Saturday Night (Beneath*

the Plastic Palm Trees). When the band split, vocalist Geoff Deane and bass player David Jaymes formed Modern Romance, aiming for a salsa and funk-based sound inspired by the Blitz scene that was the buzz of London at the time. The band hit the top twenty twice in 1981 with *Everybody Salsa* and *Ay Ay Ay Ay Moosey*, songs that did the band's credibility no good but did manage to add to the office party atmosphere.

Queen of the Rapping Scene was the last single from their debut album and was without a doubt the most outstanding song on it. For a short time, it seemed Modern Romance might be able to salvage their reputation with the track, a choice piece of pop-funk. The first half of the song featured vocals by Deane and concerned the end of a relationship and the start of a fresh, superior one, until the song morphed into a rap by French national Juliet Hetreed. Neither the lyrics in the first half, or the words of the rap were particularly memorable, but what was interesting is that for many people in the United Kingdom this would have been one of the first examples of rap they had heard.

The common story is that rap emerged from the streets of New York in the late 1970's, inspired by Jamaican immigrants who brought with them sound-systems and *toasting*. Whilst there is a large amount of truth in this, rap had existed without a name for hundreds of years before in the form of stories told over rhythms by West African griots. This style was incorporated into early jazz and blues, and can be seen in the poetry of boxer Mohammad Ali and the music of Gil Scott Heron in the 1960's. The development from rap into what we now call hip-hop on the other hand, *can* be traced to New York in the late 1970's, and from there through the work of people such as the Sugarhill Gang and Kurtis Blow, started to become both better known and influential. Rap hits in Britain, however, had so far been few and far between. *Rapper's Delight* by the Sugarhill Gang, with lyrical poetry spun on top of a rhythm taken from extended mixes of a Chic track was one of the few, along with mixed results by white artists who were some of the early absorbers of the style, such as *Rapture* by Blondie or the abominable *Ant Rap*[43] by Adam & The Ants.

Queen of the Rapping Scene was one of the more tolerable efforts of appropriation by white acts, with the DNA of the song sharing more in common with the French stylings of the previous year's *I've Seen That Face Before* by Grace Jones than New York rap.

---

[43] If there is one song I advise you NOT to check out from 1982... it would be this one. And if that is not enough to make you search for it on YouTube, then nothing will stop you.

ʊ ʊ ʊ

In the New Romantic cosmos Spandau Ballet were the top dogs, being the *house band* at the Blitz Club. Their amalgam of funk and pop over the previous couple of years had served them well, however success was now starting to dwindle. The band had been on the go under various names and styles since 1976, after being formed by guitarists Gary Kemp (who had been in all the right places at all the right times: seeing Ziggy Stardust announce his retirement in 1973, attending the Sex Pistols celebrated

Screen on the Green concert in 1976, absorbing it all) and Steve Norman. By the turn of the decade, they had settled on a line-up which also included Tony Hadley on vocals, John Keeble on drums, and Kemp's younger brother Martin on bass, the latter of whom had been asked to join because he was the coolest person they knew and was a sure-fire hit with girls wherever he went. Taking their name from the prison in Berlin where Nazi war-criminals were held after the Second World War[44] – the *ballet* was the dance they did at the end of a rope when condemned to death by hanging – the band became enmeshed in the blossoming New Romantic scene in London, and in mid-1980 they were the subject of a fierce bidding war by record companies. They eventually signed to Chrysalis Records on the condition a video was created for each release, and their debut single about male prostitution, *To Cut a Long Story Short,* went straight into the top ten. This was followed by a couple more hit singles and a top ten debut album, all produced by former singer with Landscape[45], Richard James Burgess.

The first new track from the band after this was an infective portion of funk called *Chant No. 1 (I Don't Need This Pressure)*, which reached number three, abetted by the horns from British band Beggar & Co, however in the most recent six months things were not looking so auspicious. The next single, *Paint Me Down*, only reached number thirty, and their new single *She Loved like Diamond*, peaked at number forty-nine.

It is no wonder the song failed to break the top forty, opening like the theme tune to some abysmal daytime talk show, and containing none of the determination or exhilaration that had made their early singles stand out. Even once the song got going it sounded languid, typical of *second album syndrome*. The band soldiered on, finishing the album in the overly optimistic assumption that this might halt the premature rot in their career. Amongst their club contemporaries they were now being mocked for being *bland* instead of *banned*.

Chris Wright at Chrysalis Records informed his staff that Spandau Ballet were finished.

ʊ ʊ ʊ

---

[44] Spandau Prison was used by Hitler to house opponents and critics *"for their own protection"* until they were transferred to concentration camps. After the Second World War Nazi war criminals were held there. Between 1966 and 1987 Rudolf Hess was the only remaining inmate, guarded by warden Eugene Bird. When Hess committed suicide in August 1987, to stop it becoming a Neo-Nazi shrine the prison was demolished and ground into dust before being dumped in the North Sea. A supermarket and parking lot was built on the site, which gained the nickname *Hessco*.

[45] Landscape had a hit in 1981 with *Einstein-a-Go-Go*. Their bass player went on to write the theme tune for television show *The Bill*, whilst trombone player Peter Thoms can be heard on Thomas Dolby's *Hyperactive* single.

Malcolm McLaren was always an ambiguous and chimerical character, but to see his motives and *modus operandi* you only need look at the Goldsmith's Free Festival in 1969. McLaren, a post-war baby raised by his grandmother, meandered through various art colleges in London during the 1960's, managing to get himself kicked out or becoming bored and deliberately moving on. McLaren would later self-mythologize himself into the Paris student riots of May 1968, however the truth was he visited the city in August of that year, months afterwards. Still, inspired by political revolution and the Situationists he came up with the idea of a free festival at Goldsmiths College in 1969. Advertised as featuring performances by The Rolling Stones, Pink Floyd, John Lennon, The Pretty Things, and King Crimson, readings by Alexander Trocchi and William Burroughs, dance by Lindsay Kemp, and a lecture by R.D. Laing, very few of the acts had even been booked, and the 20,000 people who turned up in place of the expected 2,000 soon over-ran the campus. McLaren hoped the large crowd's dissatisfaction at the *no-shows* would lead to insurgent disturbance, however despite the chaos the event was considered a success. McLaren, himself, was nowhere to be seen on the day.

McLaren was all about the event and the chaos, Situationist pranks, and then the disappearing act. His notoriously short attention span meant he opened a series of clothing shops with his partner Vivienne Westwood during the 1970's, retaining the same location at 430 Kings Road, London, but changing the name and style, from *Let It Rock* to *Too Fast to Live, Too Young to Die*, to *SEX*. During this he also became embroiled with The New York Dolls, an American proto-punk glam act, claiming to be their manager in 1975, a claim which everyone else involved denies.

Meanwhile, McLaren was grooming a British mob of young illiterate dropouts and petty thieves, who by 1976 were called The Sex Pistols and creating an almighty stir in the capital. Throughout that year they caused the revolution McLaren had long desired, becoming enemies of the people through their energetic and angry music, inspiring a whole movement of acts who picked up on the *do-it-yourself* attitude and disillusionment with the status quo, bands such as The Damned, The Clash, and The Buzzcocks, not to mention countless individuals who would go on to dominate the music and fashion industry over the following decade.

As their manager, McLaren courted and encouraged the controversy, however by mid-1977 when the Sex Pistols were at their commercial peak, his short attention span kicked in and he had already moved onto the idea of making a movie about the band. Or rather, about himself and how he had duped the entire music industry. By the time *The Great Rock & Roll Swindle* was completed McLaren had once again moved on, this time to Paris, and was producing soundtracks for pornographic movies, though this latest move might have been inspired by a fear of criminal prosecution.

Whilst in Paris, McLaren started writing a screenplay called *The Adventures of Melody, Lyric & Tune*, a soft-core porn rock and roll movie for kids, featuring three fifteen-year-old girls having sex at various locations in the French capital. As you would expect no one would touch the screenplay, however McLaren had also composed the lyrics to several projected songs on the soundtrack and was on the lookout for a band to write the music. That is when Adam Ant approached McLaren at a wedding with a proposal. As the frontman of the punk band Adam & The Ants, the real named Stuart Goddard was frustrated by his lack of musical progress and asked McLaren for advice. McLaren agreed to provide a month of advisory help on image, music, and direction for a fee of £1,000. He partitioned Ant from the band and spent hours coaching him on his latest idea: piracy. McLaren viewed the recently invented cassette tape as an emancipating force for teenagers; they could record music direct from the radio rather than buy singles and albums, and this would generate a revolution in the industry which would eventually bring it down. In McLaren's eyes, the kids were the new pirates, plundering what did not belong to them.

Meanwhile, McLaren advised the rest of the band to start using the Burundi beat[46], drumming created by tribal musicians in Rwanda, and arranged for classically trained member of The Penguin Café Orchestra Simon Jeffries[47] to teach them African polyrhythm. McLaren also provided a tape of disparate styles, from Gary Glitter, music of Turkey, and Hare Krishna chants, to Burundi drums, which opened the band to new horizons. What subsequently happened in the rehearsal room was relatively remarkable, as in a short period of time drummer Dave Barbarossa locked in with newly joined bass player Lee Gorman[48], who brought his experience in funk bands to the sound. The two of them created a puissant rhythm section over which guitarist Matthew Ashman could improvise whatever he wanted, as long as it was influenced by surf guitar and Ennio Morricone's spaghetti western soundtracks. The band were expected to have two finished pieces of music each day by three o'clock, at which time Adam would turn up. An hour later McLaren would arrive, and over a couple of weeks the *Svengali* realised that the band, and in particular the rhythm section, were something special, but that the singer had to go.

The axe fell in January 1980 when the band were persuaded to sack Adam from his own band. The deed was done in the rehearsal room during the sort of tense scene McLaren revelled in, and Adam left in tears. The new manager chased after the singer, adding insult to injury by offering him a job as hairstylist for the band, who were now to be called Bow Wow Wow.

McLaren remained enthralled by the idea of kids and musicians as modern-day buccaneers and encouraged Westwood to start taking inspiration for her home-made clothing range from the post-revolutionary French Directory between 1795 and 1799; *les Incroyables et les Merveilleuses*. This was an outburst of luxury and decadence following the *reign of terror*, in which the upper classes re-established their prominence and gangs of dandyish perfumed boys roamed the streets. McLaren insisted on a pirate influence in the look, as Westwood spent weeks in the British Library sourcing inspiration. Her trend for dressing up (after the dressing down of punk, whose look she had invented) chimed with what was going on in London at the time in clubs such as Blitz.

As always McLaren claimed the kudos whilst Westwood put the work in, and the same was true with Bow Wow Wow. The manager was under the illusion he had written all the songs just because their lyrics were loosely based on his ideas. He would lecture them on style and music, encouraging them into sleeping with prostitutes to deliberately corrupt them into sexual perversion.

McLaren was determined to recruit a young female singer and considered Kate Garner and Kirsty McColl before discovering fourteen-year-old half-Burmese singer Annabella Lwin working in his local laundrette. McLaren immediately begin exploiting the youth of the singer, even encouraging members of the band to take her virginity.

Signing to EMI, their first single was called *C30-C60-C90-Go!* and celebrated the relatively new music format of the cassette tape. Thirty minutes, sixty minutes, and ninety minutes were the standard length of cassette tapes and were universally viewed by the industry at the time as being the paramount threat to profits, encouraging

---

[46] The drummer was ordered to lose his hi-hat, cymbals and snare drum and allow the floor tom to dominate.

[47] Simon Jeffries arranged the brilliantly effective strings for Sid Vicious and his version of *My Way*.

[48] Gorman had learned to play every instrument going when he was given free run of Marc Bolan's stage equipment. He joined 57 Men who featured Glen Gregory (later of Heaven 17) and various subsequent members of Wang Chung.

individuals to record songs from the radio rather than purchase them. Bow Wow Wow's debut single went even further, making it desirable to do this very thing by releasing it on cassette only, the first cassette single in the world, and with a blank B-side for recording onto.

Listening to Bow Wow Wow's first few singles now, one cannot help but be impressed with just how ahead of their time they were, with a percussion-led sound mixed with surf guitar and post-modern self-referential lyrics, amalgamated with aspects of numerous cultures that would ultimately come to be called *world music*. Years later, artists like M.I.A. would steal liberally from this sound.

Sowing dissent in the ranks is one of McLaren's well-tried tactics, and in spring 1981 he hired an unknown DJ from Planets Disco by the name of Boy George to be a second singer in Bow Wow Wow, mostly to frighten Lwin who was *being difficult* by expressing independent opinions. Appearing under the name Lieutenant Lush, George lasted three gigs before being thrown out of the band.

McLaren, meanwhile, tried to launch a magazine for thirteen-year-olds called *Playkids*, with articles about crime as a career option, as well as one on prostitutes, how much

they cost and where to find them. McLaren then changed the name to *Chicken*, paedophile slang for young girls, and tried to get some to pose nude. His co-editor Fred Vermorel became more and more uncomfortable with the suggestions and eventually quit, warning the music press and police about McLaren's activities.

Throughout 1981 Bow Wow Wow became an assiduously proficient band, with a formidable tight sound, and moved from EMI to RCA, who saw their potential as a chart act. Pairing them with decent producers the band became more and more like regular musicians, an angle McLaren abhorred. He started to withdraw from the band as a manager, disinterested in the day-to-day organisation of a rock and roll act. McLaren did, however, continue to push his repugnant paedophilia angle with their next album, *See Jungle! See Jungle! Go Join Your Gang Yeah, City All Over! Go Ape Crazy!* by insisting the album cover should be a recreation of Edouard Manet's painting *Le dejeuner sur l'herbe*, with fourteen-year-old Lwin posing nude at Box Hill, Surrey. This led ultimately to Lwin's mother reporting McLaren to the police for exploitation of a minor for immoral purposes, and in a different era a gentleman's agreement was made between the authorities and the manager not to push Lwin as a *sex kitten*.

The album was released in October 1981, but it was January 1982 before we saw a hit single in the form of *Go Wild in the Country*. The song, which McLaren refused to accept would ever be a hit[49], is a cry for a return to nature, "*Sick of seeing signs to eat walking down these lonely streets*". Lwin later sings "*I don't need no hamburgers, no take-away, I want my own game…I want to go hunting and fishing*" and coupled with the frenetic tribal drumming suggests a longing for something more primitive than modern life[50]. The look of the band added to the overall effect, with Lwin's Mohawk and clothes by Vivienne Westwood tapping into the primitive. By January, Lwin had

---

[49] Bill Kimber at RCA insisted the band move the chorus closer to the front, which McLaren was dead set against. Kimber and the band won that argument.

[50] McLaren's hands were all over the line "*I can get a plane, I don't need no suitcases cos truth loves to go naked*", a corruption of an 18th century proverb "*Craft must have clothes but truth loves to go naked*" which he wrongly attributed to Jean-Jacques Rousseau and considered as a name for his shop.

turned sixteen and had become independent from her mother, giving consent for the nude shots to be used on the single cover[51].

Despite all these elements feeding into the narrative, the song stands on its own as a great example of pop, with a sing-along chorus and copious amounts of vitality, one that still sounds fantastic now, particularly when played at volume.

RCA realised that the way to break Bow Wow Wow was to exploit their live sound and set up a series of tours throughout 1982. Immediately following the single release, the band headed to the United States for a tour supporting The Police, followed by European dates with Queen which they had to leave early due to a poor reception from the audience. McLaren left the day-to-day running of the operation to tour manager Andy Corrigan and assistant Rory Johnston, who then took over the job full time.

McLaren had already discovered his next venture back in 1981 when Michael Holman, a junior credit analyst on Wall Street [52], had taken him to the Bronx River Projects to see Afrika Bambaataa and the Zulu Nations perform. McLaren, ever the cultural magpie, was transfixed by the performance and asked the act to open for Bow Wow Wow at the Ritz downtown. Along with Bambaataa, Fab 5 Freddie created graffiti live on stage, alongside break-dancers the Rock Steady Crew, in an immersive hip-hop experience that thrilled the mostly white punk and new wave audience. This was the trigger for McLaren to attempt a solo musical career, signing a deal with Charisma Records early in 1982.

ʊ ʊ ʊ

Northern Ireland had always been a dilemma for the British Government, even before it was a country. When the ruling Catholic Aristocracy fled under pressure in 1607, the territory became deliberately populated by the Presbyterian Scottish and Anglican English, with any dissent violently crushed, such as the Siege of Derry and the Battle of the Boyne. After institutionalised government-enforced discrimination against Catholics for over two-hundred years, Home Rule seemed inevitable only being blocked by the House of Lords. As the act was about to be passed by parliament, the First World War broke out and it was postponed. By the end of the war in 1918, the Easter Rising two years earlier had transformed public opinion in Ireland away from Home Rule towards outright independence. The problem lay in the north east where a Protestant majority remained loyal to the British crown, and the decision was made to partition the country, with twenty-six counties granted independence and ruled by Dublin, and six remaining under British control, ruled from Belfast. Certain powers were devolved to an Ulster parliament at Stormont, which tended to be dominated by the Protestant-approved Unionist Party.

There remained a sizeable Catholic minority within these six British counties who were discriminated against in terms of housing, jobs, policing, and electoral procedures. When the Northern Ireland Civil Rights Association formed in 1967, basing itself upon the Civil Rights movement in the United States, a campaign of domestic intransigence was started. Emotions on both sides boiled over, with the Provisional Irish Republican Army (who demanded a united Ireland) and Ulster Volunteer Force (who demanded rule by London) committing appalling acts of violence. Into this came various other splinter groups such as the Ulster Defence Army and the Irish National Liberation Army, all of whom could be intensely homicidal. The British Government, army and police professed themselves neutral in the situation, however it was later confirmed they had

---

[51] I bought this single and felt the need to hide it away from my parents due to the cover.

[52] Holman was so much more than a junior analyst, being embroiled with the Downtown New York scene in the early 1980's. He was the first person to use the phrase *hip-hop* in print.

colluded with Protestant organisations in cases of murder, as had been suspected all along.

Both sides began downward-spiralling campaigns of terror determined to vanquish the other, and the 1970's in Northern Ireland had been blighted by what became known as *the troubles*. Hundreds of people, many of them civilians, lost their lives during the decade, with an amplifying helicoid of repercussions, reaching a peak in 1972 when 467 died, leading to the suspension of the Stormont parliament and direct rule from London introduced. Whilst attempts at a ceasefire met with varying degrees of success, by the late 1970's many in the country were war-weary. The IRA stepped up their political campaign in the early 1980's with a series of hunger strikes in HM Prison Maze, the result of the Special Category (Prisoner of War) Status being removed from the inmates. The strikes caused the death of ten prisoners, a couple of whom had been elected to parliament whilst incarcerated, however it became a face-off between the IRA and Margaret Thatcher which she took as a victory when it was called off in late-1981.

Whilst the many paramilitary groups in Northern Ireland would argue their causes were political, they usually operated in the same way as organised crime gangs, carving up business for themselves and keeping their own *troops* in line with intimidation and violent action. In January 1982, internal housekeeping seemed to be the order of the day, with the Ulster Defence Army shooting dead two of their own as the result of a dispute, and the Irish Republican Army executing one of their members who was suspected of being an informant.

Not that they were taking it easy on the opposition: Off-duty Ulster Defence Regiment soldier Steven Carleton was shot dead whilst at his part-time job in a petrol station in Belfast, and Loyalist John McKeague was killed by the Republican Irish National Liberation Army supposedly as a result of him about to go public regarding child abuse at the Kincora Boys Home.

ʊ ʊ ʊ

A Certain Ratio were everything the serious music critic loves: po-faced, obscure, and flying in the face of fashion. Having started out in 1977 as a Mancunian punk band, by the time they signed to Factory Records two years later the act had added a substantial funk component to their sound brought in by drummer and percussionist Donald Johnson and the slapping bass of Jeremy Kerr. Described by Factory supremo Tony Wilson as *"having all the energy of Joy Division but better clothes"* the band could be perceived as one of the frontrunners on the label when it came to dance music, having spent some time hanging out in New York clubs whilst recording their debut album in New Jersey, and even having a dancefloor hit with their single *Shack Up* the previous year. Previous releases had been overseen by Factory in-house producer Martin Hannett, who insisted they play *"faster but slower"*, however the working relationship had now come to an end, with Kerr explaining *"We'd had loads of disagreements with him. Now, I realise he was a genius, but at the time I thought he was an arsehole"*.

New album, *Sextet*, was produced by the band themselves in two weeks of solitude at a house in Cheshire, and the recruitment of new singer Martha Tilson allowed leader Simon Topping to concentrate on his trumpet playing. The funk of *Lucinda* opened the album, with Tilson's flat vocals inimical to the unkempt enthusiasm of the music. There was space in the second track *Crystal* echoing Hannett's production style, aided by Topping's reticent introspective singing, and one could hear an undeviating filament between this and what Tricky was doing fifteen years later.

The putative highlight of the album was the seven-minute *Knife Slits Water* which was re-recorded as a single before the end of the year, this time without the departed Tilson's vocals. Throughout the album Tilson's vocals seemed disconnected from the music, often hovering through them, sometimes behind the beat, and occasionally lacking a melody. The samba-party atmosphere of the drums was antonymous to the vocals which sounded like the most miserable carnival ever. Critical mass was reached with the release, which entered the album charts at number fifty-three, before slipping back out again.

Returning for a headline date in 1982 to promote the album in New York, A Certain Ratio were supported by a singer called Madonna, who insisted on them moving their equipment. *"We had never seen anyone come onstage without a band. It was just her and her two dancers"* explained Kerr, *"When she asked us to move our gear, we told her to fuck off!"*

With the departure of Tilson, the band started to fall apart with a further two members leaving before the year was out, just after their disappointing hurried third album *I'd Like to See You Again*. However, *Sextet* remained their essential declaration, and despite a long, productive, and hitless career, their embracing of *rhythm* would ultimately lead to a transformation in label-mates New Order.

ʊ ʊ ʊ

At the climax of his *Diary of a Madman* show, Ozzy Osbourne took to hurling cuts of raw meat into the audience by using a specially developed *meat catapult*. After a couple of performances, it became apparent that whenever Ozzy launched the catapult most of the offal and organs would hit him on the back of the head, enmeshing in his hair.

The next logical step was to have John Allan, a dwarf hired as a stage prop for the tour, throw the off cuts from a bucket of slop, and this worked without problems until a show at the Indiana Hulman Centre in Terre Haute, Indiana on Friday 29th January. The meat usually arrived at the venue frozen, and if not fully thawed was in danger of becoming a dangerous weapon when thrown. This night Allan found a defrosted long piece of tripe in the bucket and whirled it around his head before letting fly towards a female member of the audience. As it wrapped around her neck she screamed, prompting her boyfriend to pick up a frozen liver and launched it back towards the stage, where it hit the dwarf on the forehead, knocked him out cold. Allan was dragged off stage by a member of the roadcrew and rushed to the emergency room where he received twelve stitches.

ʊ ʊ ʊ

Like A Certain Ratio, other British acts who experienced punk and were turning to dance and funk were looking across the Atlantic for their influences, and for the past ten years dance music had been synonymous with *disco*. Disco, as a genre, had its roots in the late 1960's and early 1970's, when gay black and Latino men would frequent private clubs to dance without fear of harassment by the police or the public. In these clubs the beat became everything as disc jockeys began to have extended versions of songs pressed on twelve-inch vinyl where the expansive grooves would make the music sound more powerful than a standard seven-inch record[53]. After 1974 the genre made inroads towards the mainstream, reaching a peak with the release of the movie *Saturday Night Fever* at the end of 1977, by which point the music held dominance over the pop charts. By the end of the decade, old white rock acts such as Rod Stewart, Kiss, and The Rolling Stones dabbled in the genre, a reliable sign it was not *cool* anymore, however it was the ascent of the *Disco Sucks* movement which caused the most damage. The pinnacle of this backlash came on the 12th July 1979 when Chicago radio DJ Steve Dahl organised a Disco Demolition Night at Comisky Park, home of the Chicago White Sox baseball team, during one of their matches. He encouraged people to bring their disco records to be blown up in the centre of the pitch. Over 50,000 people turned up, mostly white and male, and joined in a riot after the demolition, ripping up seats and setting fire to parts of the stadium. Much has been made of the racist, homophobic, and misogynist motivation for the backlash: disco was considered the music of blacks, Latinos, homosexuals, and women, and it is challenging not to view things in this way. The anti-disco protestors wanted white rock and country music back in the charts and on their radio, and the media sat up and took notice. Media outlets reported on the event with elation, and within two months multitudes of disco stations had switched to rock and the genre had all-but disappeared from the Billboard Top 100. This mood of conservatism continued in the United States into the next decade, as witnessed by the swing to the right and the election of Ronald Reagan.

The death of disco did, however, have an unexpected bonus: it forced dance music back underground into the black and LGBT clubs, allowing it to modify and mature, and eventually re-emerged in Chicago and Detroit clubs, the spawn of which took over the music industry over the next thirty years.

ʊ ʊ ʊ

Fifteen-year-old Richard Skrenta loved computers and was equally fascinated with writing code. His friends were aware of his penchant for practical jokes through the various computer games discs they swapped, which when opened would often display a taunting message inserted by Skrenta.

Over his Christmas holidays, Richard had developed something else; something unique. *Elk Cloner* was a boot-sector virus, which meant it copied itself onto the operating system of a computer and from there infected every disc subsequently inserted. The virus itself was relatively harmless, merely displaying a poem on the screen announcing itself.

Richard first passed an infected disc on to a friend on Saturday 30th January, and then sat back and watched as it spread. In 1982, kids in America were continually swapping discs with games on them so the spread of the programme was quick.

A ninth grader had just invented and released the first ever computer virus.

ʊ ʊ ʊ

In January 1982, as always, there was a deluge of terrible songs in the top seventy-five, from unexceptional imports from the United States such as *Landslide* by Olivia Newton John, *Trouble* by Fleetwood Mac frontman Lindsay Buckingham, or *We've Got Tonight* by Bob Seger, to feeble disco and soul such as *Let's Celebrate* by New York Skyy, to light fluff such as future chart-topper *The Lion Sleeps Tonight* by Tight Fit, to former Motown greats now producing middle-of-the-road silage such as *Mirror Mirror*

---

[53] The wider grooves created louder music with more bass resonance. Perfect for dancefloors.

and *Tenderness* by Diana Ross and *That Girl* by Stevie Wonder. Things were not much healthier across the Atlantic where it seemed impossible to be British and score a hit if you were under the age of thirty. America still enjoyed its music to suit the conservative appetite of the mid-west, with the musicians having beards and / or Nashville credentials. The only British acts to be in the Billboard Hot 100 in January were Genesis, The Rolling Stones, the Bee Gees, Ringo Starr, Cliff Richard, and Lulu: hardly a line-up that would lead you to believe Britain was a youthful stimulating place. That is not to say the Americans did not know how to make exquisite pop songs, as demonstrated by two new entries to the British charts.

Daryl Hall[54] and John Oates had first played together in 1967 at Philadelphia's Temple University[55], but did not start working together earnestly until 1970 once Oates returned from a prolonged sojourn in Europe. The first few albums for Atlantic Records failed to find their own sound, however they became increasingly influenced by their hometown's Philadelphia soul, with an emphasis on string arrangements. This schooling in what makes a song popular and memorable helped the duo attract attention as the decade ended, and by 1981 they had racked up a string of hits in America but still not touched the top forty in Britain. Exasperated at filtering their music through an external producer in Los Angeles, the two decided to produce themselves

in New York where they both now lived. These recordings led to a run of chart toppers in the States, and breakthrough singles in Britain. The first couple, *Kiss from My Lips* and *Private Eyes* stalled just outside the top thirty, but it was the next one, *I Can't Go for That*, which took them into the top ten.

For their new album, *Private Eyes*, Hall and Oates were working with the finest session musicians around, people who had played with Peter Gabriel, David Bowie, and Michael Jackson, however for *I Can't Go for That* they stripped the sound right back, due to the way the song was written. Hall recorded the bass on a Korg organ, adding a drum machine, and then the duo built the song up around that rhythm, an offbeat way of working for old hands such as Hall and Oates. No other musicians were required, and large segments of the song were recorded before it was written, a method which would become standard practice in future years.

The song appears to deal with a relationship gone wrong, however Hall later admitted "*That song is really about not being pushed around by big labels, managers, and agents and being told what to do, and being true to yourself creatively*", whilst Oates rather more poetically claimed it was "*a metaphoric to the personal and professional pressures coming at us from every angle*". Its strength is in a mesmerizing rhythm provided by the drum machine, along with a bass line so good that Michael Jackson admitted to stealing it for *Billie Jean* later that year, where it is often cited as one of the finest bass lines ever recorded.

The song reached number eight in the British charts, and renewed interest in their *Private Eyes* album which also reached the same number over the next couple of months. The single had competition in the *American Pop* category over the next month from another hit by a veteran.

---

[54] Daryl Hall was memorably described by Dylan Jones as "*looking like a market-town hairdresser*", which was kinder than his description of John Oates as "*Super Mario's smaller, uglier brother*".

[55] Temple University has some interesting alumni besides Hall and Oates: sex offender Bill Cosby, serial killer Ted Bundy, linguist and activist Noam Chomsky, and .... Afroman.

Toni Basil was almost forty years old in 1982 and had already made a decent living from dancing and choreography. She had been a dancer on the American pop programme *Shindig!* in the early 1960's alongside best friend Teri Garr and was choreographer on several movies including The Monkees' *Head*. After appearing in *Easy Riders* Basil formed The Lockers in 1971, universally considered to be the most influential dance troupe in America, and the founders of what is now known as *street dance*. Basil continued to make a living choreographing for musicians throughout the 1970's, such as the *Diamond Dogs* tour for David Bowie and the music video for *Once in a Lifetime* for Talking Heads.

Whose idea it was for her to turn to singing has become lost in history, however her first single was a cover version of a Racey[56] album track from 1979 called *Kitty*. Basil went to work in the studio with producers Greg Mathieson and Trevor Veitch, changed

the name to *Mickey*, and added a segment in tribute to her cheerleading days in the early 1960's. The track was recorded using bass, keyboards, and guitar provided by new wave act Devo, along with respected drummer Ric Parnell[57]. Providing cheerleader vocals was Alee Willis, who would later write *I'll Be There for You*, the theme-tune to successful sitcom *Friends*.

The song was impossible to resist, from the introductory drums and incantation of "*Oh Mickey, you're so fine, you're so fine you blow my mind*", through to the twitching new wave musicianship recalling lost 1960's garage-pop hits. There was enough in this song for it to be taken different ways by different audiences, from the pre-teen girls to the hardened new-waver.

There has been a couple of myths developed around the lyrics of the song. The first is that the title was changed to *Mickey* because Basil was in love with Mickey Dolenz from The Monkees, however this turned out to be a Wikipedia contributor erroneously putting two and two together based upon her role in *Head*. The other myth concerns the line "*So come on and give it to me any way you can, any way you wanna do it I'll take you like a man*" which has been interpreted over the years to be a solicitation for anal sex. Basil of course, denies this, however her career would undoubtedly have brought her into close contact with the gay community and it is difficult to believe that she would not have realised the implications of the line.

The whole song when originally sung by a male voice was about a teasing girlfriend who ultimately exasperates her boyfriend, despite his best efforts to get her into bed. By altering gender, Basil appeared as a sexually liberated woman trying to encourage a man into bed, with lines such as "*There's something we can use, so don't say no*" referring to contraception.

The success of the song was helped by a memorable video featuring a troupe of cheerleaders, some of whom looked suspiciously like men in drag, against a white background, choreographed by Basil who appears as one of them herself. With hindsight it is hard not to see her in the clip as anything else by a very athletic over made-up middle-aged woman. Not that anyone cared at the time and the single rocketed up to number two, remaining a perennial favourite ever since.

---

[56] Racey had been a pop band who existed purely as a front for songs written by producers Mike Chapman and Nicky Chinn.

[57] Ric Parnell would later find greater fame as the ill-fated drummer Mick Shrimpton in the movie *This Is Spinal Tap*.

FEBRUARY

31st January – 6th February 1982

#1 single: Karftwerk: The Model / Computer Love
#1 album: Barbra Streisand: Love Songs

Whilst the Conservative government were determined to make swingeing financial cuts to scale down the traditional military the opposite was true when it came to a nuclear deterrent. Given the Soviet Union's enduring threat in Western Europe, Margaret Thatcher was resolved to keep some sort of missile defence, however the existing Polaris system was approaching the end of its lifespan, and it was obvious the replacement would come at great expense.

Initial discussions with President Jimmy Carter centred around the Trident missile, but when Ronald Reagan gained leadership of the United States in January 1981, his programme of modernising the strategic nuclear forces led to the development of Trident II. Like a customer who enters a showroom to buy a new car and is persuaded by the salesperson to go for the model up, Thatcher went willingly along with the upgrade. On Monday 1st February, she sent an official note to President Reagan to verify her interest in the new missiles, at a cost of £7.5 billion.

Anyone who lived through the 1980's recalls existing under the shadow of nuclear war. Ever since Hiroshima was flattened by atomic bomb *Little Boy* in 1945, the world had been in a rush for weapons of mass destruction. The Soviet Union and United States had been building a stockpile of weapons since the Second World War, both terrified the other was leading the *arms race*. Between 1945 and 1980 over 500 atmospheric nuclear weapons tests were conducted around the world, and by 1982 the United Kingdom, France, China, and India had also become nuclear states. Whilst the Reagan administration adopted a policy of not announcing future nuclear tests at their site in Nevada, the Soviet Union tested a total of thirty-five weapons in 1982, whilst the United Kingdom managed one.

Britain's desire to embrace nuclear weapons was not an ambition held by all. In 1980 thirty-three-year-old Ann Pettit had followed her husband from London to Wales and was existing as a mother and housewife, however the threat of nuclear power and the future of her two toddler sons was continually on her mind. Over the next year she involved herself in local anti-nuclear meetings and came to the realisation that "*nuclear weapons are going to get us a lot quicker*". Pettit hatched a plan to walk in protest from her home in South Wales to Greenham Common, the RAF Base at Molesworth, Cambridgeshire where Trident was due to be deployed, and began recruiting women to join her. A choice to preclude men from the protest came from a feeling that "*women felt differently about war and violence than did men, and… these feelings came from the fact that so many of us were mothers and carers for others*".

Starting at the end of August with thirty-six people the march accumulated media interest and public support. The women resolved along the way to continue the protest by chaining themselves to the fence upon arrival, in much the same way suffragettes had shackled themselves to railings outside Downing Street. A make-shift camp was set up around the perimeter of the base with temporary shelters, as the women took it in shifts to attach themselves to the fence. Many of the original walkers had left once reaching Greenham Common, however others from all over the country were drawn to the cause whilst supplies were donated by like-minded groups and organisations. Consciousness raising meetings were held at the camp daily as the women became politicised and plighted to the principles.

Some men were initially in attendance at the camp, however they were considered *"undesirables from the town"* who *"stumbled in… and wanted to buy a load of dope and cosy down for the winter"*. As time wore on it became apparent the men were more predisposed to strumming acoustic guitars and having a smoke, believing the domestic chores should be left to the women. In February 1982, after many lengthy meetings it was decided to ask the men to depart. At around this time, the land inside the base at Greenham Common began to change shape dramatically, as six silos were built to house the American missiles, turning Britain into a remote-controlled launcher.

ʊ ʊ ʊ

1982 was the wrong time for a band like REM, who specialised in good-time guitar-based music. The rise of the synthesiser had made them look dated from the moment of their formation just over a year previously, and even in their hometown of Athens, Georgia, the local music scene considered them a bit of a retro-joke. What they were skilled at, however, was travelling to bars in small towns and rocking the house for four non-stop hours, and it seems curious given how REM later evolved into a *serious* act that they were one of the premier party bands in the American Deep South, bringing the festivity wherever they played. Making people dance in small towns was not where they wanted to be, however, and a yearning for success took them to New York on Monday 1st February to record songs for RCA Records with producer Kurt Monkacsi. This was how record companies operated, paying for a potential signing to record some songs to see if they were viable. The band put down seven tracks in two days before heading back down Athens, whilst RCA swithered. REM would be a risk for the label with their sound contrary to current trends, and they decided to pass, leaving the band with the master tapes.

ʊ ʊ ʊ

Current trends being set in the United Kingdom were beginning to edge into the American Billboard Top 100, and there was a flicker of hope in the battle against facial hair and rhinestones at the lower end of the charts as Soft Cell skulked in with *Tainted Love*. The song, a chart topper in Britain the previous year, began a long lazy journey to number four, such an unhurried rise that it took nineteen weeks to even breach the top forty. For most Americans this would have been their introduction to music generated by technology and not guitars, and the first time they had been exposed to a frontman who philandered so brazenly with the limitations of sexuality. It was also the wedge, the initial foot in the door, for what would become acknowledged as the Second British Invasion. Not that singer Marc Almond was too keen on Stateside success, claiming *"America to me means manipulation, and manipulation is just not me at all. I often think that I just cannot last in America and I will not do these things that people want me to do."*

Soft Cell were the archetypal synth-pop duo, formed by Dave Ball[58], the tall reticent keyboard player, and Marc Almond, the diminutive gregarious singer, at Leeds Polytechnic in 1977. Almond was a homosexual Southport-born-and-raised child of a violent alcoholic father and had spent time in a psychiatric ward at the age of seventeen after an overly dramatic suicide attempt. Following one single financed by Ball's mother

---

[58] Ball grew up in Blackpool, attending the same school as Chris Lowe from The Pet Shop Boys. *"What was the likelihood of two 'other ones' from famous synth duos attending the same school in a northern seaside resort?"*

the band signed to Some Bizzare, a label run by the eccentric Stevo Pearce[59], which specialised in experimental electronic acts during the 1980's such as The The, Cabaret Voltaire, Psychic TV, and Test Department[60].

After a couple of unsuccessful singles, the duo was given their last chance by Some Bizzare's parent label, Phonogram, and decided to record an updated version of an obscure Northern Soul classic, *Tainted Love*. The single salvaged their career, becoming a massive world-wide hit and topping the charts in countless countries.

By January 1982 the band had hit the top five with follow-up single *Bedsitter* and their debut album, *Non-Stop Erotic Cabaret*. The title provided evidence of where Soft Cell were coming from, with songs such as *Seedy Films*, *Secret Life*, and *Sex Dwarf*. This was music from the dark hours, tunes from the late-night dives and strip clubs, words of sleaze, homosexuality, transgender, and the secret sexual rendezvous… and at the same time displayed a crisp, clean pop sound. The duo were a perfect mix of their influences: Ball was a former Northern Soul aficionado, whilst Almond loved European chanson, and they both adored early electronic music.

Their new single, the final one to be released from the album, was arguably the finest song they ever recorded. *Say Hello, Wave Goodbye* was an opioid-paced lyric-driven track which told of the aftershock of a doomed love affair between a prostitute and her lover. From the opening line "*Standing in the door of the Pink Flamingo crying in the rain*" an air of catastrophe was established with the narrator making it clear he is talking

of previously damaged goods; "*You and I, it had to be the standing joke of the year, you were a sleep-around, a lost and found*". That the subject of the song was involved in prostitution was suggested by lines such as "*You're used to wearing less*" and "*Under the deep red light*", and ultimately the narrator opted for "*a nice little housewife who'll give me an easy life*".

People love songs to tell a story, and *Say Hello, Wave Goodbye* did this intelligently, leaving gaps: it was what was *not* said between the lines that made the song so potent, and the lines which existed were unique enough to be memorable. This was not a generic verse with a catchy chorus: each line was used to drive the narrative forward, to divulge another lamina to the story. For Almond this was typical territory, as he loved writing songs "*about the underdog, the dirt under the carpet, people at the bottom of the ladder*". At five and a half minutes long, the song was an epic which Almond refused to shorten: "*It was impossible to cut the lyrics. It was dreamy and romantic.*" The video, directed by a novice Tim Pope, was populated by all sorts of characters and curiosities from the life of the band, and featured Almond sitting at a bar of a Parisian-style nightclub like the torch singer he was desperate to be.

By the time Soft Cell were hitting number four in the British charts with the single, they duo had moved to New York and were hanging out in the clubs, making discoveries about themselves which would drive their music forward.

ʊ ʊ ʊ

---

[59] Pearce installed a small chapel and confessional box in the label's office for bands to hand over their demo tapes.

[60] Test Department were an early example of Industrial music, and at various points comedian Vic Reeves and future-Daisy Chainsaw singer Katie-jane Garside were members.

The Damned continued to straddle the thin line between chaos and a career with a low-budget tour of the United States booked for February and March. Drummer Rat Scabies and newly recruited keyboard player Roman Jugg met at Heathrow Airport, and checked-in their bags. With the luggage on the plane the two had no choice but to fly, despite no-one else from the band turning up. Once in New York they proceeded straight to the booking agency, made up a story about the singer being poorly, and obtained enough money to fly home again. A few days later the whole band flew out to America with no-one mentioning the cost and mix-up of the first trip.

The tour was a success with The Damned being perceived and respected in the States as punk originators. Their accelerated tempos had an immeasurable effect on the West Coast punk scene during initial tours in 1977, and even in 1982 acts such as The Dickies, Bad Religion, TSOL, and The Replacements were lining-up to support them. One night in New York guitarist Captain Sensible was kept awake all night by a building-site jackhammer pounding, storing the palpitating rhythm in his head for future use. Upon returning to the United Kingdom, they played the Lyceum in London, however the band were all pulling in different directions, with Scabies insisting on playing 1960's garage rock, and singer Dave Vanian's obsession with 1950's sci-fi b-movies and all things soon-to-be-called gothic, however it was guitarist Captain Sensible's worship of 1960's psychedelia and pop music which was to cause the greatest threat to their future as an act.

ʊ ʊ ʊ

On Tuesday 2nd February photographer Pennie Smith was summoned to Clash frontman Joe Strummer's hotel room in Tokyo to assist him with a predicament. She found him on the floor in tears, encircled by hundreds of dolls, carvings, clothes, and even a samurai sword. "I don't know what to do" he sobbed, "I can't get them all in my suitcase" indicating the embarrassment of gifts given to him by Japanese fans. Smith tried to convince Strummer to leave some behind, however he was unrelenting in the belief that the fans had spent time and money procuring the gifts, and it would be ignominious of him not to accept them. The next couple of hours were spent stuffing them into increasingly bloated polythene bags and taping them closed, before heading to the airport and incurring an enormous excess luggage bill.

Upon arrival in Auckland, Strummer was permitted to meander through customs with an enormous samurai sword, whilst drummer Topper Headon was subjected to a four-hour interrogation due to his recent drugs bust.

ʊ ʊ ʊ

There was no nightlife on Earth more stimulating in 1982 than the clubs in New York. New wave, early hip-hop, and disco collided on the dancefloors of venues like the Mudd Club and the Roxy, consuming a diverse congregation of clubbers, punks, graffiti artists, and scenesters. Songs could become colossal club hits worldwide if they received a positive reception in these places, as other DJs around the world would trail where New York led.

One of the leading clubs was Danceteria, which had been opened in 1979 by Rudolf Piper and Jim Fouratt[61] in premises at West 37th Street. The music played there by DJ

---

[61] Fouratt was a prominent figure in New York, having been kicked out of a seminary in the early 1960's for being homosexual before taking a diligent role in the first ever anti-Vietnam protests and co-founding the Yippies, a youth-based counter-revolutionary group. In the 1970's Fouratt developed into

Mark Kamins was multifarious and on any night you may hear The Clash mixing with James Brown, or Public Image Limited followed by Bohannan. The original Danceteria had been closed by the police and fire departments in 1980 due to a lack of safety certificates, however early in 1982, real estate developer Alex Di Lorenzo decided to open a nightclub on the first floor of a building on 21st Street, hiring John Argento to overview the launch. Argento had loved the *Danceteria* club, and wasted little time recruiting Piper, Fouratt, and the name. Where the original Danceteria had been restrained within a tiny space, the new one was custom-designed with one floor of live music, one of dancing, and another acting as a *chill-out* lounge area. Video screens were installed throughout with John Sanborn hired to create specially commissioned films and important scenesters hired from other clubs, including DJ and promoter Anita Sarko, doorman Johnny Dynall, and bartender Chi Chi Valenti.

The club opened to the public on Wednesday 3rd February, and they were met with the expected eclectic mix of music, including Afrika Bambaataa, Grace Jones, Kraftwerk, and Bow Wow Wow. Basically, new British pop along with early hip-hop and modern soul were in fashion at Danceteria: if there was a beat and it sounded pioneering then it would be played. Fouratt allegorized the experience of Danceteria as visiting a

supermarket, one where the customers must be "*open to a range of experiences*". A diverse assortment of live acts were booked, from Durutti Column to Philip Glass, with the audience expected to embrace the shock of the unusual and new.

One song you were almost guaranteed to hear at Danceteria in 1982 was *I Specialize in Love* by Sharon Brown, written by Lotti Gordon and Richard Scher. Brown was the niece of Phil Medley, the co-writer of *Twist & Shout*, and had been in the music business for over a decade when she recorded the track especially for the club market. Leased to Virgin Records in the United Kingdom, the single spent nine weeks in the charts, peaking at number thirty-eight and providing a blueprint for the debut single by a young Manhattan based singer called Madonna. It was to be the height of Brown's career, and she now lives in New York working with young people and prisoners, spreading a message of non-violence.

℧ ℧ ℧

The British Phonographic Awards, later known as the Brit Awards, were first staged in 1977 to celebrate the Queen's Silver Jubilee. They were then not repeated until Thursday 4th February 1982 when the great and the good of the British recording industry reconvened at Grosvenor House in London. The ceremony did not resemble what the public would later recognise as the Brit Awards, with no televisual coverage, no performances by musicians, and a traditional host in the form of fifty-six-year-old BBC Radio veteran David Jacobs.

The 1982 awards reflected music from the previous year and winning Best Album was the massive-selling *Kings of the Wild Frontier* by Adam & The Ants, which had originally been released in 1980. The only other albums on the shortlist were *Dare* by the Human League, and Queen's *Greatest Hits*, ignoring classics by Soft Cell, Madness, The Police, OMD, and Japan. Adam also featured heavily in the Single of the Year category with his chart-toppers *Stand & Deliver* and *Prince Charming* making the shortlist,

---

one of the foremost gay rights activists, forming the Gay Liberation Front following his involvement in the Stonewall Riots.

alongside winner *Tainted Love* by Soft Cell, whilst chart-toppers by The Specials, The Police, The Human League, Queen & David Bowie did not even get a mention. Soft Cell snubbed the ceremony, refusing to attend, choosing instead to spend the night sulking at the Columbia Hotel, whilst manager Stevo turned up to accept the award on their behalf.

The Human league triumphed as Breakthrough Artist over nominees Depeche Mode, Lynx, Soft Cell, and Toyah, whilst Randy Crawford and Cliff Richard won best Female and Male, with Sheena Easton, Toyah, Elvis Costello, and Shakin' Stevens being runners-up.

Best Group saw The Police prevailing over Adam & The Ants and Madness, with Martin Rushent awarded Best Producer for his work with The Human League. The Outstanding Contribution to Music Award was belatedly awarded to John Lennon.

7th – 13th February 1982
#1 single: The Jam: Town Called Malice / Precious
#1 album: Barbra Streisand: Love Songs

There is a myth that music was more dogmatic in the past, that it has since been neutered by generic platitudes, however a look at the charts in early 1982 would appear to show the opposite, where most acts were more concerned with partying than proselytization. Compared to the previous few years, music in 1982 tended to be non-political. Following incendiary remarks in 1976 by Eric Clapton in support of right-wing politician Enoch Powell and black repatriation, many in the music world leapt into (re)action, forming organisations such as Rock Against Racism, Rock Against Sexism, and the Anti-Nazi League. As an increasingly extreme right-wing recruited disillusioned youths, these organisations held a whole slew of events and concerts to raise awareness of tolerance and acceptance, whilst many of the larger critically acclaimed acts of the day came out in support, offering their services. With the election of Margaret Thatcher and a right-wing Conservative government in May 1979, these organisations solidified into what was generally a left-wing oppositional mindset. By 1982 however, the art of protest seemed to have gone underground, certainly as far as the charts were concerned. The anti-racist music of Two-Tone and anti-sexist agenda of a whole number of the female punk stars was absent from the charts. You would be hard pushed to find much in the way of *protest* in the top forty this year, replaced instead by hedonism, blind ambition, and aspiration. It seemed the pop stars of 1982 were too busy clawing their way up the ladder of success to care about *issues*. There would be little change in this attitude throughout the decade, despite high-profile tentpoles such as *Band Aid* and *Live Aid*, which despite the altruism of those involved had the added benefit of record sales and an increased profile.

As unemployment in the United Kingdom increased to a post-war record of 3,070,621, The Jam were one of the few voices addressing issues such as the jobless and poverty, and they were about to have their greatest year in an extremely successful career.

The Jam had been formed ten years previously in Woking by fourteen-year-old singer and guitarist Paul Weller, bass player Bruce Foxton, and drummer Rick Buckler, signing to Polydor in 1977. The band learned their trade playing 1950's rock and roll around working men's clubs, before Weller discovered long-dead Mod culture through the David Essex movie *That'll be the Day*. These 1960's influences remained a major factor with the band, even as they aligned themselves with the emerging punk movement in 1976, allowing Weller to mature into an exceptionally gifted songwriter, marrying great tunes with socially-conscious lyrics. Over masterpiece singles such as *Eton Rifles, Going Underground*[62], *That's Entertainment*, and *Down in the Tube Station at Midnight* they became *a band that mattered*. They were a perfect example of the handful of groups who emerged from punk, bands that encouraged unconditional devotion from their fans, the type of band that changed people's lives. Along with acts such as The Clash and The Specials, The Jam became a way of life for many young kids, one they stuck to for the rest of their lives. Not that Paul Weller would have tolerated anything other than complete dedication: he was possessively jealous of his own band and would often become irate if friends extolled another act.

The key to understanding Weller's personality and drive is his relationship with his father, John. Weller senior was an ex-boxer turned taxi driver who had managed Paul's career from the very first day. Weller junior was the golden boy[63], everything was

organized around him: The Jam were merely a vehicle for his success. It was as well he had an immense precocious talent when it came to songwriting, one that allowed him to create an enviable body of work in a short period of time. The Jam refused to be categorized during their career: first they were playing R&B, then they were a punk band, then a new wave band, then a mod band, none of which they would have classified themselves as, and by 1982 they were quite simply a very successful pop band. Just as their fans were settling into an inflexible lifetime of devoutness, the band themselves had spent the previous

year moving from their roots, heading out in soul and R&B directions, adding manifest funk and northern soul influences, whilst recording their new album, *The Gift*, at the end of 1981. The first single to be taken from the album was a double A-side, coupling *Town Called Malice* with *Precious*, and was released at the end of January. Such was the following of the band that the single entered the charts at the coveted number one position by the end of the week, an achievement tremendously uncommon in those days.

The better known of the two songs was *Town Called Malice*[64], three minutes of perfect pop, with the drums and bass displaying a distinct Motown influence. On top of this the track was conspicuous for the lack of trademark Weller guitar, supplanted instead by a full-bodied organ hook. The guitar was there if you were prepared to listen carefully, it was just not playing Townsend power chords but chorus-driven funk lines instead. Weller chose to nudge the guitar back in the mix to ensure the lyrics, which were a critique of the effects of Thatcherism on a working-class town, were clearly audible. Weller later claimed *"[Thatcher] was well into her stride by that time. The country was being depleted and the working classes were being shat on. It was a very desolate time. You couldn't help but be touched by the politics of the time, you were either for or against it and I was reflecting what I saw around me"*. He had recently turned one-hundred-and-eighty degrees in his political stance, having formerly stated *"Next time round we'll be voting Conservative"* in a 1977 interview with punk fanzine *Sniffin' Glue*. It was a cavalier proclamation made in the middle of supporting The Clash on their *White Riot* tour, as a rejoinder against the left-wing politics dominating

---

[62] When *Going Underground* went straight in the charts at the top position my mother dismissed modern bands because they recorded their songs a bit at a time. I thought she meant they recorded one second of the song at a time and then put it together, rather than recording one instrument at a time.

[63] One old friend described them as being like Spike the bulldog and his son Tyke in old *Tom & Jerry* cartoons, chuckling and proudly saying *"That's my boy"*.

[64] I bought this single at the time. Loved it then, love it now.

those dates, but it was a declaration that would haunt the band for years. With the specified right-wing voting intentions and use of the Union Jack onstage it was easy to see how the band were construed as *little Englanders*, and it took years of left-wing activism by Weller during the 1980's before his socialist credentials were re-instated. Within *Town Called Malice*[65] you could not mistake Weller's acrimony regarding the effects of Thatcher's policies on the working class, with lines such as "*Time is short but life is cruel*" and "*It's enough to make you stop believing when the tears come fast and furious*". Weller, when painting a picture of "*lost laughter in the breeze*" and "*rows and rows of disused milk floats*", was going beyond lamenting the loss of industry to the squandering of a nation. This was a desolate viewpoint where to "*either cut down on beer or the kid's new gear*" was the choice facing the working classes. With lyrics like these, many people would have been forgiven for being turned off, however the beat and melody drew them in. The song lacked a detectible chorus but made up for this by returning to the titular line at the end of each verse, as well as providing a sing-along *ba-ba-ba* verse.

Turning the single over you found the funk-driven horn-filled *Precious*, lyrically, back on secure boy-girl terrain, however the music was a considerable step for a band like The Jam. In recent months Weller had been influenced by Pigbag, a new act on the scene who specialized in instrumental funk workouts, and he took their sound wholesale for the single. Drummer Rick Buckler was not impressed with the song, taking a cassette version along to a local disco and watching the DJ play it without announcing the artist. The message the drummer took from the song filling the dancefloor was not that the public liked it, but that it was "*just another run-of-the-mill disco song*."

For some fans, Weller had sold out and created *pop music*, whilst for others such as *Smash Hits* it was not pop enough, with Mark Ellen claiming that despite the Motown pastiche it was "*a pity he didn't nick a tune while he was at it.*"

ʊ ʊ ʊ

Depeche Mode had something to prove at the start of 1982.
After being formed by Basildon school friends Vince Clarke and Andrew Fletcher, both of whom had been converted to the electronic cause by the sound of Orchestral Manoeuvres in the Dark and The Human League, they conscripted Dave Gahan and Martin Gore in spring 1980. With three keyboard players balancing their instruments on beer crates and Gahan singing, their rise was dizzying once a track had been

featured on a Some Bizarre compilation album alongside Soft Cell, The The, and Blancmange. This led to a deal with the recently established Mute Records, and by the turn of the year Depeche Mode were in the top seventy-five with their debut single, *Dreaming of You*.

1981 was a momentous year for the band as singles *New Life* and *Just Can't Get Enough* stormed the upper reaches of the charts, featuring their brand of infectious sanguine electronic pop written by Clarke. Just as the band released their debut album *Speak & Spell* in October Clarke made the decision to leave. Despite having the ability to write perfect synth-pop songs, he was not interested in being a *pop star*, and when the teen magazines started to ask about the colour of his socks Clarke decided

---

[65] Weller apologised to Madness before *Town Called Malice* was released, claiming to have been heavily influenced by their song *Embarrassment*.

it was time to go, later claiming "*I didn't feel happy, or contented, or fulfilled, and that's why I left*". He also expressed privately to friends at the time his frustration with the limitations of Gahan's voice, whilst label boss Daniel Miller reckoned "*He was like a technology hoover; he realised that with the technology at his fingers he could do everything, without being in a band.*"

Most anticipated the loss of their principal songwriter would result in the creative end of Depeche Mode, and a deal was even attempted whereby Clarke would continue to write for the band. This was deemed impracticable, and they parted company but not before they rejected the offer of a freshly written song called *Only You*.

Depeche Mode went straight into the studio and started recording, with the songwriting onus falling upon Martin Gore purely because he had previously written a couple of formulaic album tracks. Gore later confessed he had been embarrassed by some of Clarke's lyrics which had been written to fit around the music, almost as an add-on. February saw the first fruits of this move with the release of the single *See You*. Whilst not as instantly infectious as their previous singles, it became their largest hit to date, reaching number six in the charts and was generously trumpeted by Vince Clark as "*their best ever*".

Listening to *See You* with the hindsight of Depeche Mode's future path it appeared as a very circumspect and timorous track. Lyrically, there was naivety in lines such as "*I remember the way we used to laugh and play and look in each other's eyes*" and the chorus "*All I want to do is see you, don't you know that it's true*", however maybe we should not hold that against them: the lyrics under Clarke's reign were hardly radical.

The song appeared to be a straight-forward love song and had apparently been written by Gore when he was sixteen years old after meeting a girl on a school exchange trip to Heiligenhaus, a town near Dusseldorf in Germany. Upon returning, Gore would pay the song in Norman and the Worms, the band he had formed with school-friend Phil Burdett. At the time, Gore was very heavily involved with the church, along with Fletcher and Clarke, attending events several times a week, as well as playing at various religious festivals and gatherings. Forearmed with this knowledge transforms how we look at several early Depeche Mode songs, where the object of love could easily be alternated between a person and a deity.

Musically, the track was mid-paced, building upon an itinerant bass line and unassuming descending xylophone notes, travelling through a typical structure before fading out. There was nothing of the *pop-thrill* in the track, no head rush, no danceable beat, no peak, or trough. Even Gahan seemed hesitant in his vocals, conveying them with no real determination, matching the timidity of the music. Instead of a heroic spring headlong into a new electronic age there were even allusions to past rock and roll, with an ascending blues note in the chorus melody, layered vocal *ahhhs* from The Beatles' *Twist & Shout*[66] and a keyboard riff lifted from The Crystals *And Then He Kissed Me*.

A video was shot quickly by Julian Temple with semi-decent production values but little content, featuring Gahan trying to find a girl, played by Martin Gore's fiancé Anne Swindell. The band were never satisfied with the single, being caught between the Vince Clarke-era Depeche Mode and the future harder sounding act, and they never played it live after 1984, however it helped the band stabilize themselves and demonstrate they had another songwriter in the ranks. To buy time they recruited Alan Wilder as a hired-hand through an advert in the Melody Maker and embarked on a mini-tour taking in the United Kingdom, mainland Europe, and North America, ending in the middle of May. Wilder was not enthusiastic about the music but was willing to keep his opinions to himself for a wage of £100 per week. Mute Records, meanwhile,

---

[66] Dave Gahan was born at exactly the same date and time The Beatles were signing their record contract with Parlophone.

were gearing up to take the band global, with distribution deals in place in most territories.

℧ ℧ ℧

Calling themselves The Fun Boy Three when their lead singer was renowned for his dourness was an ironic act by Terry Hall, Lynval Golding, and Neville Staples, the trio who had fragmented from The Specials the previous summer. Rapidly releasing their debut single *The Lunatics Have Taken Over the Asylum*, the trio had moved away from

the ska of the Specials, taking on-board a more percussion-focused sound with overtly political lyrics about the Reagan administration in the United States[67]. The success bought them enough time to write and record their debut album.

In January Lynval Golding and Neville Staples had been caught in a fight between two rival gangs in a nightclub in Coventry resulting in the former receiving thirty-two stitches in his throat. Whilst in hospital the local paper printed his home address, which was promptly burgled. Staples, meanwhile, had to undergo a minor throat operation, leaving him unable to speak or sing for a couple of months.

Despite all the negative news, the trio espoused a *pop* outlook, returning in February with a new single, teaming up with a female trio called Bananarama to release a cover version of the jazz classic *It Ain't What You Do (It's the Way That You Do It)*.

Bananarama had come together in London during 1979 when Bristol childhood friends Sara Dallin and Keren Woodward teamed up with fashion journalism student Siobhan Fahey. Moving into the rat-infested former rehearsal room of The Sex Pistols in Denmark Street, the trio began singing backing vocals for the London new wave scene, mostly live and infrequently unsolicited, performing with acts such as The Jam, The Monochrome Set, and Department S. It was a world of extreme poverty with no running water, only made tolerable by the initial interest of Boomtown Rats manager, Fachtna O'Kelly, and then future Girls Aloud representative Hillary Shaw, before they decided to manage themselves. By 1981 Bananarama were being assisted by former Sex Pistols drummer, Paul Cook, and signed to Demon Records for their debut single, *Aie a Mwana*. This, and a photo shoot in which they wore moccasins, brought them to the attention of the moccasin-loving Terry Hall who requested the three contribute backing vocals to the debut album by The Fun Boy Three[68].

After starting their career with such a marvelous single The Fun Boy Three appeared to have run out of ideas, and much of their eponymous debut album released in March comprised half-finished chants, furnished with percussion and not much else, bar the infrequent piano. *It Ain't What You Do* turned out to be one of the more substantial tracks on the album, a song with a history of being sung by jazz greats like Ella Fitzgerald. Bananarama and The Fun Boy Three took turns singing, with the girls taking the chorus and the boys the verses. Given that they could disregard having to write a song and concentrate on putting together a virulent swinging rhythm, it is no surprise it turned out to be a great pop single.

---

[67] The Specials recorded their own version of *The Lunatics* on their 2019 comeback album *Encore*. It seemed even more pertinent during the Trump administration.

[68] At the same time Bananarama were being courted by former Sex Pistols manager Malcolm McLaren but were put off by his determination that they should sing sexually suggestive material to court controversy. Failing to ensnare them, he turned his attention to Bow Wow Wow instead.

The Fun Boy Three were determined to live up to their name, and footage of them shows a whole new side, one where they are dressed in khaki hunting gear and dungarees, larking around and dancing enthusiastically with Bananarama. This fun approach saw the act attract a lot of the public who would have missed out on The Specials, younger pop fans who helped send the single into the top five and push their

album to number seven. The combined six piece spent the next couple of months travelling across Europe appearing on television shows and being interviewed by the press.

The Fun Boy Three's follow up single, *The Telephone Always Rings*, was one of the more complete tracks on the album, and paradoxically also the one they had stripped most of their layers of percussion from, electing instead to work with a simple programmed drum pattern and snare. The repetition helped add to the accumulating paranoia of the song, which was further re-enforced by lyrics in which the band paralleled their hum-drum existence to that of someone who appeared to be living a much more fascinating lifestyle. The ringing of an unanswered telephone enhanced the portentous atmosphere, and helped it rise to number seventeen in the charts. The trio were glad to be in the charts at all, with Terry Hall later explaining "*Commercial success takes a lot of pressure from the band.*"

ʊ ʊ ʊ

By February Italy's Banco Ambrosiano was facing a severe financial predicament following the withdrawal of Olivetti money, and chairman Roberto Calvi was starting to contemplate incautious measures. He formulated plans to bribe the Italian magistrate, and approached Opus Dei, once described as "*executive class Catholics*", to persuade them to take on part of the debt owed the bank by the Vatican. Oddly enough, the meeting between Calvi and the Catholic church was set up by the Italian Freemasons, but the deal fell through when the bank became caught up in a power struggle between Pope John Paul II, Opus Dei, and some top Cardinals.

The President of Banco Ambrosiano Overseas, Pierre Siegenthaler, was on a sailing holiday when the request came in on Tuesday 9th February from the head branch in Milan to transfer $14 million to six numbered accounts in Switzerland belonging to well-connected entrepreneur Flavio Carboni and his girlfriend. Bank Treasurer Calvin Knowes contacted head office for more details, fearing he was being drawn into illegal financial activities, and was assured the money would be repaid within forty-eight hours. Instead, the money disappeared into a black hole, having been used by Calvi to pay Carboni for stolen jewels.

ʊ ʊ ʊ

The Clash arrived in Sydney for the Australian leg of their tour on Tuesday 9th February, and were almost immediately evicted from their élite hotel, having to make do instead with dilapidated accommodation in the red-light district. After the imposed drugs-free tour of Japan, frontman Joe Strummer had continued to abstain from smoking, becoming obsessed with what he called *the cult of the body*, running at six o'clock each morning, swimming in the ocean every day, and spending spare time in his hotel room lifting the television like a set of weights.

Strummer's support of the beleaguered classes caused trouble for the band when they invited an aboriginal land-rights campaigner onstage at the Capitol Theatre to rap about his cause. From that moment on the reception for the band became reserved, and even the hotel bar refused to serve them, as a stagehand at the theatre told their tour manager that aborigines were "*like dogs, mate*". Further trouble followed a few days later in Brisbane when an aboriginal dancer was asked on stage by the band. By the time he returned home later that night, his house had been burned down in protest.

ʊ ʊ ʊ

The J Geils Band had spent more than a decade touring and releasing records in their native United States, patiently building a following whilst becoming increasingly successful with each subsequent release, and by the second half of 1981 they were ready to release their tenth album *Freeze-Frame*. Normally, fifteen years into a career bands tend to sound lackluster, however the J. Geils Band were just hitting their creative and commercial peak, epitomized by the success of the lead single from the album, *Centerfold*.

The single had soared to the top of the American Billboard Charts and was starting a run of six weeks there at the start of February. Such success could not be ignored in Britain and the song picked up airplay, finally entering the chart on the 7th February.

Centerfold was a phenomenal pop song featuring a problem at the very core: the lyrics. Written by keyboard player Seth Justman the music was commercial dynamite, lashing forward with earworms throughout, and an infuriating but addictive "*na-na-na-na-na-na*" refrain that was generated for singing along to. Then you got to the lyrics which

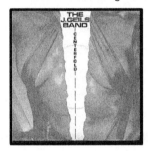 recount the tale of a man discovering his High School crush posing in a pornographic magazine. The first verse revealed his discovery of the photographs and his shock was understandable, however the hypocrisy of looking in the magazine in the first place is apparent. The second verse saw the narrator reminiscing about his infatuation of this woman whilst at High School and explains how his unwillingness to speak to her led to him creating an impossibly undefiled image of her in his mind. His objectification of women by perusing a "*girly magazine*" did not concern him until the object of his gaze is someone he recognized. Did this lead him to examine his thought process and morals? No, in the third verse he simply transformed the woman into a further object of desire, stating "*We'll take your car and drive it… to a motel room and take* [your clothes] *off in private*". She remained a passive commodity in his private fantasy.

The whole song was a perfect example of Sigmund Freud's Madonna-Whore complex, what he labelled *psychic impotence*, whereby men segregate women into two categories: saintly pure or debased prostitutes. The singer once saw the woman affectionately, but the "*years go by*" and allow the time required for him to see her as an object of sexual desire.

As the decade advanced it became manifest there was also a double standard in society's analysis of how women were portrayed in music by white and black musicians. *Centerfold* sat at the top of the American charts for six weeks and reached number three in Britain without anyone commenting on the portrayal of a woman as a simplified sexual object, yet there was great outrage at the representation of women in rap music. Dana Williams, in her essay *Beyond Rap: Musical Misogyny* stated "*There has always been objectification and misogyny against women in music, yet we focus on the black artists, not the rockers and not even the white executives who are making the big money from this kind of music*". Cynthia Fuchs sees this as a problem of authenticity, with white artists being part of "*the flamboyance of rock* [which] *is understood to be a performance, rather than from the perspective of personal feelings*", whereas with rap and hip-hop "*the mainstream takes it to represent real life, so it's seen as more threatening*". In the twenty-first century it is hard to put all these arguments aside, to simply say that it was acceptable in the eighties, and it is these lyrics which stop *Centerfold* from being an absolute classic.

℧ ℧ ℧

With record numbers of unemployed, the only way to claim benefits was by filling in the notoriously difficult Unemployed Benefit Form 40. It seemed appropriate, therefore, given their unemployed status that a Birmingham band would take the shorthand for the form as their title.

UB40 were formed in 1978 by vocalist and guitarist Ali Campbell, who financed instruments for the entire outfit after receiving a substantial compensation claim following a serious assault at the Red Lion Pub two years previously, from which he almost lost the sight in his left eye. Recruiting a cast of black and white friends, including Jimmy Brown (drums), unemployed plasterer Earl Falconer (bass), Yemeni-Welsh out-of-work carpet-fitter Norman Hassan (percussion), former electrical apprentice Brian Travers (saxophone), toaster Astro, and Mickey Virtue (keyboards), they began jamming dub and reggae around the city pubs.

Campbell persuaded his brother, former apprentice toolmaker Robin (vocals / guitar), to complete the line-up, and after being discovered playing in a pub by Chrissie Hynde, they were invited to join The Pretenders as tour support. The Campbells were the sons of the celebrated Scottish folk singer and Marxist, Ian Campbell[69], and had been brought up with an acute understanding of politics and the working class which they put to good use in their music.

After turning down an offer from Two-Tone Records because "*we considered ourselves to be a reggae band, not revivalists concentrating on music which was a decade old*",

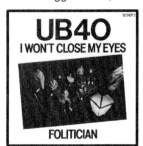

UB40's debut single, *Food for Thought*, comparing the excess of Christmas and the starving of Africa, was released on local independent label Graduate Records, and climbed into the top five. A run of mid-paced, dub influenced singles and a couple of albums followed, each of them tackling serious subjects such as 1981's *One in Ten*, named after the rate of unemployment in Britain at the time. UB40 had the makings of shrewd entrepreneurs, forming their own label DEP International and building their own studio in Birmingham, whilst licensing their songs to major labels, thus maintaining control of artistic output. However, they were also useless with money and between splitting it between their many members and being unstinting with their friends UB40 seemed endlessly to be on the brink of bankruptcy.

Early in 1982 they set about recording a new album at Windmill Studios in Dublin, and the first track to be released from these sessions was a single entitled *I Won't Close my Eyes*. On this, their now usual dub leanings were capped with a rebellious call-to-

---

[69] Born in Aberdeen, Campbell moved to Birmingham as a teenager. The Ian Campbell Folk Group at various points had Spencer Davis, Christine Perfect (Fleetwood Mac), Dave Swarbrick and Dave Pegg (both Fairport Convention) as members. They once sold out the Albert Hall, and when Simon & Garfunkel recorded his song, *The Sun is Burning* for their *Bridge Over Troubled Water* he looked to be financially set for life, however the recording was pulled from the album at the last minute. Campbell's strong Marxist beliefs forced him to continue living in a council house, but not to sharing a packet of biscuits with his four sons.

arms lyric proclaiming that *"Our strength's in our bite and not in our back"*. The band, however, were playing to an ever-shrinking audience with this single only reaching number thirty-two, their worst showing in the charts so far. Ali Campbell later stated *"It's one of our best songs, but I'm so out of tune it's unbelievable. Totally depressing."*

14th – 20th February 1982

#1 single: The Jam: Town Called Malice / Precious
#1 album: Barbra Streisand: Love Songs

It was not all wall-to-wall glistening pop music in 1982; some musical styles refused to be replaced, and one of those was hard rock. Disco and punk-influenced music had been the prevailing style for the past few years in the United Kingdom, and yet hard rock had continued to flourish. It appeared to be indestructible with a ceaseless stream of cannon-fodder pubescent males agreeable to shaking their heads at ear-piercingly loud concerts. These fans had not a care what was fashionable; they knew what they

enjoyed, and if the band were rocking, heavy, and loud then all was okay with the world. The bands they followed tended to do well in the charts without ever seeming to inconvenience the top ten. These were the days before rock bands started glamming-up in America, before giant hair and spandex, and the bands dressed like their fans; in denim and leather, a look that reflected working class pedigrees with pride.

Many rock acts in 1982 had features in common, one of which was that many of them had been around a long time, from UFO who reached number sixty-two with their single *Let It Rain*, to Black Sabbath[70] at number thirty-seven with *Turn up the Night*, both in February 1982, and both of whom were formed in the last couple of years of the 1960's. These singles entered the charts at the highest position they achieved: in other words, they were purchased by fans in the first week of release and no-one else. Crossing over from a rock audience to the chart crowd was something a lot of rock bands had difficulty in doing. For rock acts, singles were merely a means of promoting the album, and the album was a means of selling tickets for money-spinning live tours. The live arena was where these bands prospered, being able to mount superb shows of musicianship. They correspondingly, for some reason, sold a lot of records in places like Japan and South America.

Keeping UFO and Black Sabbath company in the charts in February were other veterans like Thin Lizzy with *Hollywood*, Alice Cooper with *Seven and Seven Is* and Kiss with *A World Without Heroes*. Whilst the veteran rockers were continuing to have minor hits, there was a new generation of British acts also enjoying success. Coined the New Wave of British Heavy Metal (or NWOBHM), the movement was populated by rock bands who took the vitality and DIY attitude of punk, merging them into a homogenous blend. Academic research (yes, there is such a thing) shows the audience were overwhelmingly young, male, white, and working class, with a *"collective affirmation of heterosexuality"*. Unlike punk, however, virtuoso musicianship was appreciated whilst political interests were eschewed. The whole movement, and many

---

[70] Black Sabbath were, of course, Ozzy Osbourne's original band, and had carried on without him. In 1982 their singer was Ronnie James Dio, former frontman of Rainbow.

of the bands, were ripe for satirizing, which was done fantastically in the 1984 rockumentary *This Is Spinal Tap*.

There was an eclectic assortment of acts lumped together under the NWOBHM label, from Motörhead-influenced speed rockers to melodic marketable metal such as Def Leppard. In June 1981 the publishers of *Sounds* magazine saw a niche in the market and launched a new title called *Kerrang* which was to become a weekly bible for the movement.

One of the most successful of the new wave of metal bands to emerge were Iron Maiden, who had built their reputation over two hit albums before dismissing vocalist Paul Di'Anno[71] due to his ballooning drug use. They enlisted Bruce Dickinson, formerly of Samson, in September 1981 and wasted no time writing and recording their third album.

By February 1982 Iron Maiden had a dazzling new single *Run to the Hills* ready for release. Written by bass player Steve Harris the song goes beyond being a rock track,

 and effortlessly meets the requirements for a great *pop* track, something their fans might recoil from. The song looks at the colonisation of North America expressed from two viewpoints: that of the Native Americans and then at a faster pace, that of the European colonisers. The entire track crackles with urgency, but the killer hook is in the chorus where the band exploit the same sixth interval as Frank Sinatra's *My Way* to create a superb sing-along. By having the music fast and the vocals half the pace they satisfied those who sought to rock *and* those wanting to sing. As the song climbed to number seven in the charts, the band returned to what they did best, and headed out on a 184-date world tour lasting the rest of the year.

ʊ ʊ ʊ

London band Madness were about to have their most prosperous year of an incredible decade. Before they progressed, though, their record company decided to release one final single from the previous album *7*.

Madness had been formed in 1976 by Lee Thompson (saxophone), Chris Foreman (guitar), and Mike Barson (keyboards). Barson was the most musically proficient of the three, having been educated in rock and roll by his brother who had been the singer with Bazooka Joe[72]. Throughout the next couple of years and several line-up changes, they added Graham McPherson (vocals, known as Suggs), Daniel Woodgate (drums), and Mark Bedford (bass), and began performing under the name The Invaders, becoming progressively influenced by ska. By the start of 1979, the band had changed their name to Madness, after the Prince Buster 1960's ska song, and built a following on the London gig circuit, before being noticed by The Specials and signed to their Two-Tone label. Former member Carl "Chas" Smyth who spent his spare time turning up to their gigs and dancing onstage uninvited, was made a formal member of the band in the summer, moving around the stage and interjecting vocals.

---

[71] Di'Anno has not had the most stable life, being married five times and spending time in prison for benefit fraud worth £45,000. In the 1990's he converted to Islam but gave it up because he could not stand being sober.

[72] Bazooka Joe also featured Stuart Goddard, the future Adam Ant, and provided The Sex Pistols with their first ever live appearance.

Debut single *The Prince* climbed into the top twenty, and amid considerable record company interest the band signed to Stiff Records after being hired as the entertainment at label boss Dave Robinson's wedding (it was the only way he could get to see them). What followed was a streak of eight brilliant singles and three albums in the space of two years, including classics such as *Baggy Trousers*, *My Girl*, and *One Step Beyond*, an outstanding run of top ten hits which set the band up with a devoted teenage following.

Towards the end of 1979, the band came off the back of a twenty-nine date Two-Tone British tour with The Specials and The Selecter, and straight into a fructifying racist controversy. Madness had built a skinhead following over the previous year and it all came to a head in November at the Electric Ballroom in Camden, when the audience commenced hurling racist abuse at support act Red Beans & Rice, provoking Suggs to take the stage to admonish them. This did no good, and the Madness set terminated with the skinheads *sieg heil*-ing the band. Madness had not helped themselves previously, being sluggish to censure the right-wing audience despite the black Jamaican roots of the music they were playing.

Skinhead culture had first risen from the mod movement in the late 1960's amongst working class kids who rejected the middle-class hippy aesthetic, instead being influenced by ska, reggae, rocksteady, and American soul music. Throughout the 1970's, the skinhead movement died out quite significantly before being accidentally revived by punk and Two-Tone. The problem was that a considerable number of the second generation of skinheads were a whole different kettle of arseholes: usually former punks who were too moronic to grasp the point of punk, focusing instead on Sid Vicious' Nazi t-shirts and the destructive vehemence inherent in the original movement as well as the less innovative sonic copycats that followed. With the upsurge of the far-right fascist National Front Party in Britain, many of these kids were swept up with the rhetoric to be found in some areas of the British press, where even Margaret Thatcher as leader of one of the two largest parties in the country could talk about being *"afraid that this country could be rather swamped by people with a different culture"*. Of course, by the end of 1979 Thatcher was the leader of the country, and it was once again tolerable to openly utter racist sentiments.

Racist skinheads plagued all the Two-Tone bands in the early days, which seems ludicrous given the mixed-race make-up of The Specials, The Selecter, and The Beat,

 and was certainly an issue they were outspoken about. Madness on the other hand, were lethargic in their condemnation of the racists, however by the end of 1979 they had no other choice but to speak out.

Madness were one of the first acts to fully embrace the video format, producing one for each new release. The *nuttier* the video, the more popular it was with the fans, and so we had all sorts of high-jinks captured on film including saxophone solos in mid-air, frequently stimulated by alcohol. The real motivation for making the videos had been the size of the band: it could be difficult getting all seven members in the same place at the same time, so a deal was struck with *Top of the Pops* that if ever the band could not all make it to the studio the video would be shown as an alternative. These proved so popular it no longer became crucial for the band to make the effort to turn up at all.

Madness had been deliberately evolving from their ska roots towards a mainstream pop sound over the last year, which could be heard in new single *Cardiac Arrest*. The song revolved around the account of a workaholic suffering a lethal heart attack on his way to work, scarcely top forty terrain, which BBC Radio One took on board with a decision to ban it from their playlists following the death of a relative of one of the DJs. This decision, along with the earlier release on an album, accounted for the single only reaching number fourteen in the charts, ending their enviable run of top ten singles. Not that the band cared: they had their next single and album ready to go, both of which would propel them to even greater heights.

Meanwhile, the band had flew to Los Angeles to record a Japanese advert for Honda, which Chas Smash reasoned "*We were told that if we did these ads we'd be really big overseas, but it's the same as it is* [in Britain] – *people see you on ads and think you're a wanker*".

ʊ ʊ ʊ

Following the publicity surrounding the bat-biting incident, all sorts of animals started to be thrown onstage during Ozzy Osbourne's *Diary of a Madman* tour. At Fair Park Coliseum in Beaumont, Texas on Monday 15th February, bass player Rudy Sarzo noticed the body of a massive bullfrog land at his feet. Fearing another "*Ozzy bites the head off...*" headline in the press, he dropped to his knees and picked it up, tossing it over the bass amplifier towards the back of the stage.

Unfortunately, the Fair Park Coliseum was a smaller venue than many others on the tour, and the usual full-scale show of towers, drawbridges, and turrets had not been set up, meaning keyboard player Don Airey was situated behind the amplifier as well. As he looked up to see what the secondary gap in the bass playing was, the bloated bullfrog hit him, bursting on his face.

ʊ ʊ ʊ

Dundonian vocalist Billy MacKenzie and multi-instrumentalist Alan Rankine were completely smitten by the work of David Bowie. So much so that after forming The Associates from the remnants of central Scotland cabaret act Caspian, their debut single had been a cover of *Boys Keep Swinging*, released without permission just weeks after Bowie. If the object of releasing the single illegally had been to garner attention, then the duo was successful, leading to a record deal with independent label Fiction. Their debut album *The Affectionate Punch* gained them a critical reputation but no chart success in 1980, as they recruited Michael Dempsey[73] on bass and John Murphy on drums. The four-piece began 1981 without a label after The Cure's Robert Smith insisted that they be dropped from Fiction because they were getting too much press attention. The Associates set about releasing a series of seven singles over the next year on Situation 2 Records, experimenting with instrumentation and arrangement during the recording process. The band ran a scam during the recording of these singles as each one was financed by Situation 2 to the cost of £2,000, which the band gladly accepted to fund an excessive lifestyle. Meanwhile, they persuaded different record company to pay for studio time to record demos, then used this time to record the singles, presenting each subsequent company with the same inferior demonstration recordings to ensure no deal was ever offered[74].

Towards the end of 1981 the band accepted a £60,000 advance from WEA Records based upon the strength of two new songs, *Party Fears Two* and *Club Country*, and immediately put half of it down on an open-ended block booking in the studio. The rest of the money was spent on two rooms at the Swiss Cottage Holiday Inn in London; one

---

[73] Dempsey had previously played with label mates The Cure.

[74] These singles were released as a compilation, *Fourth Drawer Down*, on Situation 2 Records as the band reached critical mass in 1981.

for the band and one for MacKenzie's pet whippets Tonto and Vanda, which were fed on smoked salmon and hard-boiled eggs from room service. The band had no notion of how to spend money astutely and had a belief the record industry owed them money in advance of their genius. The most conspicuous sign of this genius was in MacKenzie's voice; sometimes operatic, sometimes histrionic, but always melodic and remarkable. MacKenzie was blessed with one of the finest voices of his (and many other) generations, and between this and the superiority of the new songs it was no

wonder a major record company was thrilled to hand over a bulky wad of cash and set the band free without restraints.

Immediately, they began nineteen hour working days at Playground Studio in Camden, with owner and former Cure and Bauhaus producer Mike Hedges overseeing the process. The first fruits of these sessions was a new recording of *Party Fears Two*. The track had been written three years earlier as *I Never Will*, with marginally different lyrics exclaiming "*Don't make me do what the athiests do*" as the hook-line. MacKenzie and Rankine knew it was a hit instantly but also were astute enough to recognize they would need to wait for the music scene to change first. Listening to the early demo version of the song it was not difficult to see what made the record company go crazy. First there was the piano hook, one of the most indelible of the decade, hitting you right at the top of the song, strong and anthemic, interplaying with a rambling funky line from Dempsey which believed itself to be a lead guitar rather than a bass. At its heart the recording was fairly orthodox with a straightforward beat and acoustic guitar also featuring, however the whole recording was cocaine-fueled into a jet-rocket of sound; glistening, sanguine, and menacing all at the same time.

On top of this there came MacKenzie's voice, soaring above before heading off into the great elsewhere at the conclusion of the song. MacKenzie would later disown his singing style on the song, asking "*How could anyone get in such a fucking state when they were singing? That's what gets me.*" Lyrically the track dealt with a fear of commitment, with the *party* of the title denoting the narrator. The fear of forming a relationship because it might turn bad drives the song with the most telling line being the brilliant "*Even a slight remark makes no sense and turns to shark*", hinting at the ferociousness and paranoia inherent in a relationship gone wrong.

The single worked its way up the chart, helped by some unforgettable *Top of the Pops* appearances with former Martha & The Muffins keyboard player Martha Ladly, the first of which featured MacKenzie in a beret because he had a new haircut and was "*too embarrassed to reveal* [it] *on the street, never mind on national television*". Bass player Dempsey was dressed as a French sailor, whilst Rankine wore a fencing suit and insisted on playing a banjo. Mackenzie obviously liked his beret, choosing to stare and smile at himself in the television monitor for most of the performance. *Party Fears Two* peaked just inside the top ten, going on to have an extended lifecycle in the hearts of many people.

A couple of weeks later, The Associates did a typically eccentric thing by recording a session for John Peel at the BBC containing no tracks from the forthcoming album, but a collection of covers and new songs instead, including Diana Ross' *Love Hangover*, and *Waiting for the Loveboat* which would not see the light of day as a single until 1985.

℧ ℧ ℧

Given Sting's later championing of indigenous people from the rainforest it seems strange The Police would agree to play a gig in Chile, a country ruled by Fascist dictator Augusto Pinochet who had been put into power by a CIA-backed coup ten years previously and had governed with an abysmal Human Rights record. Touching down the day before their scheduled appearance at the Vina Del Mar Song Festival on Friday 19th February, the band booked into their hotel, where knives were drawn between locals and the road crew. A crowd had accumulated outside the hotel, so the crew gathered at the window and used their usual sign for "*Do you have any cocaine*" which involved touching their nose with one hand and their crotch with the other. In Chile, however, this was apparently another way of saying "*Your mother sucks cocks*" and the press were quick to capture photographs which appeared in the following days papers with the headline "*THE POLICE ARE ANIMALS*".

The tension was increased during the concert when Sting refused to use the same microphone as the previous performer, insisting it be sanitized first, and the band played to a cacophony of boos and chants, leaving the country immediately afterwards with a promise never to return.

℧ ℧ ℧

After the dressing up to dress down of punk and the misery of post-punk, 1982 was a year of acts embracing the glamourous facet of pop, pretending to be rich, erudite, and urbane in much the same way that Roxy Music had in the 1970's. Sheffield's ABC were one such band, having been formed in 1977 as synthesizer act Vice Versa by Stephen Singleton and Mark White. The duo engaged Martin Fry on keyboards after he interviewed them for his fanzine, *Modern Drugs*, with White handling most of the vocals, and played a final gig at the Futurama 2 Festival in September 1980, lining up alongside The Psychedelic Furs, U2, Siouxsie & the Banshees, and Hazel O'Connor, as well as a host of interchangeable bristly post-punk acts. At the time Vice Versa had outgrown their inchoate fascination with local stars The Human League and developed a post-punk sound, something analogous to Suicide and Joy Division. Immediately

after the festival, for some unknown reason they changed their name to ABC and moved Fry to lead vocals, with Singleton playing saxophone and White on guitar. Like city-mates The Human League at around the same time it was a move which seemed like idiocy but paid substantial dividends in the longer term.

Within a year the band were unrecognizable, signed to Parlophone Records and looking every bit the chart stars they would ultimately become. Singleton would disagree with this, stating "*It never seemed like a massive shift for us. I believe that if Vice Versa had the resources to record… in a proper studio, with a great producer… and the ability to promote the songs with a decent budget we would have had hit records*".[75] The band negotiated a distribution deal for their own Neutron Records, with the aim of signing other acts afterwards, however success took up all their time and got in the way of this plan. Their Steve Brown-produced debut single, *Tears are not Enough*, was a world away from the gothic synth-pop they had been hawking a year before, and yet there were clear links. The drums and bass locked into each other in the way that many of the acts who played Futurama had, however it is what was on top of this that marked the change: Chic guitars, sparkling pianos, and Spandau Ballet horns. Fry's vocal also soared, which makes you wonder at what point the band grasped they had the wrong singer. The

---

[75] In other words, if everything had been different it would have been the same.

single reached number nineteen, but the band sought a grander, more sophisticated sound for the album, and engaged Trevor Horn, formerly of The Buggles and Yes, on the basis of his production with pop-fluff Dollar on their single *Hand Held in Black & White*, which "*was like a widescreen record… a revolutionary sound*".

Horn was one of fifteen producers the band "*auditioned*" at a rehearsal room in West London, and they connected with him straight away. Entering RAK Studios at the end of 1981 to record next single, *Poison Arrow*, Horn made his experience in playing with 1970's disco-diva Tina Charles useful, even if he thought that kind of music "*didn't have any real heart in it… it was functional music, for people to dance to*". The band recorded the song live, after which Horn asked them "*How good do you want it to be? It can be like this, or we can make it* better". Fry answered, "*We want it as good as you can make* it", so Horn went to work programming drums and bass on a Roland 808 drum machine and Minimoog synthesizer imitating the way the band had played them. Drummer Dave Palmer and bass player Mark Lickley then spent the weekend re-recording their parts to get them unerringly in time with the programmed ones. "*It was like tracing,*" Horn later explained, "*Which meant that we got it really spot on and snappy and in your face.*" Horn brought in Anne Dudley, who added the keyboard parts giving the song a classic feel, plus Karen Clayton[76] to provide a spoken word middle-eight.

In the space of just over twelve months the band had gone from being an also-ran post-punk act to an exceedingly sophisticated pop act, a remarkable turnaround. Visually, they started to play about in the dress-up box, electing to style themselves as a classic cross between 1960's James Bond and 1950's Rat Pack, all smart tuxedos, and casino-locations.

Fry, tired of emotionlessness post-punk lyrics, had made a conscious decision to start singing about love; newly found love, lost love, jealous love, old love, new love… just as long as it was love. In *Poison Arrow* it was rejected love, love not returned, as the protagonist admited "*Then I say 'I love you' and foul the situation*", yet regardless of the distress of heartbreak, the track had a driving disco beat and bass line throughout. When Fry sang "*What I thought was the fire was only the spark*" he was dealing with more than a mere frustration of desire, but a symbolic appraisal of one's deficient worth – a humiliating blow to self-esteem.

Poison Arrow gave limited voice to the rejector, as towards the conclusion of the song a female voice states "*I know enough to know that I can never love you*", depicting her as callous and unsympathetic, characteristic of the different constructed views of the rejected and the rejector, both of which are fashioned for diverse purposes: the former to restore self-esteem, the latter to deal with guilt. The rejector is a voice mostly missing from Western culture with books, songs, and movies tending to focus on the heartbroken, providing numerous role-models and familiar scripts to follow.

Of course, having a sophisticated and watchable video in which Fry attempts to woo Lisa Vanderpump[77] did the track no harm either, particularly in the United States where British acts were much quicker to embrace the medium, and as such succeeded in stealing into the charts whilst the locals were still of the belief visuals were crass propaganda for narcissists. Within the video we also saw the introduction of Fry wearing a gold lame suit, aping Elvis Presley with its shorthand for rock and roll, which becoming synonymous with him afterwards. This was music which was nostalgic and yet forward-looking at the same time, taking the best of the past but making it sound

---

[76] Karen Clayton was the girlfriend of Gary Langan, and would go on to provide the "*Oh, to be in England, in the summertime, with my love, close to the edge*" for The Art of Noise.

[77] Vanderpump would later find great fame through *The Real Housewives of Beverly Hills* and *Vanderpump Rules*.

completely contemporary, walking the fine line between commercial pop and critical acclaim.

The single climbed to number six in the charts, however with this success the band's strong image, scope, and ambition made them pop icons overnight.

℧ ℧ ℧

Ozzy Osbourne spent the entire *Diary of a Madman* tour drunk, which angered his manager and girlfriend Sharon Arden, who had tried her hardest to arrange the whole itinerary around avoiding drinking opportunities. On Friday 19th February the tour arrived in San Antonio, Texas, and after checking into the hotel Sharon stole all of Ozzy's clothes in an attempt to stop him going out to find drink before the show. If there is one thing an alcoholic is, it is inventive, and Ozzy picked out one of Sharon's dresses, a dark green frilly one, put it on and headed off into the city with journalist Allan Jones and photographer Tom Sheehan.

After wandering around for a while slugging from a bottle of Courvoisier Ozzy decided he needed the toilet and found a crumbling old wall to urinate against. In mid-stream he heard a voice behind him shouting "*You disgust me! You're a disgrace!*" Ozzy turned round and started to explain "*My girlfriend knicked my clothes, what else was I supposed to wear?*", however his sartorial elegance was not the issue, and this was explained to him in no uncertain terms, "*It ain't the dress, you limey faggot piece of dirt. That wall you're relieving yourself against is the Alamo*".

The Alamo Mission, of course, was the site of a famous siege by Mexicans in 1836 which ended with the defeat of the Texan Defenders and led to a rush to join the Texan Army by thousands hoping to seek revenge. The tale of the Alamo was central to the myth of Texas as a state, and the building itself was almost a holy site. How was Ozzy meant to know this? He soon found out, however, when he was forced face-down in the dirt by two police officers and handcuffed.

"*When you piss on the Alamo, you piss on the state of Texas*" one officer declared, to which Ozzy replied, "*Fair Enough*".

"*Would you piss over Buckingham Palace?*" the officer continued.

"*Actually, I did once*" Ozzy said, "*I got arrested*".

After three hours in prison beside a colossal Mexican who had just murdered his wife with a brick (Ozzy said he "*seemed nice enough*"), he was charged with public intoxication and released in time for the concert, with strict instructions to leave town immediately afterwards and never return.

℧ ℧ ℧

Everything was going swimmingly for XTC. They had just celebrated their most successful hit single with *Senses Working Overtime*, their new acclaimed album *English Settlement* had been released and worked its way into the top ten, and they were about to embark on a world tour which would push their level of accomplishment to new elevations. The band had even shot videos for four of the tracks on the album in preparation for release over the impending year.

Hugh Padgham had engineered the previous two XTC albums under the eye of Steve Lillywhite, however the band realized "*Hugh… was getting all the great sounds and we were making the music, so what did we need Lillywhite for?*" Front-man Andy Partridge also realized that if he deliberately wrote songs which were difficult to play live, then he may not need to tour, a prospect that was increasingly inviting.

English Settlement was a double album (though in later years it would be combined easily onto one compact disc and was released in other territories as a curtailed single album), and throughout an array of themes were explored, with an overarching analytical look at England and the English.

The album commenced with a fade-in of the mid-paced *Runaways*, relating the tale of a teenager flying the coop after "*You caught mum chasing dad with a knife, you ran away to escape from the fights, now you're lost in a maze of neon lights*". The neon lights epitomize nighttime in the city, and the track took us nicely from small-town Swindon (where the band hailed from) to the big city regeneration of *Ball & Chain*. In this, people and buildings screamed out for clemency against the developers, with "*Don't want demolition, don't want compensation, it's not just bricks and mortar*" imploring against progress, a particularly pertinent theme given the urban renewal changing the face of Britain.

The first two songs on *English Settlement* were composed by Colin Moulding, but from the third, *Senses Working Overtime*, Partridge took over. Following the commerciality of the single came *Jason & The Argonauts*, with a bass line that rose and fell like the waves beneath the Argo. Partridge adopted on the role of Jason, navigating through all sorts of human brutality, inanity, and hostility on modern British streets, searching in vain for his own Golden Fleece. The aftershock of this ugliness was examined in *No Thugs in our House*, where over a thumping beat the police turned up at a couple's house to investigate a racist attack the preceding night, with their son being the guilty party. "*We never read the pamphlets in his bottom drawer, we never read the tattoo on his arm*" the couple beseeched, as it became apparent the son held intensely fascist opinions. The real shame

of the story was revealed later when "*Her son is innocent cause dad's a judge*", the way the establishment covers up for its own. *Knuckle Down* tackled racism as well, pleading for people to "*Put aside the hoodoo and some of the voodoo about people being different*" whilst *Fly on the Wall* looked disparagingly at human life, with distorted claustrophobic vocals over a bouncing beat, concluding "*One is born and one will die...the bit that's in the middle doesn't count*".

Next up was an old-fashioned love song, or the closest that XTC could get to one, in the form of *Yacht Dance*, placing the devoted couple in opposition to those who would disparage their love, likening themselves to tiny boats, sea birds, and then pebbles skimming across the surface of the ocean, avoiding being dragged down to the depths by others. This act of defiance in love was followed by compunctions regarding the past in *All of a Sudden*, where "*In all of your hurry you've accidently locked the gate*".

There was an Afro-beat influence on the album with *Melt the Guns*, an overly ingenuous anti-gun message aimed in particular at America, where Partridge suggested that at least the *epidemic* has been confined and concentrated in the one place, an unusual choice of subject for a military enthusiast, and *It's Nearly Africa*, in which drummer Terry Chambers recorded himself playing a looped rhythm for the rest of the band to construct a song over, in much the same way that Talking Heads had worked with Brian Eno two years previously. Africa in the title was used as a metaphor for a simpler time, innocence, the Garden of Eden. The feel was continued on *English Roundabout* where the band had had enough of the treadmill of modern life, expressing disquiet and desire to give it all up over a High-Life guitar, before finishing on a personal note with *Snowman*, a song about being given the cold shoulder by your partner.

Unemployment and sexism were also tackled on the album, with *Leisure* bemoaning the fate of those who found themselves unemployed at the expense of the computerization of factories, pointing out school prepares people for the working life, but does not explain what to do when there are no jobs: "*They taught me how to work but they can't teach me how to shirk correctly"* on top of a loping beat.   *Down in the Cockpit*, meanwhile, was an contagious pro-feminist anthem encouraging women to take over from men, using *cockpit* as a double metaphor for being in charge of the airplane and also in a more sexual way, exalting women to *"pull him right out of it"* whilst stating *"Queen wants the castle back from the rascal"*.

English Settlement was without a doubt a great album and could have been a classic with a bit of trimming. Even as a double it became XTC's highest charting album, reaching number five in the United Kingdom, and was set to be their springboard to the big time. All they needed was a world tour to push it over the edge.

21st – 27th February 1982
#1 single: The Jam: Town Called Malice / Precious
#1 album: Barbra Streisand: Love Songs

Whilst the *Diary of a Madman* tour was eventful, it was not always Ozzy Osbourne who caused the chaos. On Sunday 21st February at Corpus Christi Memorial Centre, support act UFO had just finished their set and were waiting behind guitarist Paul Chapman's wall of Marshall amplifiers to re-emerge for an encore. Fraught tempers caused by weeks on the road spilled over as bass player Phil Way and singer Phil Moog started fighting, knocking over the amplifiers, and revealing their scuffle to the cheering audience. As the crowd started chanting *"Fight! Fight! Fight!"* the band arranged themselves at their instruments and played the encore. The fight continued in the dressing room immediately afterwards, as former British Junior boxing champion Moog single-handedly caused $10,000 of damage.

ʊ ʊ ʊ

Evilspeak, which was released this week into cinemas in the United States, was a nondescript horror movie concerning a tale of Satanism and revenge. When it came to be released on VHS video in the United Kingdom, however, scenes of gore and Satanic rituals brought it to the attention of British Board of Film Classification, who instantly banned it.

In the early 1980's a loophole existed which meant video cassettes did not need to be presented to the British Board of Film Classification. A campaign led by the puritan moral campaigner Mary Whitehouse resulted in the Director of Public Prosecutions producing a list of 154 films believed to violate the *Obscene Publications Act 1959*. Amongst these were undeniable classics such as *Suspiria*, *The Thing*, *Night of the Living Dead*, *Scanners*, *Friday the 13th*, and *The Evil Dead*, along with other titles which benefitted from being on the list by making them desirable: *Cannibal Apocalypse*, *I Spit on Your Grave*, and *Zombie Flesh Eaters*. To be on the list gave notoriety, and guaranteed thousands of illegal sales.

Caught up in the puritan rush, police began to prosecute producers, distributers, and retailers indiscriminately, however the lure of notoriety was too much for some. Distributers could gain publicity by sending a copy of their title to Mary Whitehouse and the National Viewers and Listeners' Association with a carefully worded letter complaining about their own film, and the ensuing publicity and ban would guarantee a huge boost in black market sales. When the outcry in the press became so loud in 1982 the government introduced *The Video Recordings Act* requiring certification for VHS tapes.

Whitehouse, seventy-two-years-old, was a former art teacher who had found a bit of notoriety in the 1950's by writing an article for the *Sunday Times* in which she illustrated how a mother might "*best avoid...pressurising her sons towards* [homosexual] *orientation*". From 1964 she launched the *Clean Up TV* campaign and described the BBC Director General as "*the devil incarnate... [who] more than anyone else [is] responsible for the moral collapse in this country*". Whitehouse objected to any negative analysis of war, accusing television of being the "*ally of pacifism*", and crusaded against a whole host of television programmes throughout the 1970's, including *Doctor Who* which she memorably characterised as "*teatime brutality for tots*". Her organisation did, however, make time to present serial-paedophile Jimmy Saville an award for "*wholesome family entertainment*".

In the early 1970's Whitehouse set up the *Festival of Light* alongside Lord Longford[78], Malcolm Muggeridge[79], and Cliff Richard. When Margaret Thatcher came to power in May 1979, Whitehouse saw an accomplice in her argument, writing that "*already one senses a lifting of the spirit*".

In 1982 VHS tapes were far from being the dominant format for home video. Betamax, developed by the Sony Corporation offered better quality image and were cheaper to manufacture and buy, however VHS offered a longer recording time and cheaper video players. At the end of the day, it was price of the machines which won out, as well as JVC's (who had developed VHS) willingness to licence the technology to other companies. By 1982, Betamax only owned 25% of the market, and was effectively on the way out.

Initially, movie companies retailed pre-recorded videos at a high price, expecting them to only be purchased by hire shops, however upon realising that people would want to own a copy of their favourite film, the price dropped significantly. VHS remained the home entertainment format of choice until the release of DVD in 1997, after which it rapidly disappeared.

Meanwhile, most of the films placed on the *banned* list have since passed censorship uncut.

ʊ ʊ ʊ

Whilst XTC were looking backwards to pop art for inspiration, in America The B52's were also working with analogous influences. Formed in Athens, Georgia in 1976 by Cindy Wilson and her brother Ricky by enlisting keyboardist and vocalist Kate Pierson, vocalist Fred Schneider and drummer Keith Strickland, and combining new wave, surf music, B-movies, and dance into a 1960's-styled party act, their first single, *Rock Lobster* became an instantaneous cult-classic upon release in 1978, and a genuine worldwide smash hit single upon a re-release by Island Records the subsequent year.[80] With an astuteness beyond their experience the band split their list of songs into two, recording half for their self-titled debut album in 1979, and the other half for their next release *Wild Planet* in 1980, thus guaranteeing they did not suffer from second album syndrome. Of course, this just kicked the second album syndrome further down the

---

[78] Longford found homosexuality "*nauseating*" and considered homosexuals as "*handicapped people*".

[79] Muggeridge was partial to a threesome with Kingsley Amis and George Orwell's widow, and was described as a "*compulsive groper*" with the initials NSIT next to his name on BBC documents, which stood for "*not safe in taxis*".

[80] The single, seven minutes of Dada surf-rock, impelled ex-Beatle John Lennon to come out of retirement, though quite why he then recorded a middle-of-the-road album like *Double Fantasy* remains a mystery.

road to the third album, which they started to record in September 1981 with Talking Heads front-man David Byrne producing.

The situation was not ideal, with the band initially wanting to write more songs but being pressurized into recording a follow-up by their manager Gary Kurfist. Byrne, on the other hand, was simultaneously occupied by the soundtrack to a dance project, *The Catherine Wheel*, recording that during the day and The B52's at night, with little sleep in-between. Byrne brought world music and horn sections to the recordings, but either through artistic differences or lack of sleep, the sessions broke down, leaving Kurfist in a difficult position as he had promised the label a new album sooner rather than later. A compromise was reached, and in early 1982 a six-track mini album called *Mesopotamia* was released.

On the introductory track, *Loveland*, the band sacrificed lucidity and a decent song for mood and atmosphere, whilst the influence of Byrne was obvious on *Deep Sleep*, sounding more like his collaboration album with Brian Eno, *My Life in the Bush of Ghosts*, than the B52's. Kate Pierson's vocals were set back in the mix and High-Life guitars strummed throughout. The rest of the album continued in a similar manner, with the songs mostly being undistinguished, a consequence of not being complete at the time of recording.

The band then took a whole bunch of tracks they had been working on and spent the necessary effort finishing them in time for their next album, the much more consistent *Whammy*, released in 1983. Meanwhile, they headed out on the road for an extensive American tour, re-establishing themselves as the country's foremost party band.

After *Whammy* the band suffered a writing block which was further compounded by the death of guitarist Ricky Wilson from AIDS in 1985, aged thirty-two. Following the 1986 album *Bouncing off the Satellites* the band went into hibernation, before returning in 1989 with their largest worldwide hit single *Loveshack* cementing a place as floor-fillers. Since then, the albums and singles have been sporadic and often successful, but it is as a live act that The B52's have continued to shine, certain to bring the party to whatever venue they play.

ʊ ʊ ʊ

The United States continued to produce hits by acts who, to British ears, sounded more antediluvian with each passing month. One of these was by Journey who had been formed in 1970's hippie San Francisco by former members of Santana and Frumious Bandersnatch. Initially cultivating a jazz-fusion furrow, the epitome of the 1970's notion

of musicianship-over-songs, a deficiency of sales saw the band switching to an even blander Adult-Oriented Rock, comparable to that of Boston and Foreigner. The rest of the decade was spent building their profile and chart success, culminating in 1981's massive-selling album *Escape*, which topped the Billboard charts and sold in excess of ten-million copies.

It was from this album that their most celebrated song was released as a single. *Don't Stop Believin'* only reached number sixty-two in Britain upon its release in February 1982, and then the slice of AOR was forgotten for twenty-five years until it was featured at the finale of television show *The Sopranos*, and then dredged up for talent show *The X Factor*. Further exposure through the American series *Glee* saw the song climb into the British top ten, to be treated like a long lost and much-loved standard, and therein lies an admonitory truth: the songs you consider abysmal now will be reclaimed by future generations as classics. Future music consumers will not care that Take That were a manufactured boy band, Rick Astley was the latest in a lengthy line of puppets from the stable of Stock, Aitken & Waterman considered at the time to be indicative of all that was wrong with contemporary music, Abba were the most disposable pop you could find, or "*disco sucked*" in the late-1970's. No, they will treat the kitsch and the cool with equivalence, permit them an equal opportunity to be heard, initially in an ironic way but then with true and profound love. Your offspring will embrace and reclaim the music you find inconsequential and incidental, whilst failing to comprehend that which appealed to you, and there will be nothing you can do about it.

ʊ ʊ ʊ

Writing and performing uncompromising confrontational music with touches of punk, funk and dub from their beginnings in 1978, Killing Joke had created a following who loved their controversial and provoking live shows and cover artwork. Singer and keyboard player Jeremy "Jaz" Coleman was an enigmatic figure, half-English half-Bengali, who had a privileged upbringing studying piano in Leipzig and Cairo, and had teamed with Paul Ferguson, Geordie Walker, and Martin "Youth" Glover. By the time they recorded their third album in Cologne with Krautrock legend Conny Plank, Killing Joke were poised to break through to a modicum of mainstream success without compromising their sound or image.

Completing their latest British tour at Brighton Top Rank on Wednesday 24th February, Coleman went berserk onstage, angered at the amount of people in the audience spitting on him. Storming from the stage he exclaimed "*I hate them! I hate them! Why do they spit at me? I will never go on again!*"

The rest of the band had no idea what Coleman was planning and two days later, on his twenty-second birthday, the singer went missing.

ʊ ʊ ʊ

Through our twenty-first century eyes hitting a child with a belt or a cane seems barbaric and cruel, yet institutionalised ritual beatings were the norm to be expected for school pupils in 1982. Children were at the mercy of a teacher who could randomly hand out physical pain without justification. Getting something wrong in class could result in being caned in England or given the belt in Scotland. Asking for a guarantee her six-year-old son would not be physically abused, Scottish mother Grace Campbell was told by the school this was impossible. Further protests to local councillors, Members of Parliament, and the government fell upon deaf ears, and so in 1976 she took the fight to the European Court of Human Rights in Strasbourg.

To explain how ingrained corporal punishment was in the United Kingdom at the time, you only need look at the reaction to this move: many people were outraged and refused to talk to Campbell ever again, abusive graffiti was sprayed across her front door, bricks were thrown through the window, and the family telephone was tapped by the government. Not that pupils were complaining, with one youth explaining to *Sunday Times* features writer Ian Jack "*The only thing school taught me was how to doss... we used to walk around during the lessons and the teachers couldn't do nothing about it... some of us only turned up for our school dinners... if they hit you in school you'd have your dad up, wouldn't you?*"

After six years of legislation, on Thursday 25th February Campbell and co-campaigner Jane Cosans finally achieved success by getting the European Court of Human Rights to ban corporal punishment in schools.

Education would never be the same again.

ʊ ʊ ʊ

The press chose to ignore Gay Related Immune Deficiency, apprehensive to report on anything associated with gay sex. Any initial reports of the disease as being *"gay"* and incurable led to a massive increase in victimisation, with homosexual men in New York being evicted from their apartments by baseball bats, and in one case set on fire. It was also around this time suggestions started to be made by some in the gay community that the use of condoms could help prevent the spread of the disease, an opinion initially based on personal hunches rather than medical evidence.

The approach of the American press was encapsulated on Thursday 25th February when the Wall Street Times finally dedicated sixteen paragraphs to the disease, but only because it had started to turn up in women and heterosexual males.

ʊ ʊ ʊ

The Clash concluded their tour of the Far East on Saturday 27th February, arriving in Bangkok the day before to find they were number one in the charts. The elation only lasted until they discovered the charts were invented each week by the local promoter to suit whoever was in town. A few minutes before taking to the stage at the university that night, their road manager announced that, by law, every show in Thailand was obliged to begin with the national anthem. Frontman, Joe Strummer, picking up the incorrect meaning, went into a rage, screaming *"How the fuck are we meant to learn the national anthem in the next few minutes?"*

Topper Headon's heroin addiction once again became a problem, as after being required to go cold turkey in Japan, he had taken up the habit again in Australia before flying to Thailand where he presumed it would be easy to score. Instead, he found himself without drugs and spent the days itching, irritated, and in withdrawal.

On Sunday 28th February the band journeyed into the Thai countryside with photographer Pennie Smith to capture the cover shot for their forthcoming album, posing hastily on the railway line which led to the Bridge over the River Kwai, before Headon hurried to the airport for the first available flight back to London and drug salvation.

Meanwhile, bass player Paul Simonen was rushed to hospital with a suspected twisted colon and was about to have part of his intestine removed when the tour manager demanded a second opinion. A Swiss doctor was brought in and confirmed the bass player had caught a bug from jumping into puddle of mud a couple of days previously and being immediately attacked by a swarm of flies. The delay whilst he was in hospital allowed the rest of the band to relax for a couple of days before returning to London.

ʊ ʊ ʊ

Urinating on the Alamo had turned Ozzy Osbourne into Public Enemy Number One in Texas, and subsequent shows in the state were met with death threats and protests. Before the concert at Amarillo Civic Centre on Saturday 28th February, the promotor received what he considered to be a credible threat to shoot Ozzy whilst he was onstage from an armed vigilante group. Security was heightened, however lax laws regarding where and when guns could be carried made for an extremely jittery show. Throughout the performance the audience was treated to the spectacle of Ozzy moving around the stage more than normal, only for the band members to scarper away from him at every opportunity in case they were caught by a stray bullet.

MARCH

28th February – 6th March 1982
#1 single: Tight Fit: The Lion Sleeps Tonight
#1 album: Barbra Streisand: Love Songs

When first punk appeared in 1976 the original hard-core of followers were drawn to the vigour but were motivated by the concept rather than the sound to give it a go themselves. Bands were formed whose solitary motivation and grandest aim was to play a live gig. Some broke up immediately afterwards whilst others continued and developed, however the idea of a *career* remained anathema to them, except for one person, in whom punk rock collided with raw ambition: Billy Idol.

Born as William Broad in London in 1955, his family emigrated to the United States not long after, providing his first recollections to be strained through an American sensibility, a viewpoint which never left him. Upon returning to England a few year later the family settled in London peripheral town Bromley[81], where a teenage Idol met locals Steven Bailey and Susan Ballion. The three bonded over a love of Roxy Music, The Velvet Underground, and David Bowie, until stumbling upon the Sex Pistols in early 1976 and becoming coverts. Known as the Bromley Contingent[82] they followed the band throughout the determinative year and were inspired to form or join their own acts. Bailey and Ballion became Steve Severin and Siouxsie Sioux and formed the Banshees, whilst Idol[83] and Tony James played guitar and bass in the band Chelsea, backing vocalist Gene October. After a handful of gigs, Idol and James appropriated drummer John Towe and formed Generation X, with Idol as the frontman and Derwood Andrews on guitar. The four helped set up Britain's first punk venue in early 1977 at the Roxy and became the house band whilst sharpening their live set. Signing to Chrysalis Records they scored some minor hits, and abetted by Idol's matinee good looks, like a blonde sneering Elvis crossed with Billy Fury, the band became a regular on television and in magazines.

During the first Generation X recording session, veteran producer Phil Wainman had suggested to Idol he was a future solo star[84], and this idea was further accentuated when he was sent to the United States solo in 1978 for promotion purely because the record company could not afford to send the whole band. It almost seemed unavoidable that Idol would become a solo artist, with a resolute determination and pin-up looks. He refused to be limited by punk's *year zero* dogma, declaring there was no way he was giving up Gene Vincent, and throughout his time in Generation X had brought all sorts of classic rock and roll influences to the sound. This mixture of rock and roll through a punk filter led to a couple of hefty hits in the shape of *King Rocker* and *Valley of the Dolls*.

At the turn of the decade, Idol and James recognised the future lay in a more electronic direction and tried to recruit Giorgio Moroder to produce their third album. Moroder

---

[81] H.G. Wells described Bromley as a *"morbid sprawl of population"* and refused the freedom of the town. Frankie Boyle added to this by saying Bromley was *"a lobotomy made out of bricks"*.

[82] As well as these three, the contingent also contained Soo Catwoman, Simon Barker, Marcus Herbert, Debbie Wilson, Linda Ashby, Philip Sallon, Simone Thomas, Bertie Marshall, Tracie O'Keefe, and Sharon Hayman.

[83] Idol took his new name after a former chemistry teacher wrote *"William is I-D-L-E"* on a school report.

[84] Wainman had been the producer for The Sweet and The Bay City Rollers. What he actually said to Idol was *"You're absolutely bloody talentless, but you look great!"*

was too busy but recommended his erstwhile assistant Keith Forsey[85], who helped them record a new song called *Dancing with Myself*. At this point the drummer and bass player had been expelled, and they were helped by former Clash drummer Terry Chimes, along with guitarists Steve Jones (from The Sex Pistols), Steve New (from The Rich Kids), Danny Kustow (from The Tom Robinson Band) and John McGeoch (from Magazine). An album was put together and released under the designation of Gen X, partly because they were in a legal battle with their manager for the rights to the old name, and partially to indicate they were moving on musically. Both *Dancing with Myself* and the album flopped in Britian, however the single was picking up a substantial amount of exposure on dancefloors in the United States, and it was this which persuaded Idol to fly to New York in March 1981 with nothing but a suitcase, a guitar, an idea to be a solo artist, and a raging heroin addiction.

Idol set himself up in the city, right in the marrow of rap and disco, existing in an unadorned room with only a mattress, a kettle, and a black and white television. He also owned a stereo with only one speaker and upon listening to The Doors albums on stereo vinyl could only hear Jim Morrison's vocals. It was years before he realised there was music to accompany the singing. Ingratiating himself into the New York scene, Idol began working with Kiss manager Bill Aucoin, selling America the idea of a cartoon British punk star, a *Punkle Tom* character. The first recruit on the journey was guitarist Steve Stevens, who brought glam-punk to the sound. Despite being the primary songwriter in Generation X, Idol was uncertain he could write without the help of Tony James and suggested recording a version of *Mony Mony*, originally by Tommy James & The Shondells. The song had been playing on the radio when a sixteen-year-old Idol has lost his virginity, and he was convinced that a dance / rock hybrid could be successful. Flying out to Los Angeles to work with Forsey again, Idol and Stevens recorded some tracks for an introductory solo EP, along with *Hot in the City*. The record company decided this last track was too good to be buried on an EP, substituting it instead with *Dancing with Myself*, a move which led a lot of people to believe the latter was a Billy Idol solo single.

By the end of 1981 Idol and Stevens had recruited Phil Feit and Steve Missal, and were beginning to play some live dates around New York. The record company saw enough potential in the first release to make plans for a debut album. There was just one problem: Idol did not have enough songs. A meeting was arranged in January 1982 with Lou Reid to see if they could write together. Reid, who had been a hero to Idol, perched in the shadows whispering a stipulation he be paid an immoderate sum of money for each half hour spent collaborating. Idol turned him down, vowing never to meet his heroes again.

Idol flew out to Los Angeles on Monday 1st March 1982, and immediately became embroiled in a high-speed car chase with the police when his driver, high on Percodan from a dental visit, started driving erratically. Once they stopped, hitting a gatepost, the occupants of the car were held on their knees at gunpoint whilst Idol put on his poshest English accent and tried to talk his way out of the whole thing. Finding no drugs in the car, the police let them off with a fine for the damaged gatepost and sent them on their way.

ʊ ʊ ʊ

---

[85] Forsey had been the drummer on Donna Summer's disco hits. He would go on to write *Flashdance (What a Feeling)* for Irene Cara and *Don't You Forget About Me* for Simple Minds, which had originally been meant for Billy Idol.

Synth-pop pioneer Gary Numan's career had been drifting for a while, with his singles no longer guaranteed a top ten placing, however he still far from spent.

Air-travel obsessed Numan had initially found success with his band Tubeway Army in 1978, fabricating pseudo-dystopian music which benefited from a chance encounter with an early synthesizer in the studio, but was essentially put together with traditional instruments such as drums and bass guitar. Lyrically, Numan incorporated science fiction influences, sound-tracking these with a Minimoog synthesizer, and hit the top of the charts in 1979 with the single *Are "Friends" Electric*. Numan reacted to success by promptly relinquishing the group and recording all future releases under his own name. Over the next eight singles and three albums, he developed a dispassionate impassive personality analogous to that of an automaton, a move forced upon him by a combination of undiagnosed Asperger's Syndrome, an absence of stage movement brought about by stage-fright, and insipid white skin, the consequence of endeavoring to conceal his acne with heavy make-up.

By early 1982, Numan continued to have hits, but his critical reputation had been destroyed by autistic aloofness and his vocal support for the detested Thatcherite Conservative government. The previous year he had moved away from a synth-based sound, embracing elements of jazz and the idiosyncratic fretless bass sound of Japan's

Mick Karn. As he started work on the next album Numan conscripted an entirely new band, including veteran drummer Chris Slade who had spent years playing with Tom Jones during the 1960's, and new-bass-player-on-the-block Pino Palladino. A single from the first sessions, *Music for Chameleons* climbed to number nineteen in the UK charts.

There is a much about *Music for Chameleons* to be ridiculed, from its conceited title purloined from a recently published Truman Capote novel you suspect Numan never read, to the calculatingly ambiguous lyrics, and right through to the fretless bass guitar sound. It is not for no reason that when Steve Coogan chose to highlight his horrendous and preposterous character Alan Partridge playing air guitar, that he chose the bass part on this song. There is no getting away from it… fretless bass guitars are only played, and liked, by wankers. That is not to take anything away from Palladino as a musician, and over the decades he became the bass player of choice for acts as diverse as The Who and Richard Ashcroft, making a decent living. It is not for nothing that Trent Reznor of Nine Inch Nails called him the "*best bass player in the world*". However, nothing dates a record more than the fretless bass sound that slunk around the edges of the charts in the early 1980's.

Despite all these flaws, *Music for Chameleons* is a decent pop record[86], skillfully realized in the studio, with numerous hooks throughout. Numan celebrated by having a hair transplant which he then dyed blonde.

ʊ ʊ ʊ

In what would be an eventful week for Billy Idol, Tuesday 2nd March saw Keith Forsey lock him in a room at Westlake Studios with an acoustic guitar and a drum machine, ordering him not to come out until he had written a song. Twenty minutes Idol emerged from the room with *White Wedding*, the lyrics based upon the dilemma of his sister, who had recently gotten married whilst pregnant, a situation still surrounded by social

---

[86] Thereza Bazar of Dollar sang backing vocals on the B-side.

stigma in the early 1980's. The duo recorded a twenty-minute demo version which could then be abridged by the band, retaining the best bits.

Idol decided to celebrate, returning to his room at the Sunset Marquis and breaking the phone by kicking it through the window. The hotel manager was called and after being placated by a made-up explanation about being frustrated by his grandmother's health back in Britain, agreed to overlook the destruction on the condition the other members of the band were behaving responsibly in their own rooms. Unfortunately, the first room they visited had been trashed by guitarist Steve Stevens so they were compelled to move across the road to the Château Marmont.

℧ ℧ ℧

The Nazis had obliterated the Cripplegate area of London during *the Blitz* of the Second World War, and it remained a bombsite for twenty years afterwards. The whole zone was eventually developed by architects Chamberlin, Powell & Bon with Brutalist tower blocks, and re-named Barbican, taken from the Latin for *fortified outpost*. Brutalism, named after the French for *raw concrete*, had become popular in the 1960's and was a style unconcerned with looking comfortable or easy, emphasizing the function rather than the form and often utilizing repeated modular units. Basically, if you have even seen an aesthetically unpleasant building made of concrete, you have seen Brutalist architecture.

With over 140 different types of accommodation making up the 2,000 homes, the blocks of housing in the Barbican Estate provided a new type of community, with people moving between buildings as their social standing rose. Much maligned for a lack of individualism the estate became a desirable place to live, mainly due a strong residents' association which kept control of the area.

On Wednesday 3rd March Queen Elizabeth officially opened the latest addition to the estate. The Barbican Centre contained an assortment of art galleries, cinemas, restaurants, conference halls, and a library, and became the home to both the Royal Shakespeare Company and the London Symphony Orchestra.

The Barbican campus has divided opinion ever since, and in 2001 became a Grade II listed building, whilst two years later was voted London's ugliest building. In the new millennium, ballooning property prices made the Barbican an enticing place to live once again due to its proximity to the financial district. Penthouse apartments now sell for over £4 million, and the service charges alone can be up to £16,000.

Meanwhile, four miles away Robin Hood Gardens, which had been built a stone's throw from Canary Wharf at the same time as the Barbican and in a similar Brutalist style, was torn down for redevelopment in the new millennium. The distinction between the two estates: Barbican was privately owned whilst Robin Hood Gardens consisted of *social housing*. One suited the high-finance image London was looking to project, whilst the other did not turn a profit. *The Guardian* summed up when they stated *"Housing providers are being forced to take an increasingly commercial approach to their assets. The fate of the residents often takes second place"*.

Meanwhile, as part of the redevelopment of the London docklands, the London Docklands Development Corporation had persuaded housebuilders Wimpey, Barrett, Broseley, and Comben to construct new homes, with offers of cut-rate land at half the market price. The resulting development was named Savage Gardens, after the Victorian housing activist J.P. Savage, and three months of frantic construction saw 600 erected.

A week previously, Secretary of State for the Environment Michael Heseltine formally opened the development in hammering rain, with a speech which was interrupted throughout by left-wing demonstrators. The activists were outraged that old council housing had been torn down and replaced by private accommodation, foreseeing the

day when inexpensive affordable rented accommodation in London would become scarce.
The social cleansing of London had begun.

ʊ ʊ ʊ

Despite his relative absence from the charts in 1982, the effect of David Bowie could be heard everywhere. The *Thin White Duke* had spent most of the preceding year missing from the music scene, electing instead to appear on Broadway as the title character in *The Elephant Man*, as well as a BBC production of Bertolt Brecht's 1918 play *Baal*, for which he was paid the union standard of £1000. For the latter of these Bowie journeyed to his old stomping ground, Berlin, in September 1981 to record five Brecht songs with Tony Visconti, all of which were released as an extended play single

to coincide with the broadcast of the play. Regardless of being a wildly uncommercial release, such was Bowie's reputation the EP managed to reach number twenty-nine in the charts, with songs mirroring his 1970's European inspirations.

Bowie found himself in a peculiar place in 1982, only a couple of years from one of his most successful albums, *Scary Monsters...and Super Creeps*, but far enough for people to be speculating where he had gone. After an extraordinarily fecund decade in the 1970's, during which he had changed styles more rapidly than fans could follow, the new decade saw his shadow cast long on contemporary music and there was scarcely a new white act which did not cite him as an influence. With so many copycats and admirers in the charts, how could he move ahead of the curve again? It is perhaps this predicament which forced him to seek fresh challenges on the stages of theatres rather than concert halls. In the two-and-a-half-year gap since his last studio album, the public had to make do with one-off single releases such as the *Baal* EP, or his subsequent title track to Paul Schrader's film *Cat People*.

Bowie had recorded this in Montreux, Switzerland the previous summer by simply adding lyrics and vocals in less than an hour and two takes to an already recorded track by disco producer Giorgio Moroder, before nipping over to Queen's studio and knocking out *Under Pressure*.

Cat People (Putting Out Fire) was an atmospheric piece suited to Bowie at his most theatrical, providing a role-model for innumerable goth vocalists over the decade whilst building towards a glorious chorus. The single stalled at number twenty-six in Britain but was a chart topper in Scandinavia and New Zealand. Bowie, however, must have had some issues with the production and arrangement, and by the end of the year had re-recorded it in his own style for his next album, *Let's Dance*.

Bowie also spent part of 1982 performing in Tony Scott's horror movie, *The Hunger*, sharing some screen time with another act he strongly influenced: Bauhaus. *The Hunger* was a script considered terrible by everyone who saw it until screenwriter Adrian Lynne was introduced to MTV by his daughter. He announced to Scott he was "*going to do an MTV movie of this piece of shit*", and the two of them owned up to stealing liberally from Nic Roeg's movies and Helmut Newton's photographs. The movie almost killed Scott's career and it was another three years before he was trusted to make a film again.

Bowie played the role of a 300-year-old vampire, the make-up for which allowed him to nip to the pub for a drink unrecognized, whilst after hours he initiated an affair with co-star Susan Sarandon which continued in a non-exclusive way for the next three years.

ΰ ΰ ΰ

In February the band Bauhaus took advantage of a new-found association with their hero Bowie by re-releasing one of their more outstanding tracks.

Initially formed in late 1978 under the name *Bauhaus 1919* by Daniel Ash, and brothers Kevin and David J. Haskins, the band drafted acquaintance Pete Murphy on vocals purely because he looked awesome. Within four weeks of their debut gig on New Year's Eve 1978 the band recorded first single, *Bela Lugosi's Dead*, a nine-minute pillar of perdition and dub which kick-started the Goth rock movement of the 1980's, even though it was written with tongues firmly in cheeks.

Goth rock was *au courant* on the alternative scene in the early 1980's, with Bauhaus one of the preeminent lights. The phrase was first used in the late 1970's by music journalist Nick Kent in a revue of punk act Siouxsie & the Banshees, referring to the debt owed to bands such as The Doors and The Velvet Underground, acts who had caroused in crepuscular lyrics which were pompously over-poetic. With Magazine and Joy Division also leading the charge the sound of the scene remained disparate whilst

at the same time having some recurring sonic and lyrical *leitmotifs* such as tribal drums and the use of flanged guitars. The acts were inclined to revel in lyrical themes that were a blend of otherworldly qualities and doom, camouflaged by the kind of pseudo-poetry only scholars of Romanticism could appreciate, or at least those that had read J.G. Ballard and Anne Rice.

Over the first couple of years of the eighties, Bauhaus cemented their reputation through the release of two albums and a handful of singles, none of which had perturbed the top forty. The closest they had come had been a year previous when a song entitled *Kick in the Eye* reached number fifty-nine. Record company Beggars Banquet clearly felt the track merited more and re-released it in February 1982, as part of the EP *Searching for Satori*.

Beggars Banquet were correct: *Kick in the Eye* did deserve to be a massive hit, from the beat taken directly from the New York dancefloors to the funk-influenced bass line, both of which provided the spine of the track. Over this Daniel Ash provided dissonant guitar lines which did their best not to get in the way of the song, whilst Pete Murphey's lyrics addressed the notion of *Satori*, the Japanese Buddhist idea of *awakening*. Unfortunately, the public were not prepared to be awoken, and whilst the song improved upon the previous year's placing, it could still only reach number forty-five.

ΰ ΰ ΰ

John Belushi loved drugs, loved to party, and was never happier than when he could combine the two. In recent times the American actor and comedian had moved into Bungalow Number Three at the luxury Château Marmont in Los Angeles, where he could make noise and entertain however many guests as desired.

Coming up through Chicago's comedy scene, Belushi had been one of the original young comedians on NBC's *Saturday Night Live*. Like many of the *SNL* cast, Belushi's next logical step was movies, starring in commercial hits *Animal House* and *The Blues Brothers*, and was currently working on an early script for what would become *Ghostbusters*. Also like many stars from the 1970's Belushi liked wild living, however in recent months this lifestyle had started to affect his health.

Concerns about his health were such that when he visited his manager's office on Thursday 4th March to request money, Bernie Brillstein turned him down, fearing he wanted it to acquire drugs. Belushi returned later in the day, and this time Brillstein relented. That night he hooked up with former backing singer for The Band and heroin addict Cathy Smith, ingested huge amounts of alcohol and cocaine, and hit the town. Near midnight, the duo retreated to Château Marmont to shoot up speedballs, a mixture of cocaine and heroin, and sat around in a state of beatitude. Comedian Robin Williams paid a visit soon after, departing after snorting a couple of lines, and then at three in the morning actor and neighbor Robert DeNiro turned up for a short while. Smith then showered a wasted Belushi and put him to bed, before taking off in his Mercedes having enjoyed another typical night.

℧ ℧ ℧

Overjoyed with his newly written song, Billy Idol spent Wednesday 3rd March recording a proper version of *White Wedding*, along with an electronic dance mix, after which the band played an impromptu gig at what would later become the Viper Rooms.

On Thursday 4th March, high on Tequila and heroin, Idol demolished his room at the Château Marmont in the middle of the night. Once again, the manager was called, and Idol was given his marching orders with instructions to leave in the morning. Upon waking naked amongst fragments of shattered furniture and glass the subsequent morning Idol noticed the police approaching the apartment, and assuming they were coming for him decided to go out in a blaze of glory. Meeting them, still naked, outside his door with a joint in his hand he was perplexed when they passed by, heading towards Apartment Number Three further down the row.

Here, having been alerted by personal trainer Bill Wallace, the police found the body of thirty-three-year-old John Belushi in a foetal position, tongue lolling from of his mouth, with his face discoloured on one side where the blood had settled. Cathy Smith was later arrested and charged with first degree murder for supplying and injecting the speedball which killed him, before bargaining this down to manslaughter and a sentence of eighteen months.

Meanwhile, the recording of Billy Idol's debut solo album proceeded throughout March with the songs written in the studio. Once complete the band flew back to New York, but not before Idol got himself a tattoo on his arm of the Russian cartoon character *Octobriana*. In the early 1980's tattoos were still very much the dominion of convicts, bikers, and sailors, so it seemed an egregious thing for a young musician to do, however within a few years no rock star worth their weight in hairspray would be without one, especially in Los Angeles.

℧ ℧ ℧

In the days before rap, black British kids were more likely to find success with funk or soul. One of the most popular was a twenty-five-year-old from Wandsworth, London called Norman Giscombe, who had commenced his professional singing career providing backing vocals for one of Britain's great R&B acts of the early 1980's: Lynx. In late 1981 Giscombe signed a solo deal with Mercury Records, persuading them that he could be the British riposte to an artist who was just beginning to make waves across the Atlantic: Prince. The label loved the idea of an autonomous black artist, writing and producing their own material, but insisted on two things: like Prince he would only use one name, and so Norman was branded as Junior, and that he co-write with Lynx keyboard player, Bob Carter, as a safe pair of hands.

The two of them set about writing and recording with one of the first results being a track entitled *Mama Used to Say*, a dazzling piece of funk-pop equaling anything being created by the likes of Prince or Michael Jackson. The song was born from a tête-à-tête he had with his mother about remaining true to who he was, but also not to be in a haste to have life pass by, with sagacious fragments of advice dispersed throughout the chorus, such as "*Take your time, young man*" and "*Don't you rush to get old*".

With a sure-fire hit, a clean-cut image, and a song heavily influenced by American rhythm and blues, it only seemed natural the record company would push the single across the Atlantic, however when he first travelled to the continent Junior discovered there was a clear distinction between *white* and *black* music. Labels had different A&R staff for white and black artists, and for a record to break nationwide the onus was on the head of black A&R to persuade the head of white A&R the song had merit.

The mainstream radio and television remained resolutely segregated in the United States, and regardless of the success of Motown, Stax, or disco, black artists were still expected to appeal only to a black audience. Six months into its life, MTV was a citadel of white rock with no black faces on the channel. Co-founder Les Garland[87] has since denied there was a *blackout*, instead asserting that MTV was set up as a *rock* channel,

and black artists were not, in the main, making *rock* music in those days. In the first eighteen months of MTV roughly 750 videos were aired of which fewer than 24 were by black artists, a move that seemed committed to returning black artists to the station of James Baldwin's *invisible men* in society.

Junior encountered a supplementary problem when his own black A&R guy claimed the song was *too white, too rock* for black audiences, and ordered a re-mix by Tee Scott. This new version took off in inner-city areas such as Chicago, leading audiences back to the original British

version which began to cross over into the mainstream chart.

As the song climbed the Billboard charts, the driving bass line and infectious chorus also began to take off in Britain, reaching number seven, however just as Junior was on the verge of becoming an international star, he peaked commercially. Giscombe continued to work within the music business writing songs for many other artists while sustaining a spasmodic solo career throughout, but never again grasped the altitudes he had in 1982. He remained true to his muse throughout, walking away from a potentially lucrative partnership with Stock Aitken & Waterman at their height because he "*wasn't feeling it*". In later years Giscombe suffered a broken spine in a car accident as well as the death of both his spouse and daughter from Multiple Sclerosis, however Junior remained true to his musical calling, staying positive about life and music.

The other considerable British R&B act in spring 1982 was Imagination, formed the previous year by former singing waiter Leee John and Ashley Ingram. At the turn of the decade John was working as a backing vocalist on tours with end-or-career acts such as Chairmen of the Board and The Delfonics, when he met guitarist and bass player Ingram, and formed a songwriting partnership under the name of Fizzz. A single was recorded with Trevor Horn, but remained unreleased, and altering their name early 1981 to Imagination in memory of the recently assassinated John Lennon, the band added lyrics to a demo tape of a track written by white producers Steve Jolly and Tony Swain, to create *Body Talk*.

Jolly and Swain were a curious choice for the trio to work with, having almost no previous experience with black music. The two had met in 1975 when Swain was working as a cameraman on *The Muppet Show*, and had formed a band called Chaser who released a self-penned novelty tribute to the famous race-horse *Red Rum* on Polydor Records, before splitting. In 1980 the two joined forces again in writing material

---

[87] Les Garland was the voice of the DJ in Starship's *We Built This City*.

for Irish showband singer Joe Dolan, and it was not long after they started work with Imagination.

In producing *Body Talk* the duo were able to bring their studio expertise, claiming a share of the songwriting in the process. With Morgan Kahn of dance label Streetsounds sitting at their side offering advice, the kick drum and bass were pushed  through a DBX 160 compressor for maximum punch in a club atmosphere, and the ponderous pace of the track meant it was both danceable and sleazy. As the single took off, Jamaican drum veteran Errol Kennedy was recruited to be the third member.

In spring 1982 Imagination released the first track from their forthcoming second album, the trance-like *Just an Illusion*. Starting with a single note keyboard riff, the song broke into a leg-humping beat with synth bass and handclaps throughout before John's sultry falsetto took us on a hypnagogic journey. The song dealt with a male fantasy of an unattainable partner and the happiness this would provide, with the punchline at the end of each verse being this is *"just an illusion"*, the object of desire remaining sacrosanct. With John's homosexuality the song took on another dimension, with the entity of yearning possibly being a straight male: their relationship could only ever be fulfilled in his dreams.

Imagination spent as much time at the gym working on their dance moves as they did in the studio recording, and striking appearances on *Top of the* Pops featuring exotic outfits and a nebula of hedonism pushed the song to number two in the charts, selling over a million copies throughout the year and only being kept from the top spot by The Goombay Dance Band's excruciating *Seven Tears*. Imagination's look was reminiscent of George Clinton's Parliament / Funkadelic, with gold and silver lamé, African prints, and reams of flesh exposed, outrageous and yet not out of step with 1982. According to John *"the new wave kids were exploding out of… this bleak background of Thatcherism"* in one direction, whilst the black funk reaction was to be more extravagant in the face of poverty. Britain's R&B / funk scene's link with club culture indulged a more open approach towards sexuality than the British reggae scene, and it was this gay flamboyance which Imagination tapped into, with John proclaiming unconvincingly *"We don't do anything that you wouldn't see in a normal club"*. It was a time of change within black British culture, and Isaac Julien wrote *"Young black men did play with representations* [of what it meant to be a black male] *… the whole construction of the young black soul boy who was interested in dressing in a particular way which was then considered to be effeminate.* [Imagination] *offered up a different, softer image of black masculinity"*.

Britain's R&B scene of the late 1970's was the first undeniably British black music, one which formed its own identity, separate from parents or tradition. The musicians were often second-generation immigrants who felt restricted by the institutionalized racist expectations of musical tastes and chose to align themselves with the pop market. Unfortunately, the pop market assigned a narrow channel for these artists, only accepting a standard *pop* subject matter, removing any social comment or protest from their voice.

ʊ ʊ ʊ

There was a cultural chasm between the Downtown art world in New York and the art being created on the streets, subway trains, and abandoned buildings by people like

Keith Haring[88], Fab Five Freddy[89], Lee Quinones[90] and Jean-Michel Basquiat. These artists were predominantly untrained, living on a meagre amount of money, heavily involved with the club scene, and producing large-scale colourful art in public spaces. Freddy had even made inroads into the Manhattan *cool set* with an appearance and shout-out in Blondie's number-one hit *Rapture*, and the time had now come for the others as well.

Basquiat was a twenty-two-year-old of Haitian and Puerto Rican descent. Having run away from home at the age of fifteen, he had spent years sleeping rough in Manhattan, acquiring a raging heroin addiction in the process. At the turn of the decade, Basquiat had become involved in the nascent graffiti scene in the city using the tag SAMO, and in 1981 had been invited to hold his first exhibition in Italy.

On Saturday 6th March Basquiat opened his first domestic solo exhibition at the Annina Nosei Gallery, where he displayed paintings on found objects from the streets, such as old doors. The show was a sensation with one critic describing him as "*a child of the streets gawked at by the intelligentsia… Basquiat reminds me of Lou Reed singing brilliantly about heroin to nice college boys*".

Not that the artist was around to enjoy the press reaction, having been invited back to Italy to paint in Modena for a second solo Italian show. Basquiat soon rebelled against what he described as the "*factory conditions*" of being forced to paint on demand and slashed all his canvases before returning to New York.

℧ ℧ ℧

John Allan, the dwarf providing extra theatrics on tour with Ozzy Osbourne during the *Diary of a Madman* tour suffered a lot of abuse but seemed indestructible. During a show at Boutwell Memorial Auditorium in Birmingham, Alabama on Saturday 6th March, Allan was hoisted high in the air during the song *Goodbye to Romance*, and secure in a safety harness was subjected to his nightly fake execution by hanging. In his haste to prepare this night the harness was not properly secured, and as he slipped out of it, Allan began to choke for real. The roadie whose job it was to hoist him up figured his struggling body was hamming it up for the audience, and he began swing the rope furiously.

At this stage Ozzy observed the swinging dwarf, and to the delight of the crowd directed the spotlight to follow him back and forth until the end of the song. It was only when Allan was lowered the crew realized something was wrong and carried him to the dressing room, laying the body on a table. Whilst they stood around wondering who was going to administer CPR, Allan came to, leapt from the table, and flipped them all the middle finger before returning to the stage.

℧ ℧ ℧

---

[88] Keith Haring had one of the most distinctive styles of all the graffiti artists working in New York in the late 1970's / early 1980's and earned a deserved worldwide reputation as an artist before his early death in 1990 of AIDS.

[89] Fab Five Freddy was a graffiti artist who, with his posse The Fab Five, had spent years tagging the New York subway trains. He introduced Blondie to rap, and in return they immortalised him on their *Rapture* single. In 1982 Freddie released a single *Change the Beat*, which has been sampled over one thousand-times since then, making a realistic claim for being the most sampled song of all time.

[90] Lee Quinones was also a member of the Fab Five, and later became a respected painter. Eric Clapton bought his entire 1985 solo exhibition.

Producing perfect pop whilst also attaining critical acclamation was the ambition in 1982, and one of the acts pursuing the dream, Haircut 100, released their debut album *Pelican West* at the start of March. With two top ten hits under their belts already and a winsome front man there was no way the album, named after a wharf in London, could possibly fail. Produced by Bob Sergeant who had previously worked with The Beat and was chosen by Haircut 100 because "*he was John Peel's producer at the Beeb*", the album was one of the first recorded on digital equipment, which accounts for the lucidity and elegance of the sound. The band could record their parts over and over until seamless without ruining the tape usually employed in analogue recordings. That, however, was as far as the technology went with Haircut 100 eschewing synthesizers for real instruments throughout and insisting on playing everything themselves instead of employing session musicians.

This was the type of music Paul Morley had in mind when he coined the phrase *New Pop*. "*When Haircut 100 and Altered Images came along they didn't seem as teenybop as they've been hindsighted to be*" he explained years later, "*They just seemed like really interesting pop that had an unusual edge to it... at the time there seemed to be very little difference between Orange Juice and Haircut 100.*"

The album was overflowing with exceedingly amiable numbers, and even when intermittently wandering into jazz-funk territory, managed to stay the right side of pop. Lyrically however, the whole thing was naïve with nonsense rhymes and couplets throughout. Given the band's primary audience were not purchasing the records for a treatise on Roland Barthes considerations of Structuralism, none of this really mattered. In fact, the band could have been singing about anything, and often were in tracks with titles like *Lemon Firebrigade* and *You're my Little Steam Whistle*. *Marine Life*, for example, was about the ice-cream shop across the road from the studio, but listeners were only there for the singles and to behold Nick Heyward's face.

What surprises people about *Pelican West* is the level of musicianship throughout, and Heyward believed he "*hit* [his] *stride with rhythm guitar on the song Kingsize. It grooves. I overdubbed picking on my Fender Stratocaster* [and] *it sounds like Nile Rogers.*" Maybe not, but elsewhere *Baked Bean* was little more than a percussion breakdown with added lyrics, whilst *Milk Film* was whimsy *in extremis*, with Heyward proud that he was the only one "*writing about the ins and outs of the leather straps of a picnic basket.*"

Surprise Me Again was Haircut 100 at their most indebted to Orange Juice, and the Postcard connection was further accentuated in the subject matter of *Love's Got Me in Triangles*, written about Heyward's girlfriend. Heyward had flown to Glasgow to find Clare Grogan and ended up dating her best friend, Marion Killen. He explained that within the song "*The trombone is the sound of an aeroplane flying up to Glasgow and then returning to Heathrow.*"

The Gered Mankowitz photograph on the cover featuring the band lying in arran sweaters upon a bed of autumn leaves looking pensively off camera, added to the sense this was pastoral music rejoicing in an aspect of twee-ness hitherto forgotten about since the days of *Brideshead*, and it is this branch of English eccentricity that made the album an unqualified pleasure to listen to. Overlook the difficulties with the lyrics, and bathe in the luminous blend of funk, tropicalia, and jazz. This was feel-good summer music, an almost faultless debut album which had arrived fully formed and reached number two in the charts.

7th – 13th March 1982

#1 single: Tight Fit: The Lion Sleeps Tonight
#1 album: Barbra Streisand: Love Songs

On Monday 8th March Ozzy Osbourne and his guitarist Randy Rhodes were sitting in a bar in Chicago, contemplating the next date on their *Diary of a Madman* tour. The band were in the middle of a ten-day break and were due to start again in Atlanta on the 17th March. Rhodes inquired of Ozzy how long it would take to drive to Atlanta, to which a confused Osbourne replied *"Why would you want to drive when there's a wonderful invention called an airplane?"* Rhodes admitted he had become terrified of flying following an Air Florida crash in Washington D.C. in January and would never get back inside an airplane unless he absolutely had to.

ʊ ʊ ʊ

Steve Strange had been born Steven Harrington in late 1950's Caerphilly, Wales, the son of a violent womanizing father, and had his Northern Soul world turned upside down by seeing The Sex Pistols play his hometown during summer 1976. The rest of the year was spent perfecting his misfit status and promoting gigs by punk bands in South Wales[91], before moving to London, squatting on the couches of members of the punk scene such as Glen Matlock, whilst working his way into the affections of Malcolm McLaren and forming The Moors Murderers with punk icon Soo Catwoman. Over the

next six months their provocative name saw the band obtain press coverage for all the wrong reasons, whilst a series of musicians passed through the ranks. All this notoriety backfired when Strange was recognised and assaulted on Oxford Street in January 1978, prompting him to split the band.

Strange and flatmate Rusty Egan began organising weekly Bowie and Roxy Music nights in autumn 1978 at Billy's, a gay club in the basement of Gossips in Dean Street, London, which attracted an heterogeneous throng of young oddities dressed in outrageous and epicene regalia, including fashion students Stephen Jones[92], Darla Jane Gilroy, and John Galliano[93], artist Grayson Perry[94], musicians Spandau Ballet, Marilyn[95], Jeremy Healy, Billy Idol and Tony James, Scottish dancer Michael Clark, cultural commentator Robert

---

[91] During which he claims to have lost his homosexual virginity to Stranglers bass player Jean Jacques Burnel.

[92] Jones was a Liverpudlian milliner, who had his first salon financed by Steve Strange. He designed hats for Princess Diana, Grace Jones, Diana Ross, Madonna, and Culture Club amongst many others, and in 2010 was awarded an OBE.

[93] Galliano has four times been named British Designer of the Year. In 2011 he was arrested in Paris after an anti-Semitic rant in a café during which he shouted at a group of women *"I love Hitler... People like you would be dead. Your mothers, your forefathers would all be fucking gassed."*

[94] Perry, as a child, created a fantasy world based around his teddy to escape the reality of his divorced parents. He is now, of course, a national treasure, and I will not hear a word against him.

[95] Marilyn was Peter Robinson, a Marilyn Monroe impersonator, who was best friends with and insanely jealous of Boy George. He had his own hit in 1984 with *Calling you Name.*

Elms[96], film-maker Derek Jarman[97] and performance artist Leigh Bowery[98]. With Egan playing a fusion of Krautrock, electronica, New York dance, and No-wave, Boy George working the cloakroom, and Strange monitoring the door determining who was dressed resplendently enough to gain entry, the Tuesday Night Club moved to the Blitz in Great Queen Street, Covent Garden, becoming the highlight of the week for regulars with many of them spending the previous seven days creating a costume which would only be worn once. The press searched for a name for this new movement, initially using *The Blitz Kids*, before *Sounds* described them as *New Romantics* and a movement was born.

There was soon, often coincidently, club nights up and down the country playing a similar mix of Bowie and Roxy Music, along with Giorgio Moroder disco and new synth-pop hits, from the Rum Runner in Birmingham, Pips in Manchester, Cagney's in Liverpool, and the Adelphi in Leeds. These places provided liberation for outsider kids, somewhere to dress up and dance for people who were catalysed by punk but hated the violence and phlegm. It was an escape from the drab reality of Thatcher's Britain whilst at the same time tapping into the aspiration of the era. When Blitz became too successful, they moved to the Barracuda Club on Baker Street in May 1981, which they renamed *Club for Heroes*.

Meanwhile, since 1979 Strange and Egan had been writing songs together under the name Visage. Egan had been drummer in The Rich Kids, a band put together by former Sex Pistols bass player Glen Matlock and had also recently filled in on the stool for The Skids. The duo recruited another former Rich Kids member, Midge Ure, who had launched his career in the 1970's equivalent of a boy-band, Slik, with whom he had enjoyed a chart-topper with the song *Forever and Ever*. Ure had just returned from playing guitar on an American tour for Thin Lizzy and was able to bring his songwriting and studio proficiency, as well as keyboard player Billy Currie from Ultravox, who Ure had also joined. Other musicians were enlisted in the shape of Barry Adamson, Dave Formula, and John McGeoch, all of whom were members of post-punk band Magazine, and a debut single *Tar* was recorded for independent label Radar Records. According to Ure, the band was mostly him, stating "*I conceived it, I drew the graphics, I designed the Visage logo, I did all of that. I had to sing the songs first and then pump my voice into* [Steve Strange's] *ear, and what came out was a close enough representation.*"

In 1980, Strange's public profile was elevated significantly when he appeared in the video for David Bowie's *Ashes to Ashes* single, alongside other Blitz regulars. This sanctification by the *grande dame* helped propel the movement into the public eye and Visage sign to Polydor Records, releasing their eponymous debut album in late 1980. Three singles from the album charted over the next year, all of them relying heavily on synthesisers and betraying the influence of Ure's songwriting, sounding not unlike the reinvigorated and newly successful Ultravox.

Recording a second album was made problematic by the various members obligations to Ultravox, Magazine, and Siouxsie & the Banshees (whom McGeoch had recently joined), however in Autumn 1981 they reconvened at Mayfair Studios, London. *The Anvil* was named after a notorious gay club in New York and was released in March 1982. It featured a moody monochromatic front cover image of Strange taken by

---

[96] I once accidently read a fiction book by Robert Elms called *In Search of the Crack*. I think I enjoyed it, but all I can remember is there was a chapter called *A tea-towel for your tears*.

[97] Jarman made films which caused critics to go into spasms of praise, but in general are unwatchable. God knows, I've tried.

[98] Bowery was an inspirational figure in the underground scene, as a performance artist and pop musician, but was perhaps just a little bit too *out there* to ever be successful.

celebrated photographer Helmut Newton[99], the cost of which ended up in excess of £170,000 due to costumes, make-up, hair artists, top models, and a decision to shoot at the George V Hotel in Paris and fly everyone over in a private Lear jet. The shoot was not without drama as Newton was partial to slapping anyone, including the models, if they dared to question him, whilst Ollie O'Donnell claimed *"He was like Benny Hill, this big chubby German guy just talking about how big the models' tits were."* Strange was not bothered about the cost, having received his first royalty cheque for £250,000, and under the mistaken assumption this would happen every three months for the rest of his life. He never received another royalty cheque anywhere near this size again.

The Anvil lacked the focus of the first album which is not surprising given the musicians were busy with their day-jobs and Strange was continuing to run *Club for Heroes*, now moved to the Camden Palace, and another members-only club at Kensington Roof Gardens, the site of the 1970's hotspot *Regines*, where Jeremy Healy was the DJ. The album exhibited the influence of funk and soul, taking the music in a more dance-orientated direction, even if the singers voice and tuning was suffering from too many nights out and too much cocaine.

The first single from the album was *The Damned Don't Cry*[100], a slick piece of synth-pop featuring the backing vocals of Perri Lister[101]. The song was an outsider's lament, talking of desolate streets and a lack of connection, an unusual subject given Strange had been the centre of London nightlife for the past two years, but one that perhaps betrays the anxiety at the core of his character. Accompanied by a moody black and white video directed by Midge Ure at Tenterden Town Railway Station over a freezing cold January day and night, it climbed to just outside the top ten. The clip hoped to capture the glory of the Orient Express and featured various surreal dream sequences with partygoers in fedoras and diamante diadems, consuming champagne, bringing the Helmut Newton vision to life.

When the Blitz Club first took off Strange and Egan launched a second club night called *Hell* at Mandy's Club in Henrietta Street, Covent Garden, along with friend and

scenester from Merthyr Tydfil, Chris Sullivan. Sullivan was also the frontman of Spandau Ballet's theoretical principal challengers on the London club scene: Blue Rondo à la Turk. The act was formed in 1981 when Sullivan escaped from South Wales to London, and he utilised them as a vehicle for his vision of jazz and salsa grounded pop. *"I very much wanted to do something different,"* he would later explain, *"I was fed up of people wandering around with make-up and big shoulder pads and frills, fed up of electro music. I wanted to something with men with big moustaches, in suits, without a synthesizer in sight."* Following hype on the London club scene during which the band insisted on played invitation-only gigs, they signed to Virgin Records and recorded their debut single *Me & Mr Sanchez* with veteran keyboard player Pete Wingfield. Despite momentum the single stalled at number forty, however it did top the Brazilian charts for three months.

---

[99] During the Second World War Newton was interned by both the Germans and the British for being Jewish and German respectively. He died in a car crash in 2004 whilst exiting the Château Marmont in Los Angeles.

[100] By happenstance, *The Damned Don't Cry* is also the title of a 1950 film-noir starring Joan Crawford in which she leaves her husband, a character by the name of R(oy) Egan.

[101] Lister was a former member of Hot Gossip who was soon to join Kid Creole & The Coconuts whilst being the significant other of Billy Idol.

After returning to the studio with a series of producers including Clive Langer, Alan Winstanley, and Mike Chapman, their second challenge on the charts was a single produced by ex-10cc members Kevin Godley and Lol Crème. *Klactoveesedstein* was named after a Charlie Parker be-bop tune and is German slang for *Goodbye to the Blues*. Once again, they delivered a slice of pop-à-la-mode with call-and-response verses, however it fared even worse in the charts, only reaching number fifty. Quite why Blue Rondo failed to find success is a bit of a mystery: they were a tight, rousing band playing catchy dance music with a strong image, everything required in 1982, however they may have been missing a good-looking frontman, something which became progressively essential throughout the year as pop music was once again aimed at the lower teens.

ʊ ʊ ʊ

When Treasury Minister Geoffrey Howe unveiled the British government's budget in the House of Commons, and you would never have known the economic vexation of the past two years had ever existed.

Thatcherism was a mercurial array of policies which depended on the Prime Minister's individual aims at any given time, always based upon her much vaunted values of *good housekeeping* and *hard work*. The first Thatcher government had several key aims, including the loosening of legislation seen as limiting the private sector, a curtailment of public spending, and major trade union reform. Under the influence of right-wing American economist Milton Friedman, Thatcher followed a strict monetarist policy, controlling and limiting the flow of cash to areas such as social spending, education, and health. The theory behind this was the less the government spent, the more the free market would regulate these areas, making them more financially efficient. This of course meant the private sector were strongly encouraged to intervene, and personal profit became a desired virtue. In Thatcher's view, social good was best derived from the conflict between self-interest groups. One complication with this approach was great swathes of society had to be side-lined, with high unemployment and the decline of heavy industry seen as an acceptable cost for the flourishing free market. Those employed in manufacturing dropped from over seven million to just over five million in the first half of the 1980's, hitting the young hardest. There were over eight million people aged between thirteen and twenty-one at the beginning of 1982, fifteen per cent of the population, with two-thirds of them defined as working class. Males outnumbered females by 200,000, and whilst a quarter of boys would be convicted of a crime, a quarter of the girls will be married by the age of twenty. Significantly over one-million young people under the age of twenty-four were claiming unemployment benefit, with over 600,000 of them between the age of sixteen and nineteen.

The Chancellor, however, believed the country was "*moving in the right direction*" and allowed National Insurance contributions from employers to be cut. The press and public in general found themselves welcoming the budget: given the hardship of the previous two years any good news was refreshing.

ʊ ʊ ʊ

Whilst the halcyon days of the New Romantic fantasy were ending, some acts were still clinging to the dream. Classix Nouveau had been formed in mid-1979 from the vestiges of punk originals and deliberate underachievers X-Ray Spex by Jack Stafford (guitar) and B.P. Hurding (drums). Where X-Ray Spex revelled in an engagingly amateur attitude to music, the new line-up implemented a more proficient approach by recruiting vocalist Sal Solo[102] and bass player Mik Sweeney through an advert in the Melody Maker. Heavy make-up saw them promptly associated with the burgeoning New Romantic scene, along with a constructed sound of sparse guitar, fretless bass, and overwrought vocals, not unlike what Bauhaus were creating at the same time. By the end of the year Stafford had been replaced by Gary Steadman who introduced a synthesizer to the mix, pushing them further towards the *Blitz Kids* and a pop-based sound. Signing to Liberty Records and releasing their debut album in 1981, along with four singles which skirted around the outside the top forty without breaking, Classix Nouveaux were ready with their second self-produced album, *La Verite*. Lead single *Is It a Dream* was originally an instrumental until someone at the record company saw potential, and it finally provided them with a genuine hit reaching number eleven in the charts. It was to be their only top forty hit, as follow-up *Because You're Young* once again stalled outside the top forty in May.

American producer Alex Sadkin was brought in for a third album the following year, by

which point the only original member was Sal Solo, but despite the presence of hot 1980's producers Phil Thornalley and Steve Churchyard in the studio, nothing managed to break through, leaving Solo to... go solo before turning to religion and becoming increasingly involved in Catholic youth organisations.

Classix Nouveau never manged to break through in any consequential way in Britain, however they did enjoy success in other parts of the world, in particular Poland where they became the first Western band to tour as part of the post-Solidarity government *"bread and circus"* policy. They were deficient in killer songs and, more significantly, a good-looking frontman. Solo could best be described as a body double for *Nosferatu*, and the rest of the band were nameless and faceless, to the extent Steadman later joined A Flock of Seagulls and no-one noticed.

ʊ ʊ ʊ

Since arriving in Liverpool at the supposed invitation of Julian Cope, seventeen-year-old Americans Courtney Love and Robin Barbur hung around Probe Records listening to *Club Country* by the Associates or sat on the front step drinking cider. Throughout the day the two would visit the clothes shop at the back of Probe, and ostentatiously annoy owner Pete Burns, who claimed *"She had a piercing voice, so I didn't want to be noticed by her"*.

Love had lost her virginity the previous month *"in a council house, listening to 'Isolation' by Joy Division, to a guy called Michael Mooney"*, a man described by *The Liverpool Echo* as one of the city's greatest ever guitarists.[103] Mooney has since vehemently denied the story and given Love's false claims about her past, tales such as being employed to make the tea for U2 whilst they recorded the *October* album, it is possible. Then again, given Peter Burns claims that she was *"like when a baby throws a rattle across the room and screams because it can't communicate"*, what benefit is there in claiming to have lost her virginity to someone no-one had heard of?

ʊ ʊ ʊ

---

[102] The singer took his name from SALvador Dali and Napoleon SOLO.

[103] Mooney was later a member of Spiritualized

Working more like a mass-collective than an orthodox band, and heavily influenced by African rhythms and chants, The Thompson Twins had released their debut album *A Product Of...* independently in 1981. Originally from Yorkshire, frontman Tom Bailey had been joined by seven members and, motivated by punk's do-it-yourself philosophy,

moved to London, squatting in abandoned buildings and stealing electricity from neighbouring houses. A second album for Arista Records was produced by Steve Lillywhite, assisted by Thomas Dolby on synthesizers chiefly because no-one else knew how to work them. The sound on the album, entitled *Set*, was more refined than previously, particularly in the opening track, *In the Name of Love*, which had been written by Bailey as a filler, experimenting with dance beats and keyboards. Arista recognised the potential in the song and released it as lead single, where it lingered outside the British top seventy-five, lanced by an inexplicable deficiency of radio play. In the United States, however, the song gained exposure on dancefloors and rose to the top of the Billboard Club Charts, staying there for five weeks throughout May and June. The American record label put together a compilation of the first two albums to capitalise on this success, also entitled *In the Name of Love*, and this also broke into the Billboard charts. Bailey, along with New Zealand born journalist Alannah Currie and London theatre designer Joe Leeway, was prescient in observing the direction music was taking, as well as the complications of such a large and unwieldy band and hatched a plan to break away as a trio under the name *The Bermuda Triangle*. Buoyed by success in America and appreciating a full band was not required for a new dance direction, they instead decided to retain the Thompson Twins name. In April 1982, whilst *In the Name of Love* was starting to show potential in the dance charts, the other members were informed the band were splitting. Each was paid £500 and were permitted to retain their instruments in exchange for agreeing to never perform under the name The Thompson Twins again. Becoming a trio was a deliberately measured move away from *rock and roll*, vowing not to use guitars but to embrace technology as the future.

ʊ ʊ ʊ

The accomplishments of The Jam in the late 1970's, together with the release of the movie *Quadrophenia*[104], helped to initiate a mod revival at the turn of the decade.

Mixing punk brashness with elements of original 1960's bands, acts such as The Purple Hearts, The Chords, and The Lambrettas gained limited success to match their restricted musical outlook, and by 1982 the scene had run its course. None of the bands had the capacity or capability to match their hero, Paul Weller, something which cannot be held against them given his gargantuan song-writing ability.

One of the foremost acts of this revival, Secret Affair, were on the verge of splitting in 1982, having been formed in 1977 as a punk band by vocalist Ian Page and guitarist

---

[104] *Quadrophenia* was a 1979 film based upon a 1973 rock opera by The Who. It starred Toyah and Sting, but on the other hand it had Timothy Spall, Phil Daniels, and Ray Winstone as well. It served as a fine piece of nostalgia for the second wave of mods.

David Cairns under the name The New Hearts and signed to CBS. After a couple of singles, the band split, with Page and Cairns remaining together as a song-writing partnership aided by sustained record company backing. Under the spell of The Jam they recruited bassist Dennis Smith and drummer Seb Shelton and changed their name to Secret Affair, reaching the top twenty with debut single, *Time for Action*. By 1982 relationships had become strained within the band, particularly between Page and Cairns, alongside a mounting disenchantment with the music industry caused by their waning career. Following a prolonged American tour Secret Affair set about recording their third album at the end of 1981, releasing a new single *Lost in the Night* in January 1982. The single was their first not to reach the top seventy-five, and by the release of the album *Business as Usual* a few weeks later the writing was on the wall. Secret Affair had a vision, however, and set off on some dates with a full Motown-style review, including backing vocalists The Wealthy Tarts[105]. After a final date in April, they split, eventually reforming in 2002 and appreciating a longer career in the 21st Century playing scooter rallies and mod revival nights.

Also caught up on the peripheries of the Mod revival were London blues band Nine Below Zero, named after a Sonny Boy Williamson song. Fronted by vocalist and guitarist Dennis Greaves, they signed to an offshoot of A&M Records in 1980, and a concerted bout of gigging around the capital along with a live album saw them pull fans in from the blues, mod, and rock scenes. A second studio-based album in 1981, along

with support slots on tours with The Kinks and The Who, and regular television exposure saw the band poised to break through in 1982. Although styling themselves as a blues band, Nine Below Zero looked more like a mod band. More specifically, they looked like the rhythm section of The Jam.

Nine Below Zero recorded their new album *Third Degree* with Glyn Jones at his studio in West Sussex, and although it contained their most well-known song (*11+11*) along with a David Bailey photo-session on the cover, the album only reached number thirty-eight, far poorer than the break-through anticipated. The band continued to gig throughout the year, performing on the opening episode of sitcom *The Young Ones* in November, before splitting.

Greaves went on to form The Truth, who enjoyed a couple of top forty singles, and like everyone else they later reformed and have been recording and touring ever since.

℧ ℧ ℧

Dr Robert Runcie[106], the Archbishop of Canterbury, had just started his sermon at St Nicholas's Church in Liverpool on Thursday 11th March when a section of the congregation revealed hidden placards and began to shout "*traitor*" and "*Judas*". The rationale for the protest was the forthcoming visit to Britain by Pope John Paul II, and the warmth with which Runcie was willing to welcome him. Amongst the dissenting

---

[105] The Wealthy Tarts were Maz Roberts and Kim Lesley, who first found success in Jools Holland's band The Millionaires and would later join Paul Young. Roberts would later marry bass player Pino Palladino.

[106] Runcie was quite unique for an Archbishop of Canterbury in that he had killed people, having served in the Second World War and won a Military Cross for acts of bravery. He was appointed with the approval of Margaret Thatcher, but soon became a thorn in the side of the Conservative government with his criticisms of their policies.

voices raised throughout the country were the Free Church of Scotland, the right-wing Conservative politician Enoch Powell, and the Reverend Ian Paisley in Northern Ireland whose opinion was encapsulated by his accusation the BBC was in "*spiritual fornication and adultery with the Anti-Christ*".

As the voices in Liverpool increased, Runcie tried to recite the *Lord's Prayer*, but even that was interrupted, and he was forced to retreat. The following month, Runcie expressed his hope that the Church of England and the Roman Catholic Church would be re-united by the end of the century.

ʊ ʊ ʊ

Soft Cell had first visited New York in October 1981 when they spent a month recording their debut album with Mike Thorne. Whilst keyboardist Dave Ball spent time in the studio, Marc Almond partied all night, surfacing late in the day to add vocals. On his third night in the city, he met Cindy, the self-proclaimed exclusive supplier of a new party drug called MDMA, or Ecstasy. Almond was immediately hooked, loving the lack of inhibition provided, and spent the next few weeks smiling and hugging everyone he encountered. From that moment on, Almond and Ball wanted to spend as much time in New York as possible, trailing round nightclubs such as Studio 54 and Danceteria, and even held the launch for the album in the city. Almond accumulated a troupe of fellow revellers, including Marilyn Monroe impersonators, photographers, a Puerto Rican topless dancer, and Cincy Ecstasy (as she became known), enmeshing with veterans of the city such as Andy Warhol.

As *Tainted Love* climbed the American charts, the band spent more and more time across the Atlantic. To aid progress, a performance was booked on the *Merv Griffin Show* in Los Angeles in March. Worried the duo would go astray, the record company chaperoned them everywhere, however Soft Cell decided to rebel against this by dropping acid in the limousine on the way to the studio. When the acid kicked in, the Hollywood sign began to melt, and one of the two record company executives accompanying them morphed into Lucille Ball, whilst the other one started eating his own head. Sweating and terrified, Almond stared out of the window at the city whilst manager Stevo turned into a rotting Buddha. At the studios, the singer sat in his dressing room staring at himself in the mirror as blisters and spots broke out on his face in front of his eyes. Layer after layer of make-up was applied in a failed attempt to cover this, whilst his hair turned into snakes and could only be tamed by putting on a headscarf, at which point he turned into a Latin Al Pacino. A knock at the door brought American chart-reading legend Casey Kasem[107] to the door, who to Almond's eyes looked like a troll… then a garden gnome… then a monkey.

"*Who the fuck are you? Piss off out of my dressing room!*" Almond screamed on the edge of hysteria, thus losing the support of one of the most influential and important people in American pop music.

When it came time to perform the duo had to endure an interview with the host, while Almond drooled, twitched, and giggled whilst trying to avoid Griffin's false teeth which were chattering around his head. Finally, they got to the stage to perform *Tainted Love*, where the unexpected sight of high kicking dancers appearing from the side to accompany them threw Almond, and he missed the opening line of the song.

Not that this mattered, as the song rose to number eight on the Billboard charts, paving the way for the second British invasion.

---

[107] Kasem provided the voice of *Shaggy* in the *Scooby Doo* cartoon series. He was a vegan who quite the *Scooby Doo* role after an argument about voicing and advert for *Burger King*. He would only return to the role when negotiating Shaggy to be a vegetarian.

ʊ ʊ ʊ

REM were aware they fell between two camps: too commercial for independent labels and too raucous for the majors. The one label they had set their heart on, who would fit them perfectly, was I.R.S. started by Miles Copeland III[108], the son of a CIA agent and brother to Stewart Copeland, drummer from The Police. Copeland's other brother, Ian ran his own talent agency booking alternative bands into venues across the United States and had worked with REM before, so through this contact they managed to get some recordings to the label, which was already working with The Cramps, The Dead Kennedys, The Go Go's, Oingo Boingo, and Wall of Voodoo.

On Friday 12th March, the Georgia four-piece were booked into one of a seemingly ceaseless run of dates in small bars across the Southern States, The Beat Exchange in New Orleans, which turned out to be a *"junkies haven"* with a crowd in single figures. REM gave it their best shot, but when the in-house soundman disappeared halfway through the night, they finished the set in a squall of feedback. Sitting morose backstage afterwards, singer Michael Stipe noticed a well-dressed young man.

"Hi, I'm Jay Boberg from I.R.S. Records" he said offering a hand.

"I was afraid of that" replied Stipe.

Boberg's girlfriend was attending university in New Orleans, and he had jumped at the opportunity to visit her and have the record company pay for the privilege. All he needed to do was check out the band whilst in town. Three songs into the set, he turned to his girlfriend and proclaimed, *"I'm going to sign that band"*.

Just over two months later REM signed to I.R.S. Records.

ʊ ʊ ʊ

Entering the charts this week was one of the foremost buried singles of the decade: *Ain't No Pleasing You* by cockney duo Chas & Dave. In 1982, the two were considered something of an anomaly, performing a melange of music-hall, pub sing-a-longs, and boogie-woogie, with a line-up of Chas Hodges on piano and Dave Peacock on bass. They had been playing together for well over a decade, with Hodges having previously backed the likes of Jerry Lee Lewis and Gene Vincent, whilst being a member of Cliff Bennett & The Rebel Rousers and The Outlaws.[109] In the 1970's the duo had worked as session musicians, even providing backing for a Labi Siffre track which was later sampled by Eminem for his *My Name Is...* single.

When they first joined forces in the early 1970's, the idea had been to combine the high energy of early rock and roll with the sing-songs of London pubs during the blitz, a move which led to them being characterized as a novelty act thanks to hits such as 1979's *Gercha'* and *Rabbit*. What most people missed, including their manager and press agent, was the straightforward rock and roll backing on the tracks, a genre in which the two were steeped.

It came as an epiphany for the public to hear their new single, a serious ballad soaked in strings. If the song had been written and performed by Fats Domino it would now be considered a stone-cold original rock and rock classic to match *Blueberry Hill* or *Ain't That a Shame*, however this was a couple of bearded pub singers from the east end of London who were known for gimmick records, and so were disregarded by many. Still,

---

[108] Copeland's mother was an architect who once found what was considered to be another Dead Sea Scroll, but it disintegrated when her husband took it to the roof to see it in a better light.

[109] The Outlaws featured Ritchie Blackmore on guitar and were the backing band on several Joe Meek-produced singles.

enough people liked the song to help it rise to number two in the charts, the duos biggest hit single.

The song itself had been knocking around for a couple of years, initially having been written in a cottage just outside Peterborough. Hodges took the idea from a song he had heard as a child about a man returning home to no lights in his house and finding his wife dead, having committed suicide. Instead, Hodges made the reason for the  lights being the wife has left, however the new surrogate lyrics were soon to be ejected in favour of the final draft. Although the song sounded like a Fats Domino single, the inspiration was John Lennon's *(Just Like) Staring Over*, even though Hodges who had played on the same bill as The Beatles many times in the early 1960's did not rate them as musicians[110].

Once recorded, the duo ran a quick guide mix so they could listen at home, only to find it impossible to recreate the feel of this rough take during final mixing, and so the demo tape became the single, with an added out-of-time drum fill at the beginning spliced on from an alternative take. Initially, Hodges had asked Eric Clapton to play guitar on the song, however this never occurred, something which turned out to be a blessing according to the piano player, because "*a lot of people today would be saying... 'it only got where it did because Eric was playing on it'. And how would we have been able to prove different?*"

The duo was convinced the song was a hit, however the record company dragged their heels, not seeing potential in a *serious* Chas & Dave single. Instead, a couple more *novelty* singles were released, including the excruciating *Stars Over 45* which the two refused to ever play. *Ain't No Pleasing You* continued to go down a storm live, and when they unexpectedly performed it on television show *The Comedians* the phone started ringing at the record company with requests for the song.

14th – 20th March 1982
#1 single: Tight Fit: The Lion Sleeps Tonight
#1 album: The Jam: The Gift

In March Virgin Records were trying their hardest to pretend one of their hottest signings had not broken up, however as far as the members of Japan were concerned, the band was over. Tensions within the act had achieved boiling point just before the release of their last studio album *Tin Drum* when bass player Mick Karn had lost his Japanese girlfriend, photographer Yuka Fujii, to singer David Sylvian. Sylvian in later years claimed Karn had asked Fujii to leave, and with nowhere else for her to go he had taken her in, mitigating this by saying "*Anyone who knows Mick knows this was... his modus operandi: ask his partners to leave and, once gone, claim them back. It got him in some deep water over the years*". At the time Sylvian was openly claiming "*Mick... has an ego that won't let anyone supervise his work and that's a shame*". This was further compounded by manager Simon Napier-Bell concurrently whispering Faustian-fantasies of solo stardom in both Karn and Sylvian's ears. Karn was keen to keep the band together as a safety net just in case his own solo career miscarried, but Sylvian asked him to choose one or the other. Sylvian later said "[Karn] *claimed he*

---

[110] He later changed his mind about Paul McCartney.

couldn't, so I chose for him". Karn saw things differently, at the time stating *"All of us have been suppressed by David's personality for a while… I don't feel I can trust or believe anything he says"*.

Napier-Bell, dreading his cash-cow was to be sacrificed just as it was about to start earning decent money, especially the £200,000 he had personally invested, convinced the band to stay together in the public eye for another year, whilst they went about setting up their respective solo careers, which would allow them to gain from the *"status of being part of a top group"*. Grudgingly, they acquiesced and immediately set about writing and recording separately. The pretence was kept up with the press, with Sylvian saying *"It sounds like the band has split up and don't want to work with each other, but it's not like that at all."*

Virgin Records, desperate to make back the money they had invested, released several singles from *Tin Drum*. The first two, *The Art of Parties* and *Visions of China*,

stalled outside the top forty and thirty respectively, and so a third different and wholly uncommercial track was released in March.

Ghosts was another one of those songs from the early 1980's that sounded unlike anything else ever to grace the top forty. Devoid of any sort of comprehensible beat or drums, the song's verses seemed to comprise arbitrary surges of haunting electronic noise with some monotonous, sparse, and haunting vocals on top, what *Smash Hits* called a *"fearful bloodless drone"*. Sylvian later confessed *Ghosts* was the most personal of his lyrics, recounting extreme self-doubt and his desire and propensity to destroy contentment and success. He had been building towards triumph with Japan for almost a decade and finding himself on the brink of breaking through to the big league, was troubled by the accomplishment. *"When my chance came to be king, the ghosts of my life blew wilder than the wind"* he claimed over a percussive chorus before the track descended defeated back into the torporific verses. This streak in the singer infuriated Napier Bell, who explained *"He was terrified of being condemned for being commercial. He could live with being condemned as esoteric or peculiar, but he couldn't live with commercial."*

It was an incredibly daring move by Virgin and Japan to release this track as a single, and one which could easily have been a catastrophe, however the concoction of Sylvian's pin-up status in magazines such as *Smash Hits*, and an impressive but antonymous *Top of the Pops* performance saw the single rise into the top five. The band came back together for a live performance on BBC's *The Old Grey Whistle Test*, where they were augmented by Ryuchi Sakamoto, with whom Sylvian was already recording solo material.

Virgin Records were keen to cash in on Japan's unexpected mass-success, releasing the track *Cantonese Boy* from their last album. More commercial than its predecessor, with a nagging whistling refrain throughout, the single was a succession of hooks in search of a conclusion, and spent a few weeks hovering around number thirty.

Japan were ahead of the curve when it came to the so-called New Romantic movement, and consequently spent a lot of time refuting they had anything to do with it. As acts like Duran Duran and Spandau Ballet were crossing over into mass achievement, Japan no longer sought any slice of success. Whilst they could be accused of a certain amount of cultural appropriation in the slightly racist way they lumped Japan and China together in the same creative carton, the music was much more than cod-Orientalism, truly pendent in an expanse of its own, and their mixture of traditional Eastern and electronic sounds was more to do with their closeness to

Sakamoto and the Yellow Magic Orchestra. Rather naively Sylvian would claim "*I've never actually been to China. My fascination for it is purely in terms of imagery*", going on to explain that their last album "*wasn't an album about China. It was a state of mind being presented, thoughts and moods pushed forward as bare as possible to not even reach the place where confusion enters into it.*"
Sylvian never understood why journalists made a fool of him.

℧ ℧ ℧

The problem with acidheads and drug-fiends such as the Teardrop Explodes is that when placed in a confined space for a period, things were bound to become.... *strange*. Deciding to fly for thirty-two hours to Australia the wrong way to save money was a folly of grand proportions, and as the band and their crew boarded a flight at London Heathrow on Monday 15th March, a group decision was made to take LSD. For once, frontman Julian Cope uncharacteristically decided this was not a wise idea and tried to talk everyone out of the plan, but as drummer Gary Dwyer, keyboard player Dave Balfe, bass player Ronnie Francois, and four members of the road crew took theirs, he felt he had no choice but to join them. That left guitarist Troy Tate and their sound engineer to take responsibility and herd them through check-in and customs.
On the first section of the flight, Cope became convinced he was the cartoon character Droopy Dog and immersed himself with some headphones and a cassette of Throbbing Gristle's industrial noise collages. Meanwhile the rest of the band gathered near a fire escape at the back of the airplane and debated the practicalities of making a ladder so they could climb down the 35,000 feet to reach the lakes of Newfoundland below. Rather surprisingly, a stewardess joined them, helping with their joints and enquiring if they had any cocaine. Two hours from San Francisco, half the band realised they did not have the temporary US visas required for the short lay-over on the mainland, and *the fear* set in. Upon landing, they were escorted to a windowless room and held there for four hours, whilst the rest of the entourage fed themselves on wine and oysters at the airport bar. Cope had been one of the prisoners, and upon being escorted back to the group insisted on downing everyone's leftovers, which then reacted with his stomach and caused him to vomit all the way from the American mainland to Hawaii.
At the culmination of the final section of the journey to Australia, over the international dateline where another day was lost, they touched down in Sydney and were promptly hosed down by customs authorities in crop dusting suits.

℧ ℧ ℧

One myth about The Jam is that they were a hermetically sealed inward-looking three-piece act, however Paul Weller utilized many outside musicians over the years. Even Glen Matlock, the former Sex Pistol, was asked to join as a second guitarist in 1977, a move scuppered when he refused to wear a matching suit. As 1982 proceeded, Weller increasingly relied on these additional musicians, phasing out his own guitar playing. Even by his own admission, 1981 had been a barren year when it came to songwriting, and with an idea forming in his head of ending The Jam, Weller put pressure on himself to guarantee the next album would their greatest, to go out on a high. As well as the three core members of The Jam, Weller brought in producer Pete Wilson on keyboards, Keith Thomas on saxophone, Steve Nichol on trumpet, and Russ Henderson on steel drums, as he explored his love of jazz, funk, and northern soul. Weller had spent some of the previous year frequenting the club Le Beat Route in

London, submersing himself in the soul music played there, as well as the feel of Spandau Ballet's *Chant No 1*, especially the horns provided by Beggar & Co.

Despite hopes that *The Gift* would be The Jam's crowning glory, it remained too fragmented. The rhythm section of The Jam lacked the artistry or aspiration to help Weller realize his dreams of breaking out of the guitar-based cul-de-sac. The lyrics were progressively coming from a socialist point of view, and a freshly abstemious Weller embraced a hardline clean-living régime, seen by insiders in his newfound somber side. Despite the political leanings, the overall message of the album is one of *Unity*: that together the forces against us can be subjugated.

Recorded in two stretches at AIR Studios in London between October 1981 and February 1982, *The Gift* starts with *Happy Together*, a conventional love song which would have been comfortable on any of the previous albums, followed by *Ghosts* which tackled people who have lost sight of themselves, and musically foreshadowed some of Weller's more traditional solo work from the 1990's. "*I was trying to call out to my generation, a rallying call in the name of inspiration and fulfillment*" Weller later explained, whilst the band tried to make the sound as gaunt as possible to match the title. *Trans-Global Express* took its riff from Northern Soul classic *So is the Sun*, and gave its name to the subsequent tour, whilst *The Planners Dream Goes Wrong* dealt with rundown high-rise accommodation in London, buildings that had meant to be idealistic living quarters when first planned. *Carnation* explored greed and avarice told from the viewpoint of capitalism claiming, "*I trample down all life in my wake, I eat it up and take the cake*". There are a couple of classic Jam songs on the album, such as past  and future singles *Town Called Malice* and *Just Who is the 5 O'Clock Hero*, but they were balanced by tracks such as *Circus*, a lumpen funk instrumental written by bass player Bruce Foxton and *Running On The Spot* which lived up to its title by not sounding like a band looking to develop their sound, but did become the concept around which the album cover was based.

Weller also used his fame to start two record companies of his own: *Jamming* and *Respond*. The former was run by seventeen-year-old Tony Fletcher and started with an initial investment by Weller for the first single, the profits of which would then be used to finance the next one, and so on. Jamming signed Belfast punk band Rudi, who had a reputation and were therefore expected to sell a few copies, whilst Weller's approach was extremely hands-off, some would say non-existent, after the original investment. In fact, when Fletcher turned up at Jam HQ for his first day no-one even knew he was coming. Weller's father and manager John met him with "*What the fuck are you doing here?*" Fletcher's self-confessed inexperience meant successive releases failed to sell in satisfactory numbers.

Respond was a different matter, with financial patronage from Weller's label Polydor. Their first signing was a Cambridge-based female outfit called The Dolly Mixtures. Hester Smith (drums), Debsy Wykes (bass) and Rachel Bor (guitar) had formed in 1978 in the heat of punk, before being offered tours supporting Dexy's Midnight Runners and The Beat which they had to pull out of due to a dose of glandular fever. Recording at The Kinks' London studio with The Damned's Captain Sensible producing, single *Everything and More* was released in March. Next up were young Edinburgh act The Questions[111] who had already recorded for Edinburgh label Zoom

---

[111] The Questions were fronted by Paul Barry, who would go on to write *Believe* for Cher.

Records. Weller produced their debut single, *Work'n'Play*, which was released in February 1982 but failed to chart.

ʊ ʊ ʊ

Forty-eight dates into the North American leg of the *Diary of a Madman* tour, Ozzy Osbourne and his band had just completed a concert at Knoxville Civic Coliseum on Thursday 18th March and were keen to reach Orlando as soon as possible for their scheduled gig two days later. Although travelling by bus was harsh and uncomfortable, Ozzy favoured this means of transport rather than staying in hotels and flying, reasoning his room always became the centre of the party and he would not be able to resist joining in. The absence of luxury was not helped by a defective air-conditioning unit, and as they journeyed south conditions became intolerable. The thirty-three-year-old driver Andrew Aycock proposed taking a minor detour to Flying Baron Estates, Leesburg, Florida, where the headquarters of the bus company was located, to get it repaired.

They arrived at the bus company early on Friday 19th March and upon discovering an adjacent small airstrip, Aycock decided to take a Beechcraft Bonanza F35[112] up for a spin, without the authorisation of the owner. Aycock was a qualified pilot, however his licence had lapsed, and he was also high on cocaine. The first couple of flights were without incident, however on the third he was accompanied by twenty-five-year-old guitarist Randy Rhodes, and fifty-year-old Rachel Youngblood, who doubled as make-up artist, hairdresser, and wardrobe assistant, but in reality was Sharon Arden's housemaid from California. Aycock began flying low over the tour bus, attempting to buzz his ex-wife who was on board as well as scare the crap out of his two passengers. On his third pass the wings of the light aircraft clipped the roof of the bus, and then a tree on its way to landing on a nearby white colonial-style mansion, where it burst into flames. All three passengers were killed instantaneously, having to be identified later from their dental records. Ozzy and Sharon staggered half-awake from the tour bus to find a scene of carnage. Noticing the house on fire, Ozzy grabbed a fire extinguisher and ran towards it, only to be met by the occupant of the house, an elderly deaf man who had not realised what had happened and was convinced a half-dressed madman with a metal weapon was attacking him.

ʊ ʊ ʊ

XTC set out on the world tour that was intended to push them over the edge into mega-success, however on Thursday 18th March during a date at Theatre Le Palace in Paris, front man Andy Partridge suffered what appeared to be a breakdown. A few songs into the set he broke off from singing, slumped onto the drum riser with a dejected demeanor, removed his guitar, and departed the stage. The rest of the band completed the song instrumentally, and then followed to discover the singer moaning in a foetal position backstage. Immediately preceding the concert, during a French television interview, Partridge had described being in a band and touring as "*like owning a circus*" and communicated a pining to be in more tranquil circumstances.

The singer had recently developed stage fright, brought on by withdrawal from the valium he had been prescribed since 1969. He had thrown his tablets away without medical advice and was now suffering the disastrous effects.

---

[112] The Beachcraft Bonanza was the pop star's plane of choice when it came to death, with Buddy Holly, Ritchie Valens, the Big Bopper *and* Jim Reeves all perishing in one.

The remainder of the European tour was immediately cancelled with *food poisoning* cited as the reason; however the record company persuaded that band to push ahead with their American tour in April.

ʊ ʊ ʊ

Despite having reached the top of the charts two years previously, Dexy's Midnight Runners were at a low ebb, with saxophone player Paul Speare compelled to cash in his teacher's pension just to survive and singer Kevin Rowland returning to a previous job as a hairdresser in a Birmingham salon. The group were banned from every sandwich bar in Birmingham for ordering food and then not paying, and things were not about to get any better with the release of new single, *The Celtic Soul Brothers*.
Formed from the ashes of punk band The Killjoys by guitarist Kevin Archer and Birmingham-born Irish-descended vocalist Rowland, they took their name from a slang term for central nervous system stimulant Dexedrine, popular amongst Northern Soul aficionados for staying awake and dancing at all-nighters. For this fresh band, Rowland returned to his first musical love, soul, insisting all members give up their jobs and commit themselves 100% to the band. Signing with Clash manager Bernie Rhodes, Dexy's released their debut single independently, reaching the edge of the top forty in 1979, and set out on tour supporting The Specials, where Rowland took "*pride in the fact* [the audience] *hated us*". Seeing the headline band wearing suits convinced Rowland to find an image for Dexy's, and soon after they adopted donkey jackets and woolly hats in appreciation of Martin Scorsese's film *Mean Streets*.
Early in 1980 Rowland dismissed Rhodes and signed the band to EMI Records, who initially refused to release next single *Geno*, believing it to have no marketable

prospects. Rowland insisted and the record company were proven wrong when it climbed to the top of the charts, inspiring The Specials to write *Ghost Town* in the process. Rowland used the success to negotiate a better deal with EMI, even going as far as stealing and holding ransom the master tapes of their debut album from the studio on the last day of recording. At the same time as the album was released in summer 1980 Rowland imposed a press embargo, refusing to be interviewed and communicating with the public via paid adverts in the music press. Always an eccentric, the singer had grandiose ideals for the band, once stating "*The plan was: in the first year, make records, in the second year, make a film, and in the third year we'd go into politics and blow up the Houses of Parliament. I literally couldn't understand why people kept leaving the group.*"
The ensuing singles met with diminishing commercial returns with the fourth one *Keep It* failing to make the charts at all, and by the close of 1980 most of the band had quit, fed up with Rowland's idiosyncratic despotic ways, not to mention his suggestion everyone learn new instruments. Only Rowland and Paterson were left, a duo the former christened the Celtic Soul Brothers due to his Irish and Paterson's Scottish heritage. Paterson explained "*It took Kevin about thirty years to tell me that I was his Celtic Soul Brother. It never dawned on me. Needless to say, it was one of the proudest moments of my life.*". Things got so bad that EMI gladly released them from their contract only for the band to be scooped up by Mercury Records. A new line-up of Billy Adams (guitar), Seb Shelton (drums, formerly of Secret Affair), Maurice Brummitt (alto Saxophone), Paul Speare (tenor saxophone), Mickey Billingham (keyboards), and Mick Gallick (bass) started rehearsing, as well as (at the instigation of Rowland) running together first thing in the morning to engender discipline. During

summer 1981, former member Archer let Rowland hear a demo of his new band, The Blue Ox Babes. Rowland was overcome by the mix of Motown beats and violins, and immediately began crafting a new vision for Dexy's Midnight Runners. He resuscitated his idea of the musicians learning new instruments, setting the horns the task of becoming a string section with Speare on violin, and Paterson and Brummitt on cello. This line-up recorded a new single *Liars A to E* which perfectly represented Rowland's dream of a Celtic Soul Revue, mixing horns and strings. The single flopped, failing to reach the top seventy-five, however so committed was Rowland to this vision and line-up he pushed on with the venture.

As recording of a Celtic-influenced album began it was determined a more professional sound was needed for the strings, so violinists Helen (real name: Bevington) O'Hara, Steve (Shaw) Brennan and Roger (Huckle) MacDuff were recruited on the recommendation of Archer, being christened The Emerald Express. The recruitment of strings made the horn section feel paranoid and neglected, and with the promise of waiting session work they decided to resign *en masse*. Three weeks later, Rowland phoned them individually and begged them to return until the album was complete. Recording began at the start of 1982 at Genetic Studios, owned jointly by Martin Rushent and Alan Winstanley, the later of whom produced with Clive Langer. Langer and Winstanley had previously produced Madness and The Teardrop Explodes, and were therefore perfect to bring out the pop-hooks in the new songs with enough polish to make the sound highly commercial. They were also the only producers who agreed to work with the famously recalcitrate Rowland and given their brief from the record company to resurrect Dexy's career were delighted to travel to rehearsals in Birmingham and discover there were decent songs waiting.

The first release was *The Celtic Soul Brothers*, a corybantic raggle-taggle of a song featuring the fiddles of the Emerald Express upfront as a statement of intent. The track functioned as a call-and-response manifesto for the new line-up, a love song from Rowland to his band, with an opening line of "*Introducing the Celtic soul brothers featuring the strong devoted*". The song was also Rowland's response to the technology-driven music in the charts, stating he had "*Seen what's on show and now there's no more to know*", whilst providing a backing of traditional violins, piano, acoustic guitars, and mandolins. His single-mindedness was asserted during the middle eight when he declared "*I'm not waiting for approval from you*", however confidence proved not to be enough as the song stagnated at number forty-five. Alarm bells starting ringing, with Kevin Adams explaining "*We had such high hopes... it's such a high energy, upbeat, optimistic song. A declaration of intent and arrival. It was something of a shock when the single flopped.*"

ʊ ʊ ʊ

The Falklands, 8,000 miles from the United Kingdom and almost 400 miles from Argentina, comprised 780 islands of which only two were inhabited, with a population of about 1,800 people and over 500,000 sheep. The islands were in contact with the outside world through a weekly Argentinian Air Force flight from capital Port Stanley and Comodoro Rivadavia, 600 miles across the ocean. At the beginning of 1982, most people in Britain had never even heard of the islands[113] which included South Georgia 800 miles to the east, and the South Sandwich Islands 460 miles further. The Islands had been under British province, with a modest but immoderately patriotic population,

---

[113] British Secretary of State for Defence John Knott later admitted he had to refer to a globe to find them.

since 1833 despite Argentinian claims on the land. The reason these barren inhospitable clumps of land were sought after by both was two-fold: first, they contained several deep-water harbours which would be of substantial strategic significance should the Panama Canal ever be closed, and secondly and undoubtedly more crucial, their surrounding waters were possibly rich in untapped oil supplies.

Captain Cook[114] was the first known person to set foot on the South Georgian Islands in 1775, naming them in honour of King George III. To this day there remains not much to see there other than the grave of Ernest Shackleton, and their primary use for over 100 years was as a base for whaling. In 1976 the Argentinians had established a military presence on Southern Thule, one of the South Sandwich Islands, a fact which was not disclosed to parliament until two years later. Then, in December 1981 a new military junta led by General Galtieri seized control in Argentina and took a more hard-line approach to the sovereignty of the Falklands, or *Malvinas* as they called them.

When Nicholas Ridley was a junior minister at the Foreign Office, he had informed the Argentinians that the British did not care about the Falklands, and the prognosis of Admiral Jorge Anaya, based on a year spent in England, was that the British people were either *"maricones"* (*queer*) or *"putas desesperadas"* (*frantic sluts*) who would not act. This was despite an infamous quote in the late 1970's by Prime Minister Jim Callaghan who stated *"I'm not handing over one-thousand-eight-hundred Britons to a gang of fucking Fascists"*.

The inhabitants of the islands had become distrustful of the British government over the past couple of years, with Governor Rex Hunt expressing in his annual report the feeling that *"life was deliberately being made more difficult in an attempt to bring them to heel… [the government]* were cynically allowing the Islands' economy to go downhill in order to force Islanders into the hands of the Argentines."

On Friday 19th March a faction of Argentinian scrap-metal dealers arrived at Leith Harbour on the island of South Georgia and occupied an abandoned whaling station. Protocol stated that the merchants report to the British Antarctic Survey team, and when this did not happen the Survey Team went to find them instead. The Argentinians were wearing military uniforms, had raised a national flag, covered the whaling station with patriotic graffiti, and were barbequing a local reindeer, when they were handed a message from London demanding the flag be lowered and the party depart.

What London did not know, however, was that the scrap merchants were Argentine marines in civilian clothing exploiting an agreement made by Christian Salvesen to scrap the whaling stations as cover for a small-scale invasion. The Argentinians had been probing South Georgia for some time, landing a vessel on the island just before Christmas, which had resulted in a strongly worded protest from the British government.

ʊ ʊ ʊ

Making a name for themselves on the independent music scene in March were The Marine Girls, an all-female group from the home counties. Formed in the second half of 1980 whilst still at school by Tracey Thorn, Gina Hartman, Jane Fox, and her sister Alice, they set about recording their sparse songs on a four-track tape recorder. These brought them to the awareness of Pat Bermingham who recorded an album worth of songs in his garden shed to be released on In-Phaze Records, before being rapidly re-released on Whaam! Records.

---

[114] When Cook was killed by the islanders of Hawaii in 1779, they treated his body with what was considered great respect, disembowelling him, baking him to remove the flesh, and cleaning the bones as religious items.

By this time three of the girls had left school, with Jane Fox moving to Brighton to attend Art School and Thorn moving north to study English Literature at Hull University. On her first day there, Thorn met another singer-songwriter called Ben Watts and the two became inseparable, musically and romantically. During the Christmas holidays at the end of the first term, The Marine Girls were re-united from their studies to play a few gigs in London, and Thorn took the opportunity to return to Bermingham's shed to record solo material. Meanwhile, Thorn and Watt went into Alvic Studio in West Kensington to record three acoustic songs, including a cover of Cole Porter's *Night & Day*, for an as-yet untitled musical project.

In March 1982 the Marine Girls recorded their first session for John Peel, made *Single of the Week* in the *New Musical Express*, and were cover stars of the *Melody Maker*, however there were fissures showing in the band. The  *Melody Maker* interview saw the members debating their own approach towards musicality, with Thorn jaded with the confines of amateurism the group embodied. It was this deficiency of virtuosity many people found endearing about the Marine Girls, however Thorn had been introduced by Watt to all sorts of older artists such as John Martyn and Kevin Coyne, and desired to move into a newer more jazz-influenced area, and pitiable musicianship would simply not cut it. Thorn also feared being shambolic was pandering to the music industry's notion of female groups. The others in the band, on the other hand, were militantly opposed to becoming proficient or slick. Thorn was also conscious that the post-punk ethos of obscurity was falling out of fashion as new artists were more interested in the idea of infiltrating the pop charts with classic songs.

The Marine Girls debut album was re-released under the title of *Beach Party* by Cherry Red Records, reaching number twenty-nine in the British independent charts. Meanwhile, Ben Watt recorded a single, *Summer into Winter* with Robert Wyatt guesting on piano and backing vocals, also for Cherry Red. Watt had already recorded for the label and owner Mike Alway knowing that both Thorn and Watt were due to start at Hull University at the same time had surreptitiously planned for them to meet and work together.

ʊ ʊ ʊ

On Friday 19th March, the most successful Canadian movie of all time was released. Almost expunged from movie history for valid reasons, *Porky's* was initially conceived by American Bob Clark in 1972 after spending nights on set with Christopher Plummer and James Mason who would "*regale us with ribald tales of tag-teaming Shelley Winters and Julie Andrews*". Reminiscing about his own High School days in the 1950's, Clark wrote a teenage sex-romp in reaction to Reagan's "*Morning in America*" moral-majority puritanism.

After being turned down by every studio in Hollywood, co-writer Roger Swaybill took the idea to Canada where it was financed as a tax dodge by Astro Bellevue. Made for $4 million, the film went on to earn $200 million worldwide and became the fifth best grossing film in the United States in 1982, as well as the first ever movie to make a million pounds in Ireland. Not that 20th Century Fox had any faith in the movie, already distancing themselves for what they were certain was a box office disaster, choosing to open initially in only two towns.

Very few people under a certain age are even aware of the film due to the sexual politics of various sub-plots, which involve main character Pee-Wee attempting to lose his virginity to a succession of clichéd female tropes. Seen through contemporary eyes, it seems shocking that women are cast as either *nymphomaniacs* or *ballbreakers* (one of the characters is even called *Beulah Balbricker*), however the movie was simply the first in a production-line of such films culminating in the *American Pie* series, with 1982 being described as *"Year zero in the tits and ass sex-romp belle epoque"*. American critic, Roger Ebert, called *Porky's* the latest in a series of A.C.N.E.S, which stood for *adolescent character's neurotic eroticism syndrome*, criticising it because it *"obviously doesn't like women… its sex scenes all create fear and hostility"*. The moral malfeasance did not stop there, with the movie dipping toes into shallow pools of racism, body-shaming, sexism, and homophobia throughout. Not that director Clark cared, claiming *"I didn't make it for the* [critics] *of the world, I made it for* [their] *thirteen-year-old nephews"*.

ʊ ʊ ʊ

Actively positioning themselves at the forefront of what was now in danger of becoming a rapidly antiquated New Romantic movement had perhaps not been the best decision for Spandau Ballet, whose second album *Diamonds* skulked out unceremoniously in March, peaking at number fifteen. For a band once considered and self-proclaimed the *next big thing* to stumble at the hurdle of their second album did not bode well, especially off the back of a couple of underwhelming and underachieving singles. *Diamonds* saw the band continue to work with producer, Richard James Burgess, and suffered from a severe case of second-album-syndrome whereby a band has a lifetime of experience to write their first set of songs, but only months for their second. Some acts ascend above the issue, others subside into obscurity, and with *Diamonds* the sparkle  was coming off Spandau Ballet. The band had been unsettled during the recording process, working their way through six London studios in a year, which was further exacerbated by Burgess making singer Tony Hadley the scapegoat. To curtail his strong voice the producer forced Hadley to deliver his vocals lying on his back covered by a carpet, a humiliating experience which caused the singer to walk out at least once during the process.

The album started auspiciously enough with top ten hit single *Chant No 1 (I Don't Need This Pressure On)*, however this had been written and recorded long before work had begun on the album, and as such its funk stylings were more aligned with their debut. By the third track, their lacklustre and heavy-handed minor hit *Paint Me Down*, a template had been set of anonymous white soul with nugatory lyrics and a lumpen rhythm. Not to say there was lacking any suggestion of hope, especially towards the end of side two when permitted to start experimenting with textures, in the post-punk automated taciturnity of *Pharaoh* or the Japan-aping *Innocence & Science*, where over a sparse far-Eastern instrumentation Hadley tried his laxest voiced David Sylvian impression. These, however, were also the sound of a band over-extending their welcome, trying too hard to demonstrate they were more than *just a pop band*, and nearly succeeding.

As the London boys' star waned, they were forced to watch Duran Duran rise, a band who had been a second-hand Birmingham-based copy of them just over a year ago, and who had once begged to support Spandau Ballet. Duran Duran's singer Simon Le Bon commented on *Diamonds*, saying *"They went for artistic credibility and missed by a million miles"*. Even Spandau's bass player Martin Kemp agreed when he later pronounced "*It wasn't the pop album* [the public] *wanted and certainly wasn't going to sell by the millions… our fall in the marketplace was written on the wall*" before taking a more philosophical approach: "*A band has to move on to stay alive. It has to grow and develop as a natural organism. If it stops for a moment it can become stagnant and die*".

Unfortunately, the band suffered the same problem as Japan: they were good looking boys who enticed a female teenage audience that was disinclined to follow them into more experimental areas. This was reflected in declining sales and chart positions, and the record company Chrysalis were justifiably apprehensive. To ensure their investment was secure and long-lasting, Chrysalis demanded the next single be re-mixed, and two names were proposed: Andy Hill who was having success with Bucks Fizz, and Trevor Horn who was becoming the hottest producer of the year, riding high in the charts with his quite literally epic production on singles by ABC and Dollar, specialising in colossal sounds, massive drums, and orchestral soundscapes, many of the features which would become characteristic of the 1980's. There was no choice.

Horn, brought in to work on *Instinction*, tightened the song, brought the melody to the fore, and ramped up the reverb. He had Hadley re-do his vocals, encouraging his

 voice to be released, and employed Anne Dudley to add keyboards. The song itself was one of the highpoints of the album but needed Horn's input to nudge it towards sounding more contemporary. The album version sounded more like a flat demonstration recording of the single, complete with an impotent percussion breakdown in the middle and the occasional flat vocal from Hadley. Before Horn the song seemed like funk trying too hard, but the new version had an immense sound, and the lustre of the surface helped conceal the unqualified baloney that passed for lyrics. The band now sounded reinvigorated rather than worn-out, and the ensuing top ten placing renewed their hunger for success.

For the video, Spandau Ballet decided to steer away from the pretentious art films they had previously made, and created a pop video instead, dressed in *Alpine chic*, and moving away from their earlier exclusivity they agreed to appear on any television show which would have them. This was the new self-fulfilling successful Spandau Ballet.

ʊ ʊ ʊ

Cult post-punk act The Fall travelled to Iceland in September 1981 to play a series of three concerts organised by future Sugarcubes singer, Einar Orn. Whilst there they took the opportunity to record a couple of songs in a studio with walls made of lava rock. Upon returning to Britain the band were looking for a new record label, after leaving Rough Trade who singer Mark E. Smith described as "*a bunch of amateur college wankers*"[115] and hooked up with new label Kamera Records[116]. They band were booked into the freezing cold cavernous Regal Cinema in Hitchin to work with producer Richard Mazda. *Hex Enducation Hour* was The Fall's fourth album, and the first to feature double drummers Paul Hanley and Karl Burns, alongside Steve

---

[115] Rough Trade boss Geoff Travis in retaliation said: "*A gnat or a mosquito could produce a Fall record if it was lucky enough to be in the vicinity*".

[116] The owner of Kamera Chris Youle spent most of his time in the pub, so most of the work there was done by Saul Galpern, the office junior, who would later start Nude Records.

Hanley[117] (bass), Marc Riley (guitar and keyboards), and Craig Scanlon (guitar). Of course, the main character in The Fall was, and would always remain, frontman Smith, a legendary curmudgeon and the undisputed leader and owner of the band. It had not always been that way, however, and the original line-up was much more of a democracy, which according to Paul Hanley "*is probably the reason it was destined not to last*". Smith was so disillusioned by the band's inability to make progress that he decided this album was to be his final effort, as well as two fingers up to Rough Trade, later admitting "*I went into it thinking it was the last thing we'd ever do because we were getting nowhere*".

Comprising their usual mix of lo-fi Krautrock and rockabilly, the album sounded like it was recorded live… which it deliberately was as a reaction against the technology driven times. The band set up on the stage, not concerned about instruments bleeding into one another, whilst Smith isolated himself in the projection booth where he could just about see the musicians. The album managed to have enough songs that under the gristle, were catchy enough to be loosely termed *pop*, such as *Jawbone and the Air Rifle* and *Just Step S'ways*, however it opened with a statement of intent in *The Classical*, during which Smith laid out his mantra of hate over a ramshackle groove written by Scanlon. One of the few songs on the album written specifically for the two drummers, a bi-tonal approach was taken with guitar and bass played in different keys, adding a discordance to the whole affair. Scanlon asked Hanley to "*keep the beat and be Ringo… [and for Burns] to be the heavy metal monster and do the fills*", which the latter achieved by playing with his snare switched off, turning it into something akin to the frantic conga-driven sound of German act Can. Smith's lyrics, half-spoken, half-shouted, very occasionally accidently lapsing into a melody, set the stall out for the various strands of the whole album, being an attack on the increasing commercialisation of Thatcher's Britain. This was most obvious in his reference to a Wilkinson Sword television advert airing at the time which Smith felt made assertions of excellence not matched in performance. Most troubling in the song was Smith's use of the "n" word, something which remained surprisingly uncommented upon at the time. The word had been used by John Lennon, Bob Dylan, Patti Smith, and Elvis Costello in their lyrics during the past decade in what Paul Hanley called "*an attempt to highlight their own edgy coolness, all the while uncharacteristically oblivious to the possibility that by using the word they themselves were being racist*". For Smith it was a commentary on tokenism and the music scene, however he must have been conscious of the inflammatory nature of the language, and never went out his way during the rest of his life to justify its use. From out of the clutter, towards the end Scanlon switched from his wrong key to fit in with the guitar, and a chorus of "*I've never felt better in my life*" evolved, skirting close to turning the track into an anthem, before this unprecedented territory was avoided by ending the song.

The Fall were adept at using their limited musical ability to improvise music for Smith to expatiate over, such as in *Who Makes the Nazis?* written by the singer on his four-string 1964 Selco New Beat toy Beatles guitar, which appeared as a tabulation of arbitrary insinuations over the bare skeleton of a song. Often songs were created

---

[117] Paul and Steve Hanley were brothers. The two drummers came about because Hanley had been too young to tour the United States the previous year, and now Smith could not make up his mind which one to sack. Burns was the better drummer, but was too unpredictable, whilst Hanley was very young and could be easily manipulated.

around a guitar riff by Scanlon or Riley such as *Fortress / Deer Park*, a two-part track with one half in a major key and the other in a minor. The song started with the *Rock 2* beat from a Casio VLTone 1[118], the same rhythm later used on Trio's *Da Da Da*. *Fortress* was an abstract take at on a *youth* discussion radio programme Smith had been invited onto in 1981, the *Fortress* in question being the Langham Hotel, an annex of Broadcasting House in London. As one would expect, Smith was disheartened at the naivety of the other four young left-wing people on the show and played devil's advocate throughout. At one point near the end of the song he proclaimed, "*I had to go round the gay graduates in the toilet, and Good King Harry was there fucking Jimmy Savile.*" It seems unlikely Smith witnessed paedophile Savile engaging in any sort of sexual activity in the toilets of the BBC, given he never referred to this again, and the most likely explanation is that there should have been a coma in the line, with "[It's] *Fucking Jimmy Savile*" as more of an exclamation of surprise. The rest of the song dealt with Smith's anti-metropolitan impression of London.

Smith seemed both enamoured and disgusted by modern life, and the album was shot through with references to consumer products and adverts, from Hovis Bread[119] to Bacardi[120] to Mars Confectionary. His wrath was focused on a music magazine editor on *Mere Pseud Mag. Ed.*, with a melody apparently ripped off from *Babysitters* by The Stupid Babies[121]. Smith must have been aware of this because he subsequently filed the tune with the PRS as being written by Riley in case he was sued.

Then there were the songs recorded in Iceland, including *Hip Priest*, utilizing a well-battered Elgam Snoopy piano which could only produce wheezing sounds. The song featured no clear chord structure or recurring bass line and was written by Smith as "*a bit of a joke on the group cos they're all Catholics*". Referencing Kris Kristofferson's *Sunday Morning Coming Down* with the line "*I fumbled through my closet through my clothes, and found my cleanest dirty shirt*", the song also took a pot-shot at journalist Danny Baker[122]. *Hip Priest* was later used in *Silence of the Lambs* at the insistence of Jonathan Demme, for which the band were paid £6,000. As Riley reasoned "*It's no coincidence a serial killer ends up listening to it*". The other track from Iceland was called *Iceland* and written after Smith asked for a song like Bob Dylan. Drummer Hanley explained his approach: "*I just recreated the relentless pounding in my head that Iceland's licensing laws had provided.*"[123]

Smith seemed to work better when locked into a strict riff, such as on *Jawbone and the Air-Rifle*, which had been written two years previously and honed live. Smith initially

---

[118] I owned a Casio VLTone 1 and loved it. It was bought for me by my host family when on a school exchange in Minnesota in October 1982.

[119] Hovis was a by-word for old fashioned, having found their greatest fame with a faux-nostalgic advert directed by Ridley Scott.

[120] Of course, the only *real* Bacardi is that still made in Cuba. A friend once gave me a bottle of Cuban Bacardi Rum which was so full of alcohol that it needed a flame-guard on the bottle.

[121] The Stupid Babies were the first group of future rave star Adamski. He was eleven years old at the time and played a plastic guitar whilst persuading his five-year-old brother, Dominic, to sing. The single was released on Edinburgh's Fast Records. I was in a similar band when I was nine. My brother played guitar whilst I was the drummer. When I say drummer, I hit an upside-down *Quality Street* tin with a couple of my mum's knitting needles. We recorded one song on a cassette called *The Martian Disco*.

[122] Baker was a journalist for the *New Musical Express* at the time. He later became a brilliant radio broadcaster before being fired by the BBC for posting an ill-advised and seemingly racist statement on a recent royal birth.

[123] When The Fall first landed in Iceland they were met by Einar bearing a sign which said "*Buy Beer*". It turned out the airport duty free was the only place on the island to purchase the alcoholic beverage, and the band had to survive on unadulterated spirits.

asked for a song like *Run Rabbit Run* because it had been Winston Churchill's favourite, and within this he provided a straight linear narrative of a man escaping his family by going hunting for rabbits at night. With echoes of *Hamlet* he meets a gravedigger who gives him a cursed jawbone, with the result the rabbit-hunter loses his appetite, teeth, and then mind.

The album ended with *And This Day*, written by Riley and owing a debt to The Velvet Underground, the original performance lasting a relentless twenty-five minutes, before being edited down to ten-and-a-half minutes to ensure the album came in at exactly one hour. Even at this length it was difficult to cut the album onto vinyl due to the thinness of the grooves and the tapes had to be taken to a specialist facility in Hamburg. Scanlon would later describe the song as *"An instrument to pummel the audience with"*, and it featured Smith at his most rambling. Journalist Paul Morley was left wondering *"What if [Mark E. Smith] wasn't a genius... just an old drunken tramp that when he got really drunk started to spout phrases that made a kind of sense and we read too much into it?"*

The title of the album remains the subject of conjecture, with the use of the word *Hex* and the misspelling of *Induction*. When the band were in Iceland, Einar had taken them to see the volcano called The Heck[124] which is meant to be *the gateway to hell*, and it is thought Smith took this name and changed the spelling (*Heck's* to *Hex*).

Hex Enduction Hour turned out not to be the album that ended The Fall, but instead became their first hit record, reaching number seventy-one, and the release which turned a lot of people onto the band. Smith would later proclaim his pride in the album, whilst at the same time saying, *"There's always some cunt who wants to ask me about a masterpiece I made in 1982"*. The album was a critical hit, however as Smith later stated, *"You can't eat the reviews, you're still on the dole... still skint"*.

He was not interested in visiting the past and by summer the band rarely played any tracks from the album. As John Peel would later observe: *"The Fall: always the same, always different"*.

ʊ ʊ ʊ

Just as Killing Joke were experiencing their greatest chart success to date, there was a vacuum where their frontman Jaz Coleman should have been. The conundrum of his disappearance a couple of weeks earlier had been disentangled when it was revealed he had fled to Iceland to await and escape an impending apocalypse he believed was looming, conveniently choosing to overlook the American nuclear submarine base situated there. Coleman had spent time on the Nordic island the previous year, during which he suffered visions which shepherded him to the Hebridean retreat of Iona. The singer had become obsessed with the occult and the works of Aleister Crowley in recent months, expressing this through paranoid and grandiloquent ranting in the music press, though problems with alcohol may have had more to do with his state of mind. Coleman welcomed rather than feared any approaching holocaust, stating *"One thing you can be sure of... one of the good things about the apocalypse is the end of The Teardrop Explodes, Toyah, Theatre of Hate – people like that"*.

New single *Empire Song* had been recorded, along with the rest of their forthcoming album, in Germany with producer Conny Plank towards the end of 1981, and was a frantic full-frontal assault of tribal drums, flanged guitar, and anti-colonial class war.

---

[124] Heckla is one of the most active volcanoes in Iceland and had erupted a few months before The Fall visited. William Blake had shown Winter being banished to Heckla in his work

Finding the single edging towards the top forty, and with an invitation to appear on *Top of the Pops* the band elected to have drummer Paul Ferguson mime the song, whilst a

roadie dressed in full body nuclear fallout costume stood behind the keyboards, prodding randomly at the instrument in slow-motion. It had only been a few short weeks since guitarist Geordie Walker claimed they would never appear on the show, stating *"We don't want to have to degrade ourselves in front of the amorphous mass...jog and grin on cue".* Whilst they certainly did not either jog or grin during the performance, the sell-out was still not enough to crack the charts, with the single peaking at number forty-three.

The following month Walker joined Coleman in Iceland, a move which their manager claimed was because *"They're both nuts, not to put too fine a point on it. They're disturbed, stupid, crazy. The happiest day of their lives will be when the holocaust comes, just so they can say 'I told you so'. They're the biggest bastards under the sun".*

21st – 27th March 1982

#1 single: The Goombay Dance Band: Seven Tears
#1 album: Barbra Streisand: Love Songs

Goth rockers Bauhaus lost all their cool on the morning of Monday 22nd March when they were due to record their live performance of *Bela Lugosi's Dead* for Ridley Scott's movie *The Hunger*. The thought of appearing with and meeting their hero David Bowie meant they were up and enthusiastically ready at Heaven nightclub by seven in the morning. As they mimed to a live recording from Hammersmith Palais, Bowie entered the room in green combat fatigues, watched the band for a while, then disappeared off to make-up.

When he returned Bowie was wearing a black silk suit and black wig and headed straight for the jukebox in the corner. Choosing some records to play, he was surprised to find the band and half the extras in the club had followed him over and were waiting expectantly. Silently Bowie indicated they should all sit down in front of him, and then spent the next two hours regaling them with showbiz tales to a soundtrack of old 1960's music.

ʊ ʊ ʊ

On Monday 22nd March, Margaret Thatcher's private secretary Ian Gow[125] wrote to her explaining that the new editor of *The Times* newspaper, Charles Douglas-Home, was *"an old friend.... and a staunch admirer of the Prime Minister"*. The much-respected *Times* had been bought by right-wing Australian Rupert Murdoch and his company News International a couple of years previously, despite concerns this would give him unprecedented control over the British media. Any objections were rejected by the new Conservative government in exchange for Murdoch's tabloid titles helping Thatcher

---

[125] Despite being a Member of Parliament Gow kept his name and address in the local telephone directory. This proved to be his downfall when he was assassinated by an IRA bomb under his car in the driveway of his home in 1990.

gain power in 1979. The following day Douglas-Home telephoned Gow to ask in what way *The Times* could assist, asking for a critique of recent editorials. From now on, Conservative economic strategy would not be challenged in a large swathe of the media.

ʊ ʊ ʊ

Liverpool's response to the New Romantic movement came in the shape of A Flock of Seagulls, formed in 1980 and named after a line from a Stranglers song. Despite the supposed punk influence, the DNA of Wishbone Ash and other prog rock acts was more discernible, with former hairdresser Mike Score on vocals and keyboards, and his brother Ali on drums. They settled on a four-piece line-up with Frank Maudsley on bass and teenager Paul Reynolds on guitar and released their debut single on Bill Nelson's Cocteau Records, before signing to Jive.

I Ran (So Far Away) was their third single and had been produced by former Gong[126] member Mike Howlett, and whilst it lurked outside of the British top forty in spring 1982, in the United States it was a different story. A Flock of Seagulls were one of the first British acts to make sagacious use of MTV, helped by an American label who pushed an economically shot video on the station, making it their most played clip ever at the time. Despite a dearth of success in their homeland, A Flock of Seagulls would find

themselves at the vanguard of what became known as the Second British Invasion of America. Following a fallow period in the late seventies, by the start of the following year 30% of record sales across the Atlantic were by British artists. A year later 40% of the singles on the American Billboard Hot 100 were by British musicians, and in May 1985 80% of the top ten were from the United Kingdom.

Despite such success, A Flock of Seagulls were ridiculed in their home country in the early 1980's, never belonging to any one scene, and certainly on Merseyside they seemed to have by-passed the entire harsh-tongued *Eric's* crowd. There was just too much worth lampooning about the band, from a singer playing keyboards right at the front of the stage which was redolent of progressive rock, to his preposterous back-combed haircut and desperate attempts to fit his concept science fiction images of aliens and UFOs into the emerging New Romantic style. Even on *I Ran (So Far Away)*, which told the story of a man attracted to a woman and trying to absquatulate from his feelings, the couple are abducted by aliens by the end of the track. On the full version of the song there was a prolonged synthesizer-driven atmospheric instrumental introduction before the vocals start, however the song singularly failed to rise or fall, instead electing an orthodox sonic route right through to the end. Not that this stopped it being a hit around the world... just not in Britain.

A self-titled debut album was released at the end of April, containing eleven songs which were very much of their time, and possibly even slightly behind the curve, betraying the clear of influence of Gary Numan with added Bill Nelson-shaped guitars. There is only one shade across the whole album, with the keyboard providing nothing more than washes of colour and

---

[126] I once went to see Gong live on a guest pass. I'm not sure why.

the guitar taking a more central role than Paul Reynolds has been given credit for. A science-fiction theme was apparent in tracks such as *Messages*, *Telecommunication*, and *Don't Ask Me*, whilst *Modern Love is Automatic* apparently impressed Phil Spector[127] so much he offered to produce the next album. Elsewhere the track *DNA* distilled the sound of guitars from U2 and The Skids into a 150 second instrumental in search of a song which won a Grammy for Best Rock Instrumental Track in 1983.

Jive decided to release one of the stronger tracks, *Space Age Love Song* in May, an almost carbon copy of *I Ran*, and whilst it was a lesser song it did break into the British top forty, even if it did not chart as successfully around the world. Giving up on their homeland, the band went off to tour North America as the support act for Squeeze.

ʊ ʊ ʊ

Iran and Iraq had been at war since September 1980 when Saddam Hussein had ordered his troops over the border, supported (but not backed) by the United States *and* the Soviet Union, both of whom feared the international effect of the Islamic Revolution in Iran of 1979 under the Ayatollah Khomeini. There were a host of countries remotely involved, with Israel and Germany providing weapons to Iran, and Saudi Arabia and France backing Iraq. After a couple of months, the Iraqi army was stretched thin along a 400-kilometre front, and the war came to a standstill. 1981 was marked by infrequent skirmishes during which the Iraqi army dug-in and constructed a network of outposts. Saddam, fearing his own troops would become disillusioned and revolt, made sure they lived is relative comfort with colour televisions and fully furnished bunkers covered in pornography.

By spring 1982 the Iranians had assembled a considerable army and were ready to push back against Iraq. The attack came on Monday 22nd March, led first by waves of fourteen-year-old volunteers who drove across minefields on motorcycles whilst carrying the sword of martyrdom around their neck and wearing heavy winter coats to keep their shredded bodies together for a martyr's burial back in their home villages. With the minefields cleared, the Iranians introduced human-wave attacks, pouring thousands of troops across the battlefield, suffering high casualties whilst taking the Iraqis by surprise.

The Iranians, as they pushed forward to reclaim their own land, found former cities razed to the ground in a scorched earth policy. The Iranians were ordered to stop just before the old border, not to enter Iraq, with Khomeini declaring his intention to only recapture previously lost land.

ʊ ʊ ʊ

As the weather improved the number of women at Greenham Common Peace Camp increased, and they engaged in what was described as *"the politics of whimsey"*, weaving spider webs of wool to the fence, a symbol of both fragility and strength. Their protest, however, was still not achieving the desired level of publicity so a series of high-profile stunts were hatched, the first of which was a passive blockade at the gates on Monday 22nd March by 250 of the women. The aim was to stop building machines and construction materials gaining access to the base, and police were swiftly called in, arresting 34 of the protesters. The police would often make things difficult for any protesters arrested, deliberately releasing them in the middle of the night and going out of their way to drop them many miles from the camp.

---

[127] Obviously, this did not happen, and Spector remained inactive until being tempted out of retirement in 2003 by... Starsailor!

ʊ ʊ ʊ

Two singles entered the charts this week, two positions apart at number thirty-three and thirty-five, by two acts whose careers would become interlaced. *My Camera Never Lies* was the follow-up single to the chart-topping *Land of Make Believe* by Bucks Fizz, whilst *Give Me Back My Heart* was by the latest release by a recently rejuvenated Dollar.

The former was written by regular songwriter and producer Andy Hill alongside his partner Nichola Martin and saw Buck's Fizz reach the top of the charts for the third time in twelve months. An astoundingly mediocre track hidden beneath tight production which transported it into faux-new wave territory, all jerky rhythms and cut-up backing vocals, the lyrics told the story of a man following a woman in an attempt to catch her

cheating on him, emphasising post-punk themes of paranoia and voyeurism. The track was undoubtably the zenith of the act's relationship with the music press, receiving widespread warm reviews even in the New Musical Express who described it as "*almost too good to succeed*", as Buck's Fizz crested on the wave of *new pop*. Things were primed for the act's second album, released the following month, with top-notch session playing throughout from the likes of Graham Broad and Ian Bairnson. *Are You Ready* reached number ten, becoming the highest charting album of their career, and at the

height of a summer dominated by new pop a final single, acapella ballad *Now Those Days Are Gone* was released. Despite the song being at odds with the forward-looking lustre of the charts, being what Bob Stanley described as "*home counties, potting shed balladry of the highest order*", it climbed to number eight selling over quarter-of-a-million copies and earning writers Hill and Martin an Ivor Novello nomination.

Bucks Fizz started recording their third album in October, the first fruits of which was single *If You Can't Stand the Heat*, with the two female members of the act taking lead vocals for the first time, however the glory days of the band were over.

The band made the front pages of the news again in December 1984 when their tour bus was involved in a crash, injuring all members of the band, especially Mike Nolan who found himself in a coma after dying on the

operating table. Whilst he recuperated, Jay Aston quit the band after it emerged that she was having an affair with producer and songwriter Hill behind the back of his wife Martin.

Line-up changes continued over the next few years with Nolan and Bobby G using a series of female replacements, until 1996 when the former was replaced by Dollar singer David Van Day.

Dollar were perhaps the oddest act to garner critical acclaim during the early 1980's, built around a duo of Van Day and Thereza Bazar, who had first met as seventeen-year-olds when they became part of six-piece 1970's cabaret chart act Guys'n'Dolls. The act was brought together to capitalise on a popular jingle used in a McVitie's biscuit advert, and the two soon became a romantic item, leaving when Van Day became too belligerent for the management. Forming Dollar, they enjoyed some banal chart success in the late 1970's, but by 1981 their career was on the skids. At the end of a relationship with producer Chris Neil, Bazar approached Trevor Horn and asked him to produce them, and the three devised a plan in a Japanese restaurant to create a mixture of Kraftwerk and middle-of-the-road entertainer Vince Hill. Whilst the duo was determined to write their own material, the singles were penned by Horn and his trusted collaborators Bruce Wooley and Simon Darlow.

Dollar were the first act Horn truly produced, using a Roland TR808[128], a set of Simmons drum modules, and a Minimoog synthesiser. First, he had Bazar sing delicate *ahhh's* and *la la la's* in sixteen contrasting notes, one on each track of a tape, before using the mixing desk like an instrument to bring them in as required, explaining "*This was still the days of analogue tape, and we bounced it down so we had a beautiful bed that was 16 tracks of her*". Creating layers of backing vocals was a job which would become infinitely easier with the invention and widespread use of samplers over the next couple of years, however from here Horn built up four songs, including two singles from 1981 called *Hand Held in Black and White* and *Mirror Mirror (Mon Amour)*. In March 1982 the third of his productions, *Give Me Back My Heart*, was released and climbed the charts to number six. Horn had been halfway through recording this single when *Mirror Mirror* stalled just outside the top forty, and the record company instructed him to cease work, only to be given permission to begin again when the single crept up a few more places the following week. Such was Horn's asking price, the company were only willing to pay for these four tracks.

Give Me Back My Heart was a shimmering glass palace of a song, complete with an improvised Bazar vocal on the fade out which Horn compared to Julie Andrews. Lauded and eulogized by Paul Morley, Dollar were an example of an act propelling from light-entertainment towards the centre at the same time as left-field acts pushed from the other side, with the music created in the middle squeezed into pop diamonds by the pressure.

Their next single, *Videotheque*, originally a song recorded as a demo by Buggles, was like an amalgamate of Visage and Imagination, and peaked at number seventeen. Dwelling in its own auditory cosmos of exorbitant reverb, the song was full of the studio chicanery and tonality which would recur in studio manufactured pop music throughout the decade.

The 1982 singles may have been the apogee of Dollar's success, however for Trevor Horn they were a calling card, showcasing his dazzling production technique to the industry and leading to work with ABC, Spandau Ballet, and Malcolm McLaren. If there was any doubt regarding how much Horn was responsible for the success of Dollar, one simply had to listen at the rest of the album, written and produced by the duo themselves, a receptacle of the jejune, where as much significance is placed on *Hairstyles by Nicky Clarke*.

Bazar would admit it took her "*a bit of time to understand* [Videotheque] *it was so sophisticated. On a completely different dimension – jazz overtones, the subtleties, melodically not a powerful tune – that's not what it's about, it's more about these sounds that come at you. The use of the Fairlight was just experimental.*" The singer had sat by Horn's side throughout the recording of his tracks, soaking up everything she could and was "*Pretty devastated that* [Horn] *didn't have the time to finish the album. We didn't want to get another producer in... how do you follow Trevor Horn? It would be pointless.*" With Horn gone "*producing the album was all too much,*" admitted Bazar,

---

[128] The Roland TR808 was roundly savaged by critics upon its release in 1980 and discontinued in 1983. Musicians, it seemed, wanted a more realistic drum machine, however it found a market in rap and hip-hop and over time became a desirable piece of technology.

"*It was back to the drawing board. David wanted to change musical direction; in a direction I wasn't so sure was the right decision. We didn't see eye to eye about a few things... and then he just walked out one day.*" This came as something of a relief for

Bazar, who claimed "*I was exhausted. We were working really hard and under so much pressure. I used to look at the videos on Top of the Pops and think 'We look really sparkly and happy, life is great... why am I so tired?' It was making me feel exhausted just watching what we do.*" Having been romantically linked for years, by early 1983 Bazar and Van Day had been in each other's company far too much and split after a blazing row in Japan, with her describing him as "*That awful vain man*". Despite getting back together as an act a couple of times over the years, Van Day subsequently spent years touring as Dollar with

a succession of female singers, before throwing his lot in with a version of Buck's Fizz in the late 1990's. Van Day proved to be difficult to work with and was eventually kicked out of the act after a date in the Falkland Islands, only for him to team up with Mike Nolan under the name of.... Bucks Fizz. What followed was years of legal disputes about who owned the name, and at one time Van Day was even working under the name of Bucks Fizz with no original members. Nowadays there are various versions of the act playing at nostalgia festivals, and you never know which (if any) of the original members are going to appear.

ʊ ʊ ʊ

Jody Watley had been born in Chicago but grew up wherever her Evangelist father could find a home for his radio talk show. Surrounded by friends of the family such as

Sam Cooke and Jackie Wilson, it almost inevitable she would gravitate towards a career in music, finding employment as a dancer on American television show *Soul Train* at the age of fourteen. It was here she met fellow dancer Jeffrey Daniel, and at the behest of host Don Cornelius replaced the Motown session singers previously employed on the debut hit album by Shalamar. They were later joined by singer Howard Hewett and enjoyed a string of minor disco hits in the late 1970's, but in 1982 had not visited the British charts for well over a year. Shalamar turned to Leon Sylvers III to help write and produce their

next album, with most of the music provided by his family act The Sylvers along with James Ingram on keyboards. The first single to reach the charts from the new recordings was an engaging blend of soul and disco called *I Can Make You Feel Good*, a throwback to the 1970's with just enough 1980's alchemy to make it sound contemporary. The single entered at a lowly number fifty-seven before slowly climbing to number seven, whilst the same week their new long-player *Friends* entered the album charts, eventually climbing to number six and turning platinum in the United Kingdom.

The latest material only really found success in Britain, forcing the band to spend an extended period in the country. Daniels, when asked about his date of birth, would place it as 13th February 1982 at the Embassy Club in London. This was where, visiting the country with Shalamar, he experienced something of a *re-birth*, transferring himself from what was expected of him to what he wanted to be. He explained "*The black artist in the States is forced into one of two positions. Either you're a funkster and you wear those tight spandex suits, or you're a soul act and you wear those old-fashioned suits. It's so stiff in the States. They won't accept new ideas. When I came* [to Britain] *I found they were open to new ideas, creative concepts and energies.*" With the help of a new Chinese friend called Lillian, he toured London clothes shops and had his hair cut, falling in love with the new British pop acts.

Making in-roads to the British charts in Spring 1982 was another act who shared a similar name to Shalamar but were a million miles removed in sound: Shakatak[129]. Formed in 1980, Shakatak specialised in a soft jazz-funk crossover, taking the worse elements of both genres and merging them into the kind of music that permed second division footballers[130] liked to listen to in their Ford Cortinas. They were the kind of band who felt it was important not only to list the personnel on their album, but also which make of instruments they used. So, we know that Roger Odell used Sonor drums and Avedis Zildjian Cymbals, and Bill Sharpe played a Bosendorfer Grand Piano, a Fender Rhodes Electric Piano, and Oberheim OBX, ARP Odyssey and Prophet synthesisers, as if any of that mattered. Shakatak's March single *Nightbirds* reached number nine in the charts, sound-tracking a thousand nights in Thatcherite wine bars, whilst the album of the same name reached the top five. The musicians continued to have three more minor hits throughout the year, before Bill Sharpe joined forces with Gary Numan for an album.

We will not be mentioning them again in this book.

℧ ℧ ℧

George Michael was born Georgios Panayiotou in 1963 to a Greek Cypriot father who had fled to Britain in the 1950's to avoid national service. As the family ascended socially, Michael rejected his family's aspiration for him to attend a private secondary school, selecting Bushey Meads instead, his local comprehensive on the outskirts of London. On his first day there he encountered Egyptian-descended Andrew Ridgeley, who took the chunky curly-haired Michael under his wing, and the two became the closest of friends. Punk passed them by with their tastes vacillating instead between Elton John and disco, however when Two-Tone burst upon the music scene in 1979 it was perfect for them, mixing danceable music with sharp dressing. Initially with Ridgeley singing and Michael on keyboards, they formed a ska band called The Executive with school friends, including Ridgeley's brother on drums.

By summer 1980 it was apparent both the band and Two-Tone were transitory fads, and they split, with Michael and Ridgeley still unwavering in their plan to be successful. Reverting to their first love as soul boys, the duo spent nights in Soho at La Beat Route, where they were exhilarated to see Spandau Ballet and Steve Strange hanging out, even trying fruitlessly to convince Steve Dagger to manage them. Still at school, they were initially denied entry for looking too suburban which only encouraged them to dress much sharper and before long the duo were regulars on the dancefloor at La Beat Route and Blitz. Throughout 1981, Michael, Ridgeley, and his girlfriend Shirlie

---

[129] Ten years later I overheard three people at a Glasgow tenement house party attempting to work out the difference between Shalamar or Shakatak. I helped them out by delivering an extensive lecture on the differences and qualities of both acts. They looked appreciative.

[130] Around this time I was a twelve-year-old ball boy for perennial Scottish Second Division strugglers, East Strirlingshire FC. I was paid in pies at half-time and would spend my Saturday afternoons annoying Scottish international goalkeeper Alan Rough who had been relegated with Partick Thistle. Anyway, I remember the blond perm of East Stirlingshire striker David McCaig singing Shakatak whilst he warmed up before the game, and immediately went right off him.

Holliman worked on dance routines in their bedrooms which they would unleash at nightclubs, clearing a space on the dancefloor.

Upon leaving school in summer 1981, Michael was given six months liberty by his family to gain a recording contract before having to settle down to a more utilitarian career. Naming themselves Wham, they hired a Porta-studio and a *Dr Rhythm* drum machine in February 1982 for twenty pounds and recorded the outline of three songs at home: *Careless Whispers*, *Club Tropicana*, and *Wham Rap*. In the process of scouting the songs around every label in London, the duo would turn up unannounced at head offices, insist they had an appointment, and then castigate the receptionist for not having written the fake appointment down, until they were admitted. Despite the presence of three future top ten hits, including a worldwide chart-topper, not one record company saw any potential in the act, and by the spring of 1982 despondency had set in.

To their rescue came local lad Mark Dean[131], who had been the A&R man partially responsible for signing Soft Cell and ABC, and had persuaded CBS to finance his own label, Innervision. Dean had previously heard The Executive and had not been impressed, so with low expectations unenthusiastically gave the songs a listen. After one play he was able to hear what every other label had overlooked: great songs. Money was found for them to re-record the songs with a band featuring Brad Lang[132] on bass, along with a new track called *Young Guns (Go For It)*. The American backing singer hired for the day, Lynda Hayes, helped write a spoken word section for this new track, and with four sure-fire hits recorded Dean persuaded the band to sign one of the worst recording contracts in history. The contract which earned the duo nothing on the sale of twelve-inch singles, was signed on Wednesday 24th March, and was partly forced by the tight fiscal restrictions CBS were forcing Dean to work with, and partly by the gullibility and desperation of two seventeen-year-olds, as they gave away their future for £500 each. Michael used some of his advance to have his ears pierced.

ʊ ʊ ʊ

The Eurovision Song Contest was still considered a weighty enough music competition for millions to tune in on the evening of Wednesday 24th March to watch the process by which the song representing the United Kingdom was determined. *A Song for Europe* was presented by the safe hands of Terry Wogan and featured eight songs submitted by the Music Publishers Association.

The show opened with *Dancing in Heaven*, something of a curveball for Eurovision, being a track by synth-pop act Q-Feel[133], looking like a cross between a Jane Fonda workout and a scene from *Lazytown*. It sank without trace, later finding fame in America when included in the soundtrack of the movie *Girls Just Want to have Fun*. Next up was Paul Curtis, a veteran of Eurovision having written twenty-two entries for the competition over the years, of which only one made it to the finals. *No Matter How I Try* was standard mid-paced MOR slush, with Curtis appearing like a younger version of Cliff Richard in a bright blue suit.

A safe formula was evident in the third act, The Touring Company, following the Abba template that had been so successful for The Brotherhood of Man in the 1970's and Buck's Fizz the previous year. They performed *Every Step of the Way* slightly out of

---

[131] Michael's mother knew Dean's mother. Any connection, no matter how tenuous, was better than no connection.

[132] Lang was soon to join ABC.

[133] Bass player Martin Page later made a fortune by writing *We Built This* City for Starship.

tune and with a desperate look in their eyes of an old dog in a vet's waiting room. Lovin' Feeling were in safe hands with a song co-written by Tony Hillier, the man behind The Brotherhood of Man's biggest hits, but their performance of *Different Worlds and Different People* could only get them into fourth place[134].

Next was *Every Day of my Life* by Good Looks, a typical Eurovision two boy / two girl act featuring Lavinia and Louis Rodgers, siblings of Irish songstress Clodagh Rodgers, and claimed joint second place. The act voted last was Rich Gypsey with the forgettable ballad *You're the Only Good Thing in my Life*, which was almost as godawful as *How Long* by The Weltons.

The winners were Bardo, performing the Simon Jeffries song *One Step Further*, a male – female duo who at least looked young unlike the rest of the *been-around-the-block-*

a-couple-of-times contestants, though Sally Anne Triplett had entered the competition two years previously as part of Prima Donna[135]. The male of the duo was twenty-four-year-old Simon Fischer who had once played the role of a punk in *Rumpole of the Bailey*. Bardo were represented by Andy Hill and Nicola Martin, the same people behind Buck's Fizz[136], and after winning took the single up the charts to number two. The song was perfect for Eurovision, with an interpretative but unchallenging dance routine and male – female harmonies, though you suspect that the songwriter had hoped to write for Meat Loaf as there are touches of *Dead Ringer for Love* and *Paradise by the Dashboard Light* in the tune and arrangement.

On the same night songwriter and producer Nick Lowe was hosting a thirty-third birthday party at his house, where Elvis Costello took the opportunity to discuss his new album with producer Clive Langer, whilst doing their best to ignore *A Song for Europe* on the television in the background. Langer mentioned a song he had just written for Robert Wyatt and dragged Costello into another room with a piano to play it for him. The tune was full of minor jazzy chords with some make-shift words and Costello loved it immediately, promising to write lyrics sometime soon.

ひ ひ ひ

Although Altered Images had been on the scene for less than two years, they were already sounding fatigued by spring 1982. Formed on the south side of Glasgow in 1979 by former school friends Clare Grogan, Gerard McInulty, Michael Anderson, Tony McDaid, and Johnny McElhone[137], the band were influenced by post-punk, sending a demo tape to Siouxsie & The Banshees and securing a support slot on their *Kaleidoscope* tour. Edwyn Collins of Orange Juice had referred to them as a "*kindergarden Banshees*" a couple of years previously, however they were entertained by Postcard Records because of his infatuation with Grogan's sister, Kate. A couple of sessions for John Peel followed which were enough to gain a recording contract with Epic Records, however their first two singles failed to chart, partly due to an inharmonious production by Steve Severin from the Banshees, who boosted the reverb

---

[134]Their lead singer Bobby McVey later found a job as a member of The Fizz, a version of Buck's Fizz who had to tour under the name for legal reasons.

[135] She also performed in a circus and had presented Crackerjack on BBC television.

[136] Fisher had unsuccessfully auditioned for Buck's Fizz the previous year.

[137] His dad was the Labour MP for the Gorbals, Frank McElhone.

and played down the pop, and partly due to their debut *Dead Pop Stars* being released in the immediate aftermath of John Lennon's assassination.

By summer 1981, Epic were concerned their investment was failing and coupled them with Martin Rushent who was in the middle of his production success with The Human League. With McInulty choosing to leave[138] to be replaced by Jim McKinven[139], the band decamped to Rushent's Genetic Studios in Berkshire where they recorded the final track for the debut album, both called *Happy Birthday*. Rushent focused on the pop, pushing Grogan's marmite little-girl vocals to the front, and providing the band with a number two hit. Grogan would describe their journey towards pop as "*a natural reaction to what was happening... we were so young and overwhelmed by what was happening that we couldn't hide our joy*". That one of the hit movies of the summer, *Gregory's Girl*, starred Grogan also helped raise the profile of the band. Grogan had been fortunate to win the role having been discovered working as a waitress, not in a cocktail bar, but in Glaswegian restaurant The Spaghetti Factory[140] by director Bill Forsyth.[141]

The band and label then elected to engage Rushent for the whole of the second album, which they began recording at Genetic in November 1981. The following month saw the release of their second top ten hit, *I Could Be Happy*, an irresistible rush of pop with

guitar riffs owing a debt to Stuart Adamson's work in The Skids, along with Rushent's melodic hooks on keyboard. The song peaked at number seven in January 1982, just as Altered Images picked up the *Best New Band* award from the New Musical Express and the *Most Promising Act* award from Smash Hits.

Altered Images were running at full speed like newly enabled toddlers, having spent the last few months touring their first album, recording their second one, and fulfilling promotional duties for two top ten hit singles. In March they put the finishing touches to the second album, only six months after the release of their debut, and just as *I Could Be Happy* slipped out the charts, their new single *See Those Eyes* was released. Perfectly recorded by Rushent, the song was brimming with the guitar hooks Altered Images had made their signature, and barrelled along at a splendid pace, so fast and lacking development that the band were forced to repeat the first half of the track simply to make it long enough to release. It climbed to just outside the top ten, however already this early into their chart career, the feeling was Altered Images had nothing else to offer.

ʊ ʊ ʊ

The Social Democratic Party (SDP) were the newest kids on the block in British politics, having been founded by Roy Jenkins, David Owen, Bill Rodgers, and Shirley Williams. The four had been senior members of the Labour Party until they issued what became known as the *Limehouse Declaration* in January 1981 in disgust at the party committing

---

[138] McNulty went on to form The Wake with Bobby Gillespie, signing to Factory Records and the curse of forever becoming compared to New Order.

[139] Formerly of Glaswegian synth-pop act The Berlin Blondes, signed to EMI Records.

[140] There was a stage at the back of the restaurant where Orange Juice would occasionally play.

[141] The producers of the movie were reluctant to give her the role due to a noticeable scar on her face, the result of a smashed glass in a nightclub the year before, but Forsyth stood his ground, filming her in profile as much as possible or using mortician's wax and make-up for close-ups.

itself to nuclear disarmament and withdrawal from the European Economic Community, as well as their perception it had been infiltrated by hard-line Marxist / Trotskyist Militant members[142].

With a placing on the political spectrum somewhere between the left wing of Labour and the right wing of the Conservatives, they became known as the *Gang of Four* and floated the notion they would use the name *New Labour* before choosing the SDP. Initially twenty-eight Labour and one Conservative Members of Parliament joined the new party, which also gained tremendous support from a public weary of the dogma and extremes of the Right and Left. Although seen as a break-away from Labour, 60% of the new membership had never belonged to a political party before.

In June 1981 they formed an alliance with the David Steele-led Liberal party, which did not please everyone, with Liberal member and serial sex offender Cyril Smith[143] stating the SDP should have been *"strangled at birth"*. As a political force the alliance was seemingly unstoppable, and at the end of 1981 was achieving 50% of the vote in by-elections and polling.

In early 1982 the party disagreed over who would fight local elections, causing a minor dip in their poll ratings, but not enough to knock them from leading both Labour and the Conservatives. The most obvious problem the SDP was facing was that one of their highest profile *leaders*, the most experienced and therefore favourite to be Prime Minister should they triumph in a future general election, Roy Jenkins, was not a sitting member of parliament.

Jenkins had been born in 1920 and made much of his Welsh working-class background, however he was part of a generation of left-wing Oxford and Cambridge graduates, alongside Dennis Healey and Tony Crossland, who made much of the rights and nobility of the working class, only to be thrust in beside them in the armed forces during the Second World War and find they had little in common. Jenkins may have been from the valleys, however his former mineworker father[144] was a Member of Parliament, which certainly would have lifted his vision above a life in the pits, securing an intelligence job as a codebreaker at Bletchley Park along with Alan Turing.

Through the post-war years Jenkins served in Labour governments and shadow cabinets, holding posts as Minister for Aviation, Chancellor of the Exchequer, Deputy Leader of the Labour Party and Home Secretary. He was a liberalising force in society during the 1960's, overseeing the relaxing of laws relating to divorce and the abolition of theatre censorship, whilst being a vocal supporter of the legalisation of abortion and decriminalisation of homosexuality. On course to become leader of Labour, and eventually Prime Minister, in 1972 Jenkins defied a three-line party whip to support the Conservative government plan to take the country into the European Community. He continued to support Britain's place in Europe, leading a successful *"Yes"* campaign during the 1975 referendum on continued membership of what would become the European Union.

It was in Europe he found his natural home, becoming President of the European Union between 1977 and 1981, moving with ease between different countries and world leaders. Jenkins was once described as *"more of socialite than a socialist"* and he certainly enjoyed a lavish lifestyle, remaining married throughout his life despite having

---

[142] It is a situation Labour found themselves in again thirty-five years later when under the leadership of Jeremy Corbyn the hard-left grassroots movement *Momentum* began a campaign of purging the party of those who were deemed *"ideologically unsound"*.

[143] Even after accusations came to light, Smith was knighted.

[144] Arthur Jenkins studied at the Sorbonne, Paris and Ruskin College, Oxford, before representing Pontypool for eleven years.

affairs with Jackie Kennedy's sister Lee Radziwill and Ian Fleming's wife, Ann[145]. Whilst in Brussels, Jenkins oversaw the introduction of the European Monetary System, which eventually became the Euro.

Halfway through his tenure in Brussels, Jenkins started to look to his own future, and delivered the prestigious Dimbleby Lecture at the end of 1979 in which he argued for middle ground politics, somewhere between the hard right of Conservatism and the hard left that was in the process of taking over the Labour Party. The lecture acted as a lightning rod, and Jenkins found his stance popular with disillusioned politicians and the public.

A first attempt to return Jenkins to parliament was made during the Warrington by-election in summer 1981, which he lost to the Labour party[146]. It was then decided he would sit in the Glasgow Hillhead by-election in March 1982, which had been caused by the death of Conservative MP Tam Galbraith. It was curious seat to compete given it had been in Conservative control since 1918.

The Tories put forward local lawyer Gerry Malone who called for cuts in welfare and a re-introduction of the death penalty, whilst Labour chose David Wiseman who was known for his belief of and research into the Loch Ness Monster. The Scottish National Party were represented by George Leslie, who ran a campaign based upon Jenkins being not Scottish but Welsh, whilst the Ecology Party, a forerunner of the Green Party, put forward Nicolette Carlaw who encouraged people, if they did not choose her, to vote for Leslie on the grounds he looked after her cats when she went on holiday.

There was some confusion when an organisation called the Social Democratic Party stood Donald Parkin, who changed his name by deed poll to *Roy Harold Jenkins*. The local SDP members were given permission to stand outside voting stations with placards explaining which party was the real one[147].

Then there were the less established candidates including Protestant pastor Jack Glass[148], a good friend of Ian Paisley, who stood on a campaign of opposition to the Pope's forthcoming visit to Scotland, and Bill Boaks, who stood as "Public Safety Democratic Monarchist White Resident" and managed to achieve the British record for the least votes in a local election, polling a grand total of five, one less than the number of people who had nominated him as a candidate.

Despite traditionally being a Conservative stronghold, the seat was seen as up for grabs, and all the major parties sent their big hitters to Glasgow in the run up to the day. 76% of the public voted on Thursday 25th March, and Jenkins was declared winner with one third of the vote, with the Conservative and Labour candidates each polling a quarter.

Jenkins was back in parliament, and Liberal leader David Steel felt comfortable enough to tell party members "*Go back to your constituencies and prepare for government!*"

ʊ ʊ ʊ

In the immediate aftermath of the tragic death of his guitarist, Ozzy Osbourne had decided to call it a day, and plunged further into drink and drugs to anesthetize his existence. However, what else can a rock star do when he stops becoming a rock star?

---

[145] Then again, who didn't? Labour leader Hugh Gaitskell certainly did.

[146] It was perhaps not the stwongest idea to have a man like Woy Jenkins, who had twouble pwonouncing the letter "r", to wun in the constituency of Wawwington.

[147] One of these volunteers was future Liberal Democratic leader Charles Kennedy.

[148] Jack Glass loved to protest outside cinemas and theatres. There is no evidence of him having carried a "*Careful Now*" or "*Down with this sort of thing*" sign whilst doing so.

On Friday 26th March, one week after the catastrophic death, Osbourne appeared on *Late Night with David Letterman*, announcing a new guitarist had been found in the shape of Bernie Torme, formerly of Gillan, and that "*You can't kill rock and roll*".
Initially, bass player Rudy Sarzo called his younger brother Robert and asked him to audition. Unknown to him, however Sharon's father Don Arden[149] had contacted Torme and asked him to also turn up to the audition. Torme's style did not seem to suit the band and he did not know the songs, however it emerged Arden had already paid him in advance, and so he was hired.
Immediately after the funeral Arden approached his daughter Sharon in her house and demanded the money she had collected from the tour so far. "*It's Ozzy's money*" she argued, but that was not going to stop the seasoned hard man as he snapped "*Sharon, give me the fucking money*". Sharon went to retrieve the money and upon returning took handfuls of hundred-dollar bills from the bag and started throwing them around the courtyard of the house, screaming "*You want it? You fucking get it*". Don Arden started crawling around the floor collecting the money to be joined by his daughter's dog, Jet, who thought this was all a great game and started eating as many of the notes as possible. From one of the overlooking windows Ozzy was shrieking with laughter as Don Arden's short dressing gown revealed his hairy testicles every time he bent over to pick up money.
Retiring to her bedroom, Sharon observed her bookcase had been disturbed, and found Ozzy's cocaine stash hidden behind a couple of the volumes. Furious at what this drug had done to those around her, she rushed to her window overlooking the courtyard and called for Ozzy. The singer was hanging out in a guestroom with drummer Tommy Aldridge, and when the two emerged Sharon proceeded to blow the massive pile of powder all over the courtyard. Ozzy and Tommy started shouting "*Noooooo!*" but it was too late, leaving them no option but to rush around trying to scoop up whatever they could, at which point Jet the dog re-emerged for a new game of *lick up the white powder*. The dog started running frantically around the courtyard, alternating between licking, trying to hump a Shetland pony and projectile shitting. Sharon shouted at Ozzy "*Just look at him, running around like a fucking lunatic, foaming at the mouth, shitting. If it does that to the dog, what do you think it's doing to you?*"
Two days later the band flew to Pennsylvania for a couple of days rehearsal, and three days after that on Wednesday 1st April the tour resumed at Stabler Arena, Bethlehem, Pennsylvania.

ʊ ʊ ʊ

London was the hub of *new pop* in the early 1980's, however it was not only in the recording studios and live music venues that provocative and innovative sounds could be heard. The DIY and anarchistic side of punk had also reached comedy and a new strain of stand-up comedians were tackling the traditions of the craft. Eventually known as *alternative comedy*, the sexist, racist, and homophobic nature of traditional comics was confronted by these generally working-class, but university educated stand-ups, as the orthodox set-up / punchline approach and structure of jokes was discarded.

---

[149] Don Arden was the real manager of Ozzy Osbourne, who tasked his daughter Sharon with the day to day duties. Arden had begun in showbusiness as an Al Jolson impersonator, before becoming manager of The Small Faces, The Move, Wizzard, and the Electric Light Orchestra. His management style was… intense, employing extreme violence to get his way, including dangling people over balconies of tall buildings until they agreed to his demands. He was a hard man to argue with.

Centred on The Comedy Store Club which had been opened by Peter Rosengard and Don Ward in London's Soho in May 1979, the scene came together over the next few months. The Comedy Store initially opened on Saturday and Sunday nights at the Gargoyle Club[150] in Dean Street, and was compered by Alexis Sayle, a rambunctious, bald, and slightly overstuffed Liverpudlian in an ill-fitting suit, who controlled the inebriated and uproarious audience through a mixture of jokes, insults, pugnaciousness, and threatened violence. He was soon joined by *genuine bad boy* Keith Allen[151], whose impulsiveness made him both dangerous to book and a sensation to watch. Soon, the regular acts featured Rick Mayall, Adrian Edmundson, Andy De La Tour[152], Nigel Planer, and Peter Richardson. Just over a year later they broke away and started their own comedy revue called The Comic Strip, adding Dawn French, Jennifer Saunders, Arnold Brown[153], and Scottish hardman Robbie Coltrane[154] to the regular acts.

Over the next year the two clubs became the toast of London, as several television channels tried to bottle the lightning by proposing new shows featuring the acts, however none of the offers seemed correct for them, adhering too much to traditional comic roles.

In March 1982 the regulars from the Comic Strip Club travelled to Australia for a few live dates, in a package which included Alexis Sayle, Rick Mayall, Adrian Edmundson, Jennifer Saunders, Dawn French, Nigel Planer, and Peter Richardson. None of the assemblage had any sort of public profile, except for Sayle who had just appeared on *OTT*, an ill-fated adult version of the children's television programme *Tiswas*[155]. *OTT* was a ramshackle Saturday night show which appeared to exist without any writers or script, and whilst a kids' show thrived on the anarchy, the adult version was hopelessly exposed by such a slapdash approach.

Whilst in Melbourne, the Comic Strip crew ran into members of the Teardrop Explodes, themselves in the middle of a fraught Australian tour and strung-out on poor relationships and the wrong types of drugs. One unnamed member, ostensibly starved of a decent meal in weeks, was taken under the wings of French and Saunders, who ensured he was fed, gave him some of their daily money allowance, and put him to bed at a decent hour. No-one, however, could find out what he was called, because whenever asked he would produce a pencil drawing of a mythical creature from his pocket and insist that was his name.

---

[150] The Gargoyle Club could only be reached by taking an extremely cramped elevator to the Nell Gwyne Club on the floor above, making your way past the strippers, and descending a staircase which had been designed by Henri Matisse.

[151] Keith Allen was a Welsh Navy brat who was sent to borstal at the age of fifteen, giving him a dangerous edge which the other comedians could only dream of. He found a career as a more serious actor later and is perhaps best known to younger generations as the father of singer Lily Allen and actor Alfie Allen.

[152] Andy de la Tour is the younger brother of the cherished Frances de la Tour.

[153] Arnold Brown was a Jewish Glaswegian former accountant turned comedian, older than the others at the age of forty-six in 1982. The self-confessed highlight of his career was supporting Frank Sinatra at Ibrox Stadium in Glasgow.

[154] Robbie Coltrane was not actually a hardman. He was born as Anthony McMillan into a Glaswegian family of wealth, and after attending private boarding school in Perthshire enrolled at Glasgow School of Art. It was here he was nicknamed *Little Lord Fauntleroy* due to his accent being like that of Prince Charles.

[155] Being from a pretend-posh house, I was not allowed to watch *Tiswas*, and was much more of a *Swap Shop* person. In fact, I do not think we ever watched much on ITV at all. That was for *common people*.

In Melbourne, Julian Cope claimed the Teardrop Explodes "*all lost it*", with several members of their entourage succumbing to cheap Australian heroin. In their live dates, Cope had taken to clambering naked with his microphone into the gap between the ceiling and the outside of the building, amongst all the pipes and electrical wires, and delivering his vocal performance from there, much to the consternation and confusion of the audiences.

Whilst the Teardrop Explodes were losing it, and the comedians were making a name for themselves, a separate group of young writers and comedians were putting together a one-off comedy sketch show for Granada Television. Cambridge Footlights alumni Stephen Fry, Hugh Laurie, and Emma Thompson had been joined by Paul Shearer and Manchester University graduate Ben Elton, to write a show which combined the tradition of the Oxbridge comedy sketch stage show and the anarchic edgy material of the *alternative* performers in London. The writers decided they needed someone else, and the names of unknowns were banded about, such as Alfred Molina[156], Chris Langham[157] and Liz Lochhead[158], before a young Scottish actress, Siobhan Redmond was recruited. The show was eventually called *There's Nothing to Worry About*, and three episodes were broadcast in the North West of England.

28th March – 3rd April 1982
#1 single: The Goombay Dance Band: Seven Tears
#1 album: Barbra Streisand: Love Songs

With Paul Weller namechecking them, the additional publicity had allowed Pigbag to scrape into the charts with a new single *Getting Up*. The act could be labelled a funk collective, originally organized in late-1980 by Chris Hamlin along with several other horn players and rehearsing by jamming in parks and various public places. They soon recruited drums and bass and focused on a piece called *Papa's Got a Brand New Pigbag*, a song which had been the entire motive for bringing the act together in the first place. The band then hitched to Bristol to ask freshly departed Pop Group bass player Simon Underwood to join, and to their astonishment he agreed. Through his contacts the band landed a support slot with The Slits, and a record deal with Y Records. *Papa's Got a Brand New*

---

[156] Alfred Molina had made his debut movie appearance the previous year in *Raiders of the Lost Ark*, and wisely decided to follow a career of serious acting.

[157] Chris Langham had started out writing for *The Muppet Show*, making an unexpected appearance as the weekly special guest when Richard Pryor dropped out. He was billed as *Chris, the Delivery Boy*. Langham was also one of the original cast for the pilot of *Not the Nine O'Clock News*, but was replaced by Griff Rhys Jones for the series. In 2007 he was found guilty of child pornography and sentenced to ten months in prison.

[158] Liz Lochhead was another Glasgow School of Art alumni, who turned to poetry instead and was named the Scots Makar (the National Poet of Scotland) in 2011, taking over from Edwin Morgan, and being succeeded by Jackie Kay. She used to attend occasional tutorials and critiques of my work, where her *"Wha's like us"* Glaswegian working class bollocks annoyed the hell out of me. I don't think she liked me either, so it all balances out.

Pigbag was quickly recorded and released becoming a mammoth underground hit, selling over 100,000 copies without troubling the charts. At the end of March Stiff Records re-released *Papa's Got a Brand New Pigbag*, and as the band toured comprehensively up and down the country the hypnotic horn riff and contagious funk groove started to climb the charts, ultimately peaking at number three. It continued to boast an extended life after the chart run, re-emerging as a football terrace chant over a decade later and charting on numerous other occasions after being remixed by, amongst others, Paul Oakenfold. This was a song ahead of the times by several years, anticipating all sorts of dance and rave moves in the subsequent years, still sounding vigorous and vivacious decades later. The act appeared a couple of times on *Top of the Pops* in April, the first of which saw co-founder Roger Freeman leave the band in anger after they decided to all wear suits for the performance, and he insisted on wearing his customary donkey jacket. For the second performance he was replaced by Paul Nellee Hooper, a Bristol local who would go on to form The Wild Bunch[159] as well as becoming one of the most distinguished producers and remixers, working with the likes of Bjork, Madonna, Soul II Soul, and U2. Hooper was destined never to play on any of Pigbag's recordings, but the lineage between them and the entire electronica and trip-hop scenes was formed. Pigbag, as an act, could never live up to this one track; nothing they produced came near it in terms of excellence or impact, and by the time it was a hit single, they had already begun to fragment. One of the complications with being a collective is that everyone wants to have an equal say, and when opinions conflict people take umbrage. The new line-up retired to Abbey Road Studios in June to record their follow up, the Caribbean-influenced *Big Bean*, and then on a tour over the summer which took them across the Britain, Europe, New York, and Japan. By the time they returned the new single had stunted at number forty.

Pigbag reacted by recruiting a new member in the shape of New York jazz singer Angela Jaeger. If there was any uncertainty regarding who was now in charge of the band and making the decisions it was confirmed when bass player Simon Underwood married Jaeger in early 1983, by which point their next album had already been recorded. It was, however, not to be released during their existence as the band split in summer 1983. Subsequent releases of tracks from it reveal that the band were taking a more drum / bass driven sound, one that would come to ultimate popularity with the arrival of Chicago House music a couple of years later, and the ensuing efficacious spread of the genre around the globe.

ʊ ʊ ʊ

The 54th Academy Awards, Hollywood's most important night of the year, was held on Monday 29th March at the Dorothy Chandler Pavilion in Los Angeles. Professionally hosted by veteran Johnny Carson, with the orchestral music arranged by Bill Conti[160], it was anticipated the night would belong to Warren Beatty's *Reds*, the story of a journalist during the Russian Revolution, which had received twelve nominations.

The night started well for *Reds*, picking up *Best Supporting Actress*, *Cinematography*, and *Director*, however that is where the Oscars ended for Warren Beatty, with populist

---

[159] The Wild Bunch featured Hooper, along with future Massive Attack members Robert Del Naja, Grant Marshall and Andrew Vowles, as well as solo star Tricky.

[160] Bill Conti wrote the music for the *Rocky* movies. Admit it, the theme is going through your head now.

movies such as *Raiders of the Lost Ark* and *An American Werewolf in London*[161] collecting *Art Direction, Make-Up, Sound,* and *Editing.* An early indication of the direction the awards were going was given when William Hurt and Kathleen Turner announced *Original Score* for British movie, *Chariots of Fire,* with a memorable synth driven soundtrack by Vangelis, followed by the same film winning *Costume Design.* Later, the movie picked up *Original Screenplay,* with writer Colin Welland getting over excited and proclaiming "*The British are coming*"[162] from the podium.

Then an unexpected outsider came into play with *Adapted Screenplay* going to *On Golden Pond,* which also collected the *Actor* and *Actress* awards when the Academy recognised a couple of legends, with Henry Fonda picking up his first and Katharine Hepburn picking up her fourth Oscar. The final award of the night was for Best Picture, with *Reds* expected to win, however the Brits truly were coming when it was announced *Chariots of Fire* was triumphant.

Chariots of Fire was one of only twenty-four British films made in 1981 and was partially financed by Egyptian millionaire Dodi Fayad[163]. With the Academy Award the United Kingdom seemed on the edge of a renaissance in filmmaking, with more movies being made during the decade than at any time since the 1950's. Cinema attendances also started to rise again after a fallow decade when the big screen's dominance was challenged by television, rising admission prices, and recession. However, most of these new cinemagoers were seeing American-made blockbusters.

Chariots of Fire was later viewed as a typical Thatcherite movie, proclaiming the *superiority of Britishness,* however director David Putnam and writer Colin Welland were Labour supporters, who framed the story within the class constraints of Oxbridge and the establishment, with the main characters being portrayed as anti-establishment outsiders.

The drain of talent, acting, directing, and technical, to America had left the British film industry impoverished for decades, and Hollywood bullyboy booking tactics forced out many homegrown movies from the cinema. Where British films tended to be faithful adaptations of literature, the Americans were more likely to trash the original material, deleting characters, plots, and scenes to make a more watchable, and therefore more entertaining, movie. An uncredited character in many British movies at the time was the class system, with emotionally stilted upper-class characters or the brash crude working class being the poles filmmakers tended to gravitate towards, with nothing in between.

The 1980's could be considered a golden age of a certain type of British movie, one which dealt with social commentary from a leftist point of view. Considered by some to be the true *New Wave* of British cinema, many of the movies made throughout the decade were critical of government policy and the effect on the working classes. These movies, however, did not play well overseas where audiences wanted to see depictions of Britain's past, the clichéd views of Empire, King, and Country portrayed in *Chariots of Fire, Ghandi,* and any number of Merchant-Ivory productions. This *realism versus romanticism* remained a firm divide throughout the decade, with some brilliant movies made on either side.

---

[161] Watching at home, Michael Jackson made a mental note to watch the latter, later employing the director John Landis and make-up artist Rick Baker to work on his ground-breaking promo video for *Thriller.*

[162] "*The British are coming*" is supposedly what Paul Revere shouted as he rode through the Massachusetts countryside in 1775 to trigger the American War of Independence. Given the state was full of British patriots at the time, what he actually shouted was "*The Regulars are coming*".

[163] The lover and death partner of Princess Diana.

The real powerhouse of movie making in Britain throughout the decade was within television; both the BBC and ITN funded numerous long format dramas, often to be shown only once, and featuring writers, directors, and actors who would later make the leap to Hollywood, such as Stephen Frears and John Schlesinger. When Channel 4 started broadcasting later in the year they became a major source of funding for smaller, more serious movies, producing over 170 throughout the decade.

On the same night as the Academy Awards, at an Oscars house party in front of less than fifty people, the second Golden Raspberries[164] were announced. The undoubtable winner (or loser) was *Mommie Dearest*, the true tale of the abuse meted out by Hollywood legend Joan Crawford upon her daughter. The film starred Faye Dunaway in a performance that *Variety* described as "*beyond scenery-chewing*" and was largely responsible for the decline in her Hollywood career. *Mommie Dearest* won Worst Film, Worst Actress, Worst Supporting Actress, Worst Supporting Actor and Worst Screenplay, and a month after release, once the studio realised people were laughing at it, was re-marketed as a camp guilty-pleasure.

ʊ ʊ ʊ

By the time one of the original influences on the New Romantic movement, Roxy Music, returned to the charts in March 1982, they were far removed from the epicene Brian Eno-era band of the early to mid-1970's. Roxy had spent the second half of the 1970's moving away from their pop-culture roots[165] towards a debonaire adult-orientated sound, with a complementary lounge-lizard look and their frontman Bryan Ferry referred to in the New Musical Express as *Byron Ferrari*[166].

Their new album was recorded in late 1981 and early 1982, based upon songs half-written by Ferry during an extended stay at Crumlin Lodge, Ireland. By this point, Roxy Music were down to a nucleus of Ferry, Andy Mackay, and Phil Manzanera, but augmenting this sound with a congregation of legendary session musicians. With Rhett Davies producing, the band created a selection of songs very loosely based around the legend of King Arthur and called the album *Avalon* after his mythological resting place.

The album marked an appreciable modification in the working process of Roxy Music. Previously they had captured the band playing as close to live in the studio as possible, with completed songs and some over-dubs, but with *Avalon* Roxy wrote the tracks as they recorded them, creating *musical atmospheres* to the beat of a programmed rhythm, then requesting the various other musicians react to these, which explained the inclusion of a couple of superfluous short instrumental tracks. Initial recording was undertaken at Compass Point Studios, Nassau, before Roxy retreated to The Power Station in New York for overdubs. "*It's very beautiful music and it's very hard to go further than that*" Ferry explained at the time, "*The album is very romantic and dreamy – good escapist stuff!*"

---

[164] The Golden Raspberries had been started as a piece of fun the previous year by John J. B. Wilson and picked up enough publicity to double in size each year. They are now a fixture on the annual calendar, taking place on the eve of the Academy Awards, and it is even known for some actors and directors to turn up and collect their awards.

[165] Ferry claimed the initial glam look was "*very important. It made it more exciting for us and we performed better when we dressed up.*"

[166] Nick Kent went one step further and called him "*the George Lazenby of the Argentinian corned-beef market*".

Although Ferry had recently moved to a house in the country[167] the album was underpainted with references to the city in songs such as *Turn You On* and *True To Life*. Ferry was low in the mix, allowing the ethereal music and grooves to govern, with indications in the sonic expanse of what The Blue Nile would release later in the decade. On songs such as *The Space Between*, tempo increases sounded like New Romantic funk through a coffee bar filter, and the whole album glistened with the professional gloss which could only be provided by session musicians.

The first single from the album, *More Than This*, encapsulated everything Roxy Music had become: middle-aged, mid-paced, mullet-adorned, suit and tie wearing, *sophisticated*, and completely lacking the danger and experimentation which first catapulted them to fame. The last two minutes of the song were purely instrumental,

and you could almost hear Ferry slithering to the bar in a wine lodge whilst the band continue playing. However, it would be guileless to assume the song was without deeper meaning, and it could be interpreted in a couple of ways. The first was as a simple declaration of satisfaction, there can be nothing "*more than this*" added to life to make it better. The lyrics, however, pointed to a much less satisfying existence. Ferry was drawing upon the work of seventeenth century Dutch philosopher Baruch Spinoza who argued God and nature were interchangeable, and neither gave a hoot about humans. Spinoza was an ardent defender of Determinism, believing free will an illusion created by man to feel better about himself, which Ferry echoed with "*Fallen leaves in the night, who can say where they're blowing?*". Ferry would finally accept the vacuum of Yoda significance in the chorus with "*More than this, you know there is nothing*". Despite the lushness of the music, this was a hymn to an empty existence, with Ferry playing human rationalisation and the music mirroring nature. This may be why the singer abandoned the music during the second half of the song, leaving nature to continue elegantly uninterrupted.

The idea was emphasised on the single cover and accompanying video. The former featured Pre-Raphaelite[168] Dante Gabriel Rossetti's portrait of Alexa Wilding, his muse who was infamous for both her beauty and her lack of expression, just like nature. In the video Ferry, when not miming to camera wearing an unfetching leather jacket and bow tie, watched on a giant screen, with no control over the fate of his own destiny.

The single reached number six, and the subsequent album topped the charts, as the band set off on a world tour that lasted into the following year. At that point, Ferry must have realised the band was him and some session men, with Manzanera and Mackay relegated to bit players, and decided to release everything solo from then on. Roxy Music would occasionally get together to play some dates, but even when they thought they were working on a new album the tracks would invariably end up on Ferry's next solo album. For summer promotional performances across Europe Ferry also recruited the rhythm section and keyboard player from The Associates, John Dempsey, Steve Golding, and Martha Ladly purely because they looked so good. Once you're an aesthete, you are an aesthete for life.

℧ ℧ ℧

---

[167] By this point, Ferry had abandoned the city to live in the country, and enjoyed seasonal shooting in Scotland, "*not because I like shooting things, but just as a social event*".

[168] The Pre-Raphaelites were of course obsessed with the "*truth to nature*".

In the middle of their European tour Depeche Mode were bewildered to find themselves playing on Tuesday 30th March at the Rainbow Club in the tiny village of Oberkorn in Luxembourg, instead of the scheduled date in Brussels. Making matters worse was German TV channel RTL arranging to film the concert for broadcast, as the 250-capacity venue struggled to cope with both the television equipment and a fifteen-person touring organisation. After hours spent trying to generate enough power for all the electronics and overcoming the shock of the PA being split in half between two rooms, the band decided to place two members in one room, and two in the other.

With an extremely low stage and the cameras placed at the back of the room, the audience would be required to sit down, which they did at first until one girl rose to her feet and started to dance. Security intervened, trying to remove her from the room only for singer Dave Gahan to leapt from the stage and exchange a series of slaps with the bouncers. The woman, it turned out, was his girlfriend.

After the show, it was discovered the bus had broken down and the band were going to have to spend a couple of days in Oberkorn until either a replacement vehicle or spare parts could be located. At the local hotel they realised how isolated they were when Martin Gore requested an egg for breakfast only to be told with a shrug and a roll of the eyes by the waiter this was not possible because "*It is a small town*".

When the record company phoned and demanded a title for the instrumental B-side of their next single, Depeche Mode obliged with *Oberkorn- It's a Small Town*.

ʊ ʊ ʊ

On the early evening of Wednesday 31st March Margaret Thatcher was at work in her room in the House of Commons when she received word Defence Secretary John Nott required to see her urgently concerning the Falkland Islands. He conveyed that a substantial Argentinian fleet had left the mainland and were heading for the islands, and an invasion was impending. It was the Ministry of Defence opinion that once the islands were seized, it would be impossible to re-take them. Sir Henry Leach, the Chief of the Naval Staff was of a different belief, having blustered his way into the meeting in full regalia and without any identification after turning up at Downing Street directly from inspecting ships in Portsmouth, proclaiming he could have a fleet ready to sail within forty-eight hours.

"*How long will it take to get there?*" asked Thatcher.

"*Three weeks*" Leach replied, to which the Prime Minister said "*Surely you mean three days?*"

At this point Leach took control, stating "*We can recover the islands... and we must!*" When the Prime Minister asked "*Why?*", Leach was emphatic, "*Because if we do not, or if we pussyfoot in our actions and do not achieve complete success, in another few months we shall be living in a different country whose word counts for nothing!*" Thatcher, convinced the islands *must* remain British, ordered the fleet to be assembled.

The Argentinians had been planning to invade the Falkland Islands later in the year but had been coerced prematurely by the events in South Georgia earlier in the month, which was in danger of eradicating the element of surprise. British parliamentary debate over the past couple of weeks had been watched from the public gallery by an official from the Argentinian Embassy, who reported daily to General Galtieri[169] back in the homeland. The Argentinian troops on South Georgia had still not departed the

---

[169] Leopoldo Galtieri was a graduate from the US Army School of the Americas, an institution with an alarmingly high number of Central and South American dictators, despots, and mass-murderers amongst its alumni. I am sure this is just co-incidence.

island, camping in the hills instead, and the British hesitancy in properly dealing with this led to a belief in Argentina they would not respond to an invasion either.

Meanwhile diplomatic attempts were made to avoid the invasion, with Thatcher appealing to American President Ronald Reagan to press Galtieri to draw back. The Americans declared support for Britain but were very keen not to upset the Argentinian regime, given they were considered an important military dictatorship keeping the communists at bay.

ʊ ʊ ʊ

Dublin four-piece U2 were having a dual crisis of faith and confidence. Formed in late 1976 at Mount Temple Comprehensive School, U2 initially specialised in punk-influenced songs with a post-punk edge, however problems first arrived halfway through 1981 when singer Bono, guitarist The Edge, and drummer Larry Mullen came under the influence of a charismatic Christian group called the Shalom Fellowship. They were put under increasing pressure to quit music, with the band considered to conflict with their new beliefs, and second album *October* reflected this spiritualism with overt religious themes throughout, to the extent that it could reasonably be called *Christian rock*, a stance which crippled their relationship with the post-punk press. Bass player Adam Clayton had not joined the Fellowship and was feeling increasingly

like an outsider when the others held prayer meetings before going onstage, remaining something of an interloper throughout the band's career.

Early 1982 was spent touring North America as support to the J Geils Band, interspersed with some headline dates to promote *October* to a responsive audience. The only problem was the album contained no more obvious singles to coincide with the tour, so the band had returned to the studio in January with their usual producer Steve Lillywhite[170] and recorded a left-over song called *A Celebration*. The lyrics were still full of religious imagery, pretending to be something they were not by clouding the implications with incomplete lines, whilst the music was befitting an album track, at best. The single struggled to number forty-seven and is best remembered for the B-side, a track called *Trash, Trampoline, and the Party Girl*. Hastily half-finished on the single the song became a live favourite (under the name *Party Girl*) over the next few years, being played well over a hundred times.

A second single in a row not to reach the top forty in Britain, U2 looked to be on the skids, and £400,000 in debt to Island Records were refused any more money as the last album had been poorly received. There were some serious discussions about dropping the band from the label, however owner Chris Blackwell fought for them and it was decided to give them one final chance.

At the end of the American tour the band withdrew to a cottage in Howth, a peninsula to the north of Dublin, and started writing and rehearsing their next album, determined to "*come out the box fighting*".

---

[170] Steve Lillywhite was a producer who would become synonymous with bands in the 1980's, starting his career by producing the demo which allowed Ultravox to sign to Island Records. He became an in-demand producer during the days of New Wave, working with Siouxsie & the Banshees, XTC, The Members, The Psychedelic Furs, and Peter Gabriel. Later in the decade he produced Big Country, Talking Heads, The Pogues and Simple Minds amongst many others.

ʊ ʊ ʊ

In the early hours of Friday 2ⁿᵈ April the Argentinian fleet reached the Falkland Islands. The locals had been pre-warned and had burnt all classified papers the previous evening, as well as rounding up Argentinian nationals in the Town Hall, including a newly arrived Spanish teacher who was suspected by many of being a spy. The small troop of 79 Marines who were permanently posted on the island under the command of Major Mike Norman and had started organising fortifications, were briefed that large numbers of Argentinians were due at any time, and the marines were almost certainly going to be killed whilst defending the islands. The soldiers rose to the situation on the basis they were not going to go down without a fight.

Meanwhile Governor Rex Hunt, once described as *"a colonial governor in a Peter Sellers comedy"*, dined with his wife before sending her and their son to stay with friends. He then went to retrieve his shotgun, only to find his driver had beaten him to it and was told *"I've left the flag up tonight, sir, and I'll shoot any Argie bastard who tries to take it down"*.

At just after 6 a.m. gunfire was heard from behind Port Stanley, the opposite direction from what had been anticipated, and it became obvious the Argentinians had landed somewhere to the west and traversed the wilderness. For the next three hours shots were exchanged, during which between twenty and thirty Argentinians lost their lives, compared to no British casualties. At 9.25 a.m. Governor Hunt, operating from underneath a table, realised they were pinned down in Government House and the Argentinians were bringing in heavy artillery via the airport runway, and ordered a cessation of hostilities to arrange for surrender via a contact at the Argentine State airline. When Argentinian Rear Admiral Busser walked into the room he offered his hand to Hunt who refused to shake it. Later when General Osvaldo Garcia, head of the land forces, offered his hand Hunt again refused to shake it. *"It is very ungentlemanly of you to refuse to shake my hand"* he stated, to which Hunt replied, *"It is very uncivilised of you to invade my country"*.

The British troops were ordered to lie on the road, in which position their photograph was taken for propaganda purposes, with the Argentinian troops brandishing weapons they had been sold by the British Government a few years previously. The Argentines attempted to raise their flag, but it fell down the first time much to the noisy amusement of the British troops. The troops were then flown to Argentina and returned to the United Kingdom within a couple of days.

During the first day of the occupation Argentinian troops were somewhat taken aback to not find the locals waving flags and welcoming them, having been led to believe the inhabitants of the island were proud Spanish-speaking Argentinian patriots who were under imposed British rule.

Meanwhile, back in London the Ministry of Defence Press Officer started to be besieged by hundreds of requests from newspapers around the world for a place on board any naval fleet sailing to the area. Word came from Chief of Defence Staff, Admiral Sir Terrence Lewin in New Zealand, that no journalists would be allowed to travel with the fleet, however the Ministry, aware public opinion would be essential in any conflict, argued until a total of ten journalists was agreed upon. The Navy were incensed and demanded to know if they were meant to pack *"pens or bayonets"*. The press often seemed better informed than the government, for at 11 a.m. Foreign Secretary Humphrey Atkins told parliament that no invasion was taking place, a story repeated by Francis Pym, the Leader of the House of Commons, at 2.30 p.m. Sir Frank Cooper later admitted the government *"supplemented the wires and had a radio with the BBC World Service brought into the outer office"* to find out what was happening.

The government faced stern questioning in Parliament, from opposition and their own ranks, which became even more vociferous in a private meeting behind closed doors.

ʊ ʊ ʊ

As part of his preparations for the FIFA World Cup, Scotland manager Jock Stein had arranged to fly to New Zealand to see them play against a local league team. Due to fly out the following day, Saturday 3rd April, Stein was alarmed to see the news from the Falklands and phoned Scottish television journalist Archie MacPherson who was due to accompany him, explaining "*I don't think we should go. The war down there could get nasty and they'll end up cancelling the World Cup, or else we'll withdraw*". MacPherson, desperate to enhance his credentials with BBC London, spent time persuading Stein to make the journey.

Meanwhile in London, *The Sun* reported "*youths demonstrated outside the Argentinian Embassy in London last night. They sang 'Rule Britannia', ending with 'Don't Cry for Me, Argentina, We're Going to Nuke you*". Editor Kelvin MacKenzie[171] had made up his mind early which side of the argument he was going to take and was determined to stoke the patriotic and nationalist fires as much as possible, mixing jingoism and bingo to sell papers. A giant map of the South Atlantic and a portrait of Churchill were placed on the wall of the newspaper office, whilst MacKenzie insisted on wearing a naval officer's cap and being called *commander*.

ʊ ʊ ʊ

One of the most unique sounding singles of 1982 entered the charts towards the end of March, and then spent nine weeks fluttering just outside the top ten. *Ever So Lonely*

was the brainchild of record producer Steve Coe and bass player Martin Smith, who took George Harrison's Indian experiments with The Beatles and ran with them. Calling themselves Monsoon, they recruited sixteen-year-old London-born but of Indian descent Sheila Chandra[172] to add vocals. *Ever So Lonely* was an outstanding example of cultural crossover without becoming appropriation, constructed on pop beats mixed with tabla drums, whilst Dari Mankoo added a sitar melody on top. Chandra provided mesmerising vocals with a limited number of lyrics repeated throughout, in a sound which pre-empted a whole host of psychedelic dance music over a decade later. A lack of structural progress added to the dreamlike chimerical quality, with a percussion breakdown a feature popular with disco acts which would once again come into style during the rave years. *Ever So Lonely* may have been a bigger hit with improved promotion, however as it entered the charts Chandra found herself in hospital with a burst appendix, curtailing television duties for a couple of weeks.

Despite a second single with a video directed by Midge Ure, Monsoon did not last beyond the end of the year, falling out with record label Phonogram when they were instructed to "*lose the Indian influence*", and chose to split rather than compromise their reason for existing. A posthumous album was released the following year, and without

---

[171] There was never any doubt *The Sun* and MacKenzie would support the Conservative line in the conflict. His mother had been the press officer for the Conservative Greater London Council, and he was an enthusiastic Thatcherite. Under MacKenzie's editorship, *The Sun* printed racist, homophobic, and sexist news articles, many of which he admitted were made up. Around this time he was quoted as saying "*the reader.... He's the bloke you see in the pub, the right old fascist who wants to send wogs back, buy his poxy council house, he's afraid of the unions, afraid of the Russians, afraid of queers and the weirdos and drug dealers.*" When it came to the readership of *The Sun*, he was spot-on.

[172] Chandra had previously played the part of Sudhamani Patel in BBC children's drama *Grange Hill*.

a band to promote it failed to chart. By then Chandra and Coe were romantically linked and the decision was made for them to concentrate on her career, eventually signing to Peter Gabriel's Real World label and releasing three albums of experimental Indo-English pop throughout the 1990's.

In 2009 Chandra started to suffer the first symptoms of what was later diagnosed as *Burning Mouth Syndrome*, which left her unable to speak, sing, laugh, or cry without suffering intense pain. Rendered virtually mute, she turned to writing self-help books.

℧ ℧ ℧

Going to an Ozzy Osbourne concert was like visiting an abattoir, and it became more disorderly as the tour progressed. As part of the spectacle, buckets of butcher's offcuts were thrown into the audience, on occasion by a meat catapult, and of course it was only a matter of time before the audience started bringing their own meat to heave back at the stage. This ranged from entrails to all sorts of full dead animals, such as the infamous bat incident earlier in the year.

After the publicity for the bat biting the American Society for the Prevention of Cruelty to Animals began attending concerts, fearful of carnage and cruelty. On Friday 2nd April the ASPCA pulled Ozzy's tour bus over in Boston and jumped on board. Upon discovery of Mr Pook, Sharon Arden's pet Yorkshire terrier, they became convinced this animal would be the next to be sacrificed to Satan onstage and attempted unsuccessfully to take the dog into protective custody.

The following evening, Sharon announced extra tour dates in Japan over the summer, much to the consternation of new guitarist Bernie Torme.

"*I'm sorry, Sharon, but when Don hired me I was adamant about my availability for just a couple of months. I'm in the midst of recording my solo album*" he complained.

"*You mean you'd rather be playing shitholes on your own than to be playing arenas with Ozzy?*" asked Sharon, barely concealing her anger.

"*Sorry, Sharon, but that was my deal*" answered Bernie.

℧ ℧ ℧

At thirty-five, veteran drummer Simon Phillips[173] and thirty-nine-year-old keyboard player Tony Hymas[174] recruited relative spring chicken, thirty-one-year-old Scottish singer Jim Diamond[175], all of whom had spent the last decade playing in bands on the outskirts of fame. Calling themselves PHD after their initials, they signed to WEA Records and recorded a self-titled debut album with the help of guitarist Phil Palmer, nephew of Ray & Dave Davies of The Kinks. The album relied heavily on keyboards and synthesisers, the latter of which almost gave it a contemporary feel upon release in 1981.

The second single from the album was *I Won't Let You Down*, released in March 1982, and started to pick up airplay without anyone seeing what the band looked like, which is just as well because despite all their talent and ability they looked every one of their relative years.

---

[173] Simon Phillips had played with Jeff Beck, Gary Moore, Pete Townshend, and Jack Bruce amongst others. At the same time as PHD he was playing for Toyah and would go on to join Toto.

[174] Tony Hymas composed the theme tune for the *Mr Men* series.

[175] Jim Diamond was at the dinner party where *Father Ted* star Dermot Morgan died of a heart attack.

Carried by Diamond's distinctive voice the song ambled along with a light reggae feel, not a million miles away from what The Police were writing in the late 1970's. Diamond's *third harmony* style high vocal added to the comparison, however where Sting's compositions could bounce along in a sprightly manner, *I Won't Let You Down* was rooted to the earth, lumbering with resignation. Despite this, the single climbed to the top ten across Western Europe, peaking at number three in the United Kingdom.

It was accompanied by a video featuring Diamond, looking like a cross between a midget Rod Hull and an aged Gregory's Girl extra, following about a Benny Hill-type "*leggy blonde*" pleading with her to forgive him, and spends too long lingering on bums and legs.

ʊ ʊ ʊ

The United Nations Security Council were called to meet on a Saturday 3rd April, their first weekend in decades. *Resolution 502* was drafted and passed, demanding an immediate cessation of hostilities between Britain and Argentina as well as a demand the Argentinians withdraw from the Falkland Islands. Of the fifteen nations, ten voted for the resolution, four abstained (the Soviet Union, Poland, Spain, and China) and one against (Panama). The Argentinian government was stupefied by the vote, erroneously believing the world would be with them in striking a blow against Britain.

On the same day, the British Parliament met in an emergency session in which there was overwhelming outrage at the invasion, but also questions about a failure to foresee events. Thatcher was of the opinions that no "*common or garden dictator should rule over the Queen's subjects and prevail by fraud or violence*", whilst Enoch Powell[176] called for the marines stationed on the island who had been captured after three hours fighting to be court-martialled. Parliament was in the grip of jingoism, with very few dissenting voices. Powell later told the television news the conflict would allow us to see "*of what metal* [Thatcher] *was made*", whilst *The Sun* demanded "*Show us your iron, Maggie*" then immediately declared the BBC as being "*against the nation*".

Meanwhile, in London, Clash frontman Joe Strummer made the decision to change the name of the soon to be released new Clash album from *Rat Patrol from Fort Bragg* to *Combat Rock*, in honour of what he saw as the unavoidable forthcoming conflict. The album was currently being remixed by Glyn Johns, after guitarist Mick Jones' initial mix was rejected by everyone.

Johns' insistence on starting work at eleven in the morning meant he and Strummer had three songs already mixed by the time Jones turned up. Jones unsurprisingly hated the mixes but was told in no uncertain terms by Johns that he if he did not turn up in time his opinions would count for nothing. The hour-long initial mix was cut back significantly, and songs were shortened to create a sleeker final album.

---

[176] Powell was possessed of a brilliant mind but ruined his reputation with his infamously racist anti-immigration *Rivers of Blood* speech in 1968. It is thought in the aftermath of this speech he could easily have become leader of the Conservative Party and would have won a general election by a landslide. Margaret Thatcher was a self-proclaimed fan. Go figure.

APRIL

4th – 10th April 1982

#1 single: The Goombay Dance Band: Seven Tears
#1 album: Iron Maiden: The Number of the Beast

Everything had changed overnight for the British inhabitants of the Falkland Islands. Port Stanley was now called Puerto Argentino, British currency was no longer valid, cars suddenly had to drive on the right-hand side of the road, and all discussions were required to take place in Spanish, the new official language.

On the evening of Sunday 4th April, Reverend Bagnall held a special sermon at the Anglican Church in Port Stanley. The message was for the inhabitants of the Falklands to keep their heads down and await liberation. The parishioners then sang *Auld Lang Syne* before heading home. There was not a dry eye in the house.

ʊ ʊ ʊ

Following their success with the Fun Boy Three, Bananarama signed to London Records for a one-off single deal. Sara Dallon explained "*Clearly, nobody had a tremendous amount of faith in three young women achieving anything more than a momentary snippet of success*". Either through naivety or

else an unsuspected business acumen, the trio took no advance money from the label and in return were left to just get on with it, receiving no pressure to look or sound a certain way. The first sign of new material appeared in April with the release of another cover version, this time the Motown classic *Really Saying Something*. For this the girls did not stray too far from their last single, retaining Dave Jordan on production duties, the same man who had overseen the Fun Boy Three debut album, as well as the help of Hall, Golding, and Staples themselves. Where *It Ain't What You Do* was credited to The Fun Boy Three & Bananarama, this new single was credited to Bananarama & Fun Boy Three, an understated modification but one which permitted the girls to emerge into the charts with stabilizers.

The single itself was an orthodox version of The Velvelettes song but with obvious Fun Boy Three jungle-percussion in evidence. Just like *It Ain't What You Do*, the mélange of a classic tried-and-tested song with swinging percussion was a sure-fire hit, and sure enough it reached number five in the charts.

None of Bananarama could be called outstanding singers, but what they did have is voices that melded seamlessly into one. The voices blended so perfectly that future producers of the band would often just provide one microphone to record with, figuring there was no point on using up three tracks for what was fundamentally the same voice. On paper, London Records were prudent to hedge their bets with a short-term deal; three non-musicians with substandard voices and no songwriting ability. What they had not considered was just how much the British public would take to their hearts the sheer ebullience of the trio, a foundation upon which they could build a career.

With a second hit, London Records picked up on the option of an album, but only provided money for recording purposes, forcing Bananarama to take out a £5,000 bank loan, from which they paid themselves a weekly wage of £40. The trio were canny enough to refuse a £5,000 publishing deal, and six months later were able to negotiate ten times that amount.

ʊ ʊ ʊ

Scapegoats were required in Whitehall.

Somehow, Argentina had succeeded in seizing a piece of British territory, and the government had appeared wholly unprepared. Fingers were pointed by the British press at the Foreign Office, with *The Daily Express* calling Lord Peter Carrington[177] and John Nott[178] *"Thatcher's guilty men... they have misled everybody but the Argentinians"*. Under pressure, on Monday 5th April the Foreign Minister Carrington resigned, whilst Defence Minister Nott also offered his resignation but was turned down by Margaret Thatcher, but only after his insistence his resignation letter was published. Meanwhile, Chancellor of the Exchequer Geoffrey Howe[179] was omitted from cabinet meetings, as Margaret Thatcher was anxious to avoid any budgetary concerns when it came to decisions regarding the Falklands[180].

It was the most expeditious preparation for a war ever as over a few days the packing and organising of ships caused a burst of activity in ports throughout the country. A fleet of over 100 ships and 15,000 soldiers left from numerous ports, with the most visible sailing occurring on Monday 5th April. As well as British ports, ships were called from action elsewhere in the Mediterranean and Atlantic, with one cruise liner being used for school trips commandeered as a medical ship, whilst the pupils disembarked in Naples and were flown home. The task of moving a fleet of ships from the United Kingdom to the Falkland Islands was given the very 1980's title of *Operation Corporate*, and as the fleet left port 72% of the public were in favour of sending the task force, though only 20% actually expected them to fight once they arrived in the South Atlantic. Over half the personnel on British ships were under twenty-one years of age, and a quarter of them were younger than twenty, but that was nothing compared to the Argentinian troops. Conscription was still a rites-of-passage in the South American country, so the island was populated with several thousand untrained aggrieved Argentinian youths who despised the climate. The professional fully trained troops had all been deployed to the mountainous border with Chile for fear their neighbours would take advantage of the conflict.

Defence correspondents from the main media outlets were permitted to travel with the British fleet, however Thatcher was furious when they conveyed events from an impartial point of view, referring to the sides as *the British* and *the Argentinians*. There had been a furious scramble over the weekend to win one of the ten permitted press accreditation posts, with ageing newspaper owners making frantic phone calls and pulling in favours wherever they could. In the end, the BBC and ITV were each permitted to send one correspondent, but had to share a cameraman, sound engineer, and technician. The newspaper journalists were chosen from a hat by the wife of Newspaper Publishers' Association, and represented the *Daily Mirror, Daily Express, Daily Telegraph,* and *Daily Mail*, with the final place going to the Press Association. Once this was decided, the other major newspapers including *The Times, The Guardian,* and *The Sun*, began a strong voiced campaign of harassment towards Downing Street, with veiled threats of negative publicity for the whole endeavour

---

[177] Carrington had won a Military Cross during the Second World War.

[178] John Nott's son wrote the theme tune for *Wallace and Gromit*.

[179] Geoffrey Howe was a half-uncle to Camilla, Duchess of Cornwall.

[180] Thatcher had been advised to do this by former PM Harold MacMillan. Howe never fully forgave her for this.

resilient enough for Press Secretary Bernard Ingham[181] to intervene. Legendary war photographer Don McCullin was refused access, with the military keen to avoid any images getting back to Britain without their consent. The scamble to get to Portsmouth in time was hysterical and financially costly for the press, with private planes hired and cars abandoned near the dockyards, however as the fleet left port it brought out the patriotism in the British press, with *The Times* proclaiming *"WE ARE ALL FALKLANDERS NOW"*.

℧ ℧ ℧

The combination of ex-Beatle Paul McCartney, and soul legend Stevie Wonder seemed like inspired genius: surely these two could create some dazzling music together, merging the former's genius with a melody and the latter's funky beats. Instead, what

we got was *Ebony & Ivory*, a saccharine call for understanding between races, using a piano keyboard as a lubberly metaphor for black and white harmony, an idea which had been in use since at least the 1840's.

The song had been written by McCartney the previous year after a marital tiff with his wife Linda and was produced by former Beatles studio virtuoso George Martin as part of forthcoming album *Tug of War*. McCartney and Wonder met in February 1981 to record vocals at AIR Studios in the Caribbean and between them ended up playing every instrument on the song, with the American on drums and keyboards, and the Brit taking care of the guitars and bass. McCartney had been a long-time fan of Wonder, even putting a message to the singer in braille on the back of his *Red Rose Speedway* album, and the feeling was mutual, even if that did not stop the American from admonishing McCartney for his handclaps being out of time.

Wonder had arrived in at George Martin's studio in Montserrat with a primitive drum machine in his luggage, but it had been damaged in transit, so he asked the producer to remove the cover and plug it in. Whilst everyone watched in anxious horror, the blind singer ran his fingers over the various components one at a time, deftly avoiding the 440 watts

The idea for the song came to McCartney after watching a Peter Cook sketch where he played a segregated piano to demonstrate how ridiculous apartheid was, as well as Spike Milligan who used the line *"Black notes, white notes, you have to play the two to make harmony, folks"*. As you would expect, *Ebony & Ivory* was banned in South Africa.

A video was shot for the song, however McCartney and Wonder's work schedules meant they had to be filmed separately and spliced together using what at the time was cutting edge technology. This did not stop the song topping the charts on both sides of the Atlantic, giving McCartney his most prosperous post-Beatles single, and Wonder his most successful ever.

Recording sessions for McCartney's third solo album had started back in October 1980 and were interrupted by the death of John Lennon in December 1980. With former Beatles producer George Martin back in the control seat for the first time since the 1960's, much time and care was taken in making sure everything was impeccable.

---

[181] Let's play a game of *what did Bernard Ingham hate*. I'll go first. Scots (*"greedy as sin"*), Northerners (*"thick"*), wind power, anti-nuclear protesters, anyone who complained about the Hillsborough disaster. Your turn.

Martin was ruthless with McCartney's writing, rejecting several songs and telling him *"You're going to have to accept some stick from me, and you may not like it, because you've been your own boss for so long"*. This meticulousness meant the album was re-scheduled five times before being released as guest musicians dropped in to help, including Denny Laine from Wings and Carl Perkins, whilst McCartney employed what he considered *the best* session guys in the shape of Steve Gadd and Stanley Clarke. The album caught McCartney in the middle of a purple patch, approaching his fortieth birthday, and was his strongest set of songs for almost a decade (and for another ten years afterwards), opening with the mellow title track contemplating the meaning of life,

before single *Take it Away*, the closest you were going to get to a Beatles re-union, with Ringo Starr sharing drum duties and George Martin's guide piano being kept in the final mix. The song had originally been written for Ringo but was then kept by McCartney and reached number fifteen when it was released as a single in June, accompanied by a memorable video. The most personal track on the album, *Here Today*, was a tribute to Lennon, touching upon the dead Beatle's sarcasm and hatred for McCartney. One line referred to *"the night we cried"* which McCartney later revealed was a night in Jacksonville, when *"we stayed up all night… got drunk… talked a lot. And we got way too deep and got into each other's characters. This was probably a good thing… and we ended up crying. [The song is] just reminding myself that we got that intimate."* McCartney had not reacted well to Lennon's death, undergoing some serious soul-searching about their relationship, full of regrets he never fully made-up the most important and valuable friendship either ever had.

Elvis Costello was recording next door, and one day bass player Bruce Thomas put his head around the door to meet his hero. He found McCartney standing by the desk talking to a black kid who *"couldn't have been more than fourteen of fifteen because his voice hadn't broken yet"*. Thomas seemed surprised such a youngster had been taken on as a studio assistant, and more so when he piped up in a *"thin girly voice"*: *"Quincy didn't dig what Elvis said about James Brown"*.

In 1979 Costello had called James Brown a *"jive-ass n****r"* in a drunken bar argument in America, which had subsequently been reported in the press and curtailed his success across the Atlantic. Remembering the event, Thomas thought out loud *"Who the hell is Quincy?"*

"Quincy Jones, man" the youth replied.

"How the fuck do you know Quincy Jones?" demanded Thomas of the work experience lad.

"He produces my albums, man" was the reply. At this point Thomas was *"hit by a juggernaut of realisation… this squeaky kid is Michael Bloody Jackson!"* McCartney, sensing the tension, felt the need to step in at this point and smooth things over.

"He didn't mean anything by it" the ex-Beatle explained, *"It just the way the Brits are – it's just the way we rag each other. We do it all the time."*

"Yeah!" jumped in Thomas, *"It's like me saying… for fuck's sake McCartney, when are you going to write a decent song?"*

The frosty reception to this told Thomas it was time to leave.

ʊ ʊ ʊ

Frolicking up the charts in April and securing their place in the hearts of teenage girls, as well as establishing themselves as kings of the ecstatic and carefree summer soundtrack single, were Haircut 100 with another song from their debut album, *Pelican West*. *Fantastic Day* was a piece of startlingly infectious throwaway pop, perfect for

daytime radio, and managed to acquire an inordinate amount of airplay as the sun emerged. Lyrically it was a circumspect love song of non-sequential lines which under closer scrutiny became an orison of unrequited infatuation. Songwriter and frontman Nick Heyward described the bittersweet reaction of seeing someone he is in love with everyday whilst also realising they will never be together. Fortunately, it had a simple repeated chorus of "*Fantastic day / Fantastic day*" to distract from the pleasure, pain, and regret at the heart of the song, which helped the single rise into the top ten where it remained for several weeks. As devotees of Orange Juice, Haircut 100 made up in sonic professionalism what they lacked in knowing lyrical mischievousness, never quite ascending to the levels of arched eyebrow achieved by Edwyn Collins. The band had been on tour in the United Kingdom, playing to predominantly female audiences, but as Heyward later recalled "*the girls may have been screaming but as a band we were really on it*".

Meanwhile Heyward took himself off to Greece for a week's holiday to escape the sudden pressure of success, whilst also entering discussions with television companies to create a television series for the band, with a script co-written by comedian Chris Langham.

℧ ℧ ℧

If ever there was a consummate time for Simple Minds to break into the charts it was spring 1982. Having been formed in early 1978 by vocalist Jim Kerr, guitarist Charlie Burchill, and drummer Brian McGee[182] from the ashes of one of Scotland's first punk bands, Johnny & The Self-Abusers[183]. The new act took their name from a line in David Bowie's *Jean Genie*. and began absorbing glam and prog influences into their sound whilst recruiting keyboard player Mick MacNeil[184] and bass player Derek Forbes[185].

Over the next four years Simple Minds released five albums and a series of singles on Arista Records, some of which were minor hits without bothering the top forty.[186] An incessant touring schedule allowed the band to organically grow a following, especially in mainland Europe where they enjoyed larger hits. Over these releases the band graduated from their glam roots towards a mix of post-punk minimalism constructed around a motorik dance-orientated beat. Whilst sequenced keyboards and lead bass propelled the songs forward, Burchill's guitar was manipulated to create texture and Kerr's lyrics often reflected concerns of a modern mainland Europe. Tracks such as *I Travel* and *Love Song* became club classics, the epitome of extreme extant European anthems.

---

[182] McGee joined Endgames after leaving Simple Minds, before playing with Propaganda. His brother, Owen Paul, had a hit later in the decade with *My Favourite Waste of Time*.

[183] Johnny & the Self-Abusers followed the spirit of the punk movement by splitting the day their debut single was released. The other half of the band formed The Cuban Heels.

[184] MacNeil later formed a Simple Minds tribute act called Ex-Simple Minds along with Brian McGee and Derek Forbes.

[185] Forbes later played with Propaganda, Spear of Destiny, The Alarm, and Big Country.

[186] Seriously, check out *Love Song*, *I Travel*, and *Life in a Day*. The last of these reminds me of a Boy's Brigade twenty-four-hour sponsored table tennis marathon.

In 1981 the band switched to Virgin Records where their first release was the distilled *krautrock* of two simultaneous albums[187] which reached just outside the top ten. They still, however, had not managed to achieve a top-forty single as Jim Kerr explained "*I was listening to the radio and just thought 'we're never on the bloody thing!' We put all this enthusiasm and energy into the band. Surely, the more people who hear it, the better*". Towards the end of the year, drummer McGee left the band claiming to be exhausted by the constant touring and was replaced by Kenny Hyslop[188], who toured America and Australia with the band until the end of the year, having a huge influence on their sound through repeated playing of his cassette tapes of New York hip-hop, funk, and dance music on the tour bus. During the Australian dates some new songs were written which had a deliberately pop-orientated sound and in January 1982 Simple Minds recorded these in Rockfield Studio, produced by Peter Walsh who had been chosen for his work on Heaven 17's *Penthouse and Pavement* the previous year. The first public airing of these recordings was the single *Promised You a Miracle*, released at the start of April. Halfway through writing the song Kerr suffered a crisis of confidence, saying "*This isn't us. Then I thought 'Hang on a second, what isn't us?'*

What a terrible state to have got into if Simple Minds are all tied up in a box and finished". Brimful of wonder, elation, and optimism, the song did not hang around, crashing straight into the chorus and title. It had originally been based on a horn riff on one of Kenny Hyslop's New York cassettes, and was meant to be a demo recording, however the band and record company felt it chimed perfectly with the new pop zeitgeist, and so after being polished was foisted upon the public. Vocalist Jim Kerr, as an ardent fan of pop music and songwriting, knew all he needed was a catchy line to draw the public in, which he found in the title. After a chorus, the song promenaded into the first verse where any form of narrative broke down with a series of positive platitudes such as "*Chance as love takes a train*" and "*Love sails to a new life*". The whole song acted as a shimmering series of motivational soundbites: "*Belief is a beauty thing*" and the repeated "*Everything is possible*". After a second chorus Simple Minds took the unexpected early move of bringing in a typical 1980's pop breakdown before returning to their base camp of the title and chorus again, with Burchill seizing his moment of glory with a rare Simple Minds guitar solo.

Between the recording and release of the song, Simple Minds set out on an extensive mainland European tour during February and March, by which point Hyslop's suspicion of record companies created problems, and he had been replaced by Kilmarnock born Mike Ogiltree. As they completed the tour the single was released and crashed into the charts, propelling Simple Minds from cult act to genuine pop stars. A *Top of the Pops* appearance beckoned, and the single climbed to number thirteen during spring. Whilst the band had been working towards this sort of success for years, it also caught them somewhat by surprise, having no follow up material ready for release. Instead, they locked themselves into a huge barn in Perthshire and wrote an album. Kerr later admitted these few months were the easiest and most enjoyable of his career, where everything they tried just seemed to work, and everyone was getting on like a house on fire.

---

[187] *Sons and Fascination* and *Sister Feeling Call*: both chilled impassive classics.

[188] Hyslop had enjoyed success in *boy band* Slik during the 1970's before redeeming himself by joining Fife punks The Skids.

From here, the band moved to Townhouse Studios in London where producer Peter Walsh introduced them to session drummer Mel Gaynor[189]. Ogiltree magnanimously worked with Gaynor in helping him to preserve the beats from the Perthshire rehearsals, and was rewarded for his work with a *percussion* credit and payment on the ensuing album. After a couple of months, the recording was finished, and the band returned to live work with a series of festival dates across Europe.

℧ ℧ ℧

After their Australian tour the Teardrop Explodes flew on to New Zealand for some live dates, where it felt like they had travelled back in time to the 1950's. Keyboard player Dave Balfe, despite being distinctly average in the looks department, seemed to have a fail-safe chat-up technique when it came to women. For a couple of years frontman Julian Cope had wondered exactly what he said to them to appear irresistible. On Wednesday 7th April he finally found out whilst sitting in the bar of their hotel. Whilst passing a girl sitting at the reception, with a flick of the head Balfe said "*Are you coming upstairs?*"
"*Yeah, okay*" she replied, and they were gone.
Cope could not believe the simplicity of the approach and sharing a room with Balfe settled himself downstairs in the bar for a long wait. Ten minutes later Balfe was back, red-faced and grinning. "*Sorry I was ages, I met her mate on the stairs*" he said.
Cope had a lengthier wait the following day when it became apparent that he still did not have a work visa for the United States and had to stand outside the American Embassy to acquire the correct paperwork for the tour due to start in a couple of days.

℧ ℧ ℧

Behind the scenes, the Americans were trying to broker peace in the South Atlantic, caught between a violent South American Fascist dictatorship whom they supported to keep Communism at bay, and their long-time closest European adversaries. On Thursday 8th April Secretary of State Alexander Haig[190] flew into London in the first step of his shuttle diplomacy, only to be warned at the airport by his diplomats about Margaret Thatcher: "*If you think you can sway her, you're dead wrong*". He proposed a plan which would see the Argentinians withdraw from the island and an interim multilateral agency take charge to allow the two nations to discuss the future. The Prime Minister outright rejected this, stating "*I beg you to remember that in 1938 Neville Chamberlain sat at this same table discussing an arrangement which sounds very much like the one you are asking me to accept*".

℧ ℧ ℧

The Gay Men's Health Crisis, having been set up in January to raise money and awareness of Gay Related Immune Deficiency, held a major fundraiser at Paradise Garage in New York on Thursday 8th April. The organisers were worried about the gay community's lack of interest in the issue and had only sold 500 tickets before the event. Their worries were assuaged on the night, however, when a queue gathered around

---

[189] Gaynor was a Jamaican born drummer of African and Brazilian ancestry. He had previously been playing in rock act Samson, along with Iron Maiden's Bruce Dickenson.

[190] Haig really wanted to be president. During Nixon's last few months it was well known the general was running the government, and when Reagan was shot in 1981 Haig proclaimed to the press "*I am in control here*".

the block, with many people brandishing their chequebooks. Leader Paul Popham[191] addressed the crowd during the night, stating *"It may be that an equal measure of fear and hope has brought us together, but the great thing is* [that] *we are together… We've got to show each other and the unfriendly world that we've got more than looks, brains, talent, and money. We've got guts too, plus an awful lot of heart"*. Not everyone was greeted with cheers, however, as performer Evelyn "Champagne" King advised the crowd to avoid the bathhouses and back rooms where the disease was being easily spread, and to stick to *"One lover per person"*. She was bombarded with catcalls and a chant of *"No way!"* Despite this, the night was a great success, raising over $52,000 dollars and acting as a catalyst for the previously politically lethargic gay community in New York.

ʊ ʊ ʊ

Three of the four home nations had qualified for the FIFA World Cup finals in Spain in 1982: England, Scotland, and Northern Ireland, and as anticipation built the only thing that could possibly spoil this was the inevitable World Cup Squad singles.

England were first out of the traps, with *This Time (We'll Get it Right)*, written by Chris Norman and Peter Spencer of the band Smokie, who had previously written a hit song for England star Kevin Keegan. This was the first England World Cup song since 1970, the last time the team had managed to qualify for a World Cup tournament, and if the track was anything to go by their performance would be disappointing. The quality of the song did not hinder it in climbing to number two in the charts. On the other side of the single was *England (Fly the Flag)*, based upon a jingle for British Airways written by American Jake Holmes in the 1970's, to which song-writing credits were added for Adrian Gurvitz and Mickie Most, presumably for some new lyrics.

The single was accompanied by an album of the same title, with some excruciating cover versions contained within: Glen Hoddle[192] singing *We Are Champions*, anyone? Viv Anderson[193] and Trevor Francis assassinating *You'll Never Walk Alone*? Mike Reid[194] (from Eastenders) and his Minipops with *Bulldog Bobby*? The whole squad singing the national anthem? All these gems were included on the K-Tel release.

Not that the Northern Irish release was any better, featuring a duet with former Eurovision winner Dana called *Yer Man*. Scotland, on the other hand, had released singles for the last two world cup finals, *Easy Easy* in 1974, and *Ole Ola (Mulher*

---

[191] Popham was a former Vietnam veteran who worked as a banker on Wall Street. He died of AIDS in 1987.

[192] Hoddle was a future England manager who was dismissed from the job when he insisted disabled people were being punished for bad deeds in a previous life.

[193] Anderson was the first black player to gain a full cap for England.

[194] Mike Reid was Roger Moore's stunt double in *The Saint* until he was fired for pointing the star's thinning hair.

Brasileira[195]) in 1978. After the humiliation of the team's performance under manager Ally MacLeod in 1978, humbleness was required in 1982, and the decision was made to go with something more self-depreciating. It was announced that B.A. Robertson was writing the song before he had been asked, forcing his hand, with the threat he had to make it better than England's song. Being issued a list by the Scottish Football Association of things which could not be included in the song, number one of which

was that it was not to be *nationalistic*. Robertson tackled the failure of four years previous by making a self-conscious joke song, *We Have a Dream*, one in which the Scottish narrator, John Gordon Sinclair[196], can only ever succeed in his dreams. With a rousing chorus, the song rose to number five in the charts, and had become a perennial favourite with the Tartan Army ever since.

It was not just the national teams who were having hits in 1982, as Tottenham Hotspur F.C. took *Tottenham Tottenham* to number nineteen in preparation for their FA Cup Final performance. The song was written by proud Londoners (and Spurs fans) Chas and Dave, riding high in the charts at the time with *Ain't No Pleasing You*, and was initially based on the idea of Chubby Checker's *Let's Twist Again*. Tottenham Hotspur had won the FA Cup in 1981, and Chas Hodges idea was to win again "*like we did last summer*".

ʊ ʊ ʊ

Ascension Island[197] is merely thirty-four square miles, and at 1,000 miles from the coast of Africa is made of volcanic rock and ash. Owned by Britain, the Americans had constructed a serviceable runway there during the Second World War, which had been maintained by NASA for the past couple of decades. By the time the British Task Force began arriving on Saturday 10th April, the runway had gone from having one weekly flight to become the busiest airport in the world, with over 400 flights a day arriving and taking off. The American army was still present, and whilst officially neutral had surreptitiously been ordered to give the British as much help as possible without getting caught.

It was on this treeless island in the middle of the Atlantic that the final preparations, plans, and stocking of ships was taking place for the recovery of the Falkland Islands. The Ministry of Defence had been keen for journalists to be flown to the island to join the Task Force, however according to Sir John Fieldhouse the Navy were scared the journalists would arrive and realise "*there was no air defence… no missiles protecting the airfield*", and so they were placed amongst the boat crews straight from British ports.

Meanwhile, on board the Navy vessels, the small number of British journalists were getting bored. Many had expected upon setting sail that they would go twice round the Isle of Wight and then return home, a diplomatic solution having been found, however upon reaching Ascension Island it became clear they would be travelling onwards

---

[195] Performed by Rod Stewart and the World Cup Squad. I thought it was a great song, but apparently, I am wrong. The same year saw Andy Cameron release *Ally's Army*, which many people believe to be the superior song. They are wrong, though the B-side *I Want to be a Punk Rocker* is rather special.

[196] Sinclair had starred in the film *Gregory's Girl* alongside Clare Grogan, who he was in love with.

[197] After its discovery in 1501, the Portuguese released hundreds of wild goats onto the island to act as a food source for passing ships. It is now the site of one of the four antenna which enable GPS to work.

towards the Falklands. With a lack of stories to report so far, the number one target was Prince Andrew serving on board *HMS Invincible*.

The Sun led the charge with vague claims, such as the headline on this day stating, "*I HUNT THE ENEMY WITH ANDY: SUN MAN JOINS THE PRINCE ON SOUTH ATLANTIC COPTER PATROL*". Of course, the journalist in question, Tony Snow, had not actually flown with Prince Andrew but had been on board a second helicopter many miles away, but that was not going to get in the way of a good story.

This brought further tension between the Navy and the press, a relationship which was already strained. On *HMS Hermes*, a senior commander was furious at the reports being sent home, accusing them of providing Argentinian intelligence. The BBC cameraman, Bernard Hesketh[198] was not going to stand for this and pulled up his trouser leg to reveal a leg damaged in France during the Second World War. "*How dare you call me a spy*" he cried, "*These are the wounds I got from the Nazis*".

Not that the tension was evident in the London newsrooms, as *The Sun* gave away a free video game called *Obliterate* in which you commanded a British submarine attempting to sink Argentinian ships.

Ʊ Ʊ Ʊ

Traversing the Alps in the winter months can be unmanageable, but even in April some roads remain impassable, as Iron Maiden were finding out. On Saturday 10th April the band were due to play Grenoble at the foot of the French Alps but were having a bit of a problem with the tour bus. The band were halfway through the European leg of their *Beast on the Road* world tour, a jaunt designed to raise them into new echelons of success and bolster their place as one of the tightest and hardest rocking bands on the planet. Right now, however, everyone had to get off the bus, band and road crew alike, and attempt to push-start the vehicle which had become trapped in snow. Manager Rod Smallwood[199] took the opportunity to telephone his office in London and returned with the news that new album *The Number of the Beast* had entered the British charts at number one. It was something of a blessing the band had run out of songs to record after their second  album and were forced to spend some time writing specifically for Bruce Dickinson, meaning the tracks were tailored for his range and style.

A sense of relief rather than joy greeted this news, given they were working with a new singer. Would the fan base accept someone new at the front, and how would this affect sales? The tour and success of the album showed there was no need for disquiet, as Dickinson was proving to be a superior vocalist, and more importantly an outstanding frontman. There was an even greater sense of relief when the bus started, and the European tour rolled on.

The title track was released as a single at the end of April, climbing to number eighteen, and featuring a spoken word introduction by actor Barry Clayton. The band had first approached Vincent Price[200] for the job, however his asking fee of £25,000 proved too

---

[198] Hesketh won the *Royal Television Society Cameraman of the Year* award for his coverage of the Falkland conflict.

[199] Smallwood had previously been the manager of Steve Harley and Cockney Rebel, who he described as "*selfish, egotistical and obsessed*".

[200] As well as a brilliant horror actor, Price was also a Yale graduate and a gourmet cook. His grandfather invented baking powder!

much. Price made the money anyway when he was approached by Michael Jackson soon afterwards to complete a similar task. Some Christian groups, especially in the United States, believed the band were glamourizing Satan and organised protests outside venues whenever they played. Many burnt copies of the album, though some smashed them with hammers, scared to burn vinyl in case they breathed in the Satanic

fumes. The song came about when bass player Steve Harris suffered a nightmare after watching *Damien: The Omen II*, and what the protesters failed to understand was the difference between fiction and fact, between playing a role and *actually being Satanists*, between theatre and observance.

Protests against rock and roll were nothing new, however they took official government sponsored position during the 1980's, especially after Tipper Gore[201], the wife of Presidential hopeful Al Gore, formed the Parents Music Resource Centre in 1985. The PMRC was intended to increase parental control over music with sexual or violent lyrical content and forced the United States Senate to hold a hearing on rock and roll. The result of this was a voluntary agreement with major record labels to put *Parental Guidance: Explicit Lyrics* stickers on appropriate albums, a move which was guaranteed to boost sales.

ʊ ʊ ʊ

Toto were an American band of Valley kids from Hollywood, the sons of renowned Tinseltown backroom musicians and arrangers, who had grown up with sunshine and music, and through a mixture of practise and contacts had become in-demand session musicians themselves during the mid-1970's. Dave Paich, Jeff Porcaro, Steve Porcaro, and Steve Lukather had all previously played with Boz Scaggs, with the first two also touring with Steely Dan, whilst Texan singer Bobby Kimball had moved to the sunshine state a couple of years earlier. Releasing their first album in 1978 their sound and ethic was so against the emerging new wave that the music press crucified them, however the American public took them to their hearts, pushing it into the top ten. The next two albums did progressively worse, and by 1982 Toto were at make-or-break stage with label Columbia: the final album on the contract had to be successful or they would be dropped.

Recording began at Sunset Sound[202] in Los Angeles, with Van Halen working next door, and the first song recorded started off with a Bo Diddley beat before evolving into a shuffling pop song called *Rosanna*. After a short amount of rehearsal, the session-experienced band nailed the recording in two takes, with Kimball and Lukather sharing lead vocal. The title of the song was inspired by Steve Porcaro's girlfriend, the actress Rosanna Arquette[203], though the rest of the lyrics were not.

Rosanna opened the floodgates for writing as all members of the band started arriving daily at the studio with new tunes. Towards the end of recording, just when the band thought they had a pretty good album, Paich came in with a song he had written on his

---

[201] Now here's a weird thing... Tipper Gore played drums in a band in High School with several future members of The Grateful Dead. She even appeared on drums with Jerry Garcia's band on one date of their 2009 tour.

[202] Sunset Sound is a legendary Los Angeles studio which had first been built to record the soundtrack for Disney movies such as *Mary Poppins* and *101 Dalmations*.

[203] Peter Gabriel's *In Your Eyes* was also written about her.

new Yamaha GS1 synthesizer[204]. The keyboard player told the rest of the band the song was called *Africa*, so Jeff Porcarro added a percussion loop along with his dad, his godfather Emil Richards[205], and legendary session guy Lenny Castro, inspired by a visit to the New York World's Fair[206] when he was eleven years old. Twenty-four tracks were filled with various pieces of African percussion which was then looped and played behind the music. The lyrics were written by thumbing through *National Geographic* magazines for inspiration, perhaps the reason they managed to shoehorn the word "*Serengeti*" into a pop song. Paich explained "*I romanticized this story about a social worker that goes over there and falls in love with working in the country and doing good. But he also falls in love and has to make a choice between healing people for the rest of his life or having a family.*" He saw it as a metaphor for his own life; the balance between creating music and having a personal life. Not all the band thought *Africa* was a hit single, though, with guitarist Lukather stating that he would run naked down Hollywood Boulevard if it broke into the top forty.

Things did not go as smoothly in the studio as the music suggests, with bass player David Hungate unexpectedly announcing his departure after completing his parts, to be replaced by the third Porcaro brother, Mike. Singer, Kimball meanwhile had a drug charge hanging over him from December 1981, when he was caught selling cocaine to an undercover cop.

The album *Toto IV*[207] was released at the start of April along with the single, *Rosanna*, and both climbed into the American top five. Later in the year, *Africa* topped the Billboard charts, making Toto the most successful domestic act of the year in the United States. In Britain, however, none of the singles or albums touched the top seventy-five in 1982. Despite their pop hooks, *Rosanna* and *Africa* were out of touch with what was going on in the United Kingdom: just too many beards and session musician chops, not enough new-pop *nous*. You cannot keep a good song down, however, and the following year the two cracked the British top ten.

ʊ ʊ ʊ

Kim Wilde[208] had British music in her blood, being born Kim Smith to rock and roll star Marty Wilde and Vernon Girls[209] singer Joyce Baker. In 1980 she signed to Mickie Most's MCA Records at the age of twenty after being recommended by Jonathan

---

[204] Paich had a development deal with Yamaha to experiment with the instrument for the company.

[205] Richards played the xylophone on the opening credits of *The Simpsons*.

[206] As well all know, the 1964 New York World's Fair was a cover for the first arrival of aliens on earth, with the observation tower being built from their spaceships.

[207] The first three albums were called Toto I, Toto II, and Toto III.

[208] When I was in second year at High School, as far as I was concerned the King and Queen of the school were a couple in the senior year called Murray and Christine. They looked like Robert Smith and Kim Wilde. Their children would have been beautiful.

[209] The Vernon Girls were a sixteen-piece female choir sponsored by the pools company of the same name. In 1960 they released a single with Jimmy Savile.

King[210], and was marketed as the Britain's answer to Blondie, with an attenuated new wave feel to the music and a faceless all-male backing band. The formula worked and 1981 had been all about Wilde, with four top twenty singles written by her brother Ricky[211] and her father, including the classic *Kids in America* and an eponymous top three debut album.

Wilde was expected to break internationally during 1982, and in January started boasting about signing a deal with Columbia Records in the United States worth a potential £1.5 million[212], which then mutated into a deal with EMI Liberty worth significantly less. There was no shortage of offers coming in however, including the lead role in the film version of *Evita*[213] and an advert for B&L Bitter Lemon soft drink on the Japanese market. This advert came with a Japanese-only release of a single, *Bitter is Better*, which had been written by outside songwriters, proving something of a sticking point with the Wilde family refusing to allow it to be released anywhere else but Japan for fear that it would weaken their control over Kim.

Her last single *Cambodia* had been about South East Asia. Except it was not really. Her new single was called *View from a Bridge* and was about suicide. Except, it was

not really. Wilde was desperate to be taken more earnestly as a singer, fed up being asked in every interview about her father or if she had a boyfriend. The single was also a confessional ghost story, with the protagonist throwing herself from a bridge over a broken love affair, only to find herself at the bottom, a spirit as transparent and vapid as Wilde's strained double-tracked vocals.

As part of the usual promotional whirl Wilde visited Capital Radio on Saturday 10th April to add publicity to their *Help a London Child* campaign, providing a whole host of autographed items for auction, before visiting a restaurant. At some point during the meal her handbag was stolen only to be found four days later in Regents Park, missing cash and credit card, but luckily with passport intact. Not that money was a problem for the twenty-one-year-old, with Wilde splashing out on a North London apartment and a white BMW Cabrio.

---

[210] I was once woken up by a disconcerting early morning phone call from Jonathan King. He ran a monthly talent spotting compact disc for the music industry and wanted to include my band on it. Of course, this was before he was charged and found guilty of buggery on underage boys. King would send questionnaires about youth issues to teenagers, and those who listed sex as high on their list of interests would be further targeted by King. His bail was guaranteed by Simon Cowell. King later claimed *"The only apology I have is to say that I was good at seduction"*.

[211] Ricky was signed at the age of eleven by Jonathan King to his record label, where he was pushed as the new Donny Osmond.

[212] Of course, EVERY record deal is worth a potential £1.5 million pounds... if you sell enough records.

[213] The lead role for *Evita* was eventually taken by Madonna over a decade later.

11th – 17th April 1982

#1 single: Bucks Fizz: My Camera Never Lies
#1 album: Iron Maiden: The Number of the Beast

When Genvieve Alison Moyet placed an advert in *Melody Maker* in late 1981 offering herself as a vocalist looking for "*a rootsy soul / R&B band*", she had little idea a fellow resident of Basildon would get in touch and alter her life. Moyet had been born in 1961, coming from "*quite an aggressive French peasant family*", and after a dalliance with punk, sang in a couple of blues bands around Essex at the turn of the decade. "*I was disenfranchised and verbally uninhibited,*" she later explained, "*I couldn't hold down a job, but I wanted to front a band because I was dominant.*"

Moyet remembered the Basildon lad from school, mainly because he and his brothers would wear T-shirts declaring their Christianity and was surprised when Vince Clarke answered her advert with an unusual proposal: did she want to sing on a demo recording of a song he had written. Moyet agreed because she needed the money, worrying what people would think of her if she were to "*sing with this pretty boy*". Having recently left Depeche Mode, Clarke was worried Mute Records would not be interested in him and was keen to get something on tape as soon as possible. *Only You* had been written towards the end of his time with Depeche Mode, and to assuage his guilt about leaving had presented it to the band as a parting gift. They refused his offer.

Clarke took the recording to label boss Daniel Miller, who did not seem too interested, choosing to play around with a synthesiser throughout the playback, however once a Scandinavian publishing company showed enthusiasm his mind was changed. A week after recording the song Clarke was back in touch to tell Moyet the record company wanted them to re-record and release it as a single. The duo took a name from specialist blues label, Yazoo Records, which eventually led to a lawsuit and them becoming known as Yaz in the United States.

When Clarke first took Moyet to the Mute Records office in London, they found his former Depeche Mode bandmates there for a separate meeting. The band also knew  her from the Basildon scene and Andy Fletcher got a "*bit lairy and sniggering and… intimidating*". Moyet spoke directly to him: "*You're going to stop laughing or I'm going to kick you in the nuts*". Fletcher immediately did, later stating "*Never laugh at Alison Moyet. She will kill you on the spot.*"

Only You was released in mid-March, written on guitar by Clarke and then transposed to synthesiser, which perhaps explains the endurance of it as a song. Kev Walker, with whom Clark had been in a Christian duo in the 1970's, claimed the song sounded remarkably like one he had written at the time. The duo went into Blackwing Studios where owner Eric Radcliffe produced for them, mainly because Daniel Miller refused to. The song itself was simplicity distilled and showed music recorded on synthesisers could be emotionally powerful and abidingly corporeal, undoubtedly abetted by Moyet's soulful vocals and lyrics hinting at losing what is important. Moyet added bent blues notes to the sound, twisting against the unwaveringness of the digital instrumentation.

The only other song Clarke had at the time was *Don't Go* which the duo felt was too valuable to be buried on the B-side side of the single, so they wrote another in the studio called *Situation*. This was closer to Clarke's work with Depeche Mode, featuring an efficient synth riff throughout. Near the beginning of the song Moyet could be heard giggling having been startled by the reverb in her headphones, and it was decided to keep this impromptu sound in the final mix, with it acting as a contrast to the unsmiling tone of the lyrics in which the singer tells a lover to "*move out, don't mess around, move out, you bring me down*". The laugh was also an act of defiance, a fist shaken at a former lover, and an invitation to the audience to have fun despite the subject matter, and has since been sampled in countless dance tracks, becoming almost as synonymous as an Aretha Franklin scream or James Brown grunt.

It is hard nowadays to deny *Only You* is anything other than classic pop, however in 1982 it took three weeks before it even scraped into the charts. Over the next couple of months, the single crawled to a peak of the second top spot, becoming a perennial favourite, eventually reaching the top spot at the end of 1983 when British acapella group The Flying Pickets[214] released their own version.

It was the flipside, *Situation*, which took off over the Atlantic, initially as a club hit in downtown Manhattan. Mute, waking up to the dance potential, commissioned French born New York DJ Francois Kevorkian to re-mix the track, something Vince Clarke was strongly against. Despite his reservations and "*a cold hand-shake*" with the DJ when they visited New York, the re-mix became a hit, reaching the top of the Billboard Dance Chart, and was hugely influential in the future sound of the Chicago and Detroit dance scenes.

ʊ ʊ ʊ

The first British military presence reached the waters of the Falkland Islands on Monday 12th April in the shape of two nuclear-powered submarines. Able to travel all the way around the world without surfacing, and with the Argentines having no way to detect them, these thalassic vessels could do real damage. Their presence provided the British government with the confidence to declare a 200-mile Maritime Exclusion Zone around the islands. Any Argentinian vessels discovered within the region were now considered fair game.

ʊ ʊ ʊ

If there is one act who paralleled and epitomized the direction music was heading in 1982 it was Duran Duran. The five-piece had been formed by two Birmingham teenagers, Nigel Taylor and Nick Bates, in reaction to their analogous love of the Sex Pistols and Chic. Taylor had been the perfect age of sixteen when punk first broke nationally and like thousands of others his age was motivated to pick up a guitar and form an abysmal band. Over the next couple of years, he progressed through several more such acts before enlisting childhood friend Bates on keyboards and forming Duran Duran in 1978 with vocalist Stephen Duffy and bass player Simon Colley. Naming themselves after a misheard character in Roger Vadim's kitsch sci-fi cult classic *Barbarella*, they began following a more experimental course influenced by David Bowie's recent European dalliances. When Duffy and Colley left in early 1979

---

[214] The Flying Pickets were formed by actors from Scottish theatre group 7:84. Various members went on to other success: Brian Hibbard was in *Coronation Street*, David Brett was a member of *the Order of the Phoenix* in the *Harry Potter* films, Ron Donachie starred as Ser Rodrik Cassel in *Game of Thrones*.

to join another local act TV Eye[215], they recruited a new singer Andy Wickett and began hanging out at the *Rum Runner*, a Birmingham club that, despite having been open since 1964, had recently been given a Studio 54 inspired refurbishment by brothers Paul and Michael Berrow. Presenting the owners with a crudely recorded demo tape, the Berrow brothers saw something in Taylor and Bates, proposing to manage them as well as provide free rehearsal space in a disused part of the club. To this extent, it was decided Duran Duran were going to be successful before they even fully existed as a band, with Paul and Michael Berrow's faith becoming a self-fulfilling prophesy.

Enthralled with the burgeoning Bowie-influenced Birmingham response to London's Blitz Club in evidence at the Rum Runner, Taylor and Bates decided that they had to adopt more interesting names. Taylor dropped the *Nigel* and became *John*, taking up bass guitar in the process, whilst Bates became Nick Rhodes[216]. A new drummer and guitarist were recruited, both called Taylor as well, Roger and Andy respectively, just as Andy Wickett left (but not before he had written early versions of future hits *Girls on Film* and *Rio*).

Whilst they rehearsed and searched for a suitable singer[217], the band were given jobs at the club: John Taylor working as a glass collector and doorman, Andy Taylor as a cook, Roger Taylor as a barman, and Rhodes as resident DJ. Eventually in May 1980 Fiona Kemp, a barmaid at the Rum Runner suggested they try out her boyfriend, Simon Le Bon. Le Bon was a former child actor[218] who had spent some time in the late 1970's on a kibbutz in Israel, before returning home to study drama at the University of Birmingham. As soon as he joined, things started happening for Duran Duran, with their managers buying them onto a nationwide British tour supporting Hazel O'Connor in autumn 1980. At the end of the tour EMI won a bidding war to sign them and they were sent straight into the studio to record a debut single, barely six months after the line-up was completed.

1981 saw Duran Duran become the most successful act in Britain, with top ten hits such as *Planet Earth* and *Girls on Film* attracting the imaginations and screams of teenage girls, an audience that had lain dormant during the punk years. The sound of the band was influenced by the same things as the Blitz bands, namely punk, Bowie, Iggy Pop, and disco, with the Taylor rhythm section locking into a dance groove, guitarist Taylor adding some rock flourishes, and Le Bon's conceited lyrics only abstractly dealing with any issues.

As 1982 rolled around, and with a budget of £65,000 provided, they spent the first couple of months recording a second album with producer Colin Thurston[219] at George Martin's AIR Studios in Oxford Street[220] London during the day[221], and getting drunk

---

[215] Duffy is one of the great lost British songwriters, succumbing to a fashionable but quickly dated sound under the name Tin Tin, before following his own acoustic path with the extremely wonderful Lilac Time. He would later write some of his worst songs for Robbie Williams.

[216] Rhodes owns the rights to the name Duran Duran.

[217] At one point they rehearsed with Linlithgow born singer Gordon Sharp, however he decided to stick with his own band The Freeze, later finding a degree of success as a guest singer with This Mortal Coil.

[218] Le Bon was in a Persil advert when he was six years old.

[219] Thurston had engineered David Bowie's *"Heroes"* and Iggy Pop's *Lust For Life*.

[220] The album is credited with having a *Renate* engineering. Although no-one has confirmed, I suspect this was Elton John's soon-to-be wife, Renate Blauel. I mean, how many people called *Renate* can there have been working as engineers for AIR Studios in the early 1980's?

[221] Paul McCartney would put his head round the door at the end of each day and wish them good luck.

and high at the Embassy Club[222] at night. The album came together easily; none of the problems with a second album that many acts have, as the band tacked each song with measured simplicity. They avoided the temptation to pitch more into the mix, instead choosing to play to their strengths and ramp up the pop factor of the songs.

A meeting in New York the previous year between managers Paul and Michael Berrow and executives from MTV and woken the band to the possibility of video as a new medium. Up until then they had been making videos to be shown on screens in nightclubs, usually to accompany the *night version* of each single. This lack of expectation for televisual exposure meant the videos could be a bit more risqué, such as the soft-porn girl-on-girl wrestling of *Girls on Film*. At the meeting the executives informed the brothers that what they really wanted was "*sexy, exotic, travelogues… like James Bond movies*". If ever there was a band to fill that slot, it was Duran Duran in 1982.

On the way to fulfill an Australian tour in April, the band arranged to stop-over in Sri Lanka for a week with film maker Russell Mulcahey[223] to see what they could capture, a location chosen because manager Paul Berrow was obsessed with the country and had a plan to build temple there. Mulcahey later explained "*I was a frustrated feature film maker… and because there were no rules, no-one knew what they were meant to be. We just went off there and made them. There was no heavy deep thoughts about 'what does that mean?'*" Shooting on video tape with a moderate budget of £55,000, hours of footage were captured of the band without too much thought about how it would all fit together. They shot in the jungle, on the beach, on top of mountains, on top of elephants, with locals, and model Sheila Ming, sometimes miming to the lyrics, sometimes simply standing about or walking, and managed to put together videos for three songs in the six days, part fashion shoot, part "*Indiana Jones is feeling horny and wants to get laid*" according to Andy Taylor. These images would help define the band throughout the world as glamorous globetrotters, and to a certain degree trapped them in the mind of the public for the rest of their careers. Simon Le Bon, with a startling lack of irony, claimed before the video shoot "*The jet-set of the Western world leave their grubby fingermarks all over a place, and as soon as they get their hands on Sri Lanka, they'll mess that up as well. So we're going to get there first*".

Simon and John travelled first, whilst Nick and Andy stayed behind to finish mixing the album. The latter two caught the first plane after a night in the studio with no sleep and arrived unprepared for the climate.[224]

The following day, Tuesday 13th April, whilst filming elephants in a watering hole, Andy Taylor, high on Jack Daniels and Coke, was persuaded to climb a tree above the scene, only to fall and land in the filthy water, a large quantity of which he managed to swallow. Over the next two weeks Taylor felt progressively more ill, reaching a climax during a date at the Hodern Pavillion in Sydney where he had to rush behind his amplifier to vomit.

The next couple of Australian dates were cancelled, and when the band returned home to Britain at the start of May Taylor was rushed to hospital in Wolverhampton with

---

[222] The Embassy Club in Old Bond Street was owned by Jeremy Norman, Lady Edith Foxwell, and Stephen Hayter, and played host to the A-List stars of the day, including Princess Margaret, Freddie Mercury, and Pete Townshend. Lemmy had reserved seat downstairs at the *Space Invaders* machine.

[223] Mulcahy was the most successful video director of the era, and as well as Duran Duran was responsible for promotional clips for Spandau Ballet (*True, Instinction, Chant No 1*), Elton John (*I'm still Standing*), Kim Carnes (*Bette Davis Eyes*), Ultravox (*Vienna*) and The Buggles (*Video Killed That Radio Star*).

[224] The tight leather trousers worn by Rhodes would cause him to become de-hydrated on the four hour taxi ride to the filming location.

pyrexia and gastroenteritis from the water he had swallowed. Within a couple of days, the guitarist was transferred to a private hospital when the pressure of fans and the press became too much to cope with. The illness put paid to his plans to marry, and the wedding was rescheduled for mid-summer in the United States.

ʊ ʊ ʊ

Since leaving Squeeze at the height of their success, piano player Jools Holland had shared management with The Police and could be forgiven for expecting a blossoming solo career. His band, The Millionaires, had toured for a couple of years, but a debut album had failed to set the charts alite.

On Wednesday 14th April they found themselves at the Los Angeles Palladium ready to support XTC on the opening night of their North American tour. XTC front man Andy Partridge, having blown out their European tour the month before with a breakdown, was already making noises about the American dates, and according to Holland had spent a few days *"moaning that he was bored with music; he'd been there, done it all, and there was nothing new in it for him"*. Just before they were due to go onstage Partridge broke down again, certain he was going to die, and the rest of the world tour was cancelled.

Meanwhile, without the planned two-month American tour Jools Holland and his Millionaires were left stranded in California without the fiscal means to return home. A string of last minutes dates were arranged across the country, providing just enough cash to fly back to Britain, only to be met with the news they were being dropped by their record company A&M.

As a parting gift Holland was given a call by the A&M television promotions department and informed about a camera test for a new music program in Newcastle. Holland had done television before, presenting a one-off special on The Police as they recorded their last album, however the medium did not hold much appeal for him. Manager, Miles Copeland, suggested negotiating a fee of £500 for the audition, and having no other source of income Holland agreed.

On the train from London King's Cross to Newcastle, Holland was delighted to find himself sitting next to an old friend in the shape of Paula Yates. Yate, something of an *it girl* around London, was born in Wales to Elain Smith, a writer of erotic novels, and Jess Yates[225], the presenter of the ITV religious program *Stars on Sunday*. At the age of seventeen she started dating Bob Geldof of the Boomtown Rats, and in 1979 began writing a weekly column for the *Record Mirror*, utilising her flirtatious interview style to gain access to vain rock and pop stars. Holland had been one of those stars and was overjoyed to find her auditioning to be his co-host.

At the Tyne Tees studio the pair were tested in how they related to *young people*, during which Yates insisted on insulting them. When one admitted to being a student, she told him he was a *"work-shy yob and he should get a job"*. When they were to pretend to interview their *ideal guest* for the show, Holland mimed dragging the decaying corpse of John Lennon on stage. The two returned to London believing the audition had gone well without the knowledge Tyne Tees were using the tape as *"an example of the absolute worst type of television you could possibly have"*. Producer Andrew Wonfor, when talking about this, would always then add *"But I can't stop watching it. I've got to see it again. It's the most compelling thing I've ever seen!"*.

---

[225] She was later stunned to find out her biological father was Hughie Green, the presenter of television's *Opportunity Knocks*.

After other unsuccessful candidates were auditioned, including a young Jarvis Cocker who was driven up from Sheffield in a mini by his mum, and Boy George in a wedding dress, Holland and Yates were offered the job, starting in November on the new Channel 4.

If the cancelled XTC tour had been a hindrance to Jools Holland, XTC's label Virgin were still determined to have hits, and released *Ball & Chain* from the latest album.

The song was anti-development, using the voices of buildings pleading with demolishers to be spared, and was extremely apposite of what was going on in London's docklands.

The docks encapsulated around 5,000 acres of east London from Tower Bridge downstream and had been closed and abandoned between 1966 and 1981, leaving overgrown quays and hollow warehouses. Shipping traffic moved downriver to Tilbury, and London's pre-eminence as an international port diminished with emergent globalization. The working class who had manned and lived within the dockland area had also shrunk significantly, however by 1982 there were still 40,000 people living in terraced houses or tower blocks. These were communities glued together by decades of hardy living and a brute survival instinct, part of the old Britain about to vanish.

Chancellor of the Exchequer Geoffrey Howe described the area in a speech as "*an urban wilderness... in almost every British city one can see similar devastation. Whole industries have fallen off the edge... lack of economic success is breeding social tensions and threatening to destroy the framework of civilized existence*". He cited Hong Kong and Singapore as role-models, praising their "*absence of unnecessary regulations and social obligations*". The London Docklands Development Corporation was set up, and all sorts of protocols were abandoned or bent as Compulsory Purchase orders were sent out and much of the land acquired. Any businesses in the buildings around the perimeter were forcibly evicted, and their offices bulldozed to the ground. There was some confrontational consultation with the residents, however peoples' homes were never going to get in the way of the Thatcherite dream, and one businessman revealingly called the region "*all shady Dickens areas and immigrant areas... from the Jews to the Asiatics*". Left-wing activists argued any re-development should be structured around social needs and believed what was happening in the docklands was a microcosmic battle around national ideology.

The area was set up as an *enterprise zone* in April 1982, with tax breaks given to the private sector along with the promise that any new buildings would not require planning permission. The cost of construction could be offset against tax, and no business rates were due for the first ten years. Businesses were also told they would be free from health and safety regulations. New ideas were floated daily, many of which would never come to fruition, such as the plan to tether airships at one of the docks for public transport.

The Conservative government were determined to make the private sector prosperous in docklands, and invested almost £450 million over the next five years, an eye-watering amount which brings into question exactly how *private* a publicly funded private sector is. Over the next twenty years, the area became a bustling business zone with Canary Wharf stealing a lot of the financial power away from the City of London, and the Millennium Dome tempting hundreds of thousands of tourists.

Where Docklands led other cities followed, and hitherto abandoned industrial and shipping areas were redeveloped into great edifices of glass and metal. From the vestiges of disremembered industries grew enterprise, capitalism, and jobs. The only cost was community spirit.

ʊ ʊ ʊ

After the success of the video for *Say Hello, Wave* Goodbye, and the potential for visual accompaniments to help songs ascend the charts, Soft Cell were given a budget by their record company to create a whole album worth of them. They once-again employed Tim Pope, and shot twelve short films to complement songs from the debut album, as well as a couple of new singles.

For a whole week in April the band worked to bring their idea of a *surreal cabaret* to life. Some songs were performed with just the two members of the band, sometimes in the padded cell they had formerly used as a stage set, others featured a cast of characters in a similar style to *Say Hello, Wave Goodbye* (which was also included on the collection). When the duo managed to get out of the studio, they filmed themselves driving around in a car on ecstasy. Some of the videos featured singer Marc Almond's new muse, American drug dealer Cindy Ecstasy, who also performed a blundering rap on a remix of *Memorabilia*. Almond would admit in *Smash Hits* he had asked Cindy to marry him, and she had turned him down, which he saw as a good thing because he would "*probably regret it after a week. I don't really like the idea of being tied down*".

Future single *What* featured singer Mari Wilson sitting unimpressed on a couch in front of a pop-art background. Almond and Wilson had recently become close friends and Parlophone Records were delighted to stir false relationship rumours to deflect away from the Soft Cell singer's homosexuality.

The most controversial video was for the song *Sex Dwarf*, which featured transsexuals, transvestites, rent boys, and a dwarf, and contained scenes of bondage and sado-masochism. Meanwhile, heterosexual keyboard player Dave Ball was dressed as a butcher, cutting up a suspended animal carcass with a chainsaw. At the end of the song, director Pope threw a bucket of maggots over the ensemble, filming their genuine surprise and disgust. As Almond reached inside his leather jockstrap to remove some, it appeared as if he was starting to masturbate.

At the end of the day, the dwarf entered the editing suite requesting a copy of the film for his own personal portfolio and was naively given one. Two days later copies of the film were leaked by him to every major newspaper in the country, and press pandemonium broke out. The video was condemned as *sexist filth* and *insulting to women*, despite Almond pointing out the video did not actually feature any women, only men. The police raided the offices of Soft Cell's management and confiscated all copies of the video whilst the *News of the World* ran a false story about how Almond and the dwarf had tied girls up in a hotel room and whipped them.

With the major retailers informing the band they would not stock the video collection whilst *Sex Dwarf* was included, the duo recorded an ironic new video with them in suits conducting a school choir.

ʊ ʊ ʊ

Despite their recent success, the members of Toto were still touting themselves as session musicians for hire. At the beginning of April, guitarist Steve Lukather received what he considered to be a prank call early in the morning. A high-pitched voice yelped "*Hello*" to which Lukather snapped back "*Fuck you*" and hung up. Instantaneously, the phone rang again, and this time the high-pitched voice cried "*Hello, this is Michael Jackson*". Even more convinced his buddies were taking the piss, Lukather countered "*Fuck you, Michael Jackson*". It took a third call, and a series of quiz questions by

Lukather on the specialist subject of "*Michael Jackson*", to fully establish that, yes, it was *the* Michael Jackson speaking.

Lukather was hired, alongside band mates Steve and Jeff Porcaro and David Paich, to perform on the first recorded song for Jackson's new album, finding themselves at Westlake Studios in Los Angeles on Wednesday 14th April, alongside session men Louis Johnson, David Foster, and Greg Phillinganes.

All were ecstatic to find out they were recording not only with Jackson and producer Quincy Jones, but with living legend Paul McCartney. What they did not anticipate were all the other people in the studio, which included a camera crew, host of *American Bandstand* Dick Clark, a selection of former child stars from the 1970's, and Emmanuel Lewis from the sitcom *Webster*, who Jackson carried around the whole time. McCartney brought along his own entourage in the shape of wife Linda, Beatles producer George Martin, and engineer Geoff Emmerick, along with a small militia of security men. Following the assassination of John Lennon a year or so before, McCartney had become paranoid, and everyone in the room had to be vetted. First, though, he had to get over the awkwardness that Quincy Jones' wife was Peggy Lipton, with whom McCartney had enjoyed a brief dalliance back in the 1960's.

Jackson had first phoned McCartney of Christmas Day 1981, when the former Beatle was convinced a female fan had somehow gotten hold of his number. "*Who is this?*" he demanded. "*It's Michael Jackson*" came the reply. "*Fuck off! Who is it really?*" asked McCartney, becoming annoyed.

After a warm-up jam of Stevie Wonder's *I Was Made to Love Her*, the musicians were prepared to get down to business. The song was entitled *The Girl is Mine* and had been written by Jackson in a dream one night. Such was the musicianship in the room that the track was nailed in a few short takes, after which the members of Toto indulged in a joint with McCartney, but only after Jackson had left. McCartney had misgivings about the song, especially the "*dog-gone girl is mine*" line and a spoken middle-eight but deferred to Jackson and Jones.

℧ ℧ ℧

Following The Specials, Madness and The Selecter, the fourth band to release vinyl for Two-Tone Records was The Beat. Formed in 1978 by Black Country locals Dave  Wakeling and Andy Cox whilst installing solar panels on the Isle of Wight, they recruited Vectensian punk bass player Dave Steel, before all three moved to Birmingham. Experienced reggae drummer Everett Morton was added making them a mixed-race act playing a cross between punk and reggae. Playing live in their home city with other unsigned acts such as UB40 and The Au Pairs, the newly christened Beat were soon joined by *toaster* Ranking Roger[226] and created a skewered version of the ska sound, with *one-drop* drums and skittery guitar and bass lines. As they signed to the newly created Two-Tone label, The Beat recruited Saxa, a middle-aged Jamaican saxophonist who had played with the ska greats over twenty years previously.

---

[226] Roger Charlely was the drummer in Birmingham punk band The Dum Dum Boys who would often support The Beat. He was named after his dad's favourite actor, Roger Moore.

The Beat then chose to follow debut top ten single *Tears of a Clown* by leaving Two-Tone and forming their own label, *Go Feet*[227], signing a distribution deal with Arista worth £60,000. Success followed throughout 1980, but in 1981 their singles stopped reaching the top forty. By now joined by former lighting engineer Dave Wright on keyboards and Wesley Magoogan[228] on saxophone, their attention turned towards the United States where they were forced to call themselves The English Beat[229], and the possibilities offered by MTV and college radio. Extensive touring followed the release of *Save it for Later*, the first single from their forthcoming third album, which had been written by Wakeling before he formed the band but rejected by Steele for being too rock and *old wave*. When Steele failed to come up with much in the way of new material, the record company suggested they re-visit the song, and it took the threat of a Wakeling solo career to change the bass player's mind.

According to Wakeling, the title *"started off as a dirty schoolboy joke. The phrase 'save it for later' is meant to be 'save it', comma, 'fellator', as in 'leave it as it is, cocksucker'"*, and the song dealt with not knowing how to act like a man when you still felt like a kid, grasping for your place in the world. A mistake in blues tuning meant the song was written with all strings tuned to A or D, giving the song a drone-like quality, which Roger liked to compare to The Velvet Underground. Steele continued to loathe the song, slagging it off in the press when released as a single, a move which hastened the demise of the band, and even though it was a minor hit in Britain reaching number forty-seven, the song climbed the Dance Charts in America and nowadays earns about a third of their royalties.

ʊ ʊ ʊ

When Ian Craig-March and Martyn Ware left the Human League at the end of 1980 they took the unexpected step of forming an umbrella organisation: the British Electric Foundation (BEF). One off-shoot of the organisation was the act Heaven 17, featuring the duo alongside old friend Glenn Gregory[230] on vocals. As the Human League's star shot into the stratosphere during 1981, Heaven 17 released a series of singles from

their debut album *Penthouse & Pavement*, all of which failed to chart but garnered them much critical acclaim. Mixing electronic sounds with dance-music, and an ironic suited, pony-tailed, and briefcase-carrying corporate image, the band were a visual trial-run for the nimiety of the following decade, the *greed-is-good* Wall Street exorbitance. Of course, their irony was lost on some. Whilst Heaven 17 tried unsuccessfully to break into the charts with another single from the album in February 1982, a remixed version of *At the Height of the Fighting* featuring the horns of Beggar & Co, the trio were also putting together the finishing touches to an album of cover versions. Entitled *Music of Quality & Distinction – Volume 1*, the album displayed a miscellany of guest singers and musicians, some of whom were chosen for friendship, some because they were heroes.

---

[227] Despite having the green light to sign six other acts to the label each year, the only non-Beat release was a re-issue of The Congos 1970 album *Heart of the Congo*.

[228] Magoogan is the man behind the brilliant saxophone solo on Hazel O'Connor's *Will You*. He later lost his fingers in an accident with a circular saw.

[229] In Australia they were called The British Beat.

[230] The duo had originally wanted Gregory to sing in The Human League.

The opening track featured Tina Turner performing a version of The Temptations' *Ball of Confusion* against a hard-electronic beat and the horns from Beggar & Co[231]. Turner was in exceptional vocal form, having spent the last six years in a career malaise following a split from abusive ex-husband Ike Turner. Making a living by playing cabaret, Tina had recently decided she wanted to play arenas and hired Olivia Newton John's manager Roger Davies, who demanded she dump the supper-club band and start hiring modern rock musicians. At the beginning of 1982 Turner opened for Rod Stewart and the Rolling Stones, two acts that could remember her 1960's peak[232]. *Ball of Confusion* became a club hit across Europe throughout 1982, enabling Turner to sign with Capitol Records[233], and from there became one of the most successful acts of the decade[234].

Next up, Craig-March and Ware chose to work with a relatively unknown singer on an arcane David Bowie song, *The Secret Life of Arabia*. Billy MacKenzie of The Associates was unfamiliar to the public when the track was recorded, but by the time the album came out had broken through with *Party Fears Two*, beaming in a vocal performance from the edge of hysteria to accompany a hard electro-funk track.

After a faithful version of the Northern Soul classic *There's a Ghost in my House* by Manfred Mann singer Paul Jones, Paula Yates provided a barely audible susurrated squeak to a redundant version of *These Boots are Made for Walking*. This monstrosity still leaves a better taste in the mouth than Gary Glitter[235] performing an overwrought stomp through Elvis Presley's *Suspicious Minds*. To wash the pungent taste from your palette, Bernie Nolan[236] performed a version of *You Keep Me Hanging On*, providing a template for Kim Wilde's world dominating version a few years later, and featured the unmistakeable fluid bass runs of John Wilson who had previously been all over Heaven 17's *Penthouse & Pavement*.

Things continued to go downhill with Glenn Gregory destroying a version of *Wichita Lineman*[237], then Sandie Shaw with *Anyone who had a Heart* featuring Hank Marvin from The Shadows on guitar. Glenn Gregory almost redeemed himself with a semi-decent Lou Reed impression on *Perfect Day*.

The bulk of the album had been recorded at a studio owned by John Foxx, former singer with Ultravox, who provided guitar on Billy MacKenzie's version of Roy Orbison's *It's Over*, producing a suitably grandiose finale to the album, which the singer described as "angels flying on rainbows".

In danger of sounding like karaoke, the album failed to rise above an overly synthetic sound, only really breaching uninspired on the first two tracks. It was the kind of album utilising guest vocalists which dance music acts like The Chemical Brothers would excel at in later years, with Mark Ronson and The Gorillaz using it as their *modus operandi*. BEF's critical star was still rising, and the intriguing project earned easy publicity, allowing it to climb into the top thirty.

---

[231] Along with some post-punk guitar by John McGeoch from Siouxsie & the Banshees.

[232] Tina Turner taught Mick Jagger how to dance when she toured with The Rolling Stones in the 1960's.

[233] David Bowie, another massive fan, brokered the deal.

[234] Her comeback single was a version of Al Green's *Let's Stay Together*, produced by Heaven 17.

[235] Glitter has been found guilty of child pornography and child rape in several countries across the world.

[236] Bernie Nolan was the lead singer of The Nolans, and Irish singing sisters act. Lemmy claimed The Nolans were the only people who could drink him under the table.

[237] *Wichita Lineman* was the first song at my wedding. Not this version!

ʊ ʊ ʊ

American Secretary of State Alexander Haig had spent the past few weeks flying between Buenos Aires, London, and Washington, and now had formulated a plan which could work in the South Atlantic: the Argentinians would withdraw, and the islands would be governed equally by them, the British, and the Americans whilst negotiations for the future were undertaken. Britain had reluctantly agreed to the plan the previous evening when Haig flew into Buenos Aires on Thursday 15th April for a meeting with General Galtieri.

To his surprise, the Argentinians acceded to the plan... but with four amendments: the British fleet should turn back, the governor of the islands should be Argentinian, the Argentinian flag should continue to fly there, and the negotiations should end with the Argentinians holding sovereignty. Haig finally realised the nature of the Argentinian regime and informed them *"you are leaving us no choice but to break off our effort and throw our full support behind the British. Within a matter of days, the British fleet will be upon you. Their forces are capable of inflicting severe damage on yours* [with] *your systematic defeat by sophisticated British surface, sub-surface, and air power."* Back in Washington however, the CIA informed the Reagan administration that it would be extremely unlikely the British would be able to regain the islands through force.

ʊ ʊ ʊ

After a decade in the post-Merseybeat doldrums[238], Liverpool was once again a stimulating city musically in 1982, with a new generation of acts energized by punk and psychedelics making waves, including the Teardrop Explodes, Big in Japan, China Crisis, OMD, Echo & the Bunnymen, Wah, Dalek I Love You, Dead or Alive, Frankie Goes to Hollywood, and The Icicle Works. John Peel resolved to spend a week hosting his nightly BBC Radio One show from the exuberant city, showcasing local unsigned acts such as It's Immaterial[239] and The Pale Fountains.

Dave Balfe of the Teardrop Explodes and co-owner of record label Zoo, keen to capitalise on any potential publicity, decided to create and sign a female version of Soft Cell, and gave a Fairlight synthesizer and four-track tape recorder to seventeen-year-old Courtney Love[240], who had been hanging around demanding to be heard. Love had no idea how the machine worked and sat around writing songs concerning her *"plague coloured"* flat in Princess Avenue, where she and friend Robin Barbur had moved after being kicked out of Julian Cope's flat for having a regular delivery of LSD sent through the Royal Mail in his name. Echo & the Bunnymen drummer Pete de Freitas was given the job of delivering the eviction news but chickened out and left a note instead. The new flat was the embodiment of indigence, containing only a mattress and a couple of plastic chairs. Amongst the defective refrigerator and absent lightbulbs Love wrote her first song, all about Cope, with a chorus beginning *"Julian, Julian, where have you been?"*

---

[238] Other than solo Beatle releases, it's difficult to think of a successful Liverpool act of the 1970's. I get as far as The Real Thing, then I'm out.

[239] It's Immaterial had to wait until 1986 to have their own genuine hit single with *Driving Away From Home (Jim's Tune)*. By then, original member Henry Priestman had formed The Christians, who had their own late-1980's hit singles.

[240] Balfe denied having any memory of this to me on *Twitter*.

The following week Love's father arrived in Liverpool. Hank Harrison[241] was a self-proclaimed associate of The Grateful Dead and after a period in Ireland required £200 to fly home to the United States. He brought with him a valise full of LSD and orange pills which turned out to be the first ecstasy pills in Liverpool, and a deal was agreed whereby Harrison was *donated* the cash whilst the Teardrop Explodes were *gifted* the briefcase.

18th – 24th April 1982

#1 single: Paul McCartney & Stevie Wonder: Ebony & Ivory

#1 album: Status Quo: 1982

In previous years Spandau Ballet had refused to engage in anything as *rock and roll* as a tour, preferring instead to play one-off events such as a date on *HMS Belfast*, or else week-long residencies in Paris, New York, or San Tropez. Times had changed, however, and the relative lack of success of the new album obliged them to undertake a proper tour of the United Kingdom. It was on this tour they first noticed the screaming of teenage girls which would follow them around the world for the next few years. The girls even screamed at the support act, a young Glaswegian comedian by the name of Peter Capaldi[242].

Spandau Ballet had met Capaldi through their guitarist and songwriter Gary Kemp who was in the middle of an unrequited love affair with Altered Images' Clare Grogan. Despite having a long-term girlfriend, Kemp would regularly fly to Glasgow and visit Grogan's parents' house, where he would jostle for attention beside John Gordon Sinclair and David Band[243]. Grogan would play Kemp songs by Al Green and Marvin Gaye, rekindling his love of soul music, and gave him a copy of Nabakov's novel *Lolita*[244]. In the thrall of unreciprocated love Kemp started writing soul songs, beginning with a ballad called *True* which featured a phrase taken from the book; "*Take my seaside arms and write the next lines*".

ʊ ʊ ʊ

American vocalist and guitarist Alan Merrill was the first Western pop star in Japan when he formed glam rock act Vodka Collins in the early 1970's. Upon moving to London Merrill had joined The Arrows who signed to Mickie Most's RAK Records and enjoyed a top ten hit single with *Touch Too Much* as well as starring in their own weekly television show. Merrill was an accomplished songwriter, and it was on the show he first performed one of his compositions called *I Love Rock & Roll*. Touring the United Kingdom at the time were The Runaways, an all-female teenage band from Los

---

[241] You want to know what kind of father Hank Harrison is? He wants the police to re-open the Kurt Cobain suicide investigation so they can find his daughter guilty of foul play.

[242] At around this time Capaldi was in a band called The Dreamboys, along with Craig Ferguson. The two of them formed a comedy duo called *Dean & Bing Hitler*.

[243] Band was a recent graduate of Glasgow School of Art and designed the record sleeves for Altered Images and Spandau Ballet.

[244] What can we make of *Lolita* nowadays, a stunning piece of writing which is also essentially the story of a middle-aged professor's sexual infatuation with a twelve-year-old girl?

Angeles put together by Joan Jett, who fell in love with the song and would play it at soundchecks over the next few years.

When The Runaways split in 1979 Jett found herself in London, ostensibly looking for a solo career, and recorded a version of the song with Steve Jones and Paul Cook from the Sex Pistols, which was exactly the same as the original in terms of arrangement and sound, but with slightly more stilted drums. The session had been financed and produced by her new manager, Kenny Laguna[245], who then paid for more sessions and released her debut solo album on his own independent label. By this point, Jett was backed by a band called The Blackhearts, featuring Eric Ambel, Gary Ryan[246], and Lee Crystal, all recruited from the Los Angeles punk scene. Throughout 1980 the band made a meagre living touring the United States, selling their album from the back of the van after gigs, before former Casablanca Records owner Neil Bogart signed them to his new label, Boardwalk Records.

With a label behind them, Joan Jett & the Blackhearts entered Kingdom Sound Studios in Long Island to record their second album. Set up in the same room facing each

other, they recorded as if they were on stage, allowing the bleed between instruments to add to the energy. Working with experienced producer Glen Kolotkin, towards the end of the recording it was becoming apparent there was no hit single. Kolotkin voiced his fears to manager Laguna, who revealed they were holding one song back to work with legendary producer Roy Thomas Baker. Kolotkin was not having this, and insisted the band play the song for him. Realising the potential of *I Love Rock and Roll*, he asked them to play it again and hit the *record* button. One hour, and a couple of overdubs later (multiple vocals and handclaps in the chorus), the song was complete.

The Arrows had originally written the song in response to *It's Only Rock and Roll (But I Like It)* by the Rolling Stones, appalled at Mick Jagger's apology to the jet set for his career as a rock star, and by 1982 there was fear it sounded a little bit too passé. The record company had doubts about the line *"put another dime in the jukebox baby"* because both the idea of a jukebox and it costing a dime seemed outdated, however this did not bother the public who sent the single to the top of the Billboard charts for six weeks in spring 1982. After a slow start in the United Kingdom, the song worked its way up to number four.

The track was an archetypal rock song, with a snarling punk influence clear in the vocals, combining a memorable riff and a communal chorus. It encouraged audience participation through repeated singing and prominent handclaps, and the tight production has allowed it to become something more than a guilty classic.

ʊ ʊ ʊ

Following the release of their most successful album *Remain in Light* in 1980, New York's Talking Heads had taken time off to work on solo albums. This had not been a collective decision, but instead was enforced by frontman David Byrne choosing to

---

[245] Laguna had played on several pop hits in the 1960's including *Mony Mony*, *Simon Says* and *Green Tambourine*.

[246] Ryan's real surname was Ross, however he needed a false name because he was only fifteen when he joined the band.

record *My Life in the Bush of Ghosts*[247] with Brian Eno[248], then collaborating with dancer and girlfriend Twyla Tharp on a musical score for *The Catherine Wheel*. Guitarist Jerry Harrison recorded and released his own solo album *The Red and the Black* in 1981, which only left husband-and-wife rhythm section Tina Weymouth (bass) and Chris Frantz (drums). Unlike the others, the duo was refused a deal with their Talking Heads label Sire Records and chose instead to work at Compass Point Studios in the Bahamas for Chris Blackwell's Island Records. The resulting eponymous album *The Tom Tom Club* significantly outsold anything produced so far, whether solo or as Talking Heads, with worldwide hits in the form of *Wordyrappinghood* and *Genius of Love*[249].

Getting together in early 1982 to start work on a new Talking Heads album, a stopgap live double album entitled *The Name of This Band is Talking Heads* was released in March, and the band set out on a world tour to promote it with an extended band.

Arriving in Tokyo on Monday 19th April, the band were met by the ever-present Mr Udo, promotor of their date at the Shibuya Koukaidou Theatre the following night. The success of Tom Tom Club put pressure on them to perform as well, and it was agreed for Weymouth and Frantz to perform a short set at the top of the evening using the extra musicians from Talking Heads. Weymouth's sisters Laura and Lani recreated their singing roles from the album and were rewarded for their efforts by the newly recruited tour manager and soundman knocking on their hotel door all night. When they rebuffed his advances, he cut the time spent on their soundcheck down until it completely disappeared and when they asked for their daily allowance he would reach into his pocket, take out a crumpled Yen note, and throw it in their faces.

℧ ℧ ℧

The Sun continued to ramp up the anti-Argentinian rhetoric on Tuesday 20th April with a headline of "*STICK IT UP YOUR JUNTA*". The article urged "*every housewife NOT to buy corned beef produced in the Argentine… to show the South American bully boys what they thought*" and started referring to them as *Johnny Gaucho*. They also offered to pay five pounds for every anti-Argentinian joke published, the first of which by "*Titus Rowlandson, 9, from Brighton*" being about two British soldiers slaughtering hundreds of Argentinians. The next logical step was to start the merchandise, which they did with free badges, and T-shirts for sale with "*STICK IT UP YOUR JUNTA*" emblazoned on the front.

Elsewhere, they invented a story about Navy wives wearing underwear specially embroidered with the name of their husband's ship (*Invincible, Hermes,* etc), just so they could demonstrate such a product on a Page Three model, followed by another headline of "*GARTERS TO THE TARTARS*".

℧ ℧ ℧

The Palestine Liberation Organisation had been founded in 1964 with the resolution to achieve independence for Palestine from Israel through armed struggle. Since their

---

[247] *My Life in the Bush of Ghosts* was a truly innovative and forward-thinking record, featuring extensive sampling from exorcists and evangelical radio preachers accompanied by African-influenced dance music.

[248] Eno had produced the previous two Talking Heads albums but fell out with them over the credits.

[249] *Genius of Love* has been sampled by numerous acts, most successfully by Mariah Carey on her chart-topping *Fantasy*.

inception, the PLO had been a violent and malignant thorn in the side of Israel, operating initially from exile in Jordan, and then in Lebanon to the north. Headed by the charismatic Yasser Arafat[250], the PLO was recognised by a proliferating number of nations around the world as the "*sole legitimate representative of the Palestinian people*". The PLO had been sending members to the USSR for years to undergo specialist training, however Arafat's recent dealings with the United States now made the Soviets circumspect as official communiques stopped referring to *Comrade* Arafat, and now just called him Arafat.

Meanwhile, in early 1982 a cross-party group of MPs from the United Kingdom visited Arafat in the region. The group, which included Labour's Peter Snape and future Conservative Prime Minister John Major, found themselves caught in the middle of a literal exchange of gunfire between the Israeli army and Palestinian protesters, which found them diving for cover under their car.

With the Israeli policy of settlement[251], more than 300,000 Palestinians had flown the country over the previous decade, frequently taking up residence in Lebanese refugee camps. This created a state-within-a-state, and Israel was progressively uncomfortable with the potential menace this posed to her northern border. There were hundreds of Israeli incursions into Southern Lebanon in support of a Christian based army there in the early 1980's in contradiction of the United Nations Security Council Resolution 425, until a ceasefire was brokered in July 1981. This had been adhered to since then, though the peace could be exceedingly jittery at times, and United States Secretary of State Alexander Haig had counselled President Reagan in January that he feared the Israelis were looking for any excuse to invade.

On Wednesday 21st April the pretext was provided when an Israeli officer was killed by a landmine whilst visiting Lebanon[252]. In response, the Israeli's attacked the coastal town of Damour, killing twenty-three people in the process. The attack was launched just one hour after the Israeli announcement of their withdrawal from the Sinai Peninsula in Egypt and has long been suspected as undertaken to deflect attention away from what Jewish settlers there saw as a betrayal.

℧ ℧ ℧

Outside Visage, a source of regular income for Steve Strange and Rusty Egan were their club nights, and in late 1981 the two were approached by a company called *European Leisure* who offered to finance a new venture. A venue was located at a former theatre and cinema on Camden High Street which had been operating in the last few years as the *Music Machine*. Renamed the Camden Palace, the club opened on Wednesday 21st April with the slogan "*A club made by the people, for the people*". Police were forced to close the road and any fears regarding being open several nights a week were soon put aside as the Camden Palace became the epicentre of London pop culture in the early 1980's, even if the varnish on the floor was still wet on the opening night. Camden in 1982 was far from the fashionable rock and roll domain it would develop into fifteen years later, but was instead a grim, run-down burgh full of dipsomaniacs and the homeless. Basing the nightclub there played an important role

---

[250] The Israelis tried for years to assassinate Arafat, even going as far as to plan the shooting down of civilian aircraft over deep ocean he *may* be on. The other passengers were to be considered an acceptable price to pay.

[251] The Israelis had been making land claims for over ten years, sometimes violently evicting Palestinians from their homes.

[252] The landmine had been placed there four years previously and may even have been laid by the Israelis.

in the rehabilitation of the area, attracting aspiring rock and pop stars, and can profess to being partially responsible for the resurgence.

Strange can also lay claim to the invention of club culture as previously "*there had been the choice of small suburban discos or classy elitist nighteries such as Tramp*", whilst the Camden Palace was a place for the regular (if somewhat flamboyant) *unknowns* of the capital.

ʊ ʊ ʊ

The Clash made the wholly uncommercial decision to release *Know Your Rights* as the first single from their forthcoming *Combat Rock* album, a brave choice considering they had struggled to make the top forty in the past couple of years. *Know Your Rights*

indulged frontman Joe Strummer's love of old-style slap reverb rock and roll with a rockabilly beat, and jokey opening intonation of "*This is a public service announcement… with guitars*". The song was more akin in style to one of Woody Guthrie's dust-bowl talking blues, with punchlines set up in each of the three verses before a hit of truth is delivered. "*You have the right to food money… provided you don't mind a little investigation, interrogation*" Strummer exhorted, referring to means testing and the welfare state. Later, following a spaghetti western Duane Eddy guitar solo, he explained "*You have the right to free speech as long as you're not dumb enough to actually try it.*" With the United Kingdom one of only three democracies in the world lacking a written constitution, the illusion of free speech was tackled, particularly the government's individual approach to the Universal Declaration of Human Rights, which as Ian Hurd pointed out "*it is likely that a permit is needed to hold a public rally… so the practical experience of* [the right to protest] *depends on the terms that the state places on these permits.*"

The single stalled at number forty-three when released on Friday 23rd April, and the band were due to start their British tour three days later in Aberdeen. Instead, on Wednesday 21st April Strummer decided he would disappear. After phoning his mother to reassure her not to worry whatever she heard about him over the next short while, he caught a train to the south coast with girlfriend Gaby Salter, and then a boat to France. A friend of Salter had a small empty apartment in the Montmartre district of Paris, and the two moved in without telling anyone else.

The idea of disappearing had first been mooted by manager Bernie Rhodes, who was worried about sluggish sales of tickets for the tour. He suggested Strummer travel on his own to Texas to stay with friend Joe Ely, and call him every day, however the singer was determined to be his own man and chose the continent instead. Rhodes was furious and even a little bit worried, being forced to cancel the tour at great cost, as the press reported the story of Strummer's disappearance, speculating he had committed suicide, and a report even circulated that his body had been found in the River Clyde.

ʊ ʊ ʊ

The first landfall by British troops in the South Atlantic materialised on Wednesday 21st April, when a troop of SAS were dropped by Wessex helicopters on South Georgia. After a night in abysmal conditions, losing tents and equipment to torrential gales and snow, the soldiers were forced to radio for help. The weather situation was so bad that the first two helicopters sent crashed, fortuitously with no casualties. A third Wessex succeeded in evacuating all soldiers and crew back to HMS Antrim.

A new attempt was made two days later, on Friday 23rd April, where conditions once again forced an abandonment of the mission.

℧ ℧ ℧

Although to the public Japan seemed to still be a going concern, most of the members were angling for solo careers, not least singer David Sylvian who flew to New York for the weekend for talks with CBS Records. Other than at the most cutting-edge clubs in New York, the band had yet to make inroads in the United States, and their previous Virgin releases had been combined into an eponymous album compilation.

Sylvian was met by former Warhol Superstar Susan Blond, now head of CBS, on Friday 23rd April, and taken to the Factory at 860 Broadway. Andy Warhol had long been a hero of Sylvian, and to finally be interviewed and filmed by him, was one of the highlights of his career.

The two then hit the town, Sylvian in awe of the art legend, and Warhol in love with the young acolyte.

℧ ℧ ℧

On Saturday 24th April the public across the continent willingly sat down in front of their television sets to watch the 27th annual Eurovision Song Contest beamed live into their living rooms by the BBC from the newly opened 2,000-seater Harrogate International Centre, with added commentary by the ever-reliable Terry Wogan[253]. Expectations were high for the United Kingdom, having won the previous year with Bucks Fizz and *Making Your Mind Up*, being represented this year by Bardo, as newsreader Jan Leeming introduced the show. The event had not yet developed the ironic following and self-referential entries of later years, and in 1982 only France saw sense, withdrawing their entry at "*the absence of talent and the mediocrity of the songs*" before describing Eurovision as "*a monument to drivel*".

The performances began with Portugal's entry, four women dressed as musketeers called Doce with a song whose title translated as *Very Good*. After Luxembourg, married Norwegian couple Jahn Teigan[254] and Anita Skorgan sang *Adieu*, a tale of promising to stay on good terms after splitting up, which proved prophetic when they divorced a couple of years later.

Then came the British entry, male-female duo Bardo with *One Step Further*. Radio DJ John Peel once stated the song was his favorite British Eurovision entry, which is not to say it was actually any good. Whilst the track was memorable enough, on the night someone decided to go with a more traditional orchestral backing, conducted by Ronnie Hazelhurst[255] rather than the contemporary electronic instrumentation evident on the recorded version currently climbing the charts, and because of this the song ended up sounding dated when compared to some of the other entries, though perhaps not as dated as the Finnish entry which followed Turkey's attempt. Sung by Kojo, *Nuku Pommiin* (translated as *Sleep on the Bomb*) suggested the best way to avoid a nuclear war in Europe was to simply sleep right through it and received a total of (ground) zero points on the night.

---

[253] Let's face it, for years the only good thing about the event was Wogan's sardonic commentary.

[254] Teigan had represented Norway in Eurovision in 1978, when he gained infamy for being the first act to score *nul points*.

[255] Hazlehurst will forever have my respect for his theme tune for *Some Mothers do 'Ave Them*, which is the title spelled out in morse code played on two piccolos.

Back on safer Eurovision ground was Switzerland's Arlette Zola performing *Amour on t'aime* ("*Love, we Love You*"), and the Cypriot *Mono I Agapi* ("Only Love") by Anna Vissi, which achieved the country's greatest ever placing in fifth. Sweden was next and

still considered contenders following the success of Abba almost ten years previously. A country rock band called Chips sang *Time After Time* which sank without trace, only for one of their members Elisabeth Andreassen to later find success as a member of Bobbysocks who won the competition in 1985 with *Let It Swing*.

Austria and Belguim followed, before Spain's Lucia performed *El*, a song which caused controversy at the time by being a tango, a style of music associated with Argentina who were at war with the hosts. Denmark, Yugoslavia, Israel, the Netherlands, and Ireland ran through their unmemorable entries, before the final song was performed by a seventeen-year-old German high school pupil called Nicole. Seated on a stool and strumming a white acoustic guitar she performed *A Little Peace* with a backing band featuring a harp. The simplicity of the song and performance made the track stand out from the overblown entries that had come before, and when it was time for the judging Germany ran away with the competition, winning by a Eurovision record of over 160 points.

When called on to reprise the song Nicole made a spur of the moment decision to sing a verse each in German, English, French, and Dutch, thus sealing the popularity of the track across the continent. Upon release it reached number one in every single country in Europe[256] whilst becoming the 500th chart topper in Britain.

Public protest in France saw them lower their haughty morals and enter again the following year.

ʊ ʊ ʊ

Whilst tens of millions of people were watching the Eurovision Song Contest across the continent, Maximo Nicoletti and Antonio Latorre flew from Buenos Aires to Paris, where their luggage full of military scuba gear, a large amount of United States dollars, and Argentinian passports raised the suspicion of customs. After a quick interrogation they were permitted to fly to Malaga, where they hired a car and met up with Hector Rosales and an agent known as *Marciano*.

As soon as the Falklands conflict had escalated, the Argentinians started planning how to hit the British outside of the South Atlantic. Head of the Navy, Admiral Jorge Anaya, secretly toyed with the idea of a bombing campaign on mainland Britain, however this was ruled out because of the difficulty Argentinians would face blending in. Instead, eyes turned to the British owned strategically important peninsula of Gibraltar, whose location next to friendly state Spain made it perfect. Four former terrorist enemies of the Argentinian state were recruited, partly for their sabotage skills and experience, and partly because the Argentinians could deny all knowledge if caught, explaining them as patriots acting on their own. A plan was agreed whereby they would swim from Algeciras in Spain across the Bay of Gibraltar to place mines on the hull of a British vessel.

---

[256] Literal translations for each country: France (*Peace on Earth*), Spanish (*A Little Bit of Peace*), Russian (*A Little World*), Polish (*A Little Bit of Earth, a Little Bit of Sun*), Hungarian (*I Wish You Some Peace of Mind*).

Despite Spain being on high alert for terrorist activities due to the forthcoming football world cup, four Argentinians moving between various hotels close to a British naval base whilst paying for everything in cash did not raise any suspicion, even when they drove to the Argentinian Embassy to pick up mines which had been smuggled into the country in diplomatic packages.

Meanwhile, back in London, rather than have anything to do with Eurovision shenanigans, Margaret Thatcher arranged a special screening of *Chariots of Fire* at Chequers, her weekend retreat, to rouse patriotic spirits within her cabinet.

25th April – 1st May 1982

#1 single: Paul McCartney & Stevie Wonder: Ebony & Ivory

#1 album: Barry Manilow: Live In Britain

What do you do when your song comes seventh in the heats of Nationaal Songfestival, the competition to represent Holland in the Eurovision Song Contest, having been heard once by the population and rejected? The answer if you are an act called The Millionaires is to pass it on to the British.

An act called Tight Fit had experienced a couple of *Stars on 45*-type hit singles in 1981 sung by session singers, when Tim Friese Green[257] put together a version of the old Zulu song *The Lion Sleeps Tonight* with former City Boy drummer Roy Ward on vocals.

The City Boy connection[258] provided a link with Tight Fit, and it was agreed to release the song under the name, despite having no connection with the band. The song had a long history, having been written in the 1920's by a black South African singer, Solomon Linda as *Mbebe*, a traditional call-and-response. Appropriated by American folk act The Weavers in the 1950's[259], their mishearing of the word *uyimbube*[260] led to the song being renamed *Wimoweh*. A further version by white doo-wop group The Tokens applied lyrics to the song, renaming it *The Lion Sleeps Tonight*. As the Tight Fit version rocketed up the charts in February 1982, three people were recruited to act as the band for television and press appearances: Steve Grant from Gillingham dressed in a loincloth and was accompanied by Denise Gyngell and Julie Harris.

With the single topping the charts across Europe, Grant, Gyngell, and Harris insisted on being allowed to sing on the next single, the Eurovision rejection called *Fantasy Island*. A truly atypical and quite under-rated piece of Abba-lite, the song featured Anne Dudley on piano, and climbed to number five in the British charts, though next single *Secret Heart* only reached number forty-one and the act were finished as a chart entity. Just before their self-titled album was released, Gyngell and Harris realised they were

---

[257] Tim Friese Green was the grandson of Claude Friese Green, arguably the inventor of the motion picture camera.

[258] Tight Fit were managed by another former City Boy member, Clive Dunn.

[259] They also claimed songwriting credit for the music, earning a significant amount of money over the years.

[260] Zulu for *"You are a Lion"*.

being underpaid and left, being swiftly replaced by Vicky Pemberton and Carol Stevens.

Failed attempts at solo careers followed, and Gyngell eventually married pop producer Pete Waterman[261], whilst Friese Green co-produced Thomas Dolby's debut album later played keyboards with Talk Talk in their imperial phase.

ʊ ʊ ʊ

The first British triumph of the Falklands Conflict (*war* was never declared, and the government were careful not to refer to it as a *war*) came on Sunday 25th April when the Argentinian submarine *Santa Fe* was crippled by depth charges, followed by an air attack, whilst on the surface. The damaged submarine skulked into Grytviken on South Georgia, where British troops landed and accepted the surrender without any loss of life[262]. Most of the Argentinian troops surrendered, and in line with the rules of war began disarming the mines and booby traps set around their encampment, however a small group of Marines under the control of Alfredo Astiz waved a white flag to lure the British over a minefield. Luckily, the trigger mechanisms were frozen solid, and South Georgia was now back in British hands.

Margaret Thatcher, returning from an audience with the Queen at Windsor, appeared on the steps of 10 Downing Street to announce the news to the British press. As she finished her statement, they began shouting questions: "*What happens next?*" and "*What are your thoughts on…?*" Thatcher replied with some emphasis "*Just rejoice at that news and congratulate our forces and the marines*" before turning away towards the door. "*Are we going to war with Argentina, Mrs Thatcher?*" a journalist shouted. At the door, Thatcher turned again, and demanded with some force "*Rejoice!*"

ʊ ʊ ʊ

Following the success of *Golden Brown* The Stranglers were feeling self-assured and confident enough for bass player Jean-Jacques Burnel to insist the title track of their last album, *La Folie*, be the next single. The record company had suggested the track *Tramp*, supported by three members of the band, however Burnel rejected this for being *too commercial*. Cornwell explained: "[Jean] *had an aversion to pop and equated it with everything abhorrent about modern music. The result of this phobia was that*

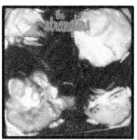

whenever we seemed to be becoming too popular… he seemed to throw a spanner in the works." EMI dithered, then acknowledged they had resisted the release of *Golden Brown* and had been erroneous regarding its commercial value, and capitulated. With *La Folie*, however, their worries had legitimacy.

A morose six-minute piece with vocals half-recited and half-sung in French about Issei Sagawa, a Japanese student who had executed, raped, and then eaten (in that order) a Dutch woman, Renee Hartevelt, the previous year, was scarcely the stuff of the top forty. In spite of being an objectively agreeable piece of background music written by frontman Hugh Cornwell, radio appropriately snubbed the single and it reached no higher than number

---

[261] Waterman's proteges Steps built their whole career on songs sounding like *Fantasy Island*.

[262] Argentinian Petty Officer Felix Artuso was shot dead the following day whilst trying to sabotage the submarine.

forty-seven despite the addition of the wonderfully beguiling old instrumental track *Waltz in Black* on the B-side[263].

As a piece of ambiguous *art* the track was noticeably in debt to Serge Gainsbourg, the French *enfant terrible* singer and musician who found some success in the 1960's, and was later re-discovered in a more heterogeneous time, juxtaposing the pretty backing track with the starkness and horror of the subject matter. The title, *La Folie*, translated as *the madness*, a title that the band were keen to elucidate was short for *the madness of love*. However much you admire the band for sticking to their artistic principles, it once again looked as if they were about to continue their journey into obscurity, even if they claimed the single was "*the most played track in French gay discos*".

ʊ ʊ ʊ

Glen Tilbrook and Chris Difford were two South London lads happily ensnared in the hippy culture of 1973 whilst clandestinely enamoured by 1960's pop music. The pair developed their love of music by forming a band called Squeeze, evolving the line-up until it consisted of Jools Holland, Gilson Lavis, and Harry Kakoulli. Specialising in three-minute spirited songs, Squeeze found their tunes were diminutive and enthusiastic enough for them to be lumped in with the post-punk new wave which arose in the late 1970's. Managed by Miles Copeland and signed to A&M, the band's debut album was produced by the sloshed and cantankerous former Velvet Underground member John Cale, who made the error of not fully realising the simple pop songs at the heart of Squeeze, trying to force them into something more experimental than the band ever wanted. Despite the success of the album, Squeeze opted for different producers in the future.

Over the next couple of years Squeeze enjoyed a succession of hits singles and albums, including lyrical and musical classics such as *Cool for Cats*, *Up the Junction*, and *Labelled with Love*, whilst increasing their profile in foreign territories. Squeeze came to the termination of their association with Miles Copeland in 1980, and at the same time parted with Holland who had been convinced by the American that immense things lay ahead for him as a solo act. From then the keyboard players changed rapidly with ex-Ace frontman Paul Carrack[264] even taking over at one point, adding vocals to their 1981 hit *Tempted*.

After commencing work on a new album with renowned producer Gus Dudgeon[265], the band chose instead to engage former Beatles engineer Phil McDonald, and spent the closing months of 1981 recording in Battersea. The ensuing album, *Sweets from a Stranger* did not capture Squeeze at their best, with lyricist Difford later acknowledging he had been exceedingly indolent in his writing (with *When the Hangover Strikes* perhaps shedding more light on the reason), and the record company ignoring the album on release in May.

---

[263] That's why I bought the single. *Waltz in Black* is dark and infectious, and reminded me of a summer at a Boys Brigade camp in the north of Scotland.

[264] Carrack is something of a go-to fill-in guy for bands. After Ace he helped out Frankie Miller and Roxy Music, after Squeeze he played with Nick Lowe, The Smiths, The Pretenders and Mike + the Mechanics (he's the singer on *The Living Years*)

[265] In 2002 Dudgeon was driving well above the drink and speed limits when he fell asleep at the wheel. The car left the road and landed upside down in a storm drain. Both Dudgeon and his wife suffered head injuries, and unable to help themselves drowned in their seats.

A month before the album, one of the highlights was released as a single. *Black Coffee in Bed* was an old-style soul song about lost love, with the protagonist trying to

substitute his former lover but being reminded of her at every turn, even when he is *"out with a friend with lips full of passion"*. The song was abetted by the Drifters-style backing vocals of Elvis Costello and future solo star Paul Young, however it stalled at number fifty-one in Britain. The band went off undeterred on a Swedish tour as a warm-up for a North American jaunt, now with Don Snow on keyboards

It does seem anomalous in a year when *catchy pop music* was so dominant in the British charts that one of the best practitioners of *catchy pop music* could not make the top forty. However, 1982 was all about catchy pop music *plus* image, and one thing Squeeze were not adept at was looking suave. This could be seen in the video for *Black Coffee in Bed*, directed by the pop visualiser of the moment Steve Barron, where the band give the impression of ungainliness, wooden and at odds with this new medium. That did not stop the track from gaining heavy rotation on MTV, raising the profile of the band significantly in the States.

ʊ ʊ ʊ

Rod Stewart had made a more than comfortable life for himself in Los Angeles, emigrating there in 1975 and embracing the world expected of a rock and pop star, complete with a string of blonde girlfriends and phallic sports cars. In 1982 he was married to model Alana Collins and settled with two small children, and whilst the first part of the year had been spent touring North America, Stewart had been back home for the last fortnight contemplating the recording of his next album and searching for a new manager.

On Monday 26th April the perennial singer took his three-year-old daughter Kimberley[266] and his secretary Martha Baher shopping, parking just off Sunset Boulevard in his 1977 Porsche. Upon returning to the Turbo-Carrera the three were met by an armed gunman who demanded the keys to the car.

Seconds later the thief was pointing the gun at Stewart again, shouting *"I can't start the car"*. The British singer was forced at gunpoint to show where the start button was, and then hand over his wallet and shopping for good measure. As the robber made off with the $50,000 vehicle Stewart phoned the Los Angeles Sheriff Office to report the crime.

Within a couple of months, he moved back to the United Kingdom.

ʊ ʊ ʊ

Just after 8 a.m. on Tuesday 27th April Roberto Rosone, deputy chairman of the troubled Banco Ambrosiano left his modest corner apartment on Via Olofredi in Milan to make the extremely brief journey to his work at a branch of the bank on the same block. As he approached the door, a short figure approached and fired a bullet into his knee. The bank had employed armed guards for several months and hearing the shots they rushed to the scene shooting dead the would-be assassin.

When the police and medical crews arrived, Rosone was taken to hospital, with the gunman identified as Roman mob boss Danilo Abbruciati. Questions began to be

---

[266] Kimberley Stewart later had a child with Benicio del Toro, although the two never dated.

asked, such as why was a mob boss carrying out such a hit when it would normally have fallen to a henchman, and what did the mafia have to do with Banco Ambrosiano? Had this been a warning or an attempted murder, who had ordered it, and for what reason?

What was clear was that the jackals were circling the ailing bank.

ʊ ʊ ʊ

After a few days moving between hotels in Algeciras, Spain, the four Argentinian former terrorists turned secret government agents found a target for their intended sabotage mission. On Wednesday 28th April a British minesweeper entered the naval port in Gibraltar, however after a long debate it was decided that the ship was too insignificant to bother with. The following day there were further discussions regarding the blowing up a non-British oil tanker, blocking the port for an extended time, however fear of the environmental effect on Spanish tourism scuppered that idea as well.

ʊ ʊ ʊ

1982 sits as a fissure between the twin paving stones of 1970's counter-culture rock star indulgence and the over-slick corporate excess of the 1980's. The rock and pop behemoths of the previous decade played little part in the story of the year: Led Zeppelin, Steely Dan and The Eagles had split, Elvis Presley and John Lennon were dead, David Bowie, Chic and The Bee Gees were missing in action, Abba and Blondie were on their last legs, and The Rolling Stones, The Who, Elton John, and Rod Stewart seemed enervated and irrelevant.

Queen spent most of the year attempting to join this list, despite having reached the top of the charts in 1981 with *Under Pressure*, their collaboration with David Bowie, as well as releasing a massively popular *Greatest Hits* compilation. The four-piece began a year as tax exiles in Munich, recording a new album on which they were resolute in being more experimental, influenced by the dance music they heard at the city's *Sugar*

Shack nightclub. The members of Queen, Freddie Mercury, Brian May, John Deacon, and Roger Taylor, were straining in disparate directions, bringing songs into the studio separately and recording them at different times of the day. This inevitably led to fractured set of recordings which were unsure what they were, as the band's interest in the night life took on more importance than the day job. As each songwriter seemed unwilling to compromise their vision, there was extreme tension in the studio.

Body Language was the first single released from the new album and took a sparse funk sound further than the band previously had, with Brian May's guitar barely audible, which *Rolling Stone* magazine harshly described as "*a piece of funk that isn't fun*". The cover of the single featured a couple of naked bodies, a factor which contributed to the single stalling in the United States, along with a Mike Hodges[267] video shot in Toronto which was the first to be banned by MTV because of excessive nudity. Lyrically, it reflected Mercury's continuing adventures in gay clubs, a pursuit still unknown to the public, however the gay bathhouses of New York and San Francisco are evident in the video. The content worried May, who later stated "*I can remember having a go at Freddie because some of the stuff he was writing was definitely on the gay side*", preferring lyrics which were

---

[267] Hodges first worked with the band on *Flash Gordon* which he directed, whilst they provided the soundtrack.

less specific, more universal. Another influence on Mercury was his personal assistant Paul Prenter, who *"very much wanted our music to sound like you'd just walked into a gay club"* according to Roger Taylor.

A few days before the album *Hot Space* was due to be released, David Bowie refused the band permission to use his backing vocals on a track called *Cool Cat*. The album was delayed whilst the track was remixed, causing the first part of the European tour to occur before the release. This caused a problem with some of the new material being met unfavourably: in Frankfurt on Wednesday 28th April the introduction of *Staying Power* was met by the crowd booing, causing Mercury to suggest that if the crowd did not want to listen, then they should *"fucking go home"*. Queen were attracting an increasingly intolerant crowd to their concerts, which led to support act Bow Wow Wow being replaced by Christian rockers After the Fire[268], which May candidly explained by saying *"Our audience is perhaps a little narrow-minded"*.

The first side of the album, dominated by songs written by Deacon and Mercury, seemed to be searching for space between the notes and a more contemporary sound. Deacon had written *Backchat* as a funk number about two people arguing, however May insisted it should have some anger in it, given the subject matter, and added resounding guitar. It was released as a single later in the year, reaching number forty. The mix of funk and pop on *Hot Space* was akin to the sound Michael Jackson would make successful within a year, however Queen's audience of white rock fans and were unready for such a move. The second side of the album featured a slightly more traditional rock and pop element, dominated by songs written by May and Taylor, including future single *Las Palabras de Amor (The Words of Love)*, a message to their South American fans in the light of the Falklands Conflict.

℧ ℧ ℧

Seemingly coming in at the arse-end of the Two-Tone movement were Bad Manners, formed at North London's Woodbury Down Comprehensive School in 1976, and fronted by larger-than-life bald singer Buster Bloodvessel[269], whose real name was Douglas Trendle. The truth of the matter was the band had been playing ska before some of the Two-Tone bands, with Bloodvessel explaining *"I went to that style because I come from Hackney and used to go to lots of West Indian shows on the weekend. They played music from that culture, Jamaican rhythms, African beats.*

Bloodvessel liked to accentuate his size[270] and reputation onstage, styling himself as having a thirteen-inch inch tongue and being able to consume thirty Big Macs in one sitting. Specialising in party ska, love songs to lager, and a high-energy version of the *Can-Can*, the band attracted a youthful audience with Bloodvessel's vivacity and

---

[268] After the Fire had a top five American hit soon after with a version of Falco's *Der Kommissar*.

[269] Bloodvessel later moved to Margate and opened a hotel called *Fatty Towers*, catering for people with larger appetites.

[270] Bloodvessel's size would become an issue over the years, and with the help of a 2004 gastric band and giving up an alcohol addiction managed to lose twenty stone of weight.

writhing tongue an easily recognisable feature. Bad Manners had been extended the opportunity to release a single on Two-Tone but turned the offer down in favour of signing with Magnet Records.

By May 1982, like many turn-of-the-decade acts, their star was fading and new single, the mid-paced reggae-glorifying *Got No Brains* was their first not to reach the top forty. It looked like things were over for the novelty ska merchants, however they had one more trick up their sleeves over the summer: a version of ska classic *My Boy Lollipop*.

The version most people are conversant with is Millie Small's 1964 worldwide hit, which itself was taken wholesale in arrangement and feel from the 1956 version by a fourteen-year-old Barbie Gray. The original featured the shuffle drums and guitar-on-the-offbeat feel of the future ska movement, and the single was introduced to the Jamaican sound systems by Island Records founder Chris Blackwell. Bad Manners changed the gender to *My Girl Lollipop*[271] and managed to reach number nine in the British charts. It was their last chart hurrah, with album *Forging Ahead* and a final couple of singles for Magnet sinking without trace.

Splitting a couple of years later, the call of the nostalgia market was too much, and a reformed version of the act have continued to tour over the years, with Bloodvessel now the only original member. Where other ska bands in the late 1970's and early 1980's tackled issues such as racism and teenage pregnancy, Bad Manners had no such interest, judging their success by a packed dancefloor with what has been described as "*the dance of the happy drunkard*". They were consistent in their good time approach, refusing to evolve or develop, and it is this which stood them in good stead over the following decades at festivals all over the world.[272]

ʊ ʊ ʊ

When Malcolm McLaren temporarily recruited Boy George to sing backing vocals for Bow Wow Wow, using him as tool to undermine Annabella Lwin's position within the band, he administered the necessary career motivation for the twenty-year-old. With his public profile vastly elevated, and tabloid features on the New Romantic scene often featuring a photograph and epigrammatic quote, an offer of a solo deal from Ashley Goodall at EMI was turned down by a savvy George, fearing he would be manipulated and moulded into something he did not want to be.

George O'Dowd had been born in 1961 in London, the son of a violent Irish Catholic immigrant builder, who grew up flamboyant on a diet of Bolan and Bowie. Not fitting in at school was a rite of passage for people like George, and he was expelled at fifteen "*unblemished by achievement*". Finding his own tribe in the nightlife of late-1970's London, O'Dowd hooked up with other congruous individuals such as Philip Sallon, under who's cattish influence he fell. In the early 1980's every city in the United Kingdom had a campy cross-dressing bitchy alpha-(fe)male, people like Martin

---

[271] The original version, as written by Robert Spencer of doo-wop group The Cadillacs, was called *My GIRL Lollipop*!

[272] I saw them at the Wickerman Festival a few years back… they were brilliant, everything I wanted them to be! And yes, I danced like a drunkard.

Degville[273] in Birmingham and Pete Burns[274] in Liverpool. With Sallon top dog in London, the town was not big enough for the two of them, and George moved in with Degville in Birmingham for a year, having bitched about too many people in the capital. Upon returning to London George shared a squat in Warren Street, frequenting Steve Strange's Bowie nights at Billy's before moving with the club to the Blitz.

The Warren Street squat was home to George, Leigh Bowery, Michael Clark, Stephen Jones, and Jeremy Healy amongst many other itinerants, and without telephones or television they were cut off from world events and trends, instead immersing themselves in a variety of creative activities and a culture of *falling apart*. These individuals were at home in Blitz, sharing the duty of cloakroom attendant between George and his friends Marilyn, Healy and Andy Polaris[275], the four of them seizing every opportunity to steal from the coats, or even the coats themselves. George found other odd jobs window dressing or modelling, waiting for opportunity in the music business under his own terms. One night whilst DJ-ing at Philip Sallon's new club Planets he was approached by a laidback black guy called Mikey Craig, a bass player

who saw a feature in the NME suggesting George was looking for a band following his exit from Bow Wow Wow. Craig, a working-class London boy, who at the age of twenty-one had already fathered two children[276], found where the singer was and approached him[277].

Next to join the band was a South London Jewish drummer called Jon Moss. Where George was flamboyant and androgynous, Moss was laddish and straight, a former boxer who had briefly played drums for The Clash, The Damned, and Adam & the Ants. Moss was a typical wheeler and dealer, the kind of character who if not for music may have ended up making a fortune on the stock exchange during the 1980's, with his love of Italian suits and BMW's, and a proud proclamation of voting Conservative. Picking up session work and touring with Jane Aire and the Belvederes, Moss blew this opportunity when he slept with the singer, losing the job, his girlfriend, and his flat as a result. Following a few months back living with his parents he received a phone call from George, who had acquired his number from Theatre of Hate's Kirk Brandon.

The final member to join was Essex hairdressing guitarist Roy Hay, as the band worked under a string of names: In Praise of Lemmings, The Sex Gang Children, The Caravan Club. Then realising they had a Jew, a cross-dressing Irish homosexual, a black man, and a straight white man in the band, this was changed to the more inclusive Culture Club. The four-piece made their debut in October 1981 at Croc's, Rayleigh[278], where Danny Goodwin from Virgin Publishing approached the band. Demo tapes were recorded for both Virgin and EMI, as the band struggled to identify their sound, and early in 1982 they signed to the former. Moss, having been burned by the music industry previously, set about arranging the business side of the band, insisting all

---

[273] Degville sold his clothes in his YaYa Boutique before becoming singer with Sigue Sigue Sputnik.

[274] Burns could only speak German for the first five years of his life. Children in Liverpool would stand outside his window and shout *"Heil Hitler"* at the house.

[275] Polaris was later the singer in band Animal Nightlife.

[276] One of his later children is professional footballer Paco Craig.

[277] George had previously asked a seventeen-year-old Tracey Emin to play bass in a band he wanted to form.

[278] In front of Depeche Mode's David Gahan.

profits including songwriting were split evenly to help avoid future resentment over earnings.

Culture Club's debut single, *White Boy*, was released on Friday 30th April, and received a significant amount of publicity due to the flamboyancy of George, but only intermittent airplay on Capitol Radio, failing to crack the top 100 and selling only 8,000 copies, mostly in London. George panicked, thinking his chance to become a pop star had gone.

The song was not a reference to race, but was instead about what George called *colourless, uninteresting boys*. Having been surrounded by outlandish people in clubland for the past few years, the singer found himself craving a *normal* partner, though he was actively discouraged by the record company from discussing sexuality in the press for fear of damaging the reputation of the band, instead adopting a policy of denying everything in interviews. The song lacked a killer hook and had the singer occasionally straining at the top of his limited vocal range, over a too prominent electronic drum, and even featured a rap by George which thankfully faded out before it could really get started.

υ υ υ

The Teardrop Explodes had worked their way east across North America, playing a limited number of dates with massive drug-fuelled drives between each one. Frontman Julian Cope, desperate to reach his new girlfriend in New York, could not be less interested in performing and sleepwalked his way through the shows. The band finally arrived in the Big Apple in time for a date at the Ritz on Friday 30th April.

Even with his girlfriend by his side, Cope still did not want to play, and backstage he forced himself to vomit in an attempt to fool the road manager into cancelling the show. It was pointed out that they could not afford to cancel or else they would not be able to raise the price of their tickets home. That sounded fine to Cope, and an hour later he had worked himself into a state where he was covered in sweat and struggling to breathe. Still no-one would indulge him, so Cope started secretly scraping his bare arm against a metal door, opening a wound. This caught the attention of keyboard player Dave Balfe who shouted "*What's all this shit? Don't be so selfish you fuckin' twat*". People ran around, finding and applying bandages, and a couple of road crew were assigned to keep an eye on the singer. To Cope it became obvious he needed to up the ante and developed even quicker breathing. "*I'm going to sit on the stairs*" he announced, which was deemed as acceptable so long as he kept the door open and could be seen. Once at the top of the staircase Cope knew what he had to do and stood on the edge of the top step before falling forward, gathering momentum with each metal platform, before landing in a heap at the bottom.

The plan worked, and the New York date was cancelled one hour after the band were due onstage, however, after a few day's rest the tour continued.

Meanwhile, across town thirty-three-year-old rock journalist Lester Bangs was alone in a messy Manhattan apartment, working freelance for anyone who would pay him. He had just finished the first draft of a book called *Rock Gomorrah*, and delivered it to his publisher on Friday 30th April, before buying a copy of The Human League's *Dare* and returning home suffering from what felt like influenza. Mixing Valium and Darvon, he planned to fall asleep listening to the album and wake in the morning refreshed. Instead, Bangs slipped into a coma from which he never recovered. When his body was discovered the next day *Don't You Want Me* was playing on repeat.

Bang had come from a troubled childhood, with a Jehovah's Witness mother and an ex-jailbird alcoholic absent father, before being sexually abused by a neighbour. Writing a scathing review of the MC5, he sent the literary assassination to *Rolling Stone* magazine with a cover letter stating "*Look, fuckheads, I'm as good as any writer you've got in there!*" and was surprised to be offered more work. Moving to *Creem* magazine in 1973, Bang took great pleasure in slaying sacred cows, with an interview style involving beginning with the most offensive question to un-nerve the subject. His gonzo-style music journalism came across like scattershot be-bop typing, pulling in cultural references wherever he could find them, and he would often invent bands and movies just so he could write a thousand words about them.

ʊ ʊ ʊ

The conflict in the South Atlantic started in earnest on Saturday 1st May with Operation Black Buck One, a meticulously planned bombing raid by a British Vulcan on the airstrip at Port Stanley. What made this operation so extraordinary were the logistics: the Vulcan took off from Ascension Island the day before, flew almost 4,000 miles, released its payload, and then flew back, the equivalent of taking off in London to bomb Chicago. No-one had ever flown such a mission before, and it involved a whole team of support aircraft: Victors flying in waves to refuel the Vulcan, or else to re-fuel the other Victors that were re-fuelling the Vulcan, or even to re-fuel the Victors that were re-fuelling other Victors that were re-fuelling the Vulcan. This was a colossal manoeuvre comprising numerous aircraft just to get the bomber to its target, and then the equivalent quantity to bring it home.

Meanwhile, strategic targets on the Falkland Islands were bombarded from sea, whilst Sea Harriers dropped *cluster bombs* onto Stanley airport. These *cluster bombs* contained 147 smaller bombs, including some which were timed to explode an hour after hitting the ground causing severe damage to any rescue services. The Argentinians protested these were outlawed by the Geneva Convention, however the British countered that the bombs were not in existence when the Convention was signed in 1977 and therefore not covered by legislation.

The British were not in a position to transmit images home from the Task Force whilst the Argentinians were, and the South Americans took full advantage of this, claiming to have shot down numerous aircraft. The British response came from BBC correspondent Brian Hanrahan who famously reported "*I counted them all out… and I counted them all back*", a phrase suggested by his cameraman when they were banned from stating exact numbers.

Elsewhere in the press the journalism was less responsible, with *The Sun* declaring "*A SUN MISSILE FOR GALTIERI'S GAUCHOS*". The story followed: "*The first missile to hit Galtieri's gauchos will come with love from The Sun… The missile will have painted on the side 'Up Yours, Galtieri' and will be signed by Tony Snow – our man aboard HMS Invincible*".

MAY

2nd – 8th May 1982

#1 single: Paul McCartney & Stevie Wonder: Ebony & Ivory

#1 album: Paul McCartney: Tug of War

The four Argentinian agents waiting across the Bay of Gibraltar were impatient to cause some damage to the British, when the frigate *HMS Ariande* sailed into port on Sunday 2nd May. Here, at last, was a target worth pursuing, and so leader Hector Rosales sought permission to attack from head of the Argentinian navy, Admiral Jorge Anaya, which was was again denied.

Earlier in the day the Irish government declared itself neutral in the conflict and voted (along with Italy) to oppose European Economic Community sanctions against Argentina. Meanwhile, President Fernando Belaunde of Peru presented a detailed peace plan to both Argentina and the United Kingdom, and hopes were high that this would resolve the conflict.

Events in the South Atlantic later the same day would render this plan null and void.

The second largest ship in the Argentinian navy, the *General Belgrano*, had formerly been an American Navy vessel called the *SS Phoenix*, and had been located at Pearl Harbour when the Japanese attacked in December 1941 before being hawked to the South Americans in 1951. A great number of ships in the Argentinian navy were British built, including the *Hercules* which had been constructed in Barrow-in-Furness and still had over £3 million outstanding to London.

The *Belgrano* was sailing with other vessels between Tierra del Fuego on the mainland and the Falkland Islands, being exceptionally vigilant to remain outside the 200-mile exclusion zone set down by the British a couple of weeks previously. She was being covertly trailed by the British submarine *Conqueror*, and there was anxiety that by heading north she would be within range of firing Exocet missiles, potentially causing severe harm to Task Force vessels. With mounting disquiet, the navy realised if the small Argentinian fleet split up then it would be infeasible to follow them, and so authorization was sought from headquarters, and then Downing Street, to engage. When granted *Conqueror* fired three torpedoes, two of which hit the *Belgrano*, causing her to explode. The decision to abandon ship was made within thirty minutes, and fifteen minutes later she sank, taking 368 with her.

When the *General Belgrano* was first hit there were pronounced cheers amongst the men on board *Conqueror*, however this transformed into an intense stillness when it became apparent the ship would sink and numerous lives would be lost. These were merely boys, just like the British sailors, and the consequences of war, especially the thin line between life and death, started to hit home.

Michael Nicholson of ITN on board the *HMS Olemeda* overheard a conversation which confirmed the *HMS Conqueror* had been the submarine responsible and broadcast this information back to London, incensing the Ministry of Defence who made it their business never to reveal the whereabouts of submarines, and the Navy made it their job not to speak to Nicholson again.

At the offices of *The Sun* newspaper in London the news broke and in response one of the staff, Wendy Henry, exclaimed "*GOTCHA!*" This was seized upon by editor Kelvin MacKenzie and used on the front page becoming the most infamous headline in the newspaper's history. As additional news came in that there may be substantial loss of life, MacKenzie began to realise the headline might be incongruous and hurried to substitute it for the second edition. *The Sun's* owner Rupert Murdoch arrived in the room at this point and expressed there was no need to change the headline, however MacKenzie persuaded him to run with *"Did 1,200 Argies Die?"* instead. This conciliation was uncommon for *The Sun*, which had decided to follow a path of what Roy Greenslade called *"cynical, jingoistic, bloodthirsty war coverage"*. Previous Falkland headlines had included *"Stick it up your Junta"* and *"Britain 6 Argentina 0"*, and when *Private Eye* did a spoof *Sun* headline of *"Kill an Argie and win a Metro"* MacKenzie was heard to ask *"Why didn't we think of that?"* From the 11th May, *The Sun* placed a banner on their front page proclaiming *"THE PAPER THAT SUPPORTS OUR BOYS"*.

The stance of the BBC was more measured, as they were criticised for saying *"British troops"* rather than *"our troops"* in news bulletins, even though this had been the agreed position between the broadcaster and the Ministry of Defence since the Second World War. That night, on BBC's *Newsnight* programme Peter Snow stated *"There is a stage in the coverage of any conflict when you can begin to discern the level of accuracy of the claims and counter-claims on either side. Tonight... we cannot demonstrate that the British have lied to us so far, but the Argentinians clearly have"*. Such a balanced approach brought howls of protest in Parliament the following day, with Conservative MP John Page claiming the line was an act of treason.

The main controversy, however, was the sinking of a ship outside the exclusion zone one which appeared to be sailing away from the area, the equivalent of being shot in the back. The Argentinians saw this as a naked act of war and correctly claimed authorization had been given from the very top: Margaret Thatcher. However, the Argentinians also maintained the action was a legitimate but regrettable act under the circumstances. A year later, Thatcher was challenged by teacher Diana Gould on this issue during a live episode of BBC television programme *Nationwide*. After a fiery altercation, Thatcher's husband Denis harangued the producer in the green room, furious his wife had been *"stitched up by bloody BBC poofs and Trots"*. The Prime Minister herself maintained the sinking had been for *"strictly military not political reasons"*, however it was a charge which would follow her through the rest of her leadership.

In the immediate aftermath of the sinking, the Argentinian navy returned to port and never put out to sea again during the conflict.

ʊ ʊ ʊ

If ever there was a band perfect for 1982 it should have been Blondie. Over the previous five years they had attained global success with a run of albums and singles convoking the vitality of punk with the summer sound, feel, and melodies of 1960's pop. They looked iconic, were musically exhilarating, and had an alluring and photogenic front-person; everything that was treasured in 1982, and yet...

Blondie were formed by former folk singer and bunny-girl Debbie Harry[279] and her boyfriend Chris Stein in 1974 New York City. The two were playing together in an act called The Stilettoes when Stein became convinced of the star potential of Harry, causing them to strike out and form a fresh act with a dazzling cool-kid drummer from New Jersey called Clem Burke and bass player Gary Valentine. The four-piece lived in poverty and played frequently at CBGB's in the East Village, alongside other new acts Talking Heads, The Ramones, Patti Smith, and Television, however they were very much viewed as the runts of the litter, particularly by the other musicians. Blondie

---

[279] Harry had been adopted as a baby, and fantasized she was the unwanted child of a pre-fame Marilyn Monroe.

enlisted keyboard player Jimmy Destri[280] in 1975 and signed to Private Stock Records with whom they released their debut single. Coming to appreciate the limitations the record company, the band bought themselves out of the contract and signed to Chrysalis instead, whilst Valentine was replaced by British bass player Nigel Harrison and second guitarist Frank Infante recruited. With Harry, Stein, Destri, Infante, and Harrison all able to write memorable pop songs which sounded amazing on radio, the band had no shortage of material, and conquered the world with multiple chart-topping hit singles such as *Sunday Girl*, *Heart of Glass*, *Atomic*, *Dreaming*, and *Call Me*, along with some judiciously chosen cover versions such as *Denis* and *The Tide Is High*.

No matter how much success they gained worldwide, at heart Blondie remained a New York band with all the *street-smarts* that advocated. Returning to the *Big Apple* at every opportunity, the band were able to submerge themselves in new musical movements as they happened, such as disco and rap, and integrate them effortlessly into their sound. This restless nature and disposition to experiment allowed Blondie to remain germane and slightly ahead of the curve, however by the end of 1981 they were a growing weary of each other as people. Harry spent the year recording a solo album, produced by Nile Rodgers and Bernard Edwards of Chic, during which she tried her best to disengage herself from the image of *Blondie*, dying her hair brown and calling herself Deborah instead of Debbie. Despite the quality being high and a significant number of Harry / Stein written tracks, the album failed to reach the altitudes Blondie had become accustomed used to.

When the band re-united to record a new album in late 1981 they were full of misgivings. Following the comparative chart failure of Harry's solo album, success no longer seemed to be a given, and having parted company with their manager were pondering where all the money from their millions of sales had gone. Stein appeared too thin and was suffering from ill health, Destri had all the indicators of a severe drug problem, Infante was absent from the sessions, as he had been during the recording of the previous album, and the band seemed to fight each other all the time. When

ISLAND OF LOST SOULS

Infante found recording had commenced without him he issued a legal writ, which was settled when he was permitted to enter the studio without the band to re-record some guitar parts. Producer Mike Chapman was brought into the Hit Factory in New York but struggled to keep the band motivated as there was little enthusiasm to continue fulfilling contractual obligations, with Harry admitting she was in "*a weird frame of mind*".

Blondie had always pushed their own boundaries, experimenting with punk, new wave, girl-group ballads, rock, reggae, and rap, and were keen to continue exploring new possibilities, most noticeable on the first single from the album, *Island of Lost Souls*. Written by Stein and Harry with a calypso flavor, the song was driven by horns and steel drums, lacking the guitars which had become an essential part of the Blondie sound. Despite this, it was an exceptionally appealing melody even if the lyrics appeared trite and forced, with lines such as "*Hey buccaneer won't you help me put my truck in gear*". What the song did betray, however, was a sense of wanting to escape; "*You want to get away, you've had it, man*", with the promise of "*no luxuries, no amenities to dull your senses*", encapsulating a band burnt out and yearning for some sort of liberty.

Despite the commercial value of the song, along with a video shot in the Scilly Isles during which they had to fly in some palm trees and Infante had been instructed by his

---

[280] Destri's uncle played in 1960's twist-kings Joey Dee and the Starliters, alongside Joe Pesci.

lawyer "*Don't talk to anyone, don't hit anyone*", the song was their least successful single in years, failing to reach the top ten in the United Kingdom.

The ensuing album was called *The Hunter*, and when released later in the month was not sympathetically received. Adrian Thrills wrote in the Melody Maker "*At a time when the best new British pop is pushing forward at an invigorating post-punk pace, Blondie could hardly sound any safer*". Their continued experimentation with genres saw a bit of Latin, calypso, new wave, pop, soul, and funk all appear on the album, assisted by some junkie Puerto Rican horn players. However, the songs just did not seem to gel, and Blondie were obviously fatigued and washed-up. The cover featured all six members of the band, including Infante who had not played a note on the final mix of the album. Harry herself, wore a high-haired ludicrous-looking blonde wig which might have made more sense if the whole concept of the cover had been realized: her face morphing with that of a lion.

The whole album was constructed around a loose concept, that of being hunted and captured, comparing Manhattan to Babylon, and even contained a redundant version of Smokey Robinson's *The Hunter Gets Captured by the Game*. The album also included a song called *For Your Eyes Only*, which had been earmarked for the latest James Bond movie, however the producers favored a Bill Conti written track with the same title, and when Blondie refused it was given instead to Sheena Easton.

ʊ ʊ ʊ

After being denied permission to bomb *HMS Ariande* the previous day, the Argentinian saboteurs in Spain knew the sinking of the *General Belgrano* would change everything. On Monday 3rd May they once again requested permission, which was given immediately. Maximo Nicoletti made a request that if they were captured, they could claim to be officially working for the Argentinians and thus be considered by the Geneva Convention as prisoners of war. This was denied, as final preparations were undertaken throughout the day.

Sleeping late the following day Hector Rosales and Antonio Latorre visited their car rental agency in the south of Spain to extend their agreement, providing them with a vehicle in which to travel north, through the south of France into Italy with the intention of flying back to Argentina following the blowing up of *HMS Ariande*. The owner of the car rental agency had become suspicious of their behaviour when he noticed they only ever paid in cash, had several sets of keys for rental vehicles, and never turned up when they said they would. The police asked him to call them when the men next appeared and to attempt to stall them, which he did on the Tuesday morning. The police arrived and arrested the two Argentinians, believing them to be part of a common criminal gang, before visiting their hotel and apprehending their still sleeping colleagues. Maximo Nicoletti caved under questioning immediately, announcing himself as an agent of the Argentinian government.

Within an hour the Spanish Minister of Interior Juan Jose Roson ordered the local police to keep the arrests quiet, and for the four to be brought to Madrid. On the way there, Nicoletti was allowed to carry their explosives, and the entire party stopped off at a roadside restaurant so he could buy the police lunch, and a shop to purchase fresh clothes. The four were then flown to the Canary Islands by the Spanish government without interrogation or charge, and from there returned to Argentina.

Damage to a British vessel may have been avoided in Spain, however that was about to change in the South Atlantic when two Argentinian Super Etendards armed with Exocet missiles took off from the mainland following information regarding the location of British ships. Engaged in searching for submarines, an attack from the sky took *HMS Sheffield* by surprise. The adjacent *HMS Glasgow* spotted the incoming airplanes and communicated a warning to all ships, however *Sheffield* assessed this as a false alarm. Meanwhile, thirty miles away the Exocets were launched, making their way across the surface of the sea, and were only spotted five seconds before hitting the side of the vessel.

HMS Sheffield had a hole torn in the hull and the subsequent explosion from the missile set fire to the insides of the destroyer. As some of the crew fought the fire, most assembled on deck to await rescue, where they broke into a chorus of Monty Python's *Always Look on the Bright Side of Life*.

In total, twenty of the crew were killed in the explosion, with a further twenty-four seriously injured. As the *Sheffield* was towed out of the Exclusion Zone it took on water through the rupture in the side and sank six days later.

Chaotic messages were broadcast back to London and rumours abounded in the corridors of power. When, at last, the government announced the news it was during the BBC Nine O'Clock bulletin and was broadcast live with Ministry of Defence spokesman Ian McDonald reading from a prepared statement. This had the effect of announcing the loss to the Navy, Members of Parliament, the public, and most importantly the wives and families of the men on board *HMS Sheffield* simultaneously. The loss of the ship and life had the effect of waking the public in Britain to the unavoidable result of war, however polls showed that support for the troops remained exceptionally high.

ʊ ʊ ʊ

After a couple of months it was becoming apparent that Killing Joke frontman Jaz Coleman and guitarist Geordie Walker were not coming back from Iceland, so drummer Paul Ferguson was persuaded to follow them. This was after weeks of Ferguson and bass player Martin "Youth" Glover bitching about Coleman, and declaring they had the rights to continue with the band name, saying of the split *"There was a shock, but now it's 'so what? Two bastards fucked off!'"* Coleman, however, had the charisma of Charles Manson, the type who could start a cult and convince everyone to drink the kool-aid, and his incessant badgering paid off. Youth, remained too bitter about the selfishness of the singer and remained in Britain, starting his own band called Brilliant.[281]

When first moving to Iceland Coleman and Walker had formed a band called Niceland, alongside local musicians from the new wave act Þeyr, who were described by Youth as being something of a Killing Joke fan club and therefore like putty in the singer's

---

[281] Brilliant also featured Jim Cauty, and were managed by ex-Teardrop Explodes member Dave Balfe, whilst being represented at their record company by ex-Teardrop Explodes / Echo & The Bunnymen manager Bill Drummond. Perversely enough, their only album was produced by Stock Aitken & Waterman, before Cauty and Drummond formed The KLF and Balfe started Food Records. Youth himself retreated to the studio where he found success with his own act Blue Pearl and their hit *Naked in the Rain*, before becoming the producer of hundreds of acts, including The Verve, U2, Crowded House, James, The Charlatans, and Erasure.

hands. By the end of May however, even Þeyr had become sick of Coleman's paranoid autocratic manner and refused to work with him anymore.

The previously recorded album *Revelations* was released in May and climbed to number twelve in the United Kingdom. The album had been recorded in Cologne with producer Conny Plank[282], though Killing Joke claimed he was no more than an engineer, stating "*If a band can't get the sound they want themselves they might as well give up*".

Revelations was Killing Joke at their most blistering, with tribal drums and chorused guitar in the vanguard. All the features of goth rock were in evidence on the album, which had been strongly influenced by Coleman's paranoid delusions and dabbling in the occult, however poor production and the increasingly maniacal delirium of the singer pulled the punch of how the band sounded live. It was an album of two halves, with the second considerably poorer. Coleman allowed his classical training to take over, explaining how on the album they were "*experimenting with fourths, because in conventional music you're never allowed to use intervals of fourths*". For Ferguson, the album was all about his drums, explaining "*This is something far older* [than rock and roll] *because drums were the basis of every civilisation*".

The music on the album was frenetic and rarely changed from a doom-riddled minor key, with even Coleman admitting "*It terrifies me to think music can be taken to that extreme*". If the end of the world was indeed coming, it now had a soundtrack.

ʊ ʊ ʊ

Depeche Mode broke from their mini-world tour to record another single, one which again caught them amid their transformation from Vince Clarke's perfect pop to Martin Gore's caliginous industrial vision. *The Meaning of Love* was, like predecessor *See You*, an inconsequential track which at least tried to head in the direction of a dancefloor. There was a danger of the band spinning into Christian rock territory within the quotidian lyrics and the cringeworthy line "*Tell me the answer, my Lord high above, tell me the meaning, the meaning of love*". Given Gore's past involvement with the church it seems feasible he was still under the influence of the Almighty, however there was also a whisper of his future goth-lite direction in the line "*Love seems something like wanting a scar*", which appeared an amputated finger amid a handful of banalities.

The cover of the single was designed by Moritz Reichelt of Dusseldorf band Der Plan, which he later described as "*a failure in psychedelic, because I had been on acid while painting it*". Aided by another goofy Julian Temple video the single climbed to number twelve in the charts, however the band were concerned that the recent massive success of Yazoo meant their time had already come and gone. Torn between craving success which would come with appearances of kids' television shows such as *Multi-Coloured Swap Shop* and *Tiswas*, and credibility, the band suffered a crisis of confidence. In the space of six months they had gone from electronic pioneers to laughable pop band, and were lampooned by Attila the Stockbroker's poem *Nigel*

---

[282] Plank started out as the soundman for Merlene Dietrich.

Wants to go and see Depeche Mode, which described them as playing "*nice bland unchallenging pop music*"[283].

They decided to hire independent public relations to combat their growing reputation as fluff. Chris Carr already looked after The Cure, Siouxsie & the Banshees, and The Birthday Party, and found the band "*somewhere between precious and naïve*" when he first met them but set to work over the next decade turning their reputation around.

ʊ ʊ ʊ

Eighteen-year-old Mancunian John Maher, the son of Irish immigrants, was already renowned as a ridiculously gifted guitarist in his home city. The *boy wonder* even made a name for himself in London when on a visit had become good friends with Matt Johnson, and the two promised to form a band called The The. No-one locally played guitar like John, however the problem was he did not have a band. Having heard Echo & the Bunnymen were in danger of splitting, Maher set his heart on ensnaring singer Ian McCulloch, lofty ambitions for an unknown teenager, but when the Liverpudlians announced gigs and a new single, Maher turned his attention elsewhere.

Having just read a book on Jerry Leiber and Michael Stoller, the duo behind many rock and roll hits in the late 1950's and early 1960's, John had become obsessed with forming his own song-writing duo, but needed a lyricist. A couple of friends, including future Theatre of Hate and Cult guitarist Billy Duffy, mentioned a local oddball called Steven Patrick Morrissey who had written a couple of reviews for the music press, but warned that he needed to be approached with prudence.

John, however, was determined, and on Wednesday 5th May caught the number 263 bus to 384 Kings Road, where Morrissey lived with his mother, and knocked on the door. His sister answered and shouted up to her brother. After what seemed an age, the twenty-two-year-old came downstairs, and John came straight out with the question "*Do you want to form a band?*"

Morrissey was waiting for fate to arrive and had even considered suicide as a career option in recent weeks. This unexpected visitor felt like destiny, and he wasted no time inviting the youth on the doorstep in.

After John chose an obscure Marvelettes B-side from Steven's collection to put on the turntable, they started writing songs together. Maher's fluid fretwork flowing around Morrissey's original lyrics, it was noted he did not seem to be able to sing but there was something in the way the words were delivered which was mesmerising.

ʊ ʊ ʊ

Following their chart debut with *Party Fears Two* in February, The Associates got down to the business of recording a new album with a down-payment on an indefinite studio booking allowing them the time to take experimentation to the extreme. Filling the studio with helium balloons, submerging drums in swimming pools, urinating into acoustic guitars, and shaking sheets of thin metal were just some of the artifices the duo tried in their exploration of innovative sound. Who knows how many of these techniques made it onto the final mix of the album, but evidence could be heard on tracks such as *Bap de la Bap* where all the toms

---

[283] Depeche Mode may have enjoyed some *schadenfreude* when in the same month Attila the Stockbroker had his electric mandolin smashed over his head by a fascist skinhead during a gig in North London.

on the drums were exchanged for various sizes of snare drum, providing an explosive sound. Despite the massive sound of the album, the recording costs were only £33,000, a deliberately small amount of money at the time for an album due to the band's licensing deal with Warners meaning they had to provide the recording costs themselves. The studio had a catalogue of potential instruments which the band utilised, as Rankine explained *"We'd look up lists of instruments and go 'what the hell is a jangle piano?' The next day this piano would suddenly arrive with all these little metal bits"*. At one-point producer Mike Hedges was persuaded to buy five-foot industrial canister of helium, which led to a false story in the press that MacKenzie could only reach the high notes with the aid of the gas.

Sulk, as the album was titled, sounded wholly unrestrained and frenetic with the band deciding to start with a climax and then build from there, the result of two obsessives over-working their craft. Upon closer scrutiny large fragments of the recording and performance were exceptionally loose, such as the drums on introductory instrumental track *Arrogance Gave Him Up*. From there the album became more concentrated on *No*, an ominous ballad straight out of a cold war spy movie, what Simon Reynolds described as *"a castle wreathed in mist"* but with lyrics which ominously betrayed desperation and suicidal thoughts (*"Shaved and cut myself again / should have let it slip down further"*). During the recording of the song Mackenzie blew the diaphragm of the microphone with the power of his singing, forcing Hedges to find a replacement. The producer asked Mackenzie to take a step back to avoid the same happening again, and when he refused the singer was informed he would have to pay for any further damage. Mackenzie asked if there were any cheaper microphones and asked to *"Put that one up – I'll save myself fifty quid"*.

By the fourth song a feeling of desolation and hopelessness had fully set in, with a half-disco cover of the standard *Gloomy Sunday*, or as it is also known: *"The Hungarian Suicide Song"*, written in 1932 then banned during wartime due to the lyrics. An urban legend grew up around the song, with the rumour that numerous individuals had committed suicide whilst listening to it, and indeed the actual songwriter took his own life in 1968. That did not stop a whole host of classic artists performing it over the years, including Billie Holliday, Sarah Vaughan, Ray Charles, and even Elvis Costello the previous year[284].

Nude Spoons had been influenced by an acid trip MacKenzie undertook when he was fifteen in which the spoons and forks in the drawer were at war with each other, whilst *Skipping* was full of flamenco guitars and elastic bass lines, the closest the band came to capturing the sound in their heads, with Mackenzie saying they had *"got the essence of what we were trying to do"*.

Alan Rankine became obsessed with guaranteeing his guitar did not repeat any of the hoary old rock and blues clichés, being extremely aware that MacKenzie sounded epic as a solo voice without any backing vocals, whilst ensuring the music could match this. New keyboard player Martha Ladly was roped in for some additional vocals, and MacKenzie insisted they record their contributions together at the same time.

The Associates were as contrary as ever, with the first side of the album featuring their most funereal material whilst saving the most marketable songs for the end, with a triple-whammy of *Party Fears Two*, *Club Country*, and an instrumental *nothinginsomethingparticular*. The release of *Club Country* at the beginning of May and its ensuing hike up the charts helped the album reach the top ten, hanging around in the charts for twenty weeks with a cover featuring a brightly coloured gel-lit

---

[284] Later, Björk was to perform a version at a memorial concert for Alexander McQueen who had also taken his own life.

photograph by Peter Ashworth taken in the fern and yukka populated conservatory of a Surrey mansion.

The album was an instant hit in the music press with Paul Morley at the New Musical Express proclaiming "*if rock music is a slow tortoise, the Associates are an elusive butterfly*" and Sounds describing the sound as "*a kitchen sink album with gold, enamelled taps*".

Club Country itself reached number thirteen and was certainly one of the oddest songs lyrically to grace the British charts. The early demo version showed the arrangement, lyrics and vocals already in place however the overall sound was profusely denser than the final version, with an overwhelming guitar resulting in a heavy-handed goth song. On the finished album the guitars had the distortion removed and a chorus effect applied, and were much further back in the mix, sounding more like disco than post-

punk. The bass once again took a lead role in the track, its effectiveness emphasised by the uncomplicated drums. As always, the star of the song was MacKenzie's voice, more measured during the verse, and then fully unbridled through the chorus, sounding, as one critic put it, like "*a trannie in a wind-tunnel*".

Deciphering the lyrics was a bit of problem, with several people putting forward suggestions, however who really knows what was meant by couplets such as "*A drive from nowhere leaves you in the cold / refrigeration keeps you young I'm told*". In the end, the early 1980's was the perfect time for artists to get away with ostentatious and enigmatic lyrics, and so it was with The Associates: no-one seemed to question what they hell they were singing about. In the end it did not matter, the public liked the mystery and helped push the song to the edge of the top ten, and The Associates to the precipice of superstardom. The truth of the matter was that the song was MacKenzie's comment on the New Romantic movement which shared his love of Bowie, however he "*felt slightly embarrassed because in one sense he felt at home there, because he wasn't surrounded by a bunch of Dundee neds and he didn't feel threatened… but at the same time he could see the complete falsehood of it*". From a Dundee scrap merchant family, MacKenzie never felt deserving of success, expressing a fear within the song that "*If we stick around we're sure to be looked down upon.*"

The band managed another couple of appearances on *Top of the Pops* with the single, the second of which saw them order two chocolate guitars from Harrods at a cost of £300 each, one of which Rankine broke and started feeding to the audience half-way through the performance. The band were continuing to live life excessively, deciding at one point to buy a *company car* rather than run up taxi bills. A 1963 Convertible Mercedes and a funereal Ford Dorchester were purchased with a business loan from the bank, the latter of which turned out to be too large to find parking for, running up thousands of pounds in parking tickets. Left out of this spending spree was drummer John Murphy, who continued to live in a squat, adrift from the rest of the band. When he was overheard criticising the band to a friend in Australia on the studio telephone Murphy was sacked, to be replaced by Steve Goulding.

The band had spent their first year's advance from Warners in twelve weeks and were forced from their life of luxury at the Holiday Inn. Blagging more money from the record company, they rented a flat in Kensington[285]. The thinking behind the excessive spending, if there was any, was to force Warners to spend so much on the act they would have no choice but to heavily promote them to earn the money back. When the

---

[285] Outbidding Yul Byrnner for the three-month let.

second lot of money ran out Mackenzie and Rankine were forced to move back to their parents' homes in Dundee and Linlithgow respectively, where the singer would help his father in the van with his furniture collecting round. In Dundee, Mackenzie found himself the target of jealous locals who saw the *pop star* as an easy and justifiable target. Mackenzie was also becoming restless with the idea of being a *pop star*, and one night at an art school disco in Dundee he confided in an old friend: "*You wouldn't believe the things that people are saying I could do, but I'm not going to do it, I'm just going to throw it all away*".

℧ ℧ ℧

On the surface everything at Banco Ambrosiano in Italy seemed to be going swimmingly, with shares in the bank due to be floated on the Italian stock market in early May. As trading began, head of the bank Roberto Calvi stood in the middle of the room watching the price of the shares plummet from 50,000 lire to 40,000 by the end of the day, a loss of 20% from the value of the bank. This was the first outward sign of the trouble Calvi had managed to get Ambrosiano into, with multiple foreign overseas shell companies and an investigation by the Bank of Italy. The fronting companies set up overseas in places like Panama and the Bahamas, as well as Lichtenstein and Luxembourg, were losing investment from foreign banks, however Calvi circumnavigated this by syphoning money illegally out of Italy through *back-to-back* loans. These involved borrowing money on international markets, then depositing it in a compliant but legal foreign bank, who would then lend the same amount to Banco Ambrosiano in South America, with a slightly increased interest rate to ensure a profit. With the Vatican, the Freemasons *and* the Italian mafia all with major interests in the bank, Calvi was becoming paranoid and had recently started carrying a pistol in his briefcase.

9th – 15th May 1982

#1 single: Nicole: A Little Peace
#1 album: Paul McCartney: Tug of War

Charlene D'Angelo was an American who had married Jeff Oliver, a teacher from England, before moving to his home country, and at the start of 1982 was happily in love and working in a sweet shop in Ilford, when her mother phoned from America at two in the morning. Her mother could never get the hang of the time difference, and from California informed her that "*Someone's trying to find you from Motown*".

D'Angelo suddenly found herself thinking back to the 1970's when she had signed to the label, only the second white woman to sign. The reticent Californian found herself hanging out with the likes of Diana Ross and Stevie Wonder, whilst releasing three albums of soulful folk on offshoot Prodigal Records, all of which disappeared without trace.

The reason for Motown getting in touch was a track sequestered on her debut album entitled *I've Never Been to Me*. D'Angelo could impersonate many of the Motown stars and would often provide the vocals on demonstration versions of songs they would later have hits with.[286] *I've Never Been to Me* felt like the first song where she had employed her own voice, but when released as a single it barely managed to scrape

---

[286] For example, she recorded the original version of *One Day in Your Life*, which Michael Jackson took wholesale and recorded his vocals on top of.

into the Billboard top 100. When her career stalled D'Angelo turned to the church, where she met her husband and settled down to a life as a footnote in the Motown story.

Then in early 1982 Scott Shannon, a local DJ in Tampa, Florida, discovered the song and started playing it on heavy rotation. Over the space of a couple of months the song spread throughout the Southern States and then nationwide, picking up airplay whenever DJs could find a copy of the long-deleted album. Shannon contacted Jay

Lasker at Motown and persuaded him to release one thousand copies of the single in Tampa. It sold out within a day, and the Motown machine went into overdrive trying to find their absent singer.

When Lasker called D'Angelo in Ilford later that day, he told her the single had been released nationwide and instructed her to catch the next Concorde to New York where she was due to appear on television show *Good Morning, America.*

D'Angelo later stated she *"got a lot of flack from women's lib, saying 'How dare you say you need a man?', 'How dare you say you need a child?'"*, however the message of the track was rooted in a deeply conservative stance. Told from the point of view of a woman looking back on her life with great regret, listing the experiences she has had, but ultimately concluding she has been lying to herself all the way through. There was a hint at an abortion in the final verse with *"I've been to cryin' for unborn children that might have made me complete"*, however the conformist viewpoint, guilt, and finger-pointing came out in the next line of *"I spent my life exploring the subtle whoring that cost too much to be free"*. The use of behaviour-shaming language seems alarming to modern sensibilities but given D'Angelo's insistence she be allowed to record a Christian album as part of her contract, it is hardly surprising. Despite her beliefs, later in the year D'Angelo released a duet with old friend Stevie Wonder called *Used to Be*, which was banned in Britain due to the line *"Have another Chivas Regal, you're twelve years old and sex is legal"*. Ignoring advice by old friends, D'Angelo signed a new contract with Motown which was very much in the favour of the record company. Despite *I've Never Been to Me* becoming a massive worldwide hit, reaching the top of the British charts in June 1982, Charlene never had another hit single, and only ever received around $13,000 from the success.

℧ ℧ ℧

Altered Images second album *Pinky Blue* was released only eight months after their debut, and the reviews made it clear that it had perhaps been a bit too rushed, a surge of inconsequential pop, lacking the intellectual deliberateness of other contemporary chart acts, and allowing too much of free reign on singer Clare Grogan's grating vocals, something which increasingly annoyed people the more they heard. The title track, which peaked at a disappointing number thirty-five when released as a single a few weeks later, was a case in point, with the voice reaching new degrees of breathlessness and tiny-

foot stomping, not helped by some of the most asinine lyrics this side of The Shadows. The rest of the album were carbon copies, seemingly played too fast for Grogan to fit any meaning, as each song tended to blend into the next.

The inclusion of a saccharine version of Neil Diamond's *Song Sung Blue* was a major misstep, a song the band had played live for a while, which may have been ironically funny and cute at early club dates in Glasgow, but on record sounded foolhardy, and exposed the inadequacies. Backing vocals were provided by producer Martin Rushent and John Peel, who was still a champion of the act despite the accusations of tweeness levelled at them. Grogan would later admit *"We did over-do the cheesy, everything's great, smiley happy people thing. I can see why the critics gave us a hard time"*.

Even with the poor reviews, the album managed to reach number twelve in the charts, but with the band pushed in a direction they did not want, drummer Michael Anderson and guitarist Jim McKinven quit. The band had one more song in 1982, the inclusion on the soundtrack album for the low-budget film *Party Party*, for which they recorded a restrained version of Del Shannon's *Little Town Flirt*.[287]

The two departing members were replaced by multi-instrumentalist Steve Lironi, and Altered Images recorded the bulk of their next album by the end of the year with producer Mike Chapman providing a more mature sound, however by the end of 1983 the band had split.

℧ ℧ ℧

Having been born and raised in the Bronx, New York during the 1950's and 1960's, Thomas Browder was exposed to a melting pot of music, instinctively ingurgitating rock and roll, salsa, jazz, big band, disco, Latin American, and Caribbean influences. After starting a career as an English teacher his hobby, Dr Buzzard's Original Savannah Band, found themselves with some success in New York, attracting the attention of RCA Records. Browder began using his middle names, August Darnell, and played bass with his half-brother Stony  Browder Jnr on guitar, Cory Daye on vocals, Mickey Sevilla on drums and Andy Hernandez on percussion. Appearing like a Miami showband of Cuban exiles from the 1940's the act scored an American hit with the irresistible Latin rhythms of *Cherchez La Femme*. Everything Darnell would utilize in his future career was already in place, from the cross-cultural musical mix, to the 1940's zoot suits and sense of theatre, but what he also brought to the party was a pride in his mixed-race heritage. Darnell claimed his brother *"had this bizarre idea that we Mulattos had been in the closet for too long… the race that was ashamed to speak its name"*, and the way to represent their mixed heritage was to infuse the patrimony of music as well in what would later be called *multiculturalism*[288]. Dr Buzzard's Original Savannah Band became the house act at Studio 54, mixing disco and big band music, delivering the good times to the exclusive coterie. Three albums brought diminishing returns as Stony became

---

[287] The soundtrack album was a curiosity, with Bad Manners covering *Yakety Yak*, Sting singing *Tutti Frutti* and Chas & Dave's version of *Auld Lang Syne*.

[288] It may have seemed a novel idea to the band however the character of the *tragic mulatto* was one which had appeared throughout American literature, the person who is not at home in either black or white culture and is therefore assumed to be sad or even suicidal. Those of mixed-race had been exploited throughout the past couple of hundred years, most noticeably at Quadroon Balls, where wealthy white men could pay to dance (and more) with quarter-black woman who could pass as white, thus making them seem more *human*. In popular culture, a Quadroon was almost always unmasked and loses everything by the end of the novel.

embroiled in drugs and August started to produce other acts, getting unexpectedly involved with the New York No-Wave movement in the process.

In 1980 he changed his name to Kid Creole, after the Elvis Presley movie, and formed The Coconuts with his Swiss wife, Adriana Kaegi, and former Savannah Band member Hernandez, who was renamed Coati Mundi[289]. Bringing on board legendary Jamaican drummer Winston Grennan[290] and a transitional assortment of musicians and Coconuts (the female backing singers), the act signed to Ze Records, a New York label formed by Michael Zilkha[291] and Michel Esteban[292]. Ze Records specialized in what it dubbed *mutant disco* and captured the sound of New York at the turn of the decade. Kid Creole & the Coconuts' first album *Off the Coast of Me* was critically acclaimed whilst the second one *Fresh Fruit in Foreign Places* boosted the vision into technicolour, being a concept album taking the act on an odyssey to numerous Caribbean islands. At the same time, Coati Mundi enjoyed a British top forty hit with *Me No Pop I*, whilst remaining a member of Kid Creole & the Coconuts.

Darnell decided his next release should be a solo album and began writing and recording at the end of 1981 for what he claimed would be *Wise Guy*. Everything changed in early 1982 when Ze Records hit some financial trouble and convinced Darnell to make his new release under the Kid Creole umbrella. Many of the tracks

had already been recorded and they were "*much more steeped in R&B than a Kid Creole record should be*" according to Darnell.

Ceding to record company demands, Darnell decided to carry on the concept of the first two albums, with the band this time shipwrecked on the imaginary island of B'dilly Bay, forced to survive for three weeks amongst the native prostitutes, thieves, and pimps.

The opening track set up the narrative with the story of a girl trying to find who her father was. Darnell played the part of the prime suspect, and whilst conceding to knowing her mother, denied being the father. *Annie, I'm Not Your Daddy* started with the party already under way, a pounding funky soca beat and memorable trombone riff. Through an ascending vocal line the narrator explained he knew the girl's mother, before explaining "*I'm telling it to you straight so you don't have to hear it in a other way*". The message was then hammered home in a Cuban calypso chorus with a repeated "*Oh Annie, I'm not your daddy*". A repeated trombone riff led to a second verse before mirroring the second chorus vocal pay-off: "*You see, if I was in your blood then you wouldn't be so ugly*".

I'm a Wonderful Thing, Baby picked up on this arrogant self-confidence, sung from the viewpoint of an egocentric lover, bearing many of the hallmarks of what rap would become: "*Take a look at me, see I couldn't look no better, girl I'm at my peak and that's a fact*". Initially written by keyboard player Peter Schott and called *It's a Wonderful Thing* until Darnell saw the storytelling opportunities in personalizing the subject. The track had an unfluctuating hypnotic beat throughout, even when Darnell started reading out his address book, starting with a list of girls beginning with the letter "*A*",

---

[289] Coati Mundi: "I have never let the lack of talent stop me from doing anything"

[290] Grennan invented the *one-drop* rhythm and played with all the Jamaican greats: Toots & the Maytals, Desmond Dekker, Bob Marley & the Wailers, Jimmy Cliff.

[291] Zilkha was the son of Selim Zilkha, the founder of Mothercare.

[292] Esteban promoted the first ever punk concerts in France before moving to New York. In 1982 he was the partner of Anna Wintour.

Imitation, close to straight-forward R&B, was Darnell's reply to constantly being told that British bands were ripping-off his previous two albums. *"Some people live off other people's dreams, reciting lines in other people's scenes"* he sang, concluding that *"Imitation, it's not for me"*. The next track *I'm Corrupt* proved to be a source of

contention on the album. Coati Mundi was already aggrieved the release was going to be under the name of Kid Creole & the Coconuts, having had little to do with the writing and recording, and a compromise was reached whereby he would have three tracks featured on the album, however in the end only an almost instrumental version of his composition *I'm Corrupt* was included.

Loving You Made a Fool Out of Me kept the pop funk flowing, with a duet between Creole and his wife, each complaining the other did not live up their promises before marriage. Creole complained he had expected her to be faithful, whilst Kaegi complained about not being treated well enough, in a piece designed to exploit the theatrical potential of the lyrics.

The highlight of the album, *Stool Pigeon*, was originally titled *Jive Talkin'* until Darnell read an article about a mafia member turned informant. After an elongated introduction, a groovy horn riff took us to the first verse, with Darnell embracing the new

format of rap, in the process turning the song from a straight-forward disco funk workout into something much more interesting. Creole's vocals were treated to sound as if they are coming through a telephone wire, emphasizing the *informant* aspect of the story.

The party continued with *The Love We Have*, before the final track, *No Fish Today*, a camouflaged tale of class struggle in which Creole took the role of a fisherman explaining to a local woman that his catch had been confiscated when *"The authorities agreed that if anyone should eat it should be the upper class"*. The chorus of *"I'm sorry ma'am, no fish today"* was broken by her pleas of *"What am I going to do? I've got a child and a mother, two little sisters and a brother"* over a lilting Caribbean beat.

The press was reluctant to go along with Darnell's new vision, and the album was slated in some corners for sounding like a weak and overly commercial version of the first two releases, however the public in Europe disagreed with the album and singles hitting the charts. Kid Creole & the Coconuts subsequently spent the rest of the year touring there with a spectacular theatrical stage show featuring full band, dancers, and fire eaters, whilst their homeland ignored the album which slithered out across the Atlantic under the original name of *Wise Guy*.

Three singles were released from the album, *I'm a Wonderful Thing* in April, *Stool Pigeon* in July, and *Annie, I'm Not Your Daddy* in October, reaching numbers four, seven and two respectively. It was to be the most glorious and successful year for Kid Creole & the Coconuts.

℧ ℧ ℧

The first evidence of Duran Duran's 1982 recording sessions to see the light of day was new single *Hungry like the Wolf*, as close to pop perfection as you can get, galloping straight into a guitar riff purloined from the T-Rex songbook on top of Rodger Taylor's pounding beat. Written by Nick Rhodes around a drum machine and his

Roland Jupiter-8 keyboard, the song came together in one day and it was perhaps this immediate short eruption of vitality which made it so alluring.

Opening with a laugh provided by Nick Rhodes' friend Elayne Griffiths[293], one of the things which surprises many people about Duran Duran is how effectual they were as musicians. In Roger Taylor they had an exceedingly robust drummer, and there is little difference between a drum machine and his playing, the dependable and unyielding

beat allowing Duran Duran to sound sensational at volume on the dancefloor. The rhythm of *Hungry Like the Wolf* was a simple 4/4 beat, but what made it rise above (and perhaps also perpetually roots it in the early 1980's) was his use of the Simmons SDS-V, the world's first fully electronic drum kit, with its idiosyncratic hexagonal pads[294], which he used to intersperse and lift the beat out of mechanism into something more human.

On the surface *Hungry like the Wolf* appeared as a song about the pursuit of love, but underneath could easily have been interpreted as being about oral sex. Certainly, there were animalistic connotations throughout with allusions to intimacy, heavy breathing, aromas, and forests. Such a risqué subject matter was kept secret from Duran Duran's core audience: screaming teenage girls. *"None of us foresaw the teenage thing. We just thought that we were going to be an album band and that we were going to have quite a serious audience, but the music we were making was transcending that"* claimed Roger Taylor, whilst other members of the band, namely John Taylor and Nick Rhodes, were more than happy to embrace the attention.

A week after the single, the album which came to define Duran Duran, and to a certain extent the whole decade, was released, named *Rio* after the opening track in which Le Bon's lyrics sum up the spirit of Brazil's party city by giving

its characteristics to a woman. Later in their career, they would assert it was a love song to North America, which undoubtedly makes more sense with lines such as *"When she smiles she really shows you all she can"* and *"From mountains in the north down to the Rio Grande"*. Even later, LeBon would claim *"I was in a restaurant in the middle of town and I saw this waitress literally swanning across the floor and that is how the lyric was born."* Musically, the track had its roots in a 1979 song called *See Me, Repeat Me* written by a previous line-up of the

band, and a TV Eye song *Steve's Radio Station*. This tended to be the way Duran Duran wrote; songs would evolve over a long period of time, sometimes even years, before the definitive version was recorded.

The title track started with a fading-in backwards piano "played" by throwing metal objects and a pixie boot belonging to Rhodes onto the strings before a scrambling dissonant introduction escorted the main verses. These played out over a funky bass line punctuated by stabbing guitar chords, and at the end of the verse the band paused before the chorus surged in with harmony vocals added by Le Bon to make it a sing-along, who cares what the lyrics mean.

After a second chorus the band employed what was becoming their trademark tool: a drum and bass breakdown. Rather than writing middle-eights, of which few exist in Duran Duran songs, they took their stimulus from disco remixes and breakdowns,

---

[293] Griffiths would be *best man* at his wedding a couple of years later.

[294] The pads were made from the same hard material as police riot shields.

especially those of Chic. After the sound of Rhodes girlfriend laughing (again), the cessation featured a saxophone solo by former Dexy's Midnight Runners horn player Andy Hamilton, delivered straight from a wine bar, perhaps located somewhere on Baker Street. The second half of the breakdown saw the band pick up the rhythm before a double chorus and final fade out, accompanied by another saxophone solo. The whole song was over five minutes long, not a length intended for daytime radio play, and even remained four and a half minutes long when released as a single later in the year.

The second track on the album was something of a cuckoo's egg. The previous November the band had released a stopgap single *My Own Way*, which in later years they would disown, omitting to include it in *Greatest Hits* compilations. It did, however, become another top ten hit, fulfilling the purpose of keeping the band in the public eye until the second album could be recorded. Rather than simply put the single version on the album the band re-recorded the track, slowing it down to make it sound less like inconsequential disco, removing the strings and ramping up the guitar and Simmons drum overdubs. Whilst the remodeling did sonically fit with the album more than the original, it still seemed out of place, a relic from earlier underdeveloped days. It may seem odd to contemporary sensibilities that the band would choose to re-record a track mere months after the original rather than simply re-mix it, however these were the days before re-mixing became *de rigueur*. In fact, Duran Duran up until now had made a habit of recording "*night versions*" of their singles, which were extended versions for playing in clubs. These were not constructed in the studio from fragments of already recorded songs, but instead would be entirely re-recorded, with the band playing a ten-minute re-arrangement of the original. *Rio* may have been better served by not including *My Own Way*, however it would seem Duran Duran only a had a limited number of new songs, as evidenced in their use of album tracks and live versions of songs on the B-sides of all released singles in 1982.

Third on the album was the mid-paced *Lonely in your Nightmare*, a song about trying to break into the world of someone who is emotionally frozen. The repeated harmony packed choruses did the uncommon thing in taking the song texturally down. Underpinning the song were sporadic lines of fretless bass, the result of John Taylor's fixation with Mick Karn, and just one of many ideas appropriated from Japan. There was never any real chance of *Lonely in your Nightmare* being released as a single, however spare footage from their Sri Lanka sojourn was edited together to create a promotional video anyway.

The pace picked up for *Hungry like the Wolf* and was maintained for the last track on side one, *Hold Back the Rain*. This could effortlessly have been a single, featuring a contagious chorus and typical Duran disco-meets-rock verse, as well as the customary instrumental breakdown. The recorded version was over ten minutes long but edited down to just under four for the album, with lyrics written by Le Bon about bass player John Taylor's mounting addiction to sex and cocaine, advising him to slow down, though you would need to search hard to be able to pick that up.

Side two kicked off with the gothic keyboard introduction of *New Religion* before settling into a funky groove. Written as a conversation between the ego and alter-ego with conflicting vocals on top of each other, Le Bon waded way out of his depth[295] and acclaimed psychoanalysis as a new religion whilst dancing in a minor key. After a run-of-the-mill sexually unsatisfied track *Last Chance on the Stairway*, came the album's big ballad, *Save a Prayer*. Constructed upon chords written on an acoustic guitar the song celebrated living in the instant, the consciousness of being young, of the

---

[295] Not the last time he would get in trouble in deep water. In 1985 he almost died when his yacht *Drum* capsized during the Fastnet Race and had to be rescued by the Royal Navy.

momentary passing of love and experience. Backed with a bamboo rim shot and featuring keyboard notes wilted into sounding like native instruments, this was a song about craving, a song set as the sun was going down, where *some people call it a one-night stand, but we can call it paradise*". It featured all the usual Duran tricks along with a simple but substantial sustained rock guitar riff at the end of the chorus, however the breakdown this time became a fade out, as the song headed into the discretion of the night.

The last track on the album *The Chauffeur* was also the last track recorded, without the help of John Taylor who was too busy partying to return to the studio. The lyrics came out of Simon Le Bon's notebook from 1978 and are told from the point of view of a driver who is in love with his passenger, as well as drawing from his experience in Israel a few years previously. He later explained "*I was on a Kibbutz it was 1979, at the end of one hot long day I watched a couple of Israeli soldier girls cooling off by driving a tractor at full speed across the flat desert.*"

The strength of *Rio* overall was the band's capacity not to overcook the songs, the awareness that keeping things simple was sometimes the best conclusion when it came to playing. Central to this was producer, Colin Thurston, as recognized by John Taylor when he claimed that "*Colin was a very firm hand at the wheel. He knew exactly how our band needed to sound*". The band never appeared this uncynical again, this detached from all going on around them, whilst at the same time wholly in touch with the zeitgeist. "*Finishing Rio marked the end of Duran Duran's innocence*" Simon Le Bon later claimed, the last time they could make an album with little in the way of expectations or apprehension about sales.

The final touch to the album was the cover, utilizing a specially commissioned painting of a woman's face by Santa Monica artists Patrick Nagel, which was then wrestled into a graphic featuring the colours of Birmingham's Aston Villa Football Club, burgundy and light blue, by designer Malcolm Garrett. The cover was iconic, achingly of its time whilst also enduring, summing up the early 80's glamour Duran Duran would forever be associated with[296].

℧ ℧ ℧

Meltdowns by Julian Cope, frontman of the Teardrop Explodes, were a weekly occurrence, and routinely ignored by the rest of the band and road crew as they were customarily the consequence of too much acid and a deficiency of sleep. Just two weeks previously he had thrown himself down a flight of stairs rather than play a date in New York City. Dave Balfe, on the other hand, had never suffered a meltdown until they reached Boston on Monday 10th May. Cope first became conscious of the keyboard player's quandary when his road manager banged on the hotel room door for half an hour until Cope could pretend to ignore him no longer. The two returned to Balfe's room and found him hunched over and rocking, eyes closed, with tears gushing down his face. After an hour of coaxing, he finally confessed that he wanted to go home, and he wanted to go home RIGHT NOW!

With a typical lack of sympathy, the band managed two more dates with Balfe sitting slumped on stage at his keyboard, staring into space, after which Cope and his girlfriend drove him the two-hundred miles to JFK Airport in New York in oppressive silence.

℧ ℧ ℧

---

[296] The painting was bought by the band for £9000 and hung in the managers' office.

On the night of Monday 10th May the BBC broadcast an episode of the news program *Panorama* discussing the Falklands crisis. The program looked at opposition to the war within Britain, with dissent from some right-wing voices as well as the usual left-wing suspects. As the programme broadcast, Margaret Thatcher, on her way to diner, stopped to watch, and left seething at the content.

The reaction within the establishment was instantaneous, with Conservative MP Sir Anthony Meyer, who had taken part in the program, being stopped in the corridors of Parliament and told *"I remember you at Eton and your mother at Datchet. You are a disgrace to your school, your regiment and my country"*. BBC Director-General Alasdair Milne[297] and Chairman Lord Howard were called before a backbench media committee, where *"a mob of vulgar Conservatives"* brayed *"Speak up!"*, *"Stand up!"* and *"Take your hands out of your pockets!"* at them.

The BBC did however prove useful to the government when the latter requisitioned one of their four transmitters on Ascension Island and began broadcasting *Radio Atlantico del Sur* on a frequency adjacent to that of Argentinian radio. The station, presented in Cuban accents, broadcast a mixture of music and *"good sound advice to surrender"* across the airwaves of the Falkland Islands.

ʊ ʊ ʊ

Buoyed by the results of their chart success with Trevor Horn, ABC threw themselves into recording their debut album during the first few months of 1982. Horn was impressed with the change in the band between the recording of *Poison Arrow* and the album. Where before they required an entire weekend to record the drums and bass alongside with the programmed 808, now the band were exceedingly tight and working at a remarkable rate, having already pre-programmed the drums and bass themselves. ABC demonstrated they were prepared to put the requisite work in to satisfy their grand ambition, and this determination was echoed in the sound of the album, the next indication of which was the release of a new single entitled *The Look of Love.*

From the opening notes the song harked back to a golden age, with 1960's Bacharach and David in the title, and a luxurious Nelson Riddle style soft-pop string arrangement throughout, whilst also bringing elements of disco and Motown to the mix. This time Martin Fry was confused by love, hinting he had been hurt once with the line *"It takes a lot to love you, you know it's true"*, before concluding *"I don't know the answer to that question, if I knew I would tell you"*. Towards the end he cautioned against false love by warning *"If you judge a book by the cover, then you judge a look by the lover"*. Throughout Fry demonstrated the band had made the prudent decision in moving him to the position of frontman, providing a dazzling vocal performance, especially in an ad-libbed final couple of choruses where he interjected standard soul phrases *"Sisters and brothers"* and *"Heavens above"*. Towards the end was delivered a spoken word interlude of *"One day, Martin, you'll find true love"*, inspired by Iggy Pop in *Turn Blue*: *"Jesus, this is Iggy"*. During the recording process David Bowie had dropped in and suggested they leave an answering machine message in the middle instead. He was rewarded by Steve Singleton *"freaking Bowie out"* by hiding his bag.

It is in this song and the accompanying video that Fry became an iconic frontman, claiming that *"Living in Sheffield you felt invisible, off radar and undetected. I guess that's where all that peacock flamboyant stuff came from. That's where the gold suit definitely came from."* The video was a cross between the animated sequences of

---

[297] There may have been some truth in the Left-wing leanings of Milne: his son, Seumas was later Jeremy Corbyn's Director of Communications.

Mary Poppins and *The Benny Hill Show*, vibrant colours and mawkish sight gags, as well as cameo appearances by Trevor Horn and music journalist Paul Morley. Whilst credit must be given to the rest of the band for embracing the concept, they looked uncomfortable on screen. Fry on the other hand looked like a star, caught between the suave insouciance of Bryan Ferry and the latter visual aloofness of Bowie. There is even a small dance routine with the band, frantically and hideously out of time with each other. This was remedied a few weeks later, on a live *Top of the Pops*, when the band once again showed how much work they were willing to put in to become the perfect pop band. As the single stormed the charts the band appeared in shiny silver suits, performing a Motown-style backing band dance routine, this time (almost) flawlessly in time, whilst Fry vamped at the front, all soul stances and dramatic hand gestures. Fair enough, there was nothing demanding in the routine, but at least it was in sync this time. That ABC had come from Alan Vega post-punk to Las Vegas glitz and dance routines in just eighteen short months was an exuberant sight, however (Fry aside), they still looked like three Northern lads, all unattractive teeth and atrocious haircuts. You could see the deliberation clearly written on their faces as they concentrated on the next rudimentary move provided by the choreographer.

Musically, the track drove along through the string arrangement with energetic drums and bass, this time an amalgamation of synthetic and human, being equal parts disco and ballad. Horn was an obsessive when it came to producing and even insisted on bringing Fry's ex-girlfriend down from Sheffield to the studio to record the word "*Goodbye*" in the second verse, figuring that *"If you're going to do things like that…you've got to make them kind of real"*. On top of this Horn had just started what was to prove a lengthy and successful professional relationship with string arranger Anne Dudley and sampler programmer J.J. Jeczalik, both of whom took the production to another level.

As the band progressed to recording the album, Horn located a weak point: bass player Mark Lickley. The producer calculated the band required a superior musician to help them accomplish the necessary disco vibe, however he did not count on the way musicians talk to each other, and the dismissal of the bass player at his command cost him the job of producing the next U2 album, with Adam Clayton quivering in his desert boots at the thought. Their new bass player was Brad Lang, and with him the band forged into a tight unit, recording most of the basic tracks for the album live in one or two takes. Meanwhile, Lickley's absence was explained as *"a case of him working from nine to five… but a lot of things happen after six"*.

ABC wanted to create music which was sophisticated yet still had the assertiveness of punk, they were fanatical about the idea of creating their own world, a world where they sounded like no-one else, and no-one else sounded like them, and on album *The Lexicon of Love* they succeeded. Fry claimed he *"like*[d] *the idea of a song being a three-minute epic"* and building their temple upon the twin foundations of Smokey Robinson and Elvis Costello, ABC were utterly committed to the project, heart and soul. They hungered for success on their own terms, but were also determined that if they failed, it would be *"a magnificent failure"*. *"The idea is to uphold standards of decency and moral conduct while everything else crumbles around you"* Fry claimed, echoing Bryan Ferry's statement a decade earlier that Roxy Music were going to be successful *"with as much dignity as possible"*.

If Fry had expressed his desire to write about love, then he succeeded with *The Lexicon of Love*[298], ten tracks that ran the gauntlet of desire. There was one theme, however, that ran through all the tracks, not of love, but of love lost. Fry had been unceremoniously discarded by his girlfriend the previous year and it was easy to follow the story of his emotional journey through the album. From love no longer reciprocated (*Show Me*), to the hazards of attempting to recapture love (*Many Happy Returns*), to disillusionment with love (*Tears are not Enough*), to resentment of love (*Valentine's Day*), to craving for love to return (*All of My Heart*), to love's built-in obsolescence (*Date Stamp*), these were not songs for swinging lovers but cries for apathetic ex-lovers,

forming an assemblage that should perhaps have been christened *The Lexicon of Heartbeak* instead. "*A love affair without a broken heart?*" he wrote on the sleeve to the *Poison Arrow* single, "[that's] *like making an omelette without breaking an egg*".

For Fry, the opening track *Show Me* "*just about sums up the whole album*", but why leave it there then you have "*The ultimate love revenge tune*" of *Poison Arrow* to follow. *Many Happy Returns* could easily have been a single, with an introduction described by Fry as "*a bit Raymond Chandler on a shoestring*" and a piano solo halfway through, "*One of the few solos permitted on the album. We were very post-punk and anti-solos. We had a manifesto.*" The album had a re-recorded version of first single *Tears Are Not Enough*, tightened up with a new harpsichord solo in the middle, followed by *Valentine's Day*, which was "*Engineered to sound great in Sheffield night spots like Penny's, Crazy Daisy, The Limit and the Penthouse.*" According to Fry "*We had a night out with Trevor* [Horn] *in Sheffield to show him the importance of the twelve-inch mix*" which paid off with a punching tight groove.

Date Stamp was a precursor to Horn's work with Frankie Goes to Hollywood in later years, with a slapped bass introduction (p)reminiscent of *Two Tribes* and a pounding beat put to better use later on in *Relax*.

The band may have been embracing the high life in London, but they were still Sheffield based lads at heart, as evidenced on the closing track *4 Ever 2 Gether*. Fry explained "*I saw the chorus lyric on the wall at Hyde Park Flats in Sheffield. Just goes to prove you can find romance in the strangest of places, there's poetry everywhere, in amongst the concrete.*"

The album was rich with string arrangements courtesy of Anne Dudley, which ambled the fine line between Nelson Riddle and the disco flourishes evident on Gamble & Huff's Philadelphia soul recordings of the 1970's, as the band attempted to capture the feel of a movie soundtrack, even down to the *Red Shoes* inspired front cover by acclaimed photographer by Gered Mankowitz[299]. Fry's vocals swooped, emulating the rollercoaster ride of love, whilst the whole package was enormously cosmopolitan, a soundtrack for young adults and new-found sophistication in the city. Despite the assuredness of the final product, Horn had trouble trying to capture the vocals, Fry having been shredded in terms of confidence by their previous producer. "*I figured out Martin wasn't a professional singer that would naturally sing the song perfectly every time*" he claimed later, "*So I got him to sing it six or seven times and I'd piece it together*", a technique which would become the industry standard in future years.

---

[298] The title came from a review of the band before they were signed by Ian Penman.

[299] Mankowitz's father wrote the screenplay for *Dr No*, then asked to have his name removed from the credits, fearing it would be a disaster.

The album was released at the end of June and debuted at number one, justifying ABC's decision to adjust direction. They were propitious with their timing as classy commercial pop music was in vogue with the critics in 1982. Or maybe that is being a bit unfair to ABC and all the other glossy pop acts that year; maybe their own ingenuity made commercial pop music irresistible in 1982. Maybe the country was fed up with the greyness of the 1970's, or with the anger of punk, and wanted something fresh and sanguine. Certainly, politically the mood of the nation was starting to improve, occasionally spilling over into mindless jingoism with the beginnings of Thatcher's golden era of big business, wealth creation, and social mobility. Pride in being working class was diminishing, and aspirational living was on the rise after spending decades being, in the words of Paul Theroux, *"seen to be a vice".*

ひ ひ ひ

Motörhead spent most of March and April touring Britain in support of their new album *Iron Fist*, before flying to North America. The first few dates in Britain had introduced the band's new stage prop: a giant fist which unfolded into an open hand. After a couple of concerts, the fist malfunctioned with only one finger unfolding. You can hazard a guess at which one it was.

After a couple of dates in Canada the band headed to New York where they played the Palladium on Friday 14th May. The following day Motörhead entered the studio with The Plasmatics, a New York punk band fronted by Wendy O. Williams[300]. The idea was to record one song by Motörhead, one by The Plasmatics, and then a duet between Williams and Lemmy on Tammy Wynette's *Stand by your Man*. Motörhead guitarist Eddie Clarke was in the producer's seat with guitar being played by the Plasmatics, however the session turned out to be challenging with Williams taking a protracted amount of time to get a vocal take in tune.

Clarke, exasperated not to be playing on the record, left the studio after some unforgiving words with Lemmy, and immediately announced he was quitting the band. The other two members of Motörhead, with tour dates booked for the rest of the year, started making panicky telephone calls to find a replacement.

ひ ひ ひ

The closer the Task Force was to the Falkland Islands the more belligerent Margaret Thatcher was becoming in her attempts to channel the spirit of Winston Churchill. In Scotland on Friday 14th May, whilst addressing the Scottish Conservatives she stated that for too long Britain had been *"drifting on the ebbing tide of history, slipping inexorably backwards under pressures we somehow felt powerless to resist… but Britain still leads the world."* She later commented *"What really thrilled me… what thrilled people was once again being able to serve a great cause, the cause of liberty".* The Iron Lady was letting it slip that she was enjoying the fight a bit too much.

ひ ひ ひ

With frontman Joe Strummer still missing, The Clash released their new album *Combat Rock* on Friday 14th May to rapturous acclaim from the critics, many of whom had judged their last triple-album overlong, self-indulgent, and bloated. *Combat Rock* could

---

[300] Williams was a former live-sex performer whose speciality was firing ping pong balls across the stage from her vagina.

have gone the same way as an initially intended double had producer Glyn Johns not trimmed the unnecessary fat to create a 46 minute single disc. Throughout 1981 The Clash had been recording songs at various locations whenever they had a break from a series of residencies in New York, Paris, and London. *Car Jamming* and *Sean Flynn* were recorded at Marcus Music, just off Westbourne Grove in London during Spring using The Rolling Stones' mobile studio, *Know Your Rights*, *Should I Stay or Should I Go*, *Inoculated City*, and *Ghetto Defendant* were recorded in Ear Studio, Notting Hill in late Summer and early Autumn, whilst final work was completed November and December in New York, after which Johns was brought in to make sense of the recordings during the mixing process.

The album was obsessed with America, and in particular its place in world politics. The influence of Francis Ford Coppolla and Martin Scorsese stood tall over *Combat Rock*, especially the films *Apocalypse Now* and *Taxi Driver*, and certainly many of the lyrics referred to the country in a post-Vietnam War identity crisis.

After an opening blast of first single *Know Your Rights*, the album settled with *Car Jamming*, abstractly following the fate of a Vietnam veteran from Missouri now forced to beg on the streets of New York, over the top of a decelerated Bo Diddley beat. The whole song viewed the streets from inside a car stuck in a traffic jam, but also from the veteran's point of view, stuck in a city of snakes, hyenas, and gorillas. Strummer saw

New York as an *"urban Vietnam"*, a jungle where souls could be lost, and the connection with Vietnam was emphasised in *Sean Flynn*, named after the son of Errol Flynn, a photographer who disappeared in 1970 whilst covering the war. The floating miasmic atmospheric ballad had obviously been influenced by the soundtrack of *Apocalypse Now*, once again having guitars replaced by jungle percussion and faint howls.

As well as looking at the American reaction to Vietnam, Strummer also showed concern with crime and poverty in New York. Lead vocals on *Red Angel Dragnet* were provided by bass player Simonon with lyrics by Strummer about the shooting dead of Frankie Melvin of the Guardian Angels[301] in the Bronx on New Year's Day, 1982. Strummer had become heavily influenced by the Beat Poets during the writing of the album, and Allen Ginsberg was on hand to lend words to a couple of the songs, providing the voice of Travis Bickle[302] (another Vietnam veteran) with a voiceover of *"someday a real rain will come and wash all the scum off the streets"*. The whole album was built upon the sound of New York City, with drums and dub bass throughout, and the guitars often mixed far back. *Ghetto Defendant* looked at the commonly held conspiracy theory that the American government, through the CIA, kept the ghettos flooded with heroin as a pacifier, both in the United States and in other areas around the third world where Communism threatened to take hold. Ginsburg was again brought in to provide additional vocals on the track, staying for a week and coaching Strummer on his lyrics, utilising the *one-drop* reggae drum technique with a call to arms for the downtrodden to rise, violently if necessary.

Larger world issues were tackled with *Overpowered by Funk* a five-minute white New York workout, featured a rap by Futura 2000 celebrating and defending graffiti artists. An ironic celebration of capitalism, the track featured a repeated chant of *"funk out"* in place of *"fuck off"*, demonstrated by the uncaring *"Food for the hungry millions, funk*

---

[301] The Guardian Angels were a self-organised alternative police force, wearing red berets and patrolling the streets and subway trains discouraging crime.

[302] Bickle was the anti-hero of Scorsese's film *Taxi Driver*, memorably played by Robert DeNiro.

out, home for the floating people, funk out". In *Atom Tan* the band attempted to deal with the aftermath of nuclear war, with mentions of bunkers, chaos in the streets, and cyanide suicides, whilst call and response shared vocals between Strummer and the band were reminiscent of what Mick Jones would later do with Big Audio Dynamite. *Inoculated City*, written and sung by Jones, looked at the chain of command in war, from the soldier to the sergeant, to the captain, to the general, to the government. Towards the end of the track a cleaning commercial was played, advertising the use of chemicals to inoculate, in reference to Agent Orange and bringing the album full circle back to Vietnam. *Combat Rock* was probably the most focussed album by The Clash, though not necessarily their best, however with its subject matter firmly set Stateside, it was the album which got them noticed in America.

16th – 22nd May 1982

#1 single: Nicole: A Little Peace

#1 album: Madness: Complete Madness

Toyah Wilcox had been born and raised in Birmingham, leaving school to study drama, first in Birmingham and then at the National Theatre in London. In the late 1970's she won roles in Derek Jarman's *Jubilee*, and *Quadrophenia*, whilst also finding work with legends such as Katharine Hepburn and Stephen Poliakoff[303]. Toyah, inspired by the punk scene, also had ambitions in music and teaming up with guitarist Joel Bogen, the singer / band released several singles for independent label Safari, finally hitting the big time in 1981 with a stream of weak top ten singles including *It's a Mystery* and *Thunder in the Mountains*. Nominations in the Brits in February suggested 1982 was going to be another successful year, however it was to instead to provide evidence of her musical limitations when pitted up against a changing scene.

Wilcox was considered a punk by the tabloids because she dyed her hair bright colours, however she had enveloped herself with veterans of prog rock[304], experienced and skilled musicians who meant the playing and production levels remained high but ultimately floundered in providing the necessary vitality required to compete in the new three-minute pop world. Many of Toyah's hits sounded thin and flaccid by comparison, almost too considered in their arrangements.

May saw the release of new single *Brave New World*, a plodding lugubrious piece accompanied by a promotional video featuring the same solarised effect Bowie had used two years previously on *Ashes to Ashes*, even utilising similar locations such as Battersea Power Station and Hastings Beach. The single struggled to number twenty-one, the first sign success was over.

The accompanying album *The Changeling* was released in June and found Toyah in a peculiar place lyrically, describing the songs as a "*mix of depression, space-age and the druids*", with the tracks taking on a futurist-apocalyptic-Celtic feel. There was a lack of gravity in the attempted earnestness of the album, one which was all too easy to

---

[303] Poliakoff's grandfather invented the paging beeper and the magnetic induction loop to allow people to hear in cinemas and theatres.

[304] She even later married King Crimson's Robert Fripp.

ridicule, and to add to the target for derision it also
featured a four-page booklet of poems written by Wilcox.
Whilst composing the songs, Wilcox was also in
negotiations for some to be included on the soundtrack to
a horror movie, a concept which fell through in the end.

1982 was an odd year for Toyah, with her maintaining the
previous year's press profile but not the chart success.
She found it easy to acquire television exposure, even
having a half-hour *Razzamatazz* special dedicated to her.
She also kept up the acting work, appearing in an episode
of *Tales of the Unexpected*, and even had a baby monkey named after her at Bristol
Zoo. Ultimately, however, Toyah turned out to be protest music for middle-class
thirteen-year-old girls to stamp their feet to, to help them rail against the injustice of
parents.

℧ ℧ ℧

Former art students Bob Last and Hilary Morrison started Fast Product in Edinburgh at
the start of 1978 with the intention of subverting the music business, favouring a type
of *mutant pop*[305]. Their first signings were Leeds act The Mekons, who seemed rather
bemused to have anyone interested in them. *"Are you sure it's us you want?"* the asked
Last, *"There's a much better band in Leeds!"* referring to The Gang of Four. Last was
intrigued and checked out the *better band* before signing them to Fast Product as well.
The Gang of Four had been formed at Leeds University in 1976 by Andy Gill, Jon King,
Hugo Burnham, and Dave Allen, and took the energy of punk welded to American funk,
with themes coming from *"the Benny Hill end of Marxism"*, creating something new in
the process: uncompromising music with a muscular rhythm section and scratchy guitar
where *"power chords* [aren't] *part of the repertoire"*, both abrasive and danceable at
the same time. Instead of guitar solos, Gill would sometimes simply stop playing and
leave the space blank, what he called *anti-solos*. In a bold move towards
egalitarianism, the drums, bass, and guitar were given equal priority within the sound,
in what Gill described as structured *"a bit like a Frank Stella painting"*. After a debut
single on Fast, they signed to EMI and released their debut album *Entertainment*,
greeted by the critics as one of the most important and innovative releases of the late
1970's.

The band were a powerful live act, making more of an impression in the United States
than at home, where there were highly influential to The Red Hot Chili Peppers, REM,
and Nirvana as they played to sold out 5,000 capacity venues, however chart success
continued to evade them through a second album. At the end of 1981 bass player
Allen left, however the dynamic had already shifted by then with Gill and King
controlling most of the power through their song-writing. Work began on their third
album with one eye on a more deliberately commercial sound, employing Mike Howlett
on production duties. The band were aware of the various ways in which the music
industry had caught up with their vision, with the likes of ABC, Heaven 17, and Scritti
Politti taking their blueprint of high concept pop music with a Marxist slant, and felt the
time was right for their own breakthrough into the public consciousness. The band took
on board bass player Sara Lee for two reasons, the first being her musical ability and
similarity in style to the departed Allen, the second being, in King's words, *"to help put
the bands feminist politics into practice"*. The continuing gender imbalance in the act

---

[305] Fast Product released The Human League and Joy Division's debut singles.

was soon addressed with the addition of female backing singers Alyson Williams[306] and Eddi Reader[307], once again synchronising with the current trends in music.

What would have been a weakness for many other acts, the pressure from a major record company to write hit singles, became a powerful weapon in the hands of The

Gang of Four, as the new album addressed commercial factors and the surrender to consumerism. Their recent experiences touring the United States helped focus the lyrics on economics, male impotence, and the military, which was most clearly expressed in the first single from the album, *I Love a Man in a Uniform*.

A deeply ironic song with the male vocals playing the part of an outdated man worrying about his manhood and lack of power when unemployed. *"Handouts, they got me down, I had to gain my self-respect, so I got into camouflage"* he sang, along with "*I had to be strong for my woman, she needed to be protected*". The newly recruited female contingent of the band punctured the machismo with "*You must be joking, Oh man, you must be joking*" as the song investigated the way the armed forces used the idea of *a real man* as a marketing tool in recruiting troops.

The single seemed certain to be a hit, receiving ample airplay and working its way into the top seventy-five, when word came from the BBC that, following new government guidelines, the song was banned. With British ships approaching the exclusion zone around the Falkland Islands, Whitehall decreed that the media would not be permitted to broadcast any song which appeared to question the armed forces or remind people of the negative aspects of war. Publicity was cut off overnight, and the song was torpedoed at number sixty-five.

With its funk-noir leanings, *I Love a Man in Uniform* became a dance hit in the cooler clubs across the Atlantic, and by the time album *Songs of the Free* was released in

June, EMI had decided it would be wise to concentrate on the American market. A new State-side manager was brought in, complete with all the clichés of cigars, fast cars, and cocaine, which allowed the record label to focus their time on Duran Duran, with their good looks and unchallenging lyrical themes a more promising prospect.

The Gang of Four's new album was a *softer* affair than the previous two, with more use of recording technology and less confrontational lyrics. Having become an inspiration to many of the acts which broke through in 1982, the Gang of Four found themselves in tune with the sound of the

times without having had to shift position too far, however they still lacked the necessary matinée looks for success.

The move to America and the compromise in their sound towards less abrasion ultimately led the band to a limbo, stuck between ideals and lack of success, disappointing both groups of supporters, and after one final poorly received album they split, only for their reputation to grow over the next thirty years, and to be recognised as innovators.

---

[306] New Yorker Williams found solo success in the late 1980's with her album *Raw*.

[307] From Glasgow, Reader was singing with Falkirk band Thrush when she answered an advert in the NME. After The Gang of Four she sang backing vocals with The Waterboys and The Eurythmics, before finding success with Fairground Attraction.

ʊ ʊ ʊ

The third wave of British punk acts continued to cluster unwanted around the lower end of the top seventy-five, with minor hits for Vice Squad, Discharge, and The Exploited. Vice Squad were Bristol punks formed from the ashes of TV Brakes and The Contingent, and featured the vocals of eighteen-year-old Rebecca Bond, who had

taken the name Becki Bondage. Being followed at gigs by violence meant they found it almost impossible to play live dates at the turn of the decade, despite a debut album which everyone, including the band, hated. Firmly anti-sexist, anti-racist, anti-meat eating, anti-war, the band became known for hardcore views, and were roundly criticized in the punk community for signing to a subsidiary of EMI in 1981. Despite this, they still considered themselves part of the genre, with Bondage claiming "*Punk will never die as long as it allows kiddies the opportunity of having their say*" before justifying their move with "*It's the small independents who are really ripping the bands off... [have you] ever tried getting royalties out of an independent* [label]*?*" With such set views, Bondage did not make things easy for herself in 1982 Britain, later complaining "*It was a lot more difficult to get vegan food back then and I used to go without food when we toured. People used to mock me for my animal rights beliefs.*"

Their second album *Stand Strong, Stand Proud* was released in May, having been recorded in Bristol by Mark Byrne, and featured a version of David Bowie's *Saviour Machine* as well as joyless minor hit single *Out of Reach*.

The album was a one-dimensional parody of punk, rarely changing tempo or failing to resemble a lobotomised Siouxsie & the Banshees but had enough followers to peak at number forty-seven. Bondage herself was not a fan of the album, describing it as "*a little bit too pop for my taste. I think ineptitude is rather charming in teenage bands but irritating in older bands who use the punk label as an excuse to be lazy.*" As part of the third wave of punk Bondage was well aware of the pitfalls, proclaiming "*Some of the problems that set in was that you had to look a certain way; a very rigid idea of how you should look, with Mohicans and everything.*" She became more disenchanted during a North American tour later in the year and announced her departure early in 1983.

Discharge from Stoke-on-Trent were a much more confrontation prospect, following a strict anarchist agenda and pioneering a loud, fast tuneless explosion of sound which would lead the way to hardcore and thrash metal. With the release of their debut album *Hear Nothing, See Nothing, Say Nothing* in May they reached a career and chart high

at number forty. Unrelenting in its grind, the album cannot be called a pleasant listen, and if words such as "*And still men and women drag out their lives in misery... the nightmare continues*" and "*Men woman and children groaning in agony from the intolerable pain of their burns*" does not cheer you, then nothing will. The band did not so much write song lyrics as T-shirt slogans for the uneducated, something they might have unwittingly acknowledged on their track *Free Speech for the Dumb*, and the saving grace of the songs were their brevity.

Possibly foremost amongst the UK82 movement of punk acts were some genuine chart stars, of sorts: The Exploited from Edinburgh had even appeared on *Top of the Pops* when their 1981 single *Dead Cities* reached number thirty-one. Fronted by the irrepressible and uncompromising ex-squaddie Wattie Buchan and with the unmistakeable figure of Big John Duncan on guitar, The Exploited were dedicated to keeping the original sound of punk alive. May saw them release a new single *Attack*, followed by an album *Troops of Tomorrow* in June, both of which were uncompromising in their sound and lyrical themes, with songs celebrating Scottish gangster Jimmy Boyle and the innocence of Sid Vicious. The music may have been intransigent in its meaning but was also relentless in the full-on sonic attack.

The single reached number fifty, and the album a heady number seventeen, the last time the band appeared in the national charts. Despite this, they have continued under the leadership of Wattie, despite heart attacks and feuds with many other bands, usually about who is most true to the spirit of punk[308].

ʊ ʊ ʊ

Thomas Dolby liked to nourish the myth of his own past by claiming to have been born in Cairo where his archaeologist father was on a dig. The more mundane truth of the matter was that he was born in London as Thomas Robertson, though his father *was* an archaeology professor at Trinity College, Cambridge. Dolby was from a distinguished family of academics and intellects, with his uncle one of the original *Monuments Men*[309] after the Second World War, and his brother a respected computer scientist.

Dolby turned away from the academia of his family, learning keyboards and joining Bruce Woolley[310] for his debut album in 1979. For the next couple of years Dolby found himself playing session keyboards and writing songs for the likes of Lene Lovich, with whom he appeared on *Top of the* Pops. During a period busking on the Paris Metro, he was contacted by producer Mutt Lange[311] and flown first class to New York to work on the latest album by Foreigner, which saw him go from penniless and busking on the street for a living to earning £500 a day plus expenses, which he then used to bankroll his own debut solo album back in London.

The Golden Age of Wireless was a truly pioneering album, recorded in 1981 and released in the first half of 1982. There was a pervading sense of post-Cold War-turned-hot running through the tracks, however Dolby used imagery from previous wars, and in particular the technology used. There was also a sense of travelling within many of the lyrics, whether by plane or car. Originally to be called *Wireless Weekly*, the album was recorded in a basement studio belonging to John Kongos[312], and then sold to EMI Records in a distribution deal which allowed Dolby to maintain a creative control. The advance was used to buy a flat and a 1964 Jaguar from *Exchange & Mart*. When Dolby had travelled by bus to Battersea to collect the second-hand Jaguar, he

---

[308] Big John Duncan later played with The Blood Uncles and Goodbye Mr MacKenzie, before becoming guitar technician for Nirvana, even playing onstage with them at one point.

[309] The Monuments Men, as represented in the frankly boring movie of the same name, were responsible for saving works of art and sculptures from the hands of the Nazis.

[310] Woolley was Trevor Horn's co-writer on *Video Killed the Radio Star* and *Hand Held in Black and White*.

[311] Rock producer extraordinaire, Lange wrote Ipswich Town's 1978 FA Cup Final single, *Ipswich Get That Goal*.

[312] Kongos was a white South African-born singer who had a hit with *He's Gonna' Step On You Again* which was later covered by The Happy Mondays as *Step On*.

met the previous owner, a retired Argentinian pilot called Carlos. Dolby was reading *Alive* at the time, the story of a Uruguayan football team who crashed in the Andes and ended up eating one of the dead to stay alive. By coincidence, Carlos knew the cousin of the pilot of the ill-fated flight, and the two got talking. The plane which crashed was a Fairchild, and from this conversation Dolby wrote *The Wreck of the Fairchild*, bringing Carlos to the studio to record a Spanish radio distress call.

A flying theme was also evident on opening number *Flying North*, with the relentless pace of air travel and the disconnect of jet lag and trans-Atlantic flights. As "*down with the landing gear* [and] *up goes a useless prayer*", Dolby was caught in the nowhere timeless world of airports and time-zones, with a cyclical keyboard riff straight from an airline advert. Dolby's childhood in a variety of locations around the world meant rootlessness was familiar to him, one where he "*never had a neighbourhood I felt I belonged to*". The sense of peripatetic travel developed on third track *Weightless*, a ballad of empty hearts where Dolby named himself as the protagonist in the first half, describing his aimless journey through an American landscape at night, longing for someone, before switching  to a second female character, at home, also lonely. The final verse hinted that the two were together, however we are left unsure if this is in the past or the future.

Although he was primarily a keyboardist playing synth pop, the album also featured a considerable amount of traditional rock and roll instruments, including Soft Boys bass player Matthew Seligman and future Bowie collaborator Kevin Armstrong on guitar. Dolby also brought in famous friends to sing backing vocals such as Lovich, Wooley, Lange, Andy Partridge, and Daniel Miller.

Europe and the Pirate Twins featured a Bo Diddley beat and infectious keyboard riff, whilst mining the same lyrical territory as Kraftwerk's *The Model*, telling of a former friend (*Europa*) who has since become famous "*on the cover of a magazine*". The two were in love when "*I was fourteen, she was twelve*", and the song stretched back to Dobly's time busking in Paris, where he had lived with Elizabeth Aumont, the daughter of a rich banker. The two had spent their nights beneath sheets, making up children's stories about themselves, taking on the name *The Pirate Twins*. Next up was *Windpower* which started with morse code before the opening line "*Switch off the mind and let the heart decide who you are meant to be*" echoed The Beatles "*Switch off you mind and float downstream*" in *Tomorrow Never Knows*. *Airwaves* was another ballad, one in which once again Dolby travelled across a landscape named as America, but much more in line with Europe, emphasised by the obvious influence of David Bowie's Berlin trio of albums, before *Cloudburst at Shingle Street* closed the album with an obvious Kraftwerk influence, and yet it was the song lyrically most in-touch with the natural world, longing for the experience of rain, something more real than the city or technology.

The only thing lacking from Dolby's career was a hit single.

ʊ ʊ ʊ

Dave Robinson, head of Stiff Records, felt bands should have a couple of *greatest hits* albums during their career, and it was now time for Madness to release their first. *Complete Madness* was released at the very end of April and was a watershed moment for the public perception of the band. Their enviable run of hits over the previous three years had been eagerly embraced by their teenage fans, helped by economically made but entertaining videos, however with the release of this album and its guaranteed "*16 *hit tracks*"[313] the wider public perceived how many wonderful songs Madness had. This was abetted by sequencing the tracks, which ran into one another without a gap, giving the appearance of an unremitting hit machine in action. The album climbed to the top spot in the charts and stayed in the top 100 for almost two years. Madness, of course, went on to have the equivalent quantity of hits again before they split (for the first time), and it is rather tempting to look at this first compilation as their *Red Album*, full of the ecstasy of short pop injections, and their later singles as a *Blue Album*, a lot more restrained and somber in character. *Complete Madness* was the first steps of the journey towards Madness being considered a national treasure.

Assisting the album to reach the top spot was the band's new single, *House of Fun*. Madness had been one of those bands who kept on recording songs in between albums without really being sure what they were going to do with them. Sometimes they became B-sides, from time to time they were reworked onto the next album, every so often they were just abandoned, but occasionally they turned out to be hit singles. Not that *House of Fun* was immediately distinguishable as such: the band had recorded all the verses one after the other and assumed the track was complete. Robinson used to listen to these vagrant recorded tracks and offer the band guidance for future recordings, and looking for a new single with which to promote the album and was certain *House of Fun* (or *Chemist Façade* as it was initially known) had potential but required a chorus. The band took a little bit more coaxing, however Robinson finally persuaded them all to get round a piano and rattle out a chorus. Being up against it in terms of time, a studio was hastily booked and the new chorus recorded once then edited in at the end of each previously recorded verse. Listening in passing to the track the edit is well camouflaged, however closer scrutiny reveals the jolt from the verse to the chorus in terms of a key change, a slight change in tempo, and a lowering of the volume of the drums.

None of this was noticeable to the public who instead fell in love with an extremely archetypal Madness single[314], one that had a nimble trace of ska, a lot of humour, and heaps of hooks. Most importantly it also had a video coalescing the usual *nutty* antics and discounted Britishness. Filmed at a funfair in Great Yarmouth and a chemist shop in Muswell Hill, London, the video told the story of the lyrics: the predicament of a sixteen-year-old boy attempting to purchase condoms for the first time. Being somewhat embarrassed by having to ask for them (this was pre-AIDS days, and the procuring of birth control was a painful but necessary experience for any teenager, a rites of passage into the adult world) the youth attempts some euphemisms such as asking for a "*box of balloons with the featherlight touch*", a "*pack of party poppers that pop in the night*" and "*a pack of party hats with the colour tips*", before being interrupted by the arrival of neighbor, Miss Clay. The pharmacist seems to misconstrue what the young protagonist is requesting and directs him to the joke shop instead (the *house of fun* of the title). The complete plot of the song was taken from one scene of the 1971 movie *Summer of '42*, which itself is based upon the

---

[313] Robinson was being a little bit mischievous, there were only twelve hits and four great album tracks that *could have been* hits

[314] Despite one music paper review saying "*It sounds like a corpse bouncing on a trampoline*".

memoirs of screenwriter Herman Raucher, in which his effort to buy condoms was interrupted by the arrival of a neighbor. Most of the public did not pick up on the meaning of the song, taking it as a bit of fairground fun instead, helping propel it to the top of the charts, the only number one single Madness ever attained amongst their enviable run of hits.

ʊ ʊ ʊ

For the past few weeks Joe Strummer and Gaby Salter had lived a blissful beatnik undercover existence in Paris, drifting around the popular tourist areas and museums without being troubled by the public, and even found time to run the Paris marathon. Strummer had a new-found love of big city marathons but never entered them officially, choosing instead to blend in shortly after the starting line and leave just before the end. Back in London, Clash manager Bernie Rhodes was corybantic. The cancelled British tour had left a considerable hole in the accounts, and a forthcoming American tour was looming which could completely wipe out the band financially. Before then, The Clash were due to headline the Lochem Festival in Amsterdam and with no news of Strummer, ticket sales were sluggish. In a string of providence, a journalist in the Netherlands mentioned in passing to the festival promoter that he had seen Strummer in a bar in Paris, who then called tour manager Kosmo Vinyl on Monday 17th May. Vinyl called Salter's brother, who supplied the name and address of her friend in Paris. Catching the next flight, Vinyl located the address and went to the nearest bar where he was greeted with the sight of a newly bearded Strummer. "*Hello, Fidel*" he said with a laugh as the two of them sat down to discuss the matter. The following day Strummer and Salter returned to London, only to head to Amsterdam twenty-four hours later for a £75,000 festival reward desperately needed to offset tour cancellation debts.

ʊ ʊ ʊ

The British had concerns about Argentinian air power in the South Atlantic, especially their Exocet missiles, which were stored at Rio Grande on Tierra del Fuego, a large island off the tip of the mainland, along with the aircraft that could deploy them. A plot was hatched which would see a Lockheed C-130 Hercules troop-carrying aircraft land on the Argentinian runway and decant fifty-five members of the SAS who would then destroy the missiles, aircraft, and airstrip, in what the troops knew would be a vainglorious suicide mission.

On Tuesday 18th May a reconnaissance flight transported a small SAS team of eight men to the mainland in a Westland helicopter. Initially it was planned to drop the troops, and then without enough fuel to return, fly to neutral Chile where the Westland would be sunk in deep water. Towards the coast visibility deteriorated to zero and they were forced to land. As the troops started the unplanned long walk to their observation point, the pilots cut holes in the bottom of the helicopter and flew it out to sea to allow it to sink. When the aircraft refused to sink, they headed back to shore to cut more holes, however an unexpected *low fuel* light blinded the pilot who was wearing night vision glasses, and they crashed onto the beach. Setting fire to the helicopter, the troops began their own long trek to Chile, where they were picked up by the military and returned to the British Embassy. With no new information gathered about the base, the whole mission was aborted.

Despite setting sail over a month before, the 18th May was also the date of the first images reaching London from the South Atlantic. The problem lay in getting photographs and film from onboard ships to the homeland. In the days before mass-satellite coverage, the press had to rely upon the Navy beaming their images back, and they were reluctant to do this because it would have jammed their satellite communication for between twenty minutes and an hour at a time. Instead, the television news had to do with John Nott making official announcements in a press room in London, and the occasional audio report from on board a ship. The journalists suspected (rightly) that the Navy could have found other ways to get the reports back to Britain but were deliberately blocking communication. Lessons had been learned from the American experience during the Vietnam War where daily reports and images of troop deaths had turned the tide of public opinion about the conflict.

℧ ℧ ℧

Cabaret Voltaire, formed in Sheffield in 1973, were a band just waiting for punk to happen, with their Brian Eno influenced approach to creating pure experimental noise going unappreciated in their home city, often leading to them being physically assaulted. Tapping into Sheffield's post-industrial history, the found kindred spirits in acts such as Clock DVA and an early version of The Human League, who fed punk's attitude not through Chuck Berry-influenced blues riffs but the filter of krautrock and electronics.

Setting up a rehearsal room in the old Socialist Workers Party Headquarters, Richard H. Kirk, Chris Watson, and Stephen Mallinder recorded over three hours of music every week, building a massive back catalogue with which to upset people. As they signed to Rough Trade instead of a deal offered by Factory Records, the trio set up their own studio, Western Works, with the aim of allowing themselves complete artistic freedom. Releasing records at a terrific rate, the band explored early uses for sampling, especially found sounds and voices, which were later to permeate the recording industry.

2 x 45 was released in May 1982 as a double album, featuring two twelve-inch singles with artwork by rising graphic artist Neville Brody. The music was experimental and groove driven, betraying their great debt to Can, with unintelligible vocals and cymbal-less drums. The first record was their last to feature Watson, who left to become one of the leading sound recordists in the United Kingdom for wildlife television programs, whilst the second album was recorded at a professional studio, and is more rhythm orientated, showing a clear path for both dance and industrial music. The album topped the Independent charts and scrapped into the official top 100 at number ninety-eight.

By the middle of the year Cabaret Voltaire were falling under the influence of Afrika Bambaataa and Grandmaster Flash, allowing John Robie to remix *Yashar* from the album for the New York clubs, where it pushed their influence further.

Later in 1982, encouraged by Stevo from Some Bizarre Records who would phone them up and shout over the sound of "*his mum doing the hoovering*", Cabaret Voltaire made a deliberate decision to become more commercial. Stevo took them, as part of a managerial deal, to Virgin Records who financed the next album, *The Crackdown*, their most successful. Virgin thought they were getting the next Human League, whilst the sound being made was probably closer to the industrial unpleasantries of Throbbing Gristle. Cabaret Voltaire never achieved the success they possibly deserved, arriving early enough to be a massive influence on the dance scene in both the Britain and United States, but too soon to benefit from the shift in mass-audience taste.

℧ ℧ ℧

Kim Wilde's second album *Select* was once again written by her brother and father, Ricki and Marty, and would not have suffered by everyone involved taking more of a gamble. The pristine production and song-writing allowed little space for the blonde singer to express personality, something which her limited vocal range may have struggled with anyway. The album cover featured only Wilde, no musicians, which was because *"the band is fairly irrelevant. If I wasn't here, there'd be no band, so why not just admit it?"*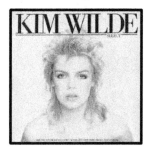
The problem Wilde had was that she was stretching a thin talent over too many songs, and the singles were beginning to sound the same, absent strong choruses and featuring verses which were instantaneously uninteresting. There was also the issue of the music being second-hand youth anthems written and marketed by people who had not been young in a long time: this was a middle-aged record executive's idea of what a young female pop star should be. At number nineteen, the album fared significantly worse than her debut, though it did sell well throughout mainland Europe, especially the Netherlands where it topped the charts. By this time, Wilde's debut single *Kids in America* had started to climb the Billboard charts, eventually reaching into the top thirty.

ʊ ʊ ʊ

Amsterdam was probably not the shrewdest place to send The Clash when they were at the height of their drug intake. After a couple of hours in the hash cafés on Thursday 20th May, the band made their way to the site of the festival they were due to headline, when an almighty rainstorm broke out. Backstage, whilst Joe Strummer was checking his stage clothes in the mirror, drummer Topper Headon removed it from the wall, laid it on the floor, and dumped a pile of cocaine on top. Unbeknownst to Headon there had been meetings behind his back during which the band expressed concern about his growing addiction, and it had been decided Amsterdam would be his final chance. For bass player Paul Simonen, Headon suffered from an outsider status in the band. *"The Clash were the only band with three frontmen,"* he would explain, *"It made it tough on Topper, because he wasn't around in the early days, and we were already a unit."*
During the performance, the festival security began beating the audience, prompting Strummer to drag the promoter onstage and demand it stop. The band's solution was to invite the fans onstage, which hundreds of them did, causing the stage to sag dangerously.
The following day, upon returning to London, the band held a meeting to inform Headon he was sacked. Headon broke down in tears, as did guitarist Mick Jones, asking who would take his place. The band did not yet know but answered that Terry Chimes, the drummer on their first album, would be joining them for their tour of the United States. Headon suggested they give Chimes his cut of the money and take him on tour as well. If he could play, he would, and if not, Chimes could stand in, however the decision had been made, and Topper was out. The press was told he was suffering from *nervous exhaustion*, though within days Strummer was telling the press the truth behind the sacking.
Not that Chimes had even been approached to join the band at the time. It was not until three days later that manager Bernie Rhodes called and offered him money to do the American tour in four days' time. Chimes had not been following the band's career closely, and not owning any of the albums, had to learn twenty-five songs in two days.

ʊ ʊ ʊ

Against the odds, Motörhead's world tour in support of their album *Iron Fist* continued at Harpo's in Detroit on Friday 21st May. Left devoid of a guitarist with the departure of Eddie Clarke a few days earlier, Lemmy had contacted former Thin Lizzy guitarist Brian Robertson in Canada and asked him to join the tour. Expecting to see a long-haired rock guitarist, they were surprised when someone with short dyed red hair appeared off the plane but reckoned that his track record spoke for itself. For the rest of the tour, and through Japan, things went brilliantly, even if Robertson refused to sign a contract for more than a year in advance.

ʊ ʊ ʊ

Temptation by New Order entered the charts on the 16th May 1982, a remarkable breakthrough for a band signed to a small, often ramshackle, independent label. Even on major labels, the idea of precision marketing, directing, and synchronizing everything for the highest possible chart entry on a certain date was foreign to the industry. Instead, a single was released around the same time as the radio stations received a copy, and with luck over the next few weeks increased radio exposure and word-of-mouth enthusiasm would see the song enter the top seventy-five, then gradually rise into the top forty, then top thirty where hopefully a *Top of the Pops* performance would propel it to the upper reaches of the charts. No-one thought to release singles in multiple formats, or to get a month's worth of advance play on the radio before release. Instead, it was left to the caprice of individual DJs and, to a certain extent, luck to decide what was a hit and what was not.

With an act like New Order, having hits was welcome but had never been the foremost intention. The band had been formed by two Mancunians, Bernard Sumner and Peter Hook, after seeing the Sex Pistols play their infamous dates at the Manchester Free Trade Hall on the 4th June and 20th July 1976. These dates had been organized by Pete Shelley and Howard Devoto of The Buzzcocks and have been called two of the most influential gigs of all time. Many hundreds of people have since claimed to be at the performances, however the number in the audience was about 30 for the first one, and just short of 200 for the second. It was what these people did subsequently that made the date so influential; the bands and record labels they would go on to form. As well as the members of The Buzzcocks, one of whom would go on to form Magazine, there was also the aforementioned Sumner and Hook, who would meet Ian Curtis at one of the gigs and form Joy Division, as well as Morrissey (The Smiths), Mick Hucknell (Simply Red), Mark E. Smith (The Fall[315]), journalist and cultural commentator Paul Morley (ZTT Records), Martin Fry (ABC), Martin Hannett (legendary Manchester producer), and Rob Gretton, Alan Erasmus and Tony Wilson (who would all start Factory Records).

Sumner, Hook, and Curtis formed The Stiff Kittens, recruiting drummer Steven Morris and changing their name to Warsaw in 1977. By early 1978 they had become Joy Division and signed a limited deal with RCA, which they had to buy themselves out of by the end of the year. Following exposure on Granada Television show *So It Goes*, they signed to newly formed Factory Records run by local TV personality and one-off

---

[315] Marc Riley, Craig Scanlon, and Steve Hanley of The Fall were also there, but nipped out for a bag of chips when The Sex Pistols played. Their *year zero* moment was seeing support acts Slaughter & The Dogs and The Buzzcocks.

eccentric Tony Wilson[316]. After a session for the John Peel show on the BBC, the band spent April 1979 recording their debut album *Unknown Pleasures* with Martin Hannett[317] producing. Hannett's technique in the studio was unorthodox, and with Joy Division he was given free-reign due to a mixture of Tony Wilson's belief in his genius and the band being naive when it came to recording. Paul Morley once described Hannett as *"the kind of man who could hear the sound of the moon moving round the earth"*, and he ripped their sound apart, creating space into which he poured synthesizer textures and the sound of disenchantment. The band despised what he had done to their powerful live sound but found it difficult to disagree that he had managed to get to the very core of the songs, and in particular the sense of displacement in the lyrics of Curtis. This, coupled with an iconic cover designed by Factory in-house artist Peter Saville, meant the album was an immediate critical hit. Live, the band were a different prospect, opting instead for a raw, full, and energetic guitar-based sound, and their shows rapidly became legendary for being powerful and mesmerizing. Catapulted into the role of the great white hopes of *alternative* music, the austerity of their sound and image as *intense young men dressed in grey overcoats* led to Joy Division being seen as the leaders of post-punk, and an enormous stimulus on the sound of the future goth movement.

As the band commenced work on a second album in early 1980, they had supplementary health issues to deal with; namely that of the snowballing regularity and intensity of epilepsy and depression suffered by Ian Curtis. This ostensibly came to a head in April when he was unsuccessful in attempting suicide, and then finally on 18th May when he took his own life at home in Manchester. It was only in the aftermath of his suicide the rest of the band listened to his lyrics with a critical ear, kicking themselves for not noticing what he had been very plainly saying all along. To them, it had just *"been Ian being Ian"*.

For many, Curtis was by far the most significant thing about Joy Division and his death sanctified him as a cult hero, someone to be studied and venerated. The rest of the band, however, were left without any direction. Losing such a significant member of their band, and a vital component of their songwriting meant the end of the band, despite the offer of U2 front man Bono to take Curtis's place. The remaining trio spent the rest of 1980 finishing tracks started by Joy Division, working on leftover material which somehow still sounded fragmentary even when complete. The lack of a lyricist with as much poetry as Ian Curtis as well as a singer added to this, as Sumner reluctantly took over the lead roll and they recruited Gillian Gilbert, the girlfriend of Morris, on keyboards and guitar. Throughout 1981, under the name of New Order they continued to attempt to crawl from under the shadow of Joy Division, a mission made more problematic by the insistence of continuing to record with Martin Hannett. Where Hannett had taken Joy Division into unmapped terrain, with New Order he started to hold them back, not helped by his open hostility towards the remaining members, making it abundantly clear that the only one he had valued was Curtis[318]. Despite this damaged working relationship, the band managed to release a couple of singles and an album, none of which revealed a huge amount of promise for the future, capturing the gloom of Joy Division with none of the poetry.

---

[316] Wilson was a Cambridge University graduate. Following his death in 2007 his gravestone was given a Factory Records catalogue number (FAC501) and was designed by Peter Saville and Ben Kelly. It describes him best: *Anthony H. Wilson. Broadcaster. Cultural Catalyst.*

[317] Hannett was a true Mancunian conundrum, having produced the first ever independent record (*Spiral Scratch* by The Buzzcocks), and was a funding director and in-house producer for Factory Records.

[318] Once Hannett told the band, as he hid in a cupboard, *"I'll come out when I hear something I like"*. He never came out.

Two things did happen, however, that at first seemed like major setbacks, but turned out to be blessings. The first was during a few American dates in September 1980, when the van holding all the band's equipment was stolen from outside their hotel in

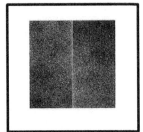

New York by a gang called *The Lost Tribe of Israel*. They had spent the previous couple of years building up specific guitars, amplifiers, effects, and drums which helped constitute the sound of Joy Division. To suddenly find all this gone turned out to be fortuitous, providing the band with a blank sonic canvas upon which to start again, or as Tony Wilson broke the news to them *"This is perfect, darlings, absolutely perfect! It's so poetic! The perfect ending!"* Once back in the Britain and with some money from Factory Records, Morris and Sumner decided to skimp on traditional instruments and buy syndrums, sequencers, and synthesizers. A lot of other acts were interested in drum machines at the time, however Morris *"moved in there and mastered it before anybody else did"*. This freed up how they wrote songs: suddenly it was all about programming rather than jamming ideas, and as 1981 progressed so did their sound, with more and more sequencing entering the recordings. The problem the band had over this period was in playing live, trying to get drum machines, synthesizers, and sequencers to all play the correct things at the right time. Digital equipment was in its infancy, and the band struggled to get any sort of coherent duplication of the songs until the technology became available which allowed for this.

The second career changing moment for New Order was when they parted company with Martin Hannett. Their growing self-confidence in the studio with electronic equipment, along with Hannett's ongoing abhorrence of the band and increasingly erratic behaviour, gave them the confidence to tell Factory Records they would not be working with him again. Initially seen by Tony Wilson as a poor decision, the band set to work recording a track to prove themselves right. Recording at Strawberry Studios in Stockport, and mixing at Avidson Studios in London during January 1982, New Order started triggering their synthesizers with voltage from the outputs on their drum machines, a move which gave them a much more controlled sound and demonstrated their new-found love of Kraftwerk and Giorgio Moroder's disco recordings. This love of dance music had been ignited by visits to New York, and in particular clubs such as Paradise Garage and Danceteria, however being a post-punk Factory Records band, they also desired to keep an uneven human aspect to the music.

The track *Temptation* had been written over the past few months and developed through live instrumental versions, occasionally with improvised vocals. For the B-side to the single, the band recorded a track called *Hurt*, within which they used their sequencers for the first time. Programming by using binary code, a system of on / off instructions, on their own home-made sequencer using Powertran parts, the band created something that was exactly what they were looking for: *stiff, precise, and robotic*. On top of all these electronic revelations, the band dubbed old-fashioned electric guitars, drums, and bass guitars, building up a wall of noise that sounded both ramshackle and precise at the same time. At the very top of the A-side was the finalized vocals by Sumner, featuring the simple but brilliant line during the break of "*Oh you've got green eyes, oh you've got blue eyes, oh you've got grey eyes*"[319]. The title of the song did not arise in the lyrics leaving the listener to work out the meaning, and it is entertaining to go online and read the differing interpretations, from temptation to drugs, womanizing, and the last thoughts of a dying man. One must keep in mind, however,

---

[319] Words which certain members of the band would use backstage many times over the years to chat up woman.

that Sumner had always been, and remained throughout his career, a dreadful lyric writer. He claimed that it was an attempt to write a love song, and that year he was taking a small daily dose of LSD at the time to open his creativity[320]. Ultimately, it remained a succession of partially connected lines, many of which, whilst throwaway, were incredibly memorable in their banality; from "*Up, down, turnaround, please don't let me hit the ground*" to "*I've never met anyone quite like you before*". If we took Sumner at face value and treated the track as a love song, then the music replicated the unadulterated ecstasy of neoteric love, with intense highs and blissed-out lows throughout, something that would become commonplace in dance music by the end of the decade and into the 1990's: the sonic build-up and then the release. Unsurprisingly, Sumner would later claim singing the song "*makes it feel to me like a prayer*" and described it as "*a very spiritual song*".

The band and the label knew they were onto something exceptional with the track, mastering it on the first ever digital editing system in Britain, and releasing both a seven-inch and twelve-inch version, both of which were different recordings from each other.[321] The song picked up a significant amount of radio play and rose to number twenty-nine in the charts, which does not seem a lofty position for such an esteemed song, however things were different for independent labels in the early 1980's. The charts were measured by what singles sold in a limited number of retailers, places such as Woolworths, R.S. McColl, and Boots, whilst bands like New Order and labels such as Factory tended to sell tens of thousands of records in smaller independent shops not included in the official count. Therefore, for any independent act to break through into the top forty at all, and this cannot be emphasized enough, was a major accomplishment. The chart success of a self-produced song utilizing a hybrid of post-punk and dance music gave New Order the boost they needed to take things further in the studio.

ʊ ʊ ʊ

Green Gartside, born and raised in South Wales in a working-class Tory family, rebelled by forming a Young Communist League at school, before finding his type of people at Art School in Leeds and having his mind scrambled by seeing the Sex Pistols on their *Anarchy in the UK* tour. An inspired Gartside formed Scritti Politti, decamping the band *en masse* to the squats of London, where they operated as a collective[322] with their first single featuring labels containing the address of the squat, stamped by the band in the kitchen. The band operated just beyond the perimeter of their ability, sounding like they were being shaken apart from the inside, and the months and years of poverty in the squat influenced health, with Greenside in particular suffering from mental exhaustion under the pressure of continually having to evaluate his every word and action. Orange Juice singer Edwyn Collins, who knew the band, was not impressed: "*Theory and semiotics were no use to songwriting; the only thing that was any use was just decent literature – plot lines, characters, the way people use*

---

[320] Microdosing psychedelics is a long-established practice whereby sub-hallucinogenic amounts of a substance are ingested, however with the prohibition of the drugs little research has been done on the subject. Some studies have shown the benefit for treating drink and drug dependency, removing end-of-life anxiety, and helping with PTSD.

[321] The twelve-inch version featured some extra whooping caused by manager Rob Gretton dropping a snowball down Sumner's back whilst completing his vocal take on a winter's day in London.

[322] Band meetings would feature whoever was in the room at the time, whether they were musicians or not.

language." Things came to a head in early 1980 whilst supporting The Gang of Four, when Gartside had a major panic attack and had to be accompanied to hospital. His family arrived from Wales to rescue him from the wards, taking him back home to recuperate.

It was in Wales that Gartside had a *road to Damascus*-type revelation regarding the direction of the band. Having fallen under the spell of Italian Marxist philosopher Antonio Gramsci and the history of Communist Bologna written by Max Jaggi, Roger Muller and Sil Schmid, both of which emphasised the new (at the time) idea that popular culture, and by extension pop music, was important to society instead of something to look down upon. In the early 1980's, this political theorising was not uncommon in musicians, many of whom saw *pure* pop music as the cultural way forward. Months were spent writing a book to convince the band the ideological correctness of embracing this *pop music*, using lines like *"No literary or culture can match the innate political strength of the pop single. It's a revolutionary text... a violent sensual sexual thing... a most glorious popular madness"*.

Gartside, having previously embraced an amateur approach to music now longed for the mainstream, writing a song called *The "Sweetest Girl"* specifically with this aim. With a loping reggae beat, he initially wanted Gregory Isaacs to sing and Kraftwerk to provide the music, and whilst the former was keen, the Germans refused to get involved, stating they hated reggae. Instead, Scritti Politti recorded their own version, recruiting Robert Wyatt to play piano, and presented it to their record company Rough Trade. Keen to infuse pop with cerebral concepts, Gartside was mesmerized by language, the capacity and nuance of words, ensuring there were inverted comas around the *sweetest girl* part of the title as a reference to the cliché of *blind love*. During the track, Gartside seemed aware of the potential controversy of his new pop direction, reciting *"sickest group in all the world, how could they do this to me"*.

Rough Trade were the politically *sound* record company of the time, not even really a record company, more a shop that would finance recordings. Started by Geoff Travis[323] in 1976, it also ran as a collective with everyone paid the same and everyone having a say in the running. This meant the opinion of the van driver was just as important as the boss when it came to the music and resulted in an eclectic output which never failed to surprise, delight, and infuriate in equal measures.

Scritti Politti were tenacious about breaking into the charts and with financial support from Rough Trade began recording a new album of pop songs at Berry Street in London. Members of the band were still not convinced by Gartside's new direction but

 took part in recording before bass player Niall Jinks left, followed in 1982 by drummer Tom Morley, who had spent most of the time programming drum machines rather than hitting things. The album took months to complete but was finally finished in the second half of 1981, but rather than release it the band decided to hold off, to put out a few singles first to build interest.

After the relative failure of *The "Sweetest Girl"* came *Faithless* in May 1982, disguised as a love song but really dealing with what happens to someone once their didactic beliefs start to fall away, as had recently happened with Gartside and Marxism, how they find a mixture of contentment at being free from dogma and restlessness at having no rock to steady themselves. Ever willing to comment on consumerism, the cover of the single *Faithless* was a pastiche of an advert for Dior's *Eau Sauvage* perfume, in the way the previous single had aped Dunhill

---

[323] *Frankly Mr Shankly* by The Smiths is reportedly about Geoff Travis.

cigarettes. The music was nonchalantly restless, with Gartside's vocal lost and adrift on a sea of backing vocals and vocoder, but just too distant from the port of a memorable tune to break through, peaking at number fifty-six.

☡ ☡ ☡

All had gone quiet around the Falkland Islands during the last couple of weeks, with the Argentinian navy consigned to port, their aircraft mounting sporadic ineffective incursions, and the British limited to launching nightly secret SAS operations onto the islands to scout the terrain. These clandestine manoeuvres came to fruition when a landing was finally attempted in Falkland Sound, the channel between the two main islands, on Friday 21st May.

The landing commenced with a small body of troops being put down beyond the Argentinian soldiers, equipped with a loudspeaker through which they urged surrender. In response, the South Americans moved towards the British, who had no alternative but to open fire in what was described as a *duck shoot*. Eventually the Argentinians surrendered, and the British were able to initiate a large-scale landing and establish a bridgehead.

These manoeuvres were conducted under fire from the air as Argentinian craft released munitions in what became branded *Bomb Alley*. With the Argentinians coming in low over land the British sea vessels had no time to lock onto targets, resulting in the hull of *HMS Ardent* being hit by two 1000lb bombs. Only one of these detonated with the loss of twenty-two lives before the ship was abandoned to burn through the night and sink. The Argentinian pilots were flying so low that Flight Lieutenant Carballo had clipped the radar antenna on *HMS Ardent* with his wing earlier in the day.

Margaret Thatcher later confessed she was "*not prepared to hold up military progress for negotiations*", and it had been crucial the British act before the end of May to avoid the unforgiving South Pacific winter months.

The conflicting approaches towards the troops by each nation was worth noting. The British Army fostered an *all-in-it-together* approach, where the officers had to earn the respect of their troops through actions, whilst the Argentine army worked the opposite way: the troops had to earn the respect of the officers, which could only be enforced through field punishments and collective beatings. Argentinian troops were shot in the head by their own officers for theft without any formal charges during May, after which the formerly rampant looting of stores in Port Stanley ended.

☡ ☡ ☡

Although he did not know it at the time, Malcolm McLaren did Adam the greatest favour of his career when he stole the Ants. After a couple of days of tears, the fear of *selling out* was abandoned and Adam emerged more resolute than ever to become successful, announcing "*cult is just another word for loser*". Recruiting guitarist Marco Pirroni[324] and the help of the man former voted as "*the prettiest punk*", drummer Jon Moss, Adam retreated to Rockfield Studios in Wales where they recorded a song called *Cartrouble*, dipping a toe into the Burundi beat that McLaren had sold him on.

Adam had started out life as Stuart Goddard in 1954, attending Hornsey College of Art in the early to mid-1970's, where he joined Bazooka Joe on bass, playing pastiche rock and roll. In late 1975 The Sex Pistols played their first ever gig as support to Bazooka Joe, and whilst Adam was not overly impressed with their sound, he was savvy enough

---

[324] Pirroni had been in the first ever line-up of Siouxsie & the Banshees, along with Sid Vicious.

to realise that what his band (and a thousand others) were doing was over[325]. The next day he quit and started the Ants, embroiling himself into the punk scene by hanging out at Malcolm McLaren's shop throughout 1976 and becoming close friends with shop assistant and punk icon Jordan[326]. Whilst other acts made breakthroughs, Adam & the Ants struggled, always the pantomime dame and never the principal boy, however blind determination allowed them to release their debut album in 1979, and for Adam to star in Derek Jarman's punk movie, *Jubilee*.

Retaining Pirroni whilst recruiting Kevin Mooney on guitar along with twin drummers Terry Lee Miall and Chris Hughes, the new sound featured heavy tribal beats with *spaghetti western* guitars and Native American chants, sonically and visually "*a fully committed look*", which attracted major interest from CBS Records. Between October 1980 and November 1981, a period of just thirteen months, Adam & the Ants released six top ten singles, and two albums, as well as three more hits with tracks re-released by old record companies. The singles were classic pop songs; *Ant Music, Kings of the Wild Frontier, Dog Eat Dog, Stand and Deliver, Prince Charming*, only ruined by a final ham-fisted and embarrassing attempt at hip-hop entitled *Ant Rap*. Adam kept a tight control over everything: the music, the image, the clothes, the record covers, and the videos, the last of which the band utilised to the utmost.

After the neutered years of punk Adam brought sex back into rock, proclaiming his as "*ant music for sex people*", whilst ignoring the music press weeklies, choosing instead to court *Smash Hits* and the tabloids. He provided a distinct image for those publications to latch on to, dressing initially as a pirate before straying into pantomime territory, whilst espousing the idea of tribalism, the concept of noble savages, and the unwritten philosophy of Geronimo.

When the *Prince Charming Revue* tour ended in January 1982, there was talk of Adam starring in a film called *Yellowbeard*, written by Peter Cook and Graham Chapman,

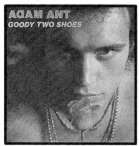

playing the son of the title character who was due to be played by either George C. Scott or Burt Lancaster. The vehicle was also due to star Christopher Reeve, Oliver Reid, and Diana Dors, and eventually came out the following year, without Adam[327]. Adam decided to split the band, fearing some members were simply going through the motions, claiming "*If they wanted to reap the benefits, they had to get in there and do the nitty-gritty. And they weren't*". Guitarist Pirroni, who stated "[we] *wanted to go back to being musicians instead of running an international corporation*" did not enjoy playing live but was kept on the payroll as a valuable songwriting partner. Adam later explained his motivation: "*I must have challenges. That's the only way I can earn people's respect*". Having been diagnosed as bi-polar seven years previously, the singer kept the black dogs at bay by becoming a workaholic, constantly hatching plans whilst fussing over every tiny detail. This work ethic got in the way when he tried to take a holiday to Barbados at the end of January and found himself lying on the beach restless and desperate to get back to work, whilst also obsessed with the idea of his on again / off

---

[325] Other members of Bazooka Joe embraced new careers as well: Daniel Kleinman has directed the opening sequences of every Bond movie since 1995, John Ellis formed punk band The Vibrators, Arabella Weir became a television comedy actor.

[326] Jordan, real name Pamela Rooke, was a true original, and an inspiration for the entire punk look.

[327] Adam's role was eventually given to Sting before the producers insisted on an American actor. One of the stars of the movie, John Cleese, described it as "*one of the worst six films made in the history of the world*".

again girlfriend, Amanda Donohue[328] sleeping with other people. His reaction to these thoughts was to fly a separate on-again / off again girlfriend, Carole Caplin[329] out to join him. Three days later, he booked early flights back home for both of them.

Instead, he threw himself into recording a new solo single, resurrecting the phrase *Goody Two Shoes* from his interview with Paul Morley back in January[330]. Working with Pirroni, and with production and drums by former Ant Chris Hughes[331], the trio put together a chart-topping pop song, starting with a driving swing beat. Over this an acoustic guitar played a staccato refrain and horns blasted an insistent line before Adam delivered the verse. Ant received some stick for the *"Don't drink, don't smoke"* line of the chorus, however as the son of a violently alcoholic father, who had also lost his favourite Aunt Ruth to lung cancer as a boy, he had lived a clean lifestyle through choice[332]. The whole song was a riposte to the press who could not get to grips with Adam's teetotal lifestyle, not being what they expected of a musician. In a triple key-changing middle Adam reflected on a Kevin Rowland and Dexy's Midnight Runners performance he had witnessed the previous year, singing *"When I saw you kneeling, crying words that you mean, opening the eyeballs, pretending you're Al Green"*. According to the singer, *"When I saw Kevin Rowland sing those words and really get into it, I think it was more honest than anything The Clash had ever done"*.

The video was filmed a couple of weeks after the release of the single, in an old Victorian sanatorium, and starred former *Hammer House of Horror* actress Caroline Munro as an uptight journalist who eventually, charmed by Adam, literally lets her hair down. The singer recreated the spirit of the video on *Top of the Pops* a couple of weeks later with a multi-stage choreographed high-energy performance, sealing the song's fate at number one.

ʊ ʊ ʊ

Factory Records had experience of running club nights at The Russel Club in Hulme between 1978 and 1980, however it was with the burgeoning success of New Order they formulated the idea of opening and owning their own space. Trips to New York, and clubs such as Danceteria and Paradise Garage had inspired Wilson and New Order manager Rob Gretton, and over the next year they hectored the band into becoming major investors.

Finding a vacant yacht salesroom, Factory Records leased the building rather than buying it, a decision which would come back to haunt them in later years. There were visionary ideals for the club: it would be open seven days a week, day and night, would have no dress code, would feature music and performance, and would supply discounted drink.

---

[328] Donohoe had moved in with Adam in 1978 when she was sixteen years old.

[329] Caplin was later a much-derided *spiritual advisor* to Tony and Cherie Blair.

[330] *The History of Little Goody Two-Shoes* was a children's story first published in 1765 about an orphan who goes through life with only one shoe and is rewarded for her virtue by the earning of a second shoe.

[331] Hughes would find more success as the producer of Tears for Fears' biggest hits.

[332] Despite a poor upbringing, Ant's mother had been Paul McCartney's cleaner during the 1960's, and Adam would often go round to the house and walk the bass player's dog, Martha.

In-house Factory designer Peter Saville turned down the offer to design the interior, overwhelmed by the assignment, so instead it went to London based Ben Kelly[333]. "*It was a big space*" he explained, "*Before that, clubs in the UK had either been shitty dirty basements or they were designed by Peter Stringfellow, with flock wallpaper and chandeliers.*" An initial budget of £70,000, of which New Order would pay half and Factory would pay the other half[334], quickly rose to £340,000 as attention was lavished on every detail. Expensive mistakes were made, such as having to completely re-build a balcony to guarantee it met building regulations or placing the stage half-way down the space which made it difficult for bands to set-up or bring in decent lighting rigs. As costs rose, more money was borrowed from Whitbread Breweries, which was balanced against any bartering power the club had for the wholesale price of alcohol.

The interior itself was striking, with everything painted a light blue-gray, and the structural elements of the building emphasized with black and yellow safety stripes rather than concealed. The dancefloor was constructed from sprung maple and the bar-tops from concrete and granite. There were issues, however, such as the nonexistence of a backroom meaning VIPs had no option but to socialize with the punters, or a DJ unit from which it was almost impossible to see the dancefloor. A high glass roof was kept, meaning not only that during the summer months the club remained light until late, but that the sound resonated around the hard surfaces and high ceilings. Two large video screens were installed, and Claude Bessy was employed to create movies to show on them, which usually included old footage of air disasters, dancing girls, and Nazi rallies.

Not everyone at Factory Records was on board: producer Martin Hannett was furious, believing the money should have been spent on creating a studio instead, saving a fortune in future recording fees. A couple of weeks before the club was due to open, he filed a lawsuit against the label to stop the venture[335].

A couple of days before opening, a New Order roadie pointed out there was no cloakroom, facilitating a desperate scramble to empty a tiny cupboard beside the front door. Then, the Licensing Board limited the club to a members-only license, so 2,000 memberships were duly printed up and sold for £5.25 each. New Order bass player, Peter Hook, later realized that someone had made extra money on this when he was asked by a fan to sign membership card number 6724.

On Friday 21st May the Haçienda had its opening night, with old-school politically incorrect comedian Bernard Manning ironically engaged to perform, which he did to a series of boos and abuse from the audience[336]. The club was mobbed on the opening night, with the audience having to circumvent the mounds of sawdust and workers tools which were still being used to finish off the interior. The following night began the series of live gigs from which the Haçienda hoped to make a living. Cabaret Voltaire played, and only 75 people turned up. A few days later, the Teardrop Explodes were paid £3,000 to play a "*secret*" gig. Everyone was sworn to secrecy, which turned out to be exceptionally effective as only eight people turned up, including Courtney Love who had arrived with the band.

---

[333] Kelly got his first publicity when he designed the front of Malcolm McLaren's *Seditionaries* store on the King's Road and was responsible for converting Badfinger's rehearsal space in Denmark Street into the headquarters for The Sex Pistols.

[334] Factory Records half was taken from the profits of New Order sales, so the band paid for everything.

[335] In typical Factory behaviour, the label gave the lawsuit a catalogue number (FAC 61). Hannett was eventually bought off for £40,000 in 1984.

[336] Manning, to his credit, then declined to take his fee, telling the owners "*Stick to your day jobs, lads, 'cause you're not cut out for clubs*".

For all involved in Factory Records, the Haçienda was an essential part of their improvised masterplan to emphasize the importance of the city, and Tony Wilson would often paraphrase historian A.J.P Taylor in his claim *"Manchester is the only city in Britain that can look London in the eye… as an alternative version of how men can live together in a community"*. There was more than money at stake with the club.

ʊ ʊ ʊ

Gary Dwyer, drummer from the Teardrops Explodes was getting married, and everyone who was anyone in the Liverpool music scene was there, including wedding-crashers Courtney Love and her friend Robin Barbur. The two arrived at the reception at Cagney's on London Road carrying a potted plant and were spotted by Dead or Alive singer Pete Burns, well known as the bitching queen of Liverpool. Burns, knowing they were not invited, approached the teenagers, and instructed them to leave, calling them *"ugly Americans"*. A furious Love dropped the plant pot, allowing it to smash on the floor, and started laying into Burns, only to be wrestled from the room by other guests. Not long afterwards, Love stole a long coat from Ian McCulloch, singer with Echo and the Bunnymen, which had some poetic justice in that he had stolen the coat from Mark E. Smith of The Fall.

ʊ ʊ ʊ

The climax of the English Football season is the F.A. Cup final, this year an all-London affair between Tottenham Hotspur and Queen's Park Rangers, held on Saturday 22nd May at Wembley Stadium. The favourites were Tottenham who had spent the season one league higher than QPR, however on the day the match was a dull affair with no scoring by full time. Ten minutes before the end of extra time Glen Hoddle[337] put Tottenham ahead, but five minutes later Terry Fenwick equalized, taking the final to a replay for only the third time in the fixture's history. Argentinian players Ossi Ardiles and Ricardo Villa were both missing from the Tottenham team, the former because he had been released early, and the later due to the extra tension of the Falklands conflict. On the same day, in Scotland, the decades old dominance of the *Old Firm*, Celtic and Rangers, continued to be challenged by an emerging force from the North. Aberdeen, under the management of Alex Ferguson, had put together an impressive squad of homegrown players, including the likes of Jim Leighton, Alex McLeish, Willie Miller, Gordon Strachan, and Mark McGhee, and was in the middle of a run of league and cup wins. In the Scottish Cup Final they came from behind at Hampden Park in Glasgow to beat a full-strength Rangers team by four goals to one. That the majority of the team were under the age of twenty-three made the victory even more impressive, as Ferguson employed the psychological tricks he would become famous for throughout his career. At half time, with the score tied, he tore into his players, asking them *"Are you happy with this? Are you in a wee comfort zone? Do you want to be watching 'Coronation Street' on a Wednesday night instead of playing European football?"* Aberdeen would go on to have an even better following season, retaining the Scottish Cup by one goal to nil against Rangers. Ferguson was now noticed on the worldwide stage as a force to be reckoned with, not least because of his live on-air rant at the end

---

[337] Hoddle was later dismissed from his job as manager of England when he espoused his belief on re-incarnation: *"You and I have been physically given two hands and two legs and half-decent brains. Some people have not been born like that for a reason. The karma is working from another lifetime. I have nothing to hide about that. It is not only people with disabilities. What you sow, you have to reap."*

of the victory over Rangers in the final of the Scottish Cup. *"We were a disgrace of a performance. Winning cups doesn't matter. Our standards have been set long ago and we're not going to accept that from any Aberdeen team. No way we should take any glory from that"* he fumed into the television camera, ignoring their victory in the European Cup Winners Cup over Real Madrid ten days earlier.

In 1986, after a short spell managing the Scottish international team after the sudden death of his Jock Stein, Ferguson took the management job at Manchester United and turned them into a world-beating force over the next twenty-seven years[338].

23rd – 29th May 1982

#1 single: Madness: House of Fun

#1 album: Madness: Complete Madness

Immediately after releasing their disappointing debut studio album, Theatre of Hate replaced Steven Guthrie and Luke Rendle with new boys Billy Duffy and Nigel Preston.

These two joined the band in the studio with Mick Jones from The Clash, to record a new single, *The Hop*, released in May.

With hindsight the song sounded like a surefire hit single: memorable and performed with passion and energy, as front man Kirk Brandon demanded a cultural revolution in the 1980's, just like the one in the 1960's. Starting with a guitar riff over a driving bass and drum, before a pedestrian verse led to a killer sing-along chorus, which was then all repeated, the whole thing was over in under three minutes, in and out again after making its point.

Somehow, it never crossed over to daytime radio play.

Theatre of Hate were located somewhere between the newly emergent goth scene, post-punk desolation, psychobilly, and catchy pop, and just needed a further push onto larger things, however next single *Eastworld* was a disappointment, with Brandon's vocals pushed to their most frenetic, aggravating, and horror-movie hysterical. The production of the next album continued sluggishly, and in early 1983 Brandon split the band to form Spear of Destiny with whom he found chart success five years later. Duffy became a trans-Atlantic guitar God when he joined The Death Cult (formerly The Southern Death Cult), who soon lost another word and became The Cult. Preston joined him for a while before dying of a drug overdose, aged twenty-nine.

℧ ℧ ℧

The major split within the Labour Party between the left and right wings was made clear at the outbreak of the Falklands conflict. Michael Foot, as leader of the party, wasted no time in supporting the government line on military action, almost before Margaret Thatcher had decided herself, whilst the hard left led by Tony Benn opposed any armed conflict.

On Sunday 23rd May many on the left wing joined a peace rally in Hyde Park, after which they marched to Downing Street to deliver a letter of protest. In Whitehall it was

---

[338] More importantly, Ferguson also invented the phrase *squeaky-bum time.*

noted that some Falkland Islanders had hung up banners calling the protesters *traitors* and *communists*. Public opinion had been influenced towards support for the conflict by the right-wing press, with the acquiescence of the government.

Foot's stance during the Falklands War drove an even greater wedge between himself and the left wing of the Labour Party, and when Tam Dalyell criticised him at a party meeting, the leader snapped back "*I know a fascist when I see one*", referring to Argentina's General Galtieri.

ʊ ʊ ʊ

Zoo Records had been started in 1978 by Bill Drummond and Dave Balfe to release a posthumous single by legendary Liverpool band Big in Japan, of whom they had both been members[339]. As two of the most well-connected men in the Merseybeat

resurrection, Drummond and Balfe released singles by other Liverpool acts, signing Echo & the Bunnymen and the Teardrop Explodes to management contracts. As these acts gained mainstream success and took up more time, the label slipped into disuse, with the final single released on Zoo Records by The Wild Swans.[340] Meanwhile, one of the principal Zoo acts and one of the brightest hopes of the independent scene, Echo & the Bunnymen, released their most commercial single yet, *The Back of Love.*

Formed in Liverpool during 1978 by Ian McCulloch, along with guitarist / short-order chef Will Sergeant and boat-building apprentice bass player Les Pattinson. Using a drum machine called Echo[341] the trio released a debut single on Zoo Records, after which Balfe insisted that they recruit Pete de Freitas, a friend of his brother, on drums. Positive press reaction led to the band signing for Warner Brothers offshoot, Korova Records, and over the next couple of years released two albums and a handful of singles which made them the darlings of the serious music press. Of course, having McCullough as a frontman greatly abetted the band as he was not averse to spouting off all sorts of arrogant verbals, willing to publicly lay into other musical acts with biting Scouse sarcasm. McCullough considered himself something of a poet in the style of Doors frontman Jim Morrison and allowed a certain empty mysticism to enter his lyrics. Depending on your opinion of the band, these were either absurd babble or allegorical poetry, as McCullough became enamoured with the idea that he was modern-day pre-Raphaelite.

The Bunnymen had been struggling to write new material at the beginning of 1982, spending unfruitful weeks in their rehearsal room, but did have one song called *Taking Advantage* which showed promise. Sergeant's flatmate and former member of Big in Japan, Ian Brodie, was roped in to produce the single under the name *Kingbird*, and the band decamped to London for this task, something manager Bill Drummond had been keen to avoid. Relationships within the band were tense and the temptations of

---

[339] Big in Japan were like a training ground for the Liverpool scene, and featured Drummond, Balfe, Holly Johnson (Frankie Goes To Hollywood), Ian Brodie (The Lightning Seeds), Budgie (The Slits / Siouxsie & the Banshees), Clive Langer, Ambrose Reynolds (who formed the original Frankie Goes to Hollywood), Jayne Casey (of Pink Military), and Steve Lindsay (ex-Deaf School)

[340] The Wild Swans eventually morphed into The Lotus Eaters and had a hit with the sublime *First Picture of You (First Picture of Summer).*

[341] Echo was the same drum machine featured on the debut OMD album.

London did nothing to help, so Drummond arranged for them to undertake a short tour of Scotland to help with the re-bonding. Drummond, always the loveable eccentric, ensured the dates, when joined on a map in the style of a dot-to-dot puzzle, made the shape of a rabbit's head and ears.

The Back of Love, as the song became, dealt with McCullough's self-diagnosed Obsessive-Compulsive Disorder, and hints at an additional bi-polar condition with the line "*Getting to grips with the ups and downs cos there's nothing in-between*". McCullough had wanted to write a love song which examined the obsessive side of the condition, whilst also staying true to his own ambition of writing "*widescreen lyrics*". "*All these chart groups seem to be writing about love in a very surface way*" he explained, "*and I wanted to write about it as a real emotional thing*". Opening with a razor-sharp staccato guitar riff, soon to be joined by determined drums and a driving bass line[342], the song powered along at a frenzied rate, never losing control despite almost collapsing into chaos at several points. Three minutes and fifteen seconds of intensity which set a blueprint for what became known as *indie music* in the 1980's, the performance of *The Back of Love* was immaculate, effortless, and at the same time inventive, marking the moment the Bunnymen went from a sparser sound to tumescence, grasping for greatness. The song was at once aggressive and transgressive, completely lost in its own existence as the band set a high bar for passion in music.

The Back of Love provided their biggest hit so far, breaking into the top forty and reaching number nineteen, something of a victory for an underground act like Echo & the Bunnymen. When the band appeared on *Top of the Pops*, they had to mime to a re-recorded version of the song to please strict *Musicians Union* rules. The re-recorded version seemed even more breath-taking, with the band looking impossibly young and cool in long coats, spiked hair, and shades.

ʊ ʊ ʊ

Siouxsie & the Banshees were survivors from the original London punk scene, formed to make up the numbers at the 100 Club Punk Festival in September 1976. That night they performed a twenty-minute version of *The Lord's Prayer* unrehearsed, with a line-up of Siouxsie Sioux, Steve Severin, Marco Pirroni, and Sid Vicious, and it was unanimously agreed they were atrocious.

Siouxsie had been born Susan Ballion in 1957, the daughter of an alcoholic Belgian father, and was raised in the quiet desperation of the London suburbs. Escaping to the city at the age of seventeen she discovered The Sex Pistols early and dedicated her life to the punk scene, becoming one of the leading *faces* as part of the so-called Bromley Contingent. With her elegant poise and exorbitant image (she would wear Swastika armbands and cup-less bras) Siouxsie became one of the three main female role models for punkettes, along with Soo Catwoman and Jordan. Whilst accompanying the Sex Pistols to a Granada Television performance in December 1976, presenter Bill Grundy came on to her live on television, prompting an abusive and foul-mouthed response from the band, helping catapult them and the punk movement into the nationwide spotlight.

Over the next few years Siouxsie & the Banshees became more serious in their approach to music, and through several line-up changes and four albums had established themselves as one of the most respected *alternative* acts in the country. Where *year-zero* punk acts took their starting point as the power chords of The Ramones, The Banshees spearheaded the jagged approach of *post-punk*, being more

---

[342] A couple of years later The Waterboys advertised in the music press for a new bass player, stating an ability to play Les Pattinson's line on *The Back of Love* as an essential requirement.

interested in moods and creating music at the margins of their abilities. By late 1981 they had enough minor hit singles under their belt to release *Once Upon a Time*, a compilation and were ready to move on to the second phase of their career.

In 1982 their line-up had settled into Siouxsie and Severin, along with former Big in Japan drummer Budgie, and Magazine / Visage guitarist John McGeoch. They had, however, just parted with manager Nils Stevenson, an ex-partner of Siouxsie whose unresolved feelings came to the fore at the commencement of her new relationship with Budgie. As they recorded a new single, Stevenson was fired, and in May they released a self-produced non-album track[343].

Fireworks may have been produced by the band however it was engineered by Mike Hedges who had been recommended by The Cure. With the inclusion of strings, it

demonstrated a direction the band were keen to explore for their next album. McGeoch wanted to use strings from a keyboard but Siouxsie and Severin insisted on the real thing. Starting with the orchestra tuning up, considered particularly naff and clichéd move by classical musicians, the strings then came in low and meticulous, with a vibrant earthy sound, clipping notes before being joined by a determined band at full pelt.

Siouxsie has since talked about the sound of the song being sexual in nature, comparing fire and heat with desire, however it came over as more of an attestation for the fructifying Goth movement, the breaking away of the arty peacock faction of punk, the Roxy and Bowie fans. This cult celebrated otherness, fabulousness in an otherwise dull world, and the lyrics chimed perfectly with this vision: "*We are fireworks burning shapes into the world*".

ʊ ʊ ʊ

With the premier of the Soviet Union, Leonid Brezhnev, looking increasingly fragile, 1982 became a year of positioning by his potential successors. Head of the KGB Yuri Andropov moved to Secretariat of the Communist Party of the Soviet Union on Monday 24th May, setting himself up as favourite. This was particularly disturbing to the United States, as Andropov had proven himself to be fervently anti-American, influencing the Politburo to set up a new intelligence operation called RYAN, devoted to finding evidence of an imminent nuclear attack by the west. Residencies around the world now became reluctant to show scepticism regarding the official line and started reporting every little thing, which led central command to conclude the increased reports were a sure sign of a forthcoming surprise attack.

ʊ ʊ ʊ

The 25th May is Argentina's National Day, celebrating the May Revolution of 1810, and so the British were not expecting the day to go devoid of some kind of occurrence in the Falkland Islands. The last couple of days had seen a continuation of Argentinian bombing raids on the British troops landed in the Falkland Sound, without an excessive amount of damage being inflicted.

HMS Broadsword had been patrolling the seawaters to the North of the islands when two Argentinian Skyhawks were spotted approaching. British Hawk Harriers were hurriedly on their tail with a certain hit in their sights but were instead ordered away by

---

[343] Siouxsie had decided to spend the year resting her voice from live work after Abba's voice specialist Dr Sanner found her voice chords to be swollen to twice their normal size.

the captain of the ship who wanted the acclaim for bringing down the aircraft with ship-fired projectiles. The only problem was that the Seawolf missiles failed to deploy correctly, and *Broadsword* found herself hit on the starboard side by a rocket which travelled clean through the hull and out the other side. Moments later a second pair of Argentinian aircraft hit the nearby *HMS Coventry* with three missiles, which this time *did* detonate. The *Coventry* keeled over on fire and commenced sinking, taking nineteen crew with her; the rest entered the water and were picked up by a damaged *Broadsword*.

Minutes later and many miles away, the *Atlantic Conveyor* was hit by an Exocet missile. The crew struggled to control the fires and the order to abandon ship was given ninety minutes later. Twelve men died, including the captain who had been the last to try to leave the ship but found the lifeboats full. He returned to the deck to find an alternative lifeboat and was never seen alive again. Three days later, the *Atlantic Conveyor* also sank.

It was a dark day for the British, and the Argentinians gained the propaganda boost for their National Day by sinking three British ships, despite their newspapers untruthfully claiming five ships and numerous aircraft.

ʊ ʊ ʊ

The Beaconsfield by-election was held on Thursday 27th May following the death in February of Conservative Sir Ronald Bell[344]. The favourite was fellow Conservative Tim Smith[345], who did indeed become the Member of Parliament with a majority of 35% over Liberal candidate Paul Tyler. Far behind, in third place, was an untested twenty-nine-year-old Labour candidate and barrister, Anthony Charles Lynton Blair, who had been encouraged to run to obtain election experience. Despite losing his deposit and pulling less than 4,000 votes the Labour party were impressed with his demeanor throughout the campaign, and the following year offered Blair the safe Labour seat of Sedgefield from where he would work towards his time as Prime Minister.

Other future leaders of the country were also busy in 1982.

Whilst thirty-nine-year-old Conservative John Major was enjoying his first term in Parliament as the member for Huntingdon, Tony Blair's future *campadre* and Prime Ministerial successor Gordon Brown had lost sight in one eye, attained two degrees, and been rector of Edinburgh University for three years by the time he was twenty-four. For the past ten years Brown had been politically active in Scotland, even standing unsuccessfully for a seat in Edinburgh in 1979. For the first couple of years of the new decade Brown had been working as a freelance producer for Scottish Television, a job which took him to the World Cup the following month to cover Scotland's efforts, travelling with the team there and back. At the age of thirty-one he was also just finishing his PhD, living in a student flat in Edinburgh, and volunteering at an educational project at Rosyth Dockyard. Later in 1982 he was to become the Vice Chairman of the Scottish Labour Party which led to him fighting and winning the Dunfermline East parliamentary seat the following year.

Meanwhile, sixteen-year-old David Cameron was sitting his 'O' Levels at Eton and had become embroiled in a drug scandal. Several pupils were found to be smoking and distributing cannabis in the school, and the normal arrangement in such a situation was for the school to inform the police whilst dealing with the matter internally. This time, however, the story broke in the national press and the police had no choice but to

---

[344] Bell died in the House of Commons, succumbing to a heart attack in his office.

[345] Smith eventually stood down from parliament when he was found guilty of accepting around £20,000 from Mohamed Al-Fayed, mostly in used fifty-pound notes stuffed into envelopes.

become involved. Many pupils were interviewed, with some permanently excluded. Cameron's was named by another pupil and when questioned he admitted to smoking but not distributing the drug, a crime for which he was punished with a school fine, 500 lines of Latin, and a refusal of leave. It was to be a turning point for the future Prime Minister, who in summer 1982 was academically average and trying to learn the drums by playing along with his favourite bands: The Jam, XTC, and Stiff Little Fingers. Not long after, he discovered an interest in politics, and never looked back.

A couple of years above Cameron at Eton, Alexander Johnson had spent his time at the prestigious school perfecting a bumbling amiable exterior which masked a keen intellect. Nearing the end of his six years, he had also persuaded everyone to call him by his middle name: Boris. In summer 1982 his teacher at the school wrote in a report that *"Boris has something of a tendency to assume that success and honours will drop into his lap. I think he honestly believes that it is churlish of us not to regard him as an exception, one who should be free of the network of obligation which binds everyone else"*. Rather than go straight to University, Boris prepared to travel to Australia for a gap year.

Cameron's successor, Theresa May, had lost both her parents within the past nine months, her father in a car crash and her mother to Multiple Sclerosis. The twenty-six-year-old Oxford Geography graduate was working for Bank of England, and relying emotionally on her husband Philip, to whom she had been introduced at University by mutual friend and future Prime Minister of Pakistan, Benazir Bhutto. May had been a volunteer for the Conservative Party in local and council elections for the past few years and had privately admitted to her husband that she wanted to become the first female Prime Minister of Britain, only to be beaten to the job by Margaret Thatcher.

Over the Atlantic Ocean, future Leaders of the Free World were also active.

The twenty-one-year-old self-styled Barry Obama had moved to New York in summer 1981 to study at Columbia University, arriving too late in the day to collect the keys for his new apartment and being forced to spend the night sleeping in an alleyway. Obama, having been born from a white mother and a black father, had transferred to New York to connect with his black heritage; it was the year he decided whether he was going to live as white or as black. In 1982 Columbia was the only remaining all-male Ivy League University, so Obama did not socialize much on campus, preferring to head out in Manhattan. In June, his mother and half-sister arrived in New York for a visit and the three spent some time visiting tourist attractions. Having been away from home for a few years now, Obama was able to see his mother in a new light, one which he found disturbing, especially when she dragged him to see the French film *Black Orpheus*. Later he would write of the experience *"I suddenly realised that the depiction of childlike blacks I was now seeing on the screen... was what my mother had carried with her all those years, a reflection of the simple fantasies that had been forbidden to a white middle-class girl from Kansas"*. The question of which race he belonged to was decided that summer.

Meanwhile, three thirty-six-year-old American males were seemingly travelling in different directions: one on the way up, one ostensibly at the top, and one apparently on the way down.

Bill Clinton was the one on the way up having become Governor of Arkansas at the age of thirty-two and was now four years later fighting for an almost unprecedented second term. During the summer of 1982 he was working on his campaign for the election at the Governor's Mansion in Little Rock when a phone call came in from the switchboard. The male voice on the line informed Clinton that he had received a message from God informing him that the Governor's main opponent in the race was *"the instrument of the Lord"*, and therefore Clinton was *"the instrument of the devil"*. It was therefore his mission to do God's will and kill Clinton. The politician was forced to wear a bulletproof vest for a few days until the police caught the culprit, and escapee from a Tennessee mental institution who had had been scouting the local stores for ammunition but was unable to provide any identification.

Donald Trump was seemingly at the top, living in New York and about to complete the crowning glory of his career so far: Trump Tower. Borrowing money based on his multi-millionaire real estate developer father's reputation, he had persuaded the city to provide tax breaks on the building on Fifth Avenue. The various permissions were granted when he told each organisation individually that contracts had been signed with all the others. Strictly speaking, this was not a lie; Trump *had* signed the contracts, but no-one else had. Originally planned to have sixty-eight floors, planning permission was only granted for fifty-eight, so Trump simply got around the problem by starting to number the floors from ten. One of the first concrete framed skyscrapers in the world, Trump Tower had a six-floor atrium, thirteen floors of office space, and thirty-nine floors of apartments which were rented to the rich and famous, including Johnny Carson, Michael Jackson, and Steven Spielberg. The concrete came by way of a connection through his lawyer Roy Cohn[346] with the notorious New York gangster Anthony Salerno, whose organisation controlled the labor and supplies of the building material. The mafia connection came in handy during summer 1982 when labor unions across the city went on strike; work at Trump Tower did not stop.

Seemingly on the way down George W. Bush was, on the outside, a successful businessman, having started his own oil drilling company called Arbusto Energy with funding from the Bin Laden family in Saudi Arabia. However, even the birth of twin daughters at the end of the previous year could not steady his excessive drinking, and the problems with alcohol threatened to derail the entire company. A change of name to Bush Exploration in 1982 still failed to attract the necessary partners to keep the company operational, and it looked likely that even help from his powerful father would not be able to stop George drinking his business away.

That father, George Bush senior, was fifty-eight and biding time as Vice President of the United States of America, desperate to eliminate Alexander Haig, his main rival for the top job. Bush was a former director of the Central Intelligence Agency and used his contacts within security to keep himself plugged in to the day-to-day business of the country. Whilst President Reagan reveled in the showbiz aspect of his position, and enjoyed an afternoon nap each day, George Bush dealt with most of the day to day running of the office.

Forty-year-old Joe Biden was the Democratic Senator from Delaware, and part of a cross-senate party who visited Israel in June at the invitation of Prime Minister Menachem Begin. On a tour of the West Bank, Biden suggested further expansion of Jewish settlements could be met with a cut in support from the United States. As the meeting became heated, Biden emphasized his point by banging a fist on the table. Begin faced him down, saying "*This table is designed for writing, not for fists!*"

ʊ ʊ ʊ

London was growing impatient with the absence of land action in the Falklands and ordered the troops to move forward to re-capture Stanley. The new strategy was to use helicopters to transfer troops to within striking distance of Stanley, however as last-

---

[346] Cohn first found success helping Joseph McCarthy persecute suspected Communists. He was also responsible for prosecuting hundreds of homosexual men, forcing them from their job and positions of power, which is ironic given he was a lifelong homosexual who later died of AIDS. Not that he would admit it, claiming instead to be "*a heterosexual man who fucks around with guys*".

minute arrangements were being made, news came in of the sinking of *Atlantic Conveyor* which had been carrying the necessary air transport. New orders came from London: the troops were to move in the direction of Goose Green and re-capture it, purely because a propaganda victory was required after such a substantial forfeiture of sea vessels on Tuesday 25th May. There was not much eagerness on the ground for the operation, with troops expected to trek over severe and desolate land, exposed to potential missile attacks, and then confront an Argentinian force which they had no idea the size of, whilst avoiding injuring any Falklands residents.

On Thursday 27th May a garrison of 42 Commando set off on an eight-mile hike, taking shelter in an outhouse. Meanwhile, in London the Ministry of Defence announced the British were approaching Goose Green, a tactical blunder which lost the element of surprise when it was reported on the BBC World Service.

The troops attacked in darkness and in silence, a common training method used by NATO troops in response to Russian air supremacy. Major Philip Neame later described the night as "*Complete chaos and confusion. We had no proper start line, no firm idea of where the enemy were, no firm idea of where* [our own troops] *were but, despite that, I think we came out of it quite well because of initiative at every level... and aggression*". By morning, the British had entered Darwin and Goose Green, apprehending Argentinian soldiers, several of whom had been curled up in foetal position in their sleeping bags at the foot of their trenches – apparently not too uncommon in combat. The fighting proceeded all day as the British worked their way foot by foot across the land, finally accepting the Argentinian surrender as the night drew in.

Once over, the British had lost seventeen men, and the Argentinians thirty-seven, though 500 British troops had captured 1,500 South Americans. It is now seen as a celebrated British victory against the odds and marked the first time the two sets of troops faced each other on the battlefield.

ʊ ʊ ʊ

Despite almost two-thousand years of Popes, not one reigning head of the Catholic Church had ever visited Britain whilst in power, when John Paul II touched down at Gatwick Airport on the morning of Friday 28th May to be met by Cardinal Basil Hume and Cardinal Cormac Murphy-O'Connor. After kissing the runway, as was his signature move in newly visited countries, the Pope was taken by rail to Victoria Station aboard the *975025 Caroline* train carriage, the same one which had taken Prince Charles and Lady Diana on their honeymoon the previous year.

Although the visit had been planned well in advance, Britain's situation in the South Atlantic almost caused a cancellation until a compromise was worked out, with the Pope making a flying visit to Argentina the following month, and the tactful cancellation of a meeting with Margaret Thatcher, who had not been enthusiastic about the visit anyway. The Pope himself had been warned by his advisors that "*the English are cold; all that fog makes them only more so; their education makes them snobbish; they will be polite but stand-offish*". The visit had further been put in doubt when the Pope had been stabbed in the back by an assailant in Portugal the previous month.

Once in London, John Paul II attended Mass at Westminster Cathedral, calling for peace in the Falkland Islands and Northern Ireland, before having lunch with the Queen at Buckingham Palace. Despite the historical animosity between their titles, the two felt a common empathy with each other, both "*two people who understood the cost of duty*".

Over the next five days, the Pope visited and held mass at Wembley, Crystal Palace, Coventry, Liverpool, York, Manchester, Edinburgh, Glasgow, and Cardiff in front of over a million people, in the largest Catholic event for over one hundred years, whilst a long-playing album called *The Pilgrim Pope* was released and spent four weeks in the charts, peaking at number seventy-one.

On his first full day in the United Kingdom, Pope John Paul II visited Canterbury Cathedral in Kent where he was met by the Archbishop of Canterbury, Dr Robert Runcie. At the Cathedral, which the Pope said reminded him of Krakow, the two knelt together in silent prayer on the spot where Thomas Beckett was murdered on the orders of Henry II, before issuing a joint statement thanking God for "*the progress that has been made in the work of reconciliation*" between the two churches. Whilst taking a short rest in the deanery, Prince Charles took the opportunity to slip into the room unexpectedly and sat awkwardly and silently by his side.

ʊ ʊ ʊ

In 1982 one of the primary sources in Britain of the substance which would become known as ecstasy was Marc Almond of Soft Cell, who was on a one-man mission to turn all onto the drug after he was introduced to it in New York the previous year. Almond would transport pockets crammed with MDMA through customs upon returning

each time from the *big apple* and dispense them to friends and acquaintances for free. It was, therefore, only a matter of time before he celebrated the sensation in song. *Torch* had been written and recorded in New York earlier in the year and was the first sign of fresh material by Soft Cell following their debut album. When the record company indicated they needed a new single, Dave Ball had locked himself in the studio with "*a Synclavier, a Roland TR-808 drum machine, a coffee machine and a gram of white lady for inspiration*" over a weekend and written the song. Produced once again by Mike Thorne, the track began with a trumpet refrain by John Gatchell, and was written after Almond had been stirred to tears by a blues singer in a bar, "*a Billie Holiday-type singer with a white gardenia in her hair and a blue sparkly dress… a person who sees his life in her song*", however halfway through the track shifted into a love song to ecstasy. Almond implored the listener to "*See her eyes, they are bright tonight… see how they light your way tonight*", as he fell under the influence of both the woman and the drug. Towards the end his dealer and voice of the drug, Cindy Ecstasy, took over the vocals in a flat imitation of an English Estuary accent, before they sang together, her the Pied Piper and him the disciple.

The single entered the top twenty and Cindy flew in from New York to appear on *Top of the Pops* with the band, wearing a stylish vintage dress. Given her absence of singing ability, viewers simply presumed she was Almond's girlfriend; very few had any idea what ecstasy was in 1982. Whilst she was in the country the band took the opportunity to record a video for the song, coaxing Cindy into wearing a bald cap to make the drug appear more androgynous. She was furious with the final video, fuming that she had been made to look *ugly*, and as a Jewish woman it reminded her of women in the concentration camps, marking the beginning of the end in their relationship. After turning her attention to Almond's musical partner, Dave Ball, and being rejected, she attached herself to Dave Balfe from the Teardrop Explodes.

Meanwhile, *Torch* climbed to second place in the charts, only being kept off the top by Adam Ant, and Soft Cell demonstrated they were destined to be more than just a flash in the pan.

ʊ ʊ ʊ

The Clash kicked off their American tour on Saturday 29th May with the first of two nights at the Convention Hall, Asbury Park, but without Topper Headon things just did not seem right. Frontman Joe Strummer later admitted "*I don't think we played a good gig after Topper was fired*". For the tour the band adopted a look somewhere between adolescent delinquent and Vietnam veteran, with camouflaged clothing styled by bass player Paul Simonon. Strummer adopted a Mohican haircut, influenced by Travis Bickle in the movie *Taxi Driver*.

During the first night a fan threw a firecracker on stage which exploded taking a slight mass of flesh from Strummer's leg, whilst he ranted at the audience to sabotage the increasing following success had brought, fearing it would dilute the message of the band. Guitarist Mick Jones, on the other hand, loved the success and was fulfilling his dreams of becoming a rock star. The two were growing increasingly apart with Jones looking to explore new directions sonically[347] and Strummer wanting to look back to Chuck Berry. On one date of the tour, Strummer became fed up with the strange new sounds coming from the guitarist, and approached him onstage, placing his hand over the frets to stop the noise. The tension between the two shifted up a gear after that.

ʊ ʊ ʊ

Both England and Scotland were impatient to prepare for the forthcoming FIFA World Cup in Spain, however they were also wary of injuring star players before the start of the tournament, and so on Saturday 29th May the annual match between the two was a restrained affair, with both sides fielding weakened teams. As the oldest international football meeting in the world the match was typically a zealous affair, and with 1982 marking the centenary of the first fixture, there was still a lot at stake. Whilst the Pope packed Wembley Stadium in London, a matching 80,000 spectators at Glasgow's Hampden Park saw a Paul Mariner goal give England a narrow victory.

Following the match Scotland manager Jock Stein gave an extremely expeditious television interview, being keen to get away and announce to the waiting players who was in the final squad for the World Cup. Entering a dressing room full of anticipation, Stein looked around before proclaiming "*We're taking all of you to Spain*". As the players started to congratulate each other, he added "*Except Tommy Burns and Ray Stewart*", and walked out. Burns, looking as if he was about follow and assault Stein was restrained by Celtic team-mate Davie Provan, but remained furious about the decision, and especially the way it was delivered, until his premature death in 2008.

---

[347] Jones was enthralled by the sound of hip-hop and electronica coming from New York. Futura 2000 was hired by the band to do live graffiti behind them onstage for this tour.

JUNE

30th May – 5th June 1982

#1 single: Madness: House of Fun
#1 album: Roxy Music: Avalon

The Cure looked as if they had split in May with the release of their fourth album, *Pornography*. The band who had been formed ten years previously at school in Crawley by Robert Smith, Michael Dempsey, and Lol Tolhurst had been motivated by the punk explosion to drive their music in more angular and murkier directions. Signing to Hansa Records in 1977[348] the trio were originally pushed to become a teen band, something which should have been obvious when the audition only required them to stand with their instruments and have a photograph taken. A stubborn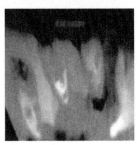
insistence on spending studio time recording their own compositions led to the contract being torn up, with Hansa being of the judgement that "*even people in prison wouldn't like these songs*". The following year saw The Cure signed to Fiction Records, a new label set up by former Polydor scout Chris Parry[349].

In 1978 the band were thrown off a Generation X tour after Tolhurst drunkenly urinated over Billy Idol whilst the front man was receiving oral relief in the toilet of a venue, however the following year another tour support proved more beneficial. A few days into the Siouxsie & the Banshees *Join Hands* tour, the drummer and guitarist from the headline act quit just hours before a date in Aberdeen. Smith was recruited to play guitar for the remainder of the tour along with Slits drummer Budgie, after which the Banshees tried to persuade him to join full-time before settling on former Magazine guitarist, John McGeoch.

Between then and 1981 the Cure released three albums, *Three Imaginary Boys*, *Seventeen Seconds*, and *Faith*, each of which reached higher in the charts than its predecessor. There was also a string of memorable singles skirting around the edges of the top forty which grew progressively gloomier with each year, from the precarious pop of *Killing an Arab* and *Boys Don't Cry*, through to the morose soundscape of *Charlotte Sometimes*.

Throughout 1980 and 1981, after recruiting another schoolfriend Simon Gallup to replace Dempsey the band increased their reputation and success by relentless touring, reaching the top ten in New Zealand and the Netherlands. Their music became more funereal, almost depressing, utilizing moods which would later impact on the goth movement whilst also creating a *catch 22* descending spiral in the mental health and disposition of the band members. The mood was further diminished halfway through 1981 when Tolhurst's mother died, plummeting the drummer into a bout of depression which he dealt with by increasing his alcohol intake. Not that the rest of the band were in a good place either, with snowballing drug use leading to Smith arriving for one Australian tour with no idea where he was.

Smith's own blackening mood influenced the recording of the next album, which he insisted on calling *Pornography* even though the name was going to stifle publicity and

---

[348] On the same day as Japan.

[349] Parry had been a pop star in New Zealand in the early 1970's before relocating to London and working for Polydor Records. Whilst there, the company refused his requests to sign The Sex Pistols and The Clash, before letting him take on board The Jam and Siouxsie & the Banshees.

press coverage. During the recording of the album in early 1982 Smith's decline into drugs made it problematic for him to clarify what he sought to realize to the rest of the band. The claustrophobic mood was increased by the band sleeping in the studio and arranging an unlimited tab at the off-licence across the road. The album was disorganized in terms of direction, with an overall feeling of dread, anxiety, and apprehension throughout, something which obviously appealed to the Cure fans who bought enough copies for it to reach number eight when released.

What became apparent during the recording of the album, however, was that any idea of The Cure being a band and not merely Smith's backing musicians was blown out of the water. Smith himself later acknowledged he was not in a good place at the time, describing himself as "*incredibly obnoxious, appalling, self-centered*", and it was this which most influenced the sound of the album. The press did not know what to make of such disconsolate music, with one review stating "*Ian Curtis, by comparison, was a bundle of laughs*".

Given the lack of good humour within the band, it was possibly imprudent for them to head off on a world tour, though that was all they had known for the past few years. Things reached crisis point at the end of the May dates across European venues way too big for them. On most dates Tolhurst described the relationships as "*morose and confrontational*", and after a concert in Strasbourg, Gallup and Smith came to blows in a nightclub, after which they both flew home separately. With dates still to satisfy Tolhurst hatched a plan to put himself and the roadies onstage in the dark and mime to the album, before both Smith and Gallup were persuaded to return and finish the

tour[350]. On Friday 11th June The Cure played their last date in Belgium, with the final song being a free-form jam featuring a roadie singing about how much of a wanker Smith was. As far as the members of the band were concerned, that was it. Smith went into hermit mode in the Lake District, Tolhurst took off to France and Spain with his girlfriend, and then did a little bit of producing back in London, whilst Gallup withdrew to Crawley.

Almost immediately the band (seemingly posthumously) released a single from the doom-laden *Pornography* album. Label boss Parry had worried about the absence of anything commercial on the album and instructed Smith and producer Phil Thornalley to polish the track *Hanging Garden* for release. Just to be on the safe side, Parry included live versions of *Killing an Arab* and *A Forest* on the B-side, and the E.P. scraped into the top forty, peaking at number thirty-four.

ʊ ʊ ʊ

President Reagan had been in discussion with the Brazilians, who had memorably defined the Falklands conflict as "*two bald men fighting over a comb*", and expressed in a late night telephone call to Margaret Thatcher on Monday 31st May their view that the best chance of peace was before the Argentinians were wholly humiliated in the fighting. This was utterly unacceptable to Thatcher and she communicated this strongly, asserting she considered it "*quite wrong… to snatch diplomatic defeat out of the jaws of military victory*". There was simply no way that Thatcher was going to pull back now, especially considering the effect the war was having on the poll ratings for both her and the Conservative Party.

---

[350] Smith had to be persuaded by his father.

Back in February, the polls had the Conservatives on only 27% of the vote, with Labour on 34% and the SDLP on 36%. Even with the potential splitting of the liberal left vote caused by the existence of the SDLP, the Conservatives were still trailing in third place. By the end of May, however, the Conservatives had almost doubled their share to 51% with Labour at 25% and the SDLP bubble bursting with only 23%. Without a doubt, the triumph and jingoism of the Falklands conflict had saved the Conservatives, and in particular the reputation of Thatcher, and from then until the General Election of 1983 they never fell below a 5% lead in the polls, often reaching as high as 20%.

℧ ℧ ℧

The re-opening of the Danceteria in New York had been almost too effortless, with the new club an even greater success than the original. Trouble, however, was brewing and within a couple of months it erupted when building owner Alex Di Lorenzo decided founder Jim Fouratt was paying the acts too much money and began arguing this through club manager John Argento. The other co-founder Rudolf Piper sided with the owner, and on Monday 31st May Fouratt found the locks changed with him on the outside. Fouratt was a self-confessed difficult individual, claiming "*I want everything done my own way*", even haranguing revered DJ Mark Kamins on his record selection. Whilst Danceteria put out a press-release stating "*Disaster mongers will be wasting their time. Danceteria will be getting better and better*", Fouratt took his claim on the ownership to the New York Supreme Court, arguing he was being denied his livelihood. Di Lorenzo argued in retaliation that the name had not been registered and the original club had been illegal, and over the next couple of months Fouratt received a couple of beatings as warnings.

To replace him Danceteria hired Ruth Polsky[351] who had been booking bands for another club, Hurrah, and was well connected with current British acts such as New Order. She started to make a couple of trips to Europe each year, paid for by the club, to book new talent and would allow touring bands to sleep in her loft apartment.

Meanwhile, across town Paradise Garage was the seasoned dancers club of choice. Ostensibly a gay venue, the Garage featured Larry Levan on the decks and played the usual mixture of soul, disco, Latin, and hip-hop, attracting the straight clubbers who differed from the usual Saturday night disco regular in their lack of homophobia. Artist Keith Haring was taken there by Fab Five Fred Braithwaite and later claimed it changed his life: "*The whole experience was very communal, very spiritual*". Levan's trick was to make left field turns with the music, playing discs which would have seen him sacked from other New York gay clubs like The Saint and The Loft.

The main competition for the gay crowd was The Saint, opened in the East Village near the New St James, the largest gay bath house in the world. The Saint featured a massive circular dancefloor situated under a giant dome onto which was projected the equivalent of a planetarium. The lights for the club were mainly the projected galaxies and stars of the roof, allowing DJs to create a celestial show in time with their music. However, the real attraction of the Saint was the ability to dance all night and then pick up some easy casual sex on the balcony behind the scrim of the planetarium screen. By 1982 the end was in sight for the Saint, as the new so-called *gay cancer* started to spread through the clientele.

---

[351] As far as British acts were concerned, Polsky was one of the most influential people on the New York music scene. She died in 1986 when a runaway cab crushed her on the steps of the Limelight Club. Two months later New Order played a benefit for her, performing *Love Will Tear Us Apart* for the first time since Joy Division split. Polsky had an on again / off again relationship with New Order bass player, Peter Hook.

ᴗ ᴗ ᴗ

The cultural musical exchange across the Atlantic between the United Kingdom and the United States continued into summer when Bow Wow Wow started to climb the

Billboard charts, whilst The Cars returned to the British top forty for the first time in four years.

The Cars typified the American idea of a new-wave band but were in reality a highly accomplished and proficient garage-rock act who had spent years coming together in Boston throughout the 1970's. Frontman Ric Ocasek was well into his thirties when they broke through in 1978 with classic pop rock hits like *My Best Friends Girl* and *Just What I Needed*. The formula, however, was becoming tired by the early 1980's, and the new album had been savaged by the critics at home, despite a Billboard top ten single with title track *Shake It Up*. The band were also getting a little bit bored with each other and following the end of their American tour in March they agreed to take some time off to work on solo projects.

And so, it was left for *Since You're Gone* to make its own way up the British charts to number thirty-seven, with Ocasek perfecting a Bob Dylan mid-70's drawl over a mechanic rhythm. The band were not gone for long, returning after solo vacations in 1984 with their most successful album, *Heartbeat City*.

Making waves in America were London's Bow Wow Wow, now more or less free from the interference of manager Malcolm McLaren. The band had recorded a version of *I Want Candy*, originally a hit in 1965 for American act The Strangeloves.[352]

Bow Wow Wow, now more interested in success rather than McLaren's preference for controversy, recruited Kenny Laguna, the man behind production and management of Joan Jett, to record a new EP called *The Last of the Mohicans*. Lead track *I Want Candy* was Bow Wow Wow at their most irresistible, clocking in at less than three minutes, full of Gretch guitar and Bo Diddley tribal beats. RCA could see the commercial potential in the recording and flew the band to the beach in Los Angeles to make a video. McLaren sent his assistant Nick Egan to keep an eye on proceedings,

and "*his only instruction was that I should make sure there were no candy canes in* [the video]. *But… I was having a great time and the video ended up being rally corny with, of course, candy canes in the shoot*". McLaren was furious, stating "*I was ashamed of* [the video]. *It wasn't anything to do with what I originally intended that group to be. I'd rather be working selling books in Foyles than have to sit through an RCA marketing meeting discussing how we'd flog 'I Want Candy'.*" With an MTV-friendly video set on a beach, the hidden drug reference of the title was overlooked as it became a gateway track for many people in America, exerting an influence over many upcoming musicians including the Red Hot Chilli Peppers and No Doubt, whilst Sofia Coppola stole Lwin's look wholesale for her film *Marie Antoinette*. In Britain, the song was released as a single on its own and reached number nine.

---

[352] The Strangeloves were a band manufactured by respected songwriters Bert Berns (*Twist and Shout*, *Tell Him* and *Piece of my Heart*), Jerry Goldstein (*Hang on Sloopy* and *My Boyfriend's Back*), and future founder of Sire Records (and writer of *Sorrow*) Richard Gottehrer. *I Want Candy* was perfect piece of 1960's pop music, for which the trio produced a fake origins story about being three Australian brothers.

RCA rush released a compilation album to capitalise on the success of the single, featuring the four tracks from the EP as well as a handful from their previous albums. The next single, *Baby Oh No*, featured a swing beat with less of the complicated Burundi drums and more slap bass, the song was as straight as Bow Wow Wow ever got, but failed to break the American top 100 and was not even released in Britain. A new version was recorded with different lyrics and released in Japan, where the retitled *Teenage Queen* was used to advertise Perky Jean cosmetics.

Unsure what role McLaren was playing in the band, bass player Leigh Gorman reversed the charges on a call from a phone box in Liverpool Street Station to New York. *"I confronted him and asked 'What the fuck is going on?'"* Gorman later explained, "*He started talking about recording his own album, things got heated and I told him to fuck off. We didn't speak again for a decade*".

It seemed as if Bow Wow Wow were about to break big in the United States, as the band spent most of the next year there touring and recording a new album with big hitter Mike Chapman, however internal conflict ripped them apart, and Lwin was fired in September 1983[353].

ʊ ʊ ʊ

The Italian financial year concluded on Monday 31st May, and as the national bank was reporting a dismal year, the deputy head of the Bank of Italy was nearing the end of his investigation into the shady dealings at Banco Ambrosiano in Milan. A letter provided by the investigator revealed knowledge of $14,000,000,000 dollars of loans to unspecified parties through banks in Panama, the Bahamas, and Luxembourg, and head Roberto Calvi was ordered to issue a copy to all directors. Calvi had managed to keep his immoral financial dealings secret from most people at Banco Ambrosiano, however this direct legal order made him realize his business could not be kept private anymore.

Calvi arranged to meet Paul Marcinkus, President of the Vatican State, in a final incautious effort to persuade the Vatican to help him out of the desperate situation he found himself in. Marcinkus informed him flatly that there was no chance of this.

ʊ ʊ ʊ

On their way to Santiago in Chile, Shakin' Stevens' backing band had been booked on a cheaper flight than the singer, and touched down in Buenos Aires where they were swiftly rounded up and thrown into an Argentinian jail as de facto *prisoners of war*. After eight hours behind bars the musicians were deported to Rio, where Stevens was waiting, having spent the day getting sunstroke on the Copacabana Beach. After a night in the airport finishing their duty free the group flew to Santiago where they met up with saxophone player John Earle, who had been allowed through Argentinian customs by the grace of having an Irish passport.

ʊ ʊ ʊ

When all-female ska act The Bodysnatchers split at the end of 1980 and vocalist Rhoda Dakar joined The Specials, the rest of the band re-grouped under the name The Belle Stars. Stella Barker, Sarah-Jane Owen, Miranda Joyce, and Judy Parsons were joined

---

[353] They may not have been working with Malcolm McLaren anymore, however the band had learned some tricks from his playbook, and Lwin only found out about being sacked when she read it in the NME.

by ex-Martha & the Muffins Clare Hurst, Lesley Shone, and vocalist Jenny Matthias[354], and signed to Stiff Records. After failing to chart with their first three self-penned singles, label boss Dave Robinson suggested they try their hand at cover versions, the first of which was released in May, a version of the old New Orleans classic *Iko Iko* which the band had been playing live from their beginnings. The band were against recording cover versions initially however Robinson explained that a couple of hits would give them the space and power to release their own material and get it played on radio. Even as they released the single they were talking it down, with Matthias claiming *"I'd like to do something like Julie London... but 'Iko Iko'... anybody could sing that"*. Shone countered this by saying *"We wouldn't release a song if we didn't think we'd put our best into it, that we'd made it a better than it originally was"*.

Iko Iko had originally been written back in the 1950's and told the story of a battle between two Native American tribes during a Mardi-Gras parade in New Orleans. Based upon tribal chants, and featuring the phrase *Jokamo*, which was a corruption of the Mardi Gras Native slang phrase *Choc-a-mo*, meaning *kiss my ass*, *Iko Iko* was

perfect Big Easy marching music, featuring West African rhythms and chants. The Belle Stars kept the instruments to a minimum, except for a saxophone solo, emphasising multi-layered rhythms instead.

Unfortunately for the Belle Stars, another version of the same song was released the same week by a twenty-six-year-old Scottish former dancer called Natasha. Born Dorothy Natasha Sherratt, she had worked for David Bowie's management at the age of seventeen and claimed her heroine was Margaret Thatcher. Marrying Bob England, the couple managed the band Darts and set up the Rockney label for Chas and Dave, whilst Natasha was also trying to find success as a singer. Teaming up with Mike Oldfield producer Tom Newman, a version of *Iko Iko* was recorded which sounded not too dissimilar to The Belle Stars. Picking up on a Buck's Fizz / Dollar vibe, accompanied by a frankly bizarre *Alice in Wonderland* influenced video, Natasha's version climbed into the top ten, whilst the Belle Star's version lumbered to number thirty-five[355].

ʊ ʊ ʊ

You could not keep Mancunian Andy Diagram away from the John Peel Radio Show on BBC Radio 1 during summer 1982. First, he completed a session as the trumpeter in Dislocation Dance, and then two weeks later his other act The Diagram Brothers, for which he played bass guitar, completed a session at the Maida Vale Studios, playing versions of *You'll Never Walk Alone* and *You've Got to Pick a Pocket or Two*. They cultivated their own inimitable style called *Discordo* which Diagram described as being *"made to a strict formula or set of rules. All the guitar chords were based on discordant notes, all the beats were very simple rock or disco, and all the words were very very straightforward and down to earth"*. In July he was back again playing trumpet for The Pale Fountains. Later in the decade Diagram went on to play trumpet for mega-stars

---

[354] Matthias auditioned by singing a version of *Stupid Cupid*.

[355] It did find an extended afterlife when included on the soundtrack of the movie *Rainman*.

James, however it was shows such as John Peel which kept him in music in the early parts of the decade.

Peel had been playing cutting edge music on the BBC since 1968, initially championing the psychedelic underground until becoming an early advocate of punk. One of his strengths was his willingness to move not so much with the times, but slightly ahead of them. He would give any type of music a spin as long as it interested him[356], and so on any given week night between ten and midnight you would be likely to find dub, early rockabilly, African High-Life, punk, poets, rap, and dancehall all rubbing up against each other, bring regular complaints that the DJ was not playing music as good as he did a couple of years ago, an accusation which followed him throughout his career, leveled by people who were not keen to move on.

An example of a typical *Peel band* was Rip, Rig + Panic, who had featured in session on 19th June, the day after their second album *I Am Cold* had been released. Formed from the ashes of The Pop Group by Bruce Smith and Gareth Sager, the Bristol based act explored post-punk, mixing the angles with jazz, funk, dub, and what would later be called *world music*. Featuring future solo star Neneh Cherry[357] on vocals, along with Sean Oliver and Mark Springer, the album was released on Virgin Records, and

featured tracks from the commercial *Storm the Reality Asylum*, to the uncommercial *Another Tampon up the Arse of Humanity*. In an act of typical Peel perversity, however, their June session featured three tracks which were not on the album, including the enticing *What are the Toads Doing so far from the Swamp?*

1982 was an unusual year for Peel in that a lot of the music he was playing was also in the top forty. What many did not appreciate is that Peel had been playing these self-same acts before they hit the charts, people like the Human League, Depeche Mode, Adam Ant, and the Teardrop Explodes. Of the eighteen acts on the Christmas Day *Top of the Pops*, eight had first been played by Peel, often in session form, and sometimes years before. After 1982 Peel ploughed his own individual furrow again, and never again coincided his playlist with the top forty.

ʊ ʊ ʊ

The concept of the medley was hardly ground-breaking in the music industry, often being utilised by cabaret acts to squeeze as many well-known numbers as possible into a limited amount of time. Many older established artists even used the technique with their own material when playing live, especially when they had too many hits to fit into one set, or a new album to foolhardily foist upon an unwilling audience.

In 1981 singles started to appear in charts around the world, kicked off by the massive global hit of *Stars On 45*, a Dutch combination of 1960's songs re-recorded by soundalike artists[358]. Soon there were Hollies and Beach Boys medleys in the charts,

---

[356] One of my proudest moments was when he played a single of mine, right after the latest by Bastard Kestrel.

[357] Cherry was born to Swedish artist Monika Karlsson and adopted by jazz trumpeter Don Cherry when the two married. Moving to London in 1979, she hooked up with The Slits when her step-father supported them on tour.

[358] The recording was overseen by Jaap Eggermont, a former member of rockers Golden Earring.

recorded by the original artists, as well as others recorded by sound-alikes such as Gidea Park[359].

It was only a matter of time before a record company released an *official* Beatles medley, and a spurious compilation album of tracks featured in their movies released in March 1982 entitled *Reel Music* was the perfect excuse. The band's American label Capitol put together a single called *The Beatles Movie Medley*, featuring *Magical Mystery Tour, All You Need is Love, You've Got to Hide Your Love Away, I Should Have Known Better, A Hard Day's Night, Ticket to Ride,* and *Get Back.* In Britain, label Parlophone refused to release the single, rightly believing it to be *tacky*, however the demand for imports forced them to change their minds. The single picked up airplay and climbed into the British top ten, to the mystification of many.

If at least we were spared a disco beat behind the selections, the segues between tracks were poor, sounding like something any unexceptional studio engineer could

have done with half an hour and a razor blade. It also remains the only Beatles single not to have been released on compact disc or digitally, and with great hindsight the record companies remain aggressive in their taking down of any appearances on YouTube, making it something unique: a hard-to-hear Beatles hit single.

One could, of course, argue that the entire second side of *Abbey Road* was a form of medley, with the songs running into each other without a break, and Paul McCartney had even put together a couple of medleys on albums by Wings, however these featured all new songs rather than

oldies. The success of this single opened the eyes of the record labels to the idea of selling an old band to a new audience, and with the twentieth anniversary of the first Beatles release approaching, ideas started to formulate.

ʊ ʊ ʊ

The British Civil Service appeared to be working against the government over the previous few days as they lobbied European leaders, through their ambassadors, to urge compromise from Margaret Thatcher's approach of *no compromise* in the Falkland Islands. New Foreign Secretary Francis Pym put forward an initiative via the state department to *internationalize* the islands, which President Reagan endorsed on Thursday 3rd June. He was then horrified when Thatcher, assuming it was Reagan's idea, rejected it outright.

The following day, Spain and Panama suggested a ceasefire resolution at the United Nations, which was vetoed by both Britain and the United States. The two nations seemed to be almost alone in their opposition to Argentinian manoeuvres in the South Atlantic, with West Germany, France, Italy, Spain, and Switzerland continuing to honour existing weapons contracts with the South Americans, whilst Belgium cancelled their contracts with the Argentine government, but conducted their business surreptitiously through Klaus Barbie[360], the *Butcher of Lyon*, instead.

---

[359] Gidea Park was Adrian Baker, whose Beach Boys release was so good that he soon joined the original band as a touring vocalist.

[360] Despite being sentenced to death *in absentia* for war crimes in France, the American government felt Barbie was too useful in their fight against Communism and recruited him. Once he moved to South

ʊ ʊ ʊ

On Thursday 3rd June Israel's Ambassador to the United Kingdom, Shlomo Argov, was shot in the head by three masked gunmen as he got out of his car at the Dorchester Hotel in London. As two of the would-be assassins drove off (the third was shot in the head by an Israeli bodyguard), Argov was rushed to the National Hospital for Neurology and Neurosurgery where he underwent brain surgery, subsequently remaining in a coma for three months. The attempted killers were arrested in a flat in London, where it was established that they were members of the Abu Nidal Organisation, an Iraqi-financed Palestinian-based terrorist collection. In fact, they had dropped their weapons off at the Iraqi Embassy on the way home.

In Israel, the news was met with a mixture of anguish and relief. Earlier that day, Foreign Minister Yitzhak Shamir had called for the elimination of the PLO in Lebanon, and now he been provided with an excuse to act.

ʊ ʊ ʊ

Seven World leaders attended the G7 Summit in Versailles between Friday 4th and Sunday 6th June where they did their best not to reference the ongoing Falkland War. On the last day, Margaret Thatcher became enraptured by President Reagan as he spoke of his economic vision for twenty minutes, ostensibly devoid of notes. The key to understanding Thatcher's relationship with Reagan is to remember that she would have been a teenage girl when he was at his pinnacle as a handsome movie star, and that to a certain extent is how she still perceived him. She was, quite simply, star-struck and in awe of whatever he said and did. Reagan, on the other hand, was overjoyed that a business-like politician and leader like Margaret Thatcher listened to and took him seriously.

Of course, shortly afterwards Reagan confessed to her that he had been reading his speech from a translucent screen in front of him, which she had assumed was there as an extra security measure.

ʊ ʊ ʊ

The British leg of Queen's European tour did not go to plan, with dates initially planned for Highbury in London and Old Trafford in Manchester, only for both to be called off when it became apparent that every portable toilet in the country had been booked for the visit of Pope John Paul II. Instead, they played two dates indoors in Edinburgh, one in Leeds, and then a night at the Milton Keynes Bowl. Further problems occurred when Queen had to delay the release of their album and were therefore unable to provide the concert promoters with the cover art for posters. Instead, a band photograph from inside their recent *Greatest Hits* album was used, which featured Roger Taylor wearing a badge with the Argentinian flag on it. Given recent events, the promotors chose to airbrush this out.

The final night of Queen's live dates at Milton Keynes on Saturday 5th June was almost called off when Freddie Mercury had a ferocious fight with his lover former lover Bill Reid, at the end of which Reid sunk his teeth into Mercury's hand between the thumb and forefinger. Medics bandaged the hand in time for the show, whilst support act The Teardrop Explodes were met with abuse from the audience. Things were not helped by Cope's use of sarcasm towards the audience: "*I hope all this V's are peace signs, maaaan!*" Frontman Julian Cope later wrote "*We were bottled mercilessly from*

America, he worked for the drug cartels whilst also providing instruction in torture techniques to various right-wing regimes.

beginning to end by heavy metal bum boys who shouted 'Fuck off, you queer' at me." Queen's audience always had an incommodious relationship with Mercury's homosexuality, either incognizant to the signs or calculatingly in denial. His *Castro Man* look of vest and moustache, camp stage-show, and one-liners seemed to sail over their heads, and in a more civil era the press declined to *out* him.

It was also the last date for a couple of members of the Teardrop Explodes, as guitarist Troy Tate and bass player Ron Francois were sacked immediately afterwards. Julian Cope had become utterly fed up with the band and wanted to split completely, however he was persuaded to stay together by manager Bill Drummond because they had a huge debt to pay off[361]. In Cope's drug addled and damaged mind, getting rid of two members was one step closer to splitting up and a step in the right direction.

Cope must, therefore, have taken great delight in the chart position of the band's latest single *Tiny Children*, which lacking both drums and a chorus and stalled at number forty-four. One more step towards obscurity.

℧ ℧ ℧

On Saturday 5th June the head of Banco Ambrosiano, Roberto Calvi, wrote an inimical letter to the Vatican in which he threatened to expose everything he knew of their secret financial dealings unless the Catholic Church helped him out of his jail sentence. What exactly did Calvi know? He knew the Vatican was laundering money from the mafia heroin trade through offshore accounts, which were being signed for by Archbishop Marcinkus. He also oversaw and had details of large illegal payments from sizeable companies to the major Italian political parties, all of which went through his bank.

Having decided to threaten and piss-off every corrupt person in Italy, Calvi instructed his daughter to pack a suitcase in readiness to leave the country.

Two days later the directors of Banco Ambrosiano filed into the boardroom realizing something important was about to happen. Calvi handed them a copy of a letter from the Bank of Italy which he had been legally required to provide. A ripple of shock ran through the room as Calvi read the contents, revealing the massive holes at the centre of the bank's finance.

℧ ℧ ℧

Just when everything was looking gleaming and gregarious in the world of British pop, Australian heroin addicts The Birthday Party arrived back in town. The band had been formed as The Boys Next Door at Caulfield Grammar, a private school in Melbourne, by Nick Cave, Mick Harvey, Tracey Pew, and Phill Calvert, and by the time Rowland Howard was added on second guitar in 1978 they had mutated into a concoction of punk, rockabilly, and blues. After hundreds of live shows and several releases they relocated to London in 1980, changing their name to The Birthday Party on the way. Signing to London independent label 4AD, the band were now in the routine of going home to Australia during the unsympathetic British winter and returning with a completed album in the spring. Unfortunately, this was not the only habit they developed, and what is conceivably most remarkable about the band is how they managed to balance live dates and recording with major heroin and alcohol addictions.

---

[361] Drummond later released a brilliant little song called *Julian Cope is Dead* in which he fantasises about killing Cope to preserve the legend of the band. It ends with *"The records weren't selling and Balfie was drooping and Gary* [Dwyer] *had a mortgage to pay"*.

Upon returning to London at the end of February 1982, they brought with them the master tapes of their next album, *Junkyard*, but left behind bass player Pew who had just started an eight-month prison sentence in Australia for drink-driving and theft[362]. His place was temporarily taken by former Magazine member Barry Adamson, with whom a couple of the tracks were re-recorded in London. When Pew was released

early for good behavior, he arrived in the country in May with his friends The Go-Betweens in tow, just as the album *Junkyard* entered the United Kingdom charts and peaked at number seventy-two.

With each release the band were re-defining themselves, and the latest album had a deliberately *"scratchy, ugly, trebly sound"* according to engineer Tony Cohen, *"We were determined to make something quite hideous. I think we succeeded."* Cohen would go on to explain the recording process: *"We made a tunnel out of corrugated iron around an amp and put mikes on the iron itself. The noise was so bad it made fillings pop out of your mouth!"* Frontman Cave was learning to apply cultural references to his ever-improving lyrics, from Shakespeare's *Hamlet* to a gold-suit wearing Elvis Presley, and many of the songs featured violent subject matter, such as the fatal car crash of *Dead Joe* and the sexually charged murder of *Six-inch Gold Blade*.

The cover featured a comic illustration by Ed *"Big Daddy"* Roth of a hot-rod car made of garbage, deliberately chosen to stand out from the many minimalist post-punk album covers designed by the like of Peter Saville. Roth took some convincing to provide the illustration, having given up *"lowering the moral standards of youth in the sixties with his artwork"* when he became a Mormon in the mid-1970's.

The Go-Betweens who had arrived in London at the same time as Pew, set about trying to find someone to release their new recordings. The band had been formed at University in Brisbane by Robert Foster and Grant McLennen in 1977 and had spent the last five years swimming against the current with their own brand of intellectual tuneful pop. A handful of singles had been released on an assortment of independent record labels, including one for Glasgow's Postcard Records. Having moved to Melbourne at the end of 1981, their story became embroiled with that of The Birthday Party, despite an obvious and significant gap in their musical styles.

Their journey to London had been financed by Geoff Travis at Rough Trade Records, and after a summer of songwriting and a radio session for John Peel, he sent them to the seaside town of Eastbourne to record a new album with producer John Brand in October. *Beyond Hollywood* was The Go-Betweens second album, but the first one they were proud of, and was released in the first half of 1983, becoming a critical favourite and leading to a major deal with Sire Records.

---

[362] Pew had been pulled over by the police in Melbourne and had given his name as Peter Sutcliffe, the name of the *Yorkshire Ripper*. He used the time in jail to temporarily kick his drug and drink addiction.

6th – 12th June 1982

#1 single: Adam Ant: Goody Two Shoes
#1 album: Madness: Complete Madness

Like waves after wave, the pretty boys with floppy hair and make-up kept crashing upon the lowland shores of the British charts. Record companies, unable to see beyond six

months ago, gathered them with increasing desperation, hoping amongst the flotsam and jetsam there would be a new Duran or Spandau.

RCA tried to push York three-piece The Mood, who had jumped unconvincingly onto the synthesised frilly shirt tails of the new romantics, even being persuaded into their own Anthony Price suits and ties. Their third single, *Paris is One Day Away* was meant to provide the breakthrough, with RCA finding a budget for a Paris-shot video. Over the summer they enjoyed a slow climb to number forty-two and were so close when invited to appear on *Top of the Pops*, however when one of the World Cup matches went into extra-time the performance was axed in a last-minute re-shuffle.

Recording at SARM East with Gary Langan, The Mood mixed with Spandau Ballet and ABC in the studio, and roped Roy Hay of Culture Club in to play some guitar. However, contacts were not enough and after a couple more singles, the finished album was shelved, and the band dropped by the record company.

MCA Records had their own version in the shape of London four-piece The Fixx, who had the extra "x" added to their name by a label worried about drug connotations. Recording their debut album with Rupert Hine producing, The Fixx failed to set the British charts alight with their first few singles or debut album, and would ultimately find success beyond their home shores, benefitting from being caught up in the second British Invasion of the United States.

Epic Records were hopeful for two-piece The Quick, whose single *Zulu* from the previous year had been a hit in various places throughout Europe, as well as a chart-topper on the American Dance Chart. Summer 1982 saw their follow-up *Rhythm of the Jungle* become a hit in the same places, just not Britain where it stalled at number forty-one. Reaching number fourteen on the American Dance Chart at the same time as

Michael Jackson was writing *Wanna' Be Startin' Something* makes the sonic and rhythmic overlap between the two songs something less than co-incidental. Arista Records hoped that being good friends with Duran Duran would be enough for Fashion, one of the more substantial challengers who had already spent a couple of years playing post-punk on IRS Records, a frenetic time for them with British tours supporting Toyah, UB40, Hazel O'Connor, Squeeze, Patti Smith, The Stranglers, U2, & The B-52's, as well as an American tour with The Police. A 1982 album, produced by German Zeus B. Held, called

Fabrique saw them moving towards a pop sound, however the lacked look to be New Romantic pop pin-ups.

Meanwhile, guitarist and keyboard player John Mulligan[363] was in the studio providing the arpeggio sequences for Duran Duran on their track *The Chauffeur*. The connection did not end there, with Mulligan and drummer Dik Davis joining former Duran Duran bass player Stephen Duffy in his new band, Tin Tin, later in the year.

Occasionally, one of the new breed would break through, such as Blue Zoo who

enjoyed their only hit single with *Cry Boy Cry* in the autumn, amidst whispered accusations of being hyped or bought into the top forty.

Starting as Modern Jazz, when they presented their debut album to label Magnet it was deemed as not commercial enough, despite being the same songs they were signed for. A name change to Blue Zoo at the record company's insistence and a string of different producers for their first few singles could not get them into the charts, not helped by statements in the music press such as singer Andy O's explanation of the name: "*This is my Zoo* [pointing across London] *and the Blue is my emotional frame.*"

Cry Boy Cry was to be their commercial peak, with a galloping beat and melody not a million miles removed from Tears for Fears who were racing them up the charts at the same time. Maybe Blue Zoo would have become successful without the record company interference, after all they were a proven live act with some of the correct attributes and influences for the decade, however a lack of a decent follow up single put paid to Blue Zoo, and they were consigned to the category of one-hit wonders.

By far the most promising of the new bands signed to Duran Duran's label, EMI, no doubt in the hope that lightning would strike twice. Talk Talk had been put together by front man Mark Hollis the previous year, tiring of playing in post-punk acts and wishing to explore his love of jazz and progressive rock instead. EMI put them out on tour supporting Duran Duran and into the studio with Colin Thurston, hoping the connection would be made, however Hollis talked this down, claiming "*people who say* [we sound like Duran Duran] *obviously haven't listened to us properly. Duran Duran's sound overall is just bass drum*".

Third single *Today* was a moody guitar-free composition, featuring a Mick Karn-styled slinky bass and thumping sing-along chorus. Described as "*Brian Ferry with clenched teeth*" singer Mark Hollis was at his most bombastic on the single, and broke through, reaching number fourteen over the summer.

Debut album *The Party's* Over was more of the same, stealing liberally from OMD on opening track *It's So Serious* and Japan on the title track and *Have You Heard the News*. One of the few fast tracks, *Another Word*, was released as a single in Germany where it had been used as the soundtrack to television detective series *Derrick*. Throughout, there was a denseness to the sound, not unlike the pounding of a migraine headache, and the lyrics were often too vague to decipher but give an overall impression of loss and depression. The album was often overlooked in the band's catalogue, especially when compared to acclaimed albums *It's My Life* and *The Colour of Spring*, and it was very much *of-it's time* in terms of sound, however it was an accomplished synth pop album, with a small number of noteworthy tracks.

---

[363] Mulligan later found work as musical director for both Bananarama and Milli Vanilla.

Talk Talk were to move on to more experimental albums, keeping their basic distinctive sound whilst becoming more sophisticated. Singer Mark Hollis explained their progress, saying *"Each album should be a definite move on from the one before it. Some people understand that and other people don't understand that. Some people think that if you have a hit with something like 'Today' then what you should do is maintain that style and that will ensure more hits"*. Talk Talk, however, had no interest in maintaining their hit making status, choosing instead to create music personal to themselves.

ʊ ʊ ʊ

Malcolm McLaren's fascination with hip-hop had developed significantly over the past few months. He saw the communal characteristic of dancing as the most consequential aspect of the genre, claiming *"I want to make the audience stars… to do a record that can really inject a lot of ideas in music, in people's cultures – and the way you do that is to get them to dance"*. Dancing was the key as far as McLaren was concerned; it was built into the human psyche. *"Rock'n'roll is jungle, it is ethnic, it's ultimately going to send you into a trance because it's magical and come from Africa where it existed long before Jesus Christ was born"* he would rant, pre-occupied with folk dances from around the world, aiming to mix this with punk and rap.

With an advance of £45,000 and a publishing deal worth £60,000 McLaren was paired up with the hottest producer in the country: Trevor Horn[364]. McLaren sold it as a trip around the world, and played old Cajun square dance music, Peruvian folk, a video of Jimmy Stewart singing *Buffalo Girls* in Frank Kapra's *It's A Wonderful Life*, Afrika Bambaataa, and Kraftwerk in an endeavour to make himself understood, however Horn still had trouble with the concept which appeared to literally encompass all styles of music. He had never met such an extravagant dresser and found it *"impossible not to be charmed by Malcolm"* and his uproarious company, becoming enamoured with the idea over time. By mid-June the initial concept of wandering around the world amassing field recordings had been abandoned, and instead McLaren decided they would travel to New York and tap into the dissimilar world cultures living side by side there. *"It's a cesspool of nations there,"* he told Horn, *"You'll love it!"*

Touching down in Manhattan, Horn and his engineer Gary Langan were left in a hotel room whilst McLaren toured the city searching for the sound he required. Whilst the production duo mucked about in the expensive Power Station studio in Hell's Kitchen during the day, McLaren would take them to clubs at night. Langan had his eyed open at Negril in the East Village, saying *"It was one of the most enlightening things I'd ever seen. It had a whole culture of entertainment there with all these different people reacting to the music. It was a pivotal moment in my life – these kids showed me that we really could do anything we wanted."* Touching base with Folkways Records, McLaren made connections with Cuban musicians, hiring a man called Kuango who provided some conventional Latin acts. Whilst McLaren enthused about the sound, Horn and Langan realised this was not what they were looking for and were given the job of sacking them. Whilst Kuango got upset and had to withdraw to the toilet, the conga player came forward and claimed to know precisely what they were looking for. The following day he returned with four other musicians, all drug addicts and alcoholics,

---

[364] Robin Scott of the band M was considered for the role of producer, as was Jona Lewie.

and charged £4,000 for the session, which turned out to be the impeccable mix of proficiency and drunken exuberance.

McLaren's rummage through Harlem and the Bronx continued to uncover musicians, including bandleader Louis Calaph and his Happy Dominicans, and two Peruvians who turned up with pan pipes and a guitar made from an armadillo shell. Horn recorded them all, still not sure how this was all going to come together.

ʊ ʊ ʊ

That the ANO, the group responsible for the shooting of Israel's Ambassador to the United Kingdom in London three days earlier was the sworn enemies of the PLO did not matter to Prime Minister Begin: it was a perfect justification for starting a war to the north with the aim of driving the PLO from their temporary base in Lebanon.

Israel began bombing Palestinian refugee camps in Southern Lebanon immediately, also concentrating on civilian cars travelling the coast road to Damour, whilst PLO leader Yasser Arafat sent a message from Saudi Arabia via President Reagan that they would not retaliate if the Israeli's did not attack. The message was disregarded and on Sunday 6th June Defence Minister Ariel Sharon launched an all-out attack across the Israeli – Lebanese border. The overtly specified purpose of the invasion was to drive the Palestinians twenty-five miles from the Israeli border, and 60,000 troops were poured into the country, however it soon became clear Israel intended to evict the PLO from the entire country. Whilst leaflets were dropped by Israeli airplanes warning the civilian population they would be bombed if they sheltered any Palestinians, Arafat hurried home to reach Beirut before the main road from Damascus was cut-off. The Saudis provided an airplane free of charge and by the end of the day Arafat was back in the Lebanese capital whilst the Israelis occupied a tenth of the country. By the following night they were only ten miles from Beirut.

The Israelis assumed they had the backing of the America, whilst United States Secretary of State Alexander Haig had come out of the same meeting the previous month with the impression that he had provided a categorical red light to any invasion of Lebanon.

ʊ ʊ ʊ

Disco may have died in the United States at the turn of the decade, however in Britain it was still possible for American acts to have hits with dancefloor fillers, and June saw two such acts do just that.

Shalamar's Jeffrey Daniels first performed a dance move which he called *the backslide* during a solo dance-routine to *A Night to Remember* on *Top of the Pops*. The solo performance was required because fellow singer Jody Watley was heavily pregnant and was unable to promote singles from the album[365]. Daniels did not think there was anything special about his dance move: "*I'd been doing the backslide since 1978, on Soul Train, so I didn't expect it to have the impact it did. I flew to Amsterdam to carry on promoting* [the single] *and suddenly the publicist was banging on my hotel door saying 'We've got to go back to the UK, everybody's talking about you'.*" A year later, Michael Jackson insisted that Daniels teach him the move, and then performed it

---

[365] Even in 1982 Watley raised some eyebrows by having a child without being married. At the time she defended herself saying "*I'm an unmarried person. At this stage in my life, having a baby seemed a natural thing to do but marriage didn't.*"

himself on the *Motown Forever: Yesterday, Today, Tomorrow* television show, renaming it the *moonwalk*. Daniels was in the audience for the performance, and afterwards said to him *"Michael, that was great, but I was surprised that it took you this long to do it."* *"I just wanted it to be perfect"* Jackson replied, and then paid Daniels

back by allowing him to do the choreography for his *Bad* and *Smooth Criminal* videos.

A Night to Remember was an extraordinary pop song, built to sound sensational both on radio and in nightclubs, and marked the peak of a successful run of singles for the act, reaching number five and enjoying a shelf-life beyond the decade, however trouble was brewing within the band.

Although Daniels and Watley had been in the band from the beginning, the management chose to push Howard Hewitt as the face of Shalamar, possibly because he was causing them less trouble. Solar management kept a tight control over the act, choosing material and musicians, whilst Daniels and Watley were under the illusion they would be given more of a say. *"We were fooling ourselves... because Shalamar was put together by the company"* Daniels explained the following year, continuing *"Recently Howard has the attitude of 'Screw you guys, piss off'."* Halfway through 1983 the trio split, before Hewitt crawled back to the record company and management and continued to work the Shalamar name. It was to be the beginning of a long battle for the brand name, with Watley ended up with the legal rights to the name, whilst Hewitt and Daniels soldiered on in the nostalgia market with their manager's daughter on vocals.

In the same month another three-piece American act, Odyssey[366], were climbing the charts with *Inside Out*, a song written by a man from the Scottish Borders. In his mid-

twenties, as a bass player from the tiny village of St Boswells, William Rae had moved to the United States with his heavy metal band, only for them to split. Rae decided to stay across the Atlantic and worked a series of odd jobs including as a runner at the New York Stock Exchange and an assistant at the Record Plant recording studio. When he literally ran into keyboard player Bernie Worrell from George Clinton's Parliament / Funkadelic organisation, Rae found himself becoming part of the extended funk family. Encouraged by the various musicians to find their own outrageous style, Rae began working under his middle name of Jesse Rae, and emphasised his Scottishness by wearing full Highland regalia, including a kilt, helmet, and claymore sword.

Taking a bass line taken from 1980 single *Watching You* by American act Slave, Rae crafted a timeless piece of disco, which in the hands of Odyssey became transcendent and otherworldly, floating in a cloud of unrequited desire. The track was irresistible to the public, rising to number three in the charts, and was the last time Odyssey hit the top forty.

ʊ ʊ ʊ

---

[366] Odyssey had their roots in the 1960's when they formed under the name The Lopez Sisters. Breaking through in 1977 with their disco classic *Native New Yorker*, Odyssey had since struggled in their homeland whilst enjoying a run of top ten hits in Britain such as *Use it Up, Wear it Out, If You're Looking For a Way Out*, and *Going Back to my Roots*.

After a couple of decades in the wilderness during which membership dropped to embarrassingly small numbers, the Campaign for Nuclear Disarmament (CND) was enjoying a renaissance, brought on by a cooling of relationships between the West and the Soviet Union. Whilst the security services were obsessed with the idea of Communist and Marxist infiltration, and the political right wing viewed the organization as naïve stooges of Moscow, Labour and the left wing embraced the concept of Nuclear Free Zones.

Back in February the final Labour-led council in Wales, Clwyd, declared itself Nuclear Free, as celebrations were held across the principality at being the first European Nuclear Free Country in Europe, a claim which may have raised eyebrows in states such as Luxembourg and Switzerland. Despite the waved daffodils and thousand yellow balloons released, the councils were powerless to stop the government transporting missiles through their borders, or even siting missiles wherever they wanted.

Labour had found themselves in a paradoxical position during the Falkland Conflict, supporting British troops in their endeavour whilst also backing unilateral nuclear disarmament. This was particularly evident at a peace rally organised by CND in London on Sunday 6th June, attended by one-hundred-and-fifty thousand people, where *The Guardian* noticed a lack of ethnic minorities and Trade Union representation amongst the broad gathering of the white middle class Labour supporters. The protesters were remonstrating against Cruise and Trident missiles, whilst also calling for peace in the Falkland Islands. Amongst the speakers on stage was Tony Benn, who stated "*We are up against a frightened bunch of world leaders who conceal their weakness behind huge armouries of weapons with which they hope to bully us into obeying them and the economic interests which they serve*" whilst the skies opened, and the rain poured down.

The fear of nuclear conflict was all too palpable in 1982, with Reagan and Thatcher's hard-line policy against Moscow supported by the press, who helped stoke up real unease amongst the public with articles about a person's chances of surviving an attack.

Released around the same time was a graphic novel, or comic book as it was then called, by Raymond Briggs entitled *When the Wind Blows*. Briggs had previously become a children's favourite for his *Fungus the Bogeyman* and *Snowman* books, and this time he turned his beautiful drawing style to the subject of nuclear war. The two main characters, based upon his parents, were Jim and Hilda Bloggs, an elderly couple who follow the government advice in their *Protect and Survive* booklet, building a make-shift fallout shelter by leaning a door against a wall. The plot follows them as they struggle with lack of electricity, water, and food[367], and as their health deteriorates rapidly due to exposure to radioactive fallout. The book ends with the couple confused this war was not like the last one, with no spirit of the blitz, as they die alone and in pain.

ʊ ʊ ʊ

During the recording of album *The Anvil* at the end of 1981, Visage founding members Steve Strange and Rusty Egan had responded to changes in London clubland with a strong New York dance influence becoming apparent at the coolest nights. This was evident in a funkier sound on many of the songs as the two former soul boys developed their interests, however as Midge Ure was responsible for most of the writing and

---

[367] At one point they smell cooking meat and mistakenly believe their neighbours to be having a barbeque, only to find the aroma is the burning flesh of their neighbours.

production, the beats could come across as slightly stiff and staid. There was an ongoing tension between the synth-pop members of Ultravox and the soul-based founding members of Visage, with the Magazine members caught in the middle, and whilst this occasionally produced some wonderful work such as the title track, it ultimately led to the splitting of the act. Egan and Strange were desperate to break into the American club market, and when terms such as "*commercial*" and "*appealing to the American market*" kept creeping up during summer 1982 Ure decided they were going in a direction he was not comfortable with, one of remixes and compromise, and he announced his departure. "*The trouble with Visage is that there were too many chefs, six* 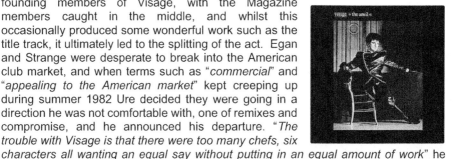 *characters all wanting an equal say without putting in an equal amount of work*" he claimed at the time. The final straw was when Strange spent a fortune hiring a camel so he could arrive atop it for a press conference at the Chase Park Club in New York. Ure said "*If you get on that fucking camel, that's it, I'm leaving the band. This is a punch and Judy show. It's just nonsense*", to which Strange replied "*Right, fuck you, leave the band then*". Strange originally wanted to hire an elephant however there were problems arranging this, so a troublesome camel which refused to leave the truck had to do. "*The reality was it rained*", Ure claimed with some glee, "*Steve's make-up ran, and the camel shat all over the floor outside the club.*" At around this time John McGeoch and Barry Adamson also gave up their place in the band, with the former continuing with Siouxsie & the Banshees and the latter helping The Birthday Party.

Throughout 1982 Strange and backing singers Perri Lister and Loraine Whitmarsh[368] did a series of personal appearances across America. These were never regular concerts, instead would often feature a fashion show, midgets, strippers, and jugglers, creating a multi-media extravaganza more suited to Las Vegas than sophisticated cities such as New York, Los Angeles, and Chicago.

The final single to feature the departing members, and the second to be released from the album, *Night Train* was a minor change in direction for the band, still containing all the features which made Visage, but with a much funkier edge and horn section driving it forward. The bass was provided at times by a synthesiser, and at other times by Barry Adamson, however it was no coincidence that James Brown had a similarly titled song, and with the intricate bass, danceable drums, and horn section, the link was made explicit.

The video was, for the first time, a band performance, bringing out a *soul review* aspect of the song, and featuring Strange's girlfriend, the future Francesca von Habsburg[369] miming backing vocals (which were sung by Lister). Strange spent most of the rest of his life hanging out with the heirs and heiresses to various fortunes, the spoilt mega-rich children of ancient European families, but no matter how much he earned it would never touch the sides of their bank accounts. Increasingly aware of the visual appeal of music, Strange had an idea of making a video for each track on the album, and even got as far as travelling to Egypt and arranging a day shoot at the Great Pyramids for

---

[368] Lister and Whitmarsh had been members of dance troupe Hot Gossip. Other notable members of the troupe are *Strictly Come Dancing* judges Arlene Phillips and Bruno Tonioli, singers Sinitta and Sarah Brightman, and Bunty Bailey, star of Aha's *Take on Me* video.

[369] She married into Austrian royalty, becoming a high-ranking member of the Habsburg – Lorraine dynasty. The Von Habsburg's were suspicious of Strange, and her father used his substantial influence to arrange for the FBI to follow Strange around and investigate his background.

the song *The Horseman*, featured the singer on horseback in a Vivienne Westwood creation.

Reaching number twelve, *Night Train* was to be the last time Visage bothered the top forty, as the remaining members released another single entitled *Pleasure Boys* in

October, however without Ure's guidance it sounded like a second-rate version of the Human League, a year too late. Strange continued with Visage through one more unsuccessful album in 1984, alongside a raging heroin addiction, and a second incarnation of the band cashed in on the growing nostalgia for the 1980's, continuing until his death from a heart attack in Egypt in February 2015.

Strange had been an important figure in the early 1980's, a catalyst for so many other creative people, however he seemed unable to move on from the sound and style of those first few years of the decade. He dated model Yasmin Le Bon (before Simon did) but was self-proclaimed as bi-sexual, and in one bizarre incident in 1999 suffered a nervous breakdown as he was caught shoplifting a Teletubbies doll for his nephew. A true maverick, Strange was the kind of figure that the early 1980's threw up, inspired by punk and simply wanting to be unique.

Strange was also a prediction of the future where he wanted fame and celebrity without having or the desire to gain any discernible talent. Even as a singer he was severely questionable, choosing to replicate Ure's guide vocal on most of the tracks. In a way the Blitz scene was a practice run for the whole *Only Way is Essex / Made in Chelsea* model of celebrity, of being famous for being famous. His real skill was in running clubs, each of which he insisted would only have a maximum lifetime of two years, despite various owners attempting to stretch it out. In 1986 he was hired by a club in Ibiza to host a party night every two weeks, hiring a private jet to transport several hundred celebrities and models to the island for each event. The following year, the rich returned along with the DJs, and the dance culture of the next twenty years was invented.

ʊ ʊ ʊ

In later years Tracey Thorn would acknowledge that everything seemed far too effortless in 1982. As well as being in an acclaimed rising band The Marine Girls, she was also studying English Literature at Hull University, had recorded a solo album due to be released in late summer, and was about to unveil a new musical project with her partner Ben Watts.

Everything But The Girl were named after a slogan on a sign for a furniture shop in Hull, and purposely worked contrary to the grain of what was in the charts. With a solid acoustic and jazz influence they recorded three songs for Cherry Red Records including a cover of Cole Porter's *Night & Day*, which was selected as the lead track on their debut single. Decent reviews followed in the

NME, Sounds, Melody Maker, and Smash Hits, together with a great evaluation on Radio 1's *Roundtable* program by Elvis Costello and Martin Fry. The single clambered to the top of the independent charts, whilst The Marine Girls new single also hung around the top ten.

Thorn's solo album *A Distant Shore*, released a month later, also garnered encouraging reviews. The songs had been recorded six months previously in a shed without Thorn having any idea what to do with them. Initially intended to be demo recordings for The Marine Girls, label boss Mike Alway pressed for them to be a solo release. Although Thorn was nervous that the understated methodology could be misinterpreted as easy listening, the press enthusiastically picked up on the starkness and immoderation of the voice and guitar approach.

At the end of summer, Thorn and Watt returned to Hull to continue their studies, a move which caused Everything But The Girl to take a hiatus before they had really begun. Paul Weller took them under his wing towards the end of the year and appeared with them at date at the ICA in London at the start of 1983, as well as coaxing Thorn to add backing vocals to the Style Council debut album.

ʊ ʊ ʊ

Following the G7 Summit in France, United States President Ronald Reagan flew by Air Force One into Heathrow on Monday 7th June, coming to a halt somewhere between the cargo terminal and the animal quarantine centre. He was met by the Duke of Edinburgh, Margaret Thatcher, and Foreign Secretary Francis Pym, and after a short discussion climbed into Marine One, a United States military helicopter specially freighted in for his visit to the United Kingdom. The helicopter took Reagan to Windsor, where he dined on haddock and mango stuffed chicken with Queen Elizabeth II, before inspecting the guard and riding on horseback. The British government had been trying to arrange for Reagan to visit for some time, but he was reluctant to agree, citing Alexander Haig's angry reception in Berlin the previous year. The actual reason for the delay in responding to the British invitation turned out to be Nancy Reagan's insistence on consulting with her astrologer before committing to anything.

ʊ ʊ ʊ

The two teenagers from Wham had little-to-no experience in the recording studio, so producer Bob Carter was brought into Maison Rouge Studios in Fulham Broadway to help them put together their debut single. *Wham Rap* was re-recorded with Junior Giscombe's backing band, as the duo signed a publishing deal with Morrison Leahy Music which was more about control than money, with George Michael insisting no-one be permitted to record a version of any of his songs without his permission, and that the music not be used in adverts or jingles.

Wham Rap had been written at Le Beat Route club when Andrew Ridgeley starting rapping "*Wham Bam I am a Man*" as a joke whilst bouncing around the dancefloor. Michael saw the potential in the gag and influenced by some of the early hip-hop being played in London clubs, expanded it into a song. In later years he was to describe the song as ironic and a "*piss-take*", however it is also easy to see how autobiographical it was at the time. With unemployment at a record high in Britain, the Left was demanding the *right to work*, a phrase coined by French socialist leader Louis Blanc[370] in the nineteenth century which was enshrined in the United Nations Universal Declaration of Human Rights, however the stance in *Wham Rap* is closer to that of Cuban revolutionary Marxist Paul

---

[370] Blanc is responsible for the phrase "*From each according to his ability, to each according to his needs*".

Lafargue[371], who wrote an essay in 1880 entitled *The Right to be Lazy*. In this, Lafargue claimed that *the right to work* was a form of enslavement for the working class, with them being subsumed unwittingly into the capitalist machine, and argued that human progress was driven forward by idleness and boredom, and the subsequent creativity these bring.

It is unlikely Michael was voicing revolutionary Marxist dogma through the track however he was celebrating the right to be unemployed. The song was a paean to having a good time at the expense of the welfare state as the lyrics explained: *"Don't give a damn cos the benefits gang are going to pay"*, expressing a self-centred view in the only way a seventeen-year-old could. It was an exuberant and funky piece of music, helped by session bass player Deon Estes[372] who had learned his instrument from James Jamerson of Motown's Funk Brothers.

Once you got past the unlikely idea of a white Greek-London teenage boy rapping, Michael made a semi-respectable job of it. At a time when rap was habitually performed to a previously recorded track by another artist, Wham produced their own music, however if the song was let down anywhere it is by some cringe-worthy lyrics such as *"Hey everybody take a look at me I've got street credibility"*. Most of the song took the format of a call-and-response, with at one point a backing vocal chanting *"D–H–S–S"*[373].

The duo was sent to New York to remix the track with Francois Kevorkian, the man responsible for D Train's "You're the One for Me" and Sharon Redd's "Can You Handle It". Missing their first flight due to a lack of work visas and Ridgely being on crutches following a football injury, they arrived in New York and booked into the Mayflower Hotel on Central Park West. The hotel staff were not happy about two men sharing the double room they had been booked into by the record company, and a couple of days later they were evicted when label Innervision forgot to pay the bill. Whilst in Manhattan, Michael took advantage of the nightlife, visiting Danceteria, The Hellfire Club, The Anvil, AM/PM, and The Peppermint Lounge.

The single was released in June with a cover provided by newly formed design company XL[374], and with parent company CBS seeing Wham as a club act they were sent on a series of personal appearances throughout London. For these, George and Andrew recruited two backing dancers: sixteen-year-old Amanda Washbourn and Ridgeley's girlfriend Shirlie Holliman. The foursome found these appearances challenging, miming to a backing track whilst drunken revellers ogled the girls and bellowed abuse at the boys. Despite this, and a single of the week in *Sounds* and *Smash Hits*, the release received no support from radio[375], mainly down its lyrics and their use of the word *"crap"*, and only reached number ninety-one.

℧ ℧ ℧

The British army had spent the past few days *yomping* across the Falklands, seizing several Argentinian lookouts without meeting much in the way of resistance, and it was perhaps this relative absence of engagement which led to complacency as troops were moved towards Port Stanley.

---

[371] Lafargue was the son-in-law of Karl Marx and ended his life in a suicide pact with his wife at the age of sixty-nine.

[372] Estes relocated from his native Detroit to Belgium with Marvin Gaye in the early 1980's, before answering the call for a bass player to play on a demo by a new young act fronted by a Greek singer.

[373] DHSS was the acronym of the Department of Health and Social Security, the government agency responsible for providing unemployment benefits.

[374] XL was run by future Pet Shop Boys, Bros, and East 17 manager Tom Watkins.

[375] Other than John Peel. Yes, Wham were a *Peel band*!

HMS Sir Galahad had already been hit by an Argentinian one-thousand-pound bomb in San Carlos Water on the 24th May, which fortuitously had failed to detonate. Once the explosive was removed, *Galahad* was used to move 350 Welsh Guardsmen to Bluff Cove to help set up a forward position in preparation for the final push to the capital. On the afternoon of Tuesday 8th June, whilst waiting to unload the troops in Port Pleasant, she was hit by two or three bombs fired by Argentinian Skyhawks, all of which exploded this time. Forty-eight soldiers and crewmen were killed in the explosion and following fire, whilst the rest abandoned ship. The *Galahad* was eventually towed out to sea and sunk as a war grave.

Sitting alongside the *Galahad*, *HMS Sir Tristram* was hit by two bombs, one of which failed to explode, whilst the other passed right through the ship. Despite the deaths of two crewmen, the *Tristram* survived, and after extensive re-building, served another twenty-three years in the Royal Navy.

One of the survivors of the *Galahad*, Simon Weston, was burned across 46% of his body. Over the next few years Weston became something of a spokesman for the veterans of the Falklands, helped by a BBC television documentary following his recovery. There is no doubt he suffered significantly, with his face becoming utterly unrecognisable, and having to be re-constructed over a process of 70 operations[376]. Understandably, Weston suffered appalling depression and post-traumatic stress, drinking, and becoming suicidal, but managed to begin a long ascent towards contentment when re-united with his old regiment, who refused to indulge his self-pity, forcing him to face up to his situation. Since then, Weston has been a spokesman for charities representing former veterans, as well as those suffering disfigurements, and has been awarded a CBE and OBE for his work.

Meanwhile, on the same day, some 450 miles off the mainland, an Argentinian Hercules spotted an oil tanker and attacked without first verifying the identity. The tanker *Hercules* turned out to be owned by New York company, however surprisingly the company and the United States government made little fuss about the incident, and as the ship was insured for $20 million, the decision was made to scupper her.

℧ ℧ ℧

To promote their new album The Birthday Party commenced a European tour in June, supported by Lydia Lunch and German act Die Haut. Lunch had first become enamored by the band in New York the previous year and had followed them to London where she held a powerful influence over various members. Lunch's performance during the tour involved ten minutes of Satanic poetry over white noise and her presence proved problematic, as Mick Harvey explained, "*Not to blame Lydia, but she did act as a distraction from a united vision which showed up the divisions which were forming about what people wanted to do.*" Cave spent most of the tour sick due to an increased use of heroin destroying his immune system. A friend of the band claimed, "*There were a lot of ego clashes* [on the tour], *they were all battling against each other and that's where a lot of problems arose.*"

As the tour, which they surreptitiously christened the "*Oops, I've got blood on the end of my shoe tour*" due to the violence perpetrated not so much by the audience as by the band themselves, reached Paris Tuesday 8th June the Birthday Party were in full self-destruct mode. To ensure the band played at Bains Douche, a former Turkish bathhouse, the promoter refused to allow them to touch the alcoholic rider before going onstage. Outraged and not really giving a fuck, the band refused to play until, on the verge of a riot in the venue, the promoter relented, and the band consumed two bottles

---

[376] At one point skin was taken from his shoulders to create eyelids.

of whiskey in five minutes then took to the stage. Before a note was played Cave threw himself into the audience, drop-kicking the first person he saw before offering to take on the entire reluctant crowd.

Afterwards, unable to score any heroin, Cave and his girlfriend Anita Lang holed up in a seedy Parisian hotel for four days, sick from withdrawal and arguing, whilst the rest of the band moved to Berlin to help Lunch record her new album.

ʊ ʊ ʊ

Morale was exceptionally low amongst the Argentinian troops on the Falkland Islands. The British had surrounded Port Stanley, the pledged rotation to the mainland had not happened, it was becoming apparent that their government had lied to them about the number of boats and troops lost by the other side, and they had been led to believe that the Falkland Islanders were desperate to be liberated and would welcome the Argentinians with open arms and parades. On the afternoon of Tuesday 8th June, their commander on the Falklands, Menendez, sent his chief of staff, Brigadier-General Daher back to the mainland to persuade General Galtieri to consider abiding by the United Nations Resolution to withdraw. Galtieri refused, however the troops on the Falklands had eaten all the sheep and were starting on the cows, and later that day the last two usable Chinooks were returned to Argentina. It was becoming apparent to Menendez that he was on the verge of an embarrassing defeat.

ʊ ʊ ʊ

Ronald Reagan was introduced to the Palace of Westminster on Tuesday 8th June by the Lord Chancellor Quinton Hogg, who claimed "*Mr President, when you come here, you are coming home*". Reagan was the first American president to address the British Parliament, and the Royal Gallery was rammed full to hear him, despite a boycott by many Labour Members of Parliament. During his speech, Reagan claimed that "*freedom and democracy will leave Marxism and Leninism on the ash heap of history*" safe in the knowledge that his country was about to develop their Strategic Defence Initiative, a system which would protect the nation from nuclear aggression whilst allowing them to attack with a hope of winning.

It brought to an end the first of three visits Reagan would make to Britain as President of the United States, during which he continued to mistakenly believe the British were enamoured with him to the same level he was with them.

ʊ ʊ ʊ

Roberto Calvi made the decision to flee Italy in the wake of the unfolding Banco Ambrosiano scandal. On Wednesday 9th June, the banker flew by private jet from Milan to Rome, having first sent his daughter to a hotel in Switzerland. In Rome Calvi visited Flavio Carboni, his partner in the illegal activities and contact between the head of the bank and both the mafia and Freemasons, and they talked over the predicament into the early hours of the morning.

The following day, Calvi visited his lawyer, giving no indication of his imminent flight from the law, whilst Carboni arranged to get him out of the country. Calvi returned to his Rome apartment, shaved off his moustache and awaited instructions.

By morning, Calvi had gone missing.

ʊ ʊ ʊ

Over the past few days, the slow but steady progress made into Lebanon by the Israelis was complicated by the presence of the Syrian troops supporting the PLO. It became clear the Israelis were determined to advance further north than their initial claims, and that the foremost target was Yasser Arafat himself, as they linked up with the Christian Lebanese Forces militia, controlled by Bashir Gemayel.

Israel had been worried about Syrian air defences for a few years, especially the Surface-to-Air missile defence system currently deployed in Lebanon. They developed plans to take out the system and named the operation *Mole 3*, based on the number of SAM batteries detected. By Wednesday 9th June the operation name had increased to *Mole Cricket 19*, and President Begin had guaranteed President Assad the previous night that no Syrian troops would be injured if they themselves did not harm Israeli troops, however Defence Minister Ariel Sharon persuaded the Israeli head of state to attack the SAM's anyway.

As the Israeli Air Force swarmed across the border the Syrians launched over 100 fighter aircraft in response, in what was the world's largest air fight since the Second World War. By the end of the day, seventeen of the nineteen batteries had been destroyed, and Israel had dominance of the air over Lebanon. With this in place, the main Beirut to Damascus road was cut, and with it any hope of Syrian assistance. Thousands of refugees flooded into Beirut as the PLO started talk of a *last stand*. Over the next two months there were over sixty ceasefires called by Israel, which they would use to consolidate their position, and in some cases advance. The PLO would then argue the Israelis were breaking the conditions of the ceasefire and would open fire, which the Israelis would then use to justify their continued bombardment of the city. When the Israelis stopped fighting, their Christian Phalangist allies would begin and vice versa, supposedly without any co-ordination between the two.

As the PLO set up their artillery beside schools and hospitals, the Israelis dropped bombs and missiles indiscriminately, not caring about civilian casualties. A minimum of 8,000 women and children died whilst cowering in the cellars of apartment blocks and public buildings. The bodies were buried in mass graves without headstones, often where they had died.

As the Israelis surrounded Beirut, they issued new identification papers to all civilians, each of which was stamped with either a square, an oblong or a circle. One represented a reliable citizen, one a neutral citizen and one a hostile citizen, however no Palestinians were ever told which was which.

The Soviet Union were watching carefully from the side-lines, normally supporters of Syria, and coming to the realisation that the West had superior military technology. According to one high ranking Soviet official, it was this Syrian defeat which led to a re-evaluation of their military power, and eventually a softened approach and *glasnost*.

ʊ ʊ ʊ

On the Falkland Islands British troops had Port Stanley surrounded, and lay in wait just beyond the hills for the precise conditions in which to move forward. Whilst the front line hunkered down in shallow water-logged trenches, they tried to dry out their socks by wrapping them around their bodies, whilst at the same time being blasted by the sub-zero wind.

The final assault commenced on the night of Friday 11th June with British troops noiselessly working their way forward through the ravines of the mountains. All was going well until section commander Corporal Milne stood on a landmine, as the explosion and his subsequent screams betrayed their position to the Argentinians. From here it was close contact fighting, with the British eventually capturing the enemy lookout points.

The Argentinians had positioned a substantial quantity of troops on the various hilltops surrounding Stanley, and the only way through was to capture them one by one. On the first night they took Mount Longdon, Two Sisters, and Mount Harriett, fighting for the territory foot by foot, with a total of 24 men killed and 65 injured, against the Argentinian total of 85 dead and 400 taken prisoner. As daylight approached, the troops crouched in ditches again, in their sodden sleeping bags.

℧ ℧ ℧

The head office of Banco Ambosiano received a telephone call at 10.30 a.m. on Friday 11th June from Luigi Mennini of the Vatican Bank. "*Where's your chairman? He was due here two hours ago*" Mennini demanded. Some frantic enquiries discovered Roberto Calvi had left his apartment the night before and was now missing. With Calvi now seemingly breaking the conditions of his bail, the bank informed the police.

Calvi, meanwhile, had caught an overnight train to Venice, travelling further from there to Trieste in the north eastern corner of Italy. That night, his friend and partner in crime Flavio Carboni arranged for Calvi to be smuggled across the Alps into Austria, crossing the border with a fake passport. Sunday was spent burning papers and preparing to leave the country.

When the stock markets opened on Monday, the value of Banco Abrosiano dropped by 15% before an uneasy halt on the slide. By that time Calvi had crossed the Alps and arrived at Innsbruck, moving on later that day with Carboni to the border between Switzerland and West Germany to meet with businessman Hans Kunz.

℧ ℧ ℧

Combat Rock had been in the shops for almost a month but was still absent a hit single when *Rock the Casbah* was released on Friday 11th June. Three days previously, The Clash had taken time before a gig in Austin, Texas to shoot a video with punk documentarian Don Letts[377]. The tension between Mick Jones and the rest of the band boiled over once again, with three of them turning up in their military stage gear, and

the guitarist wearing red long johns and Doc Martin boots. In the words of Letts, he looked "*like a fucking matchstick*". An antagonistic quarrel broke out amongst the members regarding the look, only to be resolved by Letts gently persuading Jones he would look back with remorse if he did not join in with the spirit of the shoot. Despite capitulating, Jones covered his face with a camouflage mask in protest, as the band mimed to the song in front of an oil derrick[378]. This was interspersed with a superfluous sub-plot involving an Arabian Sheik and a Hassidic Jew teaming up to go to a Clash concert.

Whilst most of the Clash songs were written by Mick Jones and singer Joe Strummer, some notable exceptions were created by other members, not least Paul Simonen's *Guns of Brixton* and in the case of drummer Topper Headon, *Rock the Casbah*. Finding himself in the studio early one day with no other members of the band, Headon set

---

[377] Letts was a London lad of Jamaican heritage and is credited with introducing reggae and dub sounds into punk. He also persuaded Bob Marley that his music and punk had a lot in common, leading to the single *Punky Reggae Party*.

[378] Towards the end of the video Strummer had had enough and ripped the mask from the face of Jones.

about recording the drums, bass, and piano for an idea he had in his head. Upon arriving, the band decided the music was complete, with Jones having difficulty finding anything interesting to play. Headon presented some lyrics about missing his girlfriend to Strummer, who scrunched them up and threw the paper in the bucket. Instead, the singer introduced his own words, based upon a story he had read about Iranians being flogged for listening to disco music.

Strummer could be accused of lazy stereotypes within the lyrics, throwing a myriad of middle eastern and north African terms into the mix, such as his use of Sharif[379], Bedouin[380], Muezzin[381], Minarets[382], and Kosher[383], not caring if cultures or religions were intermingled. In what world would a Muslim *Sheik* disapprove of and describe something as not being *Kosher*? Of course, the *kasbah* itself originated in North Africa rather than Arabia, and even today in Algiers is considered a dangerous citadel of resistance to the military regime. The use of the word spread across the Ottoman Empire and was more commonly used to describe a castle or keep at the centre of a town or city.

Throughout the song, Strummer referred to the act of throwing off oppression, symbolised by the various groups mentioned dancing and listening to Western music, which could also represent not just religious but all forms of oppression. On a more personal note, for Strummer the opening line referred to manager Bernie Rhodes, who kept on telling the band to cut out their long dub versions and go back to three-minute punk songs. In other words, "*The King told the boogiemen you've got to let that raga drop*".

Despite misgiving about the lyrics, and accusations by the small-minded of The Clash selling out by lowering themselves to creating *pop music*, the song has become a perennial favourite. As a piece of pop *Rock the Casbah* was superlative, providing a breakthrough in a United States which was dead set against pop and disco. The single is more affectionately remembered by the public than its chart position at the time would suggest, peaking at number thirty in the United Kingdom. It did, however, go top ten in Australia, New Zealand, and the United States, a feat not achieved by any of The Clash singles in their homeland whilst the band existed.

Years later, *Rock the Casbah* was used by American Forces Radio as an anthem during the first Gulf War, something which moved Strummer to tears of fury.

ʊ ʊ ʊ

Raiders of the Lost Ark had been a colossal movie success in 1981, however director Steven Spielberg had not enjoyed the process of making it at all. He felt forced into it by producer George Lucas and coerced by the Hollywood studios who demanded another hit movie after the disaster of *1941*. Spielberg could not connect with the story, but still turned in a comprehensively engaging finished product which the public cherished.

His next project, he vowed, would be more personal, claiming "*I was losing touch with the reason I became a moviemaker – to make stories about people and relationships*". He started looking back to his own childhood, and in particular feelings regarding the

---

[379] Sharif is used across the Arab world (and beyond) and generally means *noble* but is also used in some countries to refer to descendants of Mohammad.

[380] Bedouin are nomadic tribes who wander across North Africa and Arabia.

[381] A muezzin is the person responsible for the call to prayer from a mosque.

[382] Minarets are the towers build next to, or attached to, a mosque, from which the muezzin calls the faithful to prayer.

[383] Kosher is the set of dietary laws adhered to by Jews.

abandonment by his father and his own loneliness. Spielberg has since claimed the movie which became E.T. The Extra-Terrestrial was about his state of mind during the summer his parents divorced.

In the United Kingdom, divorce figures had sat in the low hundreds until just after the Second World War when the number of men returning altered from the frontline led to an upsurge to over 60,000 in 1947. The after a reduction during the 1950's numbers had been rising steadily, reaching almost 145,000 in 1982, close to the highest number recorded either before or since. In the United States the number was well over a million divorces in the same year, with over half of all marriages ending in a separation. The summer of his parents split Spielberg had yearned for a friend to talk to, to share his emotions with, even if it was a make-believe one, and from this seed he started to flesh out an idea about a boy and an alien. Unlike his previous blockbusters, Spielberg was determined to make this movie smaller, with fewer special effects and a more human aspect.

E.T. The Extra-Terrestrial can be appreciated on numerous levels. At the uppermost, it was a simple account of a boy who finds an alien in his backyard and assists him in returning to his own planet, however it could also be read as a tale of immigration, with the titular character finding themselves far from home in a foreign land, homesick, feared, and hunted. On a third level E.T. The Extra-Terrestrial is a deeply religious movie, re-telling the story of Jesus, a stranger from above who comes to Earth and is discovered in a shed, attains followers, is persecuted, dies, returns to life, and then to the sky. By Christmas 1982, Universal Studios were not shy of cashing in on this slant, producing a poster mimicking Michelangelo's Sistine Chapel image of God's finger touching the hand of Adam, with a glowing finger of E.T. and Elliot meeting above the Earth.

Spielberg's first choice of studio, Columbia had passed on the movie, seeing limited commercial potential, and when Universal picked up the option shooting began in the autumn of 1981 in the Southern California suburb of Northridge. The film was shot in sequence to ring the best emotional performance from the young actors. Spielberg shot the movie from waist height, the angle at which kids view the world, with adults as the enemy. He worked shorn of storyboards, electing instead to permit the natural responses of the children determine shots, and limited himself to a $10 million budget and two-month shoot. By Hollywood's standards this was a small movie, but when E.T. The Extra-Terrestrial was released in the United States on Friday 11th June it became an instant smash hit, staying in cinemas for over a year, and at one point personally earning Spielberg half a million dollars *a day*. Before long it surpassed *Star Wars* as the largest grossing film of all time, engaging both adults and children in equal measures. Critics were almost unanimous in their praise of the movie, delighting at such emotional depths in a simple piece of entertainment, comparing it to the effect of *The Wizard of Oz* or *It's a Wonderful Life*.

Poltergeist was released on the same day and did remarkably well at the box office for a horror, earning over $100 million from a $10 million budget. In summer 1981 Steven Spielberg had hired Tobe Hooper to make the movie, a surprising choice to direct having previously made his name with the extreme horror of *The Texas Chainsaw Massacre*.

Poltergeist told the story of a suburban family purchasing a house built on top of an old graveyard, and their subsequent haunting by restless spirits. The film has all the hallmarks of an archetypal Spielberg movie, and rumours have abounded ever since that the directing was mostly undertaken by the writer, either because he refused to let go of his creation, or else because Hooper was too under the influence of innumerable substances to do the job. Spielberg defended himself by saying "*Tobe isn't what you would call a take-charge sort of guy*", and most of the time when Hooper provided an instruction the chief cinematographer would look over his shoulder to Spielberg who would either give a nod or a shake of the head.

ʊ ʊ ʊ

Upon returning from an antipodean tour in June, and with the current Falklands conflict at the front of his mind, Elvis Costello had what he considered to be appropriate lyrics for the instrumental Clive Langer had played at Dave Edmund's birthday party back in March.  Langer had suggested the music would be perfect for "*a lyric concerned with the hours of the day*", and with Costello stuck in Australia, fourteen hours ahead of any news from the Falkland Islands, he somehow twisted the original vision into an anti-war song. Whilst waiting for Langer's own homecoming from America where he was busy producing, Costello put down a guide vocal over the previously recorded music, and then called Robert Wyatt into the studio to sing over the top. When Langer returned the two got together to mix the track. "*When I heard the final mix I just left the studio and burst into tears... the whole track was beyond my dreams*", Langer later claimed, and was justified in his enthusiasm. Wyatt was also overjoyed with the track, understanding how imperative it was to be the voice of dissent to the Falklands War, however his experienced was slightly soured when he "*asked a very young musician who worked on the song if he was happy with his contribution, and he said yes, it would look good on his CV. That was a little chill draught of the incoming Thatcherite approach to art, which said everything was to do with career*".

Shipbuilding cut a solitary figure in 1982, being one of the few genuine *protest* songs to burst the bubble of feel-good aspiration rampant in the charts. Starting with Langer's dramatic chords (played by Steve Nieve of the Attractions) before brushed drums and bass (played by Mark Bedford of Madness) came in with the vocals, Wyatt sounded fragile and vanquished, as he began with "*Is it worth it? A new winter coat and shoes for the wife, and a bicycle on the boy's birthday*". The song went on to tackle the issue of the working man on Tyneside, delighted with the news that "*within weeks they'll be re-opening the shipyards*", before the sting in the tail of "*and notifying the next of kin*". The irony was that whilst he was back in work, the ships he is helping to construct would be transporting his own son to war. Costello has since highlighted what he considers to be the most significant line as being the final one: "*Diving for dear life when we could be diving for pearls*".

The single was released in August with a cover featuring Stanley Spencer's war artist painting *Shipbuilding on the Clyde*[384], not long after the culmination of the conflict when the nation was still high on victory and sounded out of time with the dominant disposition of the country. Only when it was re-released in April 1983 did it have any impact, giving Rough Trade Records their first top forty single. Costello recorded his own glorious (and some say superior) version for his next album, featuring a trumpet solo by jazz legend Chet Baker.

ʊ ʊ ʊ

---

[384] When Spencer was working as a war artist in Port Glasgow during the Second World War, he was approached by a local woman who asked, "*Are you Stanley Spencer, the painter?*" When he replied in the affirmative, she said "*Good! I'm needing my living room painted.*" Spencer later claimed that he was tempted.

After five days of fighting, Israel and Syria agreed to a ceasefire between their troops in Lebanon on Friday 11th June. The Israelis were extremely careful to ensure this truce did not include the PLO, their primary target in the country. With the Syrian army no longer fighting, the Israelis started to make significant headway over the next twenty-four hours, and the PLO, trained for guerrilla warfare and not the full-scale war that was being undertaken, also agreed to a ceasefire the following day.

On Sunday 13th June the ceasefire fell apart and the Israelis continued their push into Lebanon. Their initial plan to have Lebanese Christian Militia take over the running of the country, under Israeli guidance of course, were dealt a blow when leader Bashir Gemayal refused to co-operate. Gemayal had a dream of uniting Christians and Muslims under his leadership and knew that being seen as an Israeli stooge would greatly diminish any chance of this ever happening.

Meanwhile, the leadership of the PLO, hidden ten stories underground in a car park, started to make plans to evacuate the country.

ʊ ʊ ʊ

After a delay of twenty-four hours to prepare, the British renewed their attack on Argentinian positions in the Falklands. The extra day on Saturday 12th June allowed the British to use new laser-guided bombs for the first time, with troops on the peak of Two Sisters directing them in once they had been released from aircraft. This was a new kind of warfare, where the enemy could be killed with extreme precision by a bomb released from an aircraft they would never even see or hear and has since become the standard mode of operation.

13th – 19th June 1982
#1 single: Adam Ant: Goody Two Shoes
#1 album: Roxy Music: Avalon

For the past couple of years, the term *goth* had been used increasingly in conjunction with music as an insult, however in summer 1982 the tide was starting to turn with the movement, if there was such a thing, solidifying and focusing on a new club which had just opened in London.

The Batcave was situated at the Gargoyle Club at 69 Dean Street, Soho, upstairs from where Billy's had been, and focused on new wave and glam rock, both of which merged beautifully into what became goth rock. The club was opened by musicians Olli Wisdom and Jon Klein, both of whom played with Specimen, a glam goth act who became the house band, advertising itself with a promise of "*absolutely no funk*". Almost immediately the Wednesday night club started attracting the misfits, the cross-dressers, and the fetish-obsessed people of the capital, as well as the *crème de la crème* of the underground alternative music scene, such as Siouxsie Sioux, Nick Cave, Marc Almond, and Robert Smith. Whilst there was something of a circus about the club, decked out with fake spider webs like Halloween and an upright coffin through which members had to pass to gain entry, it gave a focus to many post-punk bands and is acknowledged as having set what became the norms for the goth movement throughout the next decade.

On any given week you could hear Hamish McDonald spinning tracks by the likes of Specimen, Alien Sex Fiend, The Birthday Party, Siouxsie & The Banshees, The Cure, The Cramps, The Sisters of Mercy, and Bauhaus.

It was the last of these, Bauhaus, that most benefitted from the growing interest in darker themes in music and attempted once again to take advantage with the release of new single, *Spirit*. Probably the closest Bauhaus ever got to creating pop music, with an acoustic guitar in evidence throughout and a sing-along outro of "*We love our audience*", whenever the track appeared to be getting happy the band would pull it back into Bowie-esque darkness. Momentum was with Bauhaus, and there was a feeling their time was coming. Most bands were keen to avoid being lumped into one

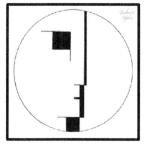

movement, despite obvious sonic similarities in their music, however Bauhaus drummer Kevin Haskins said "[We] *understand how we were tagged as such. We did all wear black, make-up, release a song about vampires and drove around in a hearse*".

It was hoped the new single which the band had recorded with Hugh Jones a couple of months earlier would be the first hit from the scene, however Bauhaus hated the final version, and would go on to record a different version for their forthcoming album. With references to their powerful live show in the lyrics, and in particular the *spirit* created

between them and their fans, singer Pete Murphy claimed "*I wear a coat of drums and dance upon your eyes*" whilst "*The stage becomes a ship in flames*" over what would in future years become known as dark pop.

The single failed and Bauhaus would need to wait for their moment.

The goth movement gathered pace over the summer, with John Peel sessions in August for Flesh for Lulu, The Sisters of Mercy, and Danse Society, whilst The Batcave did not limit itself to music, putting on mud wrestling, fire shows, drag cabaret, and old black and white horror movies, before taking the whole club out on tour around the United Kingdom in 1984. Throughout the decade, the tribe of Goth grew in Britain, with most towns and cities having their own branch. The north of England was particularly susceptible to the dark side, with strongholds in places like Leeds, Bradford, and York.

ʊ ʊ ʊ

The attack on the hills around Port Stanley resumed on Sunday 13th June, with Mount Tumbledown, Wireless Ridge, and Mount William the targets. The Scots Guard were allocated the first two, and the Gurkhas the last one. A couple of decisions were made to help with the night manoeuvres, the first of which was not to wear steel helmets, but the ceremonial berets and cap badge instead. This meant anyone wearing a helmet was the enemy and could be shot without fear of *friendly fire*. The second involved the decision not to use the standard NATO alphabet, but instead refer to the Scots Guard with "*Hey, Jimmie*" and the Gurkhas with "*Hey, Johnnie*", the reasoning being that the Argentinians could not pronounce the letter "*J*" and would be much more identifiable in the dark.

Traversing across some of the many minefields in freezing conditions, the troops came under heavy fire, and spent a long time detained in the one position, exchanging shots in the dark. After eleven hours of such fighting, Tumbledown was taken with nine British casualties.

Meanwhile, a different methodology was tried on Wireless Ridge, with a *noisy attack* making the action seem much more frantic. The sheer volume of the firepower caused many Argentinians to evacuate their positions and the ridge was captured without too much exertion. A rumour that the British had started wearing Argentinian uniforms and instructing men to withdraw in Spanish led to the order that anyone retreating without ratification by radio would be shot.

The Gurkhas had been waiting all night for Tumbledown to be taken, so they could commence their own advance on Mount William. As daylight broke, they prepared themselves for daytime action, but found as they advanced towards the target there was no Argentinians waiting, having abandoned the posts to start making their way back to Port Stanley.

ʊ ʊ ʊ

Each Football World Cup since 1966 had an official mascot, usually an animal or small child, and Spain pulled out all the stops, employing legendary artist Joan Miro to produce an emblem, which he did by choosing an anthropomorphised Orange, a typical fruit of the country, wearing a national football strip. Adidas also came up with a new version of the ball for the tournament, the *Tango Espana*, which proved itself to have poor water resistance, leading to it being changed several times during some matches[385]. For the first time, the number of nations competing in the finals was raised from sixteen to twenty-four, making the tournament truly global by allowing greater representation from Africa and Asia.

Kicking off on Sunday 13th June in front of almost 100,000 spectators at the impressive Nou Camp Stadium in Barcelona, holders Argentina played Belgium, showcasing their new attacking midfielder, Diego Maradona. The twenty-two-year-old had only just signed a world record contract of £5 million for Barcelona, and despite the expectations of many locals who turned out to see the new signing, played disappointingly in the opening match. As the Falklands War entered the finale, Argentina lost 1-0 in what was a dark couple of days for the nation.

ʊ ʊ ʊ

Whilst Trevor Horn and Gary Langan were in New York recording ethnic musicians, Malcolm McLaren headed to Knoxville, Tennessee on a whim, hoping to find some *square dance* artists. "*I honestly believe that those guys in the Appalachian Mountains calling out 'Buffalo gals go round the outside' have something in common with the rapper who lives in the South Bronx*" he would claim. A week later he telephoned the duo, and they flew out, joining him to record the Mountain Hilltoppers: a family of blind grandparents, aunts, daughters, sons, and children who turned up in a battered pick-up truck with two shotguns. They were abysmal, and their home-made instruments sounded appalling, so Horn picked up some local session men and the two groups spent a day glowering antagonistically at each other across the studio floor. When McLaren tried to pay the Hilltoppers at the end of the day, the family refused to believe there was such a thing as a $100 dollar bill and insisted on being paid in denominations of five dollars. Horn was also anxious about the quality of the studio compared to what he was used to working with in London, as well as how all this disparate music was going to be pulled together. The vague idea was that it would all gel when a rapper was brought in, however in Knoxville McLaren dropped the bombshell that he himself was going to be the lead singer. The problem with this was that McLaren had no idea of how to keep rhythm or stay in tune, turning the sessions into disarray. Horn and Langan seemed even more adrift than before.

ʊ ʊ ʊ

---

[385] This was the last fully leather ball to be used at a major tournament.

On Monday 14th June the Israeli army were on the outskirts of Beirut, where they took up positions and began a siege. Regardless of their superior firepower, the Israelis elected not to enter Beirut due to the substantial casualties street fighting would ensure. For the next seven weeks the Israelis indiscriminately fired bombs and missiles from land, sea, and air into the city. Arab agents were engaged to drive car bombs into the city, killing thousands of civilians in the process.

As the buildings and infrastructure started to disintegrate, thousands of miles away in Afghanistan a leader of the resistance to the Soviet Invasion observed the events unfolding on television. As he saw the bombed-out buildings in Beirut, an idea began to formulate in Osama Bin Laden's head: "*It occurred to me to punish the unjust the same way: to destroy towers in America*".

℧ ℧ ℧

On the morning of Monday 14th June, the Falkland Islands War was finished. The British troops had shadowed the withdrawing Argentinians down from the hills around Port Stanley, with directives not to shoot for fear of turning the day into carnage. It was also imperative that Brigadier General Menedez not be apprehended before he signed the surrender, and so a pause was ordered at the town limits.

Not that this stopped Max Hastings of the *London Evening Standard*, who dumped his camouflage and donned an anorak and walking stick before sauntering into town. Persuading an Argentinian colonel that he was from *The Times*, Hastings secured an interview and then marched back to the British troops with a press exclusive. All he had to do was get this transmitted back to London, which is where his troubles started. Eventually blagging his way on to a helicopter, Hastings made it back to *HMS Fearless* by late afternoon, only to be told there was a complete news blackout, enforced by the Ministry of Defence in London who were keen that any announcement of a surrender should first be made by the government.

There were 10,000 Argentinians in the town, with twice that many British surrounding it, and Menedez was ordered not to speak to the enemy by President Galtieri, who stated "*the only thing* [the English] *understand in the language of the gun*". A radio request was made by the British to be permitted to send a negotiating team, which was approved by Menedez, and a surrender was agreed in the afternoon. General Jeremy Moore was flown in, and the document was signed at 9 pm with no photographers present to avoid humiliating photographs of the Argentinians, after which he presented a bottle of whiskey to the inhabitants of the Stanley with an expression of regret for taking so long to get there. A toast was made to *Margaret Thatcher and the task force*, and then another to *the Queen*.

In the Houses of Parliament, the Prime Minister made an announcement: "*They are reported to be flying white flags over Port Stanley*". All parties in the house welcomed the news, congratulating both the Prime Minister and government. Upon the return to 10 Downing Street, Thatcher was met by a large crowd behind a police barrier, who sang *Rule, Britannia* and *She's a Jolly Good Fellow*.

The news blackout was finally lifted a couple of hours after midnight, allowing Hastings to be first to transmit a report back to London. Other journalists had given him copy to transmit as well, however Hastings was keen to get all the credit, and somehow *lost* the reports, causing Ian Bruce of the *Glasgow Herald* to pull out an Argentinian bayonet and threaten to kill him.

℧ ℧ ℧

Italy, one of the favoured teams in Spain, were still spiralling from a match-fixing scandal in their top division two years previously, the result of which was the banning of twenty top players. The scam had been run by restaurant manager Alvaro Trinca who was attempting to defraud the Italian pools, but when one of the Lazio players not involved found out, his jealousy led him to the police whose enquiries quickly unravelled the scandal. Such was the normal level of corruption in Italy, however, that Trinca even consulted with a lawyer to see if he had any legal position to sue the players involved for breach of contract by failing to deliver on their promise. Striker Paolo Rossi had been given a three-year ban for his role in the match fixing, which was later reduced to two years allowing him to join the Italian squad just in time for the tournament. The press and the fans were uncertain about Rossi's fitness after an absence from the game and in the opening goalless draw against Poland he was described as a "*ghost aimlessly wandering over the field*".

℧ ℧ ℧

On Tuesday 15th June the task of rounding up Argentinian prisoners started in the Falklands, as they were moved to the airfield just outside Port Stanley. The British warships remained on guard out at sea, preparing for an air attack from the mainland where the military junta had refused to recognise the surrender. To avoid the logistical nightmare of housing and feeding the surrendered troops, they were swiftly returned home on the *Canberra*, with 500 key officials being kept for an additional month as a guarantee of no further actions from the mainland.

Since the First World War, British troops had not been repatriated when killed on the battlefield, but buried instead alongside their fallen comrades, a decision made by the near unanimous vote of the fighting troops themselves. After the Falklands, however, this policy changed, with many of the families feeling the Falklands were just too far away. The majority of British fallen on land were subsequently brought back to the United Kingdom, a move that led to anti-war propaganda during the later Gulf Wars with processions of flag-draped coffins through the village of Brize Norton. The Argentinian government on the other hand, refused to accept their war dead, not wishing the public to see evidence of a disastrous campaign, and they were later re-buried on the island by the British, with full military honours.

Back on the Argentinian mainland angry crowds gathered demanding answers for the loss of the campaign and had to be dispersed violently by the police. For national leader Leopoldo Galtieri, it was too late and by the end of the week he was removed from power and held under house-arrest for the next eighteen months, before being sentenced to prison for mis-handling the Falklands War. In the meantime, Argentina was returned to democracy.

Back in Downing Street, Margaret Thatcher was collecting congratulations from everyone, with praise in the press and telegrams from many of the world leaders. One telegram came from El Salvador's Revolutionary Democratic Front, who thanked her for the unexpected withdrawal of 266 Argentinian military *advisors* from their country since the despatch of the Task Force.

Not that everyone was happy with the national mood, which playwright Alan Bennett described as "*the Last Night of the Proms erected into policy*".

℧ ℧ ℧

Unlike Britain, America did not have a problem with older rock stars, never having had the white burning heat of punk wiping away the old guard. What they did not like, however, was when their stars such as Steve Miller tried to develop their sound in new directions.

The Steve Miller Band had first formed in San Francisco in 1966, finding themselves in the middle of the psychedelic explosion and becoming one of the major break-out acts

from the scene. Throughout the 1970's they became a Classic American Rock Act, with hits such as *The Joker* and *Rock'n'me*, however by at the start of the new decade Miller, determined to move with the times, began to introduce a dance edge to the music.

Recording in 1981, Miller became obsessed with Roland synthesisers, toning down his considerable talent for playing guitar with a bunch of new songs, of which he only wrote two himself. One of these was a track called *Abracadabra*, a minor-key dance track inspired by a meeting with Diana Ross on the ski slopes of Sun Valley, Idaho. The song infuriated his long-term fans, and the record company could not see potential in it, refusing to release it as a single in his home country. Instead, the song slunk out in Europe on Phonogram, where a more forward-thinking audience propelled to the top of the charts in many countries, including a number two slot in Britain. Only then did his American label Capital release the song, to find it climbing to the top of the Billboard charts.

Now considered to be a guilty pleasure, the song was a classic pop song with no pretensions of virtuoso musicianship. Miller had everything recorded for a couple of years, except the vocals and guitar solo. Even the guitar solo was an *anti-solo*, more like a series of musical whiplashes and feedback, inspired by Miller's girlfriend mucking about with his guitar.

It was by far one of the most interesting things he ever released.

ʊ ʊ ʊ

Arrangements were made on the Swiss border by businessman Hans Kunz to help Roberto Calvi flee the European mainland, and on Tuesday 15th June he was flown on a private jet from Innsbruck to London. Calvi arrived at Gatwick Airport in the evening and breezed through customs using his fake passport before being taken to pre-arranged accommodation at Chelsea Cloisters in Sloane Square, a backstreet complex of rooms which were normally rented by the night.

Calvi had chosen London, hoping to find help and refuge in *Loggia di Londra*, the London branch of the Freemasons, however no contact was forthcoming. Instead, he settled into his spartan room, and awaited the arrival of friend and helper Flavio Carboni.

ʊ ʊ ʊ

Three home nations had qualified for the finals of the 1982 World Cup, and the first to kick off were Scotland on Tuesday 15th June. Their third World Cup finals in a row, after suffering the hubris of humiliation in Argentina in 1978 the nation was significantly less sanguine, particularly with Brazil and the Soviet Union to face in the group stages. They had a legendary club manager in the shape of Jock Stein[386], however he was still to prove himself on the international stage. The squad were taken to the Spanish - Portuguese border to acclimatise a week before the first game, where they were ordered by Stein not to sunbathe. Except for Graeme Souness, who was given

---

[386] Despite being a Celtic legend, Stein was an active member of the Freemasons.

permission because Stein considered him to be a *class act*, and as such would need a tan.

Opening opposition, New Zealand, on the other hand, spent a lot of time lounging around the pool in the sun, eating chips. The strength of Brazil and the Soviet Union made it particularly imperative that a victory was secured against the Kiwis and by half-time the Scots were three goals up and cruising to an easy victory with an inspirational performance by Gordon Strachan. Things almost went off the rails just after play was resumed with New Zealand pulling back two goals, however Scotland gathered themselves together again and scored another two before the end of the game, giving them the opening they desired. The Scots would pay dearly, however, for the lapse of concentration at the start of the second half.

England entered the World Cup finals the following day, for the first time since 1970 after what had been a disastrous decade for the national team, with a match against France. Under the management of Ron Greenwood, the team was in buoyant mood, despite having scraped through the qualifying round following an inconsistent series of results. There had been suggestions in the previous months that the home nations ought to withdraw from the tournament given the ongoing conflict with Argentina, and the British government ordered a directive that there should be no interaction between the teams and the South Americans, however when FIFA advised there was no chance defending champions would be asked to withdraw any question of a boycott disappeared. Greenwood stated that "*I would not hesitate to go along with whatever is decided. I have been through one war and I know what is important in life*". In the end, the England team were insured for £22 million against terrorism, and their players were met at the airport by armed guards and a tank.

The French national team of the early 1980's were a weak proposition, and even with their star player Michel Platini had been placed in the third pot during the draw along with Scotland and Northern Ireland.[387] England had misfortune in their squad with star players Kevin Keegan and Trevor Brooking injured, the latter of whom was being given cortisone injections for a groin injury, however they got off to a sensational start with a goal by Bryan Robson after just 27 seconds, a World Cup record for which he received an engraved gold watch. The teams went in drawing at half-time as the French clawed their way back into the game with the 110°F heat getting to the players[388], however two goals in the second half gave England the perfect start to the tournament.

Elsewhere on the same day there were more surprises as the might of reigning European champions West Germany were defeated 2-1 by Algeria, and hosts Spain were held to a 1-1 draw by Honduras, a result that led to riots in the capital Tegucigalpa when police tried to break up celebrating fans.

The third home nation in the World Cup finals, Northern Ireland, started their campaign on Thursday 17th June with a match against Yugoslavia. When you consider Yugoslavia were the combined might of Croatia, Serbia, Bosnia and Herzegovina, Macedonia, Slovenia, and Montenegro, whilst Northern Ireland were a perennially under-performing nation of less than two million people, there should have been no competition here. Instead, the Irish captained by Martin O'Neill, proved rugged opposition, surviving by the fingertips of goalkeeper Pat Jennings at times, to claim a 0-0 draw. Playing as a forward for Northern Ireland was Norman Whiteside, who at seventeen years and forty-one days became the youngest player to play at the World Cup finals, celebrating by being given a yellow card.

---

[387] Trouble was further compounded when midfielder Jean-Francois Larios left the squad early due to a rumoured affair with Platini's wife.

[388] Ray Wilkins and Terry Butcher suffering dizzy spells, and Paul Mariner lost a stone in weight.

ʊ ʊ ʊ

After an uneasy week for Banco Ambrosiano, during which there was much speculation as to the whereabouts of their head Roberto Calvi, Italy's leading financial newspaper broke the news of the letter sent from the Bank of Italy to Milan. As the value of shares in the bank fell another 18%, Consob, the authority responsible for regulating the Italian financial markets, ordered them to be suspended as lenders demanded their money back and customers rushed to withdraw everything, fearful of a collapse. The acting management retrieved letters of comfort from their vaults, letters which Calvi had extracted from the Vatican Bank, and were shocked to discover they only stated the church was aware of the debts but had not guaranteed them.

A final desperate meeting was set up between Banco Ambrosiano and the Vatican Bank on Thursday 17th June, during which the Milanese bankers begged for help. They were refused, and a quick calculation revealed debts of $1,287 million in their worldwide dealings.

Back in Milan, after wavering for almost a fortnight the board of Banco Ambrosiano acted during a midday meeting, firing missing chairman Calvi. It was then revealed the bank had bought $60 million worth of its own shares to shore up their value on the stock exchange, and the Vatican were refusing to pay back $200 million worth of loans. Tempers became strained as people apportioned the blame, and at 2.30 p.m. the meeting was suspended to allow everyone to cool down. Upon starting again, the board voted to dissolve Banco Ambrosiano, and asked the Bank of Italy to step in and take control.

Upon hearing the news, Calvi's fifty-five-year-old secretary Graziella Corrocher wrote a short note in red pen, stating *"I stand by the decision taken by the board, but I cannot stand by Calvi anymore. What a disgrace, to have run away. May he be cursed a thousand times for the harm he has done to everyone at the bank"*. Corrocher then climbed onto the ledge of her fourth-floor office and jumped to her death, landing with a loud thud on the ramp of the bank's parking garage.

In London, Calvi had been holed up in a room for two days whilst friend Flavio Carboni arrived and booked himself and his girlfriend into the luxurious Hilton Hotel on Park Lane. The two then spent the night on the town rather than meeting with Calvi. The disgraced banker phoned his daughter in Zurich several times, telling her she was in danger and would need to leave Europe for the United States with an airline ticket bought by Hans Kunz, the man who had flown Calvi himself out of Switzerland on his private jet.

Sometime before midnight, Calvi went missing from his room.

ʊ ʊ ʊ

On Friday 18th June former Beatle Paul McCartney turned forty and had recently started to become apprehensive about getting older. He quit smoking (apart from joints) and took up jogging in something approximating a mid-life crisis. Whilst looking forward, he concurrently started to look back to his childhood and commissioned animator Geoff Dunbar to create a pilot for a *Rupert the Bear* movie. McCartney had already recorded a song *We All Stand Together* for the pilot, and the job began of generating the images to complement this. He also decided the time was right to have another attempt at a project begun in the 1970's: a musical movie scripted by Willy Russel based upon the *Band on the Run* album.

The most recent in a long line of half-baked concepts from McCartney which extended back to *Magical Mystery Tour* in 1967, he decided he could write the movie himself, retaining only a couple of Russel's scenes. The plot involved the master tapes from his latest album being stolen.... and that was about it. There was no script, no screenplay, and the actors were a bunch of friends and family, including wife Linda, studio engineer Geoff Emerick, roadie John Hammel, and Ringo Starr and his wife, Barbara, who was close to being the only professional actor on set.

McCartney sought advice from film producer David Puttnam over dinner one evening, who cautioned him against even starting the project, and hired Peter Webb to direct, mainly because he was inexperienced and would do whatever the singer said. McCartney started funding the project himself, before his father-in-law brought in Harvey Weinstein who took the movie to 20th Century Fox. *Give My Regards to Broad Street* was finally released in 1984 and was comprehensively ridiculed.

℧ ℧ ℧

Malcolm McLaren's New York assistant, Ruza Blue, had shared his hip hop epiphany the previous year, and started booking rap acts on a Thursday night at a New York club called Negril. By early 1982, the night had become so popular that the fire department shut the club down, and Blue was forced to move to the much larger Roxy. The night grew from here, as rappers from uptown mixed with celebrities from downtown such as Talking Heads, Andy Warhol, The Clash, and David Bowie, along with young spoiled rich white college kids such as Rick Rubin, Adam Yauch, Michael Diamond, and Adam Horovitz. Ruza would create a collision of the rap world with the New York punk scene, booking double-dutch rope jumpers, seeing them as the female counterpart to break boys.

The opening night on Friday 18th June saw the giant roller-skating rink reduced in size by a massive graffiti curtain, with Afrika Bambaataa in charge of the music, a live performance by the Soul Sonic Force, presentations by the Double Dutch Girls, and breakdancing by the Rock Steady Crew. 300 people turned up, enough to fill the reduced space, and over the next few weeks the curtain was inched backwards until it was able to be removed when the venue was completely full.

℧ ℧ ℧

On the night of Friday 18th June thirty-two-year-old Michael Fagan was wandering the streets of central London, turning over in his head again and again that his wife Christine had just left him. Finding himself outside the walls of Buckingham Palace late at night, Fagan made a spur of the moment decision to climb into the grounds. Once inside, lacking in any sort of attention from security, he started shimmying up a drainpipe on the outside of the main building before climbing in the window of a startled maid's bedroom. When she ran to fetch security, he moved on to other rooms. The Palace guards, finding no-one in the maid's room, assumed she had imagined the whole incident. Meanwhile, Fagan wandered past doors marked "*Charles*" and *Diana*" in search of a toilet, but unable to find one was forced to urinate into a bin marked "*corgi food*". With an emptied bladder Fagan gained entry in the room marked "*Charles*", and finding it unoccupied started to help himself to the "*cheap Californian wine*" on a shelf, before finding the throne room and trying out the various seats, "*Goldilocks-style*".

As morning approached, Fagan let himself out a back door and scaled the wall back into the streets of London.

℧ ℧ ℧

After their lacklustre opening goalless draw against Poland, the Italians were expected to come up with the goods for the second match against Peru on Friday 18th June. Once again, however, the Italians were uninspiring, and the formerly disgraced Paolo Rossi was substituted at half time. The national press was now baying for blood with

Rossi seen as a folly after his two years out of football. Initially taking the lead through a Bruno Conti twenty-yard shot in the first half, the Italians did what they always do; retreated to unnecessarily boring defensive football, a gamble which failed to pay off when Peru scored with a deflected shot in the final five minutes of the match to earn a 1-1 draw.

The Italians were now in deep trouble.

The important game on this day as far as Britain was concerned was Scotland against Brazil in Seville. Before the match, whilst waiting in 100°F heat in the tunnel, the Brazilian players started to remove their tops revealing tanned and muscled bodies. Scottish players Gordon Strachan and Alex McLeish considered removing theirs as well but realised that they would only reveal "*white spotty chests*". Muscles and working out had not yet become commonplace in Britain in 1982, even amongst sportsmen.

Manager Jock Stein left star forward Kenny Dalglish on the substitute bench, perhaps as an indication that Scotland were not even going to try to win the match. The message evidently did not get through to everyone as defender David Narey scored what English commentator Jimmy Hill described as a *toe-poke* from outside the box. As Narey leapt about celebrating the rest of the team made their way back to starting positions with their heads down. As Gordon Strachan later claimed, "*Now we had annoyed them*".

From there on, Brazil delivered a masterclass in football, winning 4-1, with Stein claiming, "*It's never easy to accept defeat, but this one is different*". For the last five minutes of the game Brazilian Zico was surrounded by five or six Scottish players, all anxious to swap tops at the end.

In the crowd for the match was Rod Stewart and his family, including his Scottish father, who were spending the summer in Spain for the world cup. This meant a lot of drinking sessions, before the match, during the match, and after the match, leaving wife Alana at home with two small children. Upon returning to their villa after the Brazil – Scotland game, Stewart and his wife got into a loud screaming argument, something which had been happening all too often in the past few months. Afterwards, Stewart's father took him to one side, and said "*Doesn't she understand? This is the World Cup! Why can't the men have this one day to do what they want to do?*".

Over the next year the couple would go through a tortuous break-up, and Rod would move onto his next blonde.

ʊ ʊ ʊ

At 7.30 a.m. on Friday 18th June a postal clerk crossing Blackfriars Bridge in London saw a length of orange rope attached to the barrier. Upon investigation, the other end of the rope was found around the neck of a body which was half submerged in the water of the River Thames. Raising the alarm, the police arrived and cut down the body, finding a soggy Italian passport and £7,400 worth of currency stuffed into the pockets. The body also contained a corroded watch which had stopped at 1.52 am, and over ten pounds of stones stuffed down the trousers.

The Italian Embassy were contacted, and the consul unofficially identified the body as that of Roberto Calvi. Almost immediately the conspiracy theories started, and many in his home country believed his involvement with the Vatican, the mafia, and the freemasons gave all the clues necessary to rule out a straight suicide. Some took the stones stuffed in Calvi's pockets as a masonic message, and with the London Lodge and the bridge he was hanged from both being called Blackfriars, the finger pointed towards the organization. The disgraced banker himself, in discussions with his son, suggested it was the Vatican who were after him and would stop at nothing to silence him. Calvi intended to tell all at the appeal hearings, due four days after his body was found in London, including that he had helped the Vatican bank channel $50 million to the Solidarity movement in Pope John Paul II's home country of Poland, to help with the fight against Communism.

The British police began their investigation but were severely hampered by a lack of co-operation by officials and organizations in Italy. They were prevented from speaking to the people they needed to, and those who they could speak to knew nothing. In the days before close-circuit cameras there was no evidence from around Blackfriars Bridge overnight, and no witnesses of a man approaching the bridge, either alone or under duress.

On the evening of the 18th June Hans Kunz, the businessman who had flown Calvi out of Switzerland three days early, sent a private jet from Geneva to Gatwick and back. No-one knows who or what was being collected from London that night.

20th – 26th June 1982
#1 single: Charlene: I've Never Been to Me
#1 album: Roxy Music: Avalon

In Bilbao, England were looking increasingly confident, defeating Czechoslovakia by two goals in a boring but efficient manner to guarantee their place in the second round. The only drama surrounding the match was the question of finding new shirts. Admiral Sportswear from Leicester had provided the English kit for the tournament and after the heat of the first match it was clear the polyester shirts would not allow sweat to leave the bodies of the players. The company went into overtime putting together five new sets of shirts and shorts from an absorbent material, hand-sewing the *Three Lions* emblem at all sorts of odd angles in their haste. FIFA had decreed that team shorts should feature their playing number as well as the top, forcing Admiral to iron these on, only to have them peel off with the heat during the match.

After the match manager Ron Greenwood instructed the players to "*go and get pissed!*"

ʊ ʊ ʊ

With no record label and no live dates planned, it looked as if The Damned had split. This was further compounded when drummer Rat Scabies formed a new act in May called Foxes & Rats with former members of The Ruts.

Guitarist Captain Sensible had recorded some solo demos in the spring with Tony Mansfield producing, which were then sold to Cherry Red Records for £3000. The only problem was that Sensible had spent £10,000 finishing the songs, and so his new solo manager Andrew Miller negotiated a second deal with A&M worth £40,000, which the Captain insisted on being paid in used £1 notes. This money was used to pay off Cherry Red, Mansfield, Miller, and the musicians who had played on the recordings, leaving just enough for Sensible to buy a second-hand car.

The sessions had been successful, underlining Sensible's fascination with 1960's psychedelia, and Syd Barrett in particular. Robyn Hitchcock of The Soft Boys was brought in to add some psychedelic guitar, and Sensible protégés Dolly Mixture contributed backing vocals. Towards the end of the recording it was decided that a cover version should close the album, and after intense deliberation between *Waterloo Sunset* by The Kinks and *See Emily Play* by Pink Floyd, Mansfield told Sensible to go home and look through his parents' record collection for something whimsical to cover. The following day, he returned clutching a vinyl copy of the *South Pacific* soundtrack and was duly sent to the pub whilst Mansfield and synth player Rob Bowkett recorded a backing track for *Happy Talk*. Sensible returned drunk, late at night, and recorded

the vocal in one take, assuming this was a throw-away bit of nonsense for the end of the album.

Mansfield, manager Miller, and A&M thought otherwise. Hearing the potential in an idiosyncratic version of an already proven song they decided to release it as the first single from the album. As Vic Godard said in his *Melody Maker* review: "*You might not like it, but you'll find yourself humming it everywhere you go*".

The single picked up some airplay and scraped into the charts at number thirty-three, enough to allow Sensible to be invited onto *Top of the Pops*, after which it roared up to the top spot. Sensible now found himself monkeying around on television for a new audience, a cartoon character with a dodgy hidden past.

ʊ ʊ ʊ

Three days after his uninvited foray into Buckingham Palace, Michael Fagan was still mentally cut loose and reeling from the departure of his wife. The idea formed in his head that she had gone to Stonehenge for the summer solstice on Monday 21st June, however Fagan was without transport to get there. The solution was simple: steal a car and drive to the ancient monument in Wiltshire.

The only problem was that the police caught him, and Fagan was sent to Brixton Prison where he languished for two and a half weeks before being released on bail.

ʊ ʊ ʊ

Part of being British is subjugating yourself to a centuries-old family business built on war, greed, and the blood of peasants, or supporting the Royal Family as many know it. Some concern themselves with the stability of the royal bloodline, particularly when it comes to heirs, and these people were relieved and enthralled when on at 9.03 a.m. on Monday 21st June, William Arthur Philip Louis Windsor was born at the Lindo Wing of St Mary's Hospital in London. The pressure on his mother, Diana Spencer, had been immense in the past few months and she broke with the tradition of having royal babies at Buckingham Palace, being induced by Royal Gynaecologist George Pinker[389] to provide a child before Fleet Street went into apoplexy. Years later Diana confided to her biographer that the date had been stage managed to fit between the polo dates of her husband.

That husband, Prince Charles, was heard to mutter the words "*Oh God, it's a boy. And he's even got red hair*" in the hospital. Keen to return home for security reasons, the couple and child left St Mary's the following day, holding the baby on the steps for a press photo opportunity, even though Diana could barely walk due to the pain of the stitches. As soon as they entered the car and rounded the corner, she burst into tears. The pressure on the couple had not abated with the birth, with crowds chanting "*Nice one, Charlie, let's have another one*".

ʊ ʊ ʊ

Back in May the first single from Billy Idol's self-titled debut album, *Hot in the City*, had been released. Still unconvinced by MTV, Idol hedged his bets and made a primitive video full of the abysmal effects and awkward performances to be seen in many clips

---

[389] Pinker delivered a total of nine royal babies during his career.

from the early 1980's, which the record company did not even bother submitting to the station. Instead, Chrysalis choose to break the song the old-fashioned way, through radio play, and at one point in the song when Idol shouted "*New York*", time was spent in the studio recording over 100 other American city names to be sent to local radio

stations. The record company also initially declined to put Idol's photograph on the cover, as their research had shown that anything even vaguely to do with punk would not be played on the radio.

Despite the geographical scattering, the track was indeed a love song to Idol's new adopted home city, New York. Things had become more tolerable with the arrival of his girlfriend, English dancer Perri Lister, fresh from recording backing vocals on *The Damned Don't Cry* by Visage. In Idol's scuzzy New York apartment, the two of them sunk deeper into heroin and alcohol addiction, though both were as close to functioning addicts as it was possible to be.[390]

In Britain Idol was viewed as a bit of a has-been joke, an embarrassment from a bygone punk age, and this new *disco* inspired direction did not fool anybody with the single stalling at number fifty-eight. In the United States, however, where punk had not had any real effect on the charts he was perceived as leading the charge from a whole new generation of British acts, and the single rose to number twenty-three, providing a *bona fide* chart hit.

A second single, *White Wedding*, was released in the United States in June[391], and

White Wedding

was a genuine pop classic, written in Idol's favourite key of B, inspired by the recent wedding of his pregnant sister. The song, however, had an ancillary meaning with a *white wedding* being drug slang for a cocaine relapse, whilst to *shotgun* was to exhale the smoke of a drug into someone else's mouth[392]. The song was assisted with a video directed by David Mallet in which Lister played a bride to Idol's rock star. Full of clichés, the video became a staple on MTV, and as the channel expanded so did Idol's fame. Idol's self-titled album was released in July, and with heavy rotation on MTV for *White Wedding* and an

extensive tour of the United States over the summer, it climbed to number forty-five on the Billboard chart.

In the following few years Idol became a massive star in the United States, and subsequently the world, with hits such as *Rebel Yell* and *Eyes Without a Face* (featuring the backing vocals of Lister), concealing his acumen under a veneer of sneering rock and roll behaviour, an intellect that had seen him begin a degree in English at University before discovering punk. With the success came further helpless drug, alcohol, and sex addiction, and at one point he was even thrown out of Bangkok strapped to a medical gurney and escorted by four armed guards.

---

[390] 1982 was to prove to be a year of high profile for Lister, as she also joined Kid Creole's Coconuts, and danced topless for the video of Duran Duran's *The Chauffeur*.

[391] *White Wedding* did not come out in Britain until October and did not hit the charts until the following year.

[392] The practise had originated with US troops during the Vietnam War where they would put a marijuana cigarette into the open chamber of an unloaded shotgun and blow the smoke into each other's mouths.

Idol eventually moved to Los Angeles where he joined the ranks of the coked-up leather-wearing rock-star Harley Davidson riders, all tattoos and open highways, carving out a career for himself that was nothing more than a self-fulfilling prophesy. He will be remembered, however, for being in the of the vanguard of the second British Invasion of America, selling the idea of punk back to the States with a few great singles and videos, something which has perhaps camouflaged his song writing ability. Idol's relationship with his muse has been severely damaged by addiction through the years, and the tempestuous bond was always on shaky ground: he did not write much, but when he did, his hit rate was impressive.

ʊ ʊ ʊ

In Spain, the Northern Ireland football team had spent the previous night on the lash, but still managed to go one goal up against Honduras after ten minutes. They could, however, only manage a 1-1 draw, their second in a row, and with a final game against hosts Spain still to play it looked implausible for Billy Bingham's squad to progress any further.

Both Scotland and the Soviet Union had won against New Zealand and lost to Brazil, setting themselves up for an all-or-nothing match. Manager Jock Stein was uncertain about his team selection, and the night before asked assistant coaches Jim McLean and Andy Roxburgh to both write down on a piece of paper what they thought the team should be. After a while thinking about this, both men handed Stein their selections. According to Roxburgh, Stein "*didn't even look at them. He tore them up, threw them in a basket and said, 'Ach, I'll just pick the team myself'.*"

The Scottish fans had marched from the heart of Malaga to the stadium, beneath an enormous banner reading *Alcoholism v Communism*, as 1982 marked the beginning of their reputation as a good-time party nation rather than one which invaded and dug up the pitch at Wembley Stadium. The Scots started strong with hardman captain Graeme Souness being booked in the first five minutes, before Joe Jordan scored during a counterattack. A well-worked goal from Soviet captain Aleksandre Chivadze fifteen minutes into the second half evened the score, and with six minutes to go Alan Hansen and Willie Miller crashed into each other in the Scottish defence, allowing Ramaz Shengelia to break free with the ball and sidestep keeper Alan Rough. Two minutes later Souness equalised for the Scots, however it was too late, and the game ended in a draw, causing them to crash out on goal difference, mainly due to a weak defence and poor goalkeeping.

The Scottish fans had made themselves popular in Spain, with their good humour and willingness to party no matter the result. Upon leaving Malaga after the Russian match, the press reported "*thousands of men, women and children... waving tartan scarves and lion rampants*" came to wave them goodbye.

ʊ ʊ ʊ

On Wednesday 23rd June Margaret Thatcher travelled to New York to attend a special session of the United Nations, still euphoric about Britain's triumph in the Falklands. She was, however, irritated to find most other nations talking about world peace, expressing in her own speech that "*peace was not enough without freedom and justice, and sometimes it* [is] *necessary to sacrifice peace if freedom and justice are to prevail*". She communicated dismay at the prospect and propositions to slow down the arms race. Might was the defence policy her government now intended to pursue.

ʊ ʊ ʊ

With all teams equal after two matches, both Italy and Cameroon knew that whoever won their game on Wednesday 23rd June would advance to the next round. The Italians were under an enormous amount of pressure back home for their pitiable performance in the competition so far, and once again could not rise to the occasion, with the opening goal scored after sixty minutes by the head of Francesco Graziani, taking advantage of a slip on the surface by goalkeeper and captain Thomas N'kono. One minute later Cameroon's Gregoire M'Bida equalised with what appeared to be an offside goal, and the score remained 1-1 at full time. Despite not losing a match and with equal points and goal difference, Cameroon were eliminated by Italy having scored one more goal. The Italians could consider themselves exceptionally fortunate, being the first ever team to qualify from the opening round without winning a game, and the press and fans were still unhappy with the presence of an uninspiring Paolo Rossi.

Meanwhile, a drama was unfolding in the England training camp, as the saga of star player Kevin Keegan's back injury continued. After a day spent with John Gonzales, a specialist from a Bilbao nursing home, Keegan was willing to take desperate measure. He confronted manager Ron Greenwood at night, demanding to be allowed to fly back to his home in Hamburg to see his own personal doctor. The decision was made to attempt the journey in secret and just after midnight the footballer borrowed a Seat 500 from the receptionist at the team hotel and drove 250 miles through the night to Madrid where he caught the 7 a.m. flight to Hamburg. It was agreed not to inform the press, and the team trained the following day without Keegan, deflecting questions from journalists by saying Keegan was seeing a specialist.

Once in Hamburg, Dr Rehwinkel expressed his anger at the way the England team doctor had been treating the injury, identifying a misaligned vertebra, which he cracked back into place. After a night's sleep and some extra therapy, Keegan flew back to Madrid and drove back to Bilbao without anyone finding out.

ʊ ʊ ʊ

It did not look likely that Soft Cell would manage a new album in 1982, however, given the news that synth-pop rivals The Human League were due to release a long player of dance re-mixes, coupled with the amount of time the duo was spending in New York nightclubs, record label Parlophone suggested they try the same. *Non-Stop Ecstatic Dancing* was a mini-album and featured re-mixed tracks from their first album, *Non-Stop Erotic Cabaret*. The duo wanted to farm the tracks out to an assortment of New York producers, but in pre-remix days the record company hesitated at such a risky notion and insisted producer Mike Thorne helm the project.

In the middle of mixing, Almond and his drug dealer Cindy Ecstasy took a trip down to Florida to visit Disneyland and her parents. It was here that Almond began to comprehend that Cindy had designs on him as a husband, but he also treasured the MDMA she provided too much to confirm to her his real sexuality.

Back in New York, Cindy added a rap to *Memorabilia*, and sound effects were incorporated into the new version of *Sex Dwarf*. The record company insisted on a new track, so a version of the Judy Street northern soul classic *What* was hastily put together, a recording which Almond considered to be *feeble*. His vocals were pitched too high for an already strained voice, and the whole impression was of song that was too close to pop, and far too detached from what Soft Cell were striving for. That did not stop the song reaching number three when released as a single in August, accompanied by an opium-fuelled performance on *Top of the Pops*. The album, meanwhile, reached number six, one place lower than their debut.

ʊ ʊ ʊ

Having already qualified for the second round of the FIFA World Cup, the England soccer coach Ron Greenwood gave his team a day off on Thursday 24ᵗʰ June. After spending the day larking about in the hotel pool, and watching VHS videos of various Hollywood movies, they were treated to a cultural performance by the *London Ballet*.

When the dancers arrived, goalkeeper Peter Shilton was they first to notice the build of them. He told roommate Ray Clemence "*I know next to nothing about ballet and ballet dancers, but from the ballet I have seen on the telly… no way are these ballet dancers!*" He was proven correct when they started, and it became apparent they were go-go dancers from the *Playmodel London Ballet*. An excruciating half-hour performance followed, during which the England players tried their hardest to distance themselves from the dancers, fearing negative headlines in the newspapers back home.

The following day Greenwood fielded a weaker team, resting Bryan Robson in the final match against Kuwait, who had been eliminated by a result the day before between France and Czechoslovakia. A 1-0 victory guaranteed that England were only one of two teams to qualify into the second round with a 100% record.[393] The Kuwaiti performance was not helped by the tournament being held in the middle of Ramadan, with most players fasting and some even refusing liquids.

Meanwhile, Northern Ireland attempted the ostensibly impossible: to qualify by defeating hosts Spain. A 1-0 victory by Yugoslavia over Honduras the day before left the Irish in real jeopardy of ending up bottom of the table, and a referee selected who spoke Spanish but not English did a lot to make it look like Spain must win at all costs. The Irish, however, took a lead through Gerry Armstrong just after half time, and when Mal Donaghy was sent off after sixty minutes, they knew they were going to have to dig deep to preserve their lead. After a tense final thirty minutes the whistle blew, putting them at the top of the table and into the next round.

ʊ ʊ ʊ

Despite a lack of chart success, work began on recording Culture Club's debut album at Maison Rouge Studios in Fulham, with Steve Levine producing. Other musicians were brought in to give the band breadth, including a fourteen-year-old *toaster* who they re-named *Captain Crucial*, and experienced session keyboard player Phil Pickett, an ex-member of Sailor. It was decided that a tough female soul voice was also needed, so a friend of Phillip Salon was recruited. Helen Terry was twenty-six at the time and recruited during the Alternative Miss World competition at London gay club, Heaven.

Tempers started to fray during the recording, as would be expected for a band who had not had enough time to bond before signing a record contract. Singer Boy George left and made plans to hitch to the south of France with his friend Marilyn and do a cabaret act with George rising out of a coffin as Sarah Bernhardt. This idea fell by the wayside when George and previously stringently heterosexual drummer Jon Moss became lovers. Head over heels in love, nothing could now drag George from the band.

---

[393] The other was Brazil.

A second single about George's awareness of his own self-destructive tendencies called *I'm Afraid of Me* was released by Virgin on Friday 25th June and crept to number 100, whilst the band completed a short promotional tour to promote, with a final date at Heaven supported by Musical Youth. As the band walked on stage and began playing the single, George announced "*This wasn't a hit because you bastards didn't buy it*".

Two failures in a row put Culture Club dangerously close to be dropped by the record label. George may have been a face around London, but Culture Club would only get one more chance to prove themselves. His reputation did start to spread beyond the capital, however, and one night over the summer at Steve Strange's Camden Palace he was confronted by a furious Pete Burns, who had travelled all the way down from Liverpool. "*You ripped me off, you cunt*" he screamed, as George took refuge behind the bouncers.

Fearing their investment was not going to pay off, Virgin moved the band to the cheaper Red Bus Studios to complete the album.

ʊ ʊ ʊ

Returning from Tennessee to New York with innumerable unrelated strands of tape, Trevor Horn, Gary Langan, and Malcolm McLaren set about trying to discover somebody from the world of hip-hop to help bring their album together. When McLaren told his New York assistant Ruza Blue that he sought to create a rap record, she recommended Fab 5 Freddy as the MC, however the manager's reputation as a con-artist preceded him, and Freddy suggested a couple of radio DJs called the World-Famous Supreme Team. Consisting of Just Allah the Superstar and C. Divine the Mastermind, the duo leased late-night airtime on station WHBI where they *scratched* vinyl, took requests, and played records. Arrangements were made to fly them over to London to record their parts. Meanwhile, Terry Doktor took McLaren to see the newly released *Bladerunner*, the soundtrack and feel of which motivated him to add a futuristic Japanese synthesized aspect to the album.

In the aftermath of *Star Wars*, science-fiction movies were meant to be fast-paced and full of adventure, so when *Bladerunner* was released on Friday 25th June the deliberate pace split the critics and turned off the public. Based on Philip K Dick's 1968 novel *Do Androids Dream of Electric Sheep*, the film had been in production for over a decade, initially with Dustin Hoffman in the lead role. Taking the new name from a William S. Burroughs-penned screenplay, the script was re-written several times before Harrison Ford was recruited as lead character Rick Deckard. Director Ridley Scott was straight from the success of *Alien* and stamped his authority over the look of the film, creating a dystopian world based in parts on Fritz Lang's *Metropolis*, Hong Kong, and the industrial landscape of his childhood in South Shields.

Put simply, the film follows the fortunes of a *Bladerunner*, the name given to bounty hunters who track down and destroy androids on Earth (where they have been banned), as he attempts to find a fugitive group led by Rutger Hauer's *Roy Batty*. The film tackles some heavy themes, including genetic engineering, cloning, religion, environmental issues, globalisation, and what it means to be a human. The line is blurred between Ford's human and Hauer's replica, with both appearing to be two sides of the same coin.

Released the same day was John Carpenter's *The Thing*, a remake of the 1950's science fiction movie *The Thing from Another World*, the story of an American Research Station at the Antarctic infiltrated by a shapeshifting alien who proceeds to work through the researchers one at a time, turning them against each other through paranoia and fear. The original movie was an allegory for fear of Communism, and it was easy to see Carpenter's version as being about the newly discovered GRID virus, given the damage the creature did to the bodies of the victims.

The film was universally disliked by the critics, with one even calling it "*the most hated movie of all time*", and audiences agreed, being turned off by a nihilistic ending and the excess special effects gore. The public and critical response to the movie killed John Carpenter's promising career dead after he was labelled "*a pornographer of violence*", and he was paid by the studio not to make any more films for them.
Both *Bladerunner* and *The Thing* suffered from being released in the wake of *E.T. The Extra-Terrestrial* with the public preferring the positive ending and pure entertainment offered by Spielberg's classic when it came to their summer science-fiction. Both films, however, gained a cult following over the following decades and are now rightly seen as masterpieces in the genre, with Scott's vision becoming probably the most influential in terms of visuals.

ʊ ʊ ʊ

Alexander Haig Junior had served under the past four Presidents of the United States, as Chief of Staff for Richard Nixon and Gerald Ford, and Supreme Allied Commander in Europe under Jimmy Carter. Since the beginning of Ronald Reagan's tenure, Haig had acted as Secretary of State, overseeing diplomacy through the Falklands War and in Lebanon, both without any real success. Haig disagreed on a regular basis with many in the Whitehouse, especially Defence Secretary Casper Weinberger, and after suggesting that a nuclear warning shot in Europe might help deter the Soviet Union, his position became untenable. Offering his resignation Friday 25th June, Reagan finally accepted it almost a fortnight later, replacing him with George Schultz.
This was great news for the White House staffers under the influence of Vice President George Bush, who had been trying to displace Haig since the beginning of the Presidency, seeing him as the main contender as the next incumbent. Haig was aware of the forces inside working to bring him down, and a couple of weeks before resigning White House Chief of Staff James Baker had said "*Haig is going to go, and quickly, and we're going to make it happen*".
Almost as if by magic, three minutes after Haig announced his resignation the shelling and bombing of Beirut halted.

ʊ ʊ ʊ

The first few years of the Haçienda in Manchester were a catalogue of calamities caused by an epidemic of abysmal decisions. The club remained open every night, fully staffed, even if no-one turned up, which was frequently the case. At one point the Haçienda was selling the greatest volume of beer in the north of England, but because of their lack of bargaining power with major investors Whitbread, made no profit on this. DJs were encouraged to play black American dance acts rather than the British alternative sounds that provided the early core Factory following, and this was played through a sound system inadequate for the room. New Order bass player Peter Hook later claimed that "*on walking in, the initial impression was always 'wow', but at the end of the day concert goers don't care about the architectural style of venues, they just want to see bands play without fucking girders in the way or shit sound*". Hook made it his personal mission to sort out the appalling sound of the club and was demoralized that when the original sound system (supplied at a cost of £35,000) was taken down to find only two of the twenty speakers working.
The Factory bands and staff used the Haçienda as a gang hut, indulging themselves to what they thought was free drink and food, little appreciating that they were paying for this through unrelenting investment of their record sales. Money was being poured down the drain in the Haçienda, and such was the hubris of the club that New Order were convinced to sign personal guarantees for the bank, making the individual

members financially responsible for the debt. Profits from increasing record sales were relentlessly being streamed into the Haçienda, just to keep it afloat.

On Saturday 26th June, barely one month after the opening night, New Order played for the first time at their own club, primarily as a fund-raiser to keep it operational. They hired in a massive PA which then proceeded to blow up on the first chord of the set. The wrong type of fuse had been used on the stage power supply, which was fixed by inserting the silver paper from a Kit Kat wrapper around the fuse and having a roadie fan it throughout the performance to keep it cool.

This was the first of a whole host of benefits that New Order ended up playing over the years to support the club, not to mention the hundreds of thousands of pounds from record sales and touring that were invested. The club continued to lose money throughout the decade, remaining empty most nights, until the acid house movement at the end of the 1980's suddenly made it the hottest place to be on earth.

Throughout 1982 Factory touted the Haçienda as a live venue, and many bands included it on their tour agendas, including Orange Juice, Culture Club, Echo & the Bunnymen, Simple Minds, Bauhaus, Bow Wow Wow, The Associates, Big Country, Grandmaster Flash, and Yazoo. However, they were losing £10,000 a month, and the bar stock was being sold out the back door by opportunists as soon as it came in. Even the lighting system was stolen one piece at a time by an engineer, as missing video players, turntables and speakers were having to be replaced on an almost monthly basis.

ʊ ʊ ʊ

According to Jerry Hall, Roxy Music's new single, *Avalon*, was written following her break-up with frontman Bryan Ferry when she left him to go to Morocco with Mick

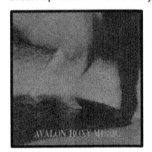

Jagger. Upon returning to the country, Ferry would not allow her back in the house to collect her belongings, which included the book she was reading called *The Mists of Avalon*.

Ferry had started out a working-class boy from Northumberland, but his ambition now was to join the upper class. During 1981 he had started dating Lucy Helmore, a socialite and the daughter of an Irish landowner, fourteen years his junior, employing her to appear wearing a helmet on the cover of the latest Roxy Music album. Their blossoming relationship took a new intensity when Helmore became pregnant early in the year, and on Saturday 26th June the couple married.

When their son Otis was born at the beginning of November Ferry signed him up for a place at Eton within a week of the birth and claimed to the Observer he was "*the first rock star to join the English aristocracy*". The transformation was complete.

27th June – 3rd July 1982
#1 single: Captain Sensible: Happy Talk
#1 album: ABC: The Lexicon of Love

British director Alan Parker[394] had made and released *Fame* two years previously, a movie which followed the fortunes of students at the High School of Performing Arts in New York. MGM Television, who owned the rights to the movie, saw the potential in the characters and commissioned a television series with the same premise. Retaining four of the actors from the film, including Lee Curreri as musician Bruno Martelli, Gene Anthony Ray[395] as dancer Leroy Johnson, and Albert Hague[396] as Professor Shorofsky, a host of new actors were brought in to fill the other roles[397]. The lead role, played by Irene Cara in the film, was filled by Erica Gimpel, who was completing her final year at the actual High School for Performing Arts whilst filming the series.

The first series aired in the United States in January, but did not appear in Britain until June, with the public taking it to their hearts immediately, whilst the title theme from the movie sung by Cara was released and climbed to become a summer number one. Written by Michael Gore[398] and Dean Pitchford[399], *Fame* was a fabulous piece of disco-rock played by top session musicians such as Leon Pendarvis[400], David Spinozza, Elliot Randall[401], Jimmy Maelen[402], and Luther Vandross. The television series also featured the song but sung by Gimpel instead.

A month after the series started in the United Kingdom, the first single from the television cast was released under the rather patronizing name of *The Kids from Fame*. *Hi-Fidelity* was wisp of featherweight fluff, and actress Valerie Lansburg claimed "*I don't think anyone ever expected Hi-Fidelity to be this huge hit single, certainly not when we recorded it. It was just this silly number that we did.*" Silly or not, the song's perky energy projected it to number five in the charts and kick started an envious chart assault. It cannot be emphasized enough how big a sway *The Kids from Fame* had over the music scene and charts in 1982 without actually having a lasting impact, with the subsequent album sitting at number one for a total of twelve weeks and remaining

---

[394] Parker's son wrote the screenplay for the movie *Moon*, which was directed by David Bowie's son.

[395] Ray's mother spent the time on set running a drugs ring, which eventually led to his dismissal from the series.

[396] Hague was a Jew who was accidently inducted into the Hitler Youth. His family fled to America, and he returned to Europe to fight the Nazis... as part of the army band.

[397] Madonna auditioned for a part later in 1982, a clip of which can be found on Youtube.

[398] Gore was the brother of singer Lesley Gore.

[399] Pitchford also wrote *Footloose*, *Holding Out For a Hero*, and *Let's Hear it For the Boy*.

[400] Pendarvis played the keyboards on Van McCoy's *The Hustle*.

[401] Randall played the guitar solo on Steely Dan's *Reelin' in the Years*, considered by Jimmy Page to be the best guitar solo ever.

[402] Maelen played with two separate acts at *Live Aid*: Dire Straits and Roxy Music.

in the charts for forty-six, becoming the second best-selling of the year[403]. A second album, the imaginatively titled *The Kids from Fame Again*, was released just a couple of months later, reaching number two, followed by a live album early in 1983.

The debut album featured songs by respected songwriters such as Carol Bayer

Sager[404], Gary Portnoy[405], Sandy Linzer[406], and Rick Springfield[407], played by session musicians like Dean Parks, Michael Landau, and Rick Schlosser. As well as these top-class performers, the cast contributed to the music, with Lee Curreri who played keyboard player Bruno Martelli adding to the songwriting. That the cast were all graduates from schools just like the one in the series and could all sing and dance to an admirable degree helped them to put together a tour in Britain. Six dates in three venues, matinee and evening performances, over the New Year period, to over 70,000 screaming pre-pubescent fans with corporate sponsorship from Doctor Pepper, were a pre-curser of what would become the norm for pop tours in the future.

A second single, the overwrought ballad *Starmaker* was performed as a tribute to the acting teacher, Mr Crandall played by Michael Thoma. There was genuine emotion in the scene as Thoma was leaving with a terminal cancer diagnosis, and as *Starmaker* climbed the charts to number three in September he died in Los Angeles.

℧ ℧ ℧

John Allan had been hired by Ozzy Osbourne to be hung every night during his *Diary of a Madman* tour. The idea had come to Ozzy whilst on holiday in Barbados that halfway through *Goodbye to Romance* they would "*execute a midget*" using a fake noose.

Allan had just appeared as a toy soldier in the movie *Bladerunner*, and when auditions were held it became obvious he was a raging alcoholic, so would be perfect for a year on the road with Ozzy Osbourne. Of course, the alcohol also made him undependable, and when on Sunday 27th June Allan was late for the flight from Los Angeles to Honolulu the tour bus was sent to collect him from the hotel. Finding Allan there, the roadie grabbed him by the back of his trousers and threw him into the luggage compartment under the tour bus. A passing woman was outraged, and shouted "*I saw what you done to that poor little man! You can't treat him like that!*" The roadie immediately replied "*Fuck off! He's MY midget!*", and at this, a little head poked out from between the suitcases and added "*Yeah, fuck off! I'm HIS midget!*"

℧ ℧ ℧

Such was the reaction to *E.T. The Extra-Terrestrial* that on Sunday 27th June Steven Spielberg was invited to show the movie at the Whitehouse to the president, his wife, and a handful of guests. By the end of the night, Nancy Reagan was in tears and

---

[403] The best-selling album of the year was Barbra Streisand's *Love Songs*.

[404] Bayer Sager wrote *A Groovy Kind of Love*, *Nobody Does it Better*, and *You're Moving Out*.

[405] Potnoy wrote the theme tune for *Cheers*.

[406] Linzer wrote *Let's Hang On*, *Working My Way Back to You*, *Native New Yorker*, and *Use It Up, Wear It Out*.

[407] Springfield, who started an affair with Linda Blair when he was twenty-six and she was fifteen, wrote *Jessie's Girl*, which I cannot hear without visualising Alfred Molina in his underpants.

Ronald Reagan *"looked like a ten-year-old kid"*. In September, Spielberg accepted an additional offer to show the film, this time to the staff at the United Nations, after which he was presented the UN Peace Medal by Secretary General Javier Perez de Cuellar[408], before the British premier was held in front of Queen Elizabeth in December. Spielberg had always retained a tight control over merchandise relating to his movies, however for the first time he signed the rights to *E.T. The Extra-Terrestrial* over to a toy company, who inundated the market with innumerable products, all of which depreciated the message of the movie bit by bit.

℧ ℧ ℧

The greatest party song of all time began with a plaintive solo violin refrain from Thomas Moore's old Irish folk song *Believe Me if all Those Endearing Young Charms* before drums and bass came in with a pounding rhythm stolen from Unit 4 + 2's *Concrete & Clay*. After a few bars, a host of musicians entered, backing an infectious violin-driven riff never visited again during the track – this song was so replete of musical ideas that it could afford not to repeat an exquisite hook.

This was a pop song about pop songs, referring to *"Poor old Johnny Ray"*, a semi-deaf singer whose tragic life as an alcoholic and secret homosexual was reflected in the sadness of his voice and songs in the early 1950's. The words were about the songs the singer's mother listened to, and the personal effect music could have on people, no matter the era. By the second verse he drew a distance between his generation and that of his parents, telling a girl that *"these people round here wear beaten down eyes sunk in smoke dried faces, they're resigned to what their fate is. But not us…. We are far too young and clever"*.

At the end of each verse the song built with the vocal and strings ascending synchronically into a chorus, and this is where the melody really hit home, bearing a striking resemblance to obscure soul classic *A Man Like Me* by Jimmy James, with a chant along title-line. Most listeners did not get beyond the chanted title, however hidden in there was an exorcism of Catholic guilt regarding sex, exploring the thin line between love and lust, with *"you in that dress, my thoughts I confess, verge on dirty"*.

Just when you thought the song had given up everything it had to offer, at the end of an extended second chorus the music paused, only to start with a slow chant, influenced by a section in *What Does Anybody Ever Think About* by The Blue Ox Babes and the *"C'mon C'mon"* section of *Leader of the Gang* by Gary Glitter[409]. This section

turned out to be the genius of the song, and was almost chopped out of the final arrangement, increasing in speed until a final couple of Bacchanalian choruses.

The song was full of key and tempo changes, counter melodies, hidden hooks in the arrangement, and multiple instruments throughout. Each section, however, felt essential to the whole, and before you knew it a fade arrived.

The song started as *Yes, Let's*, and Dexy's Midnight Runners were determined to get the track right, spending several days in a rehearsal room, learning the song in eleven major keys to see which one worked best. Co-producer Clive Langer claimed of the song that *"we recorded it as 'James, Van and Me' – James Brown, Van Morrison, and Kevin [Rowland]. That was the original chorus, singing about people who*

---

[408] In 1989 Javier Perez du Cuellar claimed to be a witness to a UFO abduction in New York.

[409] Keith Moon from The Who used to bring underage girls round to Gary Glitter's house in the 1970's.

influenced him to write the song... and then he came in one day and said I want to change the lyric completely". By the time the recording was complete the song was called *Come on Eileen*, after an attractive Swedish journalist who had interviewed Rowland and insisted on talking about spirituality whilst he was having lustful thoughts[410]. Everyone who heard the demo of the track proclaimed it to be a future hit in waiting, so a video was shot on the corner of Brook Drive and Hayles Street, near Waterloo Station in London, featured the Maire Fahey, the sister of Bananarama's Siobhan, playing the character of *Eileen*. The band appeared playing their instruments, dressed in their new image of torn denim dungarees, a sort of gypsy chic, whilst Rowland and Fahey indulge in a mini-love story. The video was most people's introduction to the new look Dexy's, and in an era of strangely dressed individuals the image became a hit, though most stopped short of copying it. Rowland insisted the band wear the new uniform on and off stage, leading to him being accused of ripping off Dexy's Midnight Runners on the bus a few times.

Knowing *Come on Eileen* was their last chance, Rowland started talking to the press again after an embargo for the past two years, but when the single was released at the end of June, credited to Dexy's Midnight Runners & The Emerald Express, it only entered the charts at the lowly position of number sixty-three. The following week it crept up to number forty-one and it looked as if they were about to have another flop. Increasing radio play pushed the single into the top forty and then a *Top of the Pops* appearance guaranteed success as it jumped to number nine, then number two, finally reaching the top on the 7th August. From there it was impossible to shift as it stayed at number one for four weeks over the summer, before a slow drop whilst selling almost one and a half million copies in Britain alone.

People who are serious about music find themselves torn by the song, with many of the opinion it is devalued by the enormous unrestricted regard in which *Come on Eileen* is held by the public. It is no fantastic assertion to claim that *Come on Eileen* is quite simply the greatest party song ever written: forty years after its release it still fills any dancefloor with people singing along and stamping their alcohol sodden feet, and yet when all and sundry know a song it becomes harder to see the magic in it.

ʊ ʊ ʊ

Bananarama were now throwing out singles at a breakneck pace, and at the end of June released *Shy Boy*, another breezy summer pop song that marked their break from working with the Fun Boy Three. After hearing *Body* Talk by Imagination, the trio

insisted on working with the team of Steve Jolley and Tony Swain, however the production duo and Bananarama did not hit it off, with the producers insisting on complete control and the girls demanding to be taken seriously. Swain and Jolley presented them with a song called *Big Red Motorbike*, a Motown pastiche which was immediately rejected due to the lyrics. *"We wanted to write lyrics from the point of view of the young women we were"* explained Sara Dallon, and the subsequent re-write produced the more acceptable *Shy Boy*. With three songs recorded, London Records relented and permitted Bananarama to write and record their own song, *Don't Call Us (Boy Trouble)* which was placed on the

---

[410] Rowland later claimed it was about childhood friend Eileen McLuskey, whose friendship had become less innocent when their sexual awareness had awoken.

B-side of *Shy Boy*, and picked up some airplay on its own terms but was hardly ground-breaking.

Shy Boy on the other hand, despite Bananarama's initial reservations, was a classic pop song in the style of 1960's Motown, however it had a frail, rapidly passé backing track and prosaic insipid vocals, whilst labouring towards a predictable fade. The accompanying video was directed by Midge Ure and Chris Cross of Ultravox, and helped the song rise to number four in the charts, giving the trio their third top five hit in as many months.

Their relationship with Swain and Jolley was about to come to a temporary halt[411] however, when Bananarama dismissed them, emboldened by their own writing and producing success with *Don't Call Us*.

℧ ℧ ℧

Lanky and balding, Joe Jackson had emerged from the south coast of England in the late 1970's, writing a similar style of edgy singer-songwriter fare as Elvis Costello and Graham Parker, whilst scoring a couple of top twenty hits with *Is She Really Going Out with Him* and *It's Different for Girls*. Since then, appearances in the charts were scarce, though each of his four previous albums had reached the top fifty in the United States. It was perhaps for this reason that twenty-eight-year-old Jackson chose to spend January and February recording in New York, with producer David Kershenbaum helping steer the sound towards the American market.

The subsequent album *Night and Day* was a love-letter to the city, from the opening *Another World* which celebrated the thrill of a new social life, to the mise-en-scène reportage of *Chinatown*. Deciding to move to the city, New York allowed Jackson to reinvent himself, and this was explored on songs which questioned the idea of masculinity, from the longing for strong arms of *A Slow Song* to the questioning of traditional gender roles in first single *Real Men*.

Where *Real Men* flopped as a single, two other tracks proved more successful. *Steppin' Out* was released in the United States during summer 1982, and in October in Britain, and climbed to number six in both countries[412]. With a simply determined beat and minimal instrumentation, Jackson sang of breaking out from mundanity and heading for the bright lights of New York, just to prove he was still alive. Follow up *Breaking Us in Two* reached the top twenty in America whilst failing to break the top forty in Britain.

With the album going top five around the world, Jackson would never again see such success, but maintained enough of a loyal following to keep him releasing albums and touring, eventually coming to terms with his sexuality in later years.

℧ ℧ ℧

West Germany against England was an international football fixture which smouldered with the ache of history, of *two world wars and one world cup*, however the opening game in the second-round group of the FIFA World Cup on the Tuesday 29th June was

---

[411] The production duo had once sent the girls home from the studio and told them to come back when they had grown up.

[412] Though *Steppin' Out* did not enter the British charts until January 1983.

a dreary and dispassionate affair. The German's, fresh from *"the disgrace of Gijon"* where they had resorted to a kick-about with Austria, both teams knowing they had to keep the score at 1-0,[413] were well-organized as expected, whilst the English appeared to be diminishing with each game played, as they both rode out a 0-0 draw.

Meanwhile Northern Ireland were riding high going into their match against Austria and dominated the first half with a header by Billy Hamilton putting them one up. Austria, requiring a victory, pulled a goal back just before half-time and then spent the break re-organising. The second half was played in intense heat and both sides wilted, however Austria went ahead through a Hintermaier goal. The Irish refused to give up, and Hamilton managed to score a second goal with his head with fifteen minutes to go. The score remained 2-2, with Northern Ireland now needing to beat France in the next game.

With Italy, Brazil and Argentina making up Group C in the second round, the promise of decidedly competitive and skilful games was on the cards. The first of these was a hitherto under-performing Italian team against world champions, Argentina, played in front of an overcrowded Sarria Stadium in Barcelona.

After a humdrum first half with the effective Italian defence of Scirea and Gentile stopping the waves of Argentinian attacks, in the second half the Italians finally started playing football to the level everybody suspected they could, scoring twice through Tardelli and Cabrini, before Argentina pulled one back in the last ten minutes.

℧ ℧ ℧

Post-punk found an intuitive home in West Germany where the disjuncture of the country and the anamnesis of a society under the influence of Adolf Hitler still haunted the parents of the nation's youth. As a rejoinder against their parent's upbringing,

young musicians in Germany had been turning away from the values of the previous generation, detaching from tradition first through the style known outside the nation as Krautrock, and then in the early 1980's in the punk influenced Neue Deutsche Welle (New German Wave). These *au courant* bands rejected Americanisms, choosing instead to sing in the harsh sounding German language and be influenced by a cold war psychosis, of which they had been brought up living on the front line. The movement especially blossomed in industrial cities, adding another hard-edged aspect to the sound amongst acts such as Spliff[414], Deutsch Amerikanische Freundschaft[415], and Trio.

The last of these had been formed in North Germany in 1979 by Stephan Remmier, Gert Krawinkel[416], and ex-circus clown Peter Behrens, and signed to German branch of Phonogram, where they were teamed up with producer Klaus Voorman[417]. Trio's

---

[413] German television commentators stopped commentating in disgust, and their Austrian counterpart ordered the viewers to switch off their sets. The system was revised after the tournament to guarantee that the final two games in each group were played concurrently.

[414] Spliff member Reinhold Heil later produced *99 Red Balloons* for Nena.

[415] John Peel considered Deutsch Amerikanische Freundschaft to be the godfathers of techno.

[416] Remmier and Krawinkel had played in a band called Just Us in the 1960's who had a residency in Hamburg's *Star Club*.

[417] Voorman was the art student who had discovered The Beatles in Hamburg and inspired their entire look to change from greasy rock and rollers to what became known as *Beatle haircuts*. He remained a

insistence on stripping their music back to instrumental basics appealed to Voorman, even though he added some bass guitar to the songs. The three scored an unexpected top ten hit across Europe with their single *Da da da, ich lieb' dich nicht du liebst mich nicht aha aha aha*, and by summer it was time for the United Kingdom to fall under its spell.

Da Da Da (as it was known in Britain) was an example of *schlager music*, the German style of pop music which was heading in a more synthesised direction in the 1980's. Whereas the real schlager artists and producers loved the new sounds and ease of recording them, believing them to be as realistic as the original instruments, Trio created a pastiche of the sound and sentiments of happy-go-lucky meaningless lyrics. Recorded using a drum beat from the tiny Casio VLT1[418] keyboard coupled with a simple snare drum played by Behrens[419], the repetitive mumbled verses were shorn of instruments, with only simple guitar and bass in the dumbly epizootic chorus. The single sold thirteen million copies worldwide, climbing to number two in Britain; not bad for a band who claimed *"our basis is rock and roll, on which we leave out everything superfluous; from star poses to bombastic instruments"*.

Of course, there was only so far that a band like Trio could take things, and they split up a couple of years later, after which Behrens did *"women, cocaine, alcohol"* until he ran out of money and returned to his previous job as a circus clown.

ʊ ʊ ʊ

Music in New York had been edging unhurriedly towards rap for a decade through black innovators in numerous nightclubs. DJ Hollywood had embraced the practice of twin turntables and pitch adjustment in 1972, before matching rhymes to instrumental segments of the records. By the following year he had appointed someone else to play the records and a couple of dancers, whilst he riled up the crowd in the disco.

The problem with DJ Hollywood and others like him was that you could only hear and see them in nightclubs, and so anyone under the age of eighteen was excluded from the scene. This changed when DJ Kool Herc, encouraged by his teenage daughter Cindy, started organising parties in the basement of his building on 168th Street. Herc is also recognised as being the first DJ to purchase two copies of each record so he could mix between them, creating extended breakdowns. It was at one of Herc's dances where Grandmaster Flash first witnessed mixing and rapping, and immediately became obsessed.

Joseph Saddler was born in Barbados and moved with his parents to New York at an early age, taking the name Grandmaster Flash in tribute to his love of kung-fu movies and the DC Comics superhero. As a small child he would place baseball cards into the spokes of his bike and spin them until he could control the speed and sync them. For two years after seeing Herc, Flash adapted the wheel technique to a couple of turntables, practising in his bedroom until he was able to mix sixteen records together in the space of two minutes, at which point he made his live debut in 1975, introducing the technique of *scratching* as well. Flash reckoned if he *"played the most exciting parts of these records one behind another… to the beat… then I should have the crowd in a total frenzy"*. Instead, the crowd stood and stared, and Flash grasped that he

---

friend with the band afterwards, joining Manfred Mann on bass and playing on solo recordings by John Lennon, Ringo Starr, and George Harrison.

[418] I had a Casio VLT-1. It doubled as a calculator.

[419] Behrens insisted that any beat he played had to be achievable whilst he was eating an apple with the other hand.

needed somebody to hype the crowd whilst he performed. Recruiting Keith "Cowboy" Wiggans, brothers Melvin "Melle Mel"[420] and Nathaniel "Kid Creole" Glover[421], Guy "Rahiem" Williams, and Eddie "Scorpio" Morris, he christened them the Furious Five. This collective soon acquired residencies at The Black Door Club and Disco Fever, where a street gang called The Casanovas intimidated their way into running the door. Motivated by the sounds being created, The Casanovas also began experimenting with music, ultimately developing into the Zulu Nation, led by Afrika Bambaataa.

By 1978 Grandmaster Flash and the Furious Five were the most popular party act in the Bronx when they were approached by Sylvia Robinson, the architect behind Sugarhill Records who ran a tight but tenacious ship. Having enjoyed success previously as one half of duo Mickey & Sylvia[422] in the 1950's and written several songs since then, including *Shame Shame Shame* for Shirley & Co[423], she was old enough and experienced enough to be called an industry veteran. After running All Platinum Records with her husband, Joe, for almost a decade, Sylvia was just across the water from hip-hop, in New Jersey, when it first started taking off in north Manhattan. It was Sylvie who had the initial idea to release a rap record, however when she approached Flash with the purpose of signing him to her new Sugarhill Records he refused, believing the idea of releasing rap on vinyl was ridiculous; this was surely a live genre which could never reproduce the feel or sound of block parties and nightclubs!

Robinson's answer was to create her own rap act, recruiting pizza delivery boy Hank Jackson to throw down some words over an instrumental version of *Good Times* by Chic, a track that was in extremely common usage almost to the point of cliché amongst Bronx DJs and rappers at the time. Jackson brought along two of his friends, Guy O'Brien and Michael Wright, and the trio became the Sugarhill Gang, cutting what many believe to be the first rap record, *Rapper's Delight*, using several lines already popularised locally by the Furious Five. Much to everybody's astonishment the single became a worldwide smash, selling over eight million copies and reaching the top ten right across Europe. Robinson, instead of sampling the original Chic song, re-recorded the music with a session band, adding an introductory section from *Here Comes That Sound Again*, written by British composer Alan Hawkshaw[424].

Rappers Delight was the song that introduced the white music industry to rap, and was taken up by punk and new wave artists quickest, with The Clash imitating the feel for *This is Radio Clash* and Blondie becoming the first act to top the Billboard charts with a section of rap in the song *Rapture*. In the latter song, the rap mentioned Grandmaster Flash ("*Flash is fast, Flash is cool*") to whom Debbie Harry had been introduced by graffiti artist Fab 5 Freddie. The video for *Rapture* featured Freddie indulging in some graffiti, and was intended to feature Flash on the turntables, but the Grandmaster did not turn up and Freddie asked his friend, the artist Jean-Michel Basquiat, to stand behind the decks and pretend to mix.

When *Rapper's Delight* hit the charts, Flash realised that he had been superseded by three unknowns, and set about releasing his own singles, which over the next couple

---

[420] Melle Mel was the first rap artist to call himself MC (Master of Ceremonies). He provided the rap for Chaka Khan's *I Feel For You*.

[421] Glover was charged with murder in 2017 after he allegedly stabbed a man to death.

[422] Mickey was Mickey Baker, a former pool hustler who had played guitar on many of the Rhythm and Blues hits of the 1950's.

[423] Singer Shirley Goodman had been a backing vocalist for The Rolling Stones on their *Exile on Main Street* album.

[424] Hawkshaw was the man who wrote both the theme from *Grange Hill* and the 30-second instrumental segment in *Countdown*.

of years, alongside releases by Kurtis Blow and further platters by The Sugarhill Gang, started to spread the word of hip-hop beyond New York. Rap, however, failed to cross over to the mainstream, and was considered by most people to be no more than a passing novelty fad.

In early 1982, Edwin Fletcher, keyboard player in the Sugarhill house band, came up with a leisurely intricate rhythm, ad-libbing the line *"It's like a jungle sometimes, it makes me wonder how I keep from going under"* over the top. Arranger James Chase instructed him to go home and complete the lyrics, which he did in his mother's basement, channelling the sounds of the street outside into words. Upon returning to the studio the next day, he jettisoned the over-complicated percussion, and added a beguiling keyboard line inspired by The Tom Tom Club.

Sylvia Robinson decided the track would be the next Grandmaster Flash & the Furious Five single. The only problem was that Flash and the Five wanted nothing to do with it: it was too slow to dance to, and the lyrics did not suggest a party which is what they believed rap should be about. Flash would state *"The shit was way too dark, way too edgy, and way too much of a downer"*, and after an animated argument they stormed out of the studio and called a cab.

The following day Melle Mel returned without notifying the others and added his vocal. It was not that he had a change of heart about the song, but instead realised that if the single was coming out with or without him, he would rather play a part than not. It was

decided to keep Fletcher's demo vocal on several of the verses, with Mel adding a verse he had written a couple of years earlier but not used.

When he found out, Flash was furious, believing he was being forced out of the group. Robinson's preference for recording the backing with a session band of Edwin Fletcher, Keith LeBlanc, Doug Wimbish, and Skip McDonald, meant that Flash's skill of providing beats and backing was fast becoming redundant. Flash described his feeling at the time as being *"this is what I was afraid of... this isn't everybody shining at the same time. This isn't about teamwork.... This is about Mel. This is about Sylvia. This is about money."*

The Message was released at the start of July and was over seven minutes of the concentrated sound of the Bronx, what Shaun Scott described as *"post-disco psychedelic peyote pulled from the urban cacti"*. In New York, unemployment was sitting at over 10%, the highest post-war level recorded, and the most affected area in the city was the Bronx. In 1975 it was suggested the entire area be demolished, such was the deterioration into slum housing, and a wave of arson by landlords trying to claim insurance money before the buildings were worth nothing meant whole blocks were left abandoned, attracting junkies and the homeless. When the city appealed to the federal government for a bail-out in 1975 President Gerald Ford stated he was *"prepared to veto any bill that has... a federal bailout for New York City"*. This was seized upon by the *New York Daily News*, who led their frontpage the following day with the headline *"FORD TO CITY: DROP DEAD"*. The underprivileged regions of the city just so happened to also be the areas where the most exciting music was fermenting, which was in turn brought downtown to clubs such as The Roxy, where hip-hop DJ's spun discs for luminaries like Andy Warhol and David Bowie. *The Message* became an instant hit on radio stations across New York, then across the nation, and then across the Atlantic.

The song was closer to the socio-conscious raps of Gil Scott-Heron or Stevie Wonder's community reflection of the mid-1970's than it was to the recently burgeoning rap scene. It was the impeccable fusion of social commentary and beats that maybe did not move your feet, but certainly touched your brain and heart.

From the opening line it did not hold back, straight in with *"Broken glass everywhere, people pissing in the street… rats in the front room, roaches in the back, junkies in the alley with a baseball bat"*, returning to a refrain of *"DON'T. PUSH. ME. COS I'M CLOSE. TO. THE. EDGE. I'M. TRYING. NOT. TO. LOSE. MY. HEAD"*, each word a struggle, each word a sentence of desperation, the whole line haunting.

The second verse concentrated on one of the victims of the city, a *"crazy lady, living in a bag, eating outta' garbage pails, used to be a fag hag"*, following her downwards spiral towards prostitution. By the fourth verse, contributed by Melle Mel, we were perceiving the story of *"a child…born with no state of mind"* who grew up in the ghetto admiring the *"number-book takers, thugs, pimps and pushers… smugglers, scramblers, burglars, gamblers"* before turning to crime and being sent to prison where his *"manhood is took…spend the next two years as an undercover fag, being used and abused"*, until one day he committed suicide in his cell.

These were areas hip hop had never dared or desired to go before, and if Chuck D would later state that *"Rap is Black America's CNN"*, then *The Message* certainly echoed the lives of millions existing in poverty. As the track progressed, the narrator became more frantic, and the music was filled with increasingly paranoid reiteration.

To keep the rest of the act contented, a closing skit was added with them gathering for a night out before being hassled and arrested by the police. The grit of the song (and skit) would in later years become fairly standard for rap music, however *The Message* lacked the bravado, swaggering, and boasting that genres such as Gangsta' Rap became notorious for, instead censuring the crime rather than celebrating it.

For Grandmaster Flash, *The Message* was the first of two massive worldwide hits, alongside the follow-up *White Lines (Don't Do It)* after which everything went sour. Flash felt that he had been edged out of the creative process of his own act, as his virtuoso performances on the turntables were forgotten with the studio singles. Sylvia Robinson once told him *"In the real world, no-one knows you from a can of paint"*, the type of attitude towards him that led Flash to eventually sue Sugarhill for unpaid royalties along with Cowboy and Raheim, whilst Cowboy, Melle Mel & Scorpio took the side of the record company.

Rap in 1982 was in danger of becoming a passing fad, having failed to wholly break through into the charts in any salient way, even attracting a parody track by comedian Mel Brooks[425] and a British comedy hit by The Brat[426]. Future Pet Shop Boys singer Neil Tennent reviewed the act in *Smash Hits* by writing *"In fifty years-time, when your grandchildren cluster round your armchair and ask 'What was rap?' you'll be at a loss to explain why the Grand Master of Rap actually sings a bunch of substandard disco songs"*. There was an issue with many of the backing tracks taken from disco, a musical genre that had well and truly fallen out of favour, and rap was in the precarious position of being dragged down with it. *The Message* went a long way to providing some longevity to the genre, however the Furious Five still dressed in a style largely influenced by George Clinton's Parliament / Funkadelic and could at times look more like Village People.

---

[425] *To Be or Not To Be (The Hitler Rap)* was a number twelve hit for Mel Brooks.

[426] The Brat was comedian Roger Kitter (who was first discovered on *Opportunity Knocks* in 1970 and had a future in BBC television sit-com *'Allo 'Allo*). Written by him, Sheena Easton's bass player Mo Foster (who himself had played on the theme tune from *Minder*), and comedy script writer Mike Walling, *Chalkdust* featured an argument between a John McEnroe type tennis player played by Kitter, and an umpire played by Kaplin Kaye, and inexplicably climbed to number nineteen.

ʊ ʊ ʊ

The Birthday Party found their spiritual home-from-home in Germany, however the chaos and in-fighting continued throughout the Teutonic leg of their European tour. On the bus between Bochum and Munich, cowboy hat wearing bass player Tracey Pew insisted on having the front seat due to him being the only non-smoker. Guitarists Rowland Howard and Mick Harvey decided to wind him up by deliberately occupying the seats, which Pew took violent exception to and started clawing at the two and pulling them from the chairs by the hair.

By the time the tour reached the Stollwerk in Cologne on Friday 2nd July, singer Nick Cave's propensity towards violence had grown, tired of people turning up to adore him. Wanting to provoke a reaction he kicked out at anyone near the stage, at one point aiming for a skinhead and accidently breaking the nose of a girl next to him. As Cave stepped outside his character and tried to apologize, an iron bar was produced from behind the bar and passed to the front of the venue, only to be wrestled from the hands of a punk as he was about to smash the singer's skull.

After the show, a local chapter of the Hell's Angels appeared backstage and demanded to use the band's equipment for their own show. Once again, a fight broke out only to be ended when Pew decided to wade into the melee with a bottle.

At the conclusion of the tour, drug consumption started to take its toll and the songwriting withered. Phil Calvert was made the scapegoat and sacked from the band, with Harvey moving from guitar to drums, and the band relocated to Berlin, a divided city more in tune with their nihilistic on-the-edge outlook, however as a creative power they were through.

By summer the band were sharing the bill and being compared to new acts such as The Sisters of Mercy, The Sex Gang Children, and The Southern Death Cult, as the idea of a unified *goth* movement crystalized. Eager to please The Birthday Party, Sisters of Mercy singer Andrew Eldritch asked for their opinion of his band. The answer came back: they were the worst band to have ever supported The Birthday Party. After a long weekend of tense discussions and soul-searching, the Sisters of Mercy decided to continue.

ʊ ʊ ʊ

The task of tidying the mess left by the collapse of Banco Ambrosiano and the death of Roberto Calvi fell to three men appointed by the Bank of Italy. On the 2nd July Alberto Bertoni, Antonino Occhiuto, and Giovanni Arduino visited Paul Marcinkus at the Vatican bank, and attempted to persuade them as major shareholders and investors to cover their portion of the debt. Marcinkus would hear nothing of it, even when Arduino threatened to go public with their involvement. *"By Monday, the name of your bank will be on the desk of every foreign bank in London, Paris, and New York"* he shouted, to which Marcinkus shrugged *"Too bad"*.

ʊ ʊ ʊ

To promote their album The Jam spent March to June touring Britain, mainland Europe, Japan, Canada, and the United States under the *Trans-Global Unity Express* title. The tour did much to push singer Paul Weller further from drummer Rick Buckler and bass player Bruce Foxton, with them hardly exchanging any conversation throughout. Wherever they went, they found themselves being watched by an audience that was not yet ready to move into the new musical directions they were exploring, resembling drunken football supporters, something which inevitably led to Weller's growing disillusionment with his status.

The Jam had recorded four cover versions back in February at Maison Rouge Studios in Fulham, with the intention of releasing these as an EP, however this idea was scrapped.[427] Instead, the band chose not to release a second single in the United Kingdom from *The Gift*, and instead *Just Who is the Five O'Clock Hero* came out as a single in a handful of European territories, an odd decision given the band's continuing lack of success on the continent. There was a precedent for this with The Jam: the Europe-only release of *That's Entertainment* from their *Sound Affects* album. Just as that single had managed to chart through the sale of imported copies, so too did *Just Who is the Five O'Clock Hero*.

Not their strongest single, the song was powered by Rick Buckler's commuter express-train drumming and an unimaginatively transparent guitar. Clocking in at just over two minutes, the track was lacking any of the usual Jam hooks, though the words were honed to perfection in their working-class anger at returning from a job "*covered in shit and aches and pains, too knacked to think*" only to find "*Prince Philip tells us we gotta' work* harder". Yet the anger was temporary as it was "*back to the lunchbox and the worker management rows*", leaving the narrator to wonder "*There's gotta' be more to this old life than this, scrimping and saving and crossing off lists*". After his dalliance with voting Conservative, Weller was now firmly on the side of the working class, explaining "*The real heroes are obviously the geezer who has to go out and do a nine to five job. So the nurses and the miners are the real heroes because they keep the country going – not pop stars*".

With almost no radio play or promotion, the imported single sold enough copies to take it to number eight, and as it peaked Weller and his girlfriend Gill Price took a short break in Italy, giving him time to reflect on his future. All he could see was a constant record – release – tour merry-go-round which completely relied on him, and he made the decision that he wanted to get off. To split what was arguably Britain's biggest band up at the height of their fame just like his beloved Beatles and Small Faces had done appealed to him, and upon returning to Britain he informed his father of the decision first.

ʊ ʊ ʊ

Early triumphs in various parliamentary seat elections along with high poll ratings made it appear as if the SDP could form the next government, if not alone then certainly in coalition with the Liberal Party. The first objective of the party, however, was to get all the *Gang of Four* back as Members of Parliament. With Roy Jenkins winning Hillhead in March, everything was in place for the party to take the country, but first they required a leader. Many considered Jenkins the natural choice given his vast experience in government and as former head of the European Union, however David Owen had recently demonstrated a ruthless determination and ambition. The two agreed not to criticise each other and were limited to a 750-word statement which was sent to all 65,000 members of the party, however their supporters made much of the dissimilarities between the candidates. Jenkins was the hoary safe hands, Owen was

---

[427] The four tracks were Curtis Mayfield's *Move On Up*, James Brown's *I Got You (I Feel Good)*, Edwin Starr's *War*, and The Chi-Lites' *Stoned Out Of Mind*, reflecting Weller's increasing fascination with soul music.

the younger more dynamic generation, Jenkins was keen to unite with the Liberals, and Owen desperately sought to keep the discrete identity of the SDP.

Ultimately, the members of the party felt they were voting for the next Prime Minister rather than somebody who desired to change the party, and Jenkins was perceived as being more statesman-like. 75% of the members voted, 56% of those voted for Jenkins, and on Friday 2nd July he was announced as leader of the Social Democratic Party.

Victory in the leadership election for the SDP was to be the highlight of Jenkins late-political career, and almost as soon as he was elected to the position his influence diminished due to three factors. Firstly, the Conservatives were in a post-Falklands jingoistic ascendancy which would ultimately steamroll all opposition for at least the next decade. Secondly, he had made an adversary of Owen in the leadership contest, who then spent the rest of the year scoring points and undermining Jenkins. Thirdly, to everybody's astonishment, Jenkins proved to be an ineffectual party leader. He was a politician of the old-school, practised in writing opinions in newspapers and delivering discourses to the public, but by the 1980's the battleground had relocated onto television, and in this Jenkins proved incapable of supplying the required soundbites, instead appearing "*old, flabby and long-winded*". In the House of Commons he failed to wound the Prime Minister during question time, having been softened by years of European Commission diplomacy and etiquettes. The hoped-for flood of Conservative MPs jumping to the SDP was not forthcoming, with most in fear of losing their lucrative business contacts.

Any momentum gained in the past year was well and truly lacking by the autumn party conference, which was held in three rolling locations: Cardiff, Derby, and Great Yarmouth, with delegates travelling between each by rail. A perfect metaphor was provided by the train transporting the members, which broke down between venues.

ʊ ʊ ʊ

Dave Murray was so exhilarated by Iron Maiden's performance supporting The Scorpions at the Chicago UIC Pavillion on Friday 2nd July that he made a spur-of-the-moment decision at the conclusion of the encore to throw his guitar into the audience. Unfortunately, in the best Spinal Tap style he forgot to unplug it first, and the ascending loop towards the crowd was cut short as the instrument clattered down upon the head of one of the security guards.

Iron Maiden were in the middle of 73 North American dates, many of which would be supporting Judas Priest, Rainbow, or Scorpions, and things were going exceedingly well. Their new album, *The Number of the Beast*, had reached number thirty-three in the Billboard charts without the accompanying Stateside release of any singles. It had also topped the charts in Britain and reached the top ten in Australia and across Europe. Their latest tour was pulling larger and larger audiences, electrified by their taut spirited live shows, special effects, and props, such as the giant animatronic head of the character Eddie who adorned their album covers.

Manager Rod Smallwood ran a tight ship, not permitting problems to get in the way of the schedule, and swiftly dealt with the situation, knowing precisely how much money to offer the security guard to make any grievances go away.

ʊ ʊ ʊ

Returning to London, Trevor Horn wrestled with the various tapes of bands he and Malcolm McLaren had recorded in New York and Tennessee. McLaren left him alone, having no real concern about the studio side of things, spending his time instead arranging a second clothes shop in St Christopher's Place, just off Oxford Street, with his partner, fashion designer Vivienne Westwood. *Nostalgia of Mud*[428] had opened in March 1982, and was deliberately designed to be difficult to access, with scaffolding at the door and mud across the floor. McLaren provided the designer with a photograph of a Bolivian dancer, and instructions to design clothes for a "*disco on Hadrian's Wall where all the kids would be folk dancing*", and Westwood had started to put together a new collection. These clothes marked the moment when Westwood really came into her own as a designer, creating muddy-coloured clothes that were roughly put together with the stitching and joins controversially becoming part of the design. Westwood recognized these designs were a leap forward from before and decided to present them on a catwalk in Paris during Fashion Week. The organisers disagreed, and turned down her application, so the *Buffalo Collection* went on show instead in a tea-room across the street, with Nick Kamen leading the first ever *street-cast* models. The critics remained unimpressed.

℧ ℧ ℧

At the Cheltenham Races on Saturday 3rd July Margaret Thatcher delivered a speech looking back upon the Falklands Conflict. "*We fought to show that aggression does not pay and that the robber cannot be allowed to get away with his swag... we have to see that the spirit of the South Atlantic – the real spirit of Britain – is kindled not only by war but can now be fired by peace*". After quoting Winston Churchill, she went on "*Now, once again, Britain is not prepared to be pushed about. We have ceased to be a nation in retreat*".

Thatcher had no truck with looking back at days of Empire, choosing instead a vision of Britain as a modern nation, a world leader. "*We have a new-found confidence – born in the economic battles at home and tested and found true 8,000 miles away. Britain found herself again in the South Atlantic and will not look back from that victory she has won*" she concluded.

℧ ℧ ℧

Whilst the PLO were only just managing to hold on in Beirut, they were being torn apart by two factions within: one which wanted to withdraw and one which wanted to fight. Leader Yasser Arafat fluctuated between the two, trying to keep the organization together, when he was summoned to the mansion of former Lebanese Prime Minister, Saeb Salam, on Saturday 3rd July. The national council made it clear that the PLO had overstayed their welcome, and the Lebanese government would no longer watch their country being bombed by the Israelis, no matter how much they supported the cause. Arafat pleaded that they could not be seen to bow down to Israeli pressure, and would rather fight to the death, however after a brief conference with the Palestinian command, a hand-written note was delivered to Salam stating the PLO would leave Lebanon.

What Arafat did not say, was *when* they would depart.

Over the next month the Americans, whilst remaining pro-Israeli, offered to transport the PLO from Lebanon aboard their Navy vessels, reckoning it would be the swiftest way to end the conflict. Immediately, the PLO command began making demands for their BMW's and Mercedes to be loaded aboard, followed by their families.

---

[428] *Nostalgia of Mud* was taken from the French *nostalgie de la boue*, which Tom Wolfe had written about ten years previously, and referred to the "*gauche thrill of taking on certain styles of the lower orders.*"

JULY

4th – 10th July 1982
#1 single: Captain Sensible: Happy Talk
#1 album: ABC: The Lexicon of Love

Northern Ireland had played the World Cup of their lives with resilient team performances and shock victories, however their good fortune and strength finally ran out against France. After an early goal by Martin O'Neill was erroneously ruled as offside, the French took control and were three goals up before the Irish pulled a consolation back through Gerry Armstrong. It gave them false optimism, and a few minutes later France scored their fourth for an unequivocal victory. Northern Ireland were going home, but they were far from humiliated, having given a superlative account of themselves and reached heights they have struggled to since.

ʊ ʊ ʊ

Declan McManus had been born in 1954, the son of Ross McManus, a singer in the Joe Loss Orchestra, ensuring the youngster had an upbringing in show-business and a wide knowledge of a range of musical styles. Throughout the early 1970's he ploughed a trade in pub rock outfit Flip City whilst building up a cache of self-written songs which eventually brought him to the attention of Stiff Records as a solo artist. Together with a new band, The Attractions, and a name change to Elvis Costello, he became swept up in new wave, where his songs of bitterness streaked with aggression felt at home. Critics in Britain were in raptures about his lyrics, full of double meaning and references, accompanied by music provided by three of the best musicians in the country. In America it was the same story magnified, where Costello was treated as the predominant face of new wave, and something of a celebrity and rock star. The secret of his success stateside was in the blend of traditional rock, referencing acts such as Bruce Springsteen and Van Morrison, and the vitality and rage of punk. What made all this unusual was how Costello looked: the school nerd with National Health glasses and his uncle's tight-fitting suit, Buddy Holly on amphetamines and bile, a sneering Pointdexter[429] for modern days.

The first five albums arrived in quick succession, recorded on the run in between relentless and excessive touring, and sealed his standing as a serious artist and lyrical poet. In 1981 Costello spent some time in Nashville indulging his genuine love of country music by recording an album of cover versions[430]. It was the first misstep of his career, sounding unwieldly and inauthentic, even though it contained one his biggest hits in the form of *Good Year for the Roses*.

Costello needed a change at the end of 1981, opting to produce himself at AIR Studios in London during October and November, with the engineering skill of ex-Beatles studio hand Geoff Emerick. The first couple of weeks did not go well, with the Attractions taking some convincing to move out of their comfort zone of playing and recording live. After a fraught fortnight, they started to open-up and experiment a bit more, encouraged by Emerick who had worked in a similar way with The Beatles through their psychedelic years. Bass player Bruce Thomas had initially suggested the bold move of asking Kate Bush to produce, which Costello took seriously until Thomas also proposed getting in another guitarist.

[429] Pointdexter is American slang for a nerd, taken from a character in a 1959 episode of *Felix the Cat*.

[430] The album was grudgingly produced by country legend Billy Sherrill.

For the first time in his career, Costello started writing in the studio, often recording backing tracks without having any idea how the vocals were going to fit on top. The freedom allowed the band meant they could experiment with other instruments such as mellotrons, marimbas, and twelve string acoustic guitars, as the album slowly came into focus by the end of the year. Costello even brought in an accordion which they struggled to play, finally laying it flat on a table whilst Steve Nieve played the keyboard and Costello moved the bellows back and forward[431]. After a date at the Albert Hall in London in January backed by the Attractions and the Royal Philharmonic, the early months of 1982 were spent by Costello working on the vocals, with Paul McCartney

next door on one side, and The Jam mixing *Town Called Malice* on the other. Costello had become obsessed with delivering more than one point of view on the album, and spent time finding other voices within himself to represent this. Initially a double album worth of material was finished, which was then whittled down to one disc, with many songs changing shape significantly at this point in the process.

Once the album was finished in March, there was a delay in the release due to contractual issues between his label F-Beat and parent company Columbia, which was resolved by appointing Costello co-owner of Demon Records and Edsel. The band filled the time by embarking on a tour of Australia and New Zealand.

The album went through a couple of name changes, initially being titled *Music to Stop Clocks*, then *This is a Revolution of the Mind*[432], before settling on *Imperial Bedroom* after a song which was eventually left off the final release. The cover featured a painting by Barney Bubbles[433] called *Snake Charmer and Reclining Octopus*, which channelled the spirit of Pablo Picasso. Costello initially resisted the idea of putting the lyrics on the inside sleeve, but eventually relented on the condition they were laid out in one block of text without any punctuation, making them more of a graphic design than something to read. A photograph of the band on the inside had been taken by David Bailey, who liked to sum people up when first meeting them with a short soundbite.

"*I see... Mad Professor?*" he said upon seeing bass player Bruce Thomas.

"*I see... moonlighting bin man?*" Thomas replied.

Opening track *Beyond Belief* set a high bar for the album, in two and a half minutes of barely contained agitation waiting to bubble over. Originally entitled *The Land of Give and Take*, the opening line sets the tone as "*History repeats the old conceits, the glib replies, the same defeats*". The narrator was a lonely pick-up artist hanging around a bar waiting to pick up, well, anyone at all, knowing no matter the outcome disappointment would be the result. Half the lines were observation of the other barflies doing the same, and half were self-criticism, which Costello recorded in multiple takes, trading lines back and forth with himself. The lyrics have been compared with the poetry of T.S. Elliot, which is not surprising as Costello took his time to avoid the obvious words: he did not say cemetery, he said "*bone orchard*", instead of bar it was "*gin palace*", instead of a hope in Hell, it was "*a hope in Hades*". The song was initially recorded without drums as Pete Thomas failed to turn up at the studio following a drunken fight with Paul Weller. When he eventually arrived Costello snarled "*Get

---

[431] A third studio engineer was drafted in to hold the instrument in place.

[432] This was a direct lift from James Brown's *King Heroin*.

[433] Bubbles committed suicide the following year by trapping gas fumes in a plastic bag and placing it over his head.

behind those fucking drums and put the headphones on – you're getting one chance at this". The effect was mostly fills until the drummer felt confident enough to come in during the outro, which helps provide tension throughout. Immediately after the take, Costello told him *"Now go home for a lie down"*.

It was not hard to read the album as being about Costello's crumbling marriage, and the whole album was very much talking to himself. *Tears Before Bedtime* was originally recorded during the sessions for the last country album, however Costello was unhappy and had another go in a different style, this time with a soul feel. The song, which started as a swing ballad, was surprisingly chirpy given it dealt with infidelity and a tumultuous relationship. For *Long Honeymoon* Costello endeavoured to get Sammy Cahn to write the lyrics, but ended up doing it himself, looking at his wife waiting at home wondering about her cheating husband. *Human Hands*, with its reference to the *"blue light of the TV"* was a deliberate allusion to Joni Mitchell's *A Case of You*, once again dealing with Costello's philandering, and a plea to his lover that he still loved her. One more song of heartbreak, *Almost Blue* has become an acknowledged late-night jazz classic, and Costello himself asserted the song owed a debt to *The Thrill is Gone* by Chet Baker[434]. For this album he had switched to composing on piano rather than guitar and it was most noticeable on this track, where the space between the notes allowed regret to seep in. Costello's repeated use of the word *almost* throughout made it clear that his new love was no substitute for his old love, as the song reflected the wee small hours self-pitying musings of the heartbroken.

The self-reflection continued on what Costello considered *"the emotional centrepiece and master stroke on Imperial Bedroom"*: a track called *Man Out of Time*. The original version was much faster and lost some of the subtleties of the lyrics, which were inspired by *"looking at my reflection in the frozen window of a Scandinavian tour bus without any idea who the hell I was supposed to be"*, and then resolved in song one morning in the garden of a Scottish hotel. *"The house which we were staying had played a very minor part in one of Britain's most notorious political scandals,"* claimed Costello, *"Apparently serving briefly as a bolt-hole for one of the disgraced protagonists"*[435]. Costello's nights of self-doubt were explained in the line *"To murder my love is crime but will you still love a man out of time"*, taken from a love letter to Bebe Buell, whom Costello had split from following her decision to have an abortion.

Costello would later claim *"the central voice of Imperial Bedroom was one filled with doubt and self-recrimination… not entirely a work of fiction"*, however he conceded *"we never sounded better as a group"*.

When Costello went out on a North American tour in mid-July it was a very different show from the last few years when the energy of punk had dictated short energetic sets. Throughout the tour the band player between thirty and forty songs per night, including a whole host of rhythm and blues cover versions. The American jaunt ended in the middle of September and the Attractions returned to Britain for the *Bedrooms of Britain* national tour. When the British tour concluded in October Costello spent a couple of weeks in the studio producing Scottish support act The Bluebells.

Whilst *Imperial Bedroom* had been a critical success it contained no top forty hit singles as Costello began his move away from chart success towards becoming a peripheral artist with an extremely dedicated demographically-precise audience: males born in the 1960's. These fans would follow him throughout the many turns and twists of his career, through albums with string quartets and blues pianos, re-unions with The Attractions and solo tours.

---

[434] Baker would collaborate with Costello on his recording of *Shipbuilding* the following year.

[435] Costello was referring to the Profumo Affair.

Around Christmas 1982 Elvis Costello and the Attractions rounded off their year with a couple of dates at the Royal Albert Hall in London. For these dates they were joined by the Imperial Horns; Big Jim Paterson, Paul Speare, and Jeff Blythe, all of whom had been the brass section with Dexy's Midnight Runners. Despite such a prestigious venue, Costello still had one eye on the future and showcased unrecorded songs from his next album, *Punch the Clock*.

Like a true artist, he was already onto the next thing.

℧ ℧ ℧

It is a common misapprehension to assume Israel is of one mind when it comes to politics. In 1982, the country was ruled by a right-wing government under Benny Begin, however there was significant left-wing opposition, and on Sunday 4th July over 400,000 of them assembled in protest in Tel Aviv. The rally was organised by the group Peace Now and was against Israel's "*War of choice*" in Lebanon. Many there likened the war to a quagmire, describing it as a middle eastern Vietnam. Amongst those speaking were several army officers back from the front, and there was no mistaking where they placed the culpability: Defence Minister Ariel Sharon's bellicose stance.

In the confusion of the situation in Lebanon, it was too easy for people to go missing. Less so for diplomats, given their immunity from prosecution and scrutiny, however on Sunday 4th July four Iranian's were travelling from the Embassy in Damascus to Beirut when their car was pulled over at a checkpoint by Lebanese Phalange Forces, a Christian army with close links to the Israeli military.

What happened next is the subject of controversy, with Iranian officials insisting the four were handed over to the Israelis and have been kept imprisoned since then, and the Israelis claiming they had been tortured and executed by the Phalangists not long after capture.

The incident has become a political rather than a judicial issue over the years, with some released Lebanese prisoners stating they had seen one of the four whilst in captivity in Israel. Israel also agreed to include an update on the fate of the four during a 2008 Israel - Hezbollah prisoner exchange agreement.

The following day the Israeli forces encircling Beirut switched off the power and water supply to the city. No-one could enter the city with food or water, and journalists reported witnessing Israeli forces confiscating food from elderly Muslim women and throwing it in a ditch. As the refugees from Southern Lebanon took shelter in office blocks, cinemas and shopping arcades, the United Nations passed a resolution calling for the restoration of power and water. The Israeli's released a communique stating they had not turned off the power and water, and then when journalists started broadcasting evidence, released a second communique denying the first communique had ever been released. The power and electricity were not restored in the following weeks, as the locals searched plans for ancient natural wells and started to drink sea water.

℧ ℧ ℧

Duran Duran had spent the spring and summer touring far off places to promote their new album *Rio*, first Australia and Japan in April and May, and then the United States in June. In between Japan and America, they had rushed home to do some television and publicity, before everyone except guitarist Andy Taylor decided to take a quick holiday in Antigua, in the West Indies. After a week in luxury, the band received a phone call from their management, telling them to stay put as the last member of the band was flying out along with film maker Russell Mulcahey and model Reema Ruspoli to shoot videos for the title track of the album, as well as *Nightboat* from their first album. The inspiration for the video shoots was a book of photographs by Cheyco

Leidmann, with models in luminous colours, often shot against a bright blue sky. Following the reaction that had met the Sri Lanka-shot *Hungry like the Wolf* video, the record company, band, and management were keen to cash in on exotic images as much as possible.

The American tour started on the East coast, and after a date in New York, Robert Palmer came backstage, hitting it off with John Taylor, a meeting that started a friendship which would eventually lead to The Power Station by the middle of the decade. The same night Taylor planted the seed of an idea into the head of Nigel Harrison, bass player with Blondie, of the two bands touring together. By the time Duran Duran had crossed the continent via a string of Canadian dates and arrived in Los Angeles, this idea had taken hold, and Duran Duran were confirmed as support on Blondie's summer tour of stadiums.

ʊ ʊ ʊ

Ozzy was head over heels in love with Sharon Arden, the daughter of notorious hard-man British music manager Don, who had previously overseen Osbourne's old band Black Sabbath. When Osbourne left the group, Sharon stepped in and offered to manage him, and it was only a matter of time before the two were sleeping together. Arden was everything to Ozzy: manager, girlfriend, lover, mother, boss, and over the last six months he had asked her to marry him seventeen times. Sometimes she said yes, sometimes she said no, however they finally decided to tie the knot on Sunday 4th July, the date chosen so that Ozzy would have a chance of remembering it.

The wedding took place in Hawaii *en route* to the Japanese leg of the tour, with a small ceremony on the Island of Maui. Sharon's father turned up, but only because he required some legal papers to be signed and insisting on talking business as he walked her down the aisle. The wedding night was a disaster with Ozzy so drunk that he passed out in the hotel corridor, and Sharon was awoken at five in the morning by the hotel manager with a request to collect her husband so the maids could gain access to the cleaning cupboard.

ʊ ʊ ʊ

Terence Higgins had been born in Wales in 1945, and recognised as a gay man he would never fit in. Making his way to London in the early 1960's, Higgins initially worked as a reporter for Hansard in the Houses of Parliament, whilst DJing at night. Throughout the 1970's he travelled to Amsterdam and New York, returning to London in 1980 suffering from a series of unidentifiable ailments. Finding employment behind the bar at gay club Heaven, Higgins collapsed at work during summer 1982 and died on Sunday 4th July of parasitic pneumonia.

Doctors at St Thomas' Hospital in London recognised some parallels with the spate of recent deaths in the United States and were able to confirm Higgins as the first British death from GRID.

Later in the year his partner Rupert Whitaker set up the Terence Higgins Trust, along with friends Martyn Butler and Tony Calvert, with the aim *"to be sure that nobody died alone and unaware of what was happening"*. Over the proceeding decades the trust changed to campaign and provide services relating to HIV and sexual health. In 1982 the Trust, like everyone else, was struggling with the deficiency of information concerning the disease. At one point it was suggested that it could be circumvented by not having sex with Americans, and their own leaflet recommended gay men *"have as much sex as you want, but with fewer people and with HEALTHY PEOPLE"*.

ʊ ʊ ʊ

During a glorious disco phase of her career Donna Summer had been the singer on one of the most influential tracks of the last decade, the Giorgio Moroder written and produced *I Feel Love*. Summer had ended up working with the producer after her touring production of anti-establishment musical *Hair* washed up in Germany and she married Helmuth Sommer, from whom she took her stage name.

In 1982 Summer had come to the end of a working relationship with Moroder, and her last album *The Wanderer* had performed poorly in the charts. A new album was

recorded, but head of her record company David Geffen was unimpressed, and the recordings were shelved. Instead, Summer was paired with Quincy Jones, whose success with Michael Jackson's *Off the Wall* album was the deciding factor. Summer was in awe of Jones, claiming *"He's a creative genius. He forced everything that's on the album to be where it is… in its proper place."* The singer did not want to be boxed in as a disco queen, stating *"I don't have a style, I am an instrument"*, and to help play this instrument the best songwriters and musicians were brought in, as Jones polished the tracks to perfection. Rod Temperton of British act Heatwave and Jones co-wrote the opening single, *Love is in Control (Finger on the Trigger)*, a perfect piece of disco pop, with clean drums, electronic funky bass, and vocoder vocals, and the freshness helped Summer achieve her first top twenty British hit single for over three years.

Elsewhere on the album Bruce Springsteen contributed a track which was originally meant to be a duet[436], whilst *Mystery of Love* was about a *"more universal love* [than my previous material] *…more about brotherly love, non-condemning, just accepting. Accepting a person in their own time and space, with their faults, and loving them for the sake of love"*.

Lush Life, an old standard closed the album, a choice which Summer did not seem happy about, later revealing *"Quincy made me do it. It was so hard to sing this song, it almost never repeats itself. There were times I wanted to give up"*, and whilst looking back was also keen to represent the modern world. *"Livin' in America"* was where Summer *"wanted to do something that was very patriotic, in the sense of revealing what this nation stands for, not allowing people to forget we are one nation under God. Having the strength as a nation to follow a dream as a unified people."*

The undoubted highlight of the album was a version of the Jon and Vangelis song *State of Independence*, which featured an all-star chorus of Michael Jackson, Kenny Loggins[437], Stevie Wonder, Dionne Warwick, Brenda Russell[438], Michael McDonald, James Ingram, and Christopher Cross[439]. With an elastic mini-moog bass line and a lolling reggae rhythm, *State of Independence* was the ultimate song of love, of hope, of optimism, of surrender to potential. Half-way through Summer's vocals became less rhythmic, smoother, and more transcendent in their tone, as she claimed *"Yes, I do know how I survive, Yes, I do know why I'm alive: To love and be with you"*.

---

[436] Springsteen originally wrote *Cover Me* for Donna Summer but was persuaded by his management to keep it for himself. Instead, he offered *Protection*, and helped with the recording of it, adding a guitar solo and backing vocals.

[437] In 1982 Loggins also fell in love with and married his *"colon therapist"*.

[438] Brenda Russell took her surname from a bloke from my hometown of Falkirk. Brian Russell moved to America and the two were married. By 1982 they had split, but she kept the name professionally.

[439] The father of singer songwriter Christopher Cross was the personal physician to President Dwight Eisenhower's grandchildren.

With chanted African influenced backing vocals, for Summer the song was "*a ploy, do we have the right to live, do we have a right to life? A very spiritual and beautiful song*". When released as a single, the track sat at the top of the Dutch charts for eight weeks, and if there had been any justice in the world would have done the same elsewhere, but instead peaked at number fourteen in Britain

Quincy Jones later claimed Michael Jackson stole liberally from this song for *Billie Jean*, which the two were recording at the same time, and many of the songwriters on Summer's self-titled album also penned songs for Michael Jackson, such as John Bettis[440], Rod Temperton, and Steve Lukather, and with Jones producing this was very much a dry run for *Thriller*. Certainly, Summer did not feel in control of the recording, later stating "*Sometimes, I feel it's a Quincy Jones album that I sang on*".

ʊ ʊ ʊ

Following their unsuccessful meeting with the Vatican three days previously, the Bank of Italy had no choice but to start dismantling Banco Ambrosiano. On Monday 5th July they ordered the bank to cut all financial help for their various affiliates in Luxembourg, Nassau, and South America. Within a couple of weeks, the satellite banking institutions started to default on payments and declare themselves bankrupt, as a wave of arrests swept across the globe.

As a rescue package was put in place by a consortium of Italian Banks, international financial institutions were assured their debts from the central Banco Ambrosiano (now to be called Nuovo Banco Ambrosiano) would be guaranteed, however any money transferred through, lent to, or invested in the overseas subsidiaries would be lost, a total of $1,287 million. At a heated meeting in London on the 29th July, International banks informed the Bank of Italy such a decision would have ramifications for Italy's financial reputation. Caretaker manager Giovanni Arduino, taking advantage of a phrase from the recent Falklands Conflict, suggested the banks create a *task force* to deal with the situation.

ʊ ʊ ʊ

With host nation Spain already eliminated from the FIFA World Cup, they only had pride to play for in their final game against England on Monday 5th July. The English, on the other hand, needed victory by two clear goals to reach the semi-finals and had been dwindling in ability throughout the tournament. Manager Ron Greenwood's predilection for attacking football had lost out to assistant coach Don Howe who believed that you only had to stop the opposition scoring by defending. With twenty-six minutes left, England's top players Kevin Keegan and Trevor Brooking finally made their debut at the finals, however it was to prove too little too late. The game was England's poorest performance of the tournament and ended in a 0-0 draw in front of a hostile home crowd who chanted "*Malvinas! Malvinas!*" throughout. As the team left the stadium the Spanish fans surrounded their bus shouting abuse about the Falkland Islands and throwing missiles. The team were ordered by the police to lie down on the floor and made an escape without any injury. England had played five games and not been

---

[440] Bettis once played banjo in a trio with Richard and Karen Carpenter, covering old-time songs at Disneyland.

defeated, but still managed to be eliminated, as Greenwood stepped down from the role of manager to be replaced two days later by Bobby Robson.

On the same day Italy met Brazil in a winner-takes-all match. With Brazil being the kings of attack, and Italy being the kings of defence, this was expected to be an exasperating one-way match. The Italian manager was immovable in his decision to place faith in shunned striker Rossi, even preventing communication between his squad and the press, and at last it paid off as he bagged the opening goal with his head after only twelve minutes. The lead was to only last seven minutes, when Socrates equalised, however Rossi had rediscovered his taste for scoring, and like a slumbering giant awoken scored his second goal after twenty-five minutes.

Brazil came out in the second half all guns blazing and were compensated with a second equaliser through a twenty-yard shot by Falcao, which would have been enough to take them through on goal difference. Rossi, however, was now on fire and completed his hat-trick with fifteen minutes to go. It was then backs-against-the-wall for Italy, and they were abetted by a miraculous save by veteran goalkeeper Dino Zoff[441] in the final minute. One minute later the Italians were in the semi-finals, and the much-maligned Rossi was once again a national hero, in a match that many believe was one of the best *ever* in world cup history.

℧ ℧ ℧

The Damned had been one of the original British trio of punk bands, along with The Sex Pistols and The Clash, but where The Sex Pistols disintegrated in early 1978, and The Clash developed their sound and stance to make a successful career, The Damned took a path somewhere in-between: on the verge of falling apart whilst somehow managing to release a stream of singles and albums, none of which provided a noticeable enough breakthrough.

Formed in 1976 by David Lett, Chris Miller, Ray Burns, and Brian Robertson, The

Damned took on the punk names of Dave Vanian ("*as in Transyl*", vocals), Rat Scabies (drums), Captain Sensible (bass), and Brian James (guitar). Signing a deal with Stiff Records mere months after forming allowed them to release what is generally considered to be the first British punk record in October, single *New Rose*, over a month before The Sex Pistols grabbed the attention with *Anarchy in the UK*. This achievement meant the Damned suffered at the hands of resentful competitors, being treated as pariahs, never one of the *in-crowd* despite their incredibly strong connections with all the original players on the scene, having previously played in acts with Mick Jones, Sid Vicious, Tony James, and Chrissie Hynde.

The first British punk album, *Damned Damned Damned*, followed in February 1977, and the band spent the rest of the year touring the United Kingdom with T-Rex and the United States. Stiff Records were keen to cash in on what they saw as the limited life of punk and released a second substandard album before the end of the year, after the band split. Various solo projects and new bands came to nothing, and by the start of 1979 The Damned had reformed, this time with Sensible on guitar instead of James, and a sequence of revolving bass players. Two acclaimed but unsuccessful albums followed, the second of which featured production by a young Hans Zimmer, along with

---

[441] When fourteen-year-old Zoff was rejected by Inter Milan and Juventus due to a lack of height, he spent five years following his grandmother's advice of eating eight eggs a day until he was tall enough.

a string of minor hit singles, but by 1982 they found themselves struggling, crushed by a public and press that saw them as nothing more than punk has-beens, as well as their own apparent inability to get organized and formulate a plan. And then there was the question of what to do about Captain Sensible's new-found success with *Happy Talk*, which acted both as a distraction from the band and as much needed attention. Back in the spring Scabies' father, John Miller, had arranged a new deal with Bronze Records. New songs were recorded in tandem with Sensible's solo album, the first of which, *Lovely Money*, was released as a single in July, and loitered just outside the top forty. Channeling Sensible's love of psychedelia, the single lacked the puissance of previous releases, sounding like the type of thing Julian Cope would make a solo career out of, whilst the extended version featured a enthused monologue by Viv Stanshall of The Dog Doo Dah Band.

ʊ ʊ ʊ

The semi-final matches in the FIFA World Cup took place on Thursday 8th July, as Poland were defeated by a revitalised Italy in Barcelona, with Rossi further adding to his rehabilitation by scoring both goals in a 2-0 victory.
All the drama, however, took place in Seville as West Germany and France simultaneously hit their peaks in the tournament. The ninety minutes of the game showed two skilful teams who could only manage one goal a side, sending the match into extra-time. The first high drama took place towards the end of regular time when German keeper Harald Schumacher launched himself with both feet flying fast and high off the ground against French player Patrick Battiston. The Frenchman was knocked unconscious for a couple of minutes, had a broken jawbone, and lost a couple of teeth. As the ball rolled out of play, Dutch referee Charles Corver saw nothing wrong with the challenge and awarded a goal kick. Battiston was stretchered off with facial damage and a broken vertebra in one of the worst fouls ever committed at this level of football. Within ten minutes of extra time France had scored twice, and it looked as if the Germans were going home. Coach Derwall made a couple of desperate substitutions, including bringing on a half-fit Karl-Heinz Rummenigge, and it paid off as he scored four minutes later. The French suddenly looked jittery, and a few minutes into the second half of extra-time Fisher scored an equaliser with a spectacular overhead kick. When the final whistle blew, the World Cup was facing its first ever penalty shoot-out. It was a cruel way for anyone to leave the competition, and it was left to West Germany's Horst Hrubesch to win the match with the final kick.

ʊ ʊ ʊ

Marc Almond flew into his spiritual home of New York to celebrate his twenty fifth birthday on Friday 9th July. A party was thrown for him at the Tavern on the Green in Central Park, where the effects of his birthday present started to kick in: a gift box of every imaginable kind of drug. The prawns in his starter salad began hopping around the plate, and then pleaded with him not to be eaten. As the party moved to The Roxy nightclub, Almond was presented with a cake featuring a naked man in bondage, before spending the night in the toilets, hunkering down between the cistern and the side of the cubicle, vomiting and crying, missing a performance by the young singer and dancer who had been booked to entertain him and was starting to appear under the name of Madonna[442].

---

[442] On the way out, Almond was introduced to Seymour Stein, who in turn introduced him to Madonna. The future superstar hung out with Almond a couple of times over the next few days, and then was put up in his bedsit flat in London when she first came to Britain to promote her single, *Holiday*.

A couple of days later Almond returned to London on Concorde, high on opium and with his pockets stuffed full of the remainder of his birthday drugs. At Heathrow Airport he breezed through customs, before being called back by one of the Customs Officers. The game was surely up as he imagined the headlines in the newspapers, and how short a time he would last in prison. As Almond arrived at the desk, the officer simply asked, *"Can I have your autograph, please?"*

At the time Almond was living at the Columbia Hotel on London's Bayswater Road, amongst every possible British pop star conceivable, where the Soft Cell after-hours parties became legendary. Almond was the heart of these, always high, and realised how out of control he was when Julian Cope had to talk him down one night. When you need to be talked down by Julian Cope, you knew you had gone too far.

It was from these parties that one of the most enduring Almond rumours came about, one that people preferred to believe through a mixture of homophobia and ghoulish voyeurism. The story went that Almond was admitted to hospital after a party, and upon having his stomach pumped it was discovered that the contents were a pint of semen, half a pint of semen, or seven different types of semen, depending on which version you heard. Of course, the story was unqualified drivel, and is a recurring myth that appears once every few years with a new name attached to it. Rod Stewart, Elton John, and David Bowie were the favourite victims in the 1970's, and in more recent years Britney Spears and Alanis Morrissette have been connected to the legend.

℧ ℧ ℧

Bass player Tina Weymouth was now appearing noticeably pregnant when Talking Heads continued their world tour with some dates in Europe. As they prepared to go onstage on Friday 9th July at the Montreux Jazz Festival, a knock at the door revealed David Bowie wearing blue jeans and a green anorak.

"May I come in?" he asked.

Talking Heads were huge fans and were delighted to welcome the living legend into their midst. After saying hello to everyone in the room, he turned his attention to the backstage buffet.

"Are you going to be eating those nuts?" he asked.

"Help yourself" replied drummer Chris Frantz.

Bowie started to pile the nuts into one of the pockets of his anorak, before turning his gaze to the other end of the table.

"How about those cheeses? Are you going to be eating those nice cheeses?" he asked whilst simultaneously stuffing them into his other pocket, before exiting with *"Well, have a good show."*

℧ ℧ ℧

Having been released on bail the previous day, Michael Fagan found himself once again wandering the streets of London in the early morning of Friday 9th July, and at the walls of Buckingham Palace decided once again to enter the grounds. As the sun rose, Fagan scaled the fourteen-foot-high wall, deftly avoiding the barbed wire and metal spikes, before entering the main building via a drainpipe just after 7.00 a.m. The alarm sensor was triggered within the security room, however the police on duty assumed it was faulty and switched it off.

Fifteen minutes later, a disheveled and shoeless Fagan entered the Queen's bedroom. Pulling the curtains back whilst holding shards of glass from an ashtray broken in an adjoining room, the started monarch exclaimed *"What are you doing here?"* Wearing an ankle length Liberty-print nightdress and barefooted, the Queen departed the room to summon security, whilst Fagan sat down on her bed.

The Page of the Backstairs, Paul Whybrew[443] was first to arrive, exclaiming "*Cor, fuckin' hell mate, you look like you need a drink*", before pouring him a glass of Famous Grouse Whiskey from the Queen's private collection. When the Palace security finally arrived, Fagan was led away and handed to police custody.

Unable to work out what to charge Fagan with (it was a civil rather than a criminal offence), he was committed for psychiatric evaluation, before being released in early 1983.

Within hours of the incident the investigation into security breaches began. The following day Home Secretary William Whitelaw declared in a closed meeting that he would have to resign but wanted to know what his colleagues thought first. Future Secretary of State for Ireland Paddy Mayhew and future Prime Minister John Major led the charge with "*No, no, no, Home Secretary, you musn't*", to which Whitelaw ended his masterful manipulation with "*I will accept the views of my colleagues*".

ʊ ʊ ʊ

As one of the most successful acts of the previous decade, Fleetwood Mac had made a soap opera of their lives, with numerous trysts, relationships, and tensions. Singer Stevie Nicks had been through long term relationships with singer and guitarist Lindsey Buckingham and then drummer Mick Fleetwood, before dating both Don Henley and Joe Walsh from The Eagles, and had just ended an affair with producer Jimmy Iovine. Meanwhile, keyboard player Christine McVie had previously been married to bass player John McVie and had just broken off a three-year engagement with Beach Boy Dennis Wilson.

It was with all this baggage that Fleetwood Mac reconvened after solo ventures at La Château, Herouville, France at the end of 1981 to record a new album *Mirage*, and the recently splintered relationships featured in songs such as *Straight Back* and *Only Over You*. Opening single *Hold Me* had been written by Christine McVie, and featured a disastrous video shot in the Mojave Desert by Steve Barron. The producer of the video, Simon Fields, later described the tension on the shoot, saying "*Four of [the band] couldn't be together in the same room for very long. Christine McVie was ten hours in the make-up trailer, but which point it was getting dark. John McVie was very drunk and tried to punch me. Stevie Nicks didn't want to walk on the sand with her platforms. Christine was fed up with all of them. Mick [Fleetwood] thought she was being a bitch, he wouldn't talk to her*". Despite the drama, the single went top five in America, whilst not bothering the top seventy-five in the Britain.

The intra-band tensions continued into the video shoot for the next single, *Gypsy*, this time written and sung by Nicks. Director Russell Mulcahy, when trying to pair band members up for scenes, was constantly being pulled to one side and told "*No, no, those two were fucking and then they split up and now he's sleeping with her. I got very confused, who was sleeping with whom*". Nicks interrupted her drug rehabilitation for the shoot, claiming "*If you watch the video you'll see I wasn't happy*", before going on to add "*We would probably have gone on to make many more great videos… had we not been so into drugs*". This second single released in September once again went top five in the United States, but only scraped in at number forty-six in Britain.

The album, which was a return to the *classic* Fleetwood Mac sound of *Rumours* after Buckingham's sonic dalliances with new wave on *Tusk,* took the band to the top of the

---

[443] Known as *Tall Paul* as opposed to *Small Paul* Burrell.

American charts, and reached number five in Britain, but with relationships at breaking point, the band only managed an eighteen-date tour of the United States, culminating in a well-paid performance at the US Festival on Labor Day weekend.

ʊ ʊ ʊ

After filming *The Hunger*, the last thing David Bowie wanted to do was make another film. In fact, having run out of nuts and cheese, he quite fancied a holiday, so when the opportunity came to make *Merry Christmas, Mr Lawrence* in New Zealand and the Cook Islands, Bowie decided to combine work and a break over the summer of 1982. The film was based on the Laurens van der Post novel about his experience during the Second World War in a Japanese prisoner of war camp, *The Seed and the Sower*, and was directed by Nagisa Oshima. Initially Robert Redford had been approached for the role of Jack Celliers, however upon the failure to secure him Bowie was approached, having been spotted in the Broadway version of *The Elephant Man*. For the role Bowie dyed his hair blonder than it currently was, and rather unconvincingly played a seventeen-year-old Celliers in some flashback scenes. The understandable lack of any female roles in the movie worried producer Paul Mayersberg who was scared that *"people would think it was a gay film"*, but Oshima told him to stop being so ridiculous. During the seven-week shoot Bowie immersed himself in old R&B records from the 1950's and 1960's, as the idea for his next album began to take shape. He had become extremely interested in making one final push for global pop mega-stardom, and approached Chic guitarist, songwriter, and producer Nile Rodgers to join him.

Their first meeting took place that summer in New York's Carlyle Hotel, where Rodgers had gone with Billy Idol to party, both high on their drug of choice. As Bowie entered the room Idol exclaimed *"Fucking hell, it's David Fucking Boooowie!"* and then immediately vomited on the floor. Rodgers played it cooler, approaching Bowie to talk, only to be surprised at his knowledge of R&B, and then shocked when he was asked to produce the next album, having not enjoyed a hit for a couple of years. The two agreed to meet up later in the year at Bowie's home in Switzerland.

11ᵗʰ – 17ᵗʰ July 1982

#1 single: Irene Cara: Fame

#1 album: ABC: The Lexicon of Love

Despite what the United States of America try to claim, the FIFA World Cup final is without a doubt the greatest single sporting occasion on earth, coming every four years and habitually including the pre-eminent player on the planet[444]. The tournament reached its culmination on Sunday 11ᵗʰ July at the Bernabeu Stadium in Madrid, as 90,000 people watched Italy take on West Germany. The Italians had been building from a sluggish start towards this match, whereas West Germany had been steady throughout and could not be written off. The match would be volatile Mediterranean passion against adroit Northern European coolness.

---

[444] The British television companies did not fare well with their theme tunes. The BBC chose a tuneless composition by Andrew Lloyd Webber, whilst ITV asked Jeff Wayne to write another forgettable piece called *Matador*.

In the end the Italian hunger won through as their famously impregnable defence played one of the best games of their careers, and for once the forward line was aggressive. On the other hand, West Germany were in disarray, with dressing room quarrels between the players which bled onto the park in the form of a team that was obviously not communicating.

Italy squandered a penalty after twenty-four minutes, with Cabrini firing wide of the goal, and the teams went in at half time tied at 0-0. It was only a matter of time, such was the supremacy of the Italians, and in the second half the scoring was opened by Paolo Rossi, who in the final three games went from resented villain to national hero with a total of six goals. This was added to by Tardelli and Altobelli, before the Germans scored a consolation goal through Breitner and the final whistle was blown. The better team had won by a country mile, in a score that at 3-1 flattered the Germans. Italy had always been favoured in competitions, and would continue to be so in the future, however this was the first time they had won the World Cup for forty-four years.

West German's whole performance at the World Cup was shrouded in controversy, from their shock opening defeat, through the disgrace of their pointless game against Austria, to the violence of the semi-final against France. For many, there was a sense of *schadenfreude* about their resounding defeat in the final, where unpredictable flair won over tedious efficiency.

On the other hand, Italy's twelve goals over seven matches was a new low for the average scored per game by a winning team. Despite this, Paolo Rossi won the Golden Boot as top goal-scorer, finding the net when it mattered with six goals in the last three games, and at forty goalkeeper Dino Zoff became the oldest player to lift the trophy.

This was also the first blatantly commercial World Cup finals, with sponsors everywhere, and the cost of flying in FIFA officials exceeding the cost of flying in the players. Stadiums were filled with corporate free-passes and would often be half-empty for the second half as complimentary food and drink was available for the sponsors in the lounges.

The day after the final, the world started preparing for Mexico in four years.

ʊ ʊ ʊ

In Lebanon, the ceasefire had failed to hold as Israeli and Christian Phalangist forces continued their missile strikes, raining phosphorus bombs down on the population of Beirut, so those not killed by the explosion were subsequently covered in a fine white powder which seared their hair and skin. One doctor in a bombed-out hospital informed journalist Robert Fisk of a pair of twins who had already died, "*I had to take the babies and put them in buckets of water to put out the flames. When I took them out half an hour later, they were still burning. Even in the mortuary, they smoldered for hours*". When the corpses were removed from the mortuary for burial the following day, they burst into flames again. The Israelis and Phalangist forces had bought the weapons from Britain, the United States, and Germany.

With indiscriminate bombing the civilians not only had to suffer burns on the outside of their bodies, but as they breathed in the white phosphorus dust they burned from the inside as well. An Israeli pilot later summed up the approach of Prime Minster Begin as "*If Hitler was in a house and there were innocent people in that house, he would bomb it.*"

ʊ ʊ ʊ

After such a massive hit with *Ain't No Pleasing You*, Chas & Dave could probably expect to have a successful follow-up single, however *Margate* only reached number forty-six. The duo had a long-standing relationship with Courage Best Bitter, a popular alcoholic drink in the south of England, and the Brewery had picked up on Chas & Dave

songs and used them successfully for adverts, including *Gertcha*, *The Sideboard Song*, and *Rabbit*. The relationship would see the duo knocking out a thirty-second version of their song, sometimes with slightly adapted words, a move which was mutually beneficial with the subsequent single helped up the chart from extra exposure to the public. *Margate* featured in the latest of these, for once having been written specifically for the advert then extended to create a full-length song. Despite the low chart position, the duo's take of a day trip to the English seaside town continued to be a popular live song and found an extended life in adverts into the next millennium.

Chas & Dave reached their commercial peak in 1982, and despite a few more minor hits, continued to tour into the next century. They were re-discovered in the 2000's by a new generation, most notably by The Libertines, and enjoyed a late career revival until Hodge died in 2018.

ʊ ʊ ʊ

Fourteen years previously, British civil servant Geoffrey Prime had been on a train travelling to his job as a translator and radio operator at RAF Gatow in West Berlin, when he tossed a message from the window at a Soviet sentry guard, offering his services as a spy. After establishing contact, Prime was swayed by the Russians to apply for a job at GCHQ in London, and over the next decade, by a series of dead letter drops in the home counties identified by secret chalk marks and discarded Coca Cola cans, passed vital information and files to the Soviet Union. In 1973 his wife discovered a substantial amount of money hidden at their home, and Prime confessed his involvement with the Russians. She shared this information with a friend, however when the women were interviewed by the British as part of regular security clearances, they chose not to disclose this.

Despite resigning from GCHQ in 1976, Prime continued to pass material to the Soviet Union, supposedly for ideological reasons, but also for a decent quantity of cash.

But Prime had another secret as well: a predatory predilection for small girls.

On Tuesday 13th July Prime attacked a young girl at her home but was frightened off by her screams and fled in his car. A nearby farmworker provided a description of Prime's distinctive car and the police paid him a visit the following day, leaving without making an arrest despite noticing his similarity to the photofit image provided. That night, Prime admitted several previous sexual crimes to his second wife, as well as his espionage for the Soviets, before visiting the police station and turning himself in.

A subsequent police search of the house turned up 2,287 index cards with details of underage girls and their parents' routines. They also found espionage equipment, which led to Prime's wife admitting to his confession.

On Thursday 15th July Prime was remanded in custody, before being found guilty during a secret court session in November of espionage and sex offences against children, and sentenced to thirty-eight years in prison, of which he served half.

ʊ ʊ ʊ

There is a myth that Martin Rushent recorded *Dare* with the Human League, realised that he had made the perfect pop album, and gave up on the basis that he would never be involved in anything as accomplished again. It is a good myth, but one that is simply not true: Rushent continued to work with artists such as Altered images, XTC, The Go-Go's, and The Associates up until 1984, after which he sold his equipment and dedicated himself to raising his children. In February he had picked up a Brit Award for his production work on *Dare*, and although the album had already been released, he did not consider his work on the tracks complete.

Rushent was a great judge of what would sell in the pop charts, having a couple of years previously attempted to set up his own label Genetic, backed financially by WEA. He had agreements to sign Spandau Ballet, Ultravox, Visage, and Joy Division, however the A&R department at WEA did not see potential in the acts.

When he first started working with the Human League, Rushent had constructed an extended remix of *Sound of The Crowd* for two reasons: firstly, to meet the record company demand for a B-side, and secondly, so he could further investigate how this new technology worked, and where the limits were. From there, Rushent began putting together longer version of all their tracks, at first with the help of the band, and then as demands upon their time grew, on his own. These new versions were compiled and released as an album in July 1982 against the advice of the record company, under the name of The League Unlimited Orchestra[445].

With the band out touring the world, Rushent had been left to finish the album, and the results went under the name *Love & Dancing*. This was an album so far ahead of the curve that it took years for everyone else to catch up with the technical innovations. *Love and Dancing* established the art of remixing extended versions of songs in the studio. At the time, caught up in the backlash of musical snootiness regarding synthesisers on one side, and the idea that the Human League had sold out by *going pop* on the other, many missed the ground-breaking nature of the album, but by the end of the decade most records were made this way, recorded and then remixed, contorted out of their initial shape by a producer.

Remixing was hardly a new phenomenon, having been practised since the invention of magnetic tape as a recording material in the 1940's. *Avant garde* artists had been manipulating sounds and cutting them up on tape for a couple of decades before Martin Rushent, however it was the Jamaican producers in the early 1970's such as King Tubby and Lee "Scratch" Perry who first began taking an existing piece of music, manipulating and extending it into something that would occasionally be recognisable from the original. Throughout the 1970's, with the rise of the disco scene, the need for longer versions of a song grew, and this was first met by the DJ mixing two separate discs together live at the decks. Realising the need for longer pre-mixed tracks, producers led by Tom Moulton[446], started to put together twelve-inch versions of disco tracks, often with a breakdown of the individual instruments included. These DJ versions were then highly instrumental in the rise of hip hop, providing beats early rappers could improvise over. What Martin Rushent added was the remix at source, purely for the band's own interests, using the original instrumentation instead of after the fact. The fact that his extended mixes sounded fantastic at modern nightclubs such as Danceteria helped.

Love and Dancing consisted of eight tracks, seven from *Dare* and one B-side (*Hard Times*), which often broke the songs down to instrumental versions, bringing out aspects of familiar music you had not noticed previously. These were not simply extended varieties of the songs, and in fact some of the remixes were shorter than the

---

[445] The name was a reference to Barry White's Love Unlimited Orchestra.

[446] Moulton was a New York DJ and mixer who was the first to put together a continuous-mix album side, when he worked on Gloria Gaynor's *Never Can Say Goodbye*.

originals but were experimental pieces of music, cooler cousins to their hit versions. Paramount to the remixes was the beat, the one thing which never wavered, electronically marching through the whole album. The whole thing is only thirty-five minutes long but included 2600 edits, all done by hand with a ruler and a tape splicer. The programming of the songs had also taken a substantial amount of time, with most instruments sounding weak until Rushent applied his engineering and mixing skills to them. The complex brass riffs on *Hard Times*, for example, took two days to programme, and three days to record, however the effort was worth it. Rushent would claim "*It sounds fantastic, even to this day. Today, it's a piece of piss. Any twat could do it because of the power of the computers*".

The tracks were rhythmically tight, but still sounded like a human was playing, designed for the dancefloor where Rushent claimed the sound was "*Right up people's backsides*". Bringing all the instruments together was a tough job. The synthesizers and Linn drum machine gave out silent time codes, but there was no way to link them up until Rushent persuaded his technicians to invent a box which would tie them together. Rushent would later claim "*Making 'Love and Dancing' was the most creative experience* [I] *ever had in* [my] *life*", and it was an experience he found difficult to top. "*It's like why astronauts go a bit loopy after they've got back from the moon*" he later explained, "*You've walked on the fucking moon. What are you gonna do now?*"

The Human League were still one of the hottest acts around, and even without their name explicitly on the record, it still reached number three and hung around the album charts for a year, and yet despite this it has become somewhat a forgotten album. Despite being aimed at the club market, the album did not fare well with black audiences, mainly due to the remaining vocals being too *white*, too *pop*.

Being too white or too pop did not hold the band back from success in the United States, however, as *Don't You Want Me* started to rise up the Billboard Top 100, finally settling at the top during the summer of 1982, and dragging the album[447] into the top three as well. Helped by heavy rotation of the video on the newly airing MTV, the Human League suddenly found themselves a world-wide phenomenon, and opened the door for many other acts to step through, leading to a second British Invasion of America.

ʊ ʊ ʊ

The high level of brutal violence in Northern Ireland would occasionally provide the means for genuine psychopathic serial killers to go about their vicious business in full view. One such person was thirty-year-old Lenny Murphy who was released from prison on the evening of Friday 16th July.

Murphy had been raised in Loyalist Belfast and despite being a Protestant, possessed a surname which suggested he may be Catholic, a factor which led to him over-compensating by joining the Ulster Volunteer Force at the age of sixteen. By the age of twenty Murphy had tortured and killed at least four Catholics, however it was only with the murder of Protestant William Pavis that charges were brought in 1973. Before the case came to trial, his accomplice Mervyn Connor was forced to write a confessional note, then committed suicide by swallowing cyanide.

Unhappy with a lack of action by the UVF, Murphy formed his own loyalist gang of around twenty men in 1975, who became known as the *Shankill Butchers* after the area in Belfast from which they operated. Over the next few months, the gang would patrol the streets at night, abducting people in Catholic areas, torturing and mutilating them before finally killing the victim by hacking at their throat with a butcher's knife, sometimes so deeply that they almost severed the spine. The bodies would then be

---

[447] With an exclamation mark added to the title by label A&M.

dumped on waste ground or in the back alleys of the city. In the next five months the gang killed at least eleven innocent people, with Murphy personally responsible for most of the violence.

In March 1976, following the shooting of a young Catholic girl, Murphy was arrested and charged with attempted murder, which he plea-bargained down to the lesser charge of a firearms offence, and was sentenced to twelve years in prison. With the police knowing he was responsible for the Shankill murders Murphy ordered the gang to keep killing whilst he was in prison to divert suspicion. Over the next year eight more people were murdered, until a botched attempt led to the arrest and imprisonment of many of the gang members, to serve a total of forty-two life sentences. Meanwhile, Detective Chief Inspector Jimmy Nisbitt *"knew this psycho was going back on the streets, and there was practically nothing we could do about it"*.

Upon release from the Maze Prison Murphy returned to his old stomping ground and began heavily drinking and holding court in the Rumford Street Loyalist Club. One of the other drinkers in the club, thirty-three-year-old Norman Maxwell who spent his life in Salvation Army hostels and had learning difficulties, apparently failed to show Murphy enough respect, and was taken out the back and severely beaten. He was then laid on the ground and a car driven over him several times before his dead body was dumped in an alley way a mile away.

Murphy was back, still with the taste for violent death, and having no contact with his wife and daughter was looking to get a new gang together.

18th – 24th July 1982

#1 single: Irene Cara: Fame

#1 album: ABC: The Lexicon of Love

Culture Club may not have broken through as had been expected, however that did not stop record companies looking for other creative acts from the same scene. One of these was Haysi Fantayzee, formed by Cambridge graduate Paul Caplan[448] when he teamed up with Wigan born model and photographer Kate Garner[449]. In 1982 both were twenty-seven-years-old, perhaps too old to be considered *young things*, and this was instrumental in Caplan choosing to stay in the background. Instead, from a fluctuating line-up of twelve people, they whittled the act down to a three piece, recruiting Jeremy Healy[450].

Healy was from Kidbrooke in London, and attended St Joseph's Academy in Blackheath, where the teachers had named him *Satan's Imp*. He took advantage of his physical similarity to the fourteen-year-old drummer of early punk band Eater, using the *"fame"* to gain access to punk gigs when he was fifteen himself. As part of the Blitz crowd, Healy developed his own look based upon a mixture of Huckleberry Finn and the Artful Dodger, or what friend Boy George described as *"Dickensian Rasta, with the emphasis on 'dick'"*.

---

[448] Caplin studied algebraic topography.

[449] Garner had previously been chased through the streets by Malcolm McLaren who wanted her to be the singer in Bow Wow Wow.

[450] Garner and Healy met when she was photographing Stephen Jones hats for the *Sunday Times*. *"He was masquerading as a hairdresser"* she reminisced, *"but he didn't even know how to put a clip into the model's hair."*

With Caplan the musician and main songwriter, EMI paid for demo recordings, which the band insisted must include a video, and led to a deal with Regard Records. Their first single *John Wayne Is Big Leggy* was released in July and took a couple of weeks to scrape into the top forty before rising to a peak of number eleven in late summer.

From an opening nonsense nursery rhyme couplet of "*Shotgun gimme' gimme' lowdown funboy, okay? Yeah, showdown*", the track thundered along at a gallop, a hybrid of country and new wave. The lyrics were caustic in their perforation of the American macho myth and white male phallic oppression of women and minorities. Having read *Bury my Heart at Wounded Knee*, Dee Brown's brilliant and influential history and take-down of white dominance of native Americans, Healy chose the most discernible representation of white America, actor John Wayne[451], as his target. "*It was an allegory for the treatment which the white settlers used on the Native American Indians.*" Healy would claim, "*I wrote like John Wayne having anal sex with a squaw*", a result of the cowboy actor's guns getting in the way of the act, and his refusal to remove them, therefore rendering him impotent without his weaponry.

Whilst the title was explained at the time as being a corruption of *John Wayne is Bow Legged* after the amount of time the actor spent on a horse in his career, the meaning of the phrase *Big Leggy* is a reference to having a large penis, the ultimate illusionary sign of masculinity.

John Wayne is Big Leggy divided the public, with most believing it to be unsufferable, and me proclaiming it a perfect pop song, full of hooks and memorable lines with not a second wasted. There was also the sound of tongues firmly in cheeks, as Caplan explained at the time: "*The last thing we want is people taking us seriously*". According to Garner, the success of the single "*was difficult to cope with because the musical foundation of our house was actually quite shaky.*"

As former friend Boy George watched the single climb up the charts "*It became the soundtrack to my despair, niggling at my psyche. I knew it was a good record too. Clever, original, and very annoying. I couldn't believe they had a video and we didn't*".

ʊ ʊ ʊ

The Stranglers were reaching the end of their recording contract with Liberty Records, owned by EMI, and were keen to move to pastures new. Identifying a get-out clause in their contract caused the label to threaten legal action, and a compromise was reached whereby the band would deliver a final song for a Greatest Hits compilation.

As is often the way when acts release a *Best Of*, a middling new track or two is included to pull in the fans who already own all the singles. What was unusual about *The Collection 1977 – 1982* compared to other acts was that the new track was exceptionally decent.

Strange Little Girl had been recorded by the band as a departing *fuck you* to the label, having initially been written in 1974 and submitted to EMI as a demo before the band were signed. EMI had originally rejected them because of the song, seeing no

---

[451] Wayne may have been a card-carrying Republican, however as an emblem of racist white supremacy he falls somewhat short, having married three women of Hispanic and Spanish American origin.

marketable value in it, so The Stranglers attitude was to force the label to accept it now. Recording with regular producer Steve Churchyard, the band sculpted the song into transcendent pop, with downbeat verses and a more upbeat chorus. The music had initially been written by early member Hans Warmling with lyrics by singer Hugh Cornwell, and the Swede was unexpectedly rewarded with a song-writing credit in a top ten single.

A sublime mid-paced melody set over an arpeggio keyboard, the song tracked the evolution of an innocent girl arriving in the city and comprehending that "*it didn't take long until she knew she'd had enough*". The role model

STRANGE LITTLE GIRL

for the girl was Cornwell's mid-1970's girlfriend, a woman from Guildford called Cathy. Though hardly *Paradise Lost*, the squandering of innocence was impeccably matched by the minor key verse and major key chorus.

The song climbed to number seven in the charts, becoming one of the bands biggest hits, and paved the way for the successful Greatest Hits compilation released in September 1982. As is the case with many bands who started having hits during the punk era, it was only once a collection of their singles was compiled that the wider public started to appreciate their body of work. Bands such as The Stranglers, Squeeze, and The Buzzcocks could at last be respected for their wonderful trail of pop nuggets.

Meanwhile, The Stranglers purchased themselves some acoustic guitars and went off in search of a new record deal.

ʊ ʊ ʊ

The medical perception of GRID being exclusively a gay disease was blown apart during the summer when an elderly man with haemophilia died from PCP, followed in the next fortnight by two more cases of haemophiliacs with the syndrome, none of whom had a history of homosexual activity. With the heterosexual population potentially being affected, the authorities began to take the condition more seriously, and the realisation that blood stock within the United States was probably contaminated.

The Centre for Disease Control in Atlanta, Georgia was keen to limit blood donations from gay men and drug users, groups where the disease was most prominent, however there was a public relations problem. The National Haemophilia Foundation was desperate for Factor VIII, the blood product which had been a lifesaver for haemophilia sufferers the world over, not to be associated with what was viewed as a homosexual disease and went to great lengths to deny the supply was infected. Meanwhile, gay leaders and community groups were outspoken in their demand that no guidelines regarding blood donations and sexual activities be introduced, stating that these would undermine the hard-won civil rights they had fought for over the past decade.

The decision was made to wait and see.

ʊ ʊ ʊ

When the Metropolitan Police announced on Monday 19th July that the Queen's bodyguard Michael Trestrail was resigning from the force due to "*personal reasons*", most assumed it was in relation to the security breach by Michael Fagan at Buckingham Palace earlier in the month. It came as something of a shock therefore when Home Secretary William Whitelaw made a short announcement in the House of Commons a couple of hours later stating the resignation was due to "*a homosexual relationship over a number of years with a male prostitute*".

The report into the affair criticized the police for having twice been informed of Trestrail's homosexuality and failing to act upon this. That these informers were acting upon nothing more than a "*gut feeling*" speaks volumes about the public view of homosexuality in 1982. The format of vetting members of the security services was questioned, with a conclusion that "*no vetting process can be proof against someone who is sufficiently determined and sufficiently skillful to keep his activities secret*". The question was asked if "*stable homosexual relationships*" were acceptable for a security job, and the answer was indecisive.

ʊ ʊ ʊ

At the end of his two-and-a-half-week Japanese tour, the newly married Ozzy and Sharon Osbourne arrived back in England on Monday 19th July. The couple moved to Ozzy's old house in Wimbledon, near to his ex-wife and children, and after a couple of days Sharon's father arrived on the scene and insisted on taking him to the pub for lunch. Once there, Don Arden started an assault on the character of Sharon, telling Ozzy all sorts of tales, some real and some made-up, to convince him his wife was a nutcase. He told Ozzy that he could arrange for the marriage to be annulled on the grounds of insanity. Ozzy returned home, drunk, and told his wife of the encounter. Sharon did not trust her father, but could not believe he would stoop this low, and immediately drove round to his house. Walking through the gates, she was attacked by the family Dobermanns, who pinned her to the ground and started to savage. After they were eventually called off, Sharon found herself bleeding from various places, including between the legs. At hospital it was discovered she had suffered a miscarriage during the attack, and in severe pain Sharon and Ozzy flew back to Los Angeles a couple of days later.

ʊ ʊ ʊ

Madonna Louise Ciccone had grown up in Detroit before moving to New York in 1978 with a dream of making it as a dancer. Instead, for the succeeding few years she found herself living in poverty, drifting from sofa to sofa, residing with friends and strangers, waitressing as well as modelling for life drawing and nude photographers just to earn enough money to eat. The one thing that she did have going for her was absolute ambition: Madonna could win anyone over in a one-to-one meeting with unalloyed zeal and persona. What she did not have was a strong singing voice, which made the resolution to commit herself to music somewhat unexpected. By 1982, having sang in a couple of bands, she had acquired a manager who attempted to market her as the new Pat Benatar. The rules were set down by the management early on, one of which was that if you slept with the singer, you would be out the band. Madonna used this to her advantage, seducing members when she wanted to get rid of them and replacing them with the people she desired, such as drummer and ex-lover Steve Bray. It was with Bray that she wrote and recorded four songs in July 1982, having split from her management, and began pursuing a dance-orientated direction. Madonna hawked this demo, especially a song called *Everybody*, around the New York nightclubs, flirting with DJs until they played it. Mark Kamins, resident at Danceteria, saw potential in the track and arranged to re-mix and overdub it with better musicians recommended by Arthur Baker. Kamins was also working A&R for Island Records and took the Madonna track to head of the label Chris Blackwell, who refused to sign her because she was his talent scout's girlfriend.

ʊ ʊ ʊ

As part of the daily Changing of the Guard procession in London, members of the Household Cavalry were proceeding on horseback along South Carriage Drive in Hyde Park on the morning of Tuesday 20th July. As they passed a parked blue Morris Marina at 10.40 a.m. an explosive inside the vehicle was triggered remotely from somewhere in the park. Eleven kilograms of gelignite propelled fourteen kilograms of nails at high speed, ripping into the soldiers and their horses. Three members of the Blues & Royals died instantly, along with seven of the horses, whilst many other troops and civilians were seriously injured.

Whilst the emergency services rushed to the scene and dealt with the horrific aftermath, the rest of London proceeded as if nothing had happened. Just over two hours later the Military Bandsmen of the Royal Green Jackets were performing selections from the musical *Oliver!* at the bandstand in Regent's Park, when a second explosive was detonated under the bandstand. Six of the bandsmen were killed instantly, with the rest as well as members of the audience being seriously injured.

The injured from both explosions were taken to Westminster Hospital, where striking staff called off their action to deal with the casualties. Meanwhile, one of the horses was rushed to veterinary hospital where he underwent eight hours of surgery for a total of 34 injuries. Sefton was given a 50% chance of survival after the operation, but over the following months made a full recovery, returning to active duty and winning *Horse of the Year*. His rider Michael Pederson was not so lucky, surviving the blast but suffering Post-Traumatic Stress Disorder for years, eventually splitting from his wife and killing both his children and himself in 2012.

The IRA claimed responsibility immediately with a statement which echoed a Margaret Thatcher speech at the outbreak of the Falklands conflict: "*The Irish people have sovereign and national rights which no task or occupational force can put down*". Two days later Thatcher rejected a call in Parliament for the return of the death penalty for terrorist murder. Throughout 1982 Irish terrorist groups murdered 111 people, mostly in Belfast.

ʊ ʊ ʊ

By 1982 the Prince's Trust Charity had been operating for ten years and decided to celebrate with a concert in the Dominion Theatre, London on Wednesday 21st July. Putting together an all-star band featuring Phil Collins, Midge Ure, and Mick Karn, the night also featured performances by Madness, Kate Bush, and Joan Armatrading. After years of anti-establishment punk and new wave acts, the music industry was once again embracing the establishment and royal family in a path which would lead to *Live Aid* in just under three years.

As the stars were tugging their forelocks to the landed gentry in London, Courtney Love realised she had outstayed her welcome in Liverpool and fed-up living in poverty on a small monthly allowance from her grandparents, caught the National Express bus to the capital. Sitting in Heathrow Airport awaiting a flight to the United States, she wrote in her diary "*There's one asset everyone has until they have spent it. Their mystique*" A couple of weeks later in San Francisco Love watched a new band called Faith No More, and afterwards berated them backstage, explaining everything wrong with their act. Love had gone to Liverpool a confident teenager but had come back ready to take on the world. She later said "*Before Liverpool my life doesn't count. Ian McCulloch and Julian Cope taught me a great deal. I owe them a lot. Liverpool had been a great school to become a rock star*"

Faith No More were so impressed and overwhelmed with Courtney, they asked her that night to be their singer.

ʊ ʊ ʊ

Sharon Osbourne knew her relationship with her father had come to an end, following his attempt to turn Ozzy against her. The couple had to move fast and flew to New York on the Thursday 22nd July to visit their record company, CBS. The company were informed that Ozzy now had nothing more to do with Don Arden, and that all monies should be frozen. When Arden's lawyer turned up at CBS an hour later to attempt the same thing, the war turned savage. Sharon and Ozzy attempted to find a lawyer, but no-one would help them, fearful for their lives following tales of Arden's strong-hand methods.

Don Arden and his wife flew into New York and tried unsuccessfully to persuade CBS of their daughter's insanity, then put around word that he intended to have her killed. Sharon and Ozzy went into hiding on the island of Hilton Head off the coast of South Carolina.

ʊ ʊ ʊ

When Madness reached the top of the charts with their greatest hits compilation *Complete Madness* and single *House of Fun*, it should have marked a watershed for the band. Most acts never progressed as creative forces beyond a *Greatest Hits* compilation, and frequently the albums were only released by record companies once a band is estimated to be past their commercial peak. Madness, on the other hand, carried on as if nothing had happened, and within a couple of months started on a new series of top ten singles.

The first of these was *Driving in my Car*, a song which simultaneously succeeded in exemplifying everything that was enchanting and irritating about Madness. The lyrics

 caught enough of the nostalgic love of everyday mundane things ("*It was made in '59 in a factory by the Tyne*"), but at the same time seemed to exist in order to create a more colourful rhyme ("*I bought it in Muswell Hill from a bloke from Brazil*"). Perhaps, the key to understanding and loving the song is the awareness that writer Mike Barson was attempting to capture the spirit of Ian Dury, and it does not necessitate too much elasticity of the imagination to hear the fellow Londoner sing the track.

If some of the lyrics existed to drive forward a video narrative, Madness did not disappoint with the visuals, which saw the band piled into an open-top car, the *Maddiemobile*, driving around the capital, interspersed with footage of the band in the garage repairing the vehicle, and in a studio miming to the track. At one point, upon mention of the A45, they pass the members of The Funboy Three, former label mates at Two-Tone, attempting to hitch a lift to Coventry.

What the song required was a killer chorus, and whilst the verses were catchy, they ultimately did not go anywhere. Perhaps more annoyingly, it was peppered with car sounds, honking horns, and roaring engines, which whilst they fitted in with the general mood of the song, did not add to the argument that it was a decent song. The band chickened out of the original idea, which was for the car radio to be switched on half-way through and tuned into a new song.

Chris Foreman, Lee Thompson, and Mark Bedford of the band had undertaken a thirty-mile charity cycle a couple of weeks previously for the BBC and managed to tie the B-side of the single in with this: a version of *Driving in my Car* with new lyrics called *Riding on my Bike*.

Around this time, Madness and their entertaining videos almost took them in a new direction as Ben Elton and Rowan Atkinson wrote a sit-com based around the band. The plot revolved around the Prime Minister being outed as an alien, and Madness being voted into power based on promises of free sweets for the kids and free beer for the adults. The BBC wisely decided not to commission the sit-com, however, according to lead singer Suggs many of the scenes and jokes eventually made their way into TV comedy series *The Young Ones*.

ʊ ʊ ʊ

The Fall's Marc Riley was becoming increasingly irked with singer Mark E. Smith's constant complaining about his guitar. *"Have you noticed that at every soundcheck and most rehearsals my guitar's too loud or it's out of time or the keyboards don't sound right?"* he complained, *"I'm only on number one. How much lower can I get?"* Smith also went out of his way to remove Riley's girlfriend from the guest list whenever she would turn up at a gig.

It was with this resentment simmering that The Fall flew to Australia without Karl Burns, one of their drummers, due to problems with a lost passport. They flew on Indonesian Airlines, which took thirty-six hours to reach Australia, by which point the band were suffering from the extreme effects of jet lag and being sprayed down with pesticides. Booking onto their run-down hotel in the King's Cross area of Sydney, they were taken straight to the first gig at the Musicians Club on Thursday 22nd July. With Smith not yet at the venue, the band proceeded to mix jetlag with Foster's lager whilst attempting to tune up by ear. *"Don't you have electric tuners in England?"* the incredulous soundman asked. When Smith finally turned up, having been taken past the Sydney Opera House three times by an opportunistic taxi driver, the band took to the stage only to find themselves entering a jetlag induced dream-like state, causing the playing to appear sloppy, sluggish, and undisciplined, and then immediately afterwards found themselves wide awake again. In their newly enlivened state, the decision was made to retire to the Mansell nightclub, where the sounds of *Town Called Malice* and *Rock the Casbah* enticed the musicians onto the dancefloor. Halfway through the new single from The Clash, Smith stormed furiously onto the floor, slapping drummer Paul Hanley. *"What the hell do you think you're doing?"* Moving on to slap guitarist Craig Scanlon, he continued *"You're not too tired to dance… but what were you like onstage?"* Next was bass player Steve Hanley, whose hit was accompanied with *"You were too fucking tired to play a decent gig, that's what!"* Smith then took it one member too far when he attempted to slap Marc Riley, who promptly punched him flat onto his back[452].

"Help! Help! I'm being attacked!" Smith yelled as he ran from the club, not to be seen again that night.

The following day, in an attempt by manager Kay Carroll to heal the rift, Smith and Riley were sent to an Australian television interview, where no amount of make-up could cover up the singer's throbbing black and purple eye.

ʊ ʊ ʊ

In regular times, when Blondie released the second single from a new album they would anticipate at least a top ten placing, however *Warchild* struggled to even break the top forty. In their native United States, the single was not even released, such was the low profile of the band. It is easy to see why the song failed to take off; it comprised

---

[452] Smith's hatred of The Clash may have stemmed from the previous year when they supported the Londoners during their residency at Bond's in New York and Joe Strummer had the nerve to be nice to him.

several of the customary Blondie features such as a disco beat and solid guitars, however the melody was simply not strong enough, and the arrangement a muddle, with the instrumentation clashing. Normally, Blondie songs were unimpeachable in their arrangements, but with *Warchild* everything seemed to have been thrown into the mix, even a horrific saxophone solo.

The band set out on a world tour, beginning with a North American leg on Friday 23rd July in Baton Rouge, by which time Frank Infante, having launched a lawsuit against the band, had been replaced by session guitarist Eddie Martinez. The peculiar consequence of this was that for the tour Infante was paid *as if he was there performing*, but Martinez was also paid because he *was there performing*. At the beginning of August, Duran Duran joined the tour as support, a fascinating amalgamation of a band on the way up and a one on the way down.

Blondie were also joined on the tour by a horn section and second keyboard player, playing a combination of material from their back catalogue, heavy on hit singles, but still only selling half the tickets for the 20,000-seater arenas.

ʊ ʊ ʊ

Wales was exposed to some first-class hard rock on Saturday 24th July when Motörhead headlined a festival at the ground of Wrexham Football Club. Playing further down the bill were a new American act called Twisted Sister, who sported make-up and played a style of glam-metal. Motörhead frontman Lemmy discerned backstage that the Americans appeared anxious and decided to take them under his wing. Fearful the hard rock audience would rip them apart due to their look, Lemmy appeared onstage before them and commanded respect from the audience. Twisted Sister nervously took to the stage, however from the first note they had the audience on board with a tight rocking set.

Throughout the day, an adjacent hospital had been complaining to the organisers about the sound, demanding the volume be turned down. The soundmen complied as much as they could, however early in the headliners set the sound became so quiet that Lemmy stated they could not continue at such a volume and Motörhead were leaving, with the parting instruction to the crowd to rip the place apart in protest. Chaos followed, with the pitch torn up and security guards fortifying themselves in a nearby building.

The following night, Motörhead played at another festival at Hackney Speedway Stadium in London, during which guitarist Brian Robertson appeared wearing green silk shorts. Lemmy was furious with this image calamity, becoming progressively conscious that perhaps the new member was not quite Motörhead material.

The festival had been poorly arranged and even worse attended, and was policed by Hell's Angels, leading to a repressive atmosphere throughout the day.

25th – 31st July 1982
#1 single: Irene Cara: Fame
#1 album: Various Artists: Fame

1982 was shaping up to be a momentous year for Sylvester Stallone as *Rocky 3*, the first of two movies starring the thirty-six-year-old actor, was released. With two previous installments, the movie was treading well-worn ground, offering nothing other than "*guys beating hell out of each other to a disco beat*", however that did not hinder it becoming a heavyweight box office success, as well as having an impact upon the music charts.

From a simple request by Stallone of "*I need a pulse*", Frankie Sullivan and Jim Peterick of Chicago rock band Survivor crafted a perennial classic. As members of Survivor, the two had been saved from a career of obscurity writing, singing, and playing on advertising jingles, signing to Atlantic Records subsidiary Scotti Brothers at the end of the 1970's. Survivor had enjoyed a couple of semi-successful American albums when the request for a theme song for *Rocky 3* came in. Sullivan explained that after reading an early copy of the script "*We turned it around fast. We wrote the music together in 10 or 15 minutes. It flowed together kind of naturally.*" The thing that took longest was the last line of the chorus, which initially read "*It all comes down to survival*", with the final word being the title of the song. When it became obvious that the opening line of the chorus was stronger, the last line and title was changed to "*The Eye of the Tiger*". When Stallone heard the demo, he complained "*It doesn't have balls. I don't care what the hell you do, I want it to kick ass.*" Sullivan explained his solution, saying "*All I did was push the faders up a single decibel and, boom, you could feel the difference. It was kicking and he loved it.*"

Stallone had first wanted to use *Another One Bites the Dust* by Queen, but was refused permission by the band, so Survivor were instructed to write something similar. Where Queen's hit had been straight forward funk and disco, *Eye of the Tiger* remained firmly in rock territory, though the two shared a pulsing beat. The track is an uplifting tale of motivation, perfectly suited for the movie which used the demo version of the song because it contained more bottom end. This rawer version suited the film however it was a smoother re-recorded version which was released as a single and rose to the top of the charts at the end of summer across the world, including in Britain where the symbiotic relationship between vinyl and celluloid kept it in the public consciousness for months.

Since then, Sullivan has undertaken several legal actions to stop Republican political candidates using the song at their rallies, including Newt Gingrich[453], Mitt Romney, and Mike Huckabee.[454]

---

[453] Many of the things Donald Trump believed in he took from Newt Gingrich, who was disparaging of the United Nations, the World Health Organization, and NATO, whilst demanding strong immigration policies and the deportation of Muslims from America. He decided to tell his wife he wanted a divorce the day after she had an operation to remove uterine cancer, telling a friend "*She's not young enough or pretty enough to be the wife of the President. And besides, she has cancer.*" It was a pattern he was to follow when he divorced his second wife just after she was diagnosed with Multiple Sclerosis. What a charmer.

[454] Mike Huckabee opposed same-sex marriage (he said it was "not a political issue...it is a biblical issue"), criticized actress Natalie Portman for having a child without getting married, opposed abortion, wanted to double military spending, and opposed gun control. What a charmer.

Stallone's second cinematic release of the year was *First Blood*, based on a novel written in 1972 by David Morrell which followed the story of returning Vietnam veteran John Rambo and his fight with a local law enforcement. The initial script was to star Steve McQueen and Gene Hackman, however the length of time in pre-production meant the lead role eventually fell to Stallone, who following his successful with the

boxing franchise had the power to demand significant rewrites. These included making the character of Rambo more sympathetic by having him not deliberately kill anyone from the police department, and more importantly for the future, not have him die at the end of the movie. Whilst the film did not receive overly positive reviews at the time, it was a box office success due to the draw of Stallone and has been re-appraised since then for the sensitivity with which it treats the violence and plight of a traumatized ex-soldier. This is in comparison to the *"violent racist power fantasy"* of *Rambo: First Blood II*, *Rambo III*, which holds the record for being the most violent film ever made and during which Stallone fights on the side of the Afghanistan Mujahideen, or *Rambo: Last Blood* which was justifiably criticized for its xenophobic representation of Mexicans.

ʊ ʊ ʊ

Following the tradition set by Bob Dylan in the 1960's of singers without a conventional voice, 1982 was a year of multiple *marmite voices*. Despite their success, many could not stand the histrionics of Dexy's Midnight Runners' Kevin Rowland, or Boy George's nasal soul-whine, and adding to this cavalcade was the gravel rake of Richard Butler, singer with the Psychedelic Furs. These types of voices were important in keeping music interesting, of avoiding what in the future would become auto-tune insipidity, and success was possible for the passionate non-singer due to industry willingness to allow an act to develop over several albums.

Described as being *"technically unruly and gratingly ugly when it was called for"*, Butler had led the London act in their journey towards mainstream success over the course of two post-punk albums, the last of which featured *Pretty in Pink*, the single which would eventually break them in America, but stalled at number forty-three in Britain.

By 1982 the line-up had settled as vocalist Butler and his brother Tim, along with John Ashton and Vince Ely, following the sacking of two original members. Ashton described

the sacking as *"a rash decision, one with no real rhyme or reason behind it, that kind of got out of hand"*. As the band wrote new material, they asked David Bowie to produce the album, which he agreed to following his filming schedule, however the Psychedelic Furs were not keen to wait that long and instead recruited Todd Rundgren.

The first single to be released was *Love my Way*, an infectious piece of marimba driven pop which managed to smooth the edges from the band and make them sound chart bound. Ashton remembered Richard Butler phoning him one night *"from the wine bar where he was drinking saying 'I've got this great song, it goes like....' And I couldn't make head or tails of it. From a guitar point of view, it's very basic, but it's the melody that's really so catchy, and the counterpoint between the marimba melody and Richard's vocals is pretty amazing"*. The marimba was played by Rundgren, replacing the keyboards of the demo version, though as he said "*It's not like I had to go rent some marimbas... I happened to have them*".

Rundgren had further influence on the tone of the song, persuading Butler to give up his "*sarcastic voice*" and sing it straight, whilst bringing in old friends Mark Volman and Howard Kaylan of the Turtles, using them to create washes of voices in the chorus, something the band were initially dead set against. Kaylan explained "*The original idea was just for us to do the fade-out of the record, and* [then] *while we were in the studio we started singing along with the chorus, just like we would've done had it been a T-Rex record. We could sing it so straight... Richard's interpretation was not straight at all, which meant that he was singing against us, and it created a very strange effect*". The duo had insisted on being allowed to sing on this one track, telling Rundgren "*We have got to sing on this one. If we don't sing on this one, we're not gonna' sing on the hit. This is the fucking hit!*"

Whilst Butler claimed not to write love songs, he did sometimes write *about* love, and *Love my Way* was his take on homosexual love. From the opening line stating "*There's an army on the dancefloor*" he looked at the heterosexual norm and the unknowing oppression it would cause someone who was gay in the early 1980's. He would later explicitly claim the song was a message of support for people who are "*fucked up about their sexuality, and basically says 'Don't worry about it'.*"

Although the song did the usual Psychedelic Furs thing and stalled at number forty-two in Britain, it became a break-through single in America, prompting the band to move there, feeling they would be better appreciated across the Atlantic.

ʊ ʊ ʊ

As Talking Heads flew into Budapest for a rare date behind the Iron Curtain on Sunday 25th July, they were forced to sit one at a time in immigration and type out a twenty-page form written completely in Hungarian. This proved too much for hired keyboard player Tyrone Downie, who suffered a breakdown in the airport, taking out his penis and waving it at the armed guards.

"*I want to go back to America where black people are black and white people are racist!*" he screamed as the guards backed off. After being talked down by the band manager, Downie was put on the next airplane to Munich to stay with friends.

ʊ ʊ ʊ

The official service of thanksgiving for the Falklands War was organised at St Paul's Cathedral in London for the evening of Monday 26th July. With the Royal family and government in attendance, the churches involved were not going to miss the opportunity to show their long-stated opposition to the war, with Cardinal Basil Hume wanting any mention of *liberation* being removed, Dr Kenneth Greet not wanting any members of the armed forces to provide a reading, and the Dean of St Paul's, Dr Alan Webster proposing half the ceremony be conducted in Spanish. A diplomatic battle was waged between the church and Whitehall, with compromise mostly being on the religious side, and the target for the press became the Archbishop of Canterbury, Robert Runcie, a former war hero and Military Cross recipient who had stated it was "*impossible to be a Christian and not to long for peace*".

The press may have made him the scapegoat, but many older members of the government who had actually been in a war agreed with the Archbishop, including William Whitelaw who had fought beside Runcie in Normandy and stated "*His words... were those of a soldier who understood war*".

ʊ ʊ ʊ

After a week in Sydney, The Fall made their way to Canberra for a show at the Civic Centre on Tuesday 27th July. Following a telling-off from manager Kay Carroll for drinking in the Irish pub next door to the venue, the musicians in the band tried to work out a way at getting back at singer and dictator Mark E. Smith. After contemplating a hunger strike, a general strike, and a vow of silence, they decided to start growing beards, something which Smith felt very strongly and vocally against.

The following day, on a visit to a nearby Koala sanctuary, Carroll confided in Steve Hanley that things were not well between her a Smith. As well as manager, the two have been a couple for years, and the singer's arrogance and insouciance was beginning to get in the way of their personal and private life. Smith was hard to live with, and even harder to work with, being "*someone who can silence a room just by sucking air*" according to Steve Hanley.

ʊ ʊ ʊ

Freddie Mercury was keen to spend as much time as possible at his New York apartment during Queen's 1982 North American tour, so when the band played Madison Square Garden on Tuesday 27th and Wednesday 28th July it allowed him an elongated stay. Not one to sit around, Mercury spent the time in the city visiting gay bathhouses and indulging in as much sex as possible. Given what is known of Mercury's health, it has been assessed these days in New York are when he was exposed to the HIV virus and became infected.

One night at the Mineshaft Club Mercury bumped into Soft Cell keyboard player Dave Ball at the bar. Recognising him, he enquired "*So David, tell me, are you and Marc [Almond] lovers?*"

Ball explained he was straight, pointing to his girlfriend Anita Sarko.

Mercury raised a surprised eyebrow and said incredulously "*Really?*" before buying Ball a bottle of Becks beer and looking for pray elsewhere. As Ball stood looking around at all the Castro clones at the bar, he decided it was time to shave off his moustache.

ʊ ʊ ʊ

Bobby Kimball, lead singer of Toto, was descending further and further into cocaine dependency, and whilst all the band indulged in the powder, no-one had allowed it to impede their performance until now. Throughout their tour in support of the album *Toto IV*, whilst they ascended to the pinnacle of the American pop charts with their singles, Kimball's performance was becoming less dependable. The problem was most noticeable in the studio, where recording his vocals took a long time due to poor pitching, but playing live Kimball was customarily spot on.

On their date at the Tennessee Performing Arts Centre in Nashville on Thursday 29th July, Kimball endeavoured to jump over the monitor, landing clumsily and breaking his leg. After hauling himself back to the edge of the stage, he performed the last song of the night before being taken to hospital. The rest of the tour was performed sitting down behind a keyboard, and with free time on his hands, Kimball began to smoke the cocaine instead.

From then on, his time in the band was limited.

ʊ ʊ ʊ

Duran Duran were determined to break America, and the traditional way to do that was through touring. Despite their videos receiving heavy rotation on MTV, the band spent the summer crossing the continent on their own and in support of Blondie. In between each date they attended radio, television, and newspaper interviews, learning to work the press like experts.

Ending their headline tour with a sold-out show at the Greek Theatre in Los Angeles on Tuesday 27th July, the band booked into the bungalows amongst the plush vegetation of the Hollywood Château Marmont[455] in preparation for guitarist Andy Taylor's wedding to his Wolverhampton-based girlfriend Tracey Wilson. The day had been postponed twice already due to band commitments, but the hairdresser and rock star finally tied the knot on Thursday 29th July overseen by the Dean of the University of California, with the rest of the band as his best men, resplendent in suits and top hats. The record company had been against the marriage, reasoning "*The fans will see the wedding and wonder who's going to be next*".

The day before, whilst the guitarist went shopping for a wedding suit, the rest of the band attended a party on... of course... a yacht, where keyboard player Nick Rhodes met his future wife, Julie Anne Friedman[456]. The following week she left home to travel with the band. A couple of days later John Taylor started dating Bebe Buell, a model and singer, the mother of Liv Tyler, former lover of Elvis Costello, and the inspiration for the Psychedelic Furs song *Pretty in Pink*[457].

ʊ ʊ ʊ

Tension within The Fall's Australian tour shifted up a gear at Geelong University on Thursday 29th July when singer Mark E Smith started ordering the band about onstage. Main nemesis Marc Riley began hammering his guitar during the songs to drown out the singer, who retaliated by unplugging the guitarist's microphone and throwing it to the back of the stage. During the next song Smith approached the bass amplifier and ran his hand across all the knobs, changing the volume and tone in one move. "*Don't you EVER touch my controls again!*" fumed bass player Steve Hanley, making a vow to himself to stand still in front of the amplifier from now on.

The following day the band found themselves playing doubles in a pool hall in Melbourne, with the musicians scratching at the stubble on their faces, the result of a beard-growing competition designed to annoy Smith. Just as things seemed about to blow again, second drummer Karl Burns arrived, having sorted his passport problem, and endured the thirty-six- hour budget airline journey from Britain. The long flight meant that Burns too had grown a three-day beard, and he immediately picked up on the tension.

"*What's up with you lot? You're all well caged-in!*" he exclaimed, "*Looks like I got here just in fucking time!*"

Smith saw his opportunity and exploded with rage, "*For fuck's sake! Will the lot of you have a fucking shave? You can't do anything unless you're all together! You dance together! You play snooker together! You can't think unless you're all in it together! And now you're all growing beards! Together! Get a fucking shave!*"

He turned to Burns, "*And now you've finally bothered to turn up, this band's like Fred Karno's army!*" before throwing his cue down and storming out.

---

[455] The Château Marmont was still covered in police tape as John Belushi's cars were still being examined in the underground garage.

[456] Friedman was the heiress to the Yonkers department store.

[457] Buell has also dated Mick Jagger, Iggy Pop, David Bowie, Jimmy Page, and Steven Tyler.

"Who the fuck is Fred Karno?" asked Burns, looking around confused and wondering what the Hell he had arrived in the middle of[458].

ʊ ʊ ʊ

Late July saw the Fun Boy Three return to the charts with their fourth hit single in the past six months, a version of the Gershwin classic *Summertime*. This track did not appear on any of their albums and at first seems quite an atypical choice for them to record and release, however upon closer examination it makes complete sense. The Fun Boy Three had chosen their cover versions wisely whilst members of The Specials, old ska songs that were brilliant but unknown outside the circle of blue-beat aficionados, such as *A Message to You*, or else appropriating them into their own material, such as *Gangsters* use of a rhythm from *Al Capone*[459], or *Too Much Too Young* stealing from *Birth Control*. Even whilst in The Specials, the trio had a track record of reaching further back into musical history than rock and roll, with covers of songs such as *Enjoy Yourself*, or *It Ain't What You Do* on their own debut album.

They insisted on adding to the original, injecting it with their own tribal drums and instrumentation, with strings and trombone now in evidence. These instruments were

played, certainly in the video and on *Top of the Pops*, by female musicians, who coincidently looked a bit like Bananarama.

All of this begs the question of why acts record cover versions. The phrase *cover* comes from the early days of rock and roll when black acts could be heard on black stations but were never permitted to break through to the more lucrative white audience. Record companies would take those songs and record an exact copy of it with a white artist singing, with the deliberately racist intention of *covering* up the original as if it had never existed. The difference between white music and black music was that the latter tended to be performance based, the singer usually give something of themselves in the song, whilst the former was more likely to be song based.

Musicians have been performing cover songs since music began, and in fact before recorded music the *cover* was generally the only way for music to be heard: you learned a song from someone other than the songwriter. Before rock and roll, a song was considered more successful the more people performed versions of it, and the charts were decided by the sales of sheet music rather than specific recordings. There has always been a complaint that the top forty is full of cover versions, stated since the beginning of the charts, and the bottom line is that cover versions sell because they are familiar. The public already know the song and if an act leaves it just long enough the audience will have forgotten what the original sounded like. This does away with troublesome hindrances such as having to write original material, and cover versions tend to be particularly popular with acts who are a front for a production team, such as boy bands. Generally, the more likely a band is to have their fans buying their singles no matter what they release, the more likely they are to record a cover version.

---

[458] To answer the question, Fred Karno was a British music hall performer from the end of the nineteenth century, who specialised in slapstick comedy and was a mentor to Charlie Chaplin and Stan Laurel. He built himself a boat, the Astoria, on the River Thames in which to live, which has since been turned into a recording studio by Pink Floyd's David Gilmour.

[459] *Al Capone* was a hit for Prince Buster and provided the inspiration for Suggs to join Madness.

Choosing the right song is essential for a cover version. Anything too modern and the public will prefer the recent original, anything too old and it may seem too out of fashion for current tastes. If an act can find a dazzling song that is also obscure, then they can find success, such as happened with Leonard Cohen's *Hallelujah*, however it is probably easier to choose something people will recognise. One thing is certain, no matter what you choose, people will always say the original was better.

During the summer of 1982 the British charts were inordinately full of cover versions, the vast majority of which were redundant. For every re-imagining such as the Funboy Three's *Summertime*, there was a *Who Put the Bomp*[460] by Showaddywaddy. There were live versions of old songs, such as The Rolling Stones' *Goin' to a Go-Go*, and an overwrought rock version of Stevie Wonder's *Living for the City* by Gillan, both of which managed to strip the soul from the originals. There were modern synth versions of old soul songs, such as Soft Cell's version of obscure Northern Soul classic *What* (which worked) and Japan's *I Second That Emotion* (which did not). There was massive success for Captain Sensible with *Happy Talk*, and much less success for Elkie Brooks with her version of *Nights in White Satin*.

From New York came a new version of Eddie Grant's fairly recent *Walking on Sunshine* by an act called Rockers Revenge, which was a project put together by twenty-seven-

year-old Boston-born New York-based producer Arthur Baker, fresh from working on the debut single by Afrika Bambaataa, and Puerto Rican DJ John Jellybean Benitez. Recruiting multi-instrumentalist Fred Zarr and reggae vocalist Donnie Calvin, the duo built a dancefloor classic, utilising drum machines in the way many more would as the decade progressed. The song sounded immense when played at volume in a nightclub, and topped the American dance charts over the summer, peaking at number four in the United Kingdom.

Older classics also found their way into the charts when Modern Romance abandoned any hope of coolness and reached number fifteen with *Cherry Pink (and Apple Blossom White)* featuring the trumpet of bald John Du Prez[461], and the lead singer of The Police, Sting, having an unexpected hit with *Spread a Little Happiness* from the 1929 musical *Mr Cinders*.[462]

You could always escape such pretentiousness by listening to The Boystown Gang's

top five hit version of *Can't Take My Eyes Off You*. San Francisco based Tom Morley and Bruce Carlton came together to cater to the city's gay crowd, miming to disco versions of old numbers at personal appearances in the first few years of the decade, initially with local cabaret singer Cynthia Manley handling lead vocals. For their second album, *Disc Charge*, Jackson Moore had replaced Manley, and their version of The Four Season's track climbed the charts over the summer. The act refused to call what they did *cover versions*, preferring *re-makes*

---

[460] *Who Put The Bomp* was a piss-take of the doo-wop style written by Barry Mann and Gerry Goffin.

[461] Du Prez would later write the score for the *Teenage Mutant Ninja Turtles* movie, as well as the musical *Spamalot*.

[462] The new version of the song was taken from the soundtrack of *Brimstone and Treacle*, a film adaptation of a Dennis Potter play, which starred the singer. He had been attracted to the role by the theme, which *"asks questions* [about] *the norms of morality, what's right and what's wrong."*

instead. It was to be their only hit in Britain, despite a career spanning a few more years performing at gay clubs.

The Belle Stars seemed to be forever trapped in a world of cover versions, following their minor hit *Iko Iko* with a version of *The Clapping Song*, originally sung by Shirley Ellis in 1965. Guitarist Stella Barker explained "*I think they (Stiff Records) had our best interests at heart when they released the covers because they wanted us to be successful. Seeing as a lot of people were releasing covers it seemed a good thing to do from a record company point of view.*" Saxophonist Miranda Joyce was not concerned with a second cover in a row, stating "*Anyone who sees us live will know we're worth more than just a glossy middle page*" as the song climbed to number eleven.

Stiff Records then took things too far with a third cover, a version of Inez and Charlie Foxx's *Mockingbird* in October, which failed to break into the charts. By now the band

were getting restless, as guitarist Sarah Jane Owen explained, "*In a way I suppose we're being manipulated, but it's for our own good. We have to make sacrifices in order to get established.*" The band flew out to Ibiza for three dates, which came with a week's stay at a villa next to a nudist beach. It was only once they were sunbathing there that it became apparent the beach was also used by the German military for manoeuvres. After scraping the bottom of the barrel as far as cover versions were concerned, things could have gone south for The Belle Stars. Luckily, they had their own composition waiting in the shape of the glorious *Sign of the Times* which hit the top three in the new year.

Also hitting the top forty were Bad Manners with *My Girl Lollipop*, Talking Heads offshoot The Tom Tom Club with *Under the Boardwalk*, and Gateshead folk act Prelude

with their versions of Neil Young's *After the Goldrush* and Roy Orbison's *Only the Lonely*.

One of the more successful covers during the summer was Ultravox frontman Midge Ure's version of the Tom Rush song *No Regrets*. Ure was in fact taking his cue from a previous version of the song by The Walker Brothers, which he "*remembered as having an enormously powerful sound but in fact it was really weak. So, I decided to do it as I remembered it*". Initially meant to be part of a whole album of covers including *Holy Holy* and *The Man Who Sold the World*, Ure made a big thing in the press of playing all the instruments himself apart from one piano note which he claimed he could not hit hard enough[463]. Riding high from his success with Ultravox and Visage, the Scotsman managed to climb to number nine in the charts[464].

ʊ ʊ ʊ

---

[463] He did not go as far as to name the person who had the required super-human finger strength to play the note.

[464] Of all the covers mentioned in this section, several were the first versions I heard. *I Second That Emotion*, *No Regrets*, *Can't Take My Eyes Off You*, *Goin' to a Go-Go*, *Under the Boardwalk* and *After the Goldrush* were stepping stones for me to discover Smokey Robinson, The Four Seasons, Neil Young, The Walker Brothers, and The Drifters, so maybe there is something to be said for cover versions?

Following Spandau Ballet's return to the top ten with *Instinction*, the band turned to the man who had remixed them to sound more contemporary: Trevor Horn. Horn turned up at Gary Kemp's parents' house and listened to him play some new songs on acoustic guitar. It was decided they would take a track called *Pleasure* forward with the aim of it being the lead single from a new album. Over the summer, Spandau Ballet began the album with Horn at George Martin's Air Studios in London, starting with a full day of trying to record John Keeble's drums. Eleven hours later Horn was still not happy with the performance. That night he phoned Kemp and expressed his dissatisfaction, suggesting they either programme the drums or else replace the drummer. By the morning Horn's position had hardened and he said he would only continue if Keeble was sacked. The band decided to stay loyal to their drummer but vowed never to tell him why the Horn recordings had ground to a halt, explaining instead that "*We couldn't have worked with Trevor because he was too overpowering, too dogmatic*". Horn was in love with technology, and would probably have insisted on programming everything on the album which the band would have resisted, however he has since said that if he had heard the track *True* he would have stayed on board and compromised this approach. Instead, Horn chose to continue working with Malcolm McLaren, mainly because the project was a challenge.

ʊ ʊ ʊ

The Some Bizarre compilation album released early in 1981 highlighted songs by unsigned synth-based acts, including Soft Cell, The The, Depeche Mode, and B-Movie,

all of whom had varying degrees of success afterwards. Tucked away at the start of side two of the album[465] was a track called *Sad Day* by a Harrow based two-piece called Blancmange.

The duo had been formed in 1979 by Lancashire singer Neil Arthur and London keyboard player Stephen Luscombe, both of whom had played in experimental bands where they would make percussion from kitchen utensils and washing machines. Arthur explained "*I'd say punk and its DIY culture was the most influential single thing in music for me. Punk released us all from the misconception that you had to be a multi-talented instrumentalist... it gave rise to the non-musician as an artist which was perfect for us*", and as former graphic designers they elected to write songs by utilising colour-coded pieces of paper.

Exposure on the album led to deal with London Records, along with opening live slots with Japan and Grace Jones, as well as spending the first part of the year as invited support on Depeche Mode's British tour, becoming close friends with the Basildon Beatles. Their debut London single was released in spring and featured *God's Kitchen* as a double A-side along with *I've Seen the Word*. The former was a mid-tempo atheist lament about the search for God, stating that he "*Ain't in my kitchen, and God ain't in my room*", over a sparse but hypnotic synth musical accompaniment. The other side was similar in style, which may suggest why it was released as a double-A side: neither song was strong enough

---

[465] The sides were called the *Fish* side and the *Eye Lamp* side. Blancmange were the opening track on the *Eye Lamp* side.

on its own. The single peaked at number sixty-five, whilst Mute Records founder Daniel Miller described Blancmange as "*the maiden aunts of electronic music*".

Over the summer they had another stab at the top forty with *Feel Me*, a vast improvement which with hindsight sounds like the kind of dancefloor filler that LCD Soundsystem specialised in over two decades later and featured backing vocals that many mistakenly assumed was Annie Lennox of The Eurythmics but was actually Madeline Bell[466]. Producer Mike Howlett was fresh from working with OMD and A Flock of Seagulls, and was by now experienced in capturing electronic music, providing a powerful dancefloor filler in search of an audience, based around a hypnotic groove with no real structure, written by Stephen Luscombe, to which vocalist Neil Arthur added the top line. Despite ample airplay, the single stalled at number forty-six.

---

[466] Bell was an American singer who had previously provided lead vocals for French disco group Space, and had sang on The Rolling Stones *You Can't Always Get What You Want*.

AUGUST

1st – 7th August 1982

#1 Dexy's Midnight Runners & The Emerald Express: Come On Eileen

#1 album: The Kids From Fame: The Kids From Fame

The success of Buck's Fizz and Bardo had given any old singer, actress, or dancer who had been around the block a few times the idea they could have a new career. Which leads us nicely to Toto Coelo. Sheen Doran, a former actress from *St. Trinian's* movies, admitted at the age of thirty-three that *"you get to an age where you can't go auditioning anymore"*, and started phoning round friends in the same position. Recruiting Anita Mahadervan, a former dancer with Legs & Co and actress in *The Benny Hill Show*, Lacey Bond a former Grange Hill actress, Lindsey Danvers, and Ros

Holness, the daughter of television presenter Bob Holness, with *"the exaggerated smile of a toothpaste advert"* the five made their debut at a Royal Wedding Night Gala party in July 1981 before supporting disco act Rose Royce and signing to Radialchoice, the same label as Toni Basil.

Teaming up with 1970's producer Barry Blue[467], who provided them with their first single, *I Eat Cannibals*, Toto Coelo insisted on sporting a home-made bin-bag style. Powered by synthetic tribal drums, the single had a nagging chorus and chanted group vocals, managing somehow to reach number eight in the charts, however success was not to last long as Toto Coelo turned out to be a one-hit novelty act[468].

Whilst Mahadervan formed Cherry Bombz with former members of Hanoi Rocks, Bond, Danvers, and Holness found work singing backing vocals in Bruce Foxton's solo band.

ʊ ʊ ʊ

Malcolm McLaren, impatient to resume his musical trip around the world, flew to South Africa at the start of August, informing producer Trevor Horn and engineer Gary Langan he would call them when he discovered something worth recording.

Visiting Soweto, where it was still perilous for white people to stray, McLaren hooked up with an ex-boxer and musician called Lulu Maseelala. A couple of weeks were devoted getting Maseelala's old band, The Boyoyo Boys, back together and rehearsing them in a room in Johannesburg. With movement of the black population restricted, getting the musicians out of Soweto also proved to be problematic and so a second room was set up closer to home.

ʊ ʊ ʊ

It had been just over ten years since considerable quantities of oil were confirmed in the North Sea, setting up a potentially lucrative source of fuel and money. When OPEC instigated an oil crisis in 1973 it became financially beneficial to start developing the vast fields a couple of hundred miles off the coast of Scotland, more of which were being discovered each year. Two years later United States Secretary of State Henry Kissinger told President Gerald Ford that Britain was *"begging, borrowing, stealing until*

---

[467] Barry Blue was actually born as Barry Green.

[468] Meanwhile, Carol Ann Holness, the sister of Ros, had signed to EMI and secured a top seventy-five hit with *No No No* at the same time.

North Sea oil comes in", a financial situation which made it imperative for the black liquid to be extracted from the seabed as quickly as possible. The previous year Britain became the first major Western nation with the ability to export oil, and annually the industry was worth £12 billion to the economy and set to grow, making it the second largest offshore producer in the world in 1982. Production in 1979 sat at almost 78 million tons, worth just over £5.5 million, whilst by 1982, 103 million tons was extracted, worth over £14 million pounds, almost 5% of the Gross Domestic Product.

The problem was getting to the oil, which was in what the Americans called "*an asshole of a field. Worse than the Canadian East Coast, worse even than fuckin' Alaska*". The Americans knew this because they had been granted almost 40% of drilling rights in politically secure waters, not to mention the manufacturing of equipment. As the Reverend Dr Andrew Ross stated, "*The only things that* [Scotland is] *supplying oilmen with are whisky and whores*". The business of drilling for oil under the sea was a relatively new one, only about thirty years old, and the technology remained unproven. Due to pressure changes divers were required to spend three weeks at a time on the seabed, working twelve hour shifts every day and sleeping in a submerged pod. For this they were paid well, however it remained extremely dangerous, with multiple deaths each year. The licenses to drill for oil were issued by the British government and many remained under state control, including the British National Oil Corporation, formed in 1975. In 1982, however, it was about to be at the forefront of Margaret Thatcher's privatisation crusade.

Privatisation was the moving of government-owned services and assets from the public to the private sector and had first been completed on a mass scale by Hitler and Nazi Germany during the 1930's as a means of raising much needed national funds. That many of these services ended up in the hands of Nazi supporting business interests also set a precedent, one which would become rampant in 1980's Britain.

On Sunday 1st August the British National Oil Company were privatised and became Britoil. At Thatcher's behest the company had been placed under the control of Sir Philip Shelbourne, a partner in the Rothschild group, who subsequently made a small fortune with the privatisation as shares were floated on the London Stock Exchange.

The successful transfer of control from public to private ownership became the test case for future privatisations, with British Telecom and Sealink Ferries following in 1984, British Aerospace and British Gas in 1986, Rolls Royce in 1987, British Leyland and British Steel in 1988, and the water authorities in 1989. The move towards reducing the state continued after the era of Thatcher, with future Conservative governments adding British Rail and the Post Office to the list.

The area where the public most felt the impact of privatisation was the *Right to Buy* policy, introduced in 1980 by Margaret Thatcher, which allowed Council tenants to purchase their rented accommodation for a sliding scale between 30% and 50% of the value, depending how long they had occupied the premises. Many Labour run local councils were against the policy, however by enshrining it in law they were legally obliged to sell. People took advantage of this in their tens of thousands, and by the end of 1982 over 440,000 people out of 6.5 million council houses, had applied to become homeowners. The Right-to-Buy policy was a shrewd one by the government, knowing that council tenants were twice as likely to vote Labour, whilst homeowners were three times more likely to vote Conservative, whilst also reducing the financial responsibilities of the state. Over the next couple of decades, the council housing stock was reduced significantly following a government ban on building new council funded houses, leading to a housing crisis, especially in the south east of England. The private sector was quick to move in, purchasing large amounts of housing through deferred transaction agreements, and by 2013 over 36% of previously council-owned properties were being rented back to councils by private companies and landlords at an inflated price.

The fetishizing of private ownership by the government had the added effect of stigmatising council rents, and with this move the make-up of council estates changed from aspirational working-class families to areas of unemployment, state benefits, and poverty. What had started out as *homes fit for heroes* now became receptacles for the poor.

℧ ℧ ℧

Releasing *Too-Rye-Ay*, their new album, whilst sitting at the top of the singles charts with *Come on Eileen* was an impeccable move by Dexy's Midnight Runners, the culmination of Kevin Rowland's Celtic soul dream, mixing horns, fiddles, Motown, and Irish folk in equal measures, whilst also managing to sound like it belonged in 1982.

The album had been onerous to make, with inter-band tensions running high. "*It wasn't a great atmosphere in the studio*" Rowland later admitted, "*Which is why the record to me is a disappointment*". Where did he put the blame? "*I think the production definitely let down the songs… and I think my performance wasn't great. How much of that is down to the production is hard to say, and how much down to the fact that half the band had left*" he would ponder. Saxophone player Paul Speare disagreed, claiming "*It was good to have producers there – Clive Langer and Alan Winstanley – who would take charge of the recording* [and] *were not prepared to be too swayed by Kevin's ideas*", whilst Winstanley felt "*The singing isn't great… but it's the sound and it works*".

Rowland had been aiming for a pietistic atheist fervour in the music, claiming at the time "*That synthesizer thing has been done to death… It's time somebody put up something different*". Twelve-hour days were spent getting everything perfect before the album was completed in five weeks during March and April. The band were valorous throughout, with Winstanley claiming "*They walked in like an army, recorded like an army, and went home like an army*".

The album was credited to *Kevin Rowland & Dexy's Midnight Runners*, an important shift in emphasis which recognised he was the only remaining original member and the undisputed driving force and leader of the band. Speare later claimed "*The whole recording of 'Too Rye Ay' was overshadowed by the tensions within the band. Jim Paterson and Brian Maurice had already gone and been brought back… there was a very strange feeling about that.*" Rowland was aware of the atmosphere, knowing "*There wasn't that unity that we had in '80 or '81. It wasn't like one for all and all for one, or anything like it.*"

Starting with a statement of intent and introduction with the previously failed single *The Celtic Soul Brothers*, the album moved promptly on to what Rowland maintained was the stand-out track, *Let's Make This Precious*. Guitarist Billy Adams agreed, saying this was "*One of the best singles that never was. It probably seemed too much in the old 'featured brass' style at the time.*" The song featured a band intensely locked into their playing, whilst Rowland indulged in an introspective call-and-response with his inner-self. Demanding unconditional commitment, he expected we "*First bare your hearts and cleanse your souls*" before we "*Sing … a record that cries pure and true, no not those guitars they're too noisy and crude.*" Whilst seemingly attempting to inflame an audience, Rowland was really singing to himself. He would later muse on the overarching themes of the album, stating "*In Catholicism… you were taught from day one you were born with sin… so you're always struggling. Those songs… they're all about struggle, alienation and redemption and talking about God and confusion".*

All in All (This One Last Wild Waltz) was a slab of Irish folk music, with backing vocals provided by the enigmatically named Sisters of Scarlet. Rowland would disown the tag, saying *"It's not that I love folk. I could not name a folk artist I like, but I think it would be a good idea for the pop scene to play acoustic music"* and felt this would have been a perfect follow-up single for *Come on Eileen*, wrong-footing people's expectations. There was a rawness to the song which may have been down to Rowland writing *"the lyrics in a wood near the studio an hour before I sang them. I had a completely different lyric up to that point but at the last minute, I decided they weren't right."* The song was an offer for previously revered master to join his servant for a final metaphorical waltz, having outgrown his lessons. Rowland had wanted Van Morrison to produce Dexy's first album, and even got as far as persuading the renowned curmudgeon to attend a band rehearsal, however the influence was to come through more discernibly on *Too-Rye-Ay*. Whilst Rowland thought the influence acceptable to peddle, the press believed otherwise, as he explained, *"There was a lot of things in the press at the time, which I took very seriously, just saying things like 'oh, Van Morrison rip-off'. They weren't saying I was influenced by Van… they were saying it was a rip off. But I made that clear, I spoke about that. I covered one of his songs for god's sake!"* That song was *Jackie Wilson Said (I'm In Heaven When You Smile)* which Rowland claimed "[Van Morrison] *quite rightly thinks it's better than his own version. I thought his version was a little bit underplayed"*. Dexy's even went as far as to invite Morrison to the studio when they were recording the song. Producer Langer described the day: *"Van came in the studio, and I said to Kevin 'Well, what's he going to sing?' And Kevin said 'Well, I don't know. Get him to sing the song'."* Winstanley then takes up the story: *"He just stood by the microphone, and we ran through it three times, and he never sang a note. Kevin went into the studio to try to nurture him along."* Ultimately, Morrison departed without adding any vocals.

Side one of the album ended with *Old*, looking at the plight of the elderly and what their knowledge and experience could provide to society, as Rowland asked *"May I sit down here and learn today? I'll hear all you say"*. The majestic and measured music had been written previously, but the melody was added by Paterson during a rehearsal break, which he considered *"My greatest moment as Kevin's song-writing partner. He trusted me to write a complete section on my own one lunchtime."*

I'll Show You was a soul march, originally intended to be the B-side to previous single *Show Me*, a paean to lost youth with Rowland listing what became of old school friends. *"I went back to see how the people I'd went to school had grown up,"* he explained, *"I've still got a soft spot for the guys in the song because they've still got it in them"*, as he sang of eternal hope and a lack of judgement.

Liars A to E had been re-recorded and re-worked from another previous single, which the record company objected to including but were over-ruled. One of the highlights of the album, the song made full use of the soulful vocals of The Sisters of Scarlet: Carol Kenyon[469], Katie Kissoon[470], and Sam Brown[471], all of whom had to be cajoled in the studio by Rowland to *"sing harder… give it some of that old southern stuff. I don't know if they were taking the piss, cos they started to wave their arms about. It worked,*

---

[469] Kenyon's greatest and most noted vocal performance was to be on Heaven 17's *Temptation*, though I have a soft spot for her work on Malcolm McLaren's *Madam Butterfly*.

[470] Katie Kissoon, along with her brother Mac, released a version of *Chirpy Chirpy Cheep Cheep* at the same time as Middle of the Road, but lost out to the Scottish act in the charts.

[471] Sam Brown was the daughter of original British rock and roller Joe Brown. She would go on to have a top five hit with the self-written *Stop* in 1989, before retiring after permanently losing her voice in 2007.

anyway". Taking lines from The Killjoys *Smoke Your Own* and *Saint Dominic's Preview* by Van Morrison, Rowland saw the song as an attack on music journalists who had doubted him in the past, claiming "*You won't look like me and you'll never think like me*". "*Sometimes I would just sit down to write a song and journalists faces would appear in my head*" Rowland would later claim, as he bared his soul.

Despite Rowlands misgivings, the album was one of the most complete ever released, a compelling concept and singular vision seen through from start to finish, one which demanded listening to in complete order, and spent four weeks sitting at an unjust number two behind the soundtrack from the television series *Fame*.

ʊ ʊ ʊ

When Duran Duran met up on Monday 1ˢᵗ August to travel to Kansas City for the first date of their support tour with Blondie, they were surprised to see Nick Rhodes bring his new girlfriend Julie Anne Friedman. The band had an unwritten rule about bringing

girlfriends on the road, and even guitarist Andy Taylor had sent his new bride home to Britain. Singer Simon LeBon approached Rhodes to ask, "*What the fuck is going on?*" "*I met her on the boat and she's coming with me*" insisted the keyboard player. Andy Taylor later explained "*We were all very English in our tastes and outlook, but suddenly we had a brash American heiress in our midst.*" The tension continued throughout the tour as Duran Duran made the most of being bought onto an arena tour, even if ticket sales were sluggish due to the waning star of Blondie. Crossing the country to Meadowlands in New Jersey, the band met Nile Rodgers and Tony Thompson of Chic, and friendships were struck that would pay dividends as the decade progressed.

Back in Britain a third single from *Rio* was released in the shape of illusory ballad *Save A Prayer*. Duran-mania was reaching a British peak and accompanied by a Sri Lankan-shot video starring model Vanya Seager[472], the song rose to number two on the charts, becoming their biggest hit to date, though it did fail to take off in other territories around the world. The band and film crew had gotten into difficulties when shooting the video, finding Sri Lanka on the verge of a civil war, and they were chased by 400 disgruntled shaven-headed monks for not treating their temple with due respect.

ʊ ʊ ʊ

Israel had never fully stopped bombing Beirut but on Wednesday 4ᵗʰ August came a torrent of fighter jets, dropping missile after missile for nine straight hours in what the government called a *tightening* of the siege. Whole streets were flattened, along with the occupants of the buildings. Philip Habib, the United States special envoy for the Middle East, was in the nearby suburb of Baabda and called Israeli Defence Minister Ariel Sharon, asking for the attack to stop on humanitarian grounds. Sharon denied the bombing was taking place, and then "*The damned man said to me on the phone that what I saw happening wasn't happening. So I held the telephone out of the window so he could hear the explosions.*" Sharon then angrily demanded "*What kind of conversation is this where you hold a telephone out of a window?*"

The Israeli military had been intercepting wireless and telephone communications to try to pinpoint the exact location of PLO leader Yasser Arafat, before confirming estimates with agents on the ground. Two days later a *vacuum bomb* hit a seven-story

---

[472] Vanya Seager later married Robson Green and named her son Taylor. Make what you want of that!

apartment block near the Lebanese Central Bank in Beirut, flattening the building and killing or wounding over 200 people inside. Arafat had been using the building temporarily but had hurriedly left a couple of minutes before the impact.

The Israeli actions were attracting an increasing voice of criticism worldwide, with the United Nations Security Council voting two days previously to call for an immediate withdrawal of the troops from Lebanese soil. As was the usual with United Nations resolutions, this was ignored.

ʊ ʊ ʊ

The attempt to save Banco Ambrosiano by a consortium of Italian banks fell through on Friday 6th August when it became clear they would not be able to raise anything near the amount needed to meet the current debts. On the same day, the five-party coalition held together by Italian Prime Minister Giovanni Spadolini started to unravel when the Socialist Party withdrew their support. With the future of the government in doubt, the Italian Treasury Minister decided to pull the plug on any attempt to salvage the bank.

As the rain poured down in Milan, Nuovo Banco Ambrosiano announced their new chairman would be Giovanni Bazoli, and after a frantic weekend transferring funds, the new bank opened for business on Monday 9th August. Initial urges to lose the *Ambrosiano* from the title were ignored, with the feeling continuity was more important than the sullied reputation of a name.

ʊ ʊ ʊ

The women at Greenham Common were constantly trying to find new ways to draw attention to their protests, and Hiroshima Day on Friday 6th August seemed like a good time to stage their next event. It was decided to commemorate the thirty-seventh anniversary of the dropping of an atomic bomb on the Japanese city by placing 100,000 stones at the war memorial at nearby Newbury, each "*a unique representation of a human life that ended on that day*".

It took a lot longer than expected to collect and count the stones, and the women had to work through the night under car headlights. In the morning they drove to Newbury with the bags of stones, and placed them carefully, whilst walking around the war memorial in silence. Some locals were furious at the protest, and a scuffle broke out with a few youths. The police arrested one of the women for "*dropping litter*", and the local paper accused them of insulting the memory of the men who had fought against the Japanese.

ʊ ʊ ʊ

Elvis Costello and the Attractions had been added to the North American tour featuring Blondie and Duran Duran, and on Saturday 7th August the show rolled into Parade Stadium in Minneapolis. As soon as he arrived Costello was told by the promoter "*Don't leave after your set, Bob Dylan is on his way*". Costello, a mammoth Dylan fan, was convinced this was a prank being played on him, having once before been caught out in Amsterdam by the same claim. After his performance, the plea was repeated, so he hung around and watched a lacklustre set by Blondie. At the end of the night, with still no sight of the legend, Costello arranged for a taxi to take him back to his hotel. As he was about to step into the cab, a white minivan hurled around the corner and screeched to a halt beside him. The side door slid open, and Bob Dylan beckoned the star-struck singer inside. The van was full, with people crouching and holding on, alongside someone in a wheelchair, and as they screamed out of the car park Dylan turned to Costello and asked in his most Dylan voice "*So, is that 'Watching the Detectives' a real show?*"

Ten minutes later Costello found himself deposited outside his hotel, wondering if the whole journey had been a dream.

ʊ ʊ ʊ

Ozzy Osbourne's mental state had declined significantly through the *Diary of a Madman* tour, and on Saturday 7th August he finally cracked. To stop the tour, Ozzy shaved his head and refused to go on stage at the Dallas Cotton Bowl. Wife and manager Sharon was having none of it, and instructed bass player Rudy Sarzo to purchase a wig and give it a haircut to match Ozzy's usual style.

"*I look like the village idiot*" Ozzy complained in front of the mirror, as his wife applied water and cut layers into the barnet.

"*That's better. You look beautiful now*" she said, standing back to admire her handiwork.

"*I still look like a bloody cunt*" moaned Ozzy, finding himself pushed onstage. At the end of the first song, he proclaimed to the audience: "*You people think I'm crazy? Well, let me show you how fuckin' crazy I am!*" before tearing the wig off to reveal a glinting bald head. The audience went wild.

The band managed one more date, the following night in New Orleans, before calling a premature end to the tour.

8th – 14th August 1982
#1 Dexy's Midnight Runners & The Emerald Express: Come On Eileen
#1 album: The Kids From Fame: The Kids From Fame

Thomas Dolby, worried about his lack of a breakthrough into the top forty, had taken to spending his days at EMI headquarters poring over radio playlists and sales graphs,

whilst Duran Duran came in to chat up the receptionists. With promotional visits across Europe, and even to Japan where he accompanied Spandau Ballet[473], he finally hit the top forty with new single *Windpower*. Although only sitting at number thirty-eight, Dolby was invited to appear on *Top of the Pops*, which was bound to springboard the song to a higher position. Musicians' Union rules stated acts had to re-record their song the night before the show to allow any session musicians to earn their fee of £56 usually involved roadies setting up the equipment until the Union representative arrived with a BBC member of staff, who would then take him to a nice restaurant for a meal and some alcohol. By the time they returned the roadies would be packing up the equipment again, and a "*new*" recording of the track which sounded remarkably like the released version was sitting

---

[473] Tony Hadley ignored him because he was in a huff about Japanese fans accidently getting marker pen on his new bespoke white suit.

in the control room. Just occasionally the Musicians' Union representative would insist on staying and a band would be caught short.

The BBC, trying to make one person on stage with keyboards look more interesting, had brought in strobe lighting and massive wind machines which blew smoke and Dolby across the stage. Afterwards, one of the *Top of the Pops* producers popped his head round the door of the dressing room and pointed out that Dolby might get some more airplay if he got to know some of the BBC executives a bit better. "*I'm having a pool party with a bunch of guys at my house next weekend, you should come and join us*" he continued. Dolby politely declined.

ʊ ʊ ʊ

The rhythm of the jackhammer which had kept Captain Sensible awake all night during The Damned's American tour earlier in the year finally came good with his new single, *Wot?* As a follow up to *Happy Talk*, it was essential Sensible avoid becoming a novelty act, and he attempted this by plugging into the hip-hop he had heard on his various Stateside tours. The song owed a great deal to *The Message* by Grandmaster Flash & the Furious Five, as well as their debt to Chic in terms of rhythm, and the lyrics concerned themselves with retelling the piledriver story. In the second verse Sensible took aim at old friend Adam Ant, declaring "*I've had a gutful of you and I'm feeling bad, you're an ugly old pirate and ain't I glad*".

Whilst the single only reached number twenty-six in Britain, it became a massive hit across Europe[474], leading to future tension between Sensible and The Damned. Sensible became a cartoon of himself, known for his red beret which had initially been worn as a protection against the tendency for punk audiences to spit on the band. "*If the stuff got in your hair, the hot stage lights would bake it into solid lumps which took ages to shampoo out*" Sensible explained. The stress came to a head during the autumn Damned British tour, which Sensible claimed "*I'd not changed, [but] the novelty single had gained me some kind of Cuddly Captain image. We heard stories of upset parents who'd brought their kids along to see The Damned thinking that because that jolly Happy Talk guy was in the band it might be a pop-tastic experience.*"

ʊ ʊ ʊ

The Associates were poised to become massive at the end of summer, with two sizeable hit singles, a top ten album, and a charismatic photogenic frontman in their arsenal. The problem was that, as good as *Sulk* was, they did not have another obvious hit single, nothing with the necessary pop hooks, no songs lacking the density and intensity displayed elsewhere on the album. The solution was to add a vocal track to the last song, a catchy instrumental entitled *nothinginsomethingparticular*. Now renamed *18 Carat Love Affair*, the new version featured recruit Martha Ladley[475] on vocals, performing what is almost a duet with Billy Mackenzie, whilst swooping and swooning during the verses.

If the instrumental was already canorous, the new version pushed things over the top with a singalong chorus in evidence, and even a decipherable narrative within the lyrics.

---

[474] Top ten in Austria, Belgium, France, Italy, the Netherlands, and Switzerland.

[475] Ladley was the girlfriend of designer Peter Saville.

Whilst it was easy to view the words as straight-forward: a man telling his mistress that they have to keep their affair secret in case his wife / fiancé / girlfriend finds out, it was also easy to see with hindsight that MacKenzie was singing about keeping his own homosexuality under wraps.

Although only twenty-five years old in 1982, MacKenzie had already been married at

seventeen whilst travelling across the United States of America. He would later claim the marriage was to acquire a green card, however his wife, a *"Dolly Parton type"* called Chloe Dummar, believed the union had been made in love. After three months MacKenzie returned to his native Dundee, and the couple were divorced in 1980.

MacKenzie was never openly gay, flirting instead with sexual yearning and ambiguity, however his bandmate Alan Rankine always just assumed he was without thinking to question why he thought that. Certainly, to see the band mime to *18 Carat Love Affair* on *Top of the Pop*, flirting with Ladley through the performance, you would believe his heterosexuality. This appearance on the show had almost not happened after MacKenzie, in full career destructing mode, had argued with the floor manager about camera angles causing the band to be kicked off the show. When replacement act Shalamar could not get to the studio in time, there was no option but to re-instate the Associates.

It is, perhaps, no surprise that MacKenzie chose to remain reticent regarding his sexuality, given the attitude towards homosexuality at the start of the 1980's, and with hindsight Rankine thought the singer was *"striving for a third sex"*. There were almost no successful *out* musicians in the charts: in the public's eye Elton John and Freddie Mercury were straight. The only openly gay musician seemed to be Tom Robinson, and his career had faltered a couple of years previously. 1982 was also a year when many gay men would be near the top of the charts, from Marc Almond to Boy George and George Michael, however none of them would *come out* for several years knowing that to be openly gay in the early eighties would have killed your career. Obviously, everyone in the business and press knew who was gay, but no-one was willing to talk about it, preferring to hold all the dirt until they needed to use it. That the public did not catch on seems incredulous to anyone born after 1978, however these were times when any good-looking male singer was called *gay* regardless of their sexuality, due to a mixture of homophobia and jealousy.

For example, Marc Almond received a huge amount of homophobic abuse, whilst simultaneously being criticised by the gay press for not coming out and being pushed back into the closet by press agent Colin Bell, who invented girlfriends, while his assistant Mariella Frostrup even tried to invent a fictional relationship with Bebe Buell. Almond later stated that *"To actually come out and say 'I'm gay' could damage my career"*, and so he encouraged the mystique of neither confirming nor denying. Almond would later reason *"Back in the seventies, even lorry drivers liked The Sweet, and you had this kind of flamboyance – male peacocks, dandies, blending masculine and feminine. But it was all play-acting."* When Almond eventually admitted publicly to his sexuality, he expressed regret, *"I liked the kind of blurring that Morrissey had. I took that from the seventies… even though you knew that Bowie and Bolan had wives, you never really knew, and that was really exciting."*

Perhaps MacKenzie also lacked the courage to come out. Certainly, he talked in later years about his feelings of unworthiness, coming from a rag-and-bone background and a rough estate on the Tay: how could he compete with the untouchable stars he looked up to? This insecurity was to be the reason for the sudden demise of the Associates' chart potential by the end of the year.

A world tour had been booked, with a nine-piece band fully rehearsed over the summer at Basing Street Studios in Notting Hill. MacKenzie, racked with self-doubt, chose to spend more and more time back home in Dundee as Rankine put the band through their paces. Bass player Michael Dempsey made an exit around this time, encouraged by MacKenzie who told him *"he planned to dismantle the band and I should stay away from what was about to happen"*. The band travelled to Edinburgh in August where they were due to begin with three nights at the Assembly Rooms as part of the Festival Fringe. After a disastrous soundcheck the day before, they retired to the bar of the George Hotel and proceeded to get drunk. Halfway through the evening, MacKenzie announced to the band he was pulling out of the tour. After much hilarity it became apparent the singer was not joking, and he was chased down George Street with Rankine hitting him on the head with a shoe. MacKenzie ended up spending the night sleeping underneath a parked car.

The following morning, finding it had not all blown over as hoped, the press was informed MacKenzie had a chest infection, and the immediate dates were to be cancelled. The press did not believe a word of this, despite MacKenzie's attempts to give the excuse some gravitas by communicating in sign language, and he was forced to flee by taxi to Dundee, leaving Rankine to get angrily drunk with the music journalists. The real reason for MacKenzie's departure has never been fully revealed, though it is thought to be a mixture of stage fright, a low boredom threshold, and an under-rehearsed band. Years later MacKenzie tried to give a reason, blaming *"Drugs. It was just cocaine frenzy. I turned into the bastard son of Frankenstein with it and hated myself"*.

The Associates initial record deal had been for the world except the United States, and with three hit singles incredible offers were coming in from across the Atlantic, however the frontman was not interested in the treadmill of touring, writing, recording, repeat. MacKenzie could also be difficult regarding *"poxy TV shows where you'd just walk on for three minutes, mime and then walk off, and he would conveniently mislay his passport"*.

After trying to talk him round, Rankine decided that he had had enough and walked away from the band, leaving MacKenzie sole rights to the name. MacKenzie wanted to become a studio-only act and had even scuppered a deal with Seymour Stein's Sire records worth £600,000 because he did not want to tour the United States. The Associates never recovered from this blow, never regained their full-blooded experimentation and bravado.

ʊ ʊ ʊ

Whilst the world believed Japan to still be an ongoing concern, especially in the light of their recently announced Autumn tour, the individual members started to record and release solo efforts.

Bass player Mick Karn had decided towards the end of 1981 to record solo material, explaining *"It didn't mean I wanted to leave Japan, it was just a little experiment that I wanted to do. I would pay for it all myself, and if Virgin Records didn't like it then I couldn't care less"*. When the rest of the band objected, the idea was shelved, however the decision to split had put a solo career back on the agenda, and Karn spent the summer in London recording his first album *Titles*. Demonstrating clearly that the fault line in Japan lay between himself and frontman David Sylvian, Karn recruited all the other members of the band, Richard Barbieri and

Steve Jansen, and as you would expect it sounded quite a bit like, well, Japan, just without Sylvian's sultry vocals. Sharing the production credits were Karn, rising studio star Colin Fairley[476], and Ricky Wilde, and the album was largely instrumental, with Karn's lymphatic bass lines assuming the starring role. With the tracks being bass-led, more time should perhaps have been spent on the rest of the instrumentation which at points had traces of Brian Eno and David Byrne's experiments with *world music* from the previous year.

The album was released in November, just as Japan announced their split, on the German subsidiary of Virgin Records, evidence that the record company had realised they were not about to get two stars from the band, and without the teen-appeal of Sylvian it did not trouble the charts.[477]

All eggs were then put into Sylvian's basket, and he breached the top forty in August with his first solo release, *Bamboo Houses*. Sylvian had been recording with Yellow

Magic Orchestra member Ryuichi Sakamoto since the start of the year, and the Japanese keyboard player had even been co-opted into the live version of Japan.

Bamboo Houses also sounded exceptionally like Japan, mostly instrumental with little in the way of Sylvian's trademark vocals, and it once again was not aimed at the teen market. A lack of accompanying video and obscure lyrics (possibly dealing with the aftermath of the atomic bombs dropped on Sakamoto's homeland) certainly kept the track away from the teenage girls' attention, and the single stalled at number thirty. "*I couldn't say I was 100% pleased with it*," Sylvian explained later, "*But that was partly because… we were only together for six days*". Sylvian did not seem in the least bit bothered by the low chart placing, by this time only interested in following his own musical path. Before then, however, he had the final Japan tour to undertake.

ʊ ʊ ʊ

When drummer Paul Ferguson re-joined Killing Joke in Iceland at the start of summer, they resumed band activities with new bass player Paul Raven. The fear of an apocalypse was obviously not strong enough to stop the band touring to support third album *Revelations*, and the rest of the summer was spent in North America. On Monday 9th and Tuesday 10th August the band's performance at Larry's Hideaway in Toronto was recorded for a live mini-album, entitled *Ha!* Which reached number sixty-six when released in November. Things remained tense during the tour with Ferguson claiming "*Jaz is becoming the focal point. I'm not going to be part of someone's fuckin' support band*". Coleman, on the other hand, rationalized "*The hate we have for each other comes out of deep respect*".

Coleman was not interested in returning to Iceland afterwards, stating "*I love the countryside, I love the place… there's no pollution, there's no army… [but] I cannot stand living among those people*". Instead, the band returned to the studio with Conny Plank at the end

---

[476] Fairley had recently been playing drums for Lonnie Donegan.

[477] Karn also branched out into sculpture in 1982, with a well-received exhibition of his work at London's Mayflower Gallery.

of summer, and recorded a new single, the sarcastic and scathing *Birds of a Feather,* marking a calmer pop sound. Criticising people for having shared beliefs, Killing Joke had an arrogant ostentation to them, the self-belief they had the answers and everything else was wrong, like modern-day keyboard warriors calling everyone *sheeple.*

It was a smugness the band retained throughout their career, as they became more polished with singles such as *Let's All Go (To the Fire Dances), Eighties,* and genuine hit *Love Like Blood,* however sonically they would have a lasting impact on the American Industrial scene, particularly acts such as Nine Inch Nails and Ministry.

ʊ ʊ ʊ

After seven weeks of siege in Beirut, during which the city had been turned to rubble by an Israeli bombardment in their attempts to kill Yasser Arafat, on Tuesday 10th August the American envoy Philip Habib sent a draft agreement to Israel asking for a ceasefire and end to the situation. Defence minister Ariel Sharon was furious at the suggestion, and ordered the further carpet bombing of the city, causing the death of hundreds of civilians. President Reagan responded angrily to the bombing, protesting to the Israeli government about what he described as "*a holocaust*". Polish-born Jewish Prime Minister Benin responded with "*Mr President, I know what a holocaust is*". The result was that Sharon was stripped of his powers, could make no further moves without the prior permission of the Israeli prime minister and cabinet, and six hours later another ceasefire was announced.

ʊ ʊ ʊ

Despite being signed to IRS Records, REM were still playing gigs in small bars and touring the country in a beat-up old van. A month worth of dates had been booked on the American West coast in August through to September, after which they would join the Gang of Four tour as support, and to help them pay their way across the 1400-mile space between Atlanta and California, the four-piece were booked into the Graham Central Station in Albuquerque, New Mexico on Wednesday 11th August. Guitarist Peter Buck was rather startled to find that they were the support for a *Hot Legs* competition in front of a thousand drunk and rowdy cowboys chanting for "*tits and ass*". The promoter looked to the band, scruffy ex-collage kids, then to the army of shit-kicking rednecks, and stated "*If you go on in front of this crowd, there is a very real chance they will kill you*". Making an on-the-spot decision to pay them *not to play*, the band found themselves $500 richer and arrived in California a day early.

The following week, their label debut was released in the United States. *Chronic Town* had mostly been recorded by Mitch Easter almost a year before, and became an instant critics' favourite, coming second in New York's influential *Village Voice* poll at the end of the year. As an introduction to the band, it was perfect, giving just enough of a flavour of what they were about, with chiming arpeggio guitars and obscure lyrics, providing the band with a solid foundation on which to release their debut album proper the following year.

Over the next decade REM provided a superlative role model of how to grow your band and brand organically, building with each album and constant touring, refusing to compromise their sound or vision. Each album outsold the previous one without them bothering the singles charts until the turn of the decade. *Murmur* reached number thirty-six in 1983, *Reckoning* number twenty-seven in 1984, *Life's Rich Pageant* number twenty-one in 1986, *Document* number ten in 1987, and *Out of Time* topped the charts worldwide in 1991. They also provided the perfect business model for a band, sharing song-writing credits and money equally, no matter who wrote or played what, and even when drummer Bill Berry left in 1997 it was on the strict condition that the other three would agree to continue without him. When they finally called it a day in 2011, it was on the best of terms, a rare feat in the music industry.

ʊ ʊ ʊ

Since Larry Kramer had set up the Gay Men's Health Crisis just over six months previously, the number of sufferers had increased much swifter than anyone had predicted. The gay community was in desperate need of help and, more importantly in Kramer's view, education regarding the disease. Kramer had made several attempts to meet Mayor Ed Koch with no success. Koch was what used to be politely called a *confirmed bachelor*, being a single man of a certain age of whom rumours swirled[478]. Koch was keen to distance himself from any hint of homosexuality, knowing the effect it would have on his ratings, and so went out of his way not to provide any funds for the epidemic.

Despite Kramer's attempts to mobilise gay voices against Koch for his inaction, the real outrage in the community was voiced against doctors such as Dan William, who had suggested that bathhouses should be required to post signs warning about the epidemic and promiscuous sex. William was attacked in the gay press and accused of "*stirring panic*".

Instead, many in the community chose to put their faith in vitamin packets called HIM (Health and Immunity for Men) which were being sold by unscrupulous opportunists as a preventative measure, and were a "*mixture of natural vitamins, minerals and herbs for the sexually active male*".

15th – 21st August 1982

#1 Dexy's Midnight Runners & The Emerald Express: Come On Eileen

#1 album: The Kids From Fame: The Kids From Fame

With the Boyoyo Boys rehearsing in Soweto, Malcolm McLaren called for Trevor Horn and his engineer Gary Langan to join him in South Africa. The two ran into trouble at the airport when it emerged that McLaren had only bought them a one-way ticket. In 1982, no-one was allowed into South Africa without a return ticket bought in advance, however a friendly air stewardess took pity and purchased them a return ticket. When Horn and Langan arrived at the Johannesburg hotel, McLaren was no-where to be seen, busy travelling to Soweto on workers' buses, spending all night in bars and sleeping all day.

On the fourth day they finally ran into McLaren in the hotel lobby by accident, and work commenced in the studio. For the next nineteen consecutive nights The Boyoyo Boys and some female Zulu singers played their music whilst Horn and Langan recorded it. McLaren started writing lyrics based on Zulu chants, Double Dutch skipping rhymes, and square dance calls, whilst the band played old tunes which Horn was led to believe copyright would be purchased for. Each night the musicians could not return to their homes as black people were not allowed on the street after 7 p.m. so they would sleep on the floor of Horn's hotel room. "*I would open my hotel door in the morning to several*

---

[478] Many knew Koch to be a closeted homosexual, and in his fight for the leadership of the city in 1977 against Mario Cuomo, posters had been placed around Manhattan with the slogan "*Vote for Cuomo, not the homo*".

surprised waiters with trolleys crammed to feed all these Zulus huddled on my floor" he fondly recalled. In the hotel room McLaren would entertain them with stories about how he took the music industry for a financial ride with The Sex Pistols.

The biggest problem was recording McLaren's vocals. Horn claims "*There was this great moment when Malcolm sang for the first time. The Zulu women were sleeping, and when Malcolm started singing they all started to wake up. And when he finished singing this little Zulu lady said 'Trevor, he can't sing'.*" Whilst trying to get a level on the microphone and headphones, a track was played back and McLaren was all over the place in terms of timing and volume, sometimes shouting, sometimes whispering. At the end of the track, he started to remove the headphones declaring himself delighted with the take. With incredulity, Langan stated "*You have to sing it again, Malcolm, because you're shouting*".

"*Shouting? I've done the song. Didn't you record it, boy?*" replied McLaren.

As Langan attempted to explain the way of the studio, with McLaren declaring "*I'm a one-take wonder*", Horn walked in and took control, explain that he had to sing the part again with timing, tuning, and feeling.

"*Hold on a minute*" said McLaren, "*You mean you want me to sing in time... sing in tune... and sing with some kind of emotion, too? That's asking a lot!*" Eventually, the songs were recorded with Horn banging McLaren on the chest to emphasise where the beat was.

With a number of songs in the can, including *Double Dutch*, *Punk It Up*, *Jive my Baby, Jive*, and *(Living on the Road in) Soweto*, McLaren got into an argument with the local branch of the record company about payment for musicians. McLaren, for once in his life not looking to exploit people, wanted to pay them the going union rate, whilst the local company wanted to pay much less because they were from Soweto. Eventually, McLaren also paid for a wedding reception for one of the musicians.

℧ ℧ ℧

Within the new technology being rushed into recording studios around the world was the seed of popular music's demise, in two different ways. Firstly, over the next three decades computer games replaced music in the hearts of many children and teenagers. Initially, game arcades full of consoles replaced the tradition jukebox as a place for youths to gather, then when games moved into the home the writing was on the wall for music. Deliberately designed to be addictive, games started to easily outsell albums by the turn of the millennium, with titles like *Minecraft* and *Grand Theft Auto V* selling more than 100 million copies. Teenage boys started to congregate in person or online to play the latest game release rather than obsess over bands.

Secondly, the very migration of music from analogue to digital in terms of recording and product made it inevitable that music would cease to hold such a favoured place in peoples' lives. For a couple of decades, the format of choice for record companies and the consumer had been the vinyl record, however in 1982 the industry was terrified by the rise of the cassette. These small plastic boxes contained magnetic tape and came in a pre-recorded format (with an album on them), or else in blank versions with either 30, 46, 60, 90, or 120 minutes of recording time. It was these blank cassettes which bothered the industry, with them correctly believing that people would simply record their favourite songs from the radio instead of buying the singles. A campaign was started by the British Phonographic Industry with the slogan *Home Taping is Killing Music*, however blank cassettes continued to sell in their millions. The real break away from vinyl came with the invention of the Sony Walkman, a portable cassette player with headphones which provided a far greater quality of sound than most would have expected. The Walkman was revolutionary in the way music was consumed. Where before the listening of a new album had often been a communal experience, it now became personal and private. The portable aspect of the music provided a soundtrack to the listeners' every moment, and a sonic soundscape to their physical landscape. The headphones were a barrier to the outside world and contact with others, providing permission to ignore everyone else as you wished. Before long, people were indulging their own musical tastes travelling to work, in work, even whilst out doing this new form of exercise which *People* magazine five years previously had christened *jogging*.

The cassette and the Walkman entered a symbiotic relationship as kids started to create their own soundtracks by curating tracks from a variety of sources, often ones which they had not actually paid for themselves. By 1982 over thirty million blank cassettes were being sold each year in America, very few of which were being used for dictation.

Cassettes and home taping also marked the beginning of the end for the traditional album. The public made it clear they would rather record a selection of the best songs from each album, preferably an album owned by a friend to save themselves the inconvenience of purchasing the product. Often the songs would be recorded from the radio, with tens of thousands of teens tuning in to the top forty on a Sunday, fingers poised over the *record* button. The selection of these individual tracks led to diminishing respect for the complete album, and to 1982 when the pop single dominated. The record industry went into decline in the early 1980's, with Columbia Records firing 300 employees in August 1982 in response to the drop in sales.

The move to digital came when Sony and Phillips teamed up in 1979 to develop disc technology. The *compact disc* was demonstrated on BBC TV programme *Tomorrow's World* in 1981, and the first commercial release of a CD was released on Tuesday 17th August 1982: Abba's *The Visitors*, pressed at the Philips Factory in Langenhagen in West Germany. For some reason Scotland seemed to be first to embrace the technology, with Jimmy Mack, Ken Bruce, and Eddie Mair at BBC Scotland becoming the first disc jockeys to play a compact disc on air in October 1982, followed by Jay Crawford on Edinburgh's Radio Forth. The album played was *Love Over Gold* by Dire Straits and as the decade wore on this band became synonymous with the technology, with *Brothers in Arms* being used as a demonstration disc in hi-fi stores up and down the country: "*Just listen to the quality of the hi-hats*". As the 1980's progressed compact discs became more common[479], and by the end of the 1990's they were the dominant music format, persuading the public to buy their record collection over again, and kick-starting the idea of looking backwards to classic rock[480]. Magazines, radio stations, and festivals sprung up around this trend, as music became more about re-living your youth than pushing onwards to new pastures. However, the very strength of compact discs also became their weakness: the digital format files contained on the disc could be easily replicated and converted to other formats such as MP3. They were easily copied, cutting into the profits, and then when the internet came along, they were downloaded for free by millions of people. Almost overnight, the money to be made from record sales disappeared, and ticket prices for concerts doubled and trebled as bands could only pay for their pensions with live work. An increasing number of vintage bands successfully charged a fortune for people to see them live before they died, playing greatest hits sets to the middle-aged and multi-generational.

---

[479] I had to buy a CD player when I won a boxset of Rolling Stones albums in 1990. The boxset would have cost more than the player.

[480] The last vinyl album I bought was *Parklife* by Blur. I remember standing in a record store with the vinyl in one hand and the compact disc in another, wondering which one to go for. I regretted choosing the vinyl a week later when it scratched.

More symbolically, the Compact Disc *"demystified music and in so doing reduced the status of those who made it"* claimed David Hepworth. The packaging reduced in size, and where once an album had been something you could carry under your arm to show your musical credentials, no-one ever did that with a compact disc or cassette. However, nothing could stop the rise of the technology, and by 1993 only two million vinyl albums were sold in America, a number which was being exceeded in compact disc sales by Alanis Morrissette *every month*.

Not only did technology cut into record sales, but other areas of the music industry suffered as well. Recording costs were cut to a minimum by computers, as musicians no longer needed to fork out money to capture their music, choosing instead to record cheaply (or free if you downloaded a pirate copy of recording software). The one thing that was hard to replicate at home on the cheap was a decent drum sound, and so drum machines or samples became the norm. New acts no longer needed to pay for CD pressing and distribution without any idea if the money would ever come back, and anyone could release a track worldwide on all the major purchasing and streaming sites for less than £50. Distribution companies and pressing plants closed. New bands who could have previously existed by selling 30,000 copies of their independent single, with enough money left over to record and release another one, no longer existed.

℧ ℧ ℧

When The Fall arrived at Christchurch Airport in New Zealand on Tuesday 17th August, tensions were still running high. Guitarist Marc Riley and singer Mark E. Smith had spent the last month-long Australian leg of the tour arguing and were unprepared for semi-celebrity in New Zealand where they had reached the chart position of eleven with their latest album, *Hex Enducation Hour*. A photograph of Riley emerging from the airport, swinging his suitcases and smiling, appeared on the front page of the local newspaper the following day, with the headline *"Happy Fall Guitarist"*, which annoyed Smith even further.

However, this being the dysfunctional Fall, the anger fermented for a few months more.

℧ ℧ ℧

A coup was under way in the Teardrop Explodes.

Keyboard player Dave Balfe rejected the songs frontman Julian Cope was writing, calling them *too rock*, nothing like the Teardrop Explodes. Instead, he insisted he was going to compose the next album himself, even though he had never written a song in his life. Whilst Balfe got to work on the album in London, Cope returned to his parents' home in Tamworth, spending is days accompanying his father on his rounds as an insurance salesman.

When Balfe finally felt confident enough to call the rest of the band to the recording sessions, Rockfield Studios was block-booked. Of course, by now the only other members of the band were Cope and drummer Gary Dwyer, who spent the entire time driving through the surrounding countryside in a borrowed Cortina with one of them clinging on to the roof, often ending up in ditches.

When the two were eventually allowed into the studio they were greeted with a *"series of whirs, clicks, loops and endless synthesized noises"*. In response, Cope filled twelve mugs with coffee, dropped ten spoons of sugar in each one, then mashed up Maryland Cookies and Digestive biscuits and forced them into mixture, believing that his protest perfectly represented what he was hearing.

Cope and Dwyer returned to the outside of the studio where they invented a game called *Brick*, the rules of which involved two people standing fifteen feet apart throwing a brick at each other. Several days of the game went swimmingly, with both out of their heads on acid, amazed at the vapour trails left by the flying brick. Then Balfe insisted on joining in, and within three throws had managed to hit Dwyer on the side of the head. Cope was furious and returned to the studio to grab a shotgun belonging to the owner, which he handed to his drummer and shouted, "*You're fuckin' dead, Balfe*". The next two hours were spent at the door of the adjoining cottage, watching with binoculars whilst Dwyer chased Balfe in distant fields, punctuated by the sound of occasional gunfire.

When the two arrived back separately, Balfe's forfeiture was to pour a couple of buckets of water over his head. Except, Cope had filled up one with watery cow-dung from a nearby septic tank, which Balfe subsequently dropped onto himself.

ʊ ʊ ʊ

The Americans had a lot invested in ending the siege of Beirut, and on Wednesday 18th August a solution was finally agreed. A couple of days later a multinational task force overseen by the United Nations landed in Lebanon to oversee the removal of the PLO. Over 10,000 Palestinian guerrillas and 2,700 Syrians who had been trapped by the Israeli attack were evacuated by land and sea, with the majority relocating to Tunisia, their new base in exile. The Israeli's had achieved their goal of removing the PLO from Lebanon, however at a cost of 19,000 lives, over half of which were either Lebanese citizens or Palestinian refugees, not to mention a resolution of support for Yasser Arafat in the Arab world. On top of this, another 30,000 people were wounded, whilst Israel in return counted their casualties as 400.

The Christian Maronites wasted no time in seizing control of Lebanon, electing military commander Bashir Gemayel as president at the military academy at Fayadiye, but not until members of parliament had to be escorted at gunpoint and forced to vote. His first duty was to visit the Israeli government, where Begin and Sharon attempted to dictate policy to him. Gemayel was furious, claiming "*The way they spoke to me was as if I was a vassal. Begin called me 'boy', but I am the President of Lebanon.*" As the Israeli's demanded he sign a peace treaty, the soon-to-be Lebanese President informed Begin that he had not spent seven years fighting the Syrians and PLO for Israel to take their place as an occupying foreign nation. Gemayel insisted that he needed time to reach a consensus amongst the people, and no peace treaty would be signed without their support

Over the next three weeks, Gemayel oversaw the opening of Beirut for the first time since 1973, as well as the resumption of the economic markets and seaports. With fair treatment of all civilians, things were looking up in the Lebanon for the first time in decades.

ʊ ʊ ʊ

President of Sire Records, Seymour Stein, had spent the last few weeks in hospital recovering from open heart surgery, when a ball of energy burst into his private room in Lennox Hill, New York. Danceteria DJ Mark Kamins had been doing some casual scouting for the label and talked up the new recording he had remixed by a hopeful Madonna. Stein liked what he heard and asked for a meeting, fully expecting it to happen once he was out of hospital. Instead, that night Madonna turned up in his room.

Never lacking confidence, Madonna went straight into her pitch.

"*The thing to do now is sign me to a record deal*" she exclaimed, opening her arms, "*Take me, I'm yours. And now, you give me the money*".

Stein was instantly bowled over by the evident star quality but played hard to get for a little while longer, realising that as a gay man Madonna's flirting act could not work on him. Eventually Madonna sighed exasperated *"Look, just tell me what I have to do to get a fucking deal in this town!"*

"Don't worry, you've got your deal" Stein eventually relented. They agreed on $15,000 per single, for a total of three singles, with an option for an album. The next day Madonna quit her job at the Lucky Strike Bar in Manhattan.

ʊ ʊ ʊ

On Saturday 21st August Blondie played at JFK Stadium in Philadelphia, alongside Duran Duran, Elvis Costello and the Attractions, A Flock of Seagulls, and headliners Genesis. They were due to begin the European leg of the tour four days later, which would have taken them to France, Spain, Denmark, Sweden, and then comprehensively through the United Kingdom. Throughout the summer guitarist Stein had suffered poor health, which many close observers assumed was the result of drug addiction, however by the end of August he was too exhausted to continue. In fact, Stein did have a serious heroin addiction, as did Debbie Harry, using the drug to mask the pain his body was feeling. All future commitments were cancelled, and Stein became seriously worried he was suffering from the newly recognised GRID, but was then diagnosed with pemphigus vulgaris, a rare auto-immune disease of the skin. *"It's when the proteins that bind your skin together break down, and you just sort of dissolve,"* Stein later explained, and after a couple of years of severe illness, during which his partner Harry put everything on hold to nurse him back to health, he was able to control it with a program of steroids. Stein later claimed the disease was stress-induced, caused by a mixture of constant work and drug use. Whatever the reason, it put an end to Blondie as a functioning unit, perhaps just as their creative light was waning.

The official announcement of the split was made in November[481], by which point bad financial management had caught up with the band, as they found their manager had simply not paid tax for the first few years of their success.

Harry and Stein split a few years later, and she released a small number of semi-successful solo albums over the next seventeen years, however the two remained close and continued to write together. Then in the late 1990's, Blondie did what few other bands had achieved: they reformed and reached the top of the charts with new material, the classic single *Maria*. Since then, Blondie have continued to tour and release the occasional album, however despite the new material they are very much entrenched in the nostalgia category that they always said they would avoid: people go to see them to hear the old hits.

22nd – 28th August 1982

#1 single: Dexy's Midnight Runners & The Emerald Express: Come On Eileen
#1 album: The Kids From Fame: The Kids From Fame

As was often the case with bands in the 1980's, Haircut 100 had kept a song back from their debut album for release soon afterwards. Albums tended to have only two or

---

[481] No-one told my cousin, and he turned up at the Edinburgh Playhouse with his tickets.

three singles on them in the early 1980's, and acts were expected to release another album within the next eighteen months, with possibly one or two non-album singles in between. For Haircut 100 it was a track called *Nobody's Fool*, and whilst it did not stray musically far from their previous three hits, such was their momentum that it sailed into the top ten without any trouble.

The track had a stomping Motown beat with a repetitive lyric about being, well, nobody's fool. The rest of the words seemed to express Nick Heyward's frustration at not getting the girl that he wanted, whilst showing some awareness of his standing in the world of teenage girls by declaring "*I wander around breaking hearts everyday*".

The video featured a young Patsy Kensit[482] as Heyward's love interest and consisted of the singer driving through a pastoral English countryside collecting various members of the band. There was even an archetypical cricket match on the village green near the end; the band playing up to the cliché they had made for themselves.

Things, however, were not well in paradise. The band were keen to return to the studio late in the year, however Heyward refused to turn up, and the record label announced that their new single, *Whistle Down the Wind*, due in January 1983 was cancelled. Around this time Heyward let slip that he had been contemplating a solo career for some time and had recorded tracks with session musicians. The truth of the matter was that Heyward had been struggling with stress and depression for several months due to the pressure of being not only the face of the band, but also the main songwriter. He described the band as "*starting with three of us and then it became six, so it literally doubled. It was like a Mini Cooper S that turned into a Mini Clubman. It felt bloated*". Following an American tour, they decided to return to being a four piece and sacked their saxophone and percussion players. Feeling suicidal, Heyward was admitted to hospital, and by the time he returned the two sacked members were back in the band, with one of them handling lead vocals. Heyward was not feeling emotionally strong enough to question this and found himself without a band. Hanging around AIR Studios when Elvis Costello was recording *Imperial Bedroom* had made him obsessed with creating something with a similar artistic depth. "*I didn't think we sounded as good as ABC, but I didn't want to work with Trevor Horn*" he would later admit, as Haircut 100 continued without him, lacking his song-writing prowess and failing to break the top forty again.

Heyward, on the other hand, had a growing stockpile of songs ready to go and wasted no time recruiting the best musicians he could find, including bass maestro Pino Palladino, former Fairport Convention drummer Dave Mattacks, Elvis Costello organ player Steve Nieve, jazz pianist Bill Le Sage, and future Pink Floyd guitarist Tim Renwick. From these sessions came his solo debut album, *North of a Miracle* and three hit singles throughout 1983. None of these singles, however, reached the top ten as would be expected of such a pop phenomenon, which was blamed upon the new mature direction Heyward had taken, with slower mid-paced tracks such as *Whistle Down the Wind* (the previously announced and then cancelled Haircut 100 single) and *Blue Hat for a Blue Day*. The bottom line is that in the days before George Michael there was no role model for Heyward in making a transition from teeny-bop pop phenomenon to serious artist. Record labels did not believe it could be done and struggled to figure out how to promote him. Heyward lost his way, releasing singles for

---

[482] Kensit was the daughter of *Jimmy the Dip*, a known associate of the Kray twins. She is currently marrying he way through marrying pop stars of 1982, with Jim Kerr (1992) and Jeremy Healy (2009) already in the bag.

the next fifteen years, none of which bothered the top twenty, whilst also continuing to be troubled by depression, until having a sudden spiritual awakening in 1998, after which the releases became almost non-existent.

ʊ ʊ ʊ

Following the endeavours of the SAS during the Iranian Embassy siege of 1980, the race had been on to create a motion picture based on the events. Within thirty days of the siege James Follett had written a novelisation of an idea, each chapter of which was mailed as it was written to Reginald Rose[483] in Hollywood and turned into a screenplay.

The plot revolved around a terrorist group attached to the Campaign for Nuclear Disarmament who take hostages at the American Embassy and demand a nuclear bomb is detonated over Holy Loch in Scotland. An obvious right-wing propaganda exercise, *Who Dares Wins* was roundly savaged by many critics and attracted protest and complaints from CND and the left wing.

On Thursday 26th August the film opened in London and was met by a three-hour silent protest in the pouring rain by CND. A couple of weeks later actor Kenneth Griffith[484] was due to introduce a festival of radical films organised by Islington North Labour Party, however when it became known that he had a role in *Who Dares Win*, the invitation was withdrawn by the chosen Labour candidate for the next general election, Jeremy Corbyn.

The following day, with the sun now shining, the women at Greenham Common chose to stage their next targeted protest, running towards the sentry box at the entrance to the gates of the military base. As the security guard put out "*his arms out to stop us, like a goalkeeper*". The women managed to occupy the box, with the guard imploring them "*Come on... you don't want to be ridiculous*" to which seasoned protester Helen John replied "*I DO want to be ridiculous!*". The women then started to weave together green wool to seal the door.

Twenty-three of the women were arrested and imprisoned for three days in November for their actions. In Holloway Prison, the Greenham women tended to find the other prisoners supportive of their cause, and one of the protesters wrote in her diary which was smuggled out of prison "*The most important thing is that the women in here know something about us and have been coming to us with newspaper clippings about Greenham*".

Three days later when the women were released, the press met them at the door with champagne.

ʊ ʊ ʊ

When Simon Edwards began working for Rough Trade Records he brought with him a wealth of experience in retail, and developed the idea of joining up the various regional record companies; Factory in Manchester, Backs in Norwich, Postcard in Glasgow, Zoo in Liverpool, and countless more. These labels were the mainstays of the independent chart, set up in January 1980 by Iain McNay of Cherry Red Records, which counted sales from the smaller shops around the country, the type of shops where the staff

---

[483] Rose wrote the quite frankly brilliant play *Twelve Angry Men*.

[484] Griffith: "*In my time I've been accused of being a Marxist, a fascist, a traitor and, probably worst in most people's eyes, inconsistent. I was a radical Socialist. I'm now a radical Tory. It has been a very painful journey.*"

were equal parts impassioned and supercilious about music, but more importantly the kind of shops where an act could sell several thousand copies of a single and not be counted by the official charts. The idea of a distribution cartel started to take shape in Edwards' mind during 1981, however it was summer 1982 that the plan really came together. The first labels approached were Service in Altrincham and Red Rhino in York. *"Factory Records were obviously mad, so I didn't think it was a good idea to use them in that area"* claimed Richard Scott from Rough Trade. The idea was to carve up the country into different regions and make a shop / label responsible for each one. They would all agree to stock new records from each other, providing an instant distribution network independent of the major labels. Revolver in Bristol, Probe in Liverpool, Backs in Norwich, and Fast in Edinburgh signed up, and suddenly any act that received a play on the John Peel Show could have their record in shops nationwide within a couple of weeks.

Of course, any company run as a collective by former hippies, was always going to encounter several moral difficulties. Everything being decided by massive meetings led to one particularly difficult gathering where four hours was spent debating if it was okay to call record sales *units*, or if this was too corporate and capitalist.

SEPTEMBER

29th August – 5th September 1982

#1 single: Survivor: Eye of the Tiger

#1 album: The Kids From Fame: The Kids From Fame

It was almost certain Vince Clarke never meant to form a band with Alison Moyet, however when debut single *Only You* reached a greater chart position than anything Depeche Mode had released, Yazoo became the principal concern of Mute Records. Fortunately, they had a follow-up prepared in the shape of *Don't Go*, faster in pace and written in a minor key, adding to the sense of restlessness of dependence touched upon by the lyrics, with Moyet's blues-yearning voice driving home the desperation.

One of the benefits of being on a small label was that Yazoo were left alone to present themselves in whatever way they desired: no-one ever fashioned them or communicated to them what to say or how to stand on *Top of the Pops*. For their first performance on the show, Moyet's mother had to lend her £30 so that she could go to Basildon market and buy material to create a dress. It was this combination of Clarke's flawless pop tunes and the accessibility of everywoman Moyet that made Yazoo so alluring to many, helping the single climb into the top ten in most countries in Europe, as well as Australia and New Zealand, peaking at number three in Britain.

Whilst clambering unexpectedly to the top five with their first two singles, Yazoo were also busy recording an album. Despite album being made before the duo had even had a pint together, they had written and recorded the tracks without discussing the songs, each instinctively knowing was needed to make them work.

The album was full of classic synth-pop songs, but what was extraordinary is how many of them were written by Moyet, who had no previous track record of song-writing. Of the ten tracks, four were by the singer and are more obviously driven by a vocal performance with a utilitarian synthesizer backing, the exception being *Didn't I Bring Your Love Down (Didn't I)* which allows itself space to be a song. The Clarke written tracks, especially the two previously released singles, were themselves much more song based with a perfect mix of vocals and instrumentation.[485]

The album was recorded at Eric Radcliffe's first floor Blackwing Studios in London, from which it took its name, *Upstairs at Eric's*. Despite two hit singles, Yazoo had to take second place to fellow Mute Records act Fad Gadget who were booked to record from mid-day onwards, meaning it was recorded during mornings over several weeks and produced by Radcliffe instead of label boss Daniel Miller, who did not seem to rate the lightness of Yazoo.

---

[485] One song on the album was called *Tuesday* and had been written by Clarke a few years earlier for a previous band. At the time he called the songs after the day he wrote them, and *Tuesday* had originally been called *Thursday*.

There was a simplicity to the sound with Clarke utilising the newly released Roland MC-4 Microcomposer, which in the days before MIDI was considered one of the most accurate electronic instruments when it came to timekeeping. Clarke loved the limitations of this instrument so much that he returned to using it with Erasure in the 1990's.

As the summer ended, the album rose to the second position in the album charts.

ʊ ʊ ʊ

During his first month after release from prison Lenny Murphy went about the business of rebuilding his violent Shankill Butchers gang in Belfast, whilst the UVF, with whom he was still associated, became increasingly worried about him. The organisation was more structured than before, and with his psychopathic tendencies knowing no boundaries, Murphy was now operating outside their control. He was not tackled, however, as many within the organisation feared him and any violent action he would potentially take when given criticism.

Murphy still needed money upon his release and within a couple of weeks had decided to extort it from local businesses. First port of call was a shopkeeper on Oldpark Road who had previously been forced to pay a monthly "*protection*" fee. Murphy explained forcefully that as he had been in prison the shopkeeper was now owing the past six years of money, however with new protection in place with the UVF the proprietor refused to pay. Murphy left the premises furious and drove to a field on a mountainside near Hightown Road where he shot two horses belonging to the store owner. Sources at the time also claimed he chopped off their heads as a clear and clichéd message.

Murphy had always been known to take the law into his own hands and did this again on Sunday 29th August when he asked UVF member Jim Galway to accompany him to source a place to bury a weapon. Upon arriving at a building site in Broughshane, Murphy shot Galway in the back of the head then buried him ten feet down. The body was not found for over a year, with the official story being that Galway had gone on a two-week holiday and never returned.

ʊ ʊ ʊ

Whilst Yazoo quietly worked at their debut album, label mates Depeche Mode had spent the summer recording their second album in London with Daniel Miller producing.

 Newly recruited keyboard player Alan Wilder was informed at the beginning that he would not be needed for the recording, but to hang around for the subsequent world tour. When the album was released in October, *A Broken Frame* captured the band at a crossroads, undecided which direction to take. What was certain is that new songwriter Martin Gore was keen to move away from the straight-up pop of Vince Clarke, and even from the first couple of singles he himself composed earlier in the year, even though they had become top twenty hits. The third single from the forthcoming album, *Leave in Silence*, saw Depeche Mode move into a minor key for the first time, a place they would become increasingly comfortable in over the years.

Leave in Silence may have been mid-paced but it kept one eye on the dancefloor, driven by an incessant beat with industrial undertones and a *Franciscan monk* chant. Dave Gahan's vocals remained further back in the mix than they should have been, an indication he was still not entirely as confident as a frontman as he would later become. Lyrically, the song has been interpreted in several ways over the years. The first is a claim by Gore that it was influenced by the Falklands War and his disgust at the British government, of which upon inspection there is little evidence. A more likely reading is the obvious one; the song was dealing with the end of a particularly unhealthy relationship, one where the singer *"can't stand this emotional violence"*. Given Gore's split from his fiancé Anne Swindell at the start of summer, this seems the most likely interpretation. A third explanation which has been put forward relates to the departure of Vince Clark almost a year previous, who had offered them a final song before leaving, more than likely out of guilt. The band chose not to accept the track, preferring him to *leave in silence* instead. Whatever one of the three you choose to go with, Depeche Mode were now making steps towards Gore's vision of the band, one which would take them to crepuscular musical depths and greater heights of worldwide success by the end of the decade.

The cover of the single was one of the first deliberate steps the band by the act to be taken more seriously, employing Martyn Atkins to design it. At the time Atkins was also designing for Echo & the Bunnymen as well as Factory Records, and it was hoped that his hipness would rub off on the band.

ʊ ʊ ʊ

One of the last members of the PLO to leave Lebanon was leader Yasser Arafat, who boarded the Greek vessel *Atlantis* on Monday 30th August. After ten years building an infrastructure in the country, the PLO were now scattered across various nations, which would make organisation almost impossible over the next few years. Arafat's first port of call was Athens rather than one of his Arab neighbours who had proved lukewarm in their support, and certainly not to Syria, whose leader Hafez al-Assad had refused to even take telephone calls from him during the darkest days in Beirut. With Egypt at peace with Israel, and General Ghaddafi of Libya urging the PLO leadership to commit group suicide rather than surrender Beirut, Arafat eventually moved further along the Mediterranean to Tunisia, whilst other members of the organisation were evacuated to Jordan, Sudan, and Yemen.

Upon arriving in Athens, Arafat was visited by the Jordanian Foreign Minister, who delivered an offer by King Hussein to set up a joint diplomatic approach on either side of the River Jordan. With the threat of Israeli expansion, Hussein was keen to create a Palestinian buffer between themselves on the west bank of the river. When Arafat hesitated, and then asked for amendments to the deal, Hussein was furious and nothing came of the plan.

At the same time, President Reagan made a peace proposal which involved the Israelis agreeing not to create any more settlements in the disputed territories. The Israelis spent two minutes looking at the proposal before rejecting it.

ʊ ʊ ʊ

By 1982 only Gary Numan's fanbase was buying his releases, and whilst this guaranteed them a brief visit to the top forty, no one else really cared. Over the summer the pasty-faced singer had released a couple of preview singles from his next album, *I Assassin*. *We Take Mystery (To Bed)* mixed Numan's newly discovered love of jazz and an unequivocal funk sound, obvious that a song was missing amongst the glissading fretless bass and spasmodic overwrought keyboards, reminiscent of Simple Minds at their most grandiose. Vocally, Numan was at the height of his obsession with David Sylvian, and whilst the lyrics only flirted with meaning, specifically his former relationship with a woman who then sold the story to the press, ultimately conceit won out. This was funk without soul, music that did not convince you of *authenticity*. You simply did not believe that Numan meant a single word he was singing. *White Boys & Heroes* was another wedge of unconvincing sinuous funk and turned out to be an accurate adumbration of the album released in October. *"I Assassin was the second worst album I ever had, so it went pretty bad, pretty quick"* Numan would later reason, and by the end of the year he was living as a tax exile in Los Angeles with a house next door to actor George Peppard.[486]   Numan kicked off a musically successful but financially draining American tour[487] organised by Miles Copeland, which worked its way through eighteen clubs during October and November, with even the small venues

failing to sell out. The proposed second part of the tour through Japan, Canada, Australia, and the Far East was scrapped, as Numan chose to start work on a new album. Numan's conservative instincts chimed with the national mood in the United States, and he found himself attracted to gun ownership, at one point aiming a repeating shotgun at a Smash Hits interviewer and declaring *"Did you know that at this distance I could cut you clean in half with just one bullet?"*

His label Beggars Banquet were keen to release *The 1930's Rust* as a single, a total change in direction with a jazz – blues feel and harmonica and saxophone, however Numan refused. Instead, the label teamed up with Palace Video and released a VHS *Greatest Hits* called *Newman Numan*, which angered fans by not featuring the full promotional videos, cutting away to interviews or footage of the singer flying a plane instead.

"There was a general decline for the next ten years," he explained, *"Each album did worse than the one before. The tours were getting harder to sell... so it was increasingly demoralising and desperate as the years went by."* Numan's popularity continued to fade as the 1980's progressed, and he had become a forgotten figure, one of scornful ridicule when his music was rediscovered in the late 1990's by American hard-core industrial acts, not least Nine Inch Nails, and then by dance acts such as Basement Jaxx, who sampled *M.E.* for their hit *Where's Your Head At.* Suddenly, everyone was claiming that they had always loved Numan's futuristic stylings, and he became the latest influential godfather of something or other.

ʊ ʊ ʊ

When Dire Straits delivered their new album to Vertigo Records in June, the label must have been scratching their heads how to promote it. With only five songs spread over forty-one minutes, none of which promised much commercially, there was consternation as to how *Love Over Gold* was ever going to get radio play. Even on songs such as opening track *Telegraph Road*, where frontman and songwriter Mark Knopfler tapped into Springsteen-esque vibes, the length of almost fifteen minutes precluded it as an obvious single. Instead, the record company decided to lead with the second track, *Private Investigations*, which itself was over six minutes long.

Starting from finger-picked acoustic guitar and flamenco flourishes, Knopfler mumbled Raymond Chandler-affected lines under descending chords, before the song changed

---

[486] Peppard once stated that his entire movie career had been spent *"charging up a hill saying 'Follow me, men! This way!'"*

[487] This was his first after announcing a *"retirement"* from live work.

pitch half-way through, bringing in distorted guitar and keyboards for an instrumental finish. This was not the sort of stuff hits were made from in 1982, and yet the single peaked at number two, the biggest chart success of their career, even topping the charts in the Netherlands.

When they formed in London in 1977 Dire Straits had been the antidote to the new wave that many craved, which given that most music listeners deplored punk was a wise move. Specialising in old-fashioned solid song writing and musical ability, the band hit the charts immediately with *Sultans of Swing*, before being rather oddly paired with Talking Heads on tour.

Love Over Gold was their fourth album, and with only two tracks on side one, the flip side went one better with three, the first of which *Industrial Disease* played upon a strong Bob Dylan influence to provide a Canadian top ten single. The whole album was *serious* song writing as a honed craft, taking great care in preserving maturity at the expense of stimulation and fun. Knopfler also held back his recently written commercial track from the album, preferring to keep *Private Dancer* for Tina Turner. Despite the seeming lack of commercial prospects, the album became Dire Straits' most successful album to date, topping the charts across the world.

ʊ ʊ ʊ

Labour leader Michael Foot was a regular face at demonstration marches, and on Friday 3rd September at a Peace and Disarmament rally in Bristol, he chose to deliver a speech as well. Within his address Foot confirmed that any future Labour government would scrap Trident and Cruise missiles, and would not allow American missiles to be staged on British soil. His belief in such a measure was based upon a meeting in Moscow with Breshnev the previous year at which the Russian premier offered to remove their own SS20 missiles from Eastern Europe. As a founder member of CND Foot had fought against the nuclear threat his entire life, and now he might have the chance to do something about it he was not going to let the opportunity pass.

ʊ ʊ ʊ

Apple Computers were starting to bring in serious money in the early 1980's and rather than pay taxes to the American government founder Steve Wozniak[488] decided he would rather stage a rock festival as a tax loss. A location was chosen just outside San Bernadino in California, and the ground prepared for three days over the Labor Day Weekend. Friday 3rd September was deemed *new wave day* with The Gang of Four, The Ramones, The Beat, Oingo Boingo, The B-52's, Talking Heads, and The Police thrilling the revellers in 43°C heat. With the taxman's loss footing the bill, no expense was spared as all bands were individually helicoptered onto the site to play to almost half-a-million people. Over the next two nights older bands took over, with

---

[488] Wozniak was going through something of a second adolescence following an airplane crash during which he suffered five-week amnesia.

performances by The Kinks, The Cars, Tom Petty & the Heartbreakers, The Grateful Dead, Jackson Brown, and Fleetwood Mac[489].

5th – 11th September 1982

#1 single: Survivor: Eye of the Tiger
#1 album: The Kids From Fame: The Kids From Fame

Scritti Politti launched another assault on the top forty with the release of *Asylums in Jerusalem* in August, backed with *Jacques Derrida* which had a hint of Marc Bolan in the vocals, over a country bass line and soulful female backing vocals. The a-side concerned itself with the extra lunatic asylums required to be built in the Holy city to house the increasing number of religious fanatics claiming to be prophets in the wake of Jesus, however this being Scritti Politti, it took a stance from the writings of Friedrich Nietzsche. The single paused just outside the top forty, forcing the album *Songs to Remember* to be released in September without a hit. Rough Trade did not have the necessary financial clout to push Scritti Politti into the upper reaches of the singles charts, or enough money to make expensive promotional videos, however Peter Walmsley from the company did

say "*more money was spent on* [them] *than was probably sensible, at the time. We had no magic formula, no guarantee any of it would work*". Head of the label, Geoff Travis, knew the next album was going to have to be a larger production, and therefor hooked up Gartside with Bob Last, the Scottish manager of the Human League and Heaven 17. At first Last was not interested, considering Scritti Politti to be anti-commercial, stating "*refuseniks did not interest me*". Travis then played a song they had recorded with Nile Rodgers from Chic and imparted the information that they were ready to make the "*most glossy records anyone on the planet was making*". Now, this was something Last could get behind: subversion from within. Last claimed "*There were more working-class people listening to* [glossy pop records] *and having their heads turned by them than there were people buying and being influenced by self-consciously revolutionary records*".

The bottom line was that *Songs to Remember* was simply too spartan: there may have been dazzling intellectual pop at the core of the melodies, however having been recorded between 1980 and 1981 their lack of gloss and ambition of sound was just too out-of-step with public taste in 1982. Post-Falklands, people wanted to party and celebrate goal-orientated initiative, not discuss philosophy and wallow in self-reflection. To break into the singles charts, which Scritti Politti did with the songs from their next album *Cupid and Psyche '85*, they needed to dream bigger. Gartside disbanded the act, keeping the name for himself, and moved to New York to immerse himself in hip-hop and black R&B, whilst signing to a major label.

℧ ℧ ℧

---

[489] Fleetwood Mac were paid $500,000 for their appearance, the equivalent of $1,300,000 today.

Upon his release from prison, Shankill Butcher leader Lenny Murphy needed a form of transport, and agreed to buy a yellow Rover from Brian Smyth, a Protestant Belfast car dealer. By Sunday 5th September Murphy had still not paid Smyth for the car when the dealer ran into him in a Belfast Club. Smyth made the mistake of reminding the psychopathic Murphy of the debt, and within a couple of hours had his drink poisoned. Asking a couple of friends to take him to the nearby Mater Hospital, the three piled into a car, but on the way to hospital were joined by a motorcyclist who fired eight shots into the car, killing Smyth.

Murphy had made his point: he expected to be given anything he wanted without question or payment.

℧ ℧ ℧

With the promotion of Phil Collins from drummer to singer in the band Genesis, and his subsequent commercial success, record companies began looking for material he had previously been involved with. Brand X were a jazz fusion act who had existed between 1975 and 1980, featuring a range of top musicians, amongst them the balding drummer. During the recording of their 1979 album *Product*, the band built up a significant collection of outtakes, which were then compiled into the posthumous release, *Is There Anything About* in 1982.

The band featured Robin Lumley[490] and Raphael Ravenscroft[491], however the real selling point was Collins, who's name helped the album reach number ninety-three in the charts.

September was proving to be a busy chart month for other various members and ex-members of Genesis, with guitarist Mike Rutherford releasing his second solo album. *Acting Very Strange* was the only album to feature lead vocals by Rutherford, a move which he immediately regretted, realising the limitations of his own voice. The album featured drums by former Glitter Band member Peter Phipps (on his way to joining XTC) and The Police's Stewart Copeland (who met Rutherford when they were in the same polo team), as well as saxophone by Gary Barnacle, who was legally obliged to play on every record in the 1980's. Rutherford was helped in the production by Nick Launey and Howard Gray, both of whom had cut their teeth in punk and new wave, which may account for the

rawer sound of the album. Afterwards, despite reaching number twenty-three, Rutherford lost confidence in his ability to sing, and formed Mike + the Mechanics for future solo work, claiming "*I had a revelation… that I'm not complete on my own. I'm much more creative and inspired when there are people around me and I'm bouncing ideas off.*"

---

[490] Lumley has a rather more famous cousin in the shape of Joanna.

[491] Despite the amusing myth that television host Bob Holness played the saxophone on Gerry Rafferty's *Baker Street*, it was Ravenscroft. There is even a myth about how the myth came about: journalist Stuart Maconie claims to have made up the story for a spoof feature in the NME in 1990, DJ Tommy Boyd claims to have made up the story as a *True or False* question in a quiz years before, whilst Ravenscroft claimed to have started the rumour after working on a Robinson's advert with Holness. Here is a true story about Bob Holness: He was the second ever person to play James Bond.

Meanwhile, former Genesis singer Peter Gabriel[492] released his fourth album, and also his fourth album called *Peter Gabriel*. Known by his fans as Peter Gabriel Four: Security, the album was recorded completely digitally utilising a mobile studio outside the singer's home in Somerset.

As usual Gabriel took a cerebral approach to his music and lyrics, whilst increasing his interest in what would soon be known as *world music*. On opening track *The Rhythm*

of the Heat, he exploited African percussion in response to Swiss psychiatrist Carl Jung's experience of tribal ritual. His empathy with other cultures was furthered on *San Jacinto* which explored Native American rituals celebrating the journey to manhood. The most commercial track on the album was *Shock the Monkey*, an abstract non-linear musing on jealousy which was released as a single in September but stalled at number fifty-eight in the United Kingdom. The album fared better, peaking at number six. Meanwhile, his old band Genesis were filling the time between studio albums by releasing *3 Sides Live*, an album of concert recordings from the past five years. The album reflected their post-Gabriel output which was slowly moving in a pop direction. Tony Banks explained this decision, saying "*It would be easy for us to just go out and do a rehash of the stuff we were doing in the early seventies because there's still a big market for that... it's more of a challenge to do a few different things that we didn't do around that time.*" He would go on to lay the change of direction at the feet of Phil Collins, claiming "*He has a very good feel for the simpler side of music.*"

1982 was a fertile time for the Norwich music scene, with the leaders of the pack being The Higsons, formed at the University of East Anglia a couple of years previously by Charlie Higson, Terry Edwards, Simon Carterton, Colin Williams, and Stuart McGeachin. Specialising in agitated punk-influenced funk, The Higsons released a smattering of singles on Norwich based Waap Records, before signing to Two-Tone in summer 1982. On the up at the same time were The Farmer's Boys, locals who had also released their first couple of singles on Waap Records and Backs Records earlier in the year.[493] The Farmer's Boys

had a more acoustic pop sound which would be most obviously influential on The Housemartins later in the decade.

Both acts often found themselves on the same bill, and in September they both produced sessions for the John Peel show. At the same time, The Higsons released a single produced in Coventry by Jerry Dammers of The Specials, called *Tear the Whole Thing Down*, watered down from the original title of *Burn the Whole Thing Down Before the Yanks Do*. By now, Two-Tone Records were waning, having lost The Selecter, The Beat, Madness, and most of The Specials, as well as finding no new successful acts.

---

[492] Gabriel wrote his first song when he was twelve years old. It was called *Sammy the Slug*.

[493] Waap and Backs were ostensibly the same label, running out of the Backs Record store in Norwich.

Founding act The Specials, now returning to their original name of The Special AKA, released another uncomfortable single in the shape of *War Crimes*. Written by Jerry Dammers as a critique of Israel's actions in Lebanon, the song made a comparison

between the concentration camps and extermination of the Second World War, and modern-day Beirut, asking *"was nothing learned?"* With such a controversial subject matter, it became impossible to hear the song, prompting Dammers to claim *"I wish they'd ban our songs, but they don't – they just ignore them"*. Not that he would have it any other way, later claiming *"We made* [War Crimes] *because we felt you have to make a point, and sometimes you have to sacrifice commercial success in order to get that point across."*

Once again, Dammers had nailed an essential message at a vital time, and it gave him the inspiration to continue with The Special AKA. Over the next couple of years, they worked on their third album, *In the Studio*, which spawned the single *Free Nelson Mandela*. For many, this was their first exposure to the fate of Mandela and was instrumental in raising awareness of the anti-apartheid movement, so much so that Dammers was honoured with the South African Order of the Companions of O.R. Tambo award by the South African nation in 2014[494].

Meanwhile, back in East Anglia, despite critical acclaim and The Farmer's Boys signing to EMI, success eluded the local bands, and by 1986 they had both split. Higsons frontman Charlie Higson moved to London where he shared a flat with Harry Enfield and old friend Paul Whitehouse, working as painters and decorators[495] whilst writing comedy, a job which provided the inspiration for Enfield's breakthrough character of *Loadsofmoney*. Higson and Whitehouse eventually found their own comedy success in front of the camera with *The Fast Show*, and even back in 1982 he was proclaiming *"I'd much rather be a writer than a singer. I've still no ambition to be a pop star... it just seemed like there was nothing better to do at the time."*

ʊ ʊ ʊ

ABC had one more single to release from their phenomenally successful album *The Lexicon of Love*, and they had saved their lushest sounding song for last. *All of my*

Heart was a towering string-soaked ballad telling a dramatic tale of lost love. Fry later called it their *Bridge Over Troubled Water* moment, however it started much smaller as he explained, *"It was like a country and western song, in the sense that it's a bit of a tearjerker, but obviously we wanted to make it sound more grandiose, widescreen and cinematic"*, and certainly by the time Trevor Horn and Anne Dudley had finished, it was as anthemic as Simon & Garfunkel. Dudley initially did not even like the song, reckoning it to be a bit weak, until a final overlong dramatic pause was added near the end

after which Fry spoke the title and timpani drums led into what Dudley called her *"English pastoral moment"*, an elongated orchestral fade-out that was amongst some

---

[494] Dammers is in good company here, alongside Mahatma Gandhi, Martin Luther King, Jessie Jackson, and Harry Belafonte.

[495] They decorated a house shared by Stephen Fry and Hugh Laurie.

of the most elegant music of the year. The band did receive some stick for releasing four singles from the same album, a move which would go unquestioned in future years.

Fry later explained "*We recorded the strings at Abby Road* [Studios]. *Trevor said that of we added full orchestra it would go to number one. He gave me an IOU for a million pounds as a guarantee. The single got to number six so I never got to cash it in.*"

When *All of my Heart* climbed into the top ten it hung around for a few weeks, just as "*The Look of Love*" started to bother the American Billboard Hot 100. The band put together a sixteen-piece band and orchestra, then set out on the road touring the album through Europe, the United States, and Japan. After the last date Dave Palmer jumped ship to join The Yellow Magic Orchestra, whilst Fry tore up his gold lamè suit and flushed it down a hotel room toilet.

Upon their return to Sheffield, ABC found that the rules of the game had changed. What had started out as role-playing had become the norm in the music industry, as other acts such as Spandau Ballet stole the suits and strings wholesale. It was all very well pretending to be suave, sophisticated, and loaded, however when you returned to your northern homeland and saw the devastation of Margaret Thatcher's policies on a former industrial heartland, and the poverty and desperation that ensued, suddenly your fake aspiration did not seem so shrewd.

ABC, however, had a final folly from *The Lexicon of Love* to indulge in. Given the albums cinematic debt, it was only natural the band would move into film. With punk film-maker Julian Temple on board as director, the result was *Mantrap*, a cold war spy thriller / live-concert footage mash-up. The film is a curiosity; at just under an hour long it was too short to qualify as a feature movie and given that the album and all singles had already been released, was too lavish and expensive to act as an elongated promotional video. The plot involved Martin Fry being set up to be recruited as the singer of a band (ABC) about to embark on a European tour. The acting is understated, closer to the level the Shadows managed in *Summer Holiday* in the early 1960's, and the plot does not quite hang together as much as the band hoped, however there is some great live concert footage, and you have to admire the ambition.

1983 saw ABC retreat from the glamour of *The Lexicon of Love* and record their second album *Beauty Stab* with session musicians. Trevor Horn was gone from the production role, to be replaced by his former assistant Gary Langan, and guitars were brought to the front. This album was a deliberate attempt by the band to redress the criticism that had been lowered at them by the music press that they were nothing more than a lightweight pop band, *walking haircuts*, but it fell miserably short, lacking the charisma or class of their debut. One by one the members left, but not before Fry had been diagnosed with, and recovered from, Hodgkin Lymphoma, and they hit the top ten again with a Motown pastiche, produced by Chic bass player Bernard Edwards, called *When Smokey Sings*.

ʊ ʊ ʊ

As Malcolm McLaren and Trevor Horn entered the final stages of recording their album, the World-Famous Supreme Team flew to London to provide the glue which was meant to hold everything together. The duo were hardened hustlers, working as pickpockets in Times Square by day, and quickly began making demands for specific pieces of equipment such as the most expensive turntable.

The duo of Divine and Justice had been brought over for their scratching skills, dropping the needle onto a vinyl record and moving it backwards and forwards at high speed. McLaren, art-school trained, loved the idea that old art would be recycled to create a sonic collage, but left the creative decisions up to Horn.

At first, they tried to get the duo to re-create their radio show in the studio, however they insisted that they needed a vinyl copy of the recorded tracks to scratch, and so one-off copies of each song was pressed onto seven-inch singles, at great expense. With Anne Dudley adding strings to the music, the duo took great pleasure in ripping up a song called *Duck for the Oyster*, a barn-dance they described as "*Ku Klux Klan shit*".

After a couple of weeks, the Supreme Team attempted to blackmail Horn, refusing to appear on the album unless McLaren made them the stars. What they were recording in London lacked the magic and sparkle of their New York radio shows, and engineer Gary Langan realised they could just use the cassette version recorded from the radio a few months previously.

ʊ ʊ ʊ

Captain Sensible's solo album *Women and Captains First* was finally released and entered the charts on the 5th September. The album was not a commercial success, only reaching number sixty-four: the people who bought novelty singles such as *Happy Talk* tended not to buy albums. However, if you looked beyond the first two singles and their novelty value, it was a collection of egregious songs, mixing Sensible's love of sixties psychedelia with eighties pop. At points owing a large debt to Syd Barrett's solo material, whilst sounding not unlike some of Julian Cope's later solo material, the album had a dexterous touch and assurance not to be expected from the guitarist in a punk band. The jewel in the crown was *Croydon*, a mid-paced slice of glorious pop with words by Sensible and music by ex-Soft Boys Robyn Hitchcock, which was only ruined by a lumpen drum machine-led production. Released as a failed single later in the year, Sensible looked back upon his youth at Stanley Technical School in the London Borough, comparing it to Los Angeles and deciding the wind and rain of England comes out on top. Hitchcock also co-wrote and added twelve-string guitar to *Brenda*, which producer Tony Mansfield attempted unsuccessfully to wrestle into a shorter pop style. If there is one album you never thought you would find yourself listening to after reading this book, it should be *Women and Captains First*. It is quite simply a mislaid paragon of intoxicating pop. Go and find it online right now.

ʊ ʊ ʊ

The self-named Neasden Queen of Soul Mari Wilson spent most of the year trying to make a breakthrough in pop music. Born to Scottish parents[496] in London twenty-eight years previously, Wilson was named *Miss Beehive 1981* by a London nightclub, styling herself as willingly stuck in the early 1960's, complete with a foot-high beehive hair-do. Inspired to "*be a singer like Judy Garland… but to dress like Shirley Bassey*", Wilson was asked by songwriter Tot Taylor to sing one of his songs, after which she recruited an eleven-piece backing band initially called The Imaginations who were forced to change their name to The Wilsations by the three-piece soul act. Consisting of six musicians and five backing singers, including future *Eastenders* actress Michelle

---

[496] Her brother was in a band with the surviving Badfinger members and wrote a couple of songs for Cliff Richard.

Collins[497], the band were given names rhyming with Mari (Harry, Barry, Larry, Gary[498], Cary... and Jim), and the highly entertaining and choreographed show was compered by someone called Hank. Whilst Wilson's ambition was to become the world's most famous diabetic, a sixty-date British tour was arranged for spring 1982, based upon the Motown revues from the 1960's. Previous singles *Beat the Beat* and *Baby, It's* True had failed to break through despite impeccable pop credentials, and it took Wilson's fifth single to finally achieve the hit she craved[499]. Claiming *"At the moment I'm a cult figure, but I don't know how much longer I want that to go on"*, new single *Just What I Always Wanted* was a song of aspiration, with the rejection of material goods serving as a sting in the chorus. Throughout the verses, Wilson listed things she has been offered for love, from a *taffeta dress*, *a pair of Picasso paintings*, *a mink from Paris* and *a ring from Rome*, however the chorus saw her choosing someone who does not *"give* [her] *anything... just yourself is good enough"*.

Written by 1960's obsessive Teddy Johns, the song toyed with vintage whilst also suffering from early 1980's production, especially with overloud and unnecessary

electronic drums, however it did manage to climb to number eight in the charts, helped by two wonderfully camp performances on *Top of the Pops*.[500]

By now various members of the band had been replaced (Though they oddly all had the same names as the previous members... Larry, Gary, Harry, etc.) and future solo star Julia Fordham had been added as a backing singer.

The single was to be the peak of Wilson's success, and she claimed that *"My records got played and* [lack of success] *wasn't because of the way I looked – they were good songs. But then* [Teddy] *ran out of steam – he was under too much pressure – and the second album never saw the light of day."* Despite a hit with a version of *Cry me a River* the following year, in 1985 Wilson walked away from her recording contract rather *"be moulded into a Hazel Dean clone"* and retreated to becoming a jazz singer in later years.

12ᵗʰ – 18ᵗʰ September 1982

#1 single: Survivor: Eye of the Tiger
#1 album: The Kids From Fame: The Kids From Fame

Depeche Mode may have been the biggest thing out of Basildon in 1982, however there was another quite different and less vaunted act in the shape of The Pinkees. Formed in 1979 and specialising in *power pop*, a form of back-to-basics guitar-based

---

[497] Aka Cindy Beale.

[498] "I only got where I am today because my name's Gary, and I know it" he claimed.

[499] The Daily Mail claimed *"Mari is dogged by the fact that her hairstyle has always been much bigger than her recording success"*.

[500] Wilson claimed at the time *"Diana Ross preaches love, I preach Tupperware"*.

music which looked to early Beatles, The Who, and The Byrds for inspiration, The Pinkees signed to Creole Records and released their second single in September.

Danger Games was an inconsequentially catchy number over and done with in under three minutes, with a nagging harmonica, guitar riff, and Beatles harmonies throughout. There was some controversy when it placed in the top forty, with accusations of chart-rigging and suspicious sales patterns, as other charts did not feature it at all, however once the band had performed on *Top of the Pops*, the single climbed to peak at number eight.

It was to be the only hit for the band, who fell apart when one of their members proved not very keen to go full time, but for a month or so their early-Beatles-with-mullet-haircuts, Rickenbacker guitars, and Squeeze-lite harmonies caught the public's taste for a little bit of Merseybeat magic which surrounded the twentieth anniversary of the original Fab Four.

ʊ ʊ ʊ

New York artists experiencing success in the Billboard Dance Charts as well as on the floors of clubs in their home city found they could have extend their prosperity in the United Kingdom, with former *Shaffer Beer Girl* and Bette Midler backing singer Sharon Redd taking the single *Never Going to Give You Up* to number twenty, duo Raw Silk hitting number eighteen with *Do It To The Music*, and the Peech Boys stumbling just outside the top forty with *Don't Make We Wait*, a track which predated the late 1980's dance music scene by over five years.

Meanwhile, Kool and the Gang celebrated their fourteenth album *As One* whilst in the middle of their most successful stretch, enjoying three top thirty hits throughout the year with *Big Fun*, *Let's Go Dancin' (Ooh La, La, La)*, and *Hi De Hi, Hi De Ho*. The album was their last with Brazilian producer Eumir Deodata[501], after which they would pursue a pop-influenced style, enjoying even greater success with hits such as *Cherish*, *Fresh*, and *Joanna*.

Former seventies disco diva and Broadway actress Melba Moore enjoyed a renaissance with the single *Love's Comin' at Ya'* which climbed to number fifteen, whilst another long-lasting act celebrated their greatest success.

Fat Larry's Band had been formed by drummer and singer Larry James, who had spent

the seventies as a session musician for Philadelphia soul acts The Delfonics and Blue Magic. Five albums in, nothing prepared the band for the scale of success the single *Zoom* generated for the band in the United Kingdom, as it climbed to number two over autumn.

The smooth soul of the track was irresistible, and although the band looked like a pastiche of refugees from a bygone disco and soul age, the music was timeless. Written by Philly soul producer Bobby Eli and former solo star Len Barry, the song also featured keyboards from new member, sixteen-year-old Bryan Hudson, who would later go on to write worldwide chart-topper *Do the Bartman*. It was to be the peak of Fat Larry's Band's career, and five years later Larry died of a heart attack at the age of thirty-eight.

---

[501] Deodata is the father-in-law of actor Stephen Baldwin, and grandfather-in-law of Justin Bieber.

ʊ ʊ ʊ

Jean-Michel Basquiat continued his rise in the New York art world, having been taken on as a client by respected agent Bruno Bischofberger. In September he was flown to Zurich, where Bischofberger collected him from the airport and drove him directly to the gallery. Immediately he told the jetlagged artist "*There's a couch if you want to lie down, but here's some canvases. I have people coming over to watch you paint*".
With tears in his eyes and a critic's description of "*a child of the streets gawked at by the intelligentsia*" in his mind, Basquiat began painting, keen to keep Bischofberger on his side because the agent also represented his hero, Andy Warhol.

ʊ ʊ ʊ

After a summer writing and recording his first solo album, Adam Ant was ready to release a new single. Written with tried-and-tested partner Marco Pirroni, *Friend of Foe* harked back to the drum-driven sound of the *Kings of the Wild Frontier* album, but with added horns provided by Geoff Daly and Martin Drover. Over the familiar tribal drums and spaghetti western guitar riff, the song set out Adam's approach to the press and public, demanding a reaction of some sort, with a chorus of "*I want those who get to*

know me to become admirers or my enemies*". A key change in the middle eight revealed a certain amount of self-awareness, as he proclaimed "*When you're a pirouetting, high-kicking, thigh-slapping cruiser... you have to be careful*".
As the song rose to number nine in the British charts, many of Adam's fans expressed their disappointment, feeling the single was straying too far away from the sound they loved.
For the first time Adam did not use his usual video director, Mike Mansfield, choosing instead to do everything himself, with varying degrees of success. Afterwards Mansfield wrote a letter explaining all the areas where he had got it wrong, and for the next single was back on board.

ʊ ʊ ʊ

Four days after the international peace keeping forces left Lebanon, elected President-in-waiting Bashir Gemayel spent the afternoon of Tuesday 14th September in Aschrafieh saying goodbye to the Lebanese Forces, of whom he had been leader for the past few years. Gemayel felt it was important that as President he separated himself from the military, for reasons of independence.
Just after 4 p.m. a bomb exploded in the headquarters, killing many of the people in the room. News spread that Gemayel had been taken by ambulance to hospital in Haifa, which was then changed to being taken by helicopter. The next rumour was that he had escaped the blast, but no-one knew where he now was. Finally, five hours later, an unidentified body was confirmed to be the President, being so severely damaged that it could only be identified by his wedding ring.
The day before, Habib Shartouni, a member of the Syrian Nationalist Party, had visited his sister who lived in the room above where Gemayel was due to meet. He secretly planted a bomb, and then the following day phoned his sister at 4 p.m. telling her to get out before detonating the bomb remotely from a few miles away. Shartouni was arrested when he returned to the scene of the crime to check his sister had escaped, immediately confessing, and stating Gemayel had "*Sold the country to Israel*". As many

Lebanese continued to believe the immortal Gemayel was not dead but merely gone to later return, the Phalangists did not execute the culprit. How could they shoot someone for murdering a man most did not believe was dead?

ʊ ʊ ʊ

U2 had taken a couple of weeks off writing their next album in August to allow singer Bono to marry his childhood sweetheart, Alison Stewart. The newlyweds went on honeymoon to Jamaica, and the others went on vacation, with guitarist The Edge stayed at home and worked on his guitar parts, making significant breakthroughs in moulding the sound that would become synonymous with U2 throughout the 1980's. Whilst drummer Larry Mullen Jnr and Bono had fallen away from their religious calling Shalom, unable to reconcile that it *"would be a very unusual, maybe even perverse, God that would ask you to deny your gift"*, The Edge still had serious doubts.

Upon reconvening at Windmill Studios in Dublin in September with regular producer Steve Lillywhite, the band were ready for action and began recording tracks immediately, motivated by a £2000-per-day studio fee when they had little financial backing from their record company. One track, *New Year's Day*, started off as a love song written by Bono for his new wife, but ended up as being vaguely about the recent Solidarity movement in Poland[502]. *Sunday Bloody Sunday* dealt with the situation in Northern Ireland, and featured not only a memorable guitar riff, but the rarest of things: a drum line that was a hook itself[503]. When Kid Creole and the Coconuts swung through town on tour, U2 befriended the Coconuts, Cherly Poirier, Adriana Kaegi, Taryn Hagey, and Jessica Felton, and the night ended with everyone drunk, back in the studios, recording backing vocals for three songs.

The rhythm section of the band had tightened up in the past year as well, with Mullen being forced to play to a click track for the first time. Bass player Adam Clayton was back in favour with the band, having come precariously close to being kicked out for following a standard rock and roll lifestyle instead of the Christian abstinence of the others, and being unexpectedly asked to be best man at Bono's wedding had gone a long way to patching everything up.

By the end of October, the album was complete and U2 set out on a warm-up jaunt around Britain, preparing the new songs for the following year's mammoth world tour. The first single from the album, *New Year's Day*, was released in January 1983, finally providing them with a major British hit single, whilst the album followed within a month and topped the charts at home as well as becoming massive elsewhere around the world. However, it was the subsequent year-long tour that broke U2 as nation after nation succumbed to their powerful and passionate live performances. Everything that people love U2 for could be found in these shows, however they were also the things that people hated the band for: taking themselves too seriously, performing at a level of passion that seemed too forced, engaging in political rabble-rousing, verging on the edge of Christian rock.

The year could easily have been the end of U2, however a break whilst the shiny commercial pop filled the charts allowed them to return with what they would have considered *authentic* music and conquer the world. 1982 was simply a pause for breath.

---

[502] The song was driven forward by a bass line written by Adam Clayton when he was trying to work out how to play *Fade to Gray* by Visage.

[503] *Sunday Bloody Sunday* featured local violinist Steve Wickham who had approached The Edge at a bus stop and insisted that U2 needed a violinist. Wickham would later join The Waterboys and provide the joyful fiddle on *Fisherman's Blues*.

ʊ ʊ ʊ

After two flop singles, Culture Club were given a final chance to fulfil their potential. *Do You Really want to Hurt Me* had been written in May when Boy George started singing along to an old Studio One dub recording. Taking the song into the next rehearsal, bass player Mikey was delighted to be on home territory with some lover's rock. The song was recorded live in the studio and immediately sounded superior to everything else on the album. It was for this track that Helen Terry[504] was brought in on vocals to add more sensuousness to the sound. Producer Steve Levine was horrified afterwards to discover the tape machine was running slow, but the band refused to re-record the track as the introduction was too high for George to sing again.

The record company were convinced the song was a hit, however George dug his heels in, feeling the lyrical content was too personal, betraying a direct message to his lover, drummer Jon Moss. A Rasta called Papa Weasel was brought in, to chat over a dub version on the b-side, and insisted his name be left off the credits for fear of being associated with "*a batty boy*".

Do You Really Want to Hurt Me crept into the charts at number sixty-six on 12th September, a week after release, despite being roundly savaged by the music press, and being told by BBC Radio 1 that "*We don't interview transvestites*". It was picked

up, however, by David Hamilton on Radio 2, who made it *Single of the Week* on what at the time was a moribund and middle-aged station. This was enough to push the single just inside the top forty, too low to appear on *Top of the Pops* until Shakin' Stevens pulled out and a replacement was needed at the last minute. Exposing Culture Club, and more significantly Boy George, to twelve million people across the nation, the performance was a revelation[505]. The talk in the playground the following day included the line "*What was that?*" repeated, as teenagers tried to work out how they felt about the whole thing. Fleet

Street sat up and took notice, with the headline "*Is it a boy or is it a girl*" and began a love affair with George that would last decades.

The androgyny of Boy George fit into a long British tradition much more than it did in many other parts of the world, including the United States. From the chopped spiked hair of female punks, back through the make-up and cross-dressing of glam rock, past the long hair of The Rolling Stones, who themselves dragged up for *Have You Seen Your Mother Standing in the Shadows*, back to the pantomime dame. It was all good old-fashioned fun, and everything was acceptable as long as we did not talk of sexuality. This was especially true in music, where the public overlooked the obvious in performers such as Liberace, Little Richard, Dusty Springfield, Elton John, and Freddie Mercury, convincing themselves it was all part of the act. Even George had to tone it done publicly, famously claiming to prefer a cup of tea instead of sex, using his clothes and look to deflect from questions about his sexuality. The image was carefully cultivated to be something in between everything, neither male or female, not gay or straight, and George was complicit in reflecting a cuddlier image rather than the bitch-queen everyone in London knew him to be. Phil Oakey of the Human League once criticised the image of George at the expense of the music, saying "*Until he came along, if the record cover looked weird, the record was going to be a little more progressive,*

---

[504] Helen Terry had spent some time claiming to be the backing vocalist on Lou Reed's *Walk on the Wild Side*, a claim which fooled the band but was utterly unfounded.

[505] George appeared bare footed in homage to Sandie Shaw.

have a few more elements that you wouldn't quite expect". George himself had an alter-ego in the shape of Boy Georgina, a high-heel wearing bitch, which the band and management attempted to curb at every opportunity. George had started wearing his own clothes designs, which he created in conjunction with Sue Clowes, festooning them with religious symbols, the Star of David, the Christian cross, as well as hearts, flowers, and airplanes. This backfired in September following Israel's invasion of Lebanon, and he phoned up *Smash Hits* asking them to airbrush the Star of David from images of the band for fear that it had become a symbol of oppression.

As the year progressed George's clothes became less provocative, more asexual, as he started to wear what could only be called smocks. George had put on some weight and started dressing to cover the bulk, but this de-sexualising of George was also a deliberate move to throw people off the scent and managed to turn him into a loveable character, a cuddly toy who could appear on family television. Over the next couple of years, George was criticised by the gay community for not coming out, especially in the wake of Bronski Beat.

The rise of *Do You Really Want to Hurt Me* allowed the band to make a promotional video, directed by Julian Temple. Set initially in a courtroom, the clip showed George on trial, backed by three black backing singers and an awkward-to-modern-sensibilities jury of black and white minstrels. If we are being generous, we could take this as a statement of the white appropriation of black culture that was apparent in the dub vibes of the song. A cameo for his mother and Aunt Heather in the public gallery was not the last time they would support him in court, and from there we cut to a re-creation of the *Gargoyle Club, Soho, 1936*, the aristocrats' hang-out of choice between the wars, where George wandered round performing the song to shocked patrons, including friend and milliner Stephen Jones. The rest of the band backed him, focusing mostly on drummer Moss and guitarist Roy Hay, because Mikey Craig refused to turn up, suffering from the effects of a heavy ganga binge the previous night, and instead sent his brother to stand in on bass. Eventually, George was manhandled from the club by two bouncers.

Next, we visited the *Dolphin Square Health Club, 1957*, a swimming pool set amongst the exclusive Dolphin Square apartments in London where the likes of Harold Wilson, Oswald Mosley, David Steel, William Hague, call-girls Mandy Rice-Davies and Christine Keeler had lived, and where Carl Beech later famously and falsely claimed a paedophile ring was operated by the establishment. In the video, George emerged from the swimming pool to walk amongst people sitting at the side, flirting with the half-naked young men, whilst disgusting the older patrons. Finally, the verdict is in, and he is found guilty and led off to prison, like Oscar Wilde being taken to Reading Gaol.

The lyrics dealt with his affair with Jon Moss, a rich Jewish drummer boy who was in love with George but did not consider himself to be gay, and certainly did not want his family finding out. From the opening line of *"Give me time to realise my crime"* George painted himself as an unwitting and confused victim, of both a love affair and the public attitude at the time towards homosexuality. The song was a plea to a lover to admit to their feelings, and his confusion regarding rejection when he has so obviously *"Danced inside your eyes"*.

Despite the misgivings of George, the single climbed to the top spot in the United Kingdom in October, and stayed there for three weeks, becoming a worldwide smash by reaching number one in Australia, Ireland, France, Belgium, Germany, Canada, Sweden, and Switzerland, whilst going top ten in the United States, Spain, Norway, New Zealand, South Africa, Italy, and Denmark. Culture Club became a global phenomenon overnight on the back of this one single.

℧ ℧ ℧

When Yasser Arafat arrived in Rome on Wednesday 15th September for an audience with Pope John Paul II, he was greeted with the news that Israeli troops had begun pouring into West Beirut in response to the assassination of Lebanese leader Bachir Geyamer the previous day. Israeli Defence Force leader Raphael Eitan had flown to Lebanon the previous night and mobilised his troops. A curfew was introduced, and by noon the refugee camps of Sabra and Shatila were surrounded, with blockades set up at entrances and exits. As night fell, an uneasy peace was broken by the Israeli tanks shelling the camps indiscriminately.

ʊ ʊ ʊ

Throughout the North American leg of Queen's world tour, the band became incredibly weary of the itinerant lifestyle. Brian May refused to fly between dates even though they had hired Elvis Presley's private jet, the *Lisa Marie*, and Freddie Mercury often insisted the front row of the audience was too ugly and was putting him off. Backstage, Mercury was ensconced in his own entourage, all of whom dressed exactly like him, and would feed him spaghetti from a bowl whilst he sat on his own hands.

However, America was resistant to this new version of Queen, and the album and singles failed to chart very highly, whilst tickets for concerts remained unsold. A rock band playing music that included black influences was considered by many to be too far for middle America, and when Queen played at the Los Angeles Forum on Wednesday 15th September, no-one realised it would be their last ever North American date, except for an under-par performance of *Crazy Little Thing Called Love* and *Under Pressure* on Saturday Night Live on the 25th September, with Mercury's voice weakened from an all-night fight with lover, Bill Reid.

It became dangerously close to becoming the last date they played anywhere. Tired of touring and each other, the band took a little bit of time off, working on solo projects, before coming together a year later to write and record *The Works*, an album that re-invigorated the band and made them relevant again.

This was nothing, however, compared to what would happen in July 1985 when Queen played *Live Aid* at Wembley Stadium. If *Live Aid* was the peak of rock and roll (it wasn't), then it could feasibly be argued that Queen's twenty-minute performance is the peak of the rock and roll genre (it might have been), with the band realising that playing a selection of greatest hits would have more impact that promoting a new single or album, a simple idea most of the other performers failed to grasp. The performance was a masterclass in showmanship, and electrified the stadium, rejuvenating Queen's reputation instantly, and injecting the momentum they needed to continue their career successfully. The performance also indicated the future of rock and roll: previously bands played to their fans, the majority of whom were similar in terms of age, gender, and taste. After Queen's *Live Aid* performance, the industry (and many acts) woke up to the idea that a band with a back catalogue could play greatest hits sets to a multi-generational audience for an inflated amount of money. There were great cash rewards for providing a nostalgic jukebox experience, as suddenly rock stars had guaranteed pension funds.

ʊ ʊ ʊ

Afrika Bambaataa, one of the main movers and shakers on the hip-hop scene was in danger of remaining a local phenomenon as others hit the charts with the new genre. Born Lance Taylor in 1957 in the Bronx, and home educated by a black activist mother in both an eclectic musical taste and in-depth knowledge of the black liberation movement, his involvement in gangs led to him becoming a *warlord* with the street gang

Black Spades in the late 1970's. It was only after winning an essay competition with a prize of a visit to Africa that his whole world view changed. Forming the Zulu Nation in New York, Bam saw hip-hop as a way of raising consciousness amongst teenagers, helping them to escape the life of street-gangs whilst also educating them about their African heritage.

Where Bambaataa differed from other DJ's was in his musical choices. His turntables wandered far from black music, mixing European electronica by Kraftwerk with the drums of Charlie Watts from the Rolling Stones, or the ice-cool of Gary Numan with The Beatles *Sgt Pepper's Lonely Hearts Club Band*.

In 1981, determined to *"create the first black electronic group"*, Bambaataa formed the Soul Sonic Force and signed a deal with Tommy Boy Records, teaming up with producer Arthur Baker to create *Planet Rock*. The song, recorded at Intergalactic Studios, was built around two Kraftwerk tracks: *Trans-Europe Express* and *Numbers*, with the stated intention being to create music which would cross boundaries. Baker explained *"I was working in Long Island City, sweeping the warehouse floors of a record distributor called Cardinal One–Stop, and when we went out for lunch and sat around the projects I'd always hear 'Trans–Europe Express'. Its melody was more eerie than usual in that setting, reverberating off the buildings. Then again, on Saturdays I also used to hang out on Fulton Street in Brooklyn and I'd go into a record store called Music Factory to see what was selling. They were always playing 'Numbers' in there, which was really up–tempo, and so it was my idea to use a combination of those two numbers for Bambaataa's record, because the beat on 'Trans–Europe Express' was too slow."* Baker added a steadier beat to go with the original train sounds, however there was another problem in that *"We realised we might get sued by Kraftwerk if we used the 'Trans–Europe Express' melody, so John [Robie] performed a different string melody just in case."* Robie was a muso who hated disco and dance music for its insistence on making highly proficient musicians play below their standard, however after the first day recording the music, Baker *"knew we had done something special, and that was even before the rappers had done their thing."*

The track brought together everything that was hot in New York at the time: hip-hop, punk, and new wave, breaking away from previous rap records with their backwards looking insistence on the use of disco, and invented a new genre called electro. *"Back then"* explained Arthur Baker. *"It was basically just rapping over beats, and most of the beats that people used were either from disco tracks or funk tracks. There was no segregation between disco, funk, and rap. It was called rhyming. People were just rhyming over breaks."* The release of the single was *"laying down a challenge to Sugarhill, Def Jam and all the other labels — 'You won't be able to figure out what we're doing here.' It was an ego thing."*

When the day after completion Baker took an acetate of the track into a Brooklyn music store, after one play the owner offered him $100 for the copy, and he knew he was on to something special. In the first week of release in Spring 1982 the single sold 50,000 copies. When Malcolm McLaren delivered his keynote speech at the New Music Seminar in New York in July, he called *Planet Rock* *"the most rootsy folk music around, the only music that's coming out of New York City which is directly related to that guy in the streets with his ghetto blaster."*

A couple of weeks after *Planet Rock* entered the British top forty, on Thursday 16th September it was certified a gold disc in America, with sales of over 600,000.

℧ ℧ ℧

As morning broke on the Sabra and Shatila Palestine refugees on Thursday 16th September, the Israelis were not willing to risk the lives of their troops by entering the camp. Instead, it was decided that whilst they would ensure no-one could leave, the Lebanese Phalangist Christian forces would enter and root out the 2,000 PLO members claimed to be there. The leaders of the Lebanese militia forces were informed by 3.00 p.m. that the people responsible for the assassination of Bashir Gemayel were in the camps, and within an hour 1,500 troops were assembled at Beirut airport, driven in Israeli jeeps to the edge of the camp, and provided with Israeli weapons. One Lebanese soldier was overheard to say, "*The question we are putting to ourselves is – how to begin, by raping or killing?*"

By nightfall, the Lebanese had started making small incursions into the camp, rounding up males at random, whilst the Israeli's fired illuminating flares to light the area. At one point an officer radioed to the control asking what he should do with forty-five men he had rounded up. The answer he was given was "*Do the will of God*". A short while later, another radio communication asked what to do with fifty women and children who had been rounded up. "*This is the last time you are going to ask me a question like that: you know exactly what to do*" was the reply.

The killing in the refugee camps continued sporadically throughout the night, and by the morning of Friday 17th September over 300 deaths had been confirmed. Reports about what was going on were deliberately muddied, as both the Israeli and American governments attempted to clarify the situation, allowing the politicians to remain ignorant of what was going on until it was too late, however the Israeli troops stationed outside the camp were beginning to get uneasy. Whilst they were desperate to rid the country of terrorist groups, there were too many tales of civilian deaths emerging. When one officer questioned the killing of civilians, he was told that "*Pregnant women gave birth to future terrorists*".

Whilst the events went on in private, a couple of journalists did make it into the camps, including Robert Fisk, who later wrote "*I saw dead women in their houses with their skirts up to their waists and their legs spread apart; dozens of young men shot after being lined up against an alley wall; children with their throats slit, a pregnant woman with her stomach chopped open, her eyes still wide open, her blackened face silently screaming in horror; countless babies and toddlers who had been stabbed or ripped apart and who had been thrown into garbage piles.*" Further reports were made of young men being castrated and scalped, and bodies with the Christian cross carved into them.

The Israeli government dragged their feet during the incoming reports of the horror, but finally ordered the Phalange to halt the operation the following morning. Reports of the numbers of dead varied from 700 to 2000, depending on the source, but what can be certain is that several hundred people were slaughtered. A commission later set up by the Israeli government found that Ariel Sharon, the Defence Minister, shouldered a substantial proportion of the blame for not taking the necessary measure to prevent civilian deaths, and recommended he be removed from his job. Sharon refused to leave, eventually reaching a compromise whereby he would remain in the government as a Minister without Portfolio, and later became Prime Minister of the country.

After a short period of disbelief, condemnation came from around the world with accusations of war crimes and genocide. A week later 400,000 people marched in Israel, demanding the resignation of Prime Minister Begin.[506]

---

[506] As a young man Begin had led militant Jewish group Betar, which on a visit by him to the United States in 1948 had been denounced by Albert Einstein as "*closely akin in its organisation, methods, political philosophy and social appeal to the Nazi and Fascist parties... [with] ultra-nationalism, religious mysticism and racial superiority*".

℧ ℧ ℧

A newly relocated Berlin-based Birthday Party played their first live date at a festival in Athens on Friday 17ᵗʰ September, alongside New Order and The Fall, and fearing they would arrive with heroin hidden amongst their equipment, the promoter had his cousin in Immigration sneak them through customs. Singer Nick Cave had hooked up with two Australian girls, and caused a late-night scene by insisting they be allowed to share his hotel room. Guitarist Mick Harvey, called down from his room, appeared in reception in his pajamas and berated Cave, "*Okay, you stupid cunt, just get the fuck up to your bedroom and go to fucking sleep!*"
Taking a second to focus his drug and drink induced eyesight, Cave slurred "*Okay, I'm leaving the band*", and walked out the hotel. In his stupor he tried to get on trams by paying in German currency, convinced he was back in Berlin, and then spent the night walking around the city before falling asleep under a bush which was serendipitously across the road from the hotel.
The following day at the festival Cave started the show by pushing the security from the excessively high stage and encouraging the audience riot.

℧ ℧ ℧

In September, The Marine Girls got together to record their second album at Cold Storage Studios in Brixton, produced by Stuart Moxham of Young Marble Giants. The album, *Lazy Days*, was released in March 1983 and showed more of a jazz influence than the amateur home-made sound of their debut. The biggest problem, however, was that the band had grown apart. Tracey Thorn had become more confident about her own vocals and felt she should sing the songs she had written, however that would mean main vocalist Alice Foxx would be left without anything to do. Things came to head in August 1983 during a gig at Night Moves in Glasgow, when a member of the audience spat on Thorn, and she walked off, ending the gig early. An argument broke out amongst the band backstage as to whether they should have continued with the show, and by the end of the night The Marine Girls were no more.

19ᵗʰ – 25ᵗʰ September 1982
#1 single: Survivor: Eye of the Tiger
#1 album: The Kids From Fame: The Kids From Fame

Simple Minds had been taken by surprise by the success of their single *Promised You a Miracle* and were forced to take time to work on an album and follow up single. With the album recorded, the Glaswegians were poised to begin a lengthy world tour in support of the release. As an advert for the album, *Glittering Prize* was released as a single, the first clear sign of Simple Minds moving away from their *art rock* beginnings towards the sound of 1982, *pure pop music*.
Once again fronted by the lead bass of Derek Forbes coupled with Mick McNeil's shimmering keyboard lines, the song seemed obviously religious in content with lines such as "*In the light of his love, in the light of reflection*" and "*I saw you up on a clear day, first taking hearts then our last breath away*", however frontman Jim Kerr was keen to distance himself from something ostensibly so *uncool*, stating "*It's about getting a glimpse of something and going out on a chase for it against the odds.*" Either way, it was a song of glistening beauty, unafraid to take time unfolding, and provided a second

top forty hit for the band, climbing to number sixteen, whilst going top ten in Australia, New Zealand, and several Scandinavian countries.

A few weeks later, with two genuine hit singles under their wing, Simple Minds unleashed their album, *New Gold Dream (81-82-83-84)*. Written in a Fife barn at the start of the year and recorded over a five-month at Rockfield Studio, The Manor, and Townhouse by twenty-one-year-old Pete Walsh, the album was a statement of intent.

Originally called *Summer Song*, Kerr described *Someone Somewhere (In Summertime)* as "*not only a great album opener but probably the first of the batch we had written... [The song] gives the feeling that we'd arrived – that we'd reached some kind of maturity*". Ostensibly a love song longing for wondrous nights of passion, Charlie Burchill explained "*Jim would record us jamming on a ghetto blaster for hours. He plucked out a guitar melody which became the intro to the song, and the rest flowed from there*", with the singer claiming, "*Somewhere there is someone who can see what I see*". The underplayed song, possibly the most straightforward on the album, was released as a single in November, but stalled at number thirty-six.

Immediately after the opener, the band turned funky, with a bass-led song about jealousy, *Colours Fly and Catherine Wheel*. Whilst subsequent years have focussed on Kerr and Burchill as the core of Simple Minds, bass player Derek Forbes was often the real driving force in the early years. Kerr would later acknowledge this, stating "*When I look back I feel incredibly lucky because not only did we have Charlie Burchill to write with, but*

Derek Forbes our bass player. [He was] essentially as good a guitar player, but Derek was coming up with these bass lines which were as melodic and any guitar lead."

Whilst the songs were led by Burchill and Forbes, Kerr's lyrics tended to be less penetrable, something he addressed by saying "*Some of the songs were less influenced by the music we listening to at the time and more influenced by cinema, especially one of our favourite directors, [Werner] Herzog[507]. I felt [Burchill and Mick MacNeil] were coming up with music that would've been equally suited to movie soundtracks*". This could be seen on the lumbering, narcoleptic, restlessness of *Big Sleep*, or the instrumental *Somebody Up There Likes You*, which Burchill had based around chords by Mahler.

The title track, *New Gold Dream (81-82-83-84)*, opened the second side of the album, and set out the roadmap for Simple Minds over four years as they strove for success with greater ambition than previously. Kerr gave success and fame a character, describing how "*she is the one in front of me, the siren and the ecstasy... sun is set in front of me, worldwide on the widest screen.*" Originally called *Festival Riff*, the original ten-minute Krautrock song was edited down, and the final recording of the song took place at four in the morning, with drummers Mel Gaynor and Mike Ogiltree recording their parts facing each other.

The album flagged towards the end, with *Hunter and the Hunted* the weakest song, even featuring a redundant jazz-funk keyboard solo performed by Herbie Hancock who had been recording next door, before ending with *King is White and in the Crowd* about the assassination of Egyptian President Sadat.

---

[507] Werner Herzog once ate his own shoe when he lost a bet, which is unfortunate as he only ever owns one suit and one pair of shoes at any one time. He also knows how to hypnotize chickens.

Kerr would later proclaim the album *"our finest work. The song and the album certainly mark the point where artistically, everything fell into* place", whilst U2 frontman Bono would say that *"Without 'New Gold Dream' I don't believe there would have been 'The Unforgettable Fire' or 'The Joshua Tree'.* [They] *accessed this ecstatic music and Jim had the poetry to paint the picture"*, describing the Scots as *"trance music pioneers"*.

The band played over 100 dates throughout 1982, building upon an already impressive live reputation, whilst learning how to control and hypnotise larger and larger crowds, so when arenas and stadiums came calling a couple of years later Simple Minds were ready for them, having honed their craft. The *New Gold Dream* tour had begun in earnest at Edinburgh Coasters for three nights on the 8th September, before sweeping through the rest of the Britain, heading to Australia and New Zealand in October, and Canada in November. The year was rounded off with the second half of their British tour, supported by label-mates China Crisis, and a homecoming Glaswegian date just before Christmas. The tour continued into the following year, where between March and August 1983, the band crossed the United States twice, as well as playing extensively through Europe and the Britain.

Simple Minds' stock rose throughout the first half of the decade, and for a while it was a toss-up between themselves and U2 as to who the world dominating *rock and roll* act of the 1980's would be. In the end U2's populism and *pop nous* won through; Simple Minds simply did not have the sing-along songs to maintain a long run at the top of the charts, and the lack of humour in their music turned them into bombast rather than a bridge to human emotions. They were never sure where they fitted in, wanting massive success but also wanting to experiment. Jim Kerr showed a little bit of hometown ignorance when he stated *"We've always had an Art School tag which I didn't mind but I thought was really funny. I don't even think there is an art school in Glasgow"*. That, and the lack of good looks in the band meant they were never *Smash Hits* front page material.

Their success hit a peak in 1985 with the chart-topping *(Don't You) Forget About Me*, the theme song from John Hughes' brat-pack movie *The Breakfast Club*. It was this song, pointedly not written by the band, which broke them in the United States, and finally elevated them to the stadiums and arenas they had been playing in their heads since 1979. It was in stadiums that Jim Kerr and Simple Minds belonged, with anthems bellowed and extended, however the stadiums were also their downfall; smaller venues had allowed them to think big whilst also remaining within touch of their audience. The music the band needed to create to appear *important* in such a vast space became nugatory clichéd rhetoric, such as the pomp of *Belfast Child* or its flipside *Mandela Day*. Ultimately, Simple Minds could not escape their art rock roots, wanting to remain obscure and mysterious whilst under the glare of 70,000 pairs of eyes, an impossible task.

ʊ ʊ ʊ

Thirty-four-year-old Scott Fahlman was at the cutting edge of studies into Artificial Intelligence, as well as semantic and neural networks at Carnegie Melon University in Pittsburgh, work which would have profound influence on the modern world in the fields of facial recognition, databases, and medical diagnosis.

His most recognisable addition to the modern world, however, was contained in a post on the Carnegie Melon computer message board on Sunday 19th September. In response to people's inability to recognise joke posts, he suggested:

I propose… the following character sequence for joke markers: :-)
Read it sideways.

Actually it is probably more economical to mark things that are NOT jokes, given current trends. For this, use: :-(

Emoticons had just been added invented.

ʊ ʊ ʊ

As part of the deal to get out his contract with former manager Don Arden, Ozzy Osbourne had agreed to one final album, which was to be a live recording of Black Sabbath tracks. On Sunday 19th September Brad Gilles, Rudy Sarzo, and Tommy Aldridge met in midtown New York to rehearse the set for five days. Ozzy did not show up, being *"not very co-operative"* according to wife and manager Sharon.
Ozzy finally appeared for the soundcheck at the Ritz in New York on the day of the concert a week later, with little memory of the lyrics. To solve this, he placed a book of the lyrics on a chair next to him and hunched over to make out the words. The band were dressed casually for the shows, with Ozzy wearing sweatpants, running through the songs on two consecutive nights, as well as an afternoon performance in the empty theatre. The best versions from these three recordings were then compiled into the live album, *Speak of the Devil*, released in November.

ʊ ʊ ʊ

In September, the Conservative government cabinet met to discuss a paper suggesting an extension of charging for services on the NHS. Margaret Thatcher was horrified at the paper, but only because she feared it may be leaked and give the opposition ammunition. Of course, the paper *was* then leaked to *The Economist*, *The Observer*, and *The Times*, and the media went into a frenzy. The lesson Thatcher took from this affair was not that charging for the NHS was unacceptable, but that she could not trust her cabinet. Her *think tank* was disbanded, and she formed her own Policy Unit, led by Ferdinand Mount[508], who spent time on *"renewing the values of society"*, with the opinion that a *"two-way relationship between obedience and responsibility is what makes a free, self-governing society"*. Thatcher became increasingly worried about the *"lack of knowledge displayed by many children about our country and society, and our history and culture"*, and was convinced that private sector traits being introduced to the public sector education system was the only way to tackle this. This developed into the *Family Policy Group*, whose most important and long-lasting policies were the *"widening of home ownership through increased sales of council houses"* through the *Right to Buy* legislation, as well the introduction of the Youth Training Scheme (YTS).
The Youth Training Scheme would come to replace the Youth Opportunities Programme (YOP), which had been established by the previous Labour government under Jim Callaghan. The aim was to ensure every school leaver either found a job, a place at college or university, or a place on a training course. With over 700 applicants for every place on the YOP, the pay being only £1 more than weekly unemployment benefit, and the likelihood you would find yourself without a job at the end of the training, many young people were understandably opposed to the programme, whilst employers saw the whole thing as a means of cheap labour, failing to provide the promised training, the supposed equivalent of an apprenticeship.
Meanwhile, unemployment continued to rise and on Wednesday 22nd September 14% of the British workforce were reported to be out of work, having continued to rise from

---

[508] Mount was the cousin of the mother of future Prime Minister David Cameron.

the January record of three million, with a further 300,000 school-leavers joining the dole queue over the summer. The unemployment numbers should have played a large part in the 1983 general election, however the Conservatives and their right-wing backers in the media were successful in persuading the public to ignore it, or else see the unemployed as deserving of their fate. 43% of the public thought people were on the dole "*through their own fault*", whilst 47% believed most could get jobs "*if they tried*". On the same date as the new figures were announced, a *Day of Action* was taking place in Glasgow, with protesters marching in support of NHS workers. Attending the march was fifty-three-year-old Labour Member of Parliament for Glasgow Queen's Park, Frank McElhone. Halfway through the day, McElhone started to feel pain in his chest before collapsing and dying of a heart attack. McElhone's seat was taken over by his widow, Helen, whilst his son Johnny was bass player in Altered Images.

Friend of McElhone and Socialist stalwart Tony Benn found out about his death whilst at home in Bristol, and the news sent him further into despair at the state of the Labour Party. Three days later he recorded in his diary: "*Compared to last year, when the left was riding high with success everywhere, this year the left is very much tail-between-the-legs.*"

℧ ℧ ℧

Frederick Waite had come from Jamaica to the United Kingdom in the 1960's having been a member of ska and rocksteady act The Techniques alongside other legendary singers such as Slim Smith[509], Winston Riley[510], Pat Kelly, Dave Barker[511], and Bruce Ruffin. Raising two boys in Birmingham whilst encouraging them to play bass and drums, Waite had not given up music completely. In 1979 he recruited his sons Freddie "Junior" and Patrick alongside their friends, brothers Kelvin and Michael Grant on guitar and keyboards, respectively. With the musicians aged between eight and twelve years old, the band were given the name Musical Youth, and started playing reggae sets around West Indian working men's clubs, despite their tender years. After an independent single and a John Peel session in 1981, it became apparent that having a middle-aged singer in a band called Musical Youth was never going to work, and Waite senior made way for the fourteen-year-old Dennis Seaton, as the band continued to play live, supporting UB40, Prince Far I, and Sugar Minott

This new younger face attracted the attention of MCA Records[512], who put them in the studio with Peter Collins, fresh from his success producing a ska-lite version of *Poison Ivy* for the Lambrettas. The first single released from the session was a mash-up of three songs: the introduction of U-Roy's *Rule the Nation*, the main verse and chorus of The Mighty Diamonds *Pass the Kouchie*, and the middle-eight taken from *Gimme the Music* by U Brown. Waite senior was smart enough to claim songwriting credit on the single, however he later had to share this with rocksteady bass player Leroy Sibbles, from whom he stole the bass line.

Pass the Dutchie was a song about sharing a cannabis blunt rolled inside a Dutch Masters cigar, which the band changed from *Kouchie* to *Dutchie*, a type of cooking pot, to allow airplay on radio. With a video shot by Don Letts, the contagious jubilant vibes

---

[509] Smith died in 1973 when he tried to break into his parents' house. Cutting himself on the broken window, he bled to death.

[510] Riley wrote the classic reggae instrumental *Double Barrel*.

[511] Barker was so severely beaten by his uncle and teachers that he developed a stammer.

[512] Dennis Seaton: "*The chap who signed us to MCA told us the company laughed at him for signing schoolboys.*"

entered the charts at number twenty-six, and then shot straight to the top position the following week, going on to sell over five million copies worldwide.

Whilst sitting at the top of the singles charts, Musical Youth released their self-titled debut album, containing twelve songs written by Freddie Waite, including future hits *The Youth of Today* and *Never Gonna' Give You Up*. Despite three top-twenty hits, the album only reached number twenty-six, an indication that their audience was too young to afford a long player. In fact, a tour in November had to be cancelled due to

poor ticket sales, as the band realised that maybe matinee performances would have been more suitable for their new audience. With the band being so youthful, they were only allowed to work for forty-two days a year and were not permitted to appear live on television after 4.30 p.m. forcing *Top of the* Pops to show their videos instead.

Musical Youth's success was short-lived, and whilst they were the first black band to be interviewed on MTV, by 1984 they had been dropped by the record company, prompting Michael Grant to ask if this meant he would need to sell the BMX bike they had given him as a present.

He was allowed to keep it. Keyboard player Grant would later reminisce *"We were exposed to sex-drugs and rock'n'roll at the age of 13. We saw things like DJ's putting their hands down women's tops – they'd be sacked on the spot today."*

Tragically, bass player Patrick Waite would later become involved in a life of petty crime, before dying of a congenital heart condition at the age of twenty-four, whilst his brother Freddie suffered from mental health problems, eventually being diagnosed as schizophrenic.

℧ ℧ ℧

Once Paul Weller decided to split The Jam, he still had to inform the other members, and reconvening in July to record a new single broke the news. Any pretense that the band was a democracy were finally shattered there and then: the decision to their future lay completely with Weller. Everyone tried to persuade him to change his mind, from the record company to his own father, but the singer had made up his mind. Bass player Bruce Foxton suggested Weller take his time, do a solo album, get it out of his system, and then come back to The Jam, but failed to understand that the main problem

was the other musicians in the band, and their limited ability to adapt. At the time Foxton admitted *"It's pretty upsetting really, from my point of view"*, whilst Rick Buckler predicted *"You don't work with someone for ten years and then suddenly forget them, do you?"*

The single they recorded was *The Bitterest Pill (I Ever Had to Swallow)*, a lush ballad and a classic pop song which remains one of the least favourite amongst fans of the band. Starting with chiming guitar and descending Small Faces notes the track was drenched in strings and charted a tale of lost love, with melancholia in lines such as *"The love I gave hangs in sad coloured mocking shadows"*. Weller has stated he wrote *The Bitterest Pill* as a piss-take of all the new bands in the charts such as ABC and Duran Duran, as an ironic effort to show how straightforward it was to compose an overblown love song. It certainly was over-the-top, with a massive production reminiscent of the work Trevor Horn was doing, however time has eroded away any sense of irony from the song, and it now simply stands as a classic: albeit one that Weller is unlikely to ever play live.

The song also saw the emergence of what would become a Weller stock in trade during the decade: a single female harmony vocal, this time supplied by Jenny McKeown, vocalist with The Belle Stars. Weller would soon use Respond Records signing Tracey Young in the same role, and then later his own wife and member of Wham, Dee. C Lee. The other members of The Jam were devastated by the imminent demise of the band, with Foxton especially taking the news badly. He refused to be involved in the video shoot for *The Bitterest Pill*[513] and announced that he would take no part in any farewell dates. Weller responded by asking former Sex Pistol Glen Matlock to play the dates, a move which saw Foxton running back into the fold.

There was, however, a re-shuffle in the touring line-up of the band in September, as the horn section was jettisoned in favour of keyboard player Jimmy Telford (of Scottish act Everest The Hard Way) and backing singers Afrodiziak (featuring future Soul II Soul singer Caron Wheeler). The remaining continental dates were then cancelled when Weller contracted shingles, a sure sign of suffering stress.

℧ ℧ ℧

Before being associated with cheap food and teenagers, many fast-food chains were something of an attraction to otherwise astute adults. Following their introduction in Lebanon during the 1960's, American chain Wimpy had obtained a reputation for poor sanitation and paucity of flavour, however this did not stop the "*cosmopolitan intelligentsia*" meeting regularly at the branch on Hamra Street in Beirut.

The sight of the occupying Israeli forces also eating at the restaurant, and insisting on paying in their own currency, incensed many Lebanese nationalists, and none more so than nineteen-year-old Khaled Alwan, a member of the Syrian Socialist Nationalist Party. On the afternoon of Saturday 24th September Alwan casually opened fire in the restaurant, killing three Israeli soldiers, before serenely departing the scene.

For many in Lebanon the act marked the beginning of violent resistance against the Israeli occupying forces.

℧ ℧ ℧

It remained difficult to have a hit in 1982: single sales were high and there was no shortage of competition. Simply releasing a great song on a major label, with guaranteed radio coverage was not enough. Singles would often linger outside the all-important top forty for weeks before something, a television performance or extra radio play, would push them into *Top of the Pops* territory. Sometimes they would not even make it into the top seventy-five, and this was the fate of the debut single by a new Scottish act called Big Country.

Big Country, however, could not exactly be called new: vocalist Stuart Adamson had been the guitarist with Dunfermline punks The Skids between 1977 and 1981, writing most of their anthemic hits. When he left in spring 1981, Virgin Records made it clear they were only interested in singer Richard Jobson, leaving Adamson to retreat to his hometown. Here he recruited local guitarist Bruce Watson, and the two of them set about writing and recording demo tapes with a drum machine. These were rejected by every major label in the country and listening to them you can see why: whilst in the

---

[513] The video featured Lee Kavanagh, who had met the band after providing the *telephone voice* for *Is Vic There?* By Department S.

same vein as material by The Skids, the songs were not fully formed, and did not coincide with what was in the charts. Adamson and Watson recruited some local musicians and started playing live, supporting Alice Cooper on British dates. The band, however, did not click, and still no one was interested in signing them.

Dropping the other musicians[514] the duo recruited London session bass player Tony Butler and drummer Mark Brzezicki[515], and immediately things seemed to work. In April 1982, the four-piece played a showcase gig in London, and within weeks had signed a worldwide deal with Phonogram. They started recording with veteran producer Chris Thomas, who was juggling that with flying to Montserrat to record the new Elton John album, but the sessions were eventually scrapped, with only one single seeing the light of day.

Harvest Home was released in September and vanished without trace, with the press either ignoring or critically demolishing it, such as an NME review which described it as "*Dour declarations over an ugly Spartan beat*". The track contained the DNA of The Skids, however it also introduced what would become known as *bagpipe guitars*, an accusation which was to haunt the band throughout their career, and one which they

never fully overcame. There was more to *Harvest Home* than bagpipe guitars, however, as it dealt with the same Scottish themes as Lewis Grassic Gibbons novel *Sunset Song*: a lament for a lost nation devastated by the Highland Clearances of the late 18th century.

Despite the failure of the single, Phonogram continued to support the band, allowing time to further develop. This development proceeded at a furious pace, after all the band had only been together for six months and were still getting to know each other. Dates supporting The Who on an American tour were cancelled to allow them to support The Jam on their farewell British tour[516], which led to the band meeting Steve Lillywhite who subsequently took over production, adding an extra width and grandness to their sound. By the end of 1983 Big Country had three hit singles and a classic top ten debut album under their belts and looked as if they might become one of the most successful acts of the decade, before the law of diminishing returns set in and they faded over the next couple of decades, despite continuing as a popular live draw. Adamson struggled with an alcohol addiction, which eventually got the better of him in 2001, and after disappearing from his home in Nashville he was found in a hotel room in Hawaii, having taken his own life by hanging himself in the closet.

ʊ ʊ ʊ

On Friday 24th September the United States Centre for Disease Control and Prevention renamed GRIDS as AIDS (Acquired Immune Deficiency Syndrome). By then doctors had ascertained that AIDS was not exclusive to the gay community, however the public were slow to catch on, generally choosing to consider it as a *gay plague*. In California, bumper stickers were sold with the phrase "*AIDS: it's killing all the right people*", which a whole series of preachers were quick to label the disease *God's punishment*. Incidences of AIDS diagnosis were now doubling every six months, with a significant number of new cases appearing in Europe.

---

[514] One of whom was future MP Peter Wishart.

[515] Both had recently been working with Pete Townsend of The Who.

[516] The support slot on The Who tour was then filled by The Clash.

ʊ ʊ ʊ

New York hip-hop promoter called Russel Simmons had been manager for his friend Kurtis Blow[517] since 1979, just as rap was first breaking internationally. For the next couple of years Simmons pushed Blow on the public, whilst becoming openly frustrated about the direction the genre was heading. For Simmons, rap should only be about the beat and the words, and he viewed the music used by Afrika Bambaataa and Grandmaster Flash as a betrayal of that ideal: It should sound and look like where it came from, not the Furious Five's cowboy hats and go-go boots.

His younger brother, Joey Simmons, felt the same way and tried during his own DJ sets to stay true to this ethic. Joey had been badgering his brother Russel for quite a while to allow him and friend Darryl McDaniels to record their own rap record. Russel put together a sparse drum machine driven beat with an occasional stab of keyboard, just to see what his younger brother could do. When Joey and Darryl started with the lines *"Unemployment at a record high, people coming, people going, people born to*

die", and ended each verse with *"It's like that, and that's the way it is"*, Russell began to see the dollar signs floating in front of his eyes. After being turned down by every record company in the city, Simmons brought the tape to Profile Records in September 1982, one of the few labels that would even consider releasing rap records.[518] Cory Robbins at Profile listened to the track, which to him sounded like a lot of shouting over a drum machine, however after listening to the cassette in his car he found something about the chorus appealing and agreed to a one-off single release. Simmons demanded $4000 to re-record the song[519], taking his brother and friend to Greene Street Studios in New York's SoHo, where his hustler characteristics came into play, persuading studio owner Steve Loeb to defer payment of the $3,700 bill. A B-side was also recorded, called *Krush-Groove 1*, which the record company changed to *Sucker DJs*, and the decision was made to call the duo Run-DMC after Joey Simmons nickname and Darryl McDaniels initials.

When the single was released in March 1983 it picked up airplay immediately, as phones started lighting up no matter which side of the disc was played. As the year progressed, the song took over black airwaves, selling a quarter of a million copies and making the Sugarhill artists sound outdated. Run-DMC went on to become one of the most influential and pioneering acts of the decade, even breaking through into mainstream consciousness and charts.

---

[517] Blow would later become a born-again Christian, and now runs the Hip-Hop Church in Harlem.

[518] Most black labels would not sign rap in the 1980's, feeling that it was *too black*!

[519] Robbins agreed to half that amount.

26th September – 2nd October 1982

#1 single: Musical Youth: Pass The Dutchie
#1 album: Dire Straits: Love Over Gold

Having just left failed Bath-based ska act The Graduate, Roland Orzabel[520] and Curt Smith would have been forgiven for believing their chance had come and gone in 1982. Despite a top ten single in Spain, and a publishing deal with Tony Hatch, Orzabel had grown sick of live work, and longed to become a studio-based musician instead.

Taking the name Tears For Fears from a form of therapy developed by Arthur Janov[521], the duo worked on electronic sounding material at a studio owned by Ian Stanley, hawking the recordings around the major record labels until signing with Phonogram at

the end of 1981. Two singles, produced by David Lord[522] then Mike Howlett, failed to set the charts alight, and they were facing their last chance with the release of *Mad World* at the end of September 1982.

Mad World had been Orzabel's deliberate attempt to write a new romantic song in the style of Duran Duran's *Planet Earth* during what he called his "*teenage menopause*". Taking further inspiration from a song by Liverpool's Dalek I Love You, Orzabel explained that he had "*suffered depression in my childhood. I kept a lid on my feelings at school, but when I was eighteen* [I] *dropped out of everything and couldn't even be bothered to get out of bed. I poured all this into the song.*" Taking further inspiration from the writings of Janov, and his belief that nightmares were good because they released tension, the song was built around a chorus of "*The dreams in which I'm dying are the best I've ever had*".

Listening to recent rhythmic releases by Talking Heads and Peter Gabriel, the band built up a dense backing track of electronic squelches and a Roland CR78 drum machine, layering anodic bass bombinates on top. The sounds used were influenced by Japan's *Tin Drum* album, which the band had become obsessed with Orzabel explaining how "*We were using the same equipment as Japan, synthesizers and such, but the mind truly boggled at how they got those noises out of them. It was the way everything hung together. I was always struggling to get a similar approach – not that I ever could.*" Phonogram were not overly keen to release the single, arguing that it was not danceable, however after a low-budget video shot at Knebworth House was added, the song started to climb the charts, peaking at number three in November.

Whilst touring in support of The Thompson Twins throughout autumn, Tears For Fears overtook the headliners in popularity, and confident they had a strong album ready to go, 1983 started to look extremely promising.

ʊ ʊ ʊ

The stress of touring harnessed with alcohol problems led to tensions within Squeeze. Between April and September they had embarked on two extensive American tours, a

---

[520] Real name Raoul Jamie Orzabel de la Quintana.

[521] The duo met Janov at the height of their success later in the decade. He tried to persuade them to write a musical about him.

[522] Lord was found guilty in 2015 of keeping a brothel and given a suspended sentence.

British tour, and a European tour, with a second October and November British tour to follow, and on a train between Hamburg and Paris on Sunday 26th September, band leaders Glen Tilbrook and Chris Difford came to the similar conclusion at the same time: the band was sounding tired and it was time to call it a day.

The two kept the decision under wraps until they were boarding the plane to their final  ever gig: the Jamaica Sunsplash Festival at the end of November. The rest of the band were understandably livid, and the final couple of performances at the festival showed a band playing sloppily, with slurred vocals and wrong chords.

Meanwhile, A&M had persuaded Squeeze to release a *greatest hits* compilation, the last desperate act of a label wanting to re-claim invested money and already aware of the direction the wind is blowing. In his autobiography, Midge Ure claimed that Ultravox were the first ever band, in 1984, to include a new song on a *Greatest Hits* compilation. This is obviously not the case, as for their release Squeeze recorded *Annie Get Your Gun*, one of their weakest singles.[523] Sending a demo recording of the song to former Cliff Richard producer and songwriter Alan Tarney, the band found when they turned up at the studio he had recorded the backing tracks himself, leaving them to simply add vocals. The finished article had the type of pop sheen Tarney later added to A-ha, however it stalled at number forty-three on the charts.

The greatest hits album entitled *Singles – 45's and Under* was a true classic, with every track timeless, and reached number three in the charts, whilst going on to become the most well-known *best of* by the band.

The split did not last long with Difford & Tilbrook releasing an album together a year later, considered to be a *lost* Squeeze album, and in 1985 the band got back together properly, releasing a series of albums throughout the decade which saw them crack America. Following another split in 1999, the two eternal members Difford and Tilbrook got together as Squeeze once again in 2007 and have intermittently toured and recorded since then.

Throughout their forty-plus years, the band have revolved around Difford and Tilbrook, the prime songwriters with Tilbrook handling the music and Difford the lyrics. In their early days the duo was often called the new Lennon and McCartney, with strong melodies and close harmonies in evidence, as they churned out the type of pop songs Crowded House later conquered the world with, only with better (if occasionally sexist) lyrics.

Squeeze were an almost perfect pop band, but in 1982, the year of perfect pop they were out of tune with the times. 1982 demanded *new* pop, and Squeeze were the result of pre-punk days, without juvenile good-looking frontmen. They seemed to hark back to the days of well-crafted song writing rather than the rush of youthful exuberance in vogue.

ʊ ʊ ʊ

Leaving Visage at the start of summer turned out to be a blessing for Midge Ure, allowing him the time to concentrate on his primary act. Ultravox had been in existence since 1973 when John Foxx teamed up with Chris Cross under the name Tiger Lily,

---

[523] Madness and The Stranglers also released new tracks on their *Greatest Hits* compilations in 1982.

but by 1976 they had become Ultravox![524], taking their influences from Kraftwerk, David Bowie, and Roxy Music. Ultravox were delighted when Brian Eno agreed to produce their debut album for Island Records, whilst a second album took on the aggression of punk and featured synthesisers and one of the first drum machines on a British release. This technology pointed towards the direction of the third album in 1978, *Systems of Romance*, which became an essential futuristic soundtrack at Rusty Egan's *Blitz Club*, which was where keyboard player Billy Currie first met Ure and joined Visage in the studio.

As Foxx departed to undertake a solo career in March 1979 and the band found themselves without a record contract or singer, Currie took a job with Gary Numan's band to pay the rent, before realising that the perfect new frontman was already in his life in the shape of Ure.

Ure, meanwhile, had come from an enforced *boy band* background, but did have a small amount of credibility within punk circles as having short hair in 1975 got him an invitation from Malcolm McLaren and Bernie Rhodes to become the singer with The

Sex Pistols, a move he wisely resisted[525]. After travelling through The Rich Kids, Ure was drawn into the world of Ultravox, and his touring as guitarist with Thin Lizzy meant the band had time to work up a whole set of new songs throughout the year before anyone even knew he had joined.

Signing to Chrysalis Records, their debut album *Vienna* broke big with a well-timed melange of electronic and real instruments, especially on the title track which became an unlikely worldwide hit in early 1981, helped by a moody promotion movie shot on film rather than video by Russell Mulcahy. This and the next album, *Rage in Eden* had been produced by German Conny Plank, however the relationship had become strained by 1982, and Ultravox chose instead to work with former Beatles studio wizard George Martin at his AIR Studios. Martin turned out to be a very hands-off producer, refusing to touch the mixing desk, preferring instead to give instructions to his assistant, who then passed these on to the studio engineer. In fact, Martin was reluctant to take the job on at all due to his failing hearing, however he was persuaded by his fifteen-year-old daughter who was a fan of Ultravox.

The first single from the album was opening track *Reap the Wild Wind*, released in the middle of September. Named after a 1942 Cecil B. De Mille movie, the song featured a prolonged string motif over bass drums and piano, before dropping down to the verse and an optimistic sounding chorus. Lyrically, the song was incognizable, an assemblage of lines which do not overtly relate to each other. It has been suggested the song was about the consequences of the Capitalist system, however like almost all Ultravox lyrics it seems instead to be a bagatelle of significance. The video gave little away, set during the Second World War and featuring the band as spitfire pilots, intercut with them building a giant monument in more modern times. There is a lot of pointing to a spot

---

[524] The exclamation mark was a reference to Neu! and was dropped after the second album.

[525] McLaren and Rhodes had driven to Glasgow to sell some musical equipment stolen by Sex Pistols guitarist Steve Jones.

392 | 1982: From One Extreme to Another

in the distance coupled with eye-squinting lachrymose expressions, but not much in the way of plot.

The song and video contained the elements that made the band ostracized by the critics; grandiose lyrics, euphuistic production, and a sense of taking itself too seriously. You are supposed to think the song is suffused with deep meaning, overwrought emotions, and thoughts mere mortals could never understand.

With a cover designed by Peter Saville, the album *Quartet* followed in October and climbed to number six. When listened to with hindsight, it was an impeccably produced album featuring relatively unornamented arrangements by a band who could play these songs live. Lyrically, it touched upon some recurring themes: people gathering, proclamations, temptations, desire, and secret organisations. The songs tended to be overlong and could shift into non-related instrumental sections for no good reason, but ultimately, they had a doleful brand of pop at their core.

ʊ ʊ ʊ

With the *Diary of a Madman* tour over, Ozzy Osbourne's band flew home to Los Angeles on Tuesday 28th September. During the flight bass player Rudy Sarzo and new guitarist Brad Gillis compared notes, with Gillis philosophical regarding the treatment he had received from Ozzy, putting it down to grief over the loss of Randy Rhoades. He let Sarzo hear a cassette of his band Nightranger on a new Sony Walkman, whilst the bass player replied by playing some tracks he had recorded with Quiet Riot.

Sarzo had struggled with the second half of the tour, having lost one of his closest and oldest friends in Rhoades, and was getting no pleasure playing songs without him, whilst Ozzy delivered sub-standard vocal performances as he sank further into a haze of drink and drugs. At that moment Sarzo decided to leave the band and try his luck with Quiet Riot.

Landing in Los Angeles, the bass player called Sharon Osbourne and explained "*I don't know how to put this, but I've joined Quiet Riot. If you want me to do the* [upcoming] *UK dates I will be available...*"

"*Forget it!*" snapped Sharon, "*Nobody leaves Ozzy!*" as she slammed down the phone.

ʊ ʊ ʊ

The Commonwealth Games, a non-event ignored every four years by most of the world, were held in Brisbane in 1982, bestowed upon the Australian city when every other candidate dropped out of the bidding competition.

The opening ceremony was held in front of Prince Phillip on Thursday 30th September at the QEII Stadium and featured the Queensland Symphony Orchestra and the Sydney Philharmonic Choir, whilst children wearing colour-coordinated clothes shaped a colossal Australian flag. Later the children formed a map of Australia, which controversially neglected the island of Tasmania, followed by folk dances and the arrival of the official mascot Matilda, an enormous winking kangaroo constructed around a forklift truck, of whom it was suggested could be used after the games to tackle *tastefulness* whenever it broke out. Once she had concluded a lap of the track, her pouch opened to reveal children outfitted as joey kangaroos, who bounced towards small trampolines whilst Rolf Harris sang and played his wobble-board along to the songs *Tie Me Kangaroo Down* and *Waltzing Matilda*.

Then came the parade of competing nations, with a special cheer for Gerald Cheek[526] from the Falklands, islands which were competing for the first time.

The games were dominated by British, Australian, and Canadians, the best funded competing nations, with gold medals for Alan Wells[527], Shirley Strong[528], and Daley Thompson.[529]

Most of the controversy occurred in the swimming, where Australia and Canada continued a bitter rivalry with psychological tricks such as the North Americans pouring "*Canadian holy water*" into each of the lanes of the pool, Canada being disqualified and denied a playback of an offending change-over because the television technicians had already gone home, and then commiting a second illegal change-over after which they threw a tantrum, kicking over wooden seats and slamming a lot of doors, before retiring to the car park where they hurled a large plastic garbage bin into a lake and uprooted a number of pot plants.

There was also controversy in the women's 4 x 100 metre relay, when both Australia and Canada were disqualified, having come first and second, for not waiting until the last swimmer had reached the end of their length. This bumped the English team up to gold, and the Scottish team into silver.

The Australians insisted on doing things their own way, and the organization responsible for the testing of athletes at the Brisbane Royal Hospital were aware that the competitors were often de-hydrated and lacking the ability to urinate on demand. Being Australia, to combat this they ensured that plenty of beer was on hand to help with the process.

By the closing ceremony on Saturday 9th October, the Queen had joined her husband, and as they left the stadium the Australian team formed a *guard of honour*, running beside the car as it circled the athletics track several times. The Canberra Times also reported that the Brisbane Belles, "*a group of astonishingly mature marching girls… flaunted for all* [and] *did their best to ensure that the display never lapsed into tastefulness*".

46 nations and 1583 athletes had participated in the event, with England topping the medals table with 108, followed closely by Australia with 107. The host nation could at least take consolation that they achieved one more gold medal than the English.

The Commonwealth Games were also the ideal opportunity for protesters to make themselves heard regarding Aboriginal land rights. On Monday 4th October over 100 people were arrested in the car park of the Queen Elizabeth Stadium for chanting, even though most of them had legitimate tickets for the event. The Queensland Police Commissioner, Terry Lewis, stated "*We cannot allow the largest sporting event in our history to be interrupted and destroyed as a spectacle by a small group of malcontents*". Amongst the people arrested, were priests and nuns.

---

[526] As radio operator at Stanley Airport, Cheek had been arrested by the Argentinians and held prisoner during the conflict.

[527] Wells had won gold for Britain at the 1980 Moscow Olympics against a field weakened by a boycott.

[528] Strong picked up the gold medal in the women's 100 metres hurdles, despite a twenty-cigarettes-a-day smoking habit. After the race she explained "*Mum and I went to a hypnotist to try and kick the habit. Mum doesn't smoke anymore, and I gave it away for three months till Christmas and parties came around. But I also put on so much weight that I couldn't get over the hurdles at the indoor winter meets so I took it up again*".

[529] Thompson could afford to take things easy in the final event, the 1500 metres, where he jogged around the track and came third last but still gained enough points to win the overall gold.

ʊ ʊ ʊ

"*Clive* [Langer] *didn't think* [Come On, Eileen] *would be a hit!*" Kevin Rowland would later claim, "*He said it wasn't as good as 'Celtic Soul Brothers', and my manager didn't think it would be a hit. He said he thought it was trying too hard. The record company wanted to release 'Jackie Wilson Said'.*" Dexy's Midnight Runners management and producer Langer got their wish at the end of September when *Jackie Wilson Said (I'm in Heaven When You Smile)* was released as a single.

The song had never been a hit single in Britain for writer Van Morrison, remaining best known as a stand-out track on his peerless 1972 album *Saint Dominic's Preview*. Dexy's version was a punctilious replica of the original, but with a beefed-up sound justifying Rowland's claim that even Morrison believed it to be the better version. As

the single climbed to number five, the band were invited on *Top of the Pops* and insisted on having a massive portrait of Scottish darts player Jocky Wilson behind them. "*We thought it was hilarious*" Rowland explained, "*The producer said 'But everyone will think we've made a mistake!'*"

With a niche in the hearts of the nation Dexy's started a tour of the United Kingdom under the name *The Bridge*. Saxophonist Paul Speare mused "*I don't suppose any of us realised quite how big it was going to become, but I do remember when we first did a couple of gigs with that material and the violins, in Newcastle, and the reaction was... surprising.*" The public were ecstatic, embracing the frenetic Celtic energy, and on the final night of the tour at Belfast's Ulster Hall the audience broke the floor of the venue in the first half hour by dancing too hard. Rowland, of course, put it all down to himself, claiming "*I really do bare myself for everybody to see, and maybe that's embarrassing, but it's real*". The band had taken on a new horn section of Nick Gatfield[530], Andy Hamilton, Spike Edney, and Mark Walters during the summer, as well as replacing bass player Mick Gallick with John Edwards, and performed the whole of the new album as well as re-arranged version of old material. Applying soot to their faces before each performance, Billy Adams became disillusioned, later complaining "*I used to turn round sometimes and I'd see some of the session players, and I think they thought it was a bit of a sort of hillbilly pantomime*".

ʊ ʊ ʊ

Whilst *Love My Way* failed to reach the British top forty for The Psychedelic Furs, it took off across the Atlantic, providing a new wave role model for young Americans. The accompanying album produced by Todd Rundgren, *Forever Now*, was released towards the end of September, and climbed into the charts, peaking at number twenty.

Starting with the double-whammy of *President Gas* and *Love my Way*, the album would become one of The Psychedelic Furs' greatest achievements, distilling their

---

[530] Gatfield would later become head on Sony Records, and throughout his career oversaw the signing of Radiohead, Blur, and Amy Winehouse.

singular vision into cannisters of alternative pop. Whilst many assumed *President Gas* was a critique of Reagan, lyrics such as "*He comes in from the left sometimes, he comes in from the right*" suggest it showed Richard Butler's general disdain of all politicians. Where the first two Psychedelic Furs albums had been dark proto-goth releases, on *Forever Now* they embraced their inner pop, encouraged by Rundgren. This was a sound which could be sold to the United States as *alternative*, even possibly *post-punk*, whilst not troubling the rock fans. Whilst there was some filler, such as the deathless chug of *Merry-Go-Round*, there were also many great album tracks like the Byrds-ian chime of *Run and Run* or the frantic flange of title track *Forever Now*.

Internal arguments led to drummer Vince Ely leaving just after the completion of the album, to be replaced by Phil Calvert from The Birthday Party, as the band began a six-month world tour, consolidating their newly found role as spokesmen for the limey left field.

ʊ ʊ ʊ

Everyone believes they can do a better job than the government, and in October a few people around the world thought they would try their hand.

Democracy in Spain was fragile in the years following the 1975 death of dictator Francisco Franco, with various vested interests looking to seize control. On Friday 1st October Home Office Secretary Juan Jose Roson was made aware of a plot by three ultra-right members of the military to stage a coup the day before the national elections at the end of the month.

In the plot, nicknamed *Operation Cervantes*, the military would take control of key public buildings, railway stations, airports, radio and television transmitters, and newspaper offices, then "*neutralize*" the political elite in their homes, to stop the socialist party winning power. Roson took this information to Spanish Prime Minister Leopoldo Calvo Sotelo, and just after midnight the plotters were arrested under terrorism charges.

The elections at the end of the month brought the Socialist Workers' Party to power, the first left-wing government in the country since 1937, with Felipe Gonzalez as Prime Minister. The elections coincided with a visit to the country by Pope John Paul II, unbelievably the first pontiff ever to visit Spain.

Meanwhile, across the continent, German Chancellor Helmut Schmidt was having trouble hanging onto his control of the country. The coalition between his Social Democratic Party and the Free Democratic Party had broken down two weeks previously, and on Friday 1st October a constructive vote of *no confidence* was held in parliament, the result of which was Helmut Kohl of the Christian Democratic Union taking control of the government.

Kohl was something of a figure of fun to the political elite in Germany, who considered him to be provincial and not too bright, however his safe hands kept control for the next sixteen years, overseeing the re-unification of the nation.

Five days later in the Republic of Ireland parliament, Charlie McCreevy launched a motion of no confidence in his party leader, Taoiseach Charles Haughey. Three years previously McCreevy had been one of Haughey's staunchest supporters but had become disillusioned by the fiscal policy taken by Fianna Fail. He was supported by what became jokingly known as the *Gang of 22*, and in the subsequent vote was defeated by 58 to 22. However, Haughey's time in the top job was limited, as a December election saw the return of Garret FitzGerald to the post.

In Sweden two days later, Olof Palme was elected to the post of Prime Minister for the second non-successive time. A child of privilege, Palme had adopted a socialist viewpoint after travelling the Third World during his student years in the aftermath of the Second World War. Entering politics, he became a Swedish Socialist Democrat MP, rising to the role of Prime Minister between 1969 and 1976. After six years in opposition, Palme was re-elected as Prime Minister on 8th October 1982, a role which he held until his assassination at close quarters by an unknown assailant in 1986.

℧ ℧ ℧

September saw the debut release of a Scottish band who would go on to become influential throughout the decade. The Cocteau Twins[531] were formed in Grangemouth by Robin Guthrie and Bill Heggie, by recruiting vocalist Liz Fraser after seeing her dancing at a local club. Guthrie's brother, Brian, was the local concert promoter, so early versions of the band were awarded support slots to larger acts such as Simple Minds (from whom they took their name). Guthrie and Fraser had seen The Birthday Party supporting Bauhaus, and although painfully shy eventually got talking to the Australians after a show, who recommended they take their music to the label 4AD. The trio recorded three songs using a drum machine, a single microphone, and a cassette recorder, but such was their naivety at the time that when they had played and recorded the songs once,

they put in another cassette and played the songs again to record them. With only two (slightly different) copies of this demo cassette, Guthrie and Fraser travelled to London, where they presented one copy to Ivo Watts-Russell, the founder of 4AD Records, and the other to John Waters, the producer of the John Peel radio show. The impact was instant, with a John Peel session and a record deal with 4AD within weeks. With Fraser's timidity and the unrefined recording process burying her singing, what attracted Watts-Russell was what he thought were stratum of guitars played by Guthrie, but were instead the result of multiple effects pedals, so it was an unbelievable bonus when the trio were put into Blackwing Studios in London to find the voice which emerged from the mix. It was initially suggested that the act record a one-off single, however when the hair-raising power of Fraser's voice was discovered this was upgraded to an album. *Garlands* was recorded with a loan of a drum machine belonging to Vince Clarke and previously used on the hits of Yazoo.

It is difficult to deny a Banshees comparison on *Garlands*, and any subtleties in the guitar playing are lost in the mix and multiple layers. Certainly, one can hear some indication of the future majesty the band would display, the one the indie-minded of the 1980's fell in love with; however, the tracks were a bit too post-punk and spiky, and about a year too late.

The trio started a habit that they were to follow for the next few years, by releasing an EP of new tracks within a couple of months, which demonstrated more of the same edged music, however it is where they went next which cemented their reputation. A

---

[531] In my teenage years, the shadow of The Cocteau Twins fell long over my hometown of Falkirk. *Their* hometown, Grangemouth, was a satellite of *mine*, and from my house on the outskirts I could see the petro-chemical factories which dominated the skyline one mile away across some fields. Many people associated with the Cocteau Twins were still in town, from brother Brian Guthrie to local legends The Dead Neighbours, a psychobilly band apparently put together by the four biggest nutters in town, and who would eventually become Lowlife with the former Cocteau Twins bass player Bill Heggie in their midst. People a few years older would regale me of tales of Guthrie and Fraser. One told me of visiting the duo in their flat in Falkirk's Firs Street to find Fraser frying some eggs, in tears and apologising to the eggs for having to break them. I have no idea if that story is true, but I so want it to be.

run of dreamlike and highly melodic albums and singles followed throughout the decade and into the next, many of which were embraced by a small but enraptured following. Their singles would occasionally skim into the lower reaches of the top forty, but a low public profile, the result of shyness, meant the band never broke through to greater success.

ʊ ʊ ʊ

With the forced termination of *Multi-Coloured Swap Shop* earlier in the year when host Noel Edmonds switched over to purportedly adult television, the BBC was keen to duplicate the winning formula. On Saturday 2nd October, they unveiled *Saturday Superstore*, presented by Radio 1 DJ Mike Reid[532], and featuring Keith Chegwin, John Craven, Maggie Philbin, and David Icke[533] in regular slots, as well as musical and celebrity guests.

Over the next few weeks musical acts such as CaVa CaVa, B.A. Robertson, and Dr Hook gave way to something more akin with the taste of the viewers in the form of Musical Youth, Bucks Fizz, and Duran Duran.

Four weeks later, ITV started their weekend replacement for *Tiswas*, in the shape of *The Saturday Show*. Initially planned and advertised as *Big Daddy's Saturday Show*, the main presenter was to be Shirley Crabtree, otherwise known as the eponymous *Big Daddy*. The six-foot six-inch wrestler was at the peak of his success in the United Kingdom, having transformed himself from a fighting villain into a fan-favourite on the weekly bouts shown on a Saturday afternoon's *World of Sport*, and was in the process of positioning himself into a role as a competitor to Jimmy Savile on children's television. Then, a few days before the first episode Crabtree had a heart scare and was forced to withdraw for health reasons, as co-presenter Isla St Clair had to take over. The Grangemouth-born thirty-year-old had made the jump from respected Scottish folk singer to television star when she co-hosted *The Generation Game* with Larry Grayson but had been idle for most of 1982.

ʊ ʊ ʊ

Even at her peak, Kate Bush had been an artist out of time, however by 1982 she was never more out of step with the charts. Whilst ABC and Scritti Politti had read and understood Barthes and Derrida, their absorption of the ideas was not overtly obvious in their music, which could be taken purely at face value without worrying about structuralism, post-structuralism, or semiotics. Kate Bush, on the other hand, operated on multiple levels and a full understanding of her music was increasingly relying on the listener peeling back those layers of nuance.

Born and raised in Bexleyheath, Kent to an English doctor father and an Irish mother, who gifted her with a sardonic intellect, a liberal upbringing, encouragement to create, and a Celtic sense of incongruity, Bush came to the attention of Pink Floyd's Dave Gilmour, who paid for a professional recording at AIR Studios in London, produced by Beatles engineer Geoff Emerick, and featuring members of the London Symphony

---

[532] In 2014 Read found himself in the middle of a controversy when he wrote and released the UKIP-backed racist *UKIP Calypso*, sung in a faux-Jamaican accent. It reached number one in the independent charts.

[533] Icke's very public breakdown a few years later, with rantings about interplanetary beings, multiple dimensions, and a reptilian royal family. Nowadays, many of his beliefs have become the bread-and-butter of conspiracy theorists.

Orchestra. From this recording came a deal with EMI, who in a recherché moment of common sense for a record company, insisted on placing her on retainer for a couple of years to mature to an age when she could handle success. The teenager spent the next couple of years writing songs and studying dance and mime with Lindsay Kemp, the man who had taught David Bowie how to be stuck in a glass box.

EMI viewed Bush as an album artist, so it was to their surprise and delight when her debut single *Wuthering Heights* became a compelling and inimitable worldwide chart-topper in January 1978, with a mixture of otherworld-ness and high-pitched vocals. The following albums confirmed that Bush was a one-off; no-one else sounded or wrote songs like her.

By the start of 1982 Bush was halfway through recording her fourth album, haven given up live work a couple of years previously after a tour revolutionary in its scale, combining music with dance and theatre, pushing all three mediums to their boundaries[534]. The tour was a great success with critics and fans, but the cost of maintaining it was crippling, especially to Bush who had underwritten the whole thing to keep full creative control. She also hated that the months of rehearsal and exhausting schedule interfered with the song writing process and had forced her to rely on some old songs for third album, *Never for Ever*. During the recording of this Bush had discovered the Fairlight Computer Music Instrument, a sampling synthesizer which had been invented by Australians Peter Vogel and Kim Ryrie in 1979. At a cost of £10,000 this new instrument was out of reach for most musicians, but Peter Gabriel was enamoured enough to start a company demonstrating and selling them in Britain. Bush borrowed one and immediately saw the creative potential, installing an 8-track demo studio in her London house, and purchasing a Linn drum machine and a Yamaha CS-80, before splashing out on her own Fairlight.

Keen to move away from traditional song structure and the sound of a conventional band, the starting point of her new album was rhythm and texture. Initially choosing to work with Tony Visconti, Bush then decided it was time to really move beyond her comfort zone, electing to produce herself. However, Bush is a brilliant *user* of people in the nicest way possible: when she hears or sees something she likes, she chooses not to imitate, but to go to the source, which is what she did when recruiting Hugh

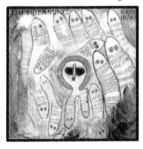

Padgham to record basic tracks at Townhouse Studios. Padgham had been one of the pioneers of the gated drum sound which became synonymous in the 1980's, and between them they recorded the tribal drum inspired single *Sat In Your Lap* which reached the top twenty in summer 1981. Soon afterwards, Padgham and Bush split with the producer using forthcoming albums by The Police, Phil Collins, and Genesis as excuse to get away from what he viewed as an unfruitful collaboration. His assistant engineer Nick Launey took over the controls, however part of the problem with Bush producing herself is that no-one was willing to say "*no*" to her, and budgets spiralled out of control as more and more tracks were filled with overdubs. The recording moved to Abbey Road Studios, at one time commandeering three separate rooms simultaneously, and then a couple of days at Windmill Lane Studios in Dublin to record members of the Irish traditional acts Planxty and The Chieftains.

---

[534] Technology had to be invented to allow the tour to happen, such as the head microphone used by many pop acts today, which was initially fashioned from a wire coat-hanger to allow Bush to move freely around the stage.

By January 1982 all the backing tracks were complete, so Bush and her partner Del Palmer locked themselves in a windowless Advision Studios for months to record the vocals. Bush was determined to sing each song on the album in a selection of different voices, and so spent time getting into character as well as drinking milk and eating chocolate to build up the mucus in her throat for a grittier sound. Mixing was finally completed in May and was the closest EMI ever got to returning an album to an artist, hearing no commercial prospects in the dense layers. In the end, the company made the decision to *accept* the album, but not to *support* it.

The first single, title track *The Dreaming*, was released in July and with no airplay scraped to number forty-eight, dealing with the plight of Australian aboriginals whose land had been shanghaied by white settlers in a search for weapons grade uranium, whilst the native population were encouraged into alcoholism to subdue them. Inspired by her memories of the Rolf Harris 1960's hit *Sun Arise*[535], Bush had written a didgeridoo part on the Fairlight, and then invited him in to record it. Harris refused to let Bush play the didgeridoo herself, stating that it was part of aboriginal law that women were not allowed to blow the instrument, much to her chagrin[536].

A promotional video featuring lasers borrowed from The Who was filmed on a soundstage made up to look like the Australian outback, which was full of all the regular Kate Bush tropes that people who dislike her could latch on to: dilettante choreography, ingenuous warbling, and hyperbolized acting. As well as controlling the music, Bush was also determined to maintain a firm hand on the visuals, however she lacked the technical expertise to fulfil the role. The head of production at EMI was furious at having spent a fortune on the video, claiming it was one of the worst promotional films he had ever seen.

The accompanying album was released in September and perplexed both reviewers and the public alike who were used to the stridulous-voiced kooky *earth mother* of previous releases. Poor reviews did not stop the album reaching number three in the charts, and Bush, realising that there was going to be very little support for the release from EMI, embarked on her own promotional tour, appearing on programmes she would not have been expected to before, such as *Pebble Mill at One* and *Saturday Superstore*, as well as a series of mimed performances across Europe. Where her previous albums had sold over a million copies each, *The Dreaming* stalled at 60,000 ensuring the extensive and protracted recording session ran at a loss for EMI.

Time has treated the album a lot kinder and it is now recognized as ground-breaking and influential, with Björk and Outkast naming it as one of their favourites. It started on the safest grounds possible, with the hit single from the previous year, *Sat in Your Lap*, before brusquely wandering into experimental territory. *There Goes A Tenner* was the tale of amateur criminals planning a big job before being overcome by paranoia, an allegory based upon Bush's own fears about her ability and talent. *Get Out of My House* was inspired by reading Stephen King's *The Shining*, using the metaphor of a possessed building intruded upon to represent her own feelings of privacy disrupted by fame. *All the Love* discussed the difficulty of opening up and allowing people into your life, whilst *Houdini*

---

[535] *Sun Arise* was produced by George Martin, and did not actually feature the didgeridoo, but eight double basses instead.

[536] So, we have a face-off of rights here: Women are forbidden to play the didgeridoo in aboriginal culture, but does cultural sensitivity trump the rights of the woman?

role-played the escapologist's wife Bess trying to communicate with him after his untimely death.

This was a deeply personal and intimate album for Bush, the first where she wrote specifically about her own feelings, albeit camouflaged by mantles of metaphor. The music and singing betrayed a hysteria which was partially deliberate, but also the result of an artist having too much freedom and too many toys in the studio.

For next single *There Goes A Tenner*, EMI instructed *The Dreaming* video director Paul Henry to cut the budget and create a more conventional promotional film that could get shown on television. When he forwarded these instructions to Bush, she was not in the slightest bit happy, choosing instead to hire the entire *Dreaming* film crew, art director, set dressers, cameramen, and wardrobe, everyone she had used on the last shoot... *except* for Paul Henry.

In a year when idiosyncratic musicians pursued their own sound Bush should have been in her element, however the shine had come off to a certain extent, and in November she dropped off the radar, exhausted by the year and a half it took to make the album and the subsequent promotional rollercoaster. The experience made her even more determined to maintain control of the process, and she built her own state-of-the-art studio in her parents' barn, a move completely in keeping with her character: Bush had always surrounded herself with her family, parents, and brothers, who in turn provided an insulating aegis[537], encouraging from an early age, allowing no negativity to creep into her self-belief.

There followed a protracted absence during which she recorded what was arguably her best album *Hounds of Love*, however a refusal to appear in public added to the perception of Bush as a recluse, an image which she did not go out of the way to disperse over the subsequent years. Albums from Bush have become infrequent, however there was a successful return to the live stage in 2014, when she staged a 22-night run at the Hammersmith Apollo with the highly theatrical *Before the Dawn* show.

She remains only one of two women to top the British singles charts with a completely self-written song.[538]

---

[537] At least one musician tells of being cut out of the *circle of trust* when he criticised a small part of a recording, never to be allowed to work with the artist again.

[538] The other is Phyllis Nelson.

OCTOBER

3rd – 9th October 1982

#1 single: Musical Youth: Pass The Dutchie
#1 album: Dire Straits: Love Over Gold

Over the past year The Beat moved away from the typical Two-Tone messages of unity and politics and embraced lyrics which dealt with more personal issues. Recent live dates in the United States had encouraged them to bring in African influences, and a further move away from the ska off-beat towards a soulful pop sound on their new album, *Special Beat Service*, was aimed at breaking America. The title was a play upon the Special Boat Service, the first British unit to land on the Falkland Islands earlier in the year.

Opening track, *I Confess* became their breakthrough hit in the United States, dealing with an unexpected pregnancy. Ageing Jamaican saxophone player Saxa had left the band in spring after being told by his doctor to give up his usual breakfast of brandy and eggs. Ranking Roger explained *"He then discovered Budweiser, renamed it Dubweiser, and lived on for another forty years"*. His place live was taken by keyboard player Dave Wright, who introduced the basic calypso piano riff from which the song was constructed. The replacement horn player was Wesley McGoogan, fresh from Hazel O'Connor's band, and he added a more jazz inflected frisson to the track. The band put together a glossy video, meant as a piss-take of the new romantic acts clogging up the charts. *"We looked like a bunch of plumbers on the unemployment line in comparison"* singer Dave Wakeling explained, but the irony of make-up was lost in the United States where the band were lumped in with all the other *British Invasion* acts, allowing MTV to push the album to into the top forty.

The party continued with *Jeanette*, a second flop single from the album, which was named after an ex-girlfriend of Wakeling who had worked in the dole office. The song momentarily took The Beat back to their ska sound, but with added French-style accordion flourishes. The album contained a variety of other influences, exhibiting a band willing to stretch themselves, from the one-drop rhythm and toasting of *Spar Wid Me* to the African High-Life guitars of *She's Going*. For *Rotating Head* the band simply played the bass line from previous hit *Mirror in the Bathroom* backwards, whilst *Pato and Roger a Go Talk* had been a previous single by Ranking Roger and Brixton-born Birmingham-based toaster Pato Banton[539].

The Beat continued to rise in America, and within six months were headlining 20,000 capacity arenas, supported by REM. The success was not to last, as they split when Wakeling persuaded Roger that the two of them were the real talent in the band. Whilst they formed General Public[540] and had some success in America, the last laugh was

---

[539] Banton had won a toasting competition which Roger had been judging. He would enjoy a chart topping single twelve years later with a version of Eddy Grant's *Baby Come Back*.

[540] General Public were something of a *supergoup*, featuring Wakeling and Roger from The Beat, Mickey Billingham and Andy Growcott from Dexy's Midnight Runners, Horace Panter from The Specials, and initially Mick Jones from The Clash.

with Dave Steel and Andy Cox who formed Fine Young Cannibals[541] and enjoyed massive worldwide success throughout the second half of the decade.

Fellow Brummies UB40 released their fourth album, *UB44*, in October, which suffered from the band moving on from their usual weed and dope to more serious drugs. As well as a cocaine dependence, frontman Ali Campbell later stated *"Certain members of the band and crew were snorting malaria tablets, Lemsip sachets, anything they could get their hands on. Then there was the acid, Supermans, Doves, magic*

mushrooms". This caused every track recorded to be too slow, *"like music made by people who were half asleep"*. Brother Robin was *"terrified of what coke was doing. It felt like everybody had gone mad around me; you know what it's like when you're the only sober one at the party."*

The album had been preceded by the single *Love is all is Alright*, responding to the *hippy aesthetic* of *"love is all you need"* the Campbell brothers had overheard throughout their childhood and adolescent years, railing against the Ku Klux Klan, racist judges, fascist brown-shirts, and bigoted police. Their conclusion was that *"Love is all is alright but you've got to find a little more hate"*, pointing out that occasionally hatred is defensible, particularly when it is directed against those who hate. Despite being snails-pace slow, the single was enormously catchy but only reached number twenty-nine. The band were progressively finding themselves at odds with what was going on musically in the United Kingdom, where the atmosphere had twisted away from *protest* towards *party*.

UB40 had other new markets to explore, such as Zimbabwe where the single sat at the top of the charts for a couple of months. To capitalize on this UB40 travelled there in summer to play a festival celebrating the second anniversary of independence. They arrived at the site to be met with an air of oppression as the armed security released vicious attack dogs on the crowd, then beat anyone in their way with sticks. As the band played, a six-month drought was ended by a sudden torrential downpour, and the government sponsored violence continued.

Robin Campbell would later claim *"Nobody knew Mugabe was about to embark on a campaign of genocide against his own people"*, but with their eyes now open to the

mood in the country, UB40 spent the rest of their time avoiding official engagements, choosing instead to visit Matopos National Park where they took great pleasure in literally dancing on the grave of Cecil Rhodes.

A third single, the minor key *So Here I Am*, expressed the frustration of the working life where *"Ten hours a day I'm grafting... making cars I'll never buy"*, an appropriate subject given Birmingham's link to vehicle manufacturing. Despite the universal sentiments expressed in the lyrics, the song crawled to number twenty-five, however bigger problems were just around the corner. CBS, who distributed the band, hated the lethargy and doom-laden sound of the album, and following them lighting up joints during a meal with the head of CBS France their contract was terminated.

The band had spent their money on building a studio in a disused slaughterhouse, doing as much of the work themselves to save money. Opening Abattoir Studios was one of the shrewdest moves UB40 ever made, cutting recording costs down to nothing,

---

[541] They first met singer Roland Gift when his band Akylykz support The Beat in January 1980.

and allowing them to record a long-mooted covers album for new label Virgin Records, including worldwide smash hit *Red Red Wine*. From there they never looked back, clocking up another forty-five British hit singles, including three chart toppers.

ʊ ʊ ʊ

See You, *The Meaning of Love*, and *Leave in Silence* had successfully bridged the gap between the departure of Vince Clarke and Martin Gore establishing himself as the primary songwriter, but it was the album *A Broken Frame* which helped seal his reputation. Despite being considered a significant step forward in the sound of  Depeche Mode, none of the songs were ever played live by the band after 1984, and Gore has since talked of his regret in recording the album.

Beyond the singles, the album dwelled in the minor keys with clearly personal songs of romantic betrayal and disillusion, not least on *Satellite* where Gahan exhorts Gore's lyrical desire to "*lock myself in a cold black room… to shadow myself in a veil of gloom*", whilst instrumental *Nothing to Fear* took the band into territory they would later explore on their more industrial albums. Influenced by Durutti Column and Der Plan, Gore had been reading a book of prophecies during the recording, and looking up his birthdate it simply said "*Nothing to fear*".

The cover of the album was designed by Martyn Atkins who had been brought in to make the band more critically acclaimed and had used Soviet imagery on the last single. He employed photographer Brian Griffin to shoot an image, with instructions to do something with a peasant and a field of wheat. Influenced by the light in the work of German Romantic painter Caspar David Freidrich, a field in Cambridgeshire just off the M11 was located and a middle-aged model hired and dressed in a peasant costume. After waiting hours for the rain to stop, a five-minute break in the clouds saw Griffin rush to catch the light, and by his own admission "*it was a one in a million* [lighting] *effect. We nearly shat ourselves when we saw the Polaroid*". The image was incredibly arresting, and later appeared on the cover of *Time Magazine* as one of the *World's Best Photographs 1980 – 1990*.

The band set off on a world tour, initially asking Sparks to support them, however the pioneering American synth duo demanded too much money. The tour served the purpose of consolidating Depeche Mode's fanbase, and confirmed they were willing to travel new directions with them. This vision was sharpened and refined on the subsequent five-month world tour starting in October, where the returning Alan Wilder brought a political influence into the lyrics and a mechanized sound to the music. Whilst the band built a reputation as a potent and powerful live act, on one date in Germany they were let down by technology when their synthesizers failed, made more embarrassing by the attendance of their heroes, Kraftwerk. The Germans left before the end of the show, believing they had no competition.

Under Gore's song-writing direction Depeche Mode would go on to sell out stadiums, as well as become a major influence on Detroit techno, British indie, synth pop, and industrial music.

ʊ ʊ ʊ

Whilst Spandau Ballet's first releases reflected their beginnings in the cutting-edge clubs of London, with the opening of the world for British bands the five-piece realised they wanted to become more global, less parochial. Main songwriter, Gary Kemp, had grown up loving pop music and was keen to move away from the pressure of working with a beat for dancing, finding his taste was moving towards soul music, influenced by Marvin Gaye, Al Green, and his unrequited love for Altered Images' Claire Grogan.

Following their failed dalliance with Trevor Horn, the band recruited Steven Jolley and Tony Swain fresh for their work with Imagination and Bananarama, entering Red Bus Studios in London to knock out a transitional filler-single called *Lifeline*. Used to writing their own material, Jolly found himself out in the cold at first, however through his catty remarks and use of *polari* he gained the trust of singer Tony Hadley and was given the job of recording and producing his vocals.

The single introduced the band's use of backing vocals to provide the main hook of a song, a trick they would utilise over the next year or so, with Kemp himself doubling up with a blue-eyed soul *"woo-hoo-hoo"*. The song also introduced saxophone to the

Spandau sound, recently learned by percussionist Steve Norman, and whilst the sound was smoother, they still managed to maintain sonic animation missing from the last album. The track was one of the band's catchiest, even if the lyrics were their usual nonsense: what exactly did *"You're living in the lifeline"* mean?

The cultural landscape had changed significantly over the past few months, as pop music picked up sales and critical acclaim, with the return of bands teenage girls could scream at. The Tory government's risky financial policies were beginning to pay off as aspiration and money became the next big things for young people to worship, and Spandau Ballet's change of direction tapped into all of these, with *Lifeline* climbing to number seven during October. The band were not hanging around to enjoy the top ten placing as they flew to the Bahamas to spend four weeks recording at Chris Blackwell's Compass Point Studios located on Love Beach on the island of North Providence, mainly because *"Robert Palmer and Talking Heads recorded there… and we could sunbathe."* Taking Jolly, Swain, and their live keyboard player Jess Bailey, it was a golden time for the band and a move that paid dividends for them and Chrysalis. They would lounge around the pool waving at Talking Heads who were mixing in the adjacent room, whilst one or two members would work on their parts indoors. With the music recorded, Swain and Jolley returned to Red Bus Studios in London to finish Hadley's vocals, followed by mixing right up the last possible minute, over-running by a few hours and intruding into the time booked by the next band. As Spandau left, they found producer Steve Levine and Culture Club waiting. *"Get the fuck out, Spandau Ballet, this is my studio time you're wasting"* spat Boy George, *"I've got some decent music to record!"*

The resultant recordings formed their next album *True*, which broke them worldwide the following year, making them one of the most successful acts of the 1980's. The band had benefited from being in the right place at the right time twice already, once in 1980 when they rode on the Blitz Club Bowie / Roxy Music influences with their debut single and album, then the following year when *Chant No. 1* had caught the London clubbing fascination with funk. In 1983 Spandau Ballet caught a third wave with British pop that appealed to screaming teenage girls, hitting the top of the charts in over twenty countries with singles such as *Communication*, *Gold*, and title track *True*, which has since racked up over five million plays on American airwaves.

Meanwhile, Gary Kemp's imagined love affair with Claire Grogan amounted to nothing more than *"one stolen kiss in a hotel elevator"*, however he gained much more from the experience in the shape of the songs that turned Spandau Ballet into a worldwide success. The turnaround for Spandau Ballet in 1982 was remarkable, with their career considered over in March and then on the verge of worldwide domination by October. By 1985 they performed a mid-afternoon slot at the Wembley leg of Live Aid, and from there it was the usual diminishing returns until their split in 1990. Tony Hadley, Steve Norman, and John Keeble then took Gary Kemp to court for song-writing royalties, losing the case and the right to use the name Spandau Ballet. Kemp and his brother Martin went into acting, playing the lead roles in the movie *The Krays*, before Gary took a role in the Whitney Houston vehicle *The Bodyguard*, and Martin found a long running role in the soap opera *East Enders*.

Like all acts, though, the lure of re-union proved too much for them in 2009, and since then they have intermittently toured until 2017 when Hadley left the band due to *"circumstances beyond my control"*. Quite what these are is unknown, however there has always been tension between Hadley and Gary Kemp, and the impression gained from their 2014 documentary *Soul Boys of the Western World* was that Kemp only just tolerated Hadley, missing no opportunity to let him know who the real talent in the band was.

ʊ ʊ ʊ

After a summer writing songs together in Manchester, John Maher and Steven Morrissey knew they were destined to move onto the next stage: forming a band. For a while, their path seemed to follow that of another unlikely young duo, George Michael and Andrew Ridgeley, as their rough demo recordings landed on the desk of Mark Dean, the owner of Innervision, who had recently signed Wham. The connection was further strengthened when the publishing duo of Morrison / Leahy showed an early interest, but instead chose to take on Michael and Ridgeley on the commercial potential value of *Careless Whispers* rather than *Suffer Little Children*.

Utilising Maher's connections a gig was booked supporting Blue Rondo à la Turk at a fashion show at Manchester Ritz on Monday 4th October, and the only problems now were to select a band name and find a rhythm section. The former came quickly with Morrissey's insistence they be called The Smiths, partly in response to the protracted moniker of the London act they were about to support, and partly because of the complete Britishness of the name.

Bass and drums were recruited from friends, with Dale Hibbert and Mike Joyce filling the posts. Maher's later recollection of the gig, which was advertised as *"An evening of pure pleasure"* was that *"Blue Rondo were a bunch of dicks, really rude and quite aggressive. They were all midgets too, which probably explains why [Steven] spent most of the night crouched down at a preposterous angle, singling into their midget height microphone"*. This was denied by Blue Rondo à la Turk frontman Chris Sullivan, who stated *"It was their first gig [so] we went out of our way to be nice to them. I was the lead vocalist and I'm 6'2". Why would I set my mike down low?"*

With Psychic TV playing a set with beatnik king William Burroughs across town at the Haçienda, very few of the *scene makers* in Manchester were at the Ritz that night. As a first gig it was unexceptional despite Steven's friend James Maker being added to the stage as a high-heeled dancer, and things had to change immediately afterwards. First to go was bass player Hibbert, to be replaced by John's friend Andy Rourke. Next, Steven announced that from now on he would only be known by his surname, Morrissey, prompting John to change his name as well. The problem was that the drummer from Mancunian punk legends The Buzzcocks was also called John Maher, and so after a slight change Johnny Marr was born.

Within a couple of weeks of the debut date everything was in place for The Smiths, from the line-up to their names, and new songs which would become nationally known within eighteen months: *What Difference Does it Make*, *This Charming Man*, and *Hand*

In Glove. These were just the beginning of a song writing relationship which would last just five years but would hold a huge influence over both music and the lives of ordinary people, those who had previously felt like outsiders. The Smiths would become the dominant British *alternative* act of the decade, one which many music lovers could not understand, but commanded everlasting loyalty from their fanatical followers.

And then Morrissey ruined it all decades later by becoming a reactionary racist bore.

ʊ ʊ ʊ

Jean-Michel Basquiat had tolerated being exhibited like a show-animal in Zurich at the behest of his agent Bruno Bischofberger the previous month, with the aim of being introduced to his hero, Andy Warhol. His dream came true in early October when the two met for lunch at Warhol's Factory studio on Union Square, New York. The two New York artists hit it off, with Warhol taking Polaroids of Basquiat with the aim of creating a silkscreened portrait. Basquiat was moved to tears by Warhol's recognition, and promptly left the studio and returned home. Two hours later a still-wet painting of the two was delivered to Warhol, prompting the elder artist to state "*I'm really jealous. He's faster than me*".

ʊ ʊ ʊ

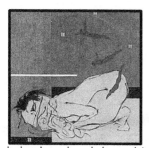

Siouxsie & the Banshees had felt a form of freedom over the summer, emancipated from punk roots to create music which dazzled, emboldened by the rising goth movement. The first result of their forthcoming self-produced album was the single, *Slowdive*, which they claimed was a twisted and failed attempt to write a dance song like *The Locomotion*, with references such as "*Do the slowdive*" and "*Revel in the dips when your backbone slips*". "*I wanted to turn the Jane Fonda Workout on its head*" explained Siouxsie in later years, and with their music now being heard and danced to in dark clubs it seemed natural for the band to produce something to force the feet to move. However, the song was more obviously a paean to female oral sex, with lines such as "*Taking honeysuckle sips from your rolling hips*", emphasised by an orgasmic whisper of "*Oh my God*" provided by violinist Anne Stephenson letting out a pained cry during the recording, which was kept in the final mix to create a false ending. The whole track was filled with unease and tension, from the opening sighs through scratching and screeching violins, as The Banshees realised they were now operating in a territory of their own, one which the public were not yet ready to follow them into with the single stalling at number forty-one.

ʊ ʊ ʊ

By the late 1970's Chrissie Hynde was the *almost-woman*, invariably on the edges of what was happening, never quite seeing them through to the end. Born in rubber capital, Akron, Ohio in 1951, Hynde had spent her teenage years obsessed with rock and roll, travelling to nearby Cleveland to see all the great bands of the 1960's without an inclination to create music herself. Enrolling at Kent State University, she was present when the National Guard opened fire on the student body, whilst also singing in a band with Mark Mothersbaugh[542], later of Devo.

After a series of dead-end jobs, Hynde's love of David Bowie and Iggy Pop, as well as the need to escape a potentially violent biker gang, took her to London in 1973 where she entered a relationship with the *enfant terrible* of British music journalism, Nick Kent.[543] Through him, she secured a job writing caustic reviews for the New Musical Express, whilst subsidising her income by working at Malcolm McLaren and Vivienne Westwood's clothes shop on the King's Road. This led her into contact with a lot of the early members of the punk scene, and she started writing songs with Mick Jones on the balcony of his gran's high rise flat overlooking the Westway, leaving when the guitarist added bass player Paul Simonen to the mix. The following week they recruited Joe Strummer and formed the Clash. Hynde was then co-opted into another band by Malcolm McLaren, initially under the name of The Masters of Backside. When she left, they became The Damned[544].

After briefly helping Steve Strange with his wilfully provocative punk act The Moors Murderers, Hynde finally put together her own band during 1978, recruiting Hereford musicians James Honeyman-Scott, Pete Farndon, and Martin Chambers. The Pretenders, as they were called, signed to Sire Records and hit the charts with their first single, a cover of The Kinks' *Stop Your Sobbing*.

As the 1980's dawned The Pretenders became massive, hitting the top of the charts all around the world with *Brass in Pocket*, and the hits continued throughout 1981 as the band released their second self-titled album and toured the globe.

The band had spent January and February 1982 touring the United States consolidating and building upon their success before heading through Japan, New Zealand, and Australia in March. Internal issues raised their head on the tour, with Farndon slipping deeper into heroin addiction and everyone else drinking heavily. It came to a head on the 14th June when he was sacked from the band, at the insistence of Honeyman-Scott. Then, out of the blue, two days later Honeyman-Scott was found dead at his girlfriend's apartment, having suffered a cocaine induced heart attack at the age of twenty-five[545].

Four days after Honeyman-Scott's death, what was left of The Pretenders entered AIR Studios in London to record a new single, recruiting former Rockpile guitarist Billy Bremner, second guitarist Robbie MacIntosh, and Big Country bass player Tony Butler who had been recording in the studio next door.

Hynde had written a new song, *Back on The Chain Gang*, at short notice in tribute to Honeyman-Scott, and veteran producer Chris Thomas was brought in with in-house engineer Steve Churchyard co-opted from the Big Country session next door. The band set up in the studio as if they were about to play live, all in the same room with

---

[542] Amongst many other things, Mothersbaugh would later compose the music for *The Rugrats*.

[543] Kent was constantly being assaulted by musicians. Sid Vicious of the Sex Pistols attacked him with a motorcycle chain, less effectively Matthew Ashman of Adam & the Ants attacked him with a pot of strawberry jam.

[544] If she had twice managed to miss out on being a member of a seminal punk act, Hynde perhaps had a lucky escape when she almost married Sid Vicious to gain a permit to stay in the country. She had initially been meant to marry Johnny Rotten, but when he pulled out Sid gallantly stepped up. Fortunately, the registry office was closed the following day, and then the day after Vicious had to appear in court on an assault charge, and so the marriage never happened. Hynde was never destined to play the role of Nancy Spungeon. Far too intelligent and streetwise, she had enough charisma and drive to realise what it was that she wanted: and that was to sit at the top table of rock and roll.

[545] Farndon was to follow him in April 1983, drowning in the bath after overdosing on heroin.

the drums on a riser, with the vocals recorded later as Hynde, hating an audience in the studio, kicked everyone out.

The song opened with a chord sequence before the band kicked in with a country guitar solo played on the spur of the moment by Bremner. Hynde started the first verse with *"I found a picture of you…hijacked my world that night"*. The picture referred to was of Ray Davies, singer with The Kinks, with whom Hynde had started a relationship and was pregnant with his child. Once Honeyman-Scott died, however, many of the lines took on a secondary meaning. Chambers and Butler added *"chain gang"* vocals to the chorus, reminiscent of Sam Cooke's song *Chain Gang*, whilst studio assistant Jeremy Allom was pressed into action to hit two studio baffle board weights together in rhythm to simulate the sound of hammers.

Given the circumstances of the recording, *Back on The Chain Gang* was a remarkable song, full of hooks and implied pain, however it only reached number seventeen in

Britain, perhaps due to the probity of a band playing together in the studio with no concessions to modern sounds being too out of touch with the current fashion.

Hynde took most of 1983 off, giving birth to a daughter, Natalie, before resuming business with The Pretenders. The hits continued throughout the 1980's and 1990's, especially in the United States with Hynde the only remaining member. The Pretenders became Hynde's alias and backing band, with a revolving door of members, which at various times featured Johnny Marr and Andy Rourke (The Smiths), Paul Carrick (Squeeze / Roxy Music), Blair Cunningham (Haircut 100), Bernie Worrell (Parliament / Funkadelic / Talking Heads), and Carlos Alomar (David Bowie). Hynde herself married Simple Minds frontman Jim Kerr in 1984, with whom she had another daughter, Yasmin, before divorcing in 1990, and enjoyed solo chart-toppers with UB40, whilst becoming a well-known animal rights activist and all-round icon.

ʊ ʊ ʊ

The protesters at Greenham Common continued to play a game of cat-and-mouse with the police and the contractors attempting to build missile silos. On Tuesday 5th October twenty of the women climbed into a ditch which had been built to hold a sewage pipe and started weaving a massive spider's web of wool on top of them, making sure some of the strands also managed to entangle their own bodies as well. When the police tried to remove them, the women made their bodies go limp, and were promptly arrested.

ʊ ʊ ʊ

With two failed singles behind them, Blancmange had saved their most commercial song for their last chance. Vocalist Neil Arthur had written a guitar line, but made a mistake when recording it, which led to the more *middle eastern* sounding riff. The duo decided to go with this, adding sitar and Indian percussion to make the song sound more exotic, creating *Living on the Ceiling* in the process. The drum pattern was unique, something *"No-one would normally program,"* explained Arthur, *"Because we did it as non-musicians but just recorded it anyway."* The single climbed to a healthy number seven on the charts, propelling Blancmange onto the pages of *Smash Hits* and the studio of *Top of the Pops*.

Despite early support from The Fall, Blancmange were ridiculed by many of the cooler acts, considered something of a commercial sell-out. Coming on the heels of Soft Cell and Yazoo, the duo faced accusations of being bandwagon jumpers. Their debut

album, *Happy Families*, had been released a couple of weeks earlier without making any mark on the charts, however with the success of the single it struggled to number thirty in October, then hung around the bottom of the top 100 for another thirty-eight weeks. Opening with the pace of *I Can't Explain* featuring the mechanic backing vocals of Joy Yates and Zambian-born Stevie Vann[546], the focus was either firmly on the ceaseless beats of the dancefloor or else the intestine miasma of a daydream. Not unlike what Depeche Mode or Yazoo were creating at their most introspective, *Wasted* provided orderly electronic contemplation, as if the whole album was the inner disquisition of a self-doubter. This reached its crest during future single *Waves*, with combers of sound washing over a synth-pop Scott Walker, written by Arthur during a summer job by the sea.

The band were somewhat taken aback by their success, with Arthur claiming "*We were two non-musicians. It's a bit like the monkeys and the typewriter, isn't it? Eventually they'll get there.*" They would go on to greater success the following year, but the spotlight was short-lived and the duo eventually split because "*the pressure – some of it self-inflicted - was destroying our friendship, so we called it a day to preserve that.*"

℧ ℧ ℧

In 1982 Bruce Springsteen was an anomaly in Britain, able to sell out six nights at the 12,500 capacity Wembley Arena on a world tour supporting his mammoth 1980 album *The River*, but still an unknown name to most music lovers in the country. Britain had not taken to his brand of *blue-collar* rock the way America had, having no real taste for the bar-room shenanigans of the likes of Springsteen, Bob Seger, Tom Petty, and many others. Britain was still a scene ruled by the three-minute titillation of the singles chart, and these artists lived in the extended world of albums, a world where themes, styles, and stories could evolve over two or more sides of vinyl.

Although Springsteen's world tour was over at the end of 1981, in his mind he was still travelling, choosing to spend night after night driving alone through the streets of his hometown, trying to work out who he was. Having turned thirty a couple of years previously, the tour had provided a welcome distraction from contemplating the ageing process, however the quietus with which he now lived was disconcerting for the artist. The minatory mood in his mind spilled into Springsteen's writing, and having become bewitched by Terence Malick's dustbowl-murder movie *Badlands*, a new set of tunes started to take shape, ones which moved from personal experience towards Steinbeck-inspired storytelling.

With a set of new songs which "*began as an unknowing meditation on* [his] *childhood*", Springsteen sat in his bedroom with a TEAC four-track recorder at the start of January and recorded fifteen of them in a twelve-hour session. These songs were then mixed onto a single cassette on a beat-box, a new

---

[546] Vann would later provide vocals for the *Bodyform* advert.

technology on the market. The aim of these recordings was to provide his backing musicians, the E Street Band, with an idea of the new music, and sessions to turn these songs into an album began optimistically enough a few weeks later, with Springsteen playing the band the demo of a song entitled *Born in the U.S.A.* about a returning Vietnam veteran. When keyboard player Roy Bittan played a keyboard riff along with the demo and drummer Max Weinberg joined in with a pounding beat, the singer was wise enough to grab his guitar. Fifteen minutes and two live takes later, the song and recording were finished. Over the next couple of days, they quickly arranged and recorded *Glory Days*, *Cover Me*, and *Darlington County*, but then the inspiration ran out when it became clear that most of the songs could not equal the intensity and intimacy of Springsteen's home recordings. The spirit and desperation of the songs was best conveyed through the sonic flaws of the late-night recordings made by the singer back in January, with their fluctuating sound quality and tempo adding to the desolation of the lyrics and music.

With the complete artistic freedom earned from huge success Springsteen decided to release the recordings as they were, mastered from a cassette tape which had been rattling around the floor of his car for a couple of months. The mastering proved to be the most difficult part of the album, with the engineers realising the singer had not cleaned the heads of the tape recorder, resulting in an intangible sound which had been recorded at the wrong speed throughout.

Nebraska was a bold move for a star of Springsteen's standing, with the expected career projection of musicians to be upwards and bigger, or at least to provide more of the same to satisfy the fans. Instead, he chose to side-step the entire machine and release a low-key poorly recorded album of bleak acoustic tracks inspired by Appalachian mountain music and the blues. The tracks told of murder, desperation, organized crime, and loss; this was the real *darkness of the edge of town* hinted at on a previous album, with no sign of salvation or redemption provided at the end. Many of the songs, such as *Mansion on the Hill*, *My Father's House*, and *Used Cars* were told from the perspective of a child, whilst all of them allowed enough space for the listener to quietly slip into the mind of the narrator.

The most commercial track on the album, *Atlantic City*, was originally titled *Fistful of Dollars*, but slowly evolved into a tale of escape and the mafia, of claustrophobic love and fate, themes which obviously made it perfect to be a failed single.

Completely out of step with what was happening in the music scene on both sides of the Atlantic, with a lack of danceable beats, synthesisers, horn sections, or glossy videos[547], despite reaching number three on both sides of the Atlantic, *Nebraska* only found a new audience for the singer over the subsequent years, people who were attracted to the raw sound and merciless honesty, especially amongst the *Alt Country* fraternity.

Meanwhile, Springsteen and the band returned to the songs first recorded during the sessions and built upon them to create their massive *Born in the U.S.A.* album a couple of years later.

In the minds of the record company, however, the album Springsteen *should* have released in 1982 was *On the Line* by rock and roll veteran Gary U.S. Bonds. With *the boss* writing seven of the eleven tracks whilst producing the album, and the E Street band providing the music, this sounded very much like a follow-up to the good-time

---

[547] *Atlantic City* had a bleak monochromatic video which did not feature Springsteen.

party songs of *The River*[548]. Springsteen even provided second vocals for many of the tracks, although his vocals were replaced on duet *Angelyne* at the insistence of Columbia Records, to be replaced by Steven Van Zandt.

The collaboration with Bonds had come about on a previous album, *Dedication*, the year before, with both Springsteen and Van Zandt being massive fans of the singer's early 1960's releases, something which can be heard on songs such as *Cherry Baby* and *Hungry Heart*. The album produced a top thirty American hit in the shape of *Out of Work*, and even a minor hit in Britain with a cover of The Box Tops' *Soul Deep*, which reached number fifty-nine.

ʊ ʊ ʊ

By the time Duran Duran toured mainland Europe in October, bass player John Taylor had moved on from Bebe Buell (who was still in love with ex-Elvis Costello anyway) and was bedding Amanda Berrow, the sister of his managers. Arranging a night out with Roxy Music in Munich on Wednesday 6th October, the band found themselves in trouble when a fight broke out against a gang with baseball bats. Despite the valiant efforts of bodyguard Simon Cook, drummer Roger Taylor took the worst of the beating whilst Bryan Ferry and John Taylor hid in the toilets. Returning from the hospital the drummer was tended to by Berrow, driving John Taylor into a raging fit of jealousy, and he returned to his room to punch his fist through a glass light fixture in anger, resulting in his own visit to hospital and several stitches, rendering him unable to play bass. As the band and crew snuck onto the tour bus in the morning, the rest of the German dates were cancelled, and everyone flew home to Birmingham.

Two days later Taylor was summoned to club headquarters the Rum Runner where the rest of the band and managers told him the band would still play the forthcoming Portuguese dates… with a session bass player. Taylor was invited along for press and publicity, but as he watched someone else do his job from the side of the stage the message was driven home: he was replaceable.

ʊ ʊ ʊ

The Teardrop Explodes managed one more tour, this time as a three piece with backing tapes. Every night Julian Cope would apologise from the stage after each song, whilst backing tapes would snap or stop and start at random times. At Manchester University on Friday 8th October, the tape went into reverse during one of the quieter numbers, and Cope completely lost it. He tore down the stage set, hauled at the lighting rig until it was hanging by one wire, threw his twelve-string guitar into the audience, pushed the monitors off the stage, tore off his shirt and kicked off his boots. He considered taking off his leather trousers, but *"the stage was already a metaphor for bad sex without introducing another soft dick into the proceedings"*.

ʊ ʊ ʊ

Madonna's first single, *Everybody*, was released on Friday 8th October on white label 12-inch vinyl marketed at the New York club market. The cover deliberately did not feature an image of the singer and the disc had a white label in the hope people would assume she was black, making her more acceptable to the dance community. Upon

---

[548] Many of the songs were re-recorded out-takes from that very album.

release one review referred to Madonna as a new duo and by the start of November it had broken into the Billboard dance chart.

Having outlived his usefulness, Madonna had split with boyfriend and producer Michael Kamins, and had started dating the new darling of the New York art world, Jean Michael Basquiat. The artist also had strong feelings for her, however when heroin is involved the partner is always going to come second. The couple, introduced to each other by video director Ed Steinberg, were immediately inseparable. She hoped some of his creativity would rub off on her, he hoped that her new payment from Sire Records would cover his rent and drugs. Whilst moving into his Lower East Side loft, which Basquiat was renting from Andy Warhol, Madonna also kept her own place… just in case.

The relationship was not to last long into 1983 as Basquiat became more interested in  his narcotic addiction and Madonna had sucked all she could from him and felt it was time to move on again.

Madonna was to go on and become the most successful female star of the decade, however the signs were not good for women in 1982. Of the 153 top ten singles in the United Kingdom during the year, 72% were by male artists and 20% by groups of mixed gender such as Kid Creole and the Coconuts and Bucks Fizz, with only 8% by female artists. The colour breakdown of the top ten was no better with 78% of acts white, and only 14% being performed exclusively by non-white artists.

Punk had provided a space for female singers to react against the stereotype of women in the music industry. Bands like The Slits (who had split in January) and The Raincoats refused to dress for the male gaze and avoided learning their instruments so as not to fall into the tired clichéd blues scales, instead creating something with which to lance the collective rock groin, something more primal. With the demise of the wave of feminist performers such as Poly Styrene from X-Ray Spex, a gap was created and there was a danger female singers may be forced back into the established and sanctioned tropes.

Into this lacuna came Madonna, a performer who was ruthless in keeping complete control of her music and image. Never pandering to male expectations, playing the industry at their own game, only showing culpability when it was to her advantage, Madonna was the perfect eidolon for an aspirational age and the epitome of empowerment, providing teenage girls with a role model and icon.

℧ ℧ ℧

As Billy MacKenzie retreated from the success of The Associates he returned to Dundee and hooked up with old friend and guitarist Steve Reid, who by now had a 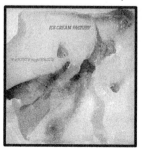 serious drug addiction and was in hiding due to a paranoid belief that he had caused the Falklands War. The two hatched a plan to write together, and persuaded Warner Brothers Records to provide £6,000 to record a single.

Released in October under the name *Billy MacKenzie Sings Orbidoig*, the song *Ice-Cream Factory*, written by Reid, had the makings of a pop song, with the singer fantasising about taking a job making ice-cream in a factory. There were hooks galore within the song, however it lacked Rankine's multi-instrumental genius, and only MacKenzie's voice lifted it above run-of-the-mill.

Despite failing to chart, Warners provided a budget of £50,000 for the next album, and recording began in November.

This album, *Perhaps*, featured three extremely minor hits and MacKenzie was dropped by the record company,[549] only to issue releases sporadically after under the Associates name as well as solo, however he never enjoyed anything near the kind of success evident in 1982. The singer was not interested in playing the game, claiming "*I don't adhere to the sweat and toil and workshop attitude of record companies.*" Tragically MacKenzie, suffering depression after the death of his mother a few months earlier, took his own life in January 1997 in the shed in Dundee where he kept his beloved whippets. By rights, with his voice and charisma, he should have been one of the biggest stars of the decade.

10th – 16th October 1982
#1 single: Musical Youth: Pass The Dutchie
#1 album: Dire Straits: Love Over Gold

Although born in Guyana in 1948, Eddy Grant had joined his parents in London when he was twelve years old, and absorbed all Britain had to offer culturally during the 1960's. With school friends he formed The Equals, the first popular inter-racial band in the United Kingdom, enjoying three years of top forty action at the end of the decade, including a chart topper in the shape of *Baby Come Back*. It took a collapsed lung and heart attack at twenty-three for him to leave the band, electing instead to spend time writing and producing at his own Coach House, the first black owned studio in Europe, as well as learning to tap dance.

Encouraged into releasing his own solo albums in the late 1970's, Grant had made a name for himself as a writer and performer of reggae-influenced political pop songs, a few of which had breached the British charts at the turn of the decade. With the advent of riots on the streets of Britain during 1981, Grant decided he had had enough, and moved to Barbados, building Blue Wave Studios for

himself. It was always Grant's approach not to stand on a soap box in his songs, explaining "*I choose melody, rhythm, harmony, and all the tools available to a songwriter to help make the message as painless as possible for people to ingest. Music is a fantastic delivery mechanism. It's like water. You want to take a serious tablet? Drink a lot of water and it will go down in some measure.*" This approach was best demonstrated in infectious new single *I Don't Wanna' Dance* and the accompanying video. The song appeared to about the singer wanting to leave an unfaithful partner, and in the video we see both, him throwing a massive strop on a raft floating off the shore of a beautiful Caribbean beach, her on the shore stamping her feet in frustration at his huff.

---

[549] When given the news over lunch MacKenzie went out of his way to ensure his A&R man did not feel bad about the decision, before asking if the record company would stand him one final taxi home on expenses. A&R man, Max Hole, felt it was the least they could do for him, however what he did not realise was that MacKenzie meant to take the taxi all the way from London to Dundee, almost 600 miles away, one final act of decadence.

And yet, the song was a vehicle for Grant to say goodbye to the United Kingdom, a country he had lived for over twenty years, where he had experienced his formative years. *"I love your personality, but I don't want our love to show"* he sings, further explaining *"The party's over for us so I'll be on my way… I won't look back even though I feel your music."* The raft in the video was Barbados, whilst on the shore Britain stomped its imperialist entitled feet. What sold the song was the music, a lilting reggae stomp with an infective chorus.

With Musical Youth sitting high in the charts, the time was perfect for another Caribbean influenced track, and *I Don't Wanna' Dance* climbed to number one, remaining there for three weeks.

ʊ ʊ ʊ

Staying alive in Berlin by winning at nightly card games, Birthday Party singer Nick Cave continued to develop his songwriting, the result of which could be heard on their

new EP, *The Bad Seed*. Recorded at Hansa Studios, the site of David Bowie and Iggy Pop's successful run of albums in the late 1970's, the songs were sparser than before with the lyrics occupying a more essential role and the vocals pushed to the front of the mix. *Deep in the Woods* had been written in the Black Forest area of South-West Germany, and was a murder ballad during which Cave proclaimed *"Love is for fools and all fools are lovers"*. The characters in the tracks were indeed *bad seeds*, from the murderer in *Fears of Gun* to the self-immolating protagonist in *Sonny's Burning*.

The songs betrayed Cave's growing fascination with older musical styles such as country and blues, a path which was to put him at odds with the direction of The Birthday Party. Tired of being lumped in with the new *goth* movement, Cave would go out of his way in interviews to disparage the other bands, declaring them as *"Paper tigers, all"*, whilst claiming *"a group that reflects anything other than their own idiosyncratic vision is not worth a pinch"*.

However, before he could follow his own vision, Cave had touring commitments to fulfill with The Birthday Party, and many around him felt this would be the final breaking point for a band already struggling to hold their own lives together, never mind a few self-destructive weeks on the road.

ʊ ʊ ʊ

As unemployment continued to rise in Britain, BBC2 responded with a new series entitled *The Boys from the Blackstuff*, first shown on Sunday 10th October. The program had begun as a one-off *Play for Today* in January 1980 and was then extended into a seven-part series. Writer Alan Bleasdale hoped to capture *"the hollowness and sense of worthlessness that a lot of people feel when they're on the dole"* and wanted to show *"urban decay, spiritual deprivation and death"*.

Following the fortunes of a group of unemployed Liverpudlian tarmac layers, the most successful episode featured Bernard Hill as Yosser Hughes, a man who has lost his job, his wife, access to his children, and is on the verge of losing his sanity. Hill brilliantly portrayed a man on the edge, fighting for his very masculinity and unable to adapt to his newfound circumstances. His repeated and increasingly desperate attempts to find work, accompanied by his mantras of *"gizza job"* and *"I can do that"*, struck a chord with the public, and at the end of the run on BB2 it was immediately repeated to a larger audience on BBC1.

ʊ ʊ ʊ

The big debate at gay nightclub The Saint in New York during Autumn was whether to completely exclude women from the venue. The Saint worked as a members-only club, however each member was allowed to sign one guest in, and recently these guests had started to include women in search of good dancing in a sexually hassle-free environment. A survey in the club newssheet revealed only 2% of members believed women should be admitted on Saturdays, whilst 52% felt they should never be allowed in. The club reached a compromise, with female guests allowed on Wednesday nights and on Sundays if they were *cleared* in advance.

It was not just women who were absent as owner Bruce Mailman marketed the venue towards the white clientele who frequented the gay Fire Island clubs during vacation time. A recent increase in membership fees further marginalised black and Latino dancers who tended to be in the wrong socio-economic bracket.

It was not long until anyone without wages found it difficult to attend any clubs in Manhattan, as Reaganomics kicked in and the financial sector took over. The gentrification of the island saw low rent apartments reducing in numbers, as developers such as Donald Trump bought and renovated former slum buildings, and an era of unparalleled nightlife came to an end.

ʊ ʊ ʊ

Marc E. Smith, keen to move on from the acclaim gathered by The Fall's *Hex Enduction Hour*, was determined the next album would be recorded quickly and be different in tone. Using the same musicians, Smith insisted they not rehearse the songs before recording for fear they learn them, and even omitted some of them on certain days by telling them they had the day off whilst everyone else met in the studio. Unhappy at the camaraderie displayed within the band during their recent tour of Australia and New Zealand, this was Smith
employing classic *divide and conquer* tactics, seeing the musicians as a close-knit Catholic cabal in contrast with his drunken Protestant atheism. He would often refer to them as "*the Jesuits*" and blame anything that went wrong on their "*mick slyness*". Even when the musicians were invited into the studio, Smith would encourage them to swap instruments, especially if they could not play them.

Room to Live (Undilutable Slang Truth) was recorded at Cargo Studios in Rochdale in June and appeared to contain Smith's comment on 1982 with songs such as *Papal Visit* and Falkland-referencing *Marquis Cha-Cha*[550]. "*We could do with taking time to turn these ideas into proper songs*" complained bass player Steve Hanley, "*Playing people off against each other is taking up the energy that should be going into the songs*". Smith, however, was having none of it, and after the critical heights of the previous album this one was described by critics as "*slapped together and half-baked.*"

---

[550] Smith spent quite a lot of interviews in 1982 defending the Falklands War, coming across as a rabid patriot in the process, complaining "*some of these moaners should get a good dose of army discipline and patriotism*". Everyone else. Not Smith himself, of course.

ʊ ʊ ʊ

There was a real sense of expectation surrounding *The Sky's Gone Out*, the new album by Bauhaus, with the burgeoning goth scene ardently anticipating one of their bands breaking through. Whilst the album is now affectionally remembered, it does sound more like a compilation than a coherent piece of work, a band caught between pleasing their audience, who perhaps would have been more contented with a recapitulation, and their own inclination to push the sound forward. This did not stop the release climbing to number four in the British charts, bolstered by a new single which did not even feature on the album.

Ziggy Stardust had been written by David Bowie in 1971 and recorded towards the end of that year for the album *The Rise and Fall of Ziggy Stardust and the Spiders from Mars*. The song was part of a conceptual cycle examining the phenomenon of pop stars and extra-terrestrials beings within a dystopian world... the perfect theme for Bauhaus! The song may have been celebrating its tenth anniversary but given music's tendency to look forward in those days it is unlikely this was the reason for Bauhaus recording their own version. The truth was they were fed up being compared to Bowie and decided to rub this lazy comparison into the critics' noses... by recording a David Bowie song, but not just any Bowie song, but the title track of his most acclaimed creation. *"There's a lot of us in that song, which is the main point"* justified David Haskins, *"Nearly everybody who hears it says it's just the same as the original, but if you go back and listen to the original, it's very different."* And to be honest, it was not too bad a version, a note for note recreation but with a post-punk edge: even the improvised *ooh's* and *ah's* were in the right place. The familiarity of the song along with the growing reputation of Bauhaus allowed it slip into the top forty, giving the band their biggest hit to date when it peaked at number fifteen. With a long-awaited breakthrough hit, Bauhaus were on

the verge of moving into the big league, as Pete Murphy began to be considered something of a pin-up, gracing the front page of *Smash Hits* usually reserved for the LeBons and Hadleys of the world. The next six months was to see them fail to reach this target with only two minor hit singles, and in summer 1983 the band split. Their appearance in the movie *The Hunger*, where they performed debut single *Bela Lugosi's Dead*, allowed Murphy to be noticed by the movie and advertising industry, and he was hired to star in a television advert for the Japanese technology company, Maxell[551].

Murphy was then stricken down by pneumonia leading to him having a reduced role in the recording of a fourth and final album, *Burning from the Inside*, and after splitting, the chisel-cheeked singer went on to form Dali's Car with Mick Karn from the band, Japan, before attempting a solo career. The rest of the band spent time playing separately with Tones on Tail and The Jazz Butcher, before a failed attempt to reform led to the formation of Love & Rockets without Murphy. This band displayed a more commercial sound and were rewarded with a top twenty hit single in America.

ʊ ʊ ʊ

---

[551] The advertising job was initially offered to David Sylvian, however Murphy was happy to *"be Marilyn Monroe for three days"*.

With the Queen out of the country opening the new $82 million National Gallery of Australia in Canberra, the official Falklands War victory parade was led on Tuesday 12th October by Margaret Thatcher, an impressive political coup which was only spoiled for her when the Archbishop of Canterbury argued for compassion for victims of the war on both sides. 300,000 people lined the mile-long route, cheering troops and military bands, the last apotheosis of jingoism from a fading empire.

ʊ ʊ ʊ

The Clash were about to complete their North American tour in September when an offer arrived from Pete Townshend, asking them to support the Who on eight dates in stadiums in front of over 80,000 people per night. With *Rock the Casbah* climbing the Billboard Hot 100, this was the perfect opportunity to consolidate success Stateside, and so at the end of September and start of October the band played a 45-minute *greatest hits* set to over half a million people. Whilst something of the communion and power of the Clash experience was lost in such a vast arena, it provided an insight into how the next album and tour would look like.

On Tuesday 12th October The Clash played Shea Stadium in New York, filmed by Don Letts for posterity and to provide a long overdue promotion clip for *Should I Stay or Should I Go*. Joe Strummer insisted they arrive in style, hiring an open-top 1956 Cadillac to transport the band from their hotel to the stadium. Despite freezing weather, the band toughed it out, looking the epitome of rock star coolness with the wind blowing through their quiffs and the Manhattan skyline in the background as they cruised the highway. At Shea, Strummer and photographer Joe Stevens explored the basement of the stadium, finding a prison containing a black kid who had been apprehended for trying to break into the gig. Strummer, always passionate about the treatment of fans, fetched food and water for the prisoner before trying unsuccessfully to persuade the authorities to release him.

Meanwhile, a double A-side single was released, containing the rough and dry commercial rock and roll of *Should I Stay or Should I Go* on one side, and *Straight to Hell* on the other. Guitarist Mick Jones had written *Should I Stay or Should I Go* about his American girlfriend, Ellen Foley[552], loosely basing the melody on *Little Latin Lupe Lu*, a song recorded in the 1960's by the Detroit Wheels. With Jones going all out to deliberately write a classic rock and roll song, Strummer decided he wanted to record parts of the song in Spanish, and with the help of Joe Ely translated the lyrics into a mongrel variant of the language. The result can be heard in the ramshackle backing vocals making declarations such as "*esta indecisión me molesta*" and the title which was sung as "*yo me enfrió o lo soplo*", which translates as "*I cooled or I blow it*". By this stage Jones and Strummer were barely talking to each other, and the song had become a comment on the guitarist's feelings towards the band.

There was a purity and fibrous rawness to the song in terms of chord progression and recording technique, which with frantic double-time choruses added to the stimulation

---

552 Foley was the woman who sang the towering female vocals on Meat Loaf's *Paradise by the Dashboard Light*.

of a *tour de force* rock and roll barrage. Despite becoming one of the best-known tracks by one of the most renowned acts, the single struggled to number seventeen[553].
I loved the song when my brother bought the single but avoided the other side because the title sounded like it would be a loud and discordant punk song. How wrong I was. *Straight to Hell* has been proven over time to be the single most impressive track recorded by a remarkable and furiously creative band.
Completed on New Year's Eve in New York, *Straight to Hell* started as a bossa nova, with the main beat provided by Strummer banging an R. White's Lemonade bottle wrapped in a towel against the front of Topper Headon's kick drum. Stummer recalled "*I'd written the lyric staying up all night at the Ironquois Hotel. We finished about twenty to midnight* [then] *took the E train from the Village up to Times Square. I'll never forget coming out of the subway exit, just before midnight, and I knew we had just done something really great.*"
Over an unhurried violin and bass guitar beat, Stummer sang a seemingly stream-of-consciousness lyrics covering a wide-range of subjects, including imperialism, the death of empire, drug addiction, and the plight of mixed-race children left in Vietnam by American troops. Starting close to home, Strummer lamented the rusting of the northern English steel mills, workers being told "*There ain't no need for you*", before going global during the second verse. The plight of *Amerasians*, the term used for children born of an Asian mother and American G.I. father, had been recognised by United States law when they passed the *Amerasian Immigration Act* in 1982, however most of these outcast children were left abandoned in the country. Despite their pleas, Strummer recognised the insurmountable cultural differences, stating "*Lemme' tell you about your blood, bamboo kid, it ain't Coca-Cola, it's rice*". Later the song brought together the common immigrant experience, claiming "*It could be anywhere, most likely could be any frontier, any hemisphere, no man's land, there ain't no asylum here*" before referencing the Molotov cocktails recently thrown at Puerto Ricans in New York's Alphabet City to encourage them to go home. The damage caused to the buildings by these acts of arson allowed developers to gentrify this part of Manhattan. The songs faded out when you did not want it to, missing a recorded final verse regarding Latino drug dealers in New York.
Straight to Hell is a song that revealed more of itself with repeated listens, even though it seemed to meander, never built to a crescendo, reflecting the never-ending drudgery of life for the disenfranchised. Strummer did not preach during the song, instead offered a series of snapshots, wisely allowing the listener to piece together their own conclusion.
Years later MIA would sample the rhythm of *Straight to Hell* for her own classic *Paper Planes*, another song which examined the immigrant experience, this time celebrating the inventiveness and ability to prosper of a migrating population. The song brought *Straight to Hell* into a new focus, with Colin Coulter comparing the two singers and their motives: "*The attempt of the son of a British diplomat to capture the plight of those enduring displacement by war is held to have drawn a stinging rebuke from the daughter of a Third World insurgent whose formative years were spent among the displaced*". There were unsupported whispers of backdated cultural appropriation, but Strummer's ability and willingness to put his money where his mouth was throughout his life was enough to quell such accusations.
At the end of the day, *Straight to Hell*, despite the despondent tone, was an enlightening track worth repeated listens, with music and lyrics to get lost in, and was one of the undisputed highlights of the decade.

---

[553] Rather surprisingly, The Clash never reached the top ten during their lifespan, though *Should I Stay or Should I Go* was re-issued on the back of a Levi's Jeans advert in 1991 and topped the charts.

℧ ℧ ℧

Once an album was released in the early 1980's it was practically considered commercially sacrosanct: nothing else could be released from it. The singles, two or three of them, would be released first, then the long player containing them would act as a sonic full stop. Very occasionally a record company would milk another single, however this was considered bad form by the industry and fans alike. That would all change before Christmas, with the release of the biggest selling album of all time, however when Culture Club hit the charts with *Kissing to be Clever* they were ready to move on. As the album

stopped at number five, the record company would probably have loved to promote it further, maybe releasing *I'll Tumble 4 Ya*, a salsa inflected commercial pop song which would go top ten in the United States when re-mixed the following year.[554]

Elsewhere, the album remained thin in terms of sound and song quality, with nothing as strong as *Do You Really Want to Hurt Me*, and even re-mixed versions of previous singles *White Boy* and *I'm Afraid of Me* sounded weak, whilst other tracks sounded too synthetic with Boy George's vocals straining at the top of their range. If we were to be generous, we could admit the album was the perfect mixture of the four members of Culture Club: Mikey Craig's dub bass, Roy Hay's funk guitar, Jon Moss' Motown / tribal drums, and George's insecurities.

℧ ℧ ℧

The John Peel show continued to expose new musical acts to the British public, with sessions throughout October by the likes of the Lotus Eaters (the well-connected Liverpudlian act who featuring ex-members of The Wild Swans and The Jazz Babies, were put together the previous months specifically for the session and would go on to have a hit single the following year with *The First Picture of You*), Strawberry Switchblade (an all-female Glaswegian act connected to Postcard Records, who would be offered a management contract from their session by Bill Drummond and Dave Balfe, and would score a top ten single in 1984 with *Since Yesterday*), skinhead Socialists The Redskins, Brilliant (featuring former Killing Joke bass player Youth), as well as more established acts such as The Undertones, The Birthday Party, Reggae legend Gregory Isaacs, and Kirk Brandon's new act, Spear of Destiny.

As well as musicians, John Peel was always keen to lend a helping hand to others, and on his show on Tuesday 12th October he read out a letter from a young Scottish exile in London who was looking for publicity for his weekly club night in Camden, at which new bands could be seen. *The Communication Club* was a great idea, however Peel paused halfway through, before castigating the letter writer for not including a date for the first night.

The young Scottish letter writer was called Alan McGee, and his music promotion career was off to a poor start.

℧ ℧ ℧

---

[554] The song was accompanied by a video for which the band learned how to tap dance, and which featured a pre-fame, pre-teen Naomi Campbell as a dancer.

Kim Wilde finally embarked on her long-promised tour, staging a low-key eight date jaunt round Denmark in September with a four-piece band, featuring brother Ricki on keyboards and guitar, future Jive Bunny arranger Graeme Pleeth on keyboards, former Gillan guitarist Steve Byrd, and Trevor Murrell on drums, as well as a horn section and Suzi Quatro's old backing singers. This was followed by an extensive British tour in October, which the press agreed struggled to ascend above average, pointing out how much the music and ageing musicians were draining any vitality from the singer. To make things worse, the crowd turned against her in Birmingham when she addressed them as "*Manchester*", and a review of the London date stated "*Clashing a couple of saucepans together couldn't be much less harmonious than the unattractive shouting she directed at the audience*".

As the tour continued through France, the Netherlands, and Belgium in November, where Wilde remained a top ten artist, she took to recording any interviews with the press, paranoid she was being misquoted.

To coincide with these dates, a new single *Child Come Away* was released, a stand-alone mid-paced, faceless single which inched to number forty-three in the charts. Over the next three years Wilde dwindled in the public consciousness until she released a hi-energy version of The Supremes' *You Keep Me Hanging On*, which reached the top ten across the world, topping the Billboard charts in America, and revitalising her career, allowing her to tour the world supporting Michael Jackson and David Bowie. In the new millennium Wilde found herself with a second career as a television gardener, balancing this with live performances on the 1980's nostalgia circuit.

υ υ υ

Watching the Falklands Victory Parade in London earlier in the week was a twenty-two-year-old who knew he had been fortunate to miss out on the whole war. Stephen William Bragg had left the army just a year before and had seen his former colleagues travel to the South Atlantic earlier in 1982.

Much has been made of Bragg's former career in the military, however the record shows he only endured the twelve-week basic training before buying himself out for £175. What this time did give him, however, was an empathetic understanding of the life and mind-set of a typical squaddie, young men who escaped bleak prospects and unemployment by enrolling for an organisation that welcomed them and provided a future. His military experience also made crystal clear where he thought his own future lay: making music.

Bragg had spent the late 1970's playing guitar in punk act called Riff-Raff, having had his *road-to-Damascus* moment whilst seeing The Clash live on the *White Riot* tour of 1977. The band released a couple of singles without achieving success and seemed set to be just another wannabe third-rate punk act when they fell apart in 1980. With no prospects, Bragg signed up for the Queens Royal Irish Hussars in May 1981, a regiment he chose because they were never sent to Northern Ireland. Upon leaving the army he set himself up playing solo gigs, accompanied only by his electric guitar and broad Essex accent. The stripped-down approach was at odds with music in 1982, where over-production and surface sheen were valued, and as such the prospects for success were extremely slim. Bragg later explained what made him take this approach, claiming "*One day I saw Spandau Ballet on Top of the Pops wearing kilts and singing…*"

and something in me snapped. I was waiting for a band to come along to play the kind of music I wanted to hear, and none was forthcoming… I finally realised it was gonna' have to be me."

During the summer of 1982 he adapted the name Spy Vs Spy, realising that he was unlikely to get gigs as a solo artist, and that a *new romantic* sounding name might help in this regard. The danger of being labelled a folk singer was warded off by Bragg's combative guitar style, usually played through a small portable amplifier, and it was this amateurish sound that made him stand out from everything else in 1982.

Spy Vs Spy made their debut in June at the Rock Garden in London, supporting a friend's band, and then spent the summer playing dates across the capital, sometimes outnumbering the audience. Dropping his first name and shortening William to Billy, Bragg recorded six tracks on a multi-track at the house of Steve Goldstein, his boss at Low Price Records where he worked during the day. These included *A New England* and *The Milkman of Human Kindness*, capturing the echinate energy of his live show. Four days after the Falklands Victory parade Bragg received a phone call from his girlfriend Katy, who worked in central London. She had picked up the newly printed copy of *Melody Maker* and discovered a review of the demo. Phoning Bragg at Low Price Records during her lunchbreak, she asked him *"Are you sitting down?"* before reading out a rhapsodising review by Adam Sweeting praising the *"Sharpest and funniest lyrics I've heard in years"*, whilst stating the *"songs put to shame most of the people who go around calling themselves songwriters"*.

In the same demo review column was a recording by Nux Vomica, which Sweeting trashed. Ironically, this was a demo of deliberately bad pop songs also recorded by Bragg with a couple of friends and sent in as a controlled scientific experiment.

17ᵗʰ – 23ʳᵈ October 1982

#1 single: Culture Club: Do You Really Want To Hurt Me
#1 album: Dire Straits: Love Over Gold

America remained in love with blue-collar rock, elevating their Bob Segar's and Bruce Springsteen's to God-like status as spokes-voices of the common man, and

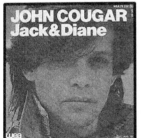

occasionally one of their heroes would break through in Britain. In October 1982 it was the turn of John Cougar Mellencamp and his single *Jack & Diane*.

The thirty-one-year-old former concrete mixer from Indiana had signed with Tony DeFries, the manager of David Bowie, and spent the 1970's moving from glam roots towards mainstream working-class rock under the name John Cougar until he had enough clout at the record company to insist that they add his birth name, Mellencamp.

Recording in Los Angeles and Miami, a fifth album called *American Fool* was put together, looking back at his upbringing in the mid-west, reflecting this in songs of small lives harshly lived. The almost auto-biographical, *Jack & Diane*, painted a nostalgic picture of young love, with the couple *"Suckin' on a chili dog outside the Tastee Freeze, Diane's sittin' on Jacky's lap, he's got his hands between her knees."* Mellencamp had been influenced by a viewing of the 1961 Warren Beatty and Natalie Wood movie *Splendor in the Grass*, providing a bleak message of failed ambition during a chorus of *"Life goes on long after the thrill of living is gone."* This was his former hero David Bowie's *Young Americans* recast into Springsteen's horizontal Badlands of the mid-west. *"Most people don't ever reach their goals"* he explained at the time, *"Failure's a part of what you're all about anyway."*

Taking Phil Coillins' *In the Air Tonight* as a sonic blueprint, Mellencamp explained to his producer Don Gehman *"This is what I want to create. I want to have a couple of verses that sound like a little folk song and then I want the big, bombastic entrance of some drums, and we'll take it to a whole new place."* The Bowie connection was furthered by using guitarist Mick Ronson in the studio, who also helped arrange the song, though a compromise was reached with the record company when it came to the lyrics. Mellencamp had originally written about an inter-racial couple but was persuaded by Riva Records to change this or else the song would not sell in the heartlands.

After reaching the top of the Billboard charts, Mellencamp turned his attention to the United Kingdom, flying in for a short promotional tour during which he made clear his disgust with the British music scene. *"I don't like the Human League cos one of those guys said eventually the guitar will become obsolete in rock and roll. In the streets where I walk, if it ain't got guitar in it, it ain't rock and roll"* he sneered in a *Smash Hits* interview, before describing Soft Cell as "A *couple of fairies, phoney and pretentious*"[555] and Public Image as *"an absolute embarrassment"*. Yet, he had been obsessed with Roxy Music in the early 1970's and had played in a glam-rock band called Trash himself, and so the newly found hatred of British music seemed to be part of a pseudo-macho American act.

The single climbed to number twenty-five, his only British top forty hit. Maybe the feeling was mutual.

ʊ ʊ ʊ

"It was twenty years ago today…" sang The Beatles in the opening line of the title track from their album *Sgt Pepper's Lonely Hearts Club Band* in 1967, and although it was

only fifteen years previously, it seemed like a threadbare message from another black and white age. This opening couplet was tenuous enough for executives at EMI to consider new ways to sell The Beatles to the public, and the twentieth anniversary of their first single seemed like the perfect and most opportunistic way to start.

Love Me Do, which had been written primarily by Paul McCartney in the late 1950's with Lennon later adding a middle section, was originally released in October 1962, peaking at number seventeen in the charts. The first version of the song had been recorded with original drummer Pete Best, but was deemed of unsuitable quality by producer George Martin. Before the second recording, Best was replaced by Ringo Starr, who appeared on the new version, but was once again considered not good enough, and so a third version was recorded with session musician Andy White playing drums. It was, however, the Starr version which was released as a single, with the White version featuring on their debut album *Please Please Me* and subsequent compilations. The Pete Best version eventually appeared on the *Anthology* album in 1995.

---

[555] Mellencamp was typically American in his attitudes: a 1982 Gallup poll discovered that 51% of Americans did not accept homosexuality as normal.

The 1982 release was marketed by EMI not as a *re-issue*, but as a *re-promotion*, retaining the same catalogue number, but this time coming in an extra seven-inch picture disc format. With media interest and the industry standard of deleting releases a short while after their peak, the market was ripe to re-discover the band, whilst those who remembered The Beatles the first time round scratched their heads and wondered what had happened to the last *twenty years*. The single raced into the top ten, peaking at number four and was followed by a twenty track greatest hits compilation later in the month.

During the summer, the city of Liverpool also celebrated twenty years of the Beatles by naming four streets John Lennon Drive, Paul McCartney Way, George Harrison Close and Ringo Starr Drive. Years later, the original drummer was also celebrated with his own Pete Best Drive.

Other old singles started to be re-issued by unscrupulous record companies, with *House of the Rising Sun* by The Animals reaching number eleven, *Love* by John Lennon halting at number forty-one, *All Right Now* by Free stopping at number fifty-seven, and *Hi-Ho Silver Lining* by Jeff Beck peaking ten places lower, as the industry woke to the idea that the past could be re-packaged and re-sold.

Meanwhile, a contemporary act from the 1960's released one final lacklustre album before splitting. *It's Hard* by The Who was an album made by a band who were not keen to release an album but were impelled by their record company to have new material for what turned out to be their farewell tour. Despite a healthy chart position of eleven, the album has been forgotten by the public, and of course, no-band ever splits up forever... not when there is nothing else for them to do. The Who reunited for intermittent live work in 1985. And again in 1988. Then for major tours in 1989, 1999, 2000, and 2002, where even the death of bass player John Entwistle on the night before the tour began could not stop them. Not to mention the 2004, 2005, 2006, 2007, 2008, and 2009 tours where a second generation of rock star kids made up their band, such as Ringo Starr's son Zak on drums and Pete Townshend's son Simon on guitar, like some kind of family franchise. And still the tours keep coming.

ʊ ʊ ʊ

Despite his first solo single topping the charts, Adam Ant still felt he had a lot to prove, and so the stakes were high with the release of album *Friend or Foe*. Stating that the aim for the album was to mix the horns of Motown with rockabilly guitars, Adam set out his stall in tracks such as *Something Girl*, a swinging pop chorus in search of a song, complete with Matt Monroe whistling. The whole album was painfully self-aware, focussing on Adam's personal and public relationships. The personal was dealt with in *Try This for Sighs* and *Place in the Country*, which took the form of an open letter to his girlfriend, referring to previous partners who had sold their stories to the tabloids, whilst claiming "*You say I'm just a stripper not afraid to strip*". Elsewhere, in the bitter *Made of Money*, he discussed his ex-wife, their recent divorce case, and his belief she was sucking him dry financially. He tried to downplay the personal aspect of the song, stating "*It's not just about marriage – it's about some relationships I've experienced since I've become successful*", however with the line "*Marriages are made in heaven so what the hell happened to mine*" it was impossible to read it any other way.

"*Since the Ants split we've got much more work done and we're much happier people*" Adam would claim at the time, however it was difficult to see any sense of calm in his discourse regarding the press. *"When you get a number one the only way is down"* he sang in *Here Comes the Grump*, whilst *Crackpot History and the Right to Lie* concerned the press tendency to knock people when they reach the top, claiming *"People lie, people hurt, like to read their Sunday dirt"*. He also used the song to take a swipe at The Who, stating *"Every rebel that I've met say they're going to die and yet I see them now and they ain't dead yet, and pushing forty-one"*.

The anti-press tirade reached its zenith on next single, *Desperate but not Serious*, which was the phrase Adam used in interviews around the time. The hatred was made explicit in the line *"Mister Pressman with your penknife, always asking about my sex life"*, and Adam obviously saw himself as an innocent victim, refusing to understand that he had courted the attention of journalists in the first place.

The album reached number five, whilst *Desperate but not Serious* became his first single for over two years not to breech the top ten, stalling at number thirty-three.

℧ ℧ ℧

Designer Vivienne Westwood had been working on her own, banning former partner Malcolm McLaren from her workshop. He may have provided the initial inspiration for her latest collection, but the creation of the garments was 100% Westwood, as 1982 was the year she stepped out from the penumbra, creating clothes that were mud brown and *"as unpackaged as possible, as close to something that has been dug up from the earth"*. Inspired by her own body, the clothes were a representation of how she felt inside, as Westwood went out of her way to employ people who were not trained haberdashers, revelling in the rough and ready joins and cuts, and distressing material, beginning with just a square of fabric to see how it hung on the body.

After the failure of her first Paris show in March, Westwood was reluctant to return to the city, however McLaren insisted, even providing music for the catwalk from initial mixes of his new recordings with Trevor Horn. This time, the fashion world fell head over heels in love with the collection, titled *Hobo / Punkature*, proclaiming Westwood as the hottest new designer in the world. Overcoming her natural shyness, the former teacher was forced onto the catwalk to take the applause at the end of the show, at which point she realised she did not require McLaren anymore.

After the show, the collection was picked up by Lucia Raffael, fashion editor of *Italian Vogue*, as well as Carlo Dimario and Giannino Malossi, who showed it in Milan where it was again a success. In London, however, Westwood could find no-one to finance her, choosing to break from McLaren and move to Italy instead. Her next collection, shown in spring 1983, was based on Haitian Voodoo and called *Witches*, *"reconceptualised fashion in terms of the effects on individual wearers"*, becoming a huge influence on the likes of Jean-Paul Gaultier and Rei Kawakubo.

The Italian connection added extra pressure on the Westwood – McLaren relationship, with him accusing her of being *Judas* for having the audacity to be influenced by people other than himself. Ultimately, McLaren treated everything he did in the same way, believing he contributed more than half of the input to Westwood's creations just because he came up with the initial inspirations. However, time and time again he fell out with collaborators when they started expressing themselves: it happened with John Lydon in The Sex Pistols, with Bow Wow Wow once they began writing their own songs and becoming talented musicians, and with Westwood when it became obvious to everyone else exactly how talented and creative she was. In later years, McLaren would see their relationship in a different light, explaining *"When I met Vivienne I saw in her a mother figure, a figure I never had. I had my life with my friends and I went home to Vivienne like you would to your mother."*

If McLaren could not control Westwood then he set out to destroy her, firing off a lawyer's letter to her newly signed Italian manufacturer, who immediately stopped production. He then changed the locks on her London workroom, and transferred all the money into his own account. Staff were told they were to answer to McLaren only, and he started prepping the newspapers with lines such as "[Vivienne] *does tend to get embroiled in spaghetti dinners and fall for Italian charm*".

In subsequent years, Vivienne Westwood became one of the giants of British fashion, always producing something original and provocative, and in the process becoming the establishment that she incipiently hated.

℧ ℧ ℧

Whilst Captain Sensible had become a proper pop star, The Damned ensconced themselves at Rockfield Studios in Wales over the summer to record their new album, *Strawberries*. Hugh Jones was called in to produce and found the inter-band arguments troublesome, with things especially fraught between Rat Scabies and bass player Paul Gray which led to one argument involving both parties and their girlfriends, after which Scabies returned to London. The rest of the band, including Sensible, then got on with recording the album in peace.

The title came from a stage comment made by singer Dave Vanian about the original fans who were reluctant to allow the band to develop, stating "*It's like giving strawberries to a fucking pig, this gig, you know?*" Those fans would not have been pleased with the mix of professionalism and experimentation evident on the album, as the Damned flexed their creative muscles, containing just enough of their old breakneck pop songs whilst also adding sitars and cellos. Psychedelic influences were introduced, especially on *Don't Bother Me* and *Life Goes On*, two tracks with Captain Sensible on lead vocals.

The next single from the album, *Dozen Girls*, failed to reach the top seventy-five, however it was in good company as Sensible's solo *Croydon* sank without trace as well.

The Damned began an autumn tour on Sunday 3rd October, and for the first time spent money and effort on a set, billing the show as The Damned Religious Service and filling the stage with a pulpit around the keyboards and three female fans dressed as nuns. Singer Dave Vanian wore a priest's dog collar as the band began to come under the sartorial dominion of their frontman, playing into his gothic Victorian gravedigger intellection. For once, Sensible was not the focus of the audience and he was quite happy to melt into the background having had enough of the spotlight, whilst also being conscious that a whole new audience had come to see him. How this pop audience dealt with The Damned live is unclear, but certainly it must have been a shock to see the Captain roaming the stage naked.

℧ ℧ ℧

Culture Club were three songs into their show at Glasgow's Nightmoves club on Monday 18th October when frontman Boy George fled from the stage. With a voice failing him, embarrassment forced his hand into cutting the set short. The Glaswegian crowd started to shout abuse and throw anything they could get their hands on, as the band sheepishly followed him offstage and back to the hotel. The three musicians did not hold back in their resentment of George's *prima donna* act, and once back at the hotel drummer Jon Moss barged into the room he was sharing with the singer, slamming the door behind.

"*Pull yourself together, what's the big deal?*" he demanded, and before long the two were trading violent blows in the tiny bedroom. It ended when George smashed a wine glass and held the sharp edge against Jon's throat, forcing the drummer to storm off to the bar.

In the morning, the two were woken by manager Tony Gordon announcing that *Do You Really Want to Hurt Me* had reached the top of the charts. The band celebrated in the van on their way to the next gig in Edinburgh, and that afternoon George and session keyboard player Phil Pickett took a walk along Princes Street, the Scottish capital's main shopping thoroughfare. In a department store George was mobbed by schoolgirls and housewives alike, all demanding a kiss or an autograph. He loved it, everything he had ever wanted had come true, however it also gave him a taste of the madness of fame. The two escaped into a black cab and back to the hotel, but from that day onwards life was never the same again.

ʊ ʊ ʊ

After the disappointing performance of their first single, the pressure was on Wham to hit the charts with the follow-up. *Young Guns (Go For It)* was cut from the same cloth as *Wham Rap*, but was a more developed piece of writing, retaining the funkiness whilst driving headfirst with a narrative, with less rapping and a catchier chorus. The duo had recorded the song a few months earlier with American backing singer Lynda Hayes helping to write a spoken word section, for which she got no credit or royalties. Not that Hayes had anything to do with the act by this point. Her place instead was taken by Ridgeley's ex-girlfriend, blonde-haired Shirlie Holliman, and Dee C. Lee. Lee was a black Londoner, born Diane Sealy, who at the age of twenty was working as an in-house session singer for EMI Publishing. She replaced sixteen-year-old Amanda Washbourn, who had been dismissed when she failed to turn up for a personal appearance in front of CBS executives. Holliman and Lee's job was to mime the female backing vocals and facilitate the dance routines, and for this they were put on a permanent wage, however it suited the act to indulge the fiction in the press that they were actual members. The foursome continued a series of personal appearances

miming to their new single in clubs until one night at Bolts, a weekend gay night at Lazer's nightclub in Haringay, London, when DJ Norman Scott put on the instrumental B-side. With live microphones the four made their first *live* performance, and from then insisted on singing live at all performances.

For the recording of the single Michael shared the production duties with Steve Brown, displaying his increasing self-assurance in a studio whilst Anne Dudley was brought in from Trevor Horn's organisation to arrange the brass section. The single was released in mid-October and looked like it was going to be another flop as it hung about outside the top forty for several weeks. After being spotted by a BBC executive during a personal appearance at Stringfellow's Nightclub, Wham were booked for Saturday Superstore, a weekend morning kids' show. The following week, despite still not being in the top forty, they were invited onto *Top of the Pops* when another act pulled out at the last minute. A band was put together featuring Deon Estes on bass, Ridgeley's brother Paul on drums, and long-time friend David Austin on guitar, to mime behind them for the show. The performance was a *tour de force*, described by Ridgely as "*the single most*

428 | 1982: From One Extreme to Another

important event in Wham's success", with the four singers acting out a routine which echoed the narrative of the lyrics, driving the story with dance steps they had practised in their bedrooms. During a break, Michael turned to David Austin and said "This is it! This is the rest of my life!" The routine was both loose enough to look home-made and tight enough to impress, and the single jumped to number twenty-four the following week, then into the top ten, finally resting at number three, selling more than 400,000 copies by the end of the year.

Whilst the song appeared a little naïve and faintly sexist, the assured confidence helped you forget Michael's faux American accent during a rap / spoken word interlude, which he attempted to retroactively justify by claiming "I just think white rap voices sound stupid – we're trying to be satiric, not comic."

The band ended the year with a performance at their old school and started 1983 with Ridgeley and Holliman splitting and another top ten hit; a re-mix of Wham Rap which was meant to be completed in New York by a famous dance producer. "We hated what he was doing" explained Ridgley, "so we sacked him and George did the remix whilst I fell asleep". He continued "We don't really care about America except for the cash", with Michael adding "People over there have absolutely no taste anyway".

Wham went on to become one of the most successful bands of the 1980's with worldwide number one hits such as Wake Me Up Before You Go-Go and Freedom, however the early club sound had been ditched by the end of 1983 in favour of an out-and-out pop direction, with traces of Motown in evidence.

Initially, as result of Michael's lack of confidence in his own looks it had been planned for him to be the musical talent behind the band, writing songs for Ridgeley to sing. By the end of the year it had become clear that George was too good to stay in the background, and his looks were proving to be an unexpected bonus to the brand. During their success Michael also released a couple of bestselling solo singles, including Careless Whisper which had been one of the tracks on the demo that got them signed. These pointed towards what would happen next, and when Wham split at the peak of their success after a farewell show at Wembley Stadium, Michael struck out as a solo artist. To a large extent his journey became the blueprint for any singer looking to move on from a successful teen band, showing musical and visual maturity which propelled him to solo superstar status throughout the world, with a string of international chart-toppers.

Despite the phenomenal success Michael became an increasingly desperate figure in private. Wrestling with his sexuality, he first came out to Ridgeley and Holliman in 1983 but kept his secret from the public for years, being romantically linked with a series of women and accentuating his playboy image within the videos. In the early 1990's he met and fell in love with Brazilian fashion designer, Anselmo Feleppa, and whilst Michael's sexuality was an open secret in the press, to the public he remained a straight man, something that seems impossible for more recent generations to believe. When Feleppa died of AIDS in 1993 Michael was devastated at losing what he considered to be the love of his life. From here on in, he played fast and loose with his talent as a singer and songwriter, and whilst his live performances were never short of spot on, his albums veered from the highly personal (Older) to the ineffectual (Songs from The Last Century). He spent a lot of his time high on cannabis and was involved in a series of bumps and incidents in motor vehicles, often under the influence of a smoke or some sleeping tablets.

Then in 1998 Michael was arrested in a toilet at the Will Rogers Memorial Park in Beverley Hills and charged with lewd conduct after propositioning a plain clothes policeman. Michael was well known in gay circles for his love of cottaging, outdoor sex with strangers, finding a thrill in the danger, however this arrest was, with hindsight rather unbelievably, the first time that the public became aware he was gay. The personal drama continued: in 2010, he was sentenced to eight weeks in Pentonville prison for possession of drugs, in 2011 he was hospitalized in a coma and almost died from pneumonia, in 2013 he suffered head injuries after falling from a fast-moving car on the M1 motorway. Then on Christmas day 2016, Michael died peacefully at home in his sleep, and the process of re-evaluating his career began. Most impressively, stories of his anonymous philanthropy started to emerge, from the millions of pounds he donated to Childline, the Terence Higgins Trust, and MacMillan Cancer Support, to the individual donations to strangers to help with their studies or IVF treatment. It was revealed he had signed the royalties of several of his singles over to various charities, thus providing an income stream beyond his death.

ʊ ʊ ʊ

Thomas Cochrane was travelling to work at a linen factory in County Armagh on Friday 22nd October when he was abducted by the Provisional IRA. A part-time sergeant in the Ulster Defence Regiment, fifty-four-year-old Cochrane was held for what the IRA claimed was *"interrogation because of his crimes against the nationalist community"*. When news of the kidnapping reached outraged Shankill Butcher leader Lenny Murphy, he hijacked a black taxi and went driving around the Falls Road in Belfast looking for revenge.[556] Just after midnight the taxi was hailed by forty-eight-year-old unemployed joiner Joseph Donegan who had just left the Pound Loney Social Club. Whilst an accomplice drove, Murphy savagely beat and kicked Donegan in the back of the taxi, before taking him to a house in Brookmount Street, Shankill, where he beat him again and extracted his teeth with pliers. Murphy then handed a shovel to an accomplice and asked him to finish the man off, but only once he had regained consciousness and they had extracted his name. The taxi was taken to another street and set on fire to destroy any forensic evidence.

Murphy phoned Nationalist councillor Cormac Boomer, claiming Donegan would be held hostage until Thomas Cochrane was released. *"We have Donegan and if the Provos do not release Cochrane by midnight we will put a bullet in his head. Do you understand?"* he demanded, to which Boomer sarcastically replied *"There's not much to choose between you and the Provos. You are all bloody heroes."* Murphy then phoned Father Desmond Wilson and threatened to dump the body of Donegan on the doorstep of the family home. Unbeknownst to everyone, Cochrane was also dead, having been shot not long after his kidnapping.

The following evening Murphy recruited a couple of acquaintances to help remove the body. As they were carrying the corpse along an alleyway towards a waiting car a young couple passed and the body was abandoned to be found the following morning by shipyard workers making their way to work. The police, upon discovering the house where the murder had taken place was a former residence of Murphy, pulled him in for questioning. The presence of his fingerprints all over the scene could be accounted for by his former occupancy, and the police knew they would not be able to find any witnesses willing to come forward. Murphy was released without charge.

Two days later Cochrane's body was found dumped on wasteland near the border, having been beaten and shot.

---

[556] The taxi driver was told to go home and not report the vehicle missing until the morning, under threat of his life.

24th – 30th October 1982

#1 single: Culture Club: Do You Really Want To Hurt Me
#1 album: The Kids From Fame: The Kids From Fame

For everyone there is a band which, for no logical reason, they cannot stand. For me, it is The Eagles. They have interminably infectious songs, played expertly by brilliant musicians... and yet there is just something about their millionaire cowboy harmonies and cocaine-induced self-belief that annoys the hell out of me. I did a quick straw poll amongst people I know. Brian, Mhairi, and Ross hate The Smiths, Stuart hates Coldplay, Kara and Denis hate Muse, Jo hates The Rolling Stones, Margaret hates The Who, Paula, Neil, and David hate Oasis, Les hates Runrig, Gerry and Lynsey hate the Electric Light Orchestra, Willie hates Nickleback, Peter hates Kasabian, Kerri hates Pink Floyd, Jill hates Deacon Blue, Allan, Lesley and Andrew hate Queen, David hates Iron Maiden, Anne hates David Bowie, Heather and William hate The Beatles, Angela hates Madness, Fiona and Alex hate Abba, Sandy hates The Monkees, Raymond hates Culture Club, Danny hates Bruce Springsteen, and Greg really, really hates Supertramp.

Or, as he would have it, Super-fucking-tramp. You can see his point: there is a lot to dislike about Supertramp. Their too-clever-for-their-own-good songs, lacking genuine humour that is not smart-ass, the whining double tracked vocals, the session man sheen of the recordings, perfecting any emotion or energy out of the music, the fact that you are fed up with the song as soon as it begins.

Supertramp themselves appeared to be fed up with each other as well in 1982. Evolving from an even more tedious prog-rock beginning, Supertramp's smug pop had conquered the world in the late 1970's with the multi-million selling *Breakfast in America*[557] album. The British act were driven by twin keyboard players and songwriters Rick Davies and Roger Hodgson, but by 1982 their relationship was

wearing thin. Hodgson had retreated to the Californian hills with his family and was reluctant to leave them at home, forcing their new album to be recorded there. Davies and Hodgson wrote estranged from each other, giving *Famous Last Words* a schizophrenic feel.

The album was advertised with the release of single *It's Raining Again*, which masqueraded as a song of lovers splitting whilst summing the relationship between the two. At no point did the lyrics mention a lover, instead stating *"Too bad I'm losing a friend"*, this was a song obsessed with the narrator, a narcissistic Hallmark motivational speech in the mirror at two in the morning, and the best thing we can say is that it eventually ends, but not before a choir of children hammer home the nursery rhyme mode of the entire track.

Whilst the single went top ten around the world, Britain saw sense and stopped it at number twenty-six.

ʊ ʊ ʊ

---

[557] *Breakfast in America* sold over twenty million copies and won a Grammy for *Best Engineered Album*. Which I suppose is a way of saying your album is *technically* good without *actually* being good.

At 7.15 on the evening of Sunday 24th October, families all over the United Kingdom gathered in front of their televisions for one of the biggest screen events of the year: *Star Wars* was showing on ITV. In the early 1980's, there was a legal five-year gap between a film's release in the cinema and it being shown on television, so for most people tuning in this was the first time they had seen the movie in a handful of years. There was no streaming, hardly anyone had video players, and even if they did, the cost of a movie was upwards of £80[558]. If you missed something at the cinema or on television in 1982, there was no way to see it again until it was shown again, which in the case of *Star Wars* was not until the 30th December 1984.

ʊ ʊ ʊ

What was it about Sheffield in 1982? Had the entire city split up with its girlfriend? The Human League were wondering *Don't You Want Me*, ABC went through the whole *Lexicon of Love*, and now Heaven 17 were pleading *Let Me Go!*

The three-piece former-Human League members were already favourites of the critics in Britain, having found acclaim with their *Penthouse and Pavement* album, but were lacking the breakthrough top forty single many believed they deserved.

Let Me Go kept just enough of the rugged funk edges evident in their previous work, whilst burnishing the overall production. Opening with calamitous drum break, a sinuous bass line provided by the new-on-the-market Roland TB303[559] intermingled

with subtle serpentine guitar runs, propelling the track into dance territory and allowing it to climb to number four on the Billboard Dance Charts. In Britain, as always, a Heaven 17 single spent six weeks lingering just outside the top forty, stubbornly refusing to climb any higher.

The band were more excited by the prospect of their next single, not due for several months, where rising chords gave the idea of building sexual tension, and a Virgin Records blank cheque meant they could hire a sixty-piece orchestra. *Temptation* had been written in singer Glenn Gregory's miserable basement flat in Ladbroke Grove, and was demoed with backing vocals by Jodi James, however Carol Kenyon was eventually chosen due to her gritty performance[560]. Knowing they had this single in the bag took the sting out of *Let Me Go* missing the charts.

ʊ ʊ ʊ

As the area around Kinnego in County Armagh had been in a state of high alert for several days, a telephone call from a local farmer to the police regarding a stolen tractor battery needed to be authenticated. The police called the farmer back on 27th October, and he confirmed that, yes, he had called in the theft, and so Constables Paul Hamilton and Alan McCloy, along with Sergeant Sean Quinn were sent to investigate and take a statement. As their car approached the farm, they triggered a massive landmine and

---

[558] The first thing I recorded with a video was a late night showing of Michael Jackson's *Thriller* promo, which would have placed it around January 1984.

[559] *Let Me Go* was the first commercial release of a song featuring the TB303, beating Orange Juice's *Rip It* Up by a few weeks. The TB303 would become synonymous with the Acid House dance movement.

[560] Kenyon and the band would fall out over money, so a model was used for the video.

the three were killed instantly. The farmer had been held at gunpoint by four members of the IRA and forced to make the call.

A police informant provided details of the four IRA men: Eugene Toman, Sean Burns, Gervaise McKerr, and Martin McCauley. However, as this was only the word of an informant, nothing could be done legally. The police started to plan other ways of gaining *justice*.

ʊ ʊ ʊ

The public continued to view homosexuality with suspicion and contempt in 1982, despite the decriminalizing in England and Wales for males over the age of twenty-one in 1967. Scotland ran years behind, only decriminalizing in 1981, whilst Northern Ireland held out until Wednesday 27th October when the Homosexual Offences (Northern Ireland) Order 1982 came into effect. The roots of the change came when Belfast shipping clerk Jeff Dudgeon was arrested by the Royal Ulster Constabulary in 1975 and questioned about his sexuality. As a gay activist Dudgeon took his treatment to the European Court of Human Rights, eventually being heard in 1981. The court found the Northern Irish government in breach of Article 8 of the European Convention on Human Rights in denying homosexual men the right to express their sexuality. The new law fell into line with the rest of the United Kingdom, with the age of consent set at twenty-one (it would only fall to eighteen in 1994, and then be equaled with heterosexuality at sixteen in the year 2000).

ʊ ʊ ʊ

October 1982 was the nadir for black music on the American Billboard charts, with the lowest number of artists since they started in the mid-1950's, or at any time afterwards. Encouraged by the *Disco Sucks* movement and by a lurch to the right following what Tim Lawrence described as Reagan's "*attack on affirmative action and social welfare programs, his firing of members of the U.S. Commission on Civil Rights who criticized his agenda,* [and] *his opposition to the introduction of sanctions against apartheid South Africa*", mainstream music in the United States had turned predominantly white. It was at this time that a relatively unknown black artist called Prince released his new album, *1999*.

Prince Rogers Nelson had been born in 1958 in Minneapolis and by his teenage years was a prodigious multi-instrumental talent. At nineteen-years-old he signed to Warner Brothers Records with complete control and the publishing rights to his own songs, an unheard-of deal for an unknown youth. From his early days Prince proved to be prolific in terms of output, and over the next four years released four albums, each of which edged him a little bit closer to mainstream success.

Finishing an extensive American tour in support of his fourth album in March 1982, Prince wasted no time in recording the follow up. Despite touring with a live band, Prince chose to play most of the instruments in the studio himself, only bringing regular guitarist Dez Dickerson in for one guitar solo and a couple of vocal lines.

Over the summer, Prince put together enough songs to inform Warners that this would be a double album, however his management felt there was not yet a knock-out first single. After being told Prince left their offices swearing in a fury before returned a week later with the song *1999*.

Prince had his heart set on crossing over to the mainstream with this album, dreaming of mashing-up Fleetwood Mac with Sly & the Family Stone, mixing gender, genres, and

race. MTV had expanded its cable coverage to New York and Los Angeles a few weeks previously, the two most important markets in the country, and Prince knew it was now essential to break into this televisual medium.

Dominated by the sound of a Linn drum machine, the album was one long orgasmic celebration of sex, music, and romance... in that order. Motor cars and airplanes were used as metaphors for Prince's purple penis throughout, especially in future hit single *Little Red Corvette*, as he attempted to get as many women to strip as possible. On *Something in the Water (Does not Compute)* Prince complained that the women he really wants always seemed to give him a hard time, and there were rumours it was based on him being turned down by an unknown dancer in Danceteria who turned out to be Madonna.

The rhythm and blues blueprint for the rest of the decade was revealed on the album, which only twice strayed from sexual conduct as a theme. The opening title track of the album was a post-apocalyptic vision of the future over a funky beat, with vocals shared between the band, and would become a party classic leading up the end of the millennium (and beyond). *All the Critics Love You in New York* was patently influenced by Talking Heads, and in particular *The Great Curve* from their *Remain in Light* album. With a new wave feel, it is unclear if Prince is admiring or is jealously resentful of the New York band's obsession with rhythm.

1999 became the breakthrough album for Prince, buoyed by hit singles and touring a powerful and well-drilled band, but could perhaps have been trimmed to a fantastic single album rather than a double. Many of the songs struggled to maintain interest for the eight minutes plus they are given, and no-one would have been upset by missing the closing two and a half minutes of the title track.

As black representation in the American charts hit an all-time low, things were only marginally better in Britain. Black musicians had been in the country for centuries, a result of trade with the colonies of the British Empire, and during the 1920's and 1930's immigrants from the Caribbean had added a calypso element to the touring American jazz bands, eventually replacing all the members when visas became difficult to acquire for the Yanks.

The arrival of the *Windrush generation* after the Second World War, encouraged by the government to fill vacancies created by loss of life, brought stable communities of black settlers to Britain, especially in London and Birmingham, and with them came traditions of music. The first generation of immigrants kept their homeland, culture, and music alive as a means of remembering where they were from, however their children considered themselves to be British, and with that came a whole new host of global influences.

In the 1970's many British-born black kids turned away from Jamaican roots reggae, which they saw as the music of their parents' homeland and seemed to be all about suffering, choosing instead music that was influenced by the joy and melody of Motown and soul. Reggae split in two in Britain, male-centric dub and roots, and the preference of the female audience: Lover's Rock. This was a singles-based medium and flew under the radar of the established British music industry, with releases occasionally selling numbers in the six figures without national radio play or troubling the charts. This was a subculture that was invisible to the (white) mainstream.

At the same time, a funk scene was developing in the cities of England, with young second-generation black kids picking up instruments after being influenced by the likes of the Ohio Players, Herbie Hancock, and Earth, Wind & Fire. Beggar & Co, Central Line, Light of the World, and Incognito emerged from this scene in the 1980's, by which point the musicians were more than proficient. They still, however, lacked an artist able to break into the British mainstream in a genre-crossing manner.

℧ ℧ ℧

When Dr Harold Jaffe met with Dr Art Ammann at a conference at the University of California in San Francisco on Saturday 30th October, the two were able to combine their individual research in the search for a definitive identification of the AIDS virus. Jaffe had three sibling children with the disease as patients, all from the same drug addict mother, however Ammann also had an infant patient with what appeared to be AIDS, whose parents were not drug addicts or involved in any homosexual activity. The child had, however, undergone extensive blood transfusions at an early age. Here, at last, was the evidence that blood transfusions were also spreading the disease.
A search of the confidential records at the Irwin Memorial Blood Bank over the next few days provided the name of someone who had died of AIDS as one of the donors. The news had an immediate response from the blood banks, who under the privatised profit-driven American healthcare system stood to lose a fortune in money and reputation, and an official line was taken that there was no connection between transfused blood and AIDS.

℧ ℧ ℧

The career of Diana Ross had been regenerated by a collaboration with Chic, and Smokey Robinson had just enjoyed worldwide solo chart success, however many other old Motown stars had been set to sea adrift on an ice floe of chart irrelevance. Only one of them, however, washed up on the shores of the small coastal city in Belgium.
The previous year Marvin Gaye had completed a European tour, and was bone-weary, drug-addicted, and corybantic with Motown Records for how they had handled his last couple of albums. Despondent in London, Gaye took advantage of an offer from his

European promotor to find refuge in Ostend, where fresh from a second divorce he cut his drug intake, started exercising, and attending church. CBS purchased his contract from Motown for one and a half million dollars, and work started on recording a new album using drum machines and synthesizers sent by the company.
Living in Europe, Gaye could not help but be influenced by what was going on musically, and incorporated elements of synth-pop, new wave, reggae, and funk into the new music, looking to push the genre of soul further, as he had done a decade previously. There was some dispute in the press as to whether this was a *comeback* album or not, but it is hard to see it in any other terms: financially or creatively.
The stand-out track, *Sexual Healing*, was released as a single at the same time, and set the template for smooth soul over the next decade and beyond. Laid on top of a slick rhythm track provided by a Roland TR808 drum machine, the song started with a whispered exhortation by Harvey Fuqua[561] to "*get up, get up, get up, get up*" and "*wake*

---

[561] Fuqua was a long-time friend of Gaye, and as a member of 1950's doo-wop outfit The Moonglows had given him is first break in the music industry.

up, wake up, wake up, wake up", before Gaye provided one of his most heartfelt vocals, a call straight from his libido. Existing and working after midnight, Gaye was used to his sexual desire being awoken in the early hours, and the song acted as a *booty call*, asking for the healing power of sexual coupling. His needs were fully explained in the fade-out when he sang "*please don't procrastinate, it's not good to masturbate*".

The single peaked at number six in Britain, giving Gaye his largest hit since *I Heard it Through the Grapevine* in 1968, whilst the album, appropriately called *Midnight Love*, was his most successful ever, selling more than six million copies.

Eighteen months later, Gaye was dead, shot through the heart by his father.

ʊ ʊ ʊ

If there was any city in the world which epitomized the 1980's, it had to be New York. Giant glass and steel edifices to affluence and commerce perched on the same island as burnt-out slums, high culture and street culture coalesced on the sidewalks, and the American dream was played out and lost every single day.

John Oates was making the most of the contradictions, living in the heart of Manhattan with his model wife Nancy Hunter, where life was a social gyre of gallery openings, meals in expensive restaurants, and visits to nightclubs. When Hunter was away on a

shoot, Oates would end up at an exclusive bar called Marylou's on Ninth Street. One night in 1982 he was with friends at a table in the inner sanctum working his way through a buffet of pasta when one of the most beautiful women he had ever seen walked in, an unnamed top model. The table went quiet as she crossed the bar towards them, a flurry of waiters seeing to her every whim. Sitting opposite Oates, the spell was broken when the woman broke into "*the most foul, crude and expletive-laced soliloquy*" he had ever heard, and a line formed in the back of the songwriters head: "*She would chew you up and spit you out*". By the end of the night the thought was joined by "*Oh-oh here she comes, she's a maneater*". Returning to his apartment alone in the early hours of the morning, and inspired by a recent trip to Jamaica, Oates began strumming a gentle reggae infused rhythm as the words formed themselves into a melody.

A few days later he played the song to multi-instrumentalist Edgar Winter, who was unimpressed, however musical partner Daryl Hall spotted the potential immediately, and added a Motown-style bass line.

Oates would later explain "*It was the juxtaposition of this great beauty with this foul mouth that really kind of sparked an idea... but neither Daryl nor I wanted to write a song that was negative toward women, so what we did was we transpose that initial idea and use New York City in the '80s as a metaphor. New York City became the maneater, the city that would chew you up and spit you out.*" He saw the saxophone solo being "*the sharp, late-day sunlight slanting off the city's steel and glass towers*"[562], *Maneater* was the sound of Wall Street in the early 1980's, of financial and narcotic excess, of the sun going down and the evening of prodigality beginning.

Whilst the single gave them their sixth American chart topper, it became their biggest hit in Britain, reaching number six and allowing the accompanying album *H20* to go top ten as well.

---

[562] The echo-laden saxophone was such a New York 1980's touch, and American hardcore act Fear even released a song called *New York's Alright if you like Saxophones*.

NOVEMBER

31ˢᵗ October – 6ᵗʰ November 1982

#1 single: Culture Club: Do You Really Want To Hurt Me
#1 album: The Kids From Fame: The Kids From Fame

A Flock of Seagulls worldwide success had been so great that Jive Records decided to send them to Compass Point on the Bahamas to record their second album, once again with Mike Howlett. The first fruit of this session was the single *Wishing (If I Had a Photograph of You)*, developed from a basic keyboard riff written by frontman Mike Score in his bedsit the previous year. Recording in a sunny climate helped to make the sound lighter and more uplifting than some of their previous material, with an extra-

long instrumental fade-out on keyboard and guitar played with an E-bow[563], an instrument which had been introduced to the band by Bill Nelson when he produced their debut single.[564] The record company splashed out an enormous (at the time) figure of £10,000 on a video, which helped push the song further into the public consciousness, and A Flock of Seagulls were finally rewarded with a top ten single in their homeland.

They only managed a couple more minor hits before fading into obscurity, being remembered as one-hit wonders and a haircut. Even in the United States, where their success was greater, the band were remembered as something of a novelty act.[565]

ʊ ʊ ʊ

It was surely what the musical world was waiting for… the first release since the multi-million selling album *Off the* Wall by Michael Jackson, coupled with former-Beatle and

all-round legend, Paul McCartney. With such a proven track record, it was bound to be the single of the year? Surely?

Try again. *The Girl is Mine* was the first single from Jackson's forthcoming album, and it was middle of the road hogwash involving two guys fighting over a love interest with a pedestrian instrumentation by Toto. The only notable part of the whole song is Jackson's cringe-worthy but memorable spoken line *"I'm a lover, not a fighter"*.

It did not bode well for the forthcoming album however the record company knew that two such big names had to be released first or else radio stations would just play it anyway.

---

[563] The E-bow was a battery powered hand-held electronic device which created a feedback loop on one string, sounding not unlike the sound of a bow on a string.

[564] Nelson had recently passed the same contraption to Big Country who were making great use of it on their debut album.

[565] Out there, somewhere, there is a version of Echo & the Bunnymen's *Lips Like Sugar*, done as a duet between A Flock of Seagulls and David Hasselhoff. If that doesn't make you scramble for YouTube, then nothing will.

Jackson and McCartney enjoyed a friendly relationship at this point, having also recorded two songs for the British singer's next album, however in later years this was to sour when Michael Jackson used his profits from this song and the *Thriller* album to purchase the rights to The Beatles enviable back catalogue. To McCartney, who had spent time advising Jackson on the importance of owning songs, this was a personal insult.

ʊ ʊ ʊ

As part of their 1979 election manifesto the Conservatives had promised to provide twenty-five hours a week of Welsh language television on the forthcoming fourth channel. Once in power, however, they rolled back on the promise, instead committing to twenty-two hours split over the channel and BBC2, and as Welsh nationalists protested, long-time Plaid Cymru leader Gwynfor Evans threatening to kill himself by hunger strike. Margaret Thatcher was persuaded of the seriousness of Evans' threat and the potential rallying call this would provide for Welsh nationalists, and in September 1980 announced S4C. In Northern Ireland, IRA inmates at the Maze Prison took notice of the effectiveness of the tactics, and five weeks later began their own ultimately fatal hunger strike.

After much preparation, S4C was launched on Monday 1st November, the day before the United Kingdom-wide launch of Channel 4. A fourth television channel for the United Kingdom had been in discussion for over fifteen years, knocked about like a political football by various governments. Since the BBC had been granted a license for a second channel in the 1960's, there had been a growing demand for an additional commercial station, which most people assumed would be under the control of ITV. For years technology companies had been manufacturing televisions with four buttons in anticipation of the new channel, with most of them labelling it *ITV 2*. The questions which had hindered progress were *what kind of programs should the channel show* and *how would it be funded*?

With Thatcher's election in 1979 the planning for the new channel started to take on some momentum, championed by William Whitelaw, with a parliamentary bill passed in February 1980 which called for specific content. "*A suitable proportion* [of programs] *calculated to appeal to tastes and interests not generally catered for by ITV*" was the first demand, followed by "*a suitable proportion of the programs* [to be of] *an educational nature*", and rather uniquely the aim was "*to encourage innovation and experiment in the form and content of programs*". Jeremy Isaacs was installed as overall controller and was keen to "*relate to various socio-political goals: woman's rights... Afro-Caribbean and Asian Britons' claims*". Unbelievably, "*young people watched little television; they had better things to do. But they deserved a service*". Where the other three channels constructed their schedules to keep the viewer tuned-in all night, Isaacs was keen to provide a varied schedule, perfectly at ease with a certain demographic tuning in for a single program and then switching either off or channel afterwards, what were called "*self-selecting minorities*". Not that the channel had any choice: BBC and ITV running costs were approximately £100,000 per hour; Channel 4 had to get by on £30,000 per hour.

New transmitters needed to be constructed across the country for the channel, and the decision was made to start broadcasting when 80% of the nation had coverage, a date which, if construction went to plan, was due to be Tuesday 2nd November.

Isaacs was keen not to prioritize one program over any other, refusing to allow any one show to represent the channel, and so rather than starting with a bang the Channel came on air at 4.45 p.m. with their regular schedule. The first program was *Countdown*, a quiz show based upon the French equivalent *Des Lettres et des Chiffres*. The program had already enjoyed a short run in the Yorkshire Television area under the name *Calendar Countdown*, where local presenter Richard Whiteley had compared, earning him the nickname *twice-nightly Whiteley* as he also presented the show *Calendar*. The format was refined for Channel 4, and has been on the air ever since, holding the record for the most episodes of a quiz show at well over 7,000.

Channel 4 took its mandate very seriously, catering for the intelligent viewer in a way that annoyed the tabloid press, who nicknamed it either *Channel Bore* or *Channel Snore*, and then *Channel Swore*. They showed non-mainstream movies, chosen by critic Leslie Halliwell from his encyclopedic knowledge, movies where the language was more reflective of that used on the streets. They devoted three consecutive Saturday nights to showing the Royal Shakespeare's nine-hour production of *Nicholas Nickleby*. They showed Pavarotti singing in *Idomeneo* from the Met. As an alternative to ITV showing the *Miss World* competition, Channel 4 they showed documentaries about women in the factories during the Second World War. The opening night also saw the first hour-long nightly news program in the United Kingdom with the award-winning Channel Four News presented by Peter Sissons and Trevor McDonald between 7.00 p.m. and 8.00 p.m.

Immediately after this on the opening night, and showing on subsequent Tuesdays and Wednesdays, was *Brookside*. The new soap opera had been thought up by Phil Redmond, a Liverpudlian scriptwriter who had previously been responsible for children's drama *Grange Hill*. Redmond convinced the channel that any soap opera they commissioned should be set in Liverpool and delivered the production within a tiny budget. A cul-de-sac of houses were built as a set, and Redmond kept a firm hand on the scripts, ensuring they remained gritty in their dealings of controversial topics. The soap was repeated in an omnibus edition at the weekend, a move soon followed by *Coronation Street* and *Eastenders*, and led to a call a month later from moral campaigner Mary Whitehouse for Isaacs to resign.

When *alternative comedian* Peter Richardson had been bumped from the cast of forthcoming sit-com *The Young Ones* he approached Channel 4 with the idea of writing and producing a six-part series of one-off comedy dramas under the title *The Comic Strip Presents*. Richardson had been running the *Comic Strip* comedy club in London for over a year along with Rick Mayall, Adrian Edmondson, Nigel Planer, Dawn French, and Jennifer Saunders, and the group held a meeting where many ideas for content were tossed around, taking a short list to Isaacs at Channel 4.

From the beginning it was decided to shoot using film rather than video, due to the former being easier to use in 1982, however this also added a touch of quality to the final product. Mayall expressed concern regarding this decision, insisting "*film makes the joke look too grand – it makes everything look too beautiful; tape makes everything look horrible, which is better for comedy*".

The first episode was broadcast on the opening night of Channel 4. Titled *Five go Mad in Dorset*, it was a spoof of both Children's Film Foundation Saturday morning films of the 1960's and 1970's, and the popular Enid Blyton *Famous Five* books, with Edmondson, French, Saunders, and Richardson playing the role of the children (the fifth of course being *Timmy the dog*).

The plot poked fun at many traditional and outdated British tropes, so whilst the five are meant to be wholesome and innocent children, they arrange to have a black railway porter arrested for nothing other than being suspiciously foreign. Their whole approach is one of elitist Little Englanders, suspicious and mistrusting of anyone who is not them, avoiding the friendship of another boy with the reasoning "*What if everybody wanted to be our friend – where would we be then?*"

Most of the furore around Channel 4 came from its use of *gratuitous language*, where films were shown uncensored causing Mary Whitehouse to write to the attorney general and ask him to "*fire a warning shot across* [their] *bows*". She followed this up by telling the public "*It's my impression that there have been more four-letter words on Channel Four in a fortnight than on any other channel in a whole year*". Swearing was heard a lot less often in British society in 1982 than it is now, with most words only being added to the *Oxford English Dictionary* within the previous decade. The day before Channel Four started broadcasting workers on the assembly line at the British Leyland car plant in Oxford had downed tools in protest at the management swearing. What they had actually said was to call the workforce "*fucking bastards and working-class pigs*".

ʊ ʊ ʊ

It is one of those often-asked questions whenever a musician dies: what kind of music would they have created in the future? What would Elvis Presley have made of major world tours once the big touring rigs were in place? What would Jim Morrison have made of punk? What kind of music would John Lennon have made in the 1980's? What would Jimi Hendrix have done with the studio technology of the 1990's? Ultimately, the reality of the answers would have been extremely depressing. Elvis would never have been allowed to tour outside the States by his manager for fear of Colonel Tom Parker's Dutch nationality and lack of visa being discovered, and if *Double Fantasy* is anything to go by, John Lennon would have continued to make middle-of-the-road pop music.

There is one act, however, that we can see beyond death: Joy Division. What would Ian Curtis have made of new technologies and ecstasy? The answer can be found in the work of New Order from 1982 onwards, conceived with *Temptation*, and birthed with album *Power, Corruption & Lies*, and especially the single they recorded in the last months of the year.

After a breakthrough single in *Temptation* New Order had spent the summer touring Italy and were now in an extremely positive state of mind about recording their new album. Booking themselves into Pink Floyd's Britannia Row studio in Islington, they began programming in earnest. The songs were still written by playing together as a band, but the major shift in approach was that they were now being transcribed onto keyboards, drum machines, and sequencers.

Power, Corruption & Lies was released in spring 1983 and featured a paradisiacal fusion of electronic and traditional equipment, however, it was the single released simultaneously which moved music onwards in one great leap.

Blue Monday was never intended to be such an advancement, initially being viewed by the band as a lesser version of the album track *5.8.6*. New Order had never liked putting singles on albums, believing it ripped off the fans, however they did realise they would need a release around the same time as the album to help promote it. The solution to this was to fulfil one of their prank ambitions: to record a fully automated track that they could then play as a "*live*" encore whilst they were living it up backstage. The recording got off to an auspicious start when someone tripped over the mains lead to the Oberheim DMX drum machine and all the initial programming by Steven Morris and Bernard Sumner was completely wiped. Bass player Peter Hook claims that he retains a lingering doubt that "*we had lost the best version* [and it] *still haunts me now*" whilst Sumner later insisted "*Even today I think about how bits of it were better on the original, kind of funkier*". The programming was re-done before the band lost the ability to remember everything they had heard and ripped off in recent visits to New York clubs.

The track soon grew into an eight-minute monster, inspired by Sylvester's *You Make Me Feel*, Kraftwerk's *Uranium*, and the disco work of Giorgio Moroder; not exactly the influences you would expect from a band who thirty months previously had been the industrial doom of Joy Division. The band had recently bought an Emulator 1 sampler and learned how to work it by *"spending hours recording farts"*, before sampling choral voices from Kraftwerk's *Radioactivity* album for use on the new song. It lacked a chorus, the title was not mentioned in the lyrics, and the whole thing was more a rhythm than a tune, however upon its release in March 1983 it began a long liaison with the charts, selling over three million copies to become the biggest selling twelve-inch record of all time.

The decision to release the song only on a twelve-inch format was taken as the wider grooves made the song sound amazing in clubs, which is where the band were hoping it would be heard. Sumner said *"I wouldn't say it was my favourite New Order track, but as a prompt to make you dance it's unsurpassed"*. New Order (and Factory Records) had never really had a large selling release, so the lack of seven-inch version or accompanying video did not seem much of a deal, and when in-house designer Peter Saville produced a cover design based upon a computer floppy disc, with three separate cut-outs on an outer and inner sleeve, they were delighted. That the sleeve would cost a few pence more than the single sold for did not bother Factory or the band, because the single was not expected to sell many copies. Three million sales later this seemed like the typical folly made by the band and label throughout their careers, where money flowed through their hands without being grasped, however what the band, label, and the Haçienda had could not be bought: credibility and foresight. In *Blue Monday* they saw and shaped the future of music, and in the Haçienda they had a major effect of the future direction of youth culture.

New Order were just about to hit their golden period, and for three or four years they were a highly creative and respected act without achieving major success. However, over time they found greater success, especially in the United States, and with this came a change in the way the band worked. Singles started to appear on albums, videos were made for the singles, re-mixes were pushed to maximise hit potential, and with increasing use of programmed drums and less and less live bass, the band eventually became little more than a vehicle for frontman Bernard Sumner.

ʊ ʊ ʊ

New York artist Jean-Michel Basquiat opened his second American solo show on Thursday 4th November at New York's Fun Gallery, a project he had committed to before becoming involved with big-time agent Bruno Bischofberger. The agent tried bullying tactics on gallery owner Patti Astor to cancel the showing, reckoning such an inconspicuous space would damage the artist's rising reputation. When this did not work, he started sending clients directly to Basquiat's studio to purchase the art. What he did not factor, however, was Astor and Basquiat's friendship through their mutual connection to the New York club scene, which kept the artist allegiant to his friends. When one rich art collector turned up at the studio, she sent her limousine driver up to his first-floor apartment with a jar of connoisseur candies. Basquiat accepted the gift, then proceeded straight to the window where he emptied the contents over the head of the waiting collector.

The show was not a success with very few paintings selling and Basquiat spending the night in the corner arguing with his girlfriend, Madonna. The problem was that Bischofberger had informed the buyers to wait until after the show and buy the art at a discounted price straight from the artist. Basquiat, however, had an unwavering awareness of his own position in the pantheon of artists, and at the end of the exhibition everything was wrapped up and put into storage to gather value.

ʊ ʊ ʊ

Banshees bass player Steve Severin and manager Dave Woods walked into The Priory pub in London on Thursday 4th November, to be greeted by the sight of ten patients from the local psychiatric ward on day release. Unexpectedly, one of the patients rose and approached them, his newly shaved bald head glistening under the lights. To their shock, they only realised when he kissed Severin on both cheeks that this was John McGeoch, the guitarist from their band. The Scottish musician had struggled with alcohol over the last couple of years, which had come to a head a week earlier when he had collapsed on stage during a date in Madrid. Upon returning to Britain, his behaviour became increasingly erratic, and his wife had him sectioned under the Mental Health Act.

As soon as he left the pub, Severin made a phone call to Robert Smith, and by the end of the day the Cure guitarist was in the band as a replacement.

The following day their fifth album, *A Kiss in the Dreamhouse*, was released. The title was taken from an infamous Hollywood whorehouse from the 1940's where the prostitutes were surgically altered to look like famous movie stars. The album had been recorded in June and July by Mike Hedges at his Playground Studios, during an intense fusillade of energy which saw the band at their most productive, working fourteen-hour days fuelled by bag after bag of white wine. Drugs were also being used, with the boys in the band injecting speed and cocaine, and singer Siouxsie experimenting with a strand of LSD called *California Sunshine*. Another influence on the sound was The Beatles *White Album*, which was listened to obsessively during the recording and helped usher in a more psychedelic feel.

Having lost her voice during a Scandinavian tour in March Siouxsie struggled with the vocals and had been advised by a doctor to give up singing altogether. There was, however, no stopping her, with a *"psycho-sexual nastiness"* to some of the lyrical themes. Ultimately, the power of the music and experimentation of the producer helped steer the mood away from a potential dark side.

Severin had been reading a lot of Baudelaire and Huysman, what he called *"late-nineteenth century decadent stuff"* and brought these influences into the recording, whilst Jerzy Koszinksi's book *Painted Bird* gave title to and informed the theme of what was a purpose-created anthem for the Goth scene. Despite their connection to the scene, author David Laurie summed things up best when he claimed "[Souixsie and the Banshees] *don't look like Goths; Goths look like them*".

Elsewhere, *Cocoon* began as a drunken comedy jazz jam at five in the morning, with Siouxsie building up vocals describing the comfort of being a baby around McGeoch's atonal piano playing. *She's a Carnival* was the first time the band had realised something was going wrong with McGeoch, as his playing was well short of the mark, but in the usual British way chose to ignore this. The album touched upon deeply personal issues, as *Circle* took a starting point from Siouxsie's way of protecting herself which she developed after being sexually assaulted at the age of nine by a stranger, and then not being believed by her family.

Exuberance got the better of the band near the end of recording when drummer Budgie shook a bottle of champagne and opened the cork, allowing the alcohol to spill over the recording console, forcing the band to move studios, choosing to try out Abbey Road. In the hallowed room, the band put together *Melt* and *Obsession*, the latter a song informed by Siouxsie's ex-boyfriend and former manager of the Banshees, Nils Stevenson, whose fixation with her after they split led to his sacking. Severin has since suggested this spilt from their manager added to the freedom of the sound; *"It felt like there were no constraints of any kind in terms of where we felt the band should be going. We kind of felt the audience would go with us wherever we went*".

A Kiss in the Dreamhouse was an astounding piece of work, a truly complete concept, which paid for this by lacking a standout track to be released as a single. Instead, the tracks had cohesion and worked as a whole rather than as individual songs. It was also McGeoch's swansong, and with lush orchestration and arrangements allowed the band to break free of the bleak post-punk prison which many of their contemporaries found themselves in.

Siouxsie and the Banshees would push their own personal boundaries further throughout the decade, becoming truly iconic, and as Dylan Jones stated about the singer, "*She transformed the role of a female frontwoman into something powerful, mysterious, and dominant.*"

ʊ ʊ ʊ

The new Channel 4 continued to provide ground-breaking television with the airing of *The Tube* on Friday 5th November. The first tolerable new music program on television for over a decade, *The Tube* was presented by former Squeeze pianist Jools Holland, music journalist Paula Yates, and Glasgow School of Art graduate Muriel Gray, providing a concoction of new and old acts playing live, along with music and media features and interviews. Broadcast live each Friday early evening from Newcastle, the show proved to be unpredictable and was not scared to showcase unsigned acts.

Yates had announced her pregnancy to the production crew a couple of days before the first episode was broadcast, causing something of a panic until producer Andrea Wonfer declared "*She's a woman. Of course she can be pregnant. If she's happy with it, then we are too!*"

Holland and Yates were the perfect couple to host the show: he would ask guests about music and she would ask about sex. Yates was altogether erratic and cared not a bit about how people viewed her; she would swear continually during rehearsals, to the extent the crew in the studio threatened to go on strike because of it. Producer Geoff Wonfor gathered them round and reasoned "*Look, you're going to seem a right bunch of tossers if you say that a tiny little girl from the South of England is making you... knock-kneed by using the odd swear word.*" The crew reluctantly agreed to return to work, only to be met by Yates declaring "*Right. Are you happy to come back now, you bunch of cunts?*"

The day of the first broadcast of *The Tube*, record companies all over the country were especially excited by the prospect of a new music programme. In the offices at Charisma Records the staff were scrambling around trying to work out how their newly purchased VHS recorder functioned, not least because their signing Peter Gabriel was due to be on the show, along with Heaven 17 and the final television performance by The Jam. As a desperate measure, they phoned a television repairman. An hour later, co-incidentally sitting in reception with a demo tape was Billy Bragg.

After his glorious review in the *Melody Maker* back in October, Bragg thought he was on the path to success, however no further progress had been forthcoming. Jeff Chegwin (the brother of television personality Keith) at music publishers Chappell had phoned and expressed his support, also stating that he did not have the finances or clout to help. What he did have, however, was a list of over two hundred contacts at record companies and publishing companies, which he sent to Bragg to help him in his search for support. Whilst he sharpened his live show during a weekly residence at the Tunnel Club in Greenwich, playing for beer money to almost no audience, Bragg continued to tout his six-song demo recording round the names on the list, with no success.

When a receptionist at Charisma Records enquired if Bragg was the TV repairman, he saw his opportunity and answered in the affirmative. Bragg's previous job at a video editing company allowed him to quickly tune the VHS recorder into the new Channel 4, after which he wandered down the hall into the office of the boss, Peter Jenner. Bragg had an easy-going manner which endeared him to everyone he met, and he also had the gift of the gab and a stand-out demo in his hand. Jenner liked him straight away and promised to listen to the cassette. The following day he did and was impressed enough to turn up at The Tunnel Club on Sunday 7th November.

As he entered the venue, Jenner noted that the atmosphere was electric, however he only arrived in time to catch the last couple of numbers. With somewhere else to go, he asked the person next to him at the bar if Bragg had been any good. "*He's been absolutely stunning*" was the answer. Jenner made straight for Bragg and promised to do something with him.

Of course, what Jenner did not know is that the atmosphere was down to a spilled pint glass immediately before he entered the room and the tension that comes just before a fight. He also never realised that the person he asked at the bar was Bragg's girlfriend. None of this mattered, as the singer recorded a mini-album for the label the following year which became a favourite of the music press and alternative radio disc jockeys. By the end of 1983 Bragg was an indie hero, moving on from Charisma Records who were going under, and signing to new label Go Discs. Throughout the decade his music became more politicised, and his low-cost live show (one man and a guitar) allowed him to play constantly, building a following. This spilled over in the early 1990's, when with a full band he started having genuine pop hits, before settling into a later life career as elder spokesman, always worth getting in touch with for a quote, with appearances on *Newsnight* and *Question Time*.

7th – 13th November 1982

#1 single: Eddy Grant: I Don't Wanna Dance
#1 album: The Kids From Fame: The Kids From Fame

Thomas Dolby had received airplay on MTV with the videos for his first few singles and was enthusiastic about the potential for the new medium. Realising he could not compete with Adam Ant, Duran Duran, or Spandau Ballet in visuals, Dolby decided to cultivate a geek-professor bearing, and started to write a treatment for a music video

which would see him placed in a psychiatric ward in a straitjacket. He wrote a title at the top of the page, *She Blinded Me with Science*, and took it to EMI who loved the idea. "*But where's the song?*" they asked.

"*I'll bring it on Monday*" replied Dolby, and then went home to write it over the weekend.

EMI sent Dolby to see Steve Barron later in the week, however the hot video director was already on a flight to Los Angeles to see Michael Jackson about making a promotional film for one of his new songs, *Billie Jean*. Instead, Dolby's contact at the video company became Baron's older sister, Siobhan, a former *Vogue* model. She encouraged Dolby to direct his own video, with her assistance, and sold the idea to EMI by telling them how much money they would save. To help Dolby understand a video shoot, she took him to see the Human League who were filming a promotional clip for their forthcoming single, *Mirror Man*.

The shoot for *She Blinded Me with Science* took place on a single day at Holme, a mansion in Regent's Park, where Dr Magnus Pyke was hired to play the part of an eccentric psychiatrist. Pyke was an eminent television scientist, famous for his spirited speech and hyperbolic gestures, but even the reward of a large pay cheque was not enough to stop him complaining about having to wear a white doctor's coat. Pyke continued to be fractious during the shoot, becoming obsessed that the car would be there to collect him at noon, and complaining about the premise of both the song and video. "*As a known scientist it would be a bit surprising if the girl blinded ME with science*" he boasted. For his tantrums, Pyke was cursed to spend the rest of his life with people shouting "*SCIENCE!*" at him wherever he went in the world and remained furious that the video was better known than his scientific work.

Despite having to write the song to demand, *She Blinded Me with Science* contains a scintillating groove, with the words unsurprisingly following the plot of the video (as opposed to the other way around). Pyke provided a voice-over with interjected shouts of "*Science*" and "*Good Heavens, Miss Sakamoto, you're beautiful*" throughout.

The single was released with another new song on the other side, possibly one of the finest written by Dolby. *One of our Submarines* dealt with a nuclear missile launch by a submarine, and the subsequent end of the British Empire. Dolby knew quite a bit about submarine warfare, as his uncle had died in a submarine during the Second World War, whilst his father worked in military intelligence, which is expressed in the line "*I can trace my history down one generation to my home in one of our submarines*". Despite two strong songs, the single only reached number forty-nine in Britain, but did become a top ten hit in the United States and topped the charts in Canada.

ʊ ʊ ʊ

The cast of the Comic Strip Club finally found a televisual vehicle that suited their style when the BBC commissioned them to write a situation comedy. To help with the writing Alexis Sayle and Rick Mayall brought on board the latter's girlfriend Lise Mayer, and his old Manchester University friend Ben Elton, fresh from his own comedy sketch show for Granada Television called *There's Nothing to Worry About*.

The six-episode series called *The Young Ones* broke many of the conventions of sit-coms at the time, disregarding plausible plotlines, breaking the fourth wall, and following random thoughts down surrealistic rabbit-holes. After a pilot filmed in January, the BBC hesitated, until the news came that Peter Richardson had approached Channel 4 with a proposal for a series of one-off stories under the title *The Comic Strip*, to feature many of the same *alternative comedy* cast. The fear of losing the next generation of talent forced the corporation's hand and the series was commissioned.

Mayall and Mayer drew upon many of the character comedians they had worked with over the years, with poetry writing Rick for the former, punk Vyvyan based upon Ade Emundson's Dangerous Brothers character, Nigel Planer bringing his hippy persona in the form of Neil, and last-minute addition Christopher Ryan[566] playing the role of Mike[567].

---

[566] Ryan was a former member of The Flying Pickets.

[567] Mike was originally meant to be played by Peter Richardson, however his subsequent falling out with director Paul Jackson led to Ryan's recruitment.

With story and plot kept to a minimum, violent slapstick, talking animals and objects took centre stage. The premise concerned four students living in a house and the exaggerated animosity between them, and whilst it could be flippant, many left-wing political statements were made regarding racism in the police, unemployment, and class stratification. Each week, a band would perform in the show, often as a loose part of any plot, with Nine Below Zero, Madness, Dexy's Midnight Runners, and Rip, Rig & Panic all appearing throughout November.

The series was aimed at people aged 18 – 30 but instead was taken up by the 10 – 14 audience following the broadcasting of the first episode on Tuesday 9th November, the people who had been raised on wacky Madness videos where anything could (and often did) happen. Almost overnight the essence of television comedy was transformed as the public began to view the old comedians as outdated. Looking back to the very fondly remembered series decades later, one is surprised to find that it has not aged well, and in fact tends to induce cringing throughout, especially if watching with someone from a younger generation. It is not that the comedy world has caught up with the humour rendering it tame, it is simply that it may not have been funny in the first place. Too many of the jokes are frozen in the time they were made, and the rest may only have been appreciated simply because nothing had been seen like it on television before. Possibly for a good reason.

The various plots over the six episodes included the flatmates finding oil in their basement, a nuclear bomb in the kitchen, and Buddy Holly hanging from a parachute upstairs. The show picked up a weekly audience of around two and a half million viewers, enough to be a success whilst still remaining cult viewing.

The left-wing stance of the original cast was compromised during a second series when they started laughing at the characters rather than with them and recruited the very Oxbridge graduates that they had set out to oppose. Alexis Sayle recalls visiting the set during the first episode of the second series to find that Stephen Fry, Hugh Laurie, and Emma Thompson[568] had roles. He approached Mayall, Meyer, and Elton and pointed out that "[the Oxbridge people] *represent systematic class oppression and the dominance of bourgeois ideology in popular culture which we have made it our mission to destroy*". The other three looked at him as if he were crazy, pointing out *"No, that was just you"*, and explaining how much they liked Fry, Laurie, and Thompson.

The new breed took very little time in joining and then becoming the establishment, as the likes of Jennifer Saunders and Dawn French became television regulars with their own safe sketch shows, whilst Ben Elton betrayed his left-wing stance by writing a juke-box musical about Queen, a band who had played South Africa's Sun City at the height of Apartheid.

ʊ ʊ ʊ

The new three-piece Thompson Twins had decided to purge themselves of all British influences, and with the record company contented to foot the bill once *In the Name of Love* was selling in the States, they claimed to voyage to Egypt[569] then the Bahamas to write and record. Washing up at Compass Point Studio in Nassau, the trio started working with head engineer Alex Sadkin, an American who had gotten his break mixing Neil Young before producing a run of ground-breaking albums for Grace Jones in the early 1980's. Jones repaid the debt by agreeing to sing backing vocals on one track (*Watching*) on an album which also featured future Cure drummer Boris Williams playing percussion. Other than that, Bailey, Currie, and Leeway provided vocals,

---

[568] Laurie & Thompson were romantically linked at university.
[569] In reality, they were in Norfolk.

percussion, and synthesizers, but most significantly, no guitars. They constructed an album of impeccable pop songs, created for dancing, with a first single released *Lies* being released at the start of November.

The song was a statement of their new direction, designed to be played loudly in a club where the digital sterility of the drum machines and bass would be most effective. The

song had traces of the old Thompson Twins, but had scraped off all agit-prop pretentions and replaced them with a sheen of pure pop. Drums and bass were relentless throughout, with a Prophet V synth providing the hooks over which frontman and main songwriter Tom Bailey sang of being betrayed by a lover.

The single was helped across the Atlantic by a memorably hallucinogenic video, seen from the point of view of a patient in a hospital bed, which although it looks clunky now would have taken a huge amount of computer generating at the time, with layer upon layer of visuals appearing. The single topped the American Dance Chart (as had their previous one) and even rose to number thirty in the Billboard countdown, however the British continued to remain immune to the charms of the Thompson Twins, peaking at number sixty-seven. This refusal to grasp them to their hearts did not last into 1983, however, when they scored three top ten hits and a number two album with the just recorded *Quick Step & Side Kick*.

The Thompson Twins became much ridiculed in later years, however, it is worth re-investigating *Quick Step & Side Kick* (or *Side Kicks* as it was called in America and Canada) to find a succinct consistent collection of dance music. The racial and gender mix of the trio (one white male, one white female, one mixed race male) extended their appeal, and in the United States they were popular in both black and white clubs and radio stations, funky enough for the former, pop enough for the latter.

The album was Bailey's show, with help from his partner and fellow member Alannah Currie. It is hard to see what third member Joe Leeway added, given that his job was visuals and live footage of the band touring show him keeping a strictly *hands-off* approach to the keyboard in front of him.

Love on your Side, their brilliant and self-referential next single in early 1983, saw them breakthrough in their home country, after which they enjoyed a few years of great success at the cost of credibility as they became more and more lost in show-business. They did, however, manage to peak in time to make an appearance at the Philadelphia leg of Live Aid in 1985, as well as release a self-titled computer game which was distributed on a flexi-disc via *Computer and Video Games Magazine*[570].

Tom Bailey was never under any illusions about the scale of ambition within the Thompson Twins, once claiming *"a multinational corporation is exactly what we are, in a business sense. We've got a monstrously big turnover internationally. A lot bigger than some of the companies that are quoted on the stock exchange."* It was a long way from their socialist agit-prop beginnings.

After the success started to dry up, Bailey and Currie moved to California where they wrote for other artists. Bailey and Currie finally married in 1991, before splitting in 2003, with Currie now married to KLF member Jimmy Cauty. Leeway moved to California, and now works as a hypnotherapist.

---

[570] The game, with terrible animation, involved the player controlling the three members of the band through a series of typed instructions whilst they found various parts of a potion. This was then given to a doctor (this was to promote the single *Doctor! Doctor!*), who combined them to reveal an answer which could win the player backstage passes to a forthcoming gig.

ʊ ʊ ʊ

For the last year, whilst the Soviet Union had been led by Leonid Brezhnev, it had been run by a cabal of Andrei Gromyko[571], Dmitriy Ustinov[572], Mikhail Suslov[573], and Yuri Andropov, making decisions as the formal leader's health deteriorated. Jostling for position as successor, Andropov was particularly active in using the KGB to spread rumors regarding Brezhnev's health, as well as stories of political corruption.

Despite having suffered a severe stroke in May, Brezhnev was a fighter and insisted on keeping the job of General Secretary of the Communist Party of the Soviet Union, and Chairman of the Presidium of the Supreme Soviet. At the age of seventy-five the Ukrainian-born leader had been a protégé of Nikita Krushchev, who he backed during a purge of the Stalinists following the leader's death in 1953. As is so often the case when power is involved, friends can easily become enemies, and Brezhnev was then involved in the removal of Krushchev in 1964, positioning himself as a supposedly temporary leader, a role he held until his death.

Under Brezhnev, personal freedoms were restricted following an easing of state control under Krushchev, whilst tanks were sent into Prague to crush a revolution in 1968, and into Afghanistan in 1979. Realizing the Soviets were far behind the United States in the arms race, Brezhnev pursued a policy of détente, whilst at the same time funding and arming guerilla armies in Third World countries. By 1982, he was in extremely poor health, suffering from insomnia, gout, leukemia, cancer of the jaw, emphysema, chronic bronchitis, memory loss, arteriosclerosis, and an addiction to sleeping pills, alcohol, and tranquilizers, all of which led to a fatal heart attack on Wednesday 10th November.

The people of the Soviet Union were not informed of the death until the following day, after twenty-four hours of deliberation by the politburo, the result of which was the awarding of the top job to Yuri Andropov.

ʊ ʊ ʊ

Sunderland-born Dave Stewart was a washed-up musician[574] with a serious drug habit when he first met Aberdonian Annie Lennox, however within days they were living together as a couple as she helped him battle the addiction. Forming a group called The Tourists, the duo bought into the new wave sound, enjoying chart success with hits *So Good (To be Back Home)* and *I Only Want to be With You*. Given their subsequent success, it is surprising to find they were not the songwriters in the group, a role which instead fell to Peet Coombs who also considered himself the lead vocalist. On a final tour of Australia, Coombes overdosed, and the band were forced to fly home[575]. Convinced the band was over, Stewart hatched a plan on the flight home to create experimental electronic music with Lennox, only to find a flaw in the plan when she promptly split with him romantically. "*I remember our conversation*" recalled Stewart years later, "*It wasn't even a long one because we were so exhausted. She goes 'Y'know what? We should probably try living separately for a second or whatever?' and we both went 'God yeah, we should', and then fell asleep.*" Stewart

---

[571] Gromyko was known at the United Nations as *Mr Nyet* for his habit of vetoing motions.

[572] In Jonathan Hickman and Nick Pitarra's graphic novel *The Manhattan Project*, Ustinov is portrayed as a brain attached to a robot body.

[573] Suslov, to be fair, died back in January, in mysterious circumstances explained as a heart attack.

[574] Stewart had been a member of Longrider, signed to Elton John's *Rocket* label in the early 1970's.

[575] The arrived back on the day John Lennon was shot dead.

had spent his last days in Australia in a hotel room in Wagga Wagga, playing around with EDP's Wasp synthesizer, and was excited about the opportunity's technology could offer.

Appreciating the creative energy they shared, the two agreed to continue working as a musical force, signing to RCA as The Eurythmics and recording their debut album in West Germany with Conny Plank producing. When the album and subsequent singles flopped, the duo persuaded the bank to lend them £5,000 to put together an eight-track recording set-up above a picture-framing store in London's Chalk Farm, complete with mixing desk, tape recorders, and basic synthesisers.

Early results, such as singles *The Walk* and *This is the House* also failed to chart, and new single *Love is a Stranger* may have been their last chance. The duo was still finding their way around the equipment which forced them to write in new ways, the result of which was a lack of obvious choruses. Working within what Stewart described as "*cold, European, hard, tough-sounding synthesizers with a soulful voice*" the song was a towering and piercing dissection of love, lust, and desire. Love was treated like a drug, to be in love a dangerous addiction, as Lennox sang through gritted teeth "*It's*

savage and it's cruel and it shines like destruction, comes in like the flood and it seems like religion. It's noble and it's brutal, it distorts and deranges, and it wrenches you up and you're left like a zombie." From the controlled sound of restless infatuation, she switched to the edge of hysteria with a repeated cry of "*I want you, I want you, I want you so, it's an obsession.*" The mood then switched to bitterness and accusations, with "*It's gilt-edged, glamorous and sleek by design, you know it's jealous by nature, false and unkind. It's hard and restrained and it's totally cool, it touches, and it teases as you stumble in the debris.*" This was no obvious love song, propelled by a pounding and relentless beat and Stewart's thrusting grunts, but was the unremitting sound of someone losing their mind.

Money was provided to produce a video, which the Eurythmics immediately used to add to the unease of the single, featuring Lennox as a high-class prostitute and Stewart as her driver. For each client she meets Lennox transforms into a different character, causing MTV to pull the plug half-way through when she removed a wig, after they assumed she was a transvestite. Stewart described Lennox's visuals at the time, saying "*Annie was toying with different stage guises before an overzealous fan managed to get on stage and pulled off her wig. Furious… Annie shaved her hair into a buzzcut and swapped the dresses she had been sporting for men's suits in order to cultivate a tougher, more aggressive stage persona*", what the singer herself called "*a gay ginger skinhead in a suit.*"

All this subversiveness caused the single to stall at number at number fifty-four, and when evicted from the space above the picture framer, Stewart and Lennox moved to the coatroom of a church building in Couch End owned by animators Bob Bura and John Hardwick[576]. It was here they put the finishing touches to a new track called *Sweet Dreams (Are Made of This)*, a song which the record company saw no potential in, once again lacking an obvious chorus and beginning with a dark, ironic opening line. As usual, the record company was wrong.

ʊ ʊ ʊ

---

[576] Bura and Hardwick had been responsible for the animation in *Captain Pugwash* and *Trumpton*.

Now that the PLO had left Lebanon, Israel might have expected a peaceful interlude, however they found a new enemy in the shape of Hezbollah, an Iranian-organised assemblage of smaller terrorist groups. On Thursday 11th November, a seventeen-year-old Lebanese boy called Ahmed Qassir parked a Peugeot car jammed with explosives outside the Israeli Defence Force headquarters in the coastal town of Tyre. Seconds later, Qassir detonated the explosives and himself, flattening the building in less than ten seconds and killing over 103 Israeli soldiers and up to 60 Lebanese prisoners. For the joint European and American forces, this was to be their first encounter with a markedly fundamentalist Iranian Islamic type of war: people who were willing to martyr themselves for their cause. As the Iranian Revolutionary Guard arrived in Lebanon, they opened an office in Beirut and started giving martyrdom lessons to children. There would be many more examples of this type of warfare in the future.

Despite overwhelming evidence to the contrary, the Israeli government insists to this day that the explosion was caused by a faulty gas cylinder.

ʊ ʊ ʊ

The official police report for an incident on Tullygally East Road, Lurgan, Northern Ireland on Thursday 11th November stated that a Ford Escort carrying Eugene Tolman, Sean Burns, and Gervaise McKerr had been stopped by officers during a routine search. The car supposedly accelerated, causing police to jump out of the way, after which a nearby patrol car pursued. When the civilians in the Escort opened fire, officers shot back, killing all three men.

Later investigations into the incident revealed a completely different version of events. The three men had been under surveillance from an RUC anti-terrorist unit for several hours, and no attempt was ever made to stop the car. A total of 108 bullets were fired by the police, from a mixture of a Sterling sub-machine gun, Ruger rifles, and a handgun[577]. None of the three civilians were armed, and the police were permitted to leave the scene immediately with their weapons, whilst forensic investigators were denied access to the weapons, clothes, and car for several days[578].

When three police officers, Sergeant Montgomery, Constable Brannigan, and Constable Robinson were eventually brought to court for the murder of Toman, they were acquitted by Lord Justice Gibson, who instead praised them for bringing the deceased men to *"the final court of justice"*[579].

It looked as if the police in Northern Ireland were now operating a shoot-to-kill policy.

ʊ ʊ ʊ

With both Haysi Fantayzee and Culture Club hitting the top ten, the question was who would be able to follow up a first hit and who would be a one-hit wonder?

First out the traps were Haysi Fantaysee with their new single *Holy Joe*, a piece of African High Life carried by Kate Garner's vocals, which superficially concerned itself with religion being sold on American television. *"Because of our [Catholic] backgrounds we feel really strongly about religion and what it does to people"* claimed Jeremy Healy at the time, whose contribution to the whole affair appeared to be some

---

[577] Most of the cartridge cases were never found. The official excuse was that they must have been swept away in the hem of the cassock of the priest who administered the last rites at the scene!

[578] Later, efforts were made to ship the car (complete with blood and bullet holes) to New York to take place in the St Patrick Day's Parade and be used as a collection box for Irish sympathizers.

[579] Gibson and his wife were later killed by a Republican car bomb in 1987.

echo-dub toasted vocal sounds in the background. Despite appearing as a lightweight pop act with little musical ability, the big guns were brought in to help during the recording of the album, including ex-Teardrop Explodes bass player Alfie Agius, future Pretenders and Paul McCartney guitarist Robbie McIntosh, and backing vocals by Afrodiziak[580], whilst Tony Visconti handled some of the production. When the single only reached number fifty-one, it looked like the wheels had come off, and despite one further minor hit the following year, Haysi Fantayzee were consigned to the scrapheap of novelty acts. Garner would go on to become an acclaimed photographer, whilst Healy found a second career as a dance-music disc jockey[581].

Meanwhile, Virgin Records did not care that Culture Club had already released three singles from their debut album *Kissing to be Clever*, and that one was still sitting high in the charts. As they searched for a new single to boost sales of the album[582] the

band staged a mini-revolution, demanding a new song be released. Virgin dug their heels in until they heard the song in question: *Time (Clock of the Heart)*.

Working once again with Steve Levine, this time with a twenty-four-piece string section, the song was a lush step forward from the rather transparent sound of the album. Opening with dub bass, the song was full of yearning for love and affection, aimed by Boy George once again at drummer Jon Moss, encouraging him to overcome his fears of being seen as gay, the problem at the root of their relationship. "*This could be the best place yet but you must overcome your tears*" he pleaded before declaring "*I felt I lost you from the start*". Reaching number three and selling half a million copies in Britain, *Time (Clock of the Heart)* is perhaps the Culture Club song which has aged best over the decades, remaining a soulful petition for love.

ʊ ʊ ʊ

Blue Rondo à la Turk continued to propel singles at the top forty throughout 1982, none of which stuck, as their debut album *Chewing the Fat* scraped the bottom of the charts for a couple of weeks. The band eventually fizzled out, with members Daniel White, Kito Ponncioni, and Mark Reilly achieving short-lived chart success a couple of years later in Matt Bianco.

Frontman Chris Sullivan had been running a Saturday night club at the Whiskey-A-Go-Go in Soho's Wardour Street, along with Ollie O'Donnell, when the new leaseholders asked them to run it full time. With the band waning it was a fortuitous request and changing the name to the Wag Club[583] whilst lowering door and drink prices they

---

[580] Afrodiziak were Caron Wheeler, Claudia Fontaine, and Naomi Thompson, and were all over the early 1980's, most famously on Special AKA single *Free Nelson Mandela*.

[581] Healy also married Patsy Kensit, her fourth husband after Dan Donovan of Big Audio Dynamite, Jim Kerr of Simple Minds, and Liam Gallagher of Oasis.

[582] The favourite was *I'll Tumble 4 Ya*, which would reach the American top ten but never be released in the United Kingdom.

[583] Whiskey-A-Go-Go = W.A.G.G. = Wag Club.

created a London institution which remained at the heart of celebrity culture and music until 2001. In November 1982 they hosted the first hip-hop night in Britain, booking Africa Bamabaataa, Fast Five Freddie, the Double Dutch Girls, and the Rocksteady Crew, as well as other New York artists. They championed bands on the verge of success, such as Sade, The Fine Young Cannibals, Swing Out Sister, and Curiosity Killed the Cat, all of whom signed after dates at the Wag Club. Anyone who was anyone turned up at the club and partied until the small hours, catching the new wave of style being pioneered by magazines such as *The Face* and *i-D*, mixing rare music with changing fashion. As you would expect, some people hated the club, with Charles Shaar Murray from the NME claiming "*I always associated the Wag Club with that very Thatcherite*  *London club culture.* [It] *was so associated with everything I hated about the eighties.*" When the club closed in 2001, it made way for an Irish theme bar.

Other than Steve Strange's Blitz and Club for Heroes, there were several other clubs crucial to the capital's cultural nightlife in the early 1980's. Le Kilt had been run on Tuesday nights at 60 Greek Street from 1981 by Robert Elms, Graham Smith, and Graham Ball, and specialised in harder funk, inspiring Le Beat Route which was held in a basement along the road at 17 Greek Street on a Friday night. At the latter Ealing's Steve Lewis would pack dancefloor to the sounds of old funk classics and New York rap, whilst O'Donnell ran the door. "*The harder I made it for people to get in… the more desperate they were to get in,*" he explained, "*More than twenty times I must have said to a very good-looking girl 'You can come in, but the guy you're with can't', and the girl would walk straight in and leave her date for the night in the street,*" The room featured Caribbean beach décor, which provided the inspiration for regulars Wham to write *Club Tropicana*, whilst the soundtrack included Kid Creole and the Coconuts, whose singer August Darnell was a visitor when in town. When Le Beat Route closed, many of the regulars moved to Dirtbox which was opened above a chemist on Earls Court Road by Phil Gray and Rob Milton, where the resident DJ was Jay Strongman.

Towards the end of 1982, 69 Dean Street in Soho, where the Batcave started, hosted a variety of different club nights, including an African Highlife night called *Gold Coast*, a jazz funk night on Fridays called *Radio Invicta*, and Saturday's popular *Roots Rock* night hosted by David Rodigan and Tim Westwood[584].

Many of the regulars at the Blitz went on to host their own club nights, including founder David Claridge who opened a fetish night called *Skin Too* in early 1983[585], Leigh Bowery who ran *Taboo* from 1985, as well as Jeremy Healy and Patrick Lilley.

 As London's nightlife was warming up, AIDS was bringing New York's golden age to an end. One of the pioneers of electronic dance music who had driven the club sound, Patrick Cowley, had teamed up with disco-diva Sylvester in San Francisco in the late 1970's. His studio skills and synthesizer wizardry meant Cowley's talents were in demand, as he joined Sylvester's live band for world tours, however his active participation in a gay San Franciscan lifestyle opened him to the danger of AIDS, and in late 1981 was mis-diagnosed with food poisoning. As his

---

[584] Sacha Baron Cohen has admitted that Westwood's white boy Jamaican patois was the inspiration for his character Ali G.

[585] Claridge gave it all up and denied any involvement when he invented Roland Rat.

health deteriorated during 1982, he struggled to record two albums, one for Sylvester and one solo. Towards the end, Sylvester dragged him out of bed, challenging him to get better, and insisted they record one final song. *Do You Wanna Funk* was a mammoth slab of high energy disco with Cowley's synthesizer parts right up front in the mix. *"If I tell you that you're really something... will you stay or will you go away?"* asked Sylvester of Cowley. Upon its release at the end of summer, the song climbed to number thirty-two in the singles charts, becoming an immediate influence on New Order who were about to record *Blue Monday*.

Do You Wanna Funk was a suitable epitaph for Cowley, who succumbed to AIDS on Friday 12th November, aged thirty-two.

ʊ ʊ ʊ

Producer Clive Langer was concerned when he turned up at the room where Madness were writing and rehearsing their new album. *"Many of the songs essentially weren't up to it"* he claimed, *"and that was maybe due to them being on the road [too long]"*. These songs had begun as a loosely linked concept around nostalgia and childhood, with all members of the band instructed to write with this in mind. Madness were fortunate in that they had six songwriters within the band, all of whom could contribute and collaborate, and so credits were split evenly across the album. Frontman Suggs tendered lyrics to five of the tracks, guitarist Chris Foreman wrote music for seven, pianist Mike Barson helped with five, backing singer and trumpet player Cathal "Chas" Smyth supplied lyrics for two, saxophonist Lee Thompson wrote three, and drummer Daniel Woodgate contributed one whole song on his own. Only bass player Mark Bedford failed to get in on the royalties gravy train.

Fourteen years after The Kinks' *Village Green Preservation Society* and twelve years before Blur's *Parklife*, *Madness Presents the Rise & Fall* squatted superlatively between them in its reflection of everyday English life. We were thrown straight in with no introduction, as the title track saw Suggs looking back on his childhood stomping ground in Liverpool, whilst future single *Tomorrow's (Just Another Day)* had Smyth trying to find optimism in the midst of a downward spiral. The album was shot-through with wistfulness, from the hidden-behind-the-lace-curtains horror of *Primrose Hill* and *Sunday Morning* to the languid multi-culturalism of *New Delhi*. Where Madness had at first considered asking Trevor Horn to produce, their decision to employ Langer and Winstanley was a wise one, allowing the natural character of the individuals to emerge. With a number one single behind them at last, the band were provided with a decent budget for the first time and utilised it by hiring strings and an expensive studio.

The tentpole of the album, opening side two of the vinyl, was *Our House*, surely the finest song recorded by a band with many classics. Identified by Langer and Alan Winstanley as a hit the first time they heard it at rehearsals, by the time the band got to AIR Studios, the producers had added a couple of presumptive key changes at the end, which caused a problem when it came to the vocals. *"When the guys did the backing vocals it was always a problem trying to pitch to come back in for the key change"* explained Winstanley, *"That was really hard, and so it took a long time to do all of the vocals and backing vocals on that song. They just couldn't get the pitch right for each upcoming key change."*

Smyth who was originally employed to dance onstage and shout "*Hey You! Don't watch that, watch this!*" was keen to justify his place in the band, and as well as providing lyrics for the song, learned the trumpet. Langer welcomed his contribution, saying "*Even though he wasn't the greatest trumpet player in the world, he played it on 'Our House'. It took him a long time to actually nail it, but he wanted to do it and we didn't say 'Nah, bollocks, let's just get a session guy in.' On some of the tracks, including 'Our House', we actually did have a brass section, but Lee and Carl played*

as a part of that section, and on other songs Carl played the trumpet on his own. So, he really evolved from being the kid who just did the nutty dancing to someone who played the trumpet, learned to play the guitar and also wrote songs, including one of their biggest hits; certainly, their biggest hit in America."

Thompson was self-taught on the saxophone, and his lack of technical understanding of the instrument helped add to the sound of Madness. Once again Langer welcomed this aspect, stating "*It was all part of the charm. In fact, when Lee taught himself to play sax, he didn't realise that it's a B flat instrument. We eventually discovered that his fingering was a semitone out, so he was kind of blowing and moving the mouthpiece to try to compensate for that. It's because he wasn't quite on the note that he always sounded slightly out of tune, and that aspect of Madness was very exciting.*"

Trying to keep the amateur *old pub* style of Madness could be quite a convoluted business, and on *Our House* Mike Barson played a grand piano, which had to be double tracked at slightly different speeds to make it sound old and battered.

The final recording appeared flawless, with not a thing superfluous or out of place, and contained one of the finest opening builds to a song ever. With a short backwards fade approaching like a bullet, the drums and piano provided a run through the chords, before bass and horns were brought in next time round, then Western-style strings, and finally an ascending five note Duane Eddy-style guitar line brought you to the opening verse. The song suffered from an attention deficit, always keen to move to the next section, cutting choruses short by a beat, ignoring tension built by verses, giving the overall impression of the chaos of a large family in a small house. At less than three and a half minutes it did not overstay its welcome or wallow in nostalgia, realising "*Something tells me that you've got to move away*". We were taken from specific observations about family members to a personal moment with Smyth, who gave the impression of taking us to one side to quickly explain in double time "*I remember way back then when everything was true and when we would have such a very good time, such a fine time, such a happy time. And I remember how we'd play, simply waste the day away, then we'd say nothing would come between us: Two dreamers*"

In a stiff Christmas market, *Our House* reached number five, going on to become one of their most beloved songs, however in the United States it became their biggest hit single, reaching number seven, thanks to heavy rotation of another of their typically anarchic videos on MTV.

The song marked the watershed between the nutty-Madness of the early 1980's, and the more mature song writing of the next three years which eventually ran out with their split in 1986. Madness never left, though, and would spend quite a few Decembers in the 1990's undertaking a British tour or playing their own one-off summer festivals. Forever remembered fondly in the minds and hearts of a generation, they were finally installed as national treasures when they played *Our House* on top of Buckingham

Palace in 2012 for the Queen's jubilee, accompanied by a stunning visual projection on the front of the façade[586].

The Rise & Fall only reached number ten, a sign that Madness were considered a singles rather than an album band, however they had a much better album to come in the shape of 2009's *The Liberty of Norton Folgate*, which I recommend you listen to right now[587].

14th – 20th November 1982

#1 single: Eddy Grant: I Don't Wanna Dance
#1 album: The Kids From Fame: The Kids From Fame

Like a latecomer to the 1982 party, one who sits in the corner refusing to have fun, China Crisis were on hand to provide some sobriety and gravity to the proceedings. Their debut album, passive-aggressively called *Difficult Shapes & Passive Rhythms, Some People Think It's Fun to Entertain*, was released on Virgin Records in November, and was at striking odds with what was going on elsewhere.

China Crisis had been born in the bedrooms of their parents' houses in Liverpool by Gary Daly, Eddie Lundon, and Dave Reilly, choosing deliberately not to socialise with other local acts through a mixture of shyness and aloofness. Although they were

signed to Virgin the same week as Culture Club, the two acts could not be further apart in terms of outlook. The songs of China Crisis tended to be weighed down by their own solemnity, and even moments intended to demonstrate a pop-conscious lightness were dragged down by Eeyore-levels of unnecessary fretless bass guitar, pace, and earnestness. Owing a debt to the soundscapes of Japan and Brian Eno, this was exactly the kind of thing Talk Talk would earn plaudits from later in the decade.

Four producers used across the eleven tracks spoke of a searching for a commercially acceptable sound, as the first two singles *African and White* and *No More Blue Horizons (Fool, Fool, Fool)* failed to break through. A tour supporting Simple Minds helped, and early in 1983 a third single, the immersive *Christian*, provided a genuine chart hit.

ʊ ʊ ʊ

Andy Wickett, living in obscurity and poverty back in Birmingham, must have been kicking himself every time the video for *Rio* was shown on television towards the end of 1982. The excess on the screen must have gotten under his skin. How was he to know when offered £600 in exchange for signing a waiver to give up the rights to two songs he had written, one of which would become *Girls on Film* and the other of which evolved into *Rio*? It seemed like a great deal at the time and had allowed him to buy himself a keyboard.

---

[586] Let's get this straight... Brian May on top of Buckingham Palace is embarrassing, Madness on top of Buckingham Palace is brilliant. I could go into reasons for this, but as it is a fact, we'll just leave it there.

[587] Drop everything. Go and listen to this album.

The single provided Duran Duran with a number nine hit on the run up to Christmas, but it was the accompanying promotional clip which people remembered most, shot the previous June in Antigua, as it turned out to be the most indelible and successful ever made by a band who were famous for their videos. It also turned out to be highly polarizing. For many, shots of the band carousing on a tropical beach or wearing brightly-coloured Anthony Price suits whilst supping champagne and cavorting with models[588] on a yacht were a touch of alluring glamour and aspiration after the bleakness of the 1970's, whilst for others the decadence was a harbinger of uncaring self-interest whilst people in Britain faced poverty and the dole queue. The images came to epitomize many of the features of the *greed is good* Thatcher / Reagan decade, as Duran Duran embraced their new-found wealth, becoming Princess Diana's favourite band whilst resolutely refusing to align themselves with any political party or

issue; they were too busy bedding models, partying, and snorting cocaine to worry about such things. Guitarist Andy Taylor would later try to rationalize by claiming "*We were working class escapists who wanted to live out our dreams. The whole look, feel, and location of the video made a statement about the sort of lifestyle we aspired to, with the designer suits, the yachts, and the beautiful models. A desire to travel to fabulous locations and enjoy a wealthy lifestyle.*" The move from frilly shirts and New Romantic threads to Thatcherite power dressing was a deliberate decision a year before, according to Nick Rhodes. "*The moment we saw Adam Ant dressed as Prince Charming, we knew the New Romantic look was over,*" he explained, "*When EMI gave Duran Duran our first clothes budget, we went straight to designer Anthony Price and blew it on suits... I think we got the 'cute young band' discount.*" Not all the members of the band enjoyed the shoot, as Nick Rhodes suffered seasickness on the yacht. In a Lord Fauntleroy manner, he complained "*I hated that boat, wrecking my Anthony Price suit with all those dreadful waves*", before adding "*I hate boats unless they are tied up and I'm having cocktails on them.*"

Despite the flawless pop album and the faux-expensive videos, Duran Duran still had not broken through in America, and in fact sold more records in Portugal than the United States. With the help of the Abrahams Report, which highlighted exactly which sound would sell well in different states on FM radio, the band agreed to have the first side of *Rio* remixed to make it more palatable to American ears. David Kershenbaum, who had made a career of recording FM artists such as Joan Baez, was brought in to remix the tracks. The vocals were brought forward, the drums given more space by use of reverb, and guitars pushed to please the rocking mid-west. Despite being slightly appalled by the idea of comprising their sound, the band soon overcame their idealism by the promise of success and riches.

ʊ ʊ ʊ

The new leader of the Soviet Union, Yuri Andropov, took control of the organization of his predecessor's state funeral. There were some traditions for the funerals of Soviet leaders which needed to be adapted, the most obvious of which was the accompaniment of the coffin with the medals won by the deceased. Normally, each medal would be carried on an individual cushion, however Brezhnev had been an

---

[588] The model in the *Rio* video was the half-Palestinian Reema Ruspoli who would later marry an Italian Prince.

incredibly vain leader and had awarded himself over 200 medals. Forty-four senior officials were given the job of carrying several medals each during the funeral procession on Monday 15th November.

With most of Moscow sealed off by the military, some of the public were allowed a chance to file past Brezhnev's coffin which had lay in state for three days. On moving the body to the House of the Unions for this, the grossly overweight leader's body had fallen through the bottom of the coffin, forcing officials to find a metal plated replacement. Once transferred to the Lenin Mausoleum, speeches were given by top party officials before the coffin was taken to a nearby location. Whilst being lowered into the ground the pallbearers struggled to handle the weight, and the coffin crashed loudly to the bottom of the grave.

Heads of state from around the world attended the funeral, including Indira Gandhi from India, Pierre Trudeau and his son Justin from Canada, Yasser Arafat from his Palestinian exile, and Fidel Castro from Cuba. Britain sent Foreign Minister Francis Pym, whilst the United States were represented by Vice President George Bush.

℧ ℧ ℧

On a cold day in Northern Italy, the remains of disgraced banker Roberto Calvi were finally laid to rest at his parish church in Drezzo. There were very few mourners at the graveside, not even his wife and son, who had instead sent red roses from their Washington exile. The press outnumbered the mourners and crushed together to capture photographs of Calvi's two brothers and his daughter. No-one from the business world attended, not even those who had worked besides him for decades.

The following day the *Corriere* newspaper featured a small obituary notice from Calvi's wife which mentioned the "*countless injustices*" inflicted upon him, and stated "*there is no peace or comfort, only resignation*".

℧ ℧ ℧

The Teardrop Explodes officially split up on Monday 15th November, four years to the exact date of their first gig. Keyboard player Dave Balfe, who had wrestled control of the band from everyone else, gave frontman Julian Cope a copy of Blancmange's *Happy Families* album and told him it sounded like his hero Scott Walker, and that they should be playing music like this. Cope's response was "*Fuck off, no way... the singer sang heavy fake depression songs, but smiled on TV like it was a joke*". Cope was in the middle of a genuine drug induced burn-out depression and wanted nothing more than to retreat from the music industry. He took the Blancmange album home and burned it on the hob of his cooker.

A couple of weeks later Cope was called to his manager's office in London where he was ambushed by Balfe who informed him they had to finish the third album and tour just to pay off the debts. "*Finish the album and tour it? You misunderstand, my friend, there is no longer a group*" was Cope's answer. In Cope's words, "*Balfe rose up to his full height of 3'1" and spluttered 'Well, don't look at me for paying the fuckin' debt, then'.*"

Cope then decided to play the martyr and claimed "*I'll take on the debt, the whole lot*", much to Balfe's unmistakable delight. Balfe made a vague promise to contribute money once he was set up as a manager and record company owner. Cope was stunned to find out fifteen years later that Balfe did indeed pay his share, but by then as the owner of Food Records, home of Blur, Jesus Jones, and Idlewild, he could more than afford it[589].

Cope meanwhile became a solo artist and much-loved eccentric minor pop star, enjoying the occasional genuinely psychedelic hit single over the next decade, before becoming one of the world's foremost experts on Krautrock and standing stones.

ʊ ʊ ʊ

In the early evening of Tuesday 16th November Shankill Butcher leader Lenny Murphy pulled up outside the Belfast door of his girlfriend's house in the yellow Rover he had killed Brian Smyth for. A blue van roared in front of him, the back door opened, and two masked men got out and opened fire, hitting Murphy twenty-two times in the head and body.

Ten days later the IRA claimed responsibility for the killing, though it is now thought they were provided information on his whereabouts by the UVF, who saw Murphy's actions as being beyond their sworn remit and were concerned about his growing power.

Four days later, the UVF *Protestant Action Force* shot dead a Catholic civilian in Dundonald in retaliation, whilst Murphy was given a full paramilitary funeral. When the coffin stopped outside his mother's home on Brookmount Street, six masked gunmen fired a volley of shots in respect. Police were kept from the scene by a convoy of black taxis at either end of the road, and the gunmen allowed to escape.

His mother was reported as saying "*My Lenny wouldn't hurt a fly*".

21st – 27th November 1982
#1 single: Eddy Grant: I Don't Wanna Dance
#1 album: Abba: The Singles – The First Ten Years

Before leaving England for Barbados, Eddy Grant had watched the Brixton riots on television, and wrote "*Now in the street there is violence*" on a piece of paper. From this seed came the song *Electric Avenue*. "*I had been talking to politicians and people at a high level about the lack of opportunity for black people, and I knew what was brewing*" he would later profess, "*I myself might have been successful, but I could have easily been one of those guys with no hope, and I knew that when people felt they were being left behind, there was potential for violence. The song was intended as a wake-up call.*"

During the 1970's Grant had been taken under the wing of actor Norman Beaton and encouraged to attend his *Black Theatre of Brixton*. Grant explained "*On my way there, I passed a street sign for Electric Avenue, and it was like a moment from God. I instantly thought, 'Jesus, what a great title for a song'.*"

Arriving in Barbados, Grant found that British Airways had lost the luggage containing all his latest songs and was forced to re-write the entire album from scratch. This was made more difficult by finding his studio only half-complete. "*I was forced into writing the record in a studio that was not yet built*" he explained, "*I had to drag song titles out of my memory bank, and one of those was Electric Avenue.*" With the sound of workmen hammering and sawing putting paid to any idea of using acoustic instruments, the singer chose to switch to

---

[589] And of course, Balfe became the subject matter of Blur's chart-topper *Country House*.

electronic drum machines and synthesisers, sneaking back in during the night to overdub real drums. Engineer Frank Agarrat explained *"The chorus – 'Rock down to Electric Avenue' – suggested cars or motorcycles, so I looped a snare drum roll and distorted it, so it sounded like a revving motorbike."* Even working at night with no-one but local monkeys around, technical problems would still arise. Agarrat claimed *"The tape would suddenly spew out of the machine for no reason. One night, nothing would work at all. Eventually it turned out that a rat had got in through the air-conditioning and*

eaten through the wires under the floor. We spent the rest of the night running around the studio trying to catch it." Despite not being as big a hit as *I Don't Wanna' Dance*, the single became a more enduring representation of Grant's milieu, mixing pop with a political message, sweetening the pill for consumption. With *Electric Avenue*[590] reaching the number two position on both sides of the Atlantic, the parent album *Killer on the Rampage* became a worldwide smash, and with his own studio and his own label, both located far from the music business centres, Grant was a truly independent artist and could follow his own instincts over his subsequent career.

ʊ ʊ ʊ

Holly Johnson had forced his way into the Liverpool punk scene by pure force of character, joining local legends Big in Japan on bass at the age of sixteen, forming a friendship with roadie Paul Rutherford. Believing he had missed the bus to success, Johnson tried one more time with a new act which he called Frankie Goes to Hollywood after a feature in *The New Yorker* magazine about Frank Sinatra. Recruiting musicians Peter Gill, Mark O'Toole, and Brian Nash whilst sharing vocal duties with Rutherford, the act cultivated a hard-core leather and bondage look, being turned down by every record company in the country during 1982. Then, on Wednesday 24th November they found themselves in the unexpected position of recording a session for the only person likely to give them a chance: John Peel, having shared the bill with him during one of his DJ gigs in Warrington.

The opening track was a frantic and funky version of *Two Tribes*, which showed the arrangement was in place years before the song became a worldwide phenomenon. The session and rumours of their sleazy live show led to a feature on *The Tube* in January 1983 in which they performed an extremely basic version of an unfinished *Relax*, which in turn brought them to the attention of Trevor Horn, who was in the process of a new venture.

The record label Zang Tuum Tumb was formed by Horn, his wife Jill Sinclair, and music journalist Paul Morley. Morley had once given Horn's act Buggles a savage write-up at the NME titled *Dirty Old Men with Moderne Mannerisms* in which he criticised them as old dinosaurs trying to cash in on punk and new wave. Band member Geoff Downes took great exception to the line of questioning and terminated the interview half-way through, however Horn had been intrigued by Morley's intellect as well as his analytical and dogmatic approach to music. When Morley became a cheerleader for the type of music being produced by Horn with Dollar and ABC in 1982, the two engaged in a series of conversations about the nature of pop music as well as the possibilities for the future. From these intense conversations ZTT was formed, with Horn wanting to

---

[590] Grant was invited back to turn on a new illuminated street sign in Brixton and was presented with the original *Electric Avenue* sign as a gift.

create modern dance music and Morley wanting to stir things up a bit. Morley himself was *"going through a period of guilt about how as a critic all I did was comment and carp... ultimately I felt parasitical. I had this romantic idealism that I should contribute"*. Horn and Sinclair were in the middle of negotiations with Island Records for a distribution deal for their own newly formed label, Perfect, when Morley came on board. He immediately decided the name was too dull and instead chose Zang Tuum Tumb[591], named after a sound poem by Italian Futurist poet Filippo Tommaso Marinetti, describing his impression of a machine gun at the Battle of Adrianopple during the First Balkan War of 1912 – 1913. Morley took a highly intellectual approach to the label, seeing their releases as being somewhere between Dada and the Dancefloor.

The first signing to the label was the Art of Noise, consisting of the production team that Horn had already built around himself: J.J Jeczalik, Gary Langan, Anne Dudley, and Horn himself. Morley then became the fifth member of the act, being responsible for their press releases and titles, though Jeczalik later described him as the *tea boy*.

ZTT was a perfect example of *betting on the upside*, a Silicon Valley phrase which means everything is staked upon massive success. They would spend months recording singles in very exclusive studios, with teams of expensive musical experts on hand, and then spend even more money on extravagant advertising. It was a formula which would make Horn very rich: the acts used his studio, and so he got payment for the hiring of the facilities, as well as a percentage payment for being the producer, and then another one for owning the record company. He would also try his hardest to get his name on the songwriting, ensuring more money came his way: the only person making money on a flop ZTT single was Trevor Horn. What Trevor Horn did for Frankie Goes to Hollywood and their songs was provide them with some discipline, replacing guitar and bass lines with orchestration and expanding them sonically. Debut single *Relax* took months to record, months to break into the top forty, and then months to be knocked off the number one slot. Follow-up *Two Tribes* increased the bombast, selling millions at the top of the charts as well, and then third single *The Power of Love* completed a trio of number ones and an amazing 1984 for the band no-one in Liverpool thought had a chance[592].

℧ ℧ ℧

The distance between the official line and the truth continued to grow in Northern Ireland, as exemplified by events on Wednesday 24th November.

Officially, two police officers on a routine patrol witnessed a man carrying a gun near a barn, and upon investigating overheard voices and the cocking of a rifle. Shouting *"Police! Throw down your weapons!"*, the officers opened fire when nineteen-year-old Martin McCauley refused to relinquish his weapon, hitting him with fourteen rounds. The police then turned to seventeen-year-old Michael Justin Tighe, who also refused to drop his weapon, and opened fire.

The truth was far murkier and has never fully been revealed. The barn was owned by the widow of a deceased Republican and had previously been a weapons storage for the IRA. Within a couple of weeks the officers involved changed their story, instead claiming they were not on routine patrol and had not witnessed anyone with a gun. When it emerged the officers were the same as involved with the shooting of unarmed men a couple of weeks previous, and they were ordered to tell the first story to protect an informant, it became clear more was going on here than met the eye.

---

[591] Or Zang Tumb Tuum, no one was really sure of the spelling.

[592] *"How can they possibly fail?"* Pete Frame asked sarcastically in his 1982 Liverpool Rock Family Tree.

No ammunition was ever found at the barn and only three pre-war Hauser rifles recovered. What was not recovered was the MI5 tape recording from the barn, which had been bugged for months.

With such conflicting reports, sometimes from the same person, the judge refused to believe evidence from both sides.

ʊ ʊ ʊ

It should have been the hand-up needed by The Birthday Party when television cameras were sent to capture their performance at the Ace Cinema in Brixton on Thursday 25th November. In a set filled with their usual aggression and unspoken threats of violence, the band finished after forty-five minutes and returned to the dressing room. With fifteen minutes of filming still to go, it did not look as if they were willing to return to the stage, so their publicist, on instructions from the television crew, approached them backstage.

"*Are you going to go back on and do some more stuff?*" he asked.

"*What's the point?*" a surly Nick Cave replied.

"*The first four songs were new material, so let's do it!*" he tried to encourage them.

"*Why don't you go and fucking do it?*" sneered drummer Mick Harvey.

Sensing the blood of a new victim, Cave added "*Yeah, why don't you go on and play the fucking spoons*".

Eventually they were persuaded to return to the stage, though bass player Tracey Pew had trouble remembering which song they had agreed to play. Harvey decided to take control of the situation and started to pound the correct song on the drums, but still Pew could not find the notes, and the drummer eventually threw down his sticks in fury. As the two began to fight amongst the toms and cymbals, the gig was now well and truly over.

Two nights before at Nitemoves in Glasgow, the band had met with new label mates The Cocteau Twins, and had agreed to have their photograph taken with the starstruck Scots. Afterwards, the photographs hung in the shared Falkirk flat of Elizabeth Fraser and Robin Guthrie, and when friends would ask who was in the picture the two would answer "*Oh, just us with some fans of ours*".

After struggling on for another year, during which Cave and Howard stopped writing together, surviving by playing more inflammatory live shows around the world, attracting attention more on repute than anything else, the band disintegrated.

After a final date in Australia in July 1983, they flew to London where Nick Cave started to piece together a lengthy successful and respected solo career, backed by a new band, The Bad Seeds, which often featuring Mick Harvey.

Kicking the drugs would take a bit longer.

ʊ ʊ ʊ

Whilst Alison Moyet described Yazoo as being akin to "*an arranged marriage*" in terms of her relationship with Vince Clarke, they continued to produce first-class synth pop. They formed and had their first hit within a few short months, not finding the time to get to know each other, and the two hardly spoke until Clarke said "*I don't want to do this anymore*". Moyet, who Clarke described as outspoken and himself as a "*sulker*", found the sudden level of fame difficult because she was "*one of the only people I knew who wasn't desperate to get out of Basildon*". Clarke was satisfied to produce one Yazoo album and then leave things at that, however under pressure from his publishers who pointed out that leaving a second successful band within a year would look bad, the

duo started work on a new long player, working separately with Clarke recording in the morning, and Moyet in the afternoon, adding to each other's contributions.

As a stopgap, single *The Other Side of Love* was released, peaking at number eleven, and was a far finer song than either member give it credit. Moyet would later claim *"Personally, I always thought* [it] *was a bit wank. It's my least favourite track. I don't like singing it, and Vince is not bothered."*

Clarke eventually got his wish to split, and after a short-lived third project called The Assembly, formed a long-term act called Erasure who would enjoy worldwide success for decades.

ʊ ʊ ʊ

With a third single from his first solo album, *Desperate but Not Serious*[593], stalling at

number thirty-three, it looked as if Adam Ant had finally lost the magic touch which had propelled him through the past three years of success.

Having escaped from one band, Adam knew he needed new musicians to go back out on the road. For the first time in his life, he started to suffer from stage fright, panicking about playing with a new band, having to prove himself as a live act once again. He recruited dual drummers Bogdan Wiczling and Barry Watts, Cha Burns[594] on guitar, bass player Chris DeNiro, and horn section Tony Hughes, Stewart Van Blandamer, and Steve Farr, all of whom had just finished backing Paul Young in the Q-Tips. On the opening night of the tour Burns broke his wrist, and the band were loose in comparison to the old Ants. The reviews were terrible with the NME describing the Glasgow performance as a *"cockroach on a dunghill"*. If things were bad in Britain, they then got worse in the November and December tour of the United States. Adam was not a star across the pond and was starting again at the bottom, beginning with the entire band having to cram into the one car which had been sent to JFK Airport to collect them. Upon arrival in Manhattan, their rooms at the hotel were double booked, Adam caught conjunctivitis and had to wear an eye-patch (not necessarily that bad a move given his previous costumes) and his knee was starting to play up, leading to a crippling injury in early 1983 which took him off the road for months. The band found themselves playing tiny clubs, often not making it to the stage until after midnight. It was all a step down from the admiration he was used to in Britain.

However, as the tour progressed, *Goody Two Shoes* started to creep up the American charts, and the venues started to increase in capacity. The final date in Los Angeles ten days before Christmas was met with ecstatic reviews, and Doors guitarist Robbie Kreiger joining them onstage for their version of *Hello, I Love You*.

Success was to be fleeting in in America, and Ant's star waned dramatically in his home country throughout the decade. He was to suffer well-publicised mental health

---

[593] The United States managed to avoid this single, but instead were treated to a completely redundant version of The Doors' *Hello, I Love You*.

[594] Burns had played with Lene Lovich and would go on to play with Scottish rockers The Silencers.

problems, but despite this remains a powerful and enigmatic live performer, enduring album-themed tours well into the twenty-first century.

ʊ ʊ ʊ

The Vatican's role in the Banco Ambrosiano scandal continued to plague them throughout the year. An internal report completed by three representatives from the Catholic Church and three representatives appointed by the Italian government which found the Vatican bank completely innocent of any wrongdoing was released on Friday 26th November during a Cardinals' meeting in Rome. This report, however, was overshadowed by Pope John Paul II's surprise announcement that 1983 would be an official Holy Year. This decision was on the surface dedicated to the 1,950th anniversary of the death of Christ but would also have the added advantage of millions of dollars of pilgrim money flowing into the country and the Vatican at a time when millions had been lost.

Paul Markincus, the chairman of the Vatican bank and *de facto* "*mayor*" of the Vatican City, was marginalized for his role in the affair, being left off the list of fifteen new cardinals, a rank which would traditionally have gone to one in his position.

As the weeks and months progressed into 1983, numerous other officials involved in the bank were arrested and had their passports confiscated, as the Italian government attempted to get to the bottom of the labyrinthine complexities of the bank accounts.

ʊ ʊ ʊ

The Human League returned from their Spring and Summer world tour, and chart-topping success in the United States, and went straight back into Genetic Studios with producer Martin Rushent, starting work on a song they had been playing live: *Mirror Man*. A deliberate electronic pastiche of the Motown sound with the lyrics a dig at Adam Ant for his constantly changing persona, seen by Oakey as being a desperate need to be loved by his audience to the extent where he had lost touch with who he

really was, the song was the anticipated pure pop. From the shimmering synth introduction to Susan Sully and Joanne Catherall's background "*oohs*" and "*ahs*", it contained just enough *Human League-ness* to keep the new fans happy but moved on the tiniest amount to show progression.

Virgin Records were convinced it was destined for the Christmas number one position, just like *Don't You Want Me* had achieved in 1981, however after initially entering the charts at a promising number eight, *Mirror Man* stalled in second place. Even worse, it was held back in the United States until May 1983 when it was released as part of an EP with next single *(Keep Feeling) Fascination*. Eighteen months previously, the Human League and Virgin would have leapt at number two, however the failure to reach the top spot with a top-drawer song was very much seen as a result of the band having the unheard-of audaciousness to not release a single for a whole year. The worry was that the public had forgotten them.

The band attempted to rectify this by immediately releasing their next single, *(Keep Feeling) Fascination* early in 1983. By then they had parted ways with Martin Rushent, the producer who had arguably been the biggest influence on their success. The root of the break-up was a band meeting where Sully voiced an opinion that the drums, having taken up a full day, were taking far too long to program and record. Rushent disagreed, preferring to take time and get it right, at which point Sulley asked him *"What do you know about what young people want?"*. Rushent replied *"'Hang on a minute. Correct me if I'm wrong, but haven't you just had an album out called Dare that has gone platinum in just about every country in the world? And am I right in saying that I produced it for you? Still, I'll tell you what; if you think I'm not the right producer for you because I don't know what the market wants, I'll do you a favour and resign. Consider you have just been handed my resignation."* He then walked out of his own studio and despite attempts by Virgin boss Richard Branson, A&R man Simon Draper, and an apology from Sully herself, ended his partnership with the band. Joanne Catherall would later acknowledge Rushent's role in the success of the band, stating *"You can have great songs, but if you don't have a good producer – we didn't have anyone within the band who could produce – it can't get finished off to the level of loveliness that Martin did it."* Rushent himself later saw the root of the problem being everyone in the band realising the money was being made with the songwriting and demanding to have their opinion heard. He explained *"We'd had this huge global success that was completely unanticipated, and it did knock us off the straight and narrow for a while, emotionally and psychologically. Suddenly, all of your dreams come true and people's attitudes towards you change. From being just an average bloke who worked in a studio, suddenly I was Mr Superstar, and it was the same for the band. By the time we went back into the studio, Philip was more interested in playing with his new motorbike and his new remote control hi-fi system than he was in working."*

The Human League went on to have a long career, albeit one that increasingly relied on the nostalgia market, as they slimmed down to the three singers. Oakey spent half his time complaining about this, and half being thankful: *"When you're number one you're everybody's. Nobody cares about you anymore. Everyone and their grandma knows about you, so nobody wants to wear your badges anymore"*. Despite a string of different producers, the band always sounded like themselves, due to Oakey's distinctive vocals, and even reached the top of the Billboard charts again with a track called *Human* in the mid-1980's, however their days of being at the cutting edge of pop were over by the end of 1982.

ʊ ʊ ʊ

The final live date of 1982 for The Clash was at the Jamaican World Music Festival on Saturday 27th November. Frontman Joe Strummer had swapped an expensive watch for a bag of pot earlier in the day which he mixed with psilocybin mushroom tea and shared with guitarist Mick Jones and Ranking Roger from The Beat. The three sat out under the stars celebrating their *oneness* with Gladys Knight and the Pips who were performing onstage. The festival ran twenty-four hours a day with the Clash finally appearing at 4.00 a.m. and only after manager Bernie Rhodes insisted on another $20,000. This demand surprised Strummer, who assumed they were playing for free, when in fact their fee was $200,000.

This was to be the last live appearance of what could be described as the classic line-up of the band. Within six months, guitarist and songwriter Mick Jones had either left the band or been thrown out, depending on which version of the story you believed, and with his departure the spell was broken, as Strummer allowed manager Bernie Rhodes to take over for the universally reviled next album. The Clash ended at their commercial peak, and over the years the legend grew, as they lived up to their self-proclaimed *greatest rock and roll band in the world* and *last gang in town* tags. Their reputation remained undiminished right up to, and forever because of, the untimely death of Strummer in December 2002.

ʊ ʊ ʊ

Immediately following their debut album Orange Juice recruited Malcolm Ross, the former guitarist with Postcard Records labelmates Josef K, hoping "*he'd become a catalyst because we were becoming very lethargic and apathetic*". Ross was quick to perceive the tension within the act, with guitarist James Kirk being the main target for the frustration of singer Edwyn Collins. Eventually the agitation became too much, with Ross and bass player Dave McClymont deciding to leave and offering Collins the chance to join them. Drummer Steven Daly later explained "*They wanted to get rid of James, and I said: 'You can't do that, he is Orange Juice'. James was a very sensitive guy, and… I just thought it would be very damaging to cut him adrift. So Edwyn called back later and said: 'OK, you can go as well'.*" A new drummer was recruited in the shape of Zimbabwean-born Glaswegian resident Zeke Manyika who had fled to Scotland from Rhodesia in 1974, and the band began recording their second album of the year at Berwick Street Studios in London over the summer.

Collins talked of pursuing a "*sophisticated amateurism*" with the album, not wanting to lose their scrupulous naivety[595] while also looking to push their boundaries, and it could certainly be viewed as a more polished version of their debut. This was most discernable in title track *Rip it Up*, which was almost thrown away as a B-side. Taking the title from Little Richard and the groove from the Tom Tom Club, this was the funkiest thing the band had done, featuring a saxophone solo by legendary jazz musician Dick

Morrisey and a bass line stolen from Chic played by Collins on a Roland 303 Bassline machine, which had only gone on sale a week previously. The song was a call by Collins to himself in response to *new pop*, an imploration to "*rip it up and start again*", to take on board new technology and enjoy a fresh start with new members of the band. The guitar was played through a Mu-Tron BiPhase to deliberately make it sound more like *Genius of Love* by Tom Tom Club, though former guitarist Steven Daly would later cattily comment "[Edwyn] *traded in all our equity for a funny bassline*". The song was a masterclass in pop music, even containing a second chorus with the line "*I hope to God you're not as dumb as you make out*" just in case the first one was not commercial enough. The middle section featured lyrics lifted directly from *Boredom* by The Buzzcocks, who had proclaimed "*You know me – I'm acting dumb, you know the scene – very humdrum, boredom, boredom*". Collins instead ended with "*My favourite song's entitled Boredom*" before breaking into a two-note guitar solo also purloined from The Buzzcocks.

With some of the band's early quirks extricated with the departure of Kirk, producer Martin Hayles allowed Collins to bring his love of disco to the fore, resulting in a slicker and funkier sound. Tensions, however, remained, as Ross remembered "*I'd say to Edwyn, 'Do you really think we have to have a Fender Rhodes piano on every song?', and he would say, 'Well, we've got a snare drum on every song.'*"

For Collins the album was "*a good compromise between the abrasive, astringent quality of the early Postcard singles, and the lackluster, dull, bland pop sound which is necessary if you want people to listen to you.*" Collins was happy to share the vocal duties on the album, with a significant contribution made by the inimitable Paul Quinn on *Mud in Your Eye*, Ross taking lead on an old unrecorded Josef K song *Turn Away*,

---

[595] Orange Juice and their initial shambling beauty became a role model in their native Glasgow, as 1982 saw the formation of acts influenced by them such as Lloyd Cole & The Commotions, The Pastels, and Primal Scream.

and Manyika contributing his voice to the High-Life guitars and stylings of *A Million Pleading Faces*[596] and *Hokoyo*.

The album showed a professionalism previously unexpected from Orange Juice, whilst avoiding designating slickness as the main priority. Whilst glancing affectionately back at rock and roll history, and especially soul music on the Philly styled *Flesh of my Flesh* and the Four Tops handclap-referencing *I Can't Help Myself*, both of which would go on to be near hits, the album was firmly placed in the present, safeguarding itself against dating by a prudent use of technology.

The only genuine hit from the album turned out to be the title track, which reached number eight when released early in 1983. Collins found himself a reluctant pop star, a role he tried to dissuade as wife Grace explained: "*People were taking pictures of* [Edwyn] *and it looked like somebody had scrubbed* [his] *face with a Brillo pad. I remember the tour around that time,* [him] *going out onstage, and suddenly there's packs of little girls screaming 'Edwyn! Edwyn!' Now, where every other bugger can cope with that, Edwyn comes out, and he goes, 'Well, you can cut that out right away.'*"
At the end of the day, Collins best summed up his approach to success with a line in album track *Louise Louise*: "*I'll spoil your party with my punky sneer*".

Friends and latecomers to the whimsical Postcard intellectual party were an East Kilbride's Aztec Camera, led by a precocious sixteen-year-old *wunderkind* Roddy

Frame. The three-piece were Glaswegian neds, but whilst everyone else was trying to play loud and fast, Frame was gifted with the guitar-playing fingers of angels and the lyrical soul of a romantic. Inspired by punk, but obsessed with Django Reinhardt, they were infatuated by the Teardrop Explodes and Liverpool's Zoo Records, writing long letters asking for a recording contract. To placate them, they were given a couple of support slots with their heroes on the Scottish dates of their British tour. With Campbell Owens on bass and Davy Mulholland on drums, Aztec Camera signed to Postcard Records, despite some misgivings about the company being owned by *Glaswegian poshos*, and released their first couple of critically acclaimed singles.

One day, in the kitchen of Postcard Headquarters at 185 West Princes Street, Glasgow, Frame witnessed Alan Horne answer the phone with "*Fuck off, I'm having my lunch*" before hanging up, and realised that Aztec Camera could be getting courted by major labels and he would never know. Frame asked Horne who had been on the phone. "*I'm having my bloody lunch*" was the answer, and with this the decision was made: Aztec Camera moved to London and signed to Rough Trade Records.

The first fruits of this deal were recorded in Eastbourne in 1982 and released as the single *Pillar to Post*. As an introduction to the band, it was commercial enough to be noticed, but not good enough to make the charts. For Aztec Camera, it did not matter: they had one of the finest debut albums, *High Land, Hard Rain* and a decade-highlight and career making song in the shape of *Oblivious* ready to go in the new year.

---

[596] Malcolm Ross had been born in Malawi, maybe the guitar sound of the country seeped into his early unconsciousness?

THE WAITRESSES
CHRISTMAS WRAPPING

ORE YOU CAME

DECEMBER

THE STORY OF

FUN BOY THREE

THE MORE I SEE
(THE LESS I BELIEVE)

SURK

maisonettes
HEARTACHE AVENUE

SOFT CELL

CHEERS THEN

Save You
Renée &

28th November – 4th December 1982

#1 single: The Jam: Beat Surrender

#1 album: John Lennon: The John Lennon Collection

When Londoner Matt Johnson had been introduced to Mancunian Johnny Marr earlier in the year and found they had incredible simpatico, their vow to start working together

was ruined by geography and Marr falling under the spell of Morrissey. For the time being, Johnson would have to make it on his own.

Not that he was starting from the bottom, having just turned twenty-one with two unreleased solo albums, and a third on the 4AD label[597]. Johnson had also been performing as The The for three years, and it was under this name that he pushed forward with new recordings. Signing with Some Bizarre, Johnson was sent to New York to record a new single, *Uncertain Smile*, with Soft Cell producer Mike Hedges and money from London Records.

Utilising a Roland 808 drum machine, Johnson played all the instruments himself, including a toy xylimba he bought from Manny's Music[598] on 48th Street.

Upon returning to Britain, Some Bizarre label boss Stevo reneged on the London Records deal, and started a bidding war for The The. CBS Records won their signature, but only after negotiating the contract on top of a lion statue at the foot of Nelson's Column, at the insistence of Stevo.

Uncertain Smile was commercial enough for 1982, a song of unrequited longing, but with a downbeat vocal and extended piano solo by Jools Holland the single to stalled at number sixty-eight. It would take another four years for The The to make the charts, with a single from their stunning *Infected* album, and a further three years for Johnny Marr to fulfil his promise and finally joined the group.

ʊ ʊ ʊ

Rather than release another track from the phenomenally successful *Too-Rye-Ay* album, Dexy's Midnight Runners ended the year with new song *Let's Get This Straight*

from the Start. Once again working with Clive Langer and Alan Winstanley, the recording provided unexpected drama when the studio engineer introduced them to the studio autocue system which meant when the tape stopped the talk-back came on automatically. Forgetting about this, following one take of the song the band were treated to the sound in their headphones of one of the producers saying *"No, we don't want to use any of that"*, followed by a discussion of how bad the bass player was. Kevin Rowland sacked the unfortunate bass player the following day. George Chandler, Jimmy Thomas, and

---

[597] *Burning Blue Soul* was released under the name Matt Johnson, but later re-released as The The at the singer's insistence. He hated his albums not all being in the same rack in record stores.

[598] Everybody in rock and roll had bought guitars from Manny's Music: Buddy Holly, The Beatles, Jimi Hendrix, The Doors, The Who, Bob Dylan, Pink Floyd, Johnny Cash.

Simon Solace, known collectively as The Brothers Just were brought in to provide backing vocals, whilst violinist Helen O'Hara was given a co-writing credit in what was a prosaic single, one well below the high standards Rowland proclaimed to set for himself. With momentum on their side, the single climbed to number seventeen, however Dexy's were poised to find unexpected success in the United States the following year, where *Come On, Eileen* topped the charts, turning them into a one-hit wonder and novelty act instead of the serious passionate searching artists Britain knew them to be.

Rowland would never reach the same heights of success again, and an increasing paranoia and insistence of perfection relegated him to the fringes of culture, a much beloved figure, but one to be wary of.

ʊ ʊ ʊ

The track which persuaded producer Trevor Horn that Malcolm McLaren's hotchpotch of world music could work was *Buffalo Girls*, completed in early October and released as a single the subsequent month. It featured *scratching* from the World-Famous Supreme Team, as well as excerpts from their New York phone-in radio show, keyboards and drum machines programmed by J.J. Jeczalik and Thomas Dolby, backing vocals by a troupe of female Zulu singers, and McLaren leading a square-dance call.

The song was an auditory revolution, at times sparse of instrumentation, often with only a programmed hip-hop drum pattern, a sample from a live Kool & the Gang track, and  the occasional stab of synth courtesy of Anne Dudley. The traditional locale of electric guitar power-chords was supplanted by the scratching of vinyl, skilfully and fastidiously located in the music by Horn and engineer Gary Langan.

McLaren and Horn took two diametrically opposite musical styles, modern black urban hip-hop and old white rural square-dancing, and made them sound as if they had always been together, with McLaren intoning "*Two buffalo girls go around the outside*" over the top of a gravid beat. The square call was lifted from a 1949 recording of Piute Pete on Folkways Records, and the white rural influence was augmented by the fiddle playing of Joel Birchfield from the East Tennessee Hilltoppers. However, the mix of the two styles perfectly represented what modern America was: a salmagundi of different religions, cultures, and nationalities, a place where hip hop and country music could both legitimately claim to be the sound of the nation. McLaren's argument was that when it came down to it, both were forms of music for dancing to and both contained rhythmic talking instead of singing.

The cut-up approach of the track was apparent in the arrangement, which abandoned the traditional pop music approach of verse and chorus for something more experimental. Instead, the song worked by the agency of phases, initially with McLaren's square dance calling, followed by a more urban section, before returning to McLaren. Throughout, both styles are interrupted and accompanied by samples of a radio phone-in. Horn edited scratching and utilised cut-up techniques throughout the song to create new phrases, such as one section when out-takes from the Zulu choir singing "*She's looking like a hobo*" were repeated with a scratch to make it sound like "*she's... itching*", tying in beautifully with a Supreme Team radio phone-in sample of "*All that scratching's making me itch*". This technique was used again successfully when McLaren's repeated call of "*promenade*" became "*hominy*", the coarsely ground corn used to make grits, a Southern States favourite.

The record company, of course, despised the single. Radio plugger Phil Hardy "*refused to take it to the radio and declared that it was 'not music*'", whilst Charisma Records started preparing legal action against McLaren for delivering an album of unacceptable commercial value. McLaren countered by leaking a version of *Buffalo Girls* to disc jockey David Jensen on Capital Radio, and within twenty-four hours of him playing it Charisma were receiving telephone calls from radio stations across Britain demanding a copy. The record company capitulated and were rewarded with a top ten hit single, however it was a contrasting story in the United States, where MTV refused to broadcast the video because, according to McLaren "*they objected that the people in my video were the sort who would terrorise, rape, and steal from suburban, white viewers.*"

Throughout the recording Langan, Horn, Jeczalik, and Dudley had been creating music on their own to be considered for the album. Their experiments with samples and synthesizers, cutting up sounds and putting them together again, managed to create multiple out-takes which they decided to release under their own band name: The Art of Noise[599].

When the subsequent McLaren album *Duck Rock* was released in January, it was nothing short of revolutionary, mixing hip hop culture with Zulu chants, Appalachian square dancing, Hispanic disco, and a punk rock attitude. It had a colossal role in introducing *world music* to the British consciousness, paving the way for a cross-pollination of genres, sounding fresher and more relevant with each passing year. This was partly due to McLaren's vision, but mostly to Horn's brilliant production and arrangement, taking existing genres and creating something new with each one. Even the cover with its mixture of primitive cave painting imagery by Keith Haring, and modern hip-hop culture graffiti came from leftfield, drawing a line between African tribal culture and modern New York youth culture. The inside sleeve contained some information about each track, from an explanation of the track to illustrated dance steps, however what it did not contain was credits for the musicians involved, of which there were many. In fact, even Trevor Horn had to fight to get a mention on the cover art!

As far as McLaren was concerned, the entire project was his, seeing himself as a cultural anthropologist, taking the work of Franz Boas as his starting point, viewing differing ethnologies as rich in their own rights rather than on different parts of the same evolutionary timeline. What McLaren was wise enough to see, at a time when black and white culture was totally separate, was how modern technology would allow these cultures to become enmeshed in the future.

Not all musicians felt the same was as McLaren, and at the Charisma Records Christmas party he was confronted by Peter Gabriel who berated him for exploiting the work of others and cultural appropriation. Trevor Horn was quick to defend McLaren, stating "*The Africans got married on what we paid them. The Cubans charged us a lot of money; they really had their heads screwed on. The Dominicans charged us a fortune. They screwed us!*"

ʊ ʊ ʊ

Towards the end of 1982 music accountant Will Keen, having fallen out with his former employers at Virgin Records, started work at Rough Trade, where he helped their accounting system begin to make a bit more sense. There was resistance to him from many of the employees, with some seeing him as the devil incarnate, an example of

---

[599] McLaren, always keen to be involved, offered to manage them.

the man, mainly because he was a *real* accountant with one foot firmly in financial reality.

On Tuesday 30th November he delivered six months' worth of accounts, and they made an alarming read. In the past few months, the distribution wing had lost £61,000, the label had lost £54,000, the booking agency lost £43,000, and the shop had lost £30,000. They also owed money all over the place, not least £750,000 to Daniel Miller at Mute Records. A series of urgent meetings were called over the next week, during which the booking agency was partitioned to become All Trade Bookings, the shop was separated from the business and continued to trade, the Reggae Import wing (*Rough Lion*) was closed, and a deal was made with Mute Records to pay off the debt over a long period of time through an exchange of trade services. A system of stock-control was introduced for the first time, and weekly chaired meetings were instigated.

Thanks to Keen's insistence on a semblance of order, Rough Trade continued over the decades, signing acts such as Arcade Fire, The Strokes, The Smiths, Ryan Adams, Aztec Camera, Cornershop, and the Fall, whilst the shop expanded to several locations around London and continued to concentrate on music not in the mainstream.

ʊ ʊ ʊ

Musically, it would be easy could divide the 1980's into two: what came before Michael Jackson's *Thriller*, and what came after. Of the nine tracks on the album, seven were released as singles, changing the way albums were marketed. Previously the public had felt short-changed if an album contained any more than a couple of singles, but it would soon be expected that an artist would release the album first and then any number of singles from it over the next couple of years, often in re-mixed or slightly altered formats.

Songwriter Rod Temperton, engineer Bruce Swedien, and producer Quincy Jones were already an efficacious working team when they began recording *Thriller* back in April, and the dynamic in the studio soon settled into a routine, with Jackson bringing Bubbles the chimp and Muscles the twenty-foot-long boa constrictor to the studio, the latter of which terrified Jones, whilst Temperton was banished to a separate room because he smoked so much.

Jackson had a lot to live up to, having sold nine million copies of his predecessor *Off the Wall*, and on the first day he proclaimed "*I want to sell 100 million*", to which Jones responded "*Michael, calm down a bit. We'll be happy if we have another hit*". This was not good enough: Jackson wanted to break every record going, and in the fractured American music scene knew he needed to reach into numerous markets to do so. Hundreds of songs were considered for the album, scores of them were recorded, and then they were used likes pieces of a car to slot together and create the ultimate machine. The final nine tracks were chosen for their genre as much as for their quality, and so *The Girl is Mine* was the pop market, *Beat It* for the rock market, *Thriller* for the disco market, *Human Nature* was for the smooth soul market. Jackson desired airplay on all radio stations in America and beyond, regardless of their format. He was on a mission at Westlake Audio in Los Angeles to "*save the recording industry*", and both him and Jones had never been so obsessed with a project before, determined to turn in an album where every song was strong enough be a single, spending eighteen hours a day in the studio, sometimes sleeping on the couch in the control room.

Initially there was due to be fifty-six minutes of music, however engineer Swedien insisted that length would compromise the quality of the sound towards the inside of the vinyl and was proven right when the final song on each side of a test pressing was distorted. It was decided to lose a couple of tracks and edit the ones which were left. Mixing and editing was completed at the rate of one song per week, ensuring every detail was perfect, however disaster struck when the first mix of the album was rejected by CBS after a playback at Westlake Studios in Los Angeles, described as "*horrible*" by one executive. Jackson was furious, claiming "*I felt devastated. All this pent-up emotion came out. I got angry and left the room*". Jones suggested a compromise, asking for ten days delay in the release, and started mixing from scratch, one song a day, so they could meet the Christmas deadline. Further delays occurred when Jackson had a nose-job just before the shooting of the album cover.

Opening with *Wanna' Be Startin' Something*, a track written by Jackson several years earlier during the *Off the Wall* session, the feel of the song was taken directly from British act The Quick whose *Rhythm of the Jungle* single had been an American Dance hit during the recording. Building to an effective Swahili chorus stolen from Manu Dibango's *Soul Makossa*[600], Jackson tackled tabloid lies and harassment over an unrelenting furious beat, bemoaning the fact he had become nothing more than food for the press buffet.

Despite the aim of *all killer no filler*, there were dips in the album, such as the following twin trough of *Baby Be Mine* and first single *The Girl is Mine*, both of which failed to provide the assiduously edged dance beats evident elsewhere, and the closing trio of *Human Nature*, *Pretty Young Thing*, and *The Lady in my Life.*

Human Nature was ostensibly a Toto song, having been written by Jeff Porcaro and arranged by the rest of the band, however Jones insisted that guitarist Steve Lukather make it funkier, plugging the guitar straight into the desk rather than playing through an

amplifier. *Pretty Young Thing* was supplied by James Ingram and featured backing vocals by Jackson's younger sisters, La Toya and Janet, whilst *The Lady in my Life* took a while to record because Jackson could not get vocals right until Jones took him to one side and told him to beg. The title track was written by Cleethorpes resident Temperton, initially under the name of *Starlight*, then *Midnight Man*, but changed to *Thriller* overnight purely because that title was easier to visualise at the top of the charts, even if it was a difficult word to sing. Vintage horror actor Vincent Price was hired to record a spoken vocal towards the end of the track, though it was not until the night before that anyone bothered to write any of the words for him to recite, finishing them in the taxi on the way to the studio. The rhythm for the song was taken directly and deliberately from *Don't Stop 'til you get Enough* from Jackson's previous album, which had proved itself irresistible to feet on a dancefloor.

Aiming for the rock market, Jackson offered *Beat It* which he claimed was "*written with school kids in mind… it tells kids to be smart and avoid trouble*". Lyrically it evoked a dialogue between a youth's inner angel and devil, encouraging him to be sensible and wreckless. "*They're out to get you, better leave while you can*" implores the angel, whilst the devil counters "*Don't want to be a boy, you better be a man*". Later the devil argues "*You have to show them that you're really not scared*" whilst the angel reminds him "*You're playing with your life this ain't no truth or dare*". Singing along with a click track provided by Toto's Jeff Porcaro[601], fellow band member Steve Lukather added guitar and bass riffs, having to tone his sound down due to Jones' opinion that it was *too rock.*

---

[600] Jackson would later pay an undisclosed sum in royalties to Dibango.

[601] Porcaro had to try to fit in with Jackson hitting a drum case with his hands on the second and fourth beat.

1982 was a transitional time for black music, which had almost always existed in relative isolation to white music, providing a stream of influence for white artists to commandeer and sanitise for mass-consumption. In the early 1980's the river started to flow both ways, with black artists taking on board elements of rock music, hip hop borrowing liberally from European electronic music and 1970's rock riffs. Critic John Rockwell argued the *Thriller* album marked the beginning of *"the destructive barriers that spring up… between black and white music… [being] breached once again"*.

Despite Lukather's guitar being deemed *too rock*, Eddie Van Halen[602] was brought in to provide a *none-more-rock* guitar solo, for which he refused a session fee, not realising how big a deal it would become. Van Halen's solo became the talking point of *Beat It*, much to the resentment of Lukather who had provided everything else, including a memorable opening riff[603].

Opening side two of the album was *Billie Jean*, originally called *Not My Lover* because Jones thought *Billie Jean* would be mistaken for the tennis player. The song, which Jackson instinctively knew was going to be massive whilst writing, was a first-person narrative of a man who wanted nothing to do with the child he has fathered. Jackson told Jones it was inspired by a woman found in a bathing suit by his pool having climbed over the wall of his mansion who accused Jackson of being the father of one of her twins.

It was decided to record the drums with extreme separation, and the lack of sonic bleed between each microphone made them sound like a drum machine. Jackson would later claim *"the bass is the protagonist of the situation"*, and four different bass tracks recorded by Louis Johnson were combined. Jones wanted to shorten the bass and drum introduction considerably, however Jackson insisted they stay, stating *"But that's the jelly! That's what makes you want to dance!"*

The vocals were partially recorded through a five-foot tube of cardboard, as the team strove to create music unlike any before, and the search for perfection continued at the mixing stage, during which ninety-one different versions were created[604].

When released as a single in early 1983, what really sold the song was the video, considered to be on the cutting edge at the time, with Jackson dancing in a studio setting with paving stones lighting up as he steps on them. It is only with hindsight we can see that only a few of the paving stones were able to light up, and Jackson had to tailor his dancing to hit them on cue. The video featured Jackson as a well-dressed narrator in an urban setting, flipping a coin towards a homeless man, a gesture for which he received criticism from some quarters because, as Shaun Scott claims *"Under late capitalism, charity is the preferred substitute for a political commitment to the fair distribution of wealth"*. Jackson's performance and dress were seen by others as a signal of the new *Yuppie* culture, a word coined by Joseph Epstein during 1982. *Yuppie* was short for *Young Upwardly-mobile Professional* or *Young Urban Professional*, and represented the new breed of people in their twenties and thirties who were ambitious for success at all costs, those that bought into Thatcher and Reagan's financial dream. They were described by in the *Wall Street Journal* as *"a class of people who put off having families so they can make payments on the SAAB"*. One such young British person was Caroline Kellett, who in an article about Oxford students told Ian Jack of the *Sunday Times* *"If you're at all bright you know that you fuck other people before they fuck you"*.

---

[602] Van Halen thought it was a prank call when Jackson telephoned, and told him to *"fuck off"*.

[603] Also resentful of the song was Michael Sembello, whose track *Carousel* was ejected from the album at the last minute to make way for it.

[604] They ended up using the second one.

Whilst director Steve Baron was editing the video in London, Jackson secretly flew into Britain to oversee the process. In the corridor of the editing suite he bumped into Thomas Dolby, himself putting the finishing touches to his own *She Blinded Me with Science*. The two enthusiastically exchanged genuine praise for their new singles and watched the early cuts of the videos together. Jackson expressed interest in Dolby's clip, impressed with the narrative, and stated he hoped to include more of a story in future videos, then the two exchanged telephone numbers and agreed to meet up again at some point in the future.

The *Billie Jean* video may have driven the format forward significantly; however, it was met with great resistance from the industry, and especially MTV. The accusation of racism was first levelled at the station by Rick James when his *Superfreak* video was not shown, though that might have been more on the grounds of taste than racism. Carolyn Baker turned down the video "*because there were half-naked women in it, and it was a piece of crap. As a black woman I did not want that representing my people as the first black video on MTV*". Whilst Tina Turner and Musical Youth were played, the bottom line was that not many black artists were making videos, and it took pressure and an intervention from David Bowie during a live interview on the station to bring them to their senses.

Billie Jean was cleared for playing on MTV on 2nd March 1983, when chief Executive Bob Pitman finally bowed to public pressure. Despite some revisionist claims by MTV, Walter Yetnikoff at CBS would later say "*They did not want to play 'Billie Jean' and 'Beat It'. If Pittman wants to deny that, he should go back to Mississippi*".

Jackson would drive the video revolution further over the next year, with groundbreaking videos for *Beat It* and *Thriller*. CBS refused to provide any money for the latter, demanding the finances come from MTV for providing content to fill their shows[605]. The label would claim that "*It would have been a terrible precedent for us to start paying for the production of videos. So, what we did was pay for 'The Making of Thriller', and the money made from that was used to make the actual video*".

The whole concept of MTV, which had been launched on the 1st August 1981, was viewed by the American music industry with suspicion. On the other hand, British acts from The Beatles to Bowie had traditionally fussed over their visuals and had no qualms over utilising the channel. Radio stations were mystified when they started to receive requests for songs they had never played, usually by *lightweight* British acts without an ounce of old-fashioned rock and roll in their (often literal) make-up. The British groups by-passed the traditional discerning rock fan in America, and went straight for the early teens, those who were more likely to be swayed by visuals and a good-looking frontman. The effect on the American market, which accounted for roughly a third of world-wide record sales, was remarkable; by mid-1983 British acts accounted for over a third of singles sales in America.

Happy to be carried along by this new British invasion, each one of Jackson's singles from *Thriller* was backed by $100,000 in bribes to radio station controllers, or *independent promotion* as it was called in the accounts, and as the label opened their minds to the potential of videos, the unheard-of $50,000 budget for *Billie Jean* was increased to $200,000 for *Beat It* three months later.

The album started to sell early and continued throughout the year... then into the next one... and the next again, as the public embraced Michael Jackson as a global phenomenon. Ultimately, *Thriller* continued to sell for decades, and would famously

---

[605] The idea of MTV financing the video is not so outrageous, as the channel initially thought they would have to pay acts to make videos, however once a few forward-thinking record companies started giving their videos for free, other labels soon fell in behind, fearful that they would lack the same exposure for their artists.

become the biggest selling album of all time with current sales approaching seventy-million copies, earning Jackson over $700 million in the first four years alone. Jackson wanted to be bigger than the Beatles, and this financial reward helped him finally achieve this when he bought their back catalogue, the ultimate musical corporate takeover.

ʊ ʊ ʊ

Channel 4 continued to inadvertently court controversy when on Tuesday 30th November they innocently released their Christmas schedule. This included delights such as the first showing of a specially commissioned animation of Raymond Briggs' *The Snowman*, to become a world-wide perennial favourite, a season of Indian cinema, and a new program called *Treasure Hunt*. It was not these that the press focused on, however, but a single program due to be broadcast at 11 p.m. on New Year's Day called *One in Five*. This was a one-off non-sensationalist documentary on homosexual lifestyles and the *Daily Mail*, apoplectic and red faced, was simply not going to stand for it. The following day, Wednesday 1st December, their front-page proclaimed "*BAN TV4 DEMANDS ANGRY MP*", whilst the article began: "*Channel 4 provoked a new row yesterday when it announced it was to screen a homosexual entertainment program*". Conservative MP John Carlilse[606] was quoted as saying "*I am horrified at the thought of this program… the channel is an offence to public taste and decency.*"
The government's attitude to Channel 4 was later expressed plainly to controller Jeremy Isaacs during an event at the German Embassy, when Employment Secretary Noman Tebbit said "*You've got it all wrong, you know, doing all these programs for homosexuals and such. The different interests you are supposed to cater for are… golf and sailing and fishing*". Meanwhile, their greatest cheerleader within the government, William Whitelaw, confided to Isaacs that his colleagues thought the channel *too left-wing*, accusing him of "*letting the loonies on the air*".

ʊ ʊ ʊ

David Bowie had spent the year away from music, making movies instead (as well as an introduction to *The Snowman*) but was now keen to make a spectacular return. Finding himself without a record label for the first time in over a decade, it was a no-brainer to sign for EMI for a reputed $17 million and was now under pressure to recoup this money with commercial success. Luckily for all parties involved, Bowie was in a mental place where he was keen to embrace the mainstream, and when he approached Chic main-man Nile Rodgers to produce, the specific instruction was to "*make hits*". Bowie instructed Rodgers to bring a modern commercial dance component to the mix, whilst Rodgers has claimed the title track of the album *Let's Dance* was originally written on a folk-sounding twelve-string acoustic guitar. Everything clicked when Bowie said "*Nile, darling, I want the album to sound like this*" and showed Rodgers a photograph of Little Richard wearing a bright red suit getting into a red Cadillac. The aim was to create an album hyper-aware of the past but self-assured of the future.

---

[606] Carlilse was a rent-a-quote Conservative, happy to express an outraged comment to the press on demand, which encompassed his views on Feminism (he was against it), Apartheid (he was for it), homosexuality (he was against it), the European Union (against), and gun control (following the Dunblane massacre he was the voice of the gun lobby).

After three days working on a demo the duo entered the Power Station Studios in New York in December 1982 and emerged less than three weeks later with a complete album recorded and mixed, one that would go on to become Bowie's most commercially successful, selling two to three times more than any previous releases. The singer was working with musicians he was unfamiliar with, people who had been chosen by Rodgers, including bass player Carmen Rojas, Omar Hakim and Chic's Tony Thompson on drums, and blues guitarist Steve Ray Vaughan. Unusually for Bowie, he did not play a single instrument on the album.

Whilst this was going on, Bowie was back in the charts with a Christmas song released by his previous label, RCA. *Little Drummer Boy / Peace on Earth* was a duet recorded on 11th September 1977 with Bing Crosby for a British Christmas television special. This odd coupling, Bowie was thirty at the time, Crosby seventy-three, were originally

going to duet on *Little Drummer Boy*, however Bowie threw a hissy fit, stating that he hated the song. Songwriters Ian Fraser, Alan Kohan, and Larry Grossman[607] were dispatched to the basement and hastily wrote a counterpart melody and lyrics for *Peace on Earth*. After a quick rehearsal the duo recorded the song live, but not before Bowie was persuaded to remove the make-up he had turned up wearing.

Crosby died five weeks later, before the special was broadcast, and the track would probably have been forgotten about if RCA, having nothing else in the vaults, had not released it. The single began a slow climb up the charts, peaking at number three just before Christmas, and going on to become an annual favourite.

ʊ ʊ ʊ

Margaret Thatcher made no secret that she blamed high unemployment on the trade unions and had set about with Norman Tebbit to curb their power. Towards the end of 1981 they formulated the basics of a plan, introduced it to parliament in February 1982, and it came into law as the *Employment Act, 1982*, on Wednesday 1st December. This reduced the power of unions in the closed shop environment by forcing them to ballot their member on their existence and made it legal for employers to sack anyone taking part in a strike without fear of an *unfair dismissal* claim. The public support for these moves, stoked by the right-wing press, allowed the Conservatives to consider further reforms, such as stopping the union financial contribution to the Labour Party, and introducing compulsory use of secret ballots, both of which started to be written into an early manifesto for an expected general election the following year.

Margaret Thatcher and the Conservative Government had been in trouble at the start of 1982. Her obstinate insistence on pursuing a policy of monetarism, influenced by the thinking of Milton Friedman, was strangling the country with high inflation and record unemployment. Reading her own recollections of the era it becomes obvious she was obsessed with the idea that workers' wages were too high, and business profits were too low, and was determined to address these issues.

At the time, Labour Party stalwart Tony Benn wrote *"Here is a woman entirely without any human sympathy whatever, applying rigidly capitalist criteria at a time of great hardship and deliberately widening the gap between rich and poor"*. There were also many within her own party, and indeed her own cabinet, who disagreed with the policy, and she took to referring to colleagues as either *wet* or *dry*, depending on their thinking.

---

[607] Grossman was the musical director of *The Muppet Show*.

The *wets* disagreed with her, and were feeble-minded and wrong, whilst the *drys* were of one opinion and obviously *decent* people. They were also divided by Thatcher's parliamentary secretary into *heroes* and *reptiles*, with the former celebrating their unwavering stance with unpopular policies. When the arguments against the policy became too much, she simply shuffled her cabinet to ensure that there were no dissenting voices.

Although she would claim victory in the Falklands was because "*women make naturally good managers*", and much was made of her role as first female Prime Minister of Britain, Thatcher failed to promote a single woman to her cabinet during her decade long reign. *The Guardian* described her as a *queen bee*, "*one who makes it herself, and pulls the ladder up behind her*", and Thatcher seemed to enjoy being the only woman in the cabinet, revelling in the attention of the men, many who found her sexually alluring.

The Falklands changed everything, and by the end of 1982, Thatcher and the Conservatives had the public on their side, with opinion polls placing their approvement rating at 44%, 13% ahead of Labour, whilst support for the SDP / Liberal Alliance had collapsed.

ʊ ʊ ʊ

After a couple of months silence, The Cure's Robert Smith phoned drummer Lol Tolhurst to ask if he wanted to return to the studio. Tolhurst was more than relieved, believing his time in the band was over, however the dynamic had changed permanently, and it was now clearly Smith's band with hired hands and sidekicks. The first thing Smith did as leader was to move Tolhurst from drums to keyboards, accounting for the change in sound and direction the band subsequently took.

Fiction Records label boss Chris Parry knew exactly how to motivate Smith and challenged him to write a straight pop song. Whilst Smith was skeptical and dismissive

at first, Parry knew the idea of an unmet challenge would niggle at him until he accepted it. Parry could see exactly how the direction music was taking and after such a glorious year of intelligent pop, he knew that The Cure could justify staking a claim in there.

The result of this challenge was *Let's Go to Bed*, The Cure's first truly great *pop* song. Smith immediately regretted recording the track and attempted to persuade Parry to release it under a pseudonym, however the label boss pointed out that would have defeated the purpose, which was to lay the ghost of the old Cure to rest. As a compromise he made a bet with Smith that if the song were not a hit single, he would release Smith from his contract.

The single marked the beginning of a long-term working relationship with video director Tim Pope. The Cure had shot films for their songs before, but they were as doom laden as the music, whilst the video for *Let's Go to Bed* marked the beginning of a glorious phase where they created inventive, entertaining, and funny, yes funny, visual accompaniments to their music, helped by a director who understood the contradictions inherent within the character of the act. Within the video both Tolhurst and Smith danced, larked about, *and even smiled*[608].

---

[608] The video also showed that The Cure had grown their hair longer and taller, a seemingly insignificant act, but one which was to help define the band in the future, so much so that over twenty years later

The song was a continuation of the type of music The Cure had previously created, except that it was made with a greater emphasis on keyboards and melody. There were pop hooks throughout and jokes within the lyrics, such as the opening line of "*Let me take your hand, I'm shaking like milk*". The irony of all this was that Smith was being as cynical as possible, realizing that most songs were all about trying to get someone into bed, and so his *pop song* may as well be too. There are, of course, other interpretations of the lyrics, and an obvious one is that the song documents an argument between a couple. Certainly, there are lines within the track which could easily refer to this, ending with them deciding to just let it go, go to bed, to sleep on it. However, you could also interpret the song as being about the state of The Cure at the time, with "*the two of us together again, but it's just the same: a stupid game*", and given Smith's attitude towards the band, who he admitted were not his priority at the time, you can understand the cynicism.

Despite uncertainty around the lyrics, the rest of the song was highly effective, returning to an infectious *do-do-do-do* chorus at regular intervals. However, even with a lot of airplay, it failed to crack the top forty, stalling at number forty-four, and despite his promise, Parry reneged and refused to release the band from their contract. Ultimately the song turned out to be a freeing experience for Smith (and therefore The Cure). He had been keen to take a holiday from himself, and with increasing airplay for the single realized that he did not need to live up to the perceived expectations of The Cure.

At around the same time, Siouxsie & the Banshees had asked Smith to join them to replace guitarist John McGeoch, and he delighted at the opportunity to not be the front-man anymore, spending the next year recording and touring with them, as well as recording a psychedelic album with bass player Steve Severin under the name The Glove.

In between all this activity, Smith continued to push the boundaries of what it meant to be The Cure, with a couple more pop songs, the first a completely electronic track entitled *The Walk*, the second a swing number recorded in Paris called *The Lovecats*, both of which cracked the top twenty, the latter reaching number seven. The Cure had arrived as a chart act and never looked back, releasing a string of brilliant pop songs over the decade, whilst allowing themselves to indulge their lugubrious roots on the albums. Smith had found a compromise between commercial success and experimentation which suited him and followed this path for the rest of his career.

Even playing live was back on the table, more so once he left The Banshees in mid-1984. Live was where The Cure really excelled, often playing concerts of over three hours to huge crowds all over the world. Within the next couple of decades, the band built a loyal following in places like Japan, South America, and mainland Europe, becoming a truly global phenomenon without having to compromise their stance. The band itself was always based around a small rotating group of musicians, with Simon Gallup rejoining in 1985, and Tolhurst being thrown out in 1988 due to his struggles with alcohol, however the central figure has always been Smith.

Smith has become something of a cultural reference, with an easily recognizable visual style: black spiked hair and smeared lipstick, one that Tim Burton has acknowledged was influential in the design of *Edward Scissorhands*[609]. Smith (and The Cure) became shorthand for American scriptwriters to indicate a teenager was a confused and miserable outsider, with many posters appearing on the walls of bedrooms in 1980's teen-dramas. Despite being such a recognizable character, Smith has always been reticent about revealing his personal life, and as such remains a bit of an enigma to the

---

The Mighty Boosch referred to the strongest hairspray known to man as being made from the tears of Robert Smith.

[609] The Cure were approached to provide the soundtrack for *Edward Scissorhands*, but it was not to be.

public. Certainly, there are hints of autism in his personality, with controlling behaviors in evidence and a determination to stick to the same path and not see other's points of view, all of which inadvertently has made for a welcome and richer cultural experience.

ʊ ʊ ʊ

Internal personal tension drove The Fall through their November and December British tour, and when guitarist and keyboard player Marc Riley brought his fiancé with him to a date at Liverpool's Warehouse on Friday 3rd December, it infuriated singer Mark E. Smith. After the show he started shouting at Riley, "*What are you doing bringing your girlfriend to Liverpool anyway? If you worked for McVities you wouldn't have her sitting there watching you wrap Jaffa Cakes, would you?*"

"*No*" snapped back Riley, "*But I might pull strings to have her employed as the foreman*" he said, referring to Kay Carroll, Smith's partner and the manager of the band.

"*You were shit because you were fussing round your girlfriend all night and not concentrating on playing*" Smith further taunted.

"*That's ridiculous! I played like I always do!*" seethed Riley.

"*Yeah. Fucking wishy washy with no spirit!*" Smith sneered back.

With Riley gone, Smith turned his attention to former mate, Echo and the Bunnymen singer Ian McCulloch, who is hanging around at the bar. "*Look over there! Look at him and his acolytes now, arse-licking that new Radio 1 DJ*" he said, referring to Janice Long[610], "*Look at them fucking sell-outs!*"

As he approached the Liverpudlian, Smith forced a grin onto his face, opening the conversation with "*I see you got what you wanted! I saw you fucking miming on Top of the Pops. And you're ripping me off with your long overcoat. I was wearing one like that two years ago!*"

MacCulloch, always quick of wits, fired straight back "*I'm surprised you can get that overcoat on, the size of the chips on your shoulders.*"

Smith did not have to wait long for revenge on Riley, firing him over Christmas at the wedding of bass player Steve Hanley[611].

ʊ ʊ ʊ

Richard Attenborough had been trying to make a single movie for twenty years, initially with himself in the title role, and then as he grew older, as director. Enthralled by Louis Fischer's biography of Indian lawyer and anti-colonial nationalist Mohandas Gandhi, Attenborough's pre-production of the film was hindered by financing and the declaration of a state of emergency in India, but finally started shooting in December 1980. The six-month shoot featured a stellar cast including Ben Kingsley as the title character[612], as well as British legends such as Edward Fox, John Gielgud, John Mills, and Trevor Howard as the colonial establishment. There were also roles for Bernard Hill, Martin Sheen, Ian Charleston, Ian Bannen, Richard Griffiths, Nigel Hawthorne, John Ratzenberger, and Daniel Day Lewis, as well as a record-breaking 300,000 local extras for Gandhi's funeral scene.

---

[610] Fall bass player Steven Hanley attempted to talk to Janice Long that night with the one piece of information he knew about her. *"You're Keith Chegwin's sister, aren't you?"* "No" she snapped back, *"He's MY brother!"*

[611] Riley took an Elgan Snoopy electric piano without permission as part of his severance pay.

[612] Writer John Briley initially wanted John Hurt to play the title role

The three-hour eleven-minute film[613] received a British premier on Friday 3rd December at the Odeon Leicester Square in London in front of Prince Charles and Princess Diana, before a limited December release in the United States to allow it to be considered for the Academy Awards. This was a shrewd move, which paid off in 1983 when *Gandhi* collected eight Oscars, including Best Picture, Best Director, Best Actor, Best Original Screenplay, and Best Cinematography. Upon opening, the film received generally good reviews, with particular praise for Kingsley's performance, however Attenborough had chosen to focus on a particularly Western historical context rather than the manifold spiritual or moral issues surrounding Gandhi the man. It took an ancient Greek approach, one in which history is dictated by the deeds of individual men rather than a myriad of interconnecting and individual reasons, but one can forgive Attenborough for this given the complicated political and historical situation in post-war India would have warranted a much longer running time. The film was criticized outside the Western speaking world for the telling of the story mostly through the eyes of and interaction with foreigners rather than any Indian viewpoints, replacing the colonialism of the British Raj with a cultural one.

ʊ ʊ ʊ

In December Culture Club travelled to New York, their first visit to America, and the start of a campaign to break through. They were unlikely candidates for success across the Atlantic, with cross-dressing, multi-racial pop at odds with what middle-America would accept. During a flurry of interviews and a date at the Ritz on Friday 3rd December, George camped things up, asking the crowd *"Are there any poofs in the audience?"* and ending each song with *"Thank you, girls"*. The use of polari was an accepted component of British music hall, part of growing up in a repressed country which vented sexuality through cross-dressing but unthreatening entertainers, however George would soon drop these sorts of statements from the act, becoming asexual in the knowledge that other territories in the world would not accept campness.

The record company was determined to break *Do You Really Want to Hurt Me* in the States, despite there being little history of successful reggae and dub there. They decided to play down the image, issuing the single in a white sleeve, and watched in amazement as Culture Club became the most talked about and successful act in the country during 1983.

ʊ ʊ ʊ

In Britain for a sold-out December tour, Duran Duran returned to Birmingham as bass player John Taylor found himself back at his parents' house with a bout of crabs from his nightly dalliances with willing fans, providing an ideal father – son bonding activity as they crept around buying medication and boiling clothes and bedsheets behind his mother's back. Life in Birmingham seemed tedious now, and some of the band flew back to New York for the MTV New Year's Eve ball, where they were able to hang out with Andy Warhol.

As the New Year dawned, the Kershenbaum remixes seemed to be doing the job in the States, with *Hungry Like the Wolf* rising to number three and the album going top ten. From then on, the band enjoyed gobal success, and started fulfilling all the

---

[613] I sat through all three hours and eleven minutes on an uncomfortable wooden bench in
Northumberland. It was the first and only time I had ever heard the national anthem being played at the end of the night and everyone standing to attention for it.

necessary clichés of rock and roll bands: recording their next album in the South of France, dating models, touring the world, making a fortune, and acquiring drug and drink addictions.

1983 started brilliantly with their first number one single in the shape of *Is There Something I Should Know?* and ended with a successful album *Seven and the Ragged Tiger*, from which spawned their best-selling single: a Nile Rogers remix of *The Reflex*. 1984 and 1985 were their glory years, culminating in a performance at Live Aid, however by this point the band was falling apart, with John and Andy Taylor forming a side-project The Power Station alongside Robert Palmer and Chic drummer Tony Thompson, whilst the other members formed their own hobby band: Arcadia.

The band spent the next couple of decades chasing past glory with decreasing original members until they were down to a core of John Taylor, Nick Rhodes, and Simon Le Bon. Success came and went, and then in the new millennium the nostalgia market kicked in enough for the original line-up to get back together, where they were treated like the classic band that they always wanted to be.

Duran Duran had perhaps been regarded rather cruelly, still seen by some as a 1980's version of the boy band, alongside Spandau Ballet and Wham. However, this did them an injustice as they were a powerful and tight live act, comprising five musicians who were more than competent with their instruments[614], and initially had all the right influences for critical acclaim: Bowie, Iggy Pop, and Roxy Music.[615] They did themselves no favours by zealously embracing success and ambition, two things which are always going to rile serious music journalists and will be forever seen in the words of Alan Partridge as "*Thatcher Pop*"[616]. Ultimately, they will never reach dry land; forever onboard a yacht in Antigua in sharp-coloured suits and dyed hair, drinking champagne with super-models, and having a ball.

ʊ ʊ ʊ

What distinguished Ultravox from many other new synthesizer acts in the early 1980's was their ability to play live, refusing to employ pre-recorded tapes, insisting on every sound being produced on stage, to the extent that they had to pay their support act, The Messengers, to help on instrumentation. Starting a thirty-three date British tour throughout November and December the band declined to make things easy for

 themselves, transporting a huge stage set through Europe and the United States in early 1983. The set was battleship grey with all instruments painted the same colour, inspired by a play starring Rupert Everett which Midge Ure had been taken to by Paula Yates earlier in the year.

Coinciding with the tour, the band released a second single from their new album, and as the *Book of Revelations*-inspired lyrics of *Hymn* peaked at number eleven, the accompanying video contained a miscellany of imagery regarding temptation, the devil, and the fall of man, as well as a choral arrangement by producer George Martin. Music critic Paul Morley was both dismissive and grudgingly appreciative of the band, saying "*The thing is not to take them too seriously, and then for the first time you might see a point in*

---

[614] Well, maybe not Nick.

[615] Even John Peel championed their debut single.

[616] Or in the words of historian Andy Beckett: "Secret Thatcherites".

Ultravox's existence" whilst writer David Laurie summed up my own feelings regarding this single when he said *"I thought it was jaw-droppingly incredible at the time… I now see* [it is] *arse-clenchingly terrible"*.

The British tour produced the band's next album, a live recording of six songs from their Hammersmith Odeon show accompanied by a film of the performance. The release showed the band at their peak, performing with passion and creativity, especially in an extended four person drum break at the end of *The Voice*.

From there Ultravox would enjoy continued success with their next album *Lament* before Ure was press-ganged by Bob Geldof to become part of the Band Aid single at the end of 1984. Whilst the duo took joint song-writing credit for the song *Do They Know it's Christmas*, it was Ure who put it together, recording everything at his home studio before bringing in the most successful British acts to record the vocals at Trevor Horn's studio a week later. The single went on to become the biggest selling British single of all time[617], and kick-started the whole idea of the charity single, whilst Ure helped set up Live Aid and was rewarded with an early afternoon slot for Ultravox. He capitalised on his raised profile by releasing a solo album and reaching the top of the charts with single *If I Was*, and by the time Ultravox reconvened the following year everything had changed. Drummer Warren Cann was unfairly made the fall guy for things not working, and was sacked from the band he had formed, with Ultravox splitting not long after.

℧ ℧ ℧

There was a time when you could not move in Britain's High Streets without bumping into a fake South American pan pipe band. These well organised outfits would arrive

with a PA and atmospheric mellow backing tapes, spend a couple of hours blowing and hitting their odd-looking instruments carved from gourds and the shells of armadillos, whilst hawking tapes and compact discs of their relaxing mood music with names such as *Songs of the Seasons*, *Dance of the Flames*, or *Flight of the Condor*. Whenever they appeared, I would raise my fist and shout a curse at the band Incantation.

As fringe members providing challenging music for new shows of the ground-breaking and world acclaimed Rambert Dance Company, Tony Hinnigan[618], Mike Taylor, Forbes Henderson, Simon Rogers[619], and Chris Swithinbank had been commissioned to write music for *Ghost Dances*, a new production about political oppression in South America. Purchasing authentic Chilean instruments and recruiting Claudia Figuerora, Sergio Avila, and Mauricio Venegas to teach them how to play, the performance was followed by an unexpected offer of a recording contract from Coda Records.

Debut single *Cacharpaya*[620] picked up radio exposure in unusual places, enough to help the song slowly climb into the top ten, despite awkward looking *Top of the Pops* appearances by people who were so obviously not Chilean. Who knew or indeed cared

---

[617] Until Elton John's posthumous ode to Princess Diana in 1997.

[618] You have heard Tony Hinnigan play without knowing it: he is all over the soundtracks for *The Mission, Honey, I Shrunk the Kids, Braveheart, Apollo 13,* and many others.

[619] Simon Rogers gave up all the fancy stuff to join The Fall, the fool.

[620] The Chilean word for "cultural appropriation". No, not really.

how authentic the song was to the music of the Andes, the chirping strumming banging managed to embed itself in enough people's heads to sell.

Incantation have been forgotten, and an internet search for information on them almost immediately turns up an extremely unfortunate story which they had nothing to do with. It concerns a Crewe Alexandria football coach who abused young boys in the 1980's, with one complainant describing how he would play *Cacharpaya* as he abused them. "*That tune just sends chills down my spine*" he would claim in court.

Not the kind of publicity any act would welcome.

Joining Incantation in the *one-hit wonder* category in December were The Maisonettes, with the fully developed Motown sound and look of *Heartache Avenue*.

Formed by ex-City Boy singer Lol Mason[621], alongside guitarist Mark Tibbinham, drummer Nick Parry, and Tamla "*oohs*" supposedly supplied by Elaine Williams and Denise Ward[622], *Heartache Avenue* was a tour de force of retro stylings and reverb. David Virr at Graduate Records was first to fall in love with the song, setting up a label called *Ready Steady Go* specially for the band, and helping it climb to number seven in the new year. As infectious as the song was, it was to be the only hit the act had, being let down by a band who had obviously been around the block a few times and could not fit into the young ideals prevalent in the charts.

ʊ ʊ ʊ

After over a decade of funk in the form of Parliament / Funkadelic, frontman George Clinton found himself without musicians in 1982. Clinton had been born in 1941 and had worked his way up through doo-wop groups in the 1950's and a soul act in the 1960's, before combining soul, funk, rock, and psychedelics towards the end of the decade. Funkadelic were formed as a funk off-shoot of The Parliaments[623], and spent the next few years going *further out* in terms of music. With ever changing line-ups, Clinton kept both groups over the next decade, alternating albums between them, along with increasingly theatrical stage shows.

The twin damage caused by lawsuits and cocaine brought the empire to an end in July 1981 as many of the members laid claim to the brand name. With hip-hop in the ascendancy, Funkadlic's back catalogue was prime to be raided for samples as a new generation were introduced to the music without knowing who had created it. Afrika Bambaataa and Grandmaster Flash stole Funkadelic's look, and the time seemed perfect for Clinton to cash in on the new generation of musicians proclaiming him as an influence... once he had gotten over his Los Angeles based freebasing addiction whilst staying with Sly Stone.

Clinton negotiated a $300,000 record deal with Capitol, which fell apart when both Warners and CBS claimed he was still signed to them. Capitol demanded a return of the money, but Clinton refused and eventually they relented, allowing him to put together the album *Computer Games*. This featured all the familiar Funkadelic stylings brought up to date with hip-hop parlance and technology. The first sign of any new

---

[621] Mason's father invented Radio Four soap opera *The Archers*.

[622] Actually supplied by a couple of session musicians. Williams and Ward were models recruited for the video, and when it turned out they could not sing a note were replaced.

[623] Ultimately to get out of a recording contract.

recordings was a white label twelve-inch single distributed to New York clubs, with nothing but *Loopzilla* on the label.

An insistent electro beat pulsed throughout, with a chorus of *"Don't touch that radio, don't touch that radio, don't touch that knob"* and references to *Planet Rock*, it sounded achingly contemporary. Clinton was wise enough to namecheck New York's three main black radio stations – WBLS, KISS, and KTU – thereby ensuring play over the airwaves as well. In Britain the single climbed to number fifty-seven, his biggest ever hit.

Next single, *Atomic Dog*, had been recorded earlier in the year when new keyboard  player David Spradley spent five hours programming the backing track before calling on Clinton to add vocals. At that point, the song only had a backwards drum rhythm, most of which was kept in the final mix, becoming a huge influence on Detroit house music later in the decade. Clinton, still out of his head on drugs, could not find either the microphone or the backbeat, but once orientated improvised a vocal take with some unusual timings, only to return to the studio the following day and be informed that everyone else had sung harmonies over his improvisations and that the track was finished. The single was released in the United States in December 1982, and became a massive R&B hit, knocking Michael Jackson's *Billie Jean* from the top of the charts in early 1983. It sank without a trace in Britain.

ʊ ʊ ʊ

Soft Cell had been working on their new album in New York for the past few months, as keyboard player Dave Ball became obsessed with making sure the sound was more beefed up than their debut. He had started dating DJ Anita Sarko, a Detroit born lawyer  who made a living playing the most contemporary new wave and rap on New York radio and in the clubs. She was one of the most important and influential people on the New York scene, and introduced the Soft Cell to all sorts of places, finding no door was closed to them so long as Sarko was with them.

Whilst Ball laboured in the studio, Almond would spend nights touring the clubs and S&M dungeons in New York. An initiation for any journalist visiting the band would to be taken to the Hellfire Club where all sorts of depravity and exchanging of bodily fluids was taking place in full view. The club did not even have a toilet: instead it had a bath where paying punters would wait to be urinated on by anyone that needed. From there, unsuspecting journalists would be taken to the Anvil, which progressed several steps further in terms of deviant behaviour, and whilst gay and transgressive culture was at its peak in New York, the insidious shadow of AIDS was starting to be cast.

In recent months, Almond and Ball had switched their main drug of choice from ecstasy to acid, whilst also building up a sizeable cocaine addiction, and the new recordings were produced under the influence of psychedelics. The album, *The Art of Falling Apart,* showed an increased confidence in the writing, with the duo determined to move away from their accidently acquired teenage audience into ominous darker territory. *Numbers* dealt with the emptiness of multiple sexual partners, and as the 1980's progressed, the body count would sound more like a death toll. When released as a single the following year it had to be packaged with a copy of *Tainted Love* because the record company did not believe in its commercial value, angering the band who went to Phonogram headquarters and smashed the office up as best they could. *Martin* was high goth, telling the story of a boy who drained the blood of his victims, whilst Almond was still aware of his fan base by providing a couple of tracks about mis-understood teenagers, one of which was released as a single at the end of 1982.

Where the Heart Is was pure teenage rebellion and adolescent moodiness performed over a dawdling beat, and brought out the worse of Almond in terms of lyrics and vocals. An already thin voice, abused by decadent living, was stretched to the point of breaking, betraying a tone that only dedicated fans could love. *"Smiling you did your time at school, crying silently like a fool"* he complained, before unconvincingly emoting that *"Fathers never understand when children have the upper hand"*.

Soft Cell would manage one more album before splitting, with Almond enjoying varied solo success since, with a much-strengthened voice and penchant for *torch songs*. They would get back together for a final live show in September 2018 at the O2 Arena in London, simultaneously beamed live into selected cinemas throughout the country, as for the last time they waved goodbye to their public.

5th – 11th December 1982

#1 single: The Jam: Beat Surrender
#1 album: John Lennon: The John Lennon Collection

In late 1982 reports began coming into the British Embassy in Addis, Ethiopia, about the suffering of the people in the civil war-torn country. With a mixture of both drought and heavy rain, it was estimated over four million people would suffer food shortages, a figure the Embassy reported back to London. The Office for Overseas Development requested urgent aid from the treasury and was refused on the grounds that it was *"not apparently a sufficiently serious crisis"*. Government spending on overseas disaster relief had fallen from 0.52% of GDP at the start of the Thatcher government three years previously, to the current 0.31%, whilst the international target was set at 0.7%, and so millions of Africans starved to death until the BBC and Michael Buerk brought the situation to the attention of Bob Geldof two years later.

ʊ ʊ ʊ

Chart success had allowed the personal lives of Bananarama to improve throughout 1982, with a move from their damp Denmark Street residence to a council flat on the eleventh floor of Babington Court in Holborn, even if the lift did still smell of urine and the heating relied on a small grill fire in the one room. Siobhan Fahey had been dating Stiff Little Fingers drummer Jim Reilly, however this did not get in the way of their legendary drinking prowess, being able to compete on even terms with the most lairy of rock bands such as Def Leppard.

The trio had appeared unstoppable during the summer, with three top five hits in the space of five months, however that was all about to come to a precipitous end with their new single, *Cheers Then*. Having parted with production duo Jolley and Swain, the girls were partnered with Barry Blue, the early-1970's hit maker who had gone on to become a songwriter and producer for the likes of Heatwave and was riding high with a top ten hit for Toto Coelo. Despite his songwriting prowess, Bananarama's new single was self-written and intended to have a huge Phil Spector production, however once again the band came up against the limits of their own vocal ability and stalled at number forty-five.

This sudden failure prompted London Records to have a re-think, as Jolley and Swain were called back in to finish the album, *Deep Sea Skiving*, a top ten success in 1983, along with further large formulaic hits *Na Na Hey Hey Kiss Him Goodbye*, *Robert De Nero's Waiting*, and *Cruel Summer*. The trio were well connected and used this to their advantage, with songs written for them by Paul Weller ("*Doctor Love*"), Vaughn Toulouse of Department S ("*Give Us Back Our Cheap Fares*"), as well as *Young at Heart*[624], co-written by the band and Robert Hodgens from up-and-coming Glasgow act The Bluebells, who was by then Fahey's latest beau. Meanwhile, Karen Woodward

 spurned the advances of Hollywood titan Robert De Nero on a date in Pizzaland (he had heard the single and was curious), and started dating Andrew Ridgeley of Wham, who she later married[625].

In 1986 the band left Jolley and Swain again and moved to the newly emerging Stock, Aitken and Waterman production team who provided them with a worldwide smash in the shape of a version of *Venus*. This song catapulted the trio into a different arena, reaching number one across the world including the United States, and the partnership continued for a few successful years afterwards. The girls were not financially naïve and insisted on songwriting credit on most of their hits, with a large input into the lyrics, and occasionally the music. Within a couple of years Siobhan Fahey, by now married to Dave Stewart of The Eurythmics, had left and formed the triumphant Shakespears Sister with Marcella Detroit[626], by which point Bananarama were the most successful all-female act in the history of music, a title they retained until the Spice Girls came along.

ʊ ʊ ʊ

Jazz Summers had managed a few dead-end acts during the 1970's but had finally hit the charts with Blue Zoo, giving him a little bit of clout. During the summer he had heard Wham's demo tape and had insisted on meeting them. As the duo hit the charts, they became an obsession with Summers: he *needed* to become their manager. To gain even more influence, he decided to team up with Simon Napier-Bell, who with the demise of Japan was casting his eye around for something to do.

They arranged a meeting at Napier-Bell's apartment in Bryanstone Square, London, and over champagne Summers suggest they go into partnership and manage Wham and the Eurythmics.

"*No, I don't want to manage a girl and a guy, but Wham look rather good*" Napier-Bell agreed.

---

[624] *Young at Heart* later became a huge hit for The Bluebells themselves, albeit in a very different format.

[625] Woodward was also caught up in a feature run by *No. 1* Magazine the following year whereby they would set up pop stars on blind dates. Barking up the wrong tree, she was set up with Ridgeley's bandmate George Michael. Paul Young and Paul Weller protégé Tracey Young were also set up, as were Dee Snider (of Twisted Sister) and Mari Wilson. Meanwhile, future Weller wife and member of Wham, D.C. Lee actually did date Jeremy Healy of Haysi Fantayzee.

[626] Detroit, previously known as Marcy Levy, had spent the 1970's singing backing vocals for Eric Clapton. She would later marry the brother of Jay Aston from Bucks Fizz.

A meeting was set up with Wham's publishers, Morrison and Leahey, where they were told that Michael Jackson's managers were set to take over the role from their lawyer. Despite this, a meeting was arranged for the new year, and within a few weeks Summers and Napier-Bell were the new managers of the rising duo.

ʊ ʊ ʊ

To qualify for the Academy Awards, a movie had to have been shown for seven days straight at a cinema in Los Angeles within the given year. Therefore, December is not only full of festive releases aimed at children and families, but also new movies which the studios would like to be considered. Two of these were released on Friday 10th December, and neither could be considered a bundle of laughs.

The Verdict was a courtroom drama based on the book of the same name by Barry Reed, and directed by Sidney Lumet, hoping to capture some of the magic he had with *Twelve Angry Men* or *Dog Day Afternoon*. With a debut screenplay by playwright David Mamet, the film starred Paul Newman as a down-on-his-luck alcoholic lawyer who takes on a medical malpractice case and finds himself in the process. When the time came, the film picked up Oscar nominations for Best Actor, Supporting Actor, Director, Film and Screenplay.

Sophie's Choice was even less fun, adapted from the award-winning novel by William Styron, and starring Meryl Streep as the title character. The two-and-a-half-hour film is not a joyous ride, with *Variety* calling it "*astoundingly tedious*" and the *New Yorker* saying it was "*an infuriatingly bad movie*". What the critics were agreed on, however, was Streep's bravura performance, which won her the Best Actress award at the Academy Awards[627].

Much more enjoyable was *Tootsie*, directed by Sydney Pollock and starring Dustin Hoffman, which opened in the United States the following week. The plot involved Hoffman as Michael Dorsey an out-of-work actor who no-one will employ due to his argumentative temper. In desperation, he drags up and applies for a middle-aged female role in a live soap opera under the name of Dorothy Michaels. Successfully winning the part, Dorothy Michaels becomes an overnight sensation by constantly going *off-script* and calling out male behaviour in the show.

The movie was an instant success, the audience falling in love with the mixture of comedy, light social commentary, and Hoffman's spot-on performance. From a budget of $21 million, it took $177 million worldwide, becoming the second biggest release of the year after *E.T. The Extra Terrestrial*. The December release also paid off, with ten nominations for Academy Awards, of which Jessica Lange was the only winner as *Best Supporting Actress*.

At the time it was all good fun, but how do we go about viewing a film like *Tootsie* in the twenty-first century? On one level it was a crossdressing screwball classic comedy in the style of *Some Like It Hot*, however it could also be seen as a feminist movie, one in which womens' experience of sexual harassment and inequality is voiced, even if it is by a man. Dig deeper down, and the source of Dorothy Michaels' power is revealed at the end when Dustin Hoffman strips off his costume to disclose his masculinity; everyone suddenly understands where the strength comes from, and we can all return to our previous fixed mindsets regarding gender roles and power: no-one had learned anything from the entire affair.

---

[627] The film is probably now most remembered for the chilling choice of the title, a flashback to Auschwitz in which *Sophie* is forced to choose between her two children as to which one is to die and which one to survive.

Hoffman in later years talked with some passion about his first make-up test for the film, and his disappointment at not being a more attractive woman. He said the moment was a revelation to him about his own perception of women, and how many interesting and strong women he had missed out on knowing because of their outward appearance. What we make of this in the light of the multiple accusations of sexual harassment that attached themselves to the star post-Weinstein is a difficult question.

ʊ ʊ ʊ

The blood banks in America had dragged their heels all year regarding the transmission of the AIDS virus through transfusions. They argued there was no evidence for such a claim and did all they could to stop the public picking up on the theory. On Friday 10th December the Center for Disease Control were finally going public with confirmation and arranged a press conference at the University of California in San Francisco. Immediately afterwards Dr Joseph Bove from the FDA's Blood Advisory Committee went on network television and denied there was any chance of getting AIDS from infected blood. He claimed the CDC was simply exaggerating the danger to gain more funding from the government and stated that many at the FDA did not even believe that AIDS existed. This need for profit would cause the deaths of many more people over the next few years.

ʊ ʊ ʊ

With crumbling personal relationships and diminishing chart success, one of the most successful acts of the past decade were in trouble. Having worked together in various formations for years, Benny Andersson, Bjorn Ulvaeus, Agnetha Faltskog, and Anni-Frid Lyngstad first started using the name ABBA in 1973. Faltskog and Ulvaeus were already married to each other, whilst Lyngstad and Andersson lived together and would marry in 1978, around the same time as the first couple divorced. Lyngstad and Andersson would also split at the end of 1980, divorcing the following year, but

continuing to work closely amid disintegrating relationships had a substantial effect on the music produced, with more contemplative and introspective material such as *The Winner Takes It All* and *One of Us* continuing the glorious run of massive pop singles.

By the start of 1982, however, Abba seemed exhausted as a creative force, with main songwriters Andersson and Ulvaeus looking to broaden their horizons into writing for other people, and possibly for the stage, whilst Faltskog developed a whole range of constrictive fears and phobias, including flying, crowds, open spaces, and heights, making it impossible for the band to tour.

Late Spring had been spent in their own Polar Studios in Stockholm recording a handful of new songs, however the results were disappointing, and it was decided to release a double-album greatest hits compilation instead. *The Singles: The First Ten Years* could genuinely claim to be a *Greatest Hits*, with twenty-two songs, many of which had been chart toppers. Even the NME had to admit that this was "*a seam of unbroken, highly individual pop music that in lifespan terms is still unmatched*".

To make the album more appetising, a couple of new tracks were included, both of which were released as singles to coincide with some limited promotional duties. *The Day Before You Came* documented a day in the life of the singer, a banal list of everyday routines, repeated beyond the point of ennui. Nothing within the song was categorical; at no time did the singer state she did anything for certain, only that she *must have* or *probably* did. Originally called *The Suffering Bird*, the song asked us to examine a life half-lived, unfulfilled, just before the start of a relationship, and to match this the music was both unflagging and irresolute, the sound of someone floating in nothingness, detached from existence. This was emphasized by the line "*I had no sense of living without aim the day before you came*", and at the mention of the title a radiance of warm synthesised chords was introduced each time.

The song had been constructed by Andersson on top of a click track, using keyboards and a drum machine, and was the only Abba song to feature a sequencer. Ulvaeus added a sprinkling of acoustic guitar, and a snare was played by regular drummer Åke Sundqvist. For the vocals Faltskog was encouraged to sing in an aloof manner, as if playing a part rather than performing from the soul. This approach allowed the vocal to appear more like a *normal* person, with foibles and vulnerabilities, the lack of customary Abba harmonies accentuating the forlornness of the message, whilst it remained one of the few songs by the Scandinavians where a Swedish accent was clearly noticeable on certain phrases.

Whilst the song was driven forward by melancholy, underscored by the deceptively simple minor chords and almost six-minute running time, it audaciously lacked a chorus, with an unreliable narrator living a life of quiet desperation.

There was a line near the end of the song stating "*I must have read a while, the latest by Marilyn French or something in that style*" which potentially altered the whole context of the track[628]. French was a New York based radical feminist author whose most famous novel, 1977's *The Women's Room*, had a character state "*All men are rapists, and that's all they are. They rape us with their eyes, their laws, and their codes*", a quote which was often erroneously accredited as being the belief of the author. With the mention of French, we are suddenly viewing the song through feminist eyes, and no longer is the narrator lost, but waiting to be *rescued*. Malcolm Womack has pointed out what he called "*the unremarkable woman given purpose by a remarkable man… most often… through romance*" in many Abba songs, and this would appear to be the entire essence of the song. How are we to interpret songs about unfulfilled love lives written by men with the express knowledge they will be sung by a woman?

The song was what lyricist Tim Rice called "*beyond what the Abba fans expected*", a break from their anthemic choruses, but only reached a disappointing number thirty-two when released. Whilst Andersson later claimed it was one of his favourite songs, he also felt it was one of the worst Abba productions. It was an unheralded synthpop classic which could easily have been written by Soft Cell or Depeche Mode, and was in fact covered by Blancmange a couple of years later, reaching a higher position than the original.

The album was released a month later and topped the charts, as the band undertook a final round of promotional duties. On Friday 10th December they made their last ever appearance together as a band on *The Late, Late Breakfast Show*, where the response to host Noel Edmonds question about rumours of a split was a flat denial. After an awkward interview, the band performed together for the last time with a fitting acoustic version of *Thank You for the Music*.

For most of the 1980's Abba remained an embarrassingly obsolescent act in the consciousness of the younger public, until two 1990's Australia films, *Muriel's Wedding* and *Priscilla, Queen of the Desert*, kick-started a resurgence in interest, long enough away to disassociate them with context and elevate the band into the *timeless* category. From then on there was no stopping the resurgence of public adoration and recognition.

---

[628] Blancmange, with their version of the song changed this to Barbara Cartland, whilst Meryl Streep used Margaret Atwood in the *Mamma Mia* version.

ʊ ʊ ʊ

After the public announcement in October of their split, The Jam spent the last part of 1982 fulfilling commitments, with a final single, live album, and British tour during November and December. For the single Paul Weller was torn between two songs: *Beat Surrender* and *Solid Bond in Your Heart*. The latter seemed the more obvious

choice, however the singer wanted to keep it for his next band,[629] so *Beat Surrender* was released at the end of November. Not that it was in any way a compromise, being one of the more durable Jam singles in a career of classics, entering the charts at the top spot in the first week. A cross between rock and northern soul, the song had an impellent beat and all the routine Jam trademarks, however once again guitar was conspicuous by how far back it was mixed, with resolute horns and piano taking its place. A call-to-arms for surrender to the beat, to music, to feel passion about what it does, the single could also

have been the last act of a band, beating surrender on the drums. Backing vocals were provided by Respond signing Tracey Young[630], with Weller delivering an effective double-tracked call and respond with himself.

According to the terms of their contract, The Jam still owed Polydor one final album, so *Dig the New* Breed, a live album retrospective of their career was released in December, reaching number two in the charts. A live album made sense as The Jam were known for brilliant tours, keeping their faithful fans happy.

As they were unceremoniously discarded, the split left a bad taste in the mouths of bass player Bruce Foxton and drummer Rick Buckler. Weller did not speak to either one for decades afterwards, even blanking Buckler when he turned up at the studio unannounced whilst passing one day. It did not help that those around Weller were also dismissive, with one acerbically describing them as "*the finest rhythm section in Woking*". At one point Buckler phoned the Jam management headquarters to ask for

a list of fan club members so he could let them know about his new venture and was refused. Foxton enjoyed a brief solo career with a minor hit single called *Freak*, until inevitably and rather woefully the two got together again in a Jam tribute act called *From The Jam*.

The final tour was proceeded by a live performance of a handful of songs on the first episode of *The Tube*, including an interview with Muriel Gray in which Weller claimed that no-one in the band had any plans beyond the tour. A horn section was added to the line-up as fans turned up to bid a tearful goodbye to the only band that

mattered to them. In Glasgow, they received a ten-minute standing ovation before they even hit a note and filled five nights straight at the 10,000 capacity Wembley Arena. The final date was at the Brighton Centre on Saturday 11th December, ending their set with *The Gift*, before a hush descended over the audience as they left the venue in disbelief that *their* band had ended.

The Jam achieved what very few bands manage: to go out at the absolute peak of their success. 1982 had been a phenomenal year for them with four top ten singles, two of

---

[629] *Solid Bond in Your Heart* reached number eleven for The Style Council a year later.

[630] Young was one of two young female singers Weller was considering working with at the time. The other was Carol Smillie.

which had topped the charts, and two top ten albums. In their ultimate year they were without a doubt the most successful act in Britain, and yet their success was generally limited to home, unable to achieve a top ten hit single in any other country in the world. Perhaps they appeared too British, too English, and by finishing before they were past their best, The Jam left their legacy unsullied.

Weller was only twenty-five years old when The Jam split, and despite his claims on *The Tube,* had definite plans for his immediate career, wanting to break free from the confines of a three-piece rock band and the limitations that implied, whilst refusing to follow the tried-and-tested route of going solo. Instead, he recruited keyboard player Mick Talbot, a former member of Dexy's Midnight Runners and mod group The Merton Parkas, and formed The Style Council, a loose collective of musicians. Weller appeared to take himself less seriously and started having fun, both on stage and in his videos, refusing to stick to one style of music. Over the next eight years The Style Council played jazz, pop, funk, soul, rap, and ultimately an ill-fated venture into deep house which saw their core audience completely abandon them, along with the record company. Weller started the 1990's as a solo act, and with a resurgence of interest in 1960's mod culture during the Britpop years was hailed as the *Modfather* of the movement. From there, he has continued to create new music, constantly pushing his own boundaries without straying too far from a 1960's blueprint and is one of the few musicians who still produces music of worth more than forty years into his career.

12th – 18th December 1982

#1 single: Renèe & Renato: Save Your Love
#1 album: John Lennon: The John Lennon Collection

The women at Greenham Common had spent the last few months working towards an *Embrace the Base* protest on Sunday 12th December. The action was organised through word of mouth and a series of chain letters entitled *Women for Life on Earth Say "No" to Cruise Missiles at Greenham Common*, and attracted 30,000 people to the base. There was a schism in opinion amongst the protesters as to whether they were *circling the base* or *embracing the base*, but either way the women linked hands and implanted personal items in the chain-link fence, such as photographs of loved ones. With three times the expected number, the women had trouble arranging enough temporary marquees and toilets as many companies refused to hire them once they knew the client. The founder of the whole organisation, Ann Pettitt, was stunned at the sight before her in Newbury: "*The tears actually flowed down my face because it was just full of women…it was like the greatest women's show on earth*". Wheelchair bound grandmother Mary Brewer later recalled "*I'll never forget that feeling; it'll live with me forever… it was even better than holding your baby for the first time.*"

The following day, 2,000 women stayed on from the protest and blockaded the entrances and exits to and from the base. When the police removed protesters from the entrances, the press took photographs of the pained faces of women who had been pulled and kicked, printing the images the next day as *the faces of anger*.

ʊ ʊ ʊ

The lies of the British government in Northern Ireland continued on Sunday 12th December as two unarmed men were shot dead in Mullacreavie Park, Armagh City.

The official account was that the men, Seamus Grew and Roddy Carroll, broke through a random police road block, and were shot as they drove the car at officers.

The truth, once again, was very different. Grew and Carroll had been followed by the RUC for several days, driving into the Republic of Ireland and back to the north without being stopped. Near the border, the undercover army car and a routine police patrol car had accidently crashed into each other, causing a second undercover car to panic. Picking up the RUC officer from the crashed vehicle, they sped ahead and pulled to a stop in front of the civilian car. The RUC Officer left his vehicle and fired a revolver through the windscreen, then reloaded and fired more shots into the dead bodies of the two men. He was then removed from the scene, along with his weapon, before being interviewed, and instructed to tell lies to protect a source.

With this the latest in a shoot-to-kill spree by the RUC, Deputy Chief Constable John Stalker of the Greater Manchester Police was employed to lead an investigation into events, and was met with a refusal to co-operate at all levels. Stating that *"The investigation was without doubt the most serious enquiry ever undertaken by any senior officer into the conduct of other policemen. It involved possible offences of murder, perjury and conspiracy to pervert the course of justice. It seemed to encompass senior officers in the high reaches of the Force as well as relationships between the police, the Director of Public Prosecutions, coroners, the courts and governments in London and Dublin"*. Stalker would removed from the enquiry, following a false smear campaign, before his findings could be published, as they were deemed to be damaging to the police. The report into the killings has never been made public.

Pointless deaths were to continue in Northern Ireland throughout the 1980's with over 850 people killed by terrorists throughout the decade.

ʊ ʊ ʊ

Christmas is traditionally the time for novelty songs, singles which would never stand an ice cube's chance in the infernal regions at any other time of the year, and 1982 did not disappoint.

Cashing in on his popular Radio 1 weekday show *Steve Wright in the Afternoon*, which had started the previous year and featured a host of characters in what is known as a

zoo format, *I'm Alright* was released as a single under the name Young Steve & the Afternoon Boys, a throwaway cockney knees-up which would not have been out of place in an episode of *The Two Ronnies*. The single spent an inexplicable seven weeks in the charts, peaking at number forty, whilst the spirit of Chas & Dave also hung heavy over other novelty songs, with a compilation of Christmas favourites called *Sing-along-a-Santa* by Santa Claus & The Christmas Trees, which somehow managed to reach number nineteen. Then there was *Christmas Rapping* by Dizzy Heights, embarrassingly the first British record to feature rap all the way through, and the excruciating *Xmas Party* by The Snowmen[631]. Even old hands had a go, as Cliff Richard reached number eleven with a version of the carol *Little Town*, whilst ventriloquist Keith Harris hit the top five with the conceivable ingenuity of *Orville's Song*, on which he performed a duet with a *"huge gormless*

---

[631] The Snowmen had a hit with a version of *The Hokey-Cokey* the previous year, helped by rumours that it was either Ian Dury or Jona Lewie on vocals. Although the previous single had been on Stiff Records, the *mastermind* behind the act was session guitarist Martin Kershaw, who had previously played on *Dance Yourself Dizzy* and *Kung-Fu Fighting*.

falsetto-voiced green duckling sporting a nappy fastened by a giant safety pin". Or Orville, as he was known.

If you wanted to recreate the office party, then you needed look no further than Modern Romance, breaking in their new singer Michael Mullins[632] with their biggest hit, *The Best Years of our Lives*, whilst the easy listening piano stylings of smiling, winking Frenchman Richard Clayderman[633] saw his television advertised self-titled album reach number two. 1970's icon David Essex also wanted a piece of the Christmas action, releasing single *A Winter's Tale*, written at the last minute by Mike Batt[634] and Tim Rice. Batt would explain how the collaboration came together, saying *"David Essex rang me late in 1982... and asked if I could write him a Christmas hit. It was already late October, so we didn't have much time. I was due to be writing with Tim Rice the following day... so we started thinking of ideas."* The song was a tale of desperation, with Essex lamenting *"Why should the world take notice of one more love that's failed?"* however depressive reflection was obviously what the public wanted as it reached number two.

Christmas for mums everywhere was sorted by the release of *Heartbreaker*, a new Dionne Warwick album written and produced by the Bee Gees, an alliance made in harmony heaven. Like everything the brothers wrote, the songs sounded like the Bee Gees, featuring their trademark temperate close-harmony vocals, and the title track provided Warwick with her biggest British hit, peaking at number two.

By far the most curious and successful Christmas hit was sung by an Italian immigrant living in the West Midlands. Renato Pagliari had moved to Britain from Rome in 1975  and demonstrated a singing style which could easily have seen him selling cornetto ice-creams or a car insurance comparison website, best described as cod-opera. He was paired with songwriter Johnny Edward[635] in 1982, who wrote the mushy Mr Whippy kitsch of *Save Your Love* *"as a joke, to give the finger to 'Save Your Kisses for Me' by Brotherhood of Man among other tracks that made me chew the carpet."* Renato was coupled with singer and actor Hilary Lester, and the single released on independent label Hollywood Records[636], under the name Renée and Renato. Over the course of two months, it crept up the charts, eventually reaching the top spot in time for Christmas[637], by which point Lester had been replaced by a more Italian looking model for the video. How can you explain to future generations the love Britain felt for a corpulent Italian chap with a cliched moustache warbling a clinquant Caruso cast-off like a Latin lothario at the end of a middle-aged holiday romance? I have no idea, but just thinking of the song has it going round in my head in a loop, over and over again. It will probably be there all night, keeping me awake. Maybe I am in the wrong? Maybe this is a work of towering brilliance?

---

[632] Mullins would later enjoy a Christmas number one, singing backing vocals on *Mistletoe & Wine* by Cliff Richard.

[633] I once briefly convinced my wife that Clayderman played the piano on David Bowie's *Life on Mars*.

[634] Batt, who had written all the hits for The Wombles, would use a suspiciously similar melody for Alvin Stardust's 1984 hit *I Feel Like Buddy Holly*.

[635] Edward was on the verge of being cool, having played guitar with David Bowie in the 1960's. On the other hand, he invented the television show *Metal Mickey*.

[636] *Save Your Love* was the first ever independent single to top the charts in Britain.

[637] My mother bought this single and loved it. She was only thirty-eight at the time.

For me, however, the best Christmas song from 1982 did not even break into the top forty. The Waitresses were a hip New York band featuring an ex-member of Television on drums, when their label Ze Records asked them to

contribute a song to a Christmas compilation album of *cool* bands at the end of 1981. Guitarist Chris Butler hated the festive season, but needed the money, so he "*poured all my sourness into this song. The first words I wrote down were 'Bah humbug!'*" Titled *Christmas Wrapping* in honour of Kurtis Blow's *Christmas Rapping*, the song told the story of someone determined to have a terrible Christmas after "*A&P provided me with the world's smallest turkey*", only to be caught up with the festive spirit after meeting another lonely soul whilst buying cranberry.

With Tracey Wormworth's bass line a self-admitted unrelenting steal from Chic, the song was funky throughout, embellished with a celebratory horn breakdown, but the band soon forgot all about it. "*We went back on the road*" explained Butler, "*We were in Rochester, New York, a few months later when I called home and my girlfriend said 'You're all over the radio!' I thought* [new single] *'I Know What Boys Like' had finally made it* [but] *she said 'No, no. It's the Christmas song!' We put it in the repertoire that night.*"

Despite only reaching number forty-five in the charts, *Christmas Wrapping* had an afterlife which continues to see its popularity growing each December, and every year Butler makes a donation to a children's library in his hometown of Akron in the name of the first person to tell him they heard the song on the radio.

ʊ ʊ ʊ

On the bus between Chicago and Cincinnati on Sunday 12th December Prince started quizzing keyboard player Matt Fink as to why people were so attracted to blue collar rocker Bob Seger. Fink proposed it was the big ballads such as *We've Got the Night* which the public loved, and suggested Prince try writing something like that if he really wanted mass appeal.

That afternoon, during the soundcheck at the Riverfront Coliseum, the singer showed the band a chord sequence for a new song, a big ballad. Wendy Melvoin, the partner of keyboard player Lisa Coleman, started filling out the chords with suspensions, as the band jammed. At this stage there were no lyrics or melody, however everyone there immediately felt there was a power in the song that was greater than the sum of their parts.

Prince was in the habit of recording soundchecks, which could often last for hours, and where new ideas were tried out. He sent the recording of the song, over ten minutes long, to Fleetwood Mac's Stevie Nicks, and asked her to write some lyrics. Overwhelmed by the task she sent it back, forcing Prince to write the words himself. The first thing he did was find a title: *Purple Rain*.

ʊ ʊ ʊ

After fulfilling their promise to manager Simon Napier-Bell to stay together for a year to boost the commercial value of their solo careers, Japan finally bid farewell in December at the end of a limited world tour. Playing through mainland Europe and Britain in October and November, supported by Japanese synth trio Sandii & The Sunsetz and augmented by keyboard players Ryuicho Sakamoto and Masami Tsuchiya, Japan ended their Western career with six nights at Hammersmith Odeon, the last of which saw an attempted visit by David Bowie. Napier-Bell had arranged for the band to meet their hero, and he turned up at the stage door in a stretch limo.

"*Who do you think you are?*" asked the security guard.

"*I'm David Bowie*" answered the superstar.

"*Well, I'm President Reagan*" the guard sneered, "*So you can piss off.*"

From there it was off to, appropriately enough, Japan, where after a few dates they performed their swansong on Thursday 16th December at Shi Kohkaido in Nagoya. There was no heart in the performances as David Sylvian admitted "*I want to get away from everything Japan has become – everything I didn't want. Like this tour... and the live album that was meant to follow*". The mood was tense backstage, or as Napier-Bell put it "*David was being a prick. He was bringing* [ex-partner of Mick Karn] *Yuka to the dressing room... Mick just had to sit there.*"

Napier-Bell had invested a significant amount of money in the band and was only just beginning to see a return. With them about to split, he decided to take his cut of the tour profits, something which displeased the band. "*They were horrified I took my management commission. It meant they made no profit. If they hadn't broken up, I wouldn't have done it. I'd figured that once they got on that tour... they'd get back together.*" he explained, "*Of course, they didn't, so I thought 'fuck it'. I've done everything I can and these bloody stupid, pig-headed people can't see they're killing their career.*"

Like The Jam, Japan choosing to split at the peak of their career was commendable, but less so when it emerged they had spent most of the past year away from each other, barely speaking, and were only together this long for money and a bolstered future solo career. Certainly, David Sylvian believed he was carrying the band, boldly stating even at the time "*Japan was four people working together on an equal basis, but on the creative side – the concepts, writing, the way an album goes in the studio – it was mainly my project... that can't work anymore because of ego problems. People no longer want to work under me.*" That their subsequent careers never reached anything like the peak of Japan's success in 1982 is hardly surprising. Success was

never the point of Japan; they flaunted their avant-garde leanings through their career, and when those accidently coincided with the pop charts, they had some hits. Once again, unusual subjects, such as urban alienation, were taken into the charts in 1982, and made to sound appealing.

The minor hits had kept on coming throughout the year. *Life in Tokyo* had been released (for the third time) by their old label Hansa in October, albeit in a band-approved remixed version. Upon its first release in 1979, the synth-driven track produced and co-written in Los Angeles by David Sylvian and disco pioneer Georgio Moroder seemingly a desperate final unsuccessful attempt to have a hit. Despite being the most commercial recording the band ever released, the lyrics about observing the beautiful life of the rich from a distance remained obscure enough to keep people guessing, however who cared when you had such a great melody. With disco anathema in 1979, white acts trying to "*do disco*" such as Kiss, The Rolling Stones, and Rod Stewart seemed embarrassingly contrived, so what chance did five young kids wearing make-up from Lewisham have? Within a year the New Romantic movement blossomed, and *Life in Tokyo* no longer seemed so outré, to the extent that Duran Duran asked Sylvian to produce their debut album, an offer which he declined[638]. By 1982, *Life in Tokyo* sounded painfully contemporary and managed to rise to number twenty-eight. The only question that remained is why it was not a bigger hit.

Emboldened by this, Hansa released another old track in December. *Nightporter* had originally appeared on Japan's 1980 album *Gentlemen Take Polaroids*, and was influenced by French composer Erik Satie, especially his 1888 work *Gymnopedies*. The lyrics owed a debt to the 1974 Dirk Bogarde and Charlotte Rampling movie of the same name about an ex-concentration camp guard and one of his captives whom he had sexually abused, and the subsequent emergence of *Stockholm Syndrome* when the two met again in Vienna in 1957. With such a *risqué* subject matter, what is remarkable is that the beautifully moody and mournful minor key melody backed by a simple waltzing piano rose to number twenty-nine in the charts.

After the split Sylvian pursued his own idiosyncratic path, choosing to shun popular acclaim for something more personal and obscure, releasing albums with titles such as *Alchemy: An Index of Possibilities* and *When Loud Weather Buffeted Naoshima*, some of which contained nothing but instrumentals. He refused to re-visit material created by his old band, stating *"I'm neither ashamed nor proud of what Japan did. If people want to keep that period alive it's really up to them – but they are fooling themselves. What I think about the work of Japan is that at its centre, there's an emotional void"*. When he finally did get the band back together with all four original members for one final album, he insisted they go under the name of Rain Tree Cow and locked the other members out of the studio during mixing.

℧ ℧ ℧

Twisted Sister made their British television debut on Channel 4's *The Tube* on Friday 17th December, and after a couple of their own numbers introduced Lemmy and Brian Robertson from Motörhead. As both ran towards the stage, Robertson tripped and fell, much to the amusement of Lemmy who by that point had come to blows with the guitarist. Robertson increasingly distanced himself from the band, often wearing ballet shoes on stage as a statement that he was just *guesting* and not an actual member of Motörhead. Eventually, things became too much in 1983, and he *"left"* the band, however by then Motörhead's glory days were well over: their classic line-up had ended with the departure of Eddie Clark back in May.

The performance on *The Tube* was something of an omen for the future of bands like Motörhead. 1982 marked the end of a type of rock music which had dominated the scene for the past decade, that of regular denim and leather clad men with long hair, playing music as hard as they could. Many of these musicians were British, but soon the centre of *rock* moved to Los Angeles, where spandex and big hair became the norm, along with a softer more melodic brand of music.

Then something strange happened in the new millennium. It became acceptable to like Motörhead, admiring them for simply still existing, and Lemmy for his hard-drinking uncompromising ways. Motörhead, not unlike the Ramones, became the type of band that more people owned a T-shirt than bought the records, helped by Top Shop stocking the apparel of both acts as fashion items. The allure of Lemmy remains something of a conundrum. Despite alcoholism, intolerance of others, an arrogance born of fatuity, rampant homophobia and sexism, holocaust denials, and being the self-

---

[638] According to Napier-Bell, "[Duran Duran] *came day after day and begged him to produce them. Every one of them copied David's looks, so you had five David look-alikes. Then they very sensibly went off, and instead of making esoteric Japan music, they recorded good, old-fashioned four-to-the-floor disco … [and] got the hits with the Japan look"*.

confessed father of a child with an under-age girl, he is still considered something of a loveable legend by too many. They started to sell out larger venues to people who had only heard their biggest hit, *Ace of Spades*, and remained a people's favourite until Lemmy's death in 2015.

19th – 25th December 1982

#1 single: Renèe & Renato: Save Your Love
#1 album: John Lennon: The John Lennon Collection

Twenty-year-old William Bailey and his seventeen-year-old girlfriend Gina Siler arrived at Los Angeles in her beat-up car on Tuesday 21st December, having just driven from Lafayette, Indiana. Bailey had been run out of town by the local law authorities with the threat of being charged as being a habitual criminal, having been involved in a string of misdemeanors over the past three years. All the youth had was a polythene bag of some clothes and a vague dream he could be a singer in a rock and roll band, having already spent a little time in the city during the summer.

Bailey's life had been in turmoil for the past three years, ever since he had accidently discovered his biological father was not the man who had raised him. He had started to use his birth father's surname, and the move to California was the perfect excuse to make that change permanent. From now on he would be known as William Rose, until he formed a band called AXL, and adopted *that* name as his own.

ʊ ʊ ʊ

Sometimes a music scene within a city or town will revolve around a venue, and sometimes it will be a record store. In Liverpool it was Probe Records, just around the corner from Mathew Street, home of the Cavern and birth of the Beatles back in the 1960's. Probe was the kind of place you could aggrandize your musical confines by discovering Thelonious Monk or Captain Beefheart, or else could just hang out and meet people. Over the past few years Julian Cope of the Teardrop Explodes, Pete

Burns of Dead or Alive and Paul Rutherford of Frankie Goes to Hollywood had all worked behind the counter, absorbing esoteric music whilst networking with the local scene. Also working at Probe Records was the biggest Scouse networker of them all, Pete Wylie, and it placed him at the perfect location to form a band in the aftermath of punk.

The Crucial Three only existed as a band for just a couple of weeks[639] during the summer of 1977 but featured three future Liverpudlian legends: bass player Julian Cope went on to find success as singer with The Teardrop Explodes, whilst singer Ian McCulloch was the frontman of Echo & the Bunnymen. The third of the trio was guitarist Pete Wylie, and everyone who met him was convinced by his enthusiasm that he was going to be a superstar, not least Wylie himself as he wandered around the city reading excerpts out loud from Jack Kerouac's beat novel *On the Road*.

---

[639] The only thing the trio did in those weeks was organise a petition demanding local act Big in Japan disband, which was placed on the wall in Probe Records and signed by members of Big in Japan themselves.

Having frustratingly watched his two former bandmates find success in the early years of the decade, Wylie was convinced he was becoming the forgotten man, but was still driven by an unrelenting self-determination and mouth the size of the Mersey. Forming Wah! Heat with Rob Jones, Carl Washington, Colm Redmond, and Ken Bluff, he released a couple of acclaimed singles on Inevitable Records and an album under the name Wah! on Eternal Records.

Signing to WEA and working with producer Mike Hedges, Wylie raised his game with new single *The Story of the Blues*, choosing to create Phil Spector-sized pop powered by a Linn drum machine. This was a loser's lament inspired by *The Boys from the Black Stuff*, a song of eternal optimism in the face of adversity, and even if he did sing the entire thing slightly sharp, it was undoubtably one of the musical highlights of the year.

"*We were an indie band and 'Story of the Blues' was kind of an accidental hit,*" Wylie would later muse, "*And we owe it all to Duran Duran really!*" The Birmingham heart-throbs were thrown off a Granada television Christmas show for swapping tapes, and Wah were called in, pushing the single into the top forty on Christmas Day.[640] With the increased exposure, the irresistible song started a slow rise to number three in January 1983.

A song of someone down on their luck it may have been, however there is nothing cowed about *The Story of the Blues*, a piece of music where every word and note is wrenched from the soul, with a grandiose string introduction and a soaring chorus. If Edith Piaf had sung this it would have brought the roof down at the Paris Olympia.

It was to prove to be the premature pinnacle of Wylie's career, a never to be repeated epic. Wylie was not too bothered about a brand name over the years, releasing records as Wah Shambeko! and The Mighty Wah, as well as under his own name, and a couple of times aligning his singular vision with the charts. "*I sometimes think we've been ghosts in the music industry machine*" Wylie would claim in later years, a perfect description of the hint of greatness they would leave behind.[641]

ʊ ʊ ʊ

On Christmas Eve, Culture Club guitarist Roy Hay married his long-term girlfriend, Alison, at Fulham Register Office. Singer Boy George had been picking substantial press coverage, so chose to avoid the ceremony for fear of stealing the limelight. Instead, he joined them that night for a celebration at their flat in Fulham, asking drummer and boyfriend Jon Moss "*When are you going to make a decent woman of me?*"[642]

Moss and George had continued their tumultuous relationship which was built on "*power-tripping and masochism*", often fighting, sometimes physically. Culture Club's British autumn tour in 1983 had to be cancelled after one such fight, when George broke Jon's finger, although the official story was that he fell over in the tour bus. Moss

---

[640] Duran Duran were probably not that bothered. Simon LeBon spent Christmas with his girlfriend Clare, then flew to Sri Lanka to spend time with his other girlfriend. Nick Rhodes and John Taylor flew to New York to attend the MTV New Year Ball. Andy Taylor spent his first Christmas at home with his new wife.

[641] I recently looked up the video for *The Story of the* Blues on YouTube. 235,000 people had viewed it. Not bad, I thought, until I checked out Nicki Minaj's *WAP*. Over 373,000,000 had viewed it, a sign if needed, that greatness is not measured in numbers.

[642] Boy George was voted 5th Best Male Singer in the 1982 Smash Hits Poll, and 12th Best Female Singer. "*As far as I'm concerned, I'm a man. I'm not going around trying to be a woman.*" he responded.

would often sleep with women during their relationship, and George was so blinded by love that he always forgave him.

Culture Club were typical of the new breed of acts in 1982, bands who were media-savvy and wanted something more than coverage in the *Melody Maker, NME,* and *Sounds*. For bands like Culture Club, Spandau Ballet, and Duran Duran, they wanted the tabloids to cover their lives, they wanted to complete with Princess Diana and the jet-set for headlines. Statistics showed that people tended to stay loyal to a newspaper, and so the 1980's saw the tabloids courting the teen market in the hope of cultivating a future readership, with an increasing number of stories about pop stars.

Much as later bands would know how to use the internet before the record companies did, the bands of the early 1980's understood television and visuals quicker than the executives. They wanted to appear on television as much as possible, and to guarantee this they needed a video. Television responded throughout the decade, and where the 1970's were ruled by *Top of the Pops* for the teenagers, and *The Old Gray Whistle Test* for serious music fans, the 1980's saw a whole host of *youth programming* featuring pop acts. *Top of the Pops* stayed important for sales, the *Old Gray Whistle Test* became just *The Whistle Test*, but there also was *The Tube, The Chart Show, Pop Quiz, Tiswas, Swap Shop, Saturday* Superstore, *Cheggers Plays Pop, Razzamatazz, The Oxford Road Show, The Hitman & Her, The Minipops, The O-Zone, Snub TV, Network 7,* and *No Limits* to name but a few.

Boy George knew exactly what he wanted from the national press: a story in one of them every single day. It did not matter if these stories were made up, as they were most of the time, often by the band themselves, what mattered was that the profile of the band was kept high. And boy, did the press love George. He always looked his best and could provide a memorable bitchy quote on demand.

Of course, it all backfired as George eventually resented being followed by photographers and journalists twenty-four hours a day. Having lived the kind of life he had, sexually and drug-wise, it was only a matter of time before the skeletons came tumbling out of the closet. There was always someone willing to make money selling a story of some past or present scandal, and the tabloids were more than happy to pay. Over the next year, Culture Club became the biggest band on the planet, with their second album, *Colour by Numbers*, and the single *Karma Chameleon* taking over the world. In the process, however, George lost something: his cutting-edge critical respectability. Instead of being one of the freaks, he became a cuddly toy for the press. A year after their peak, they were on the scrapheap, brought down by internal fighting between the two lovers, a terrible third album, and a raging heroin habit for the singer. Eventually, in summer 1986 George was forced to confront his reality when friends sold his circumstances to the press and the front covers blazed *"only weeks left to live"* type headlines. The fall was as spectacular as the rise.

26th December 1982 – 1st January 1983
#1 single: Renèe & Renato: Save Your Love
#1 album: John Lennon: The John Lennon Collection

The Fun Boy Three, despite having great success with cover versions throughout 1982, had still not convinced they were a serious creative force. This was to change in 1983 as the band moved away from percussion-based tracks towards a more mature form of song writing. After spending most of 1982 attempting to persuade everyone that they were indeed the FUN boy three, they returned in the last week of December with one of the most serious tracks of the year.

The trio had spent the last three months in Wessex Studios, London, with Talking Heads frontman David Byrne producing, putting together the tracks which would constitute their second album, *Waiting*. These songs were a leap forward from the debut album of six months previous in terms of subject matter and song writing, and this change of direction was indicated with the release of *The More That I See (The Less I Believe)* as a single.

The most noticeable thing was that the jungle percussion and tribal chants had gone, to be replaced by a band of female musicians, including Nicky Holland[643], Ingrid Schroeder[644], Bethan Peters[645], June Miles-Kingston[646], Annie Whitehead[647], and

Caroline Lavelle.[648] The songs were now about *something*, from *The Tunnel of Love*'s sardonic look at marriage to *Our Lips Are Sealed* secret romance, and even Hall's spoken-word confession to being sexually abused by a teacher on a school trip to France.

The More That I See was Hall's take on the troubles in Northern Ireland. The song remained on edge throughout, mirroring the political situation, and took no prisoners within the lyrics, from the opening lines where "*The houses of God are full of sinners every week praying for forgiveness for those they leave to bleed*". Hall refused to choose a side, instead stating that "*They keep telling me, it's not my concern*", describing himself as "*Too ignorant to find my own conclusions*". By the third verse he was naming names, stating that "[Ian] *Paisley's getting his shirt off, Sein Fien are going insane*", before having a go at the British army with "*Another kid with a brick gets shot in the back and gets left on the pavement to bleed*". With a chorus of "*Belfast's only half an hour away*", Hall ended on the repeated plea "*Does anybody know any jokes?*", on the surface an attempt to lighten the mood after his boisterous rant, but underneath a sly dig at the anti-Irish jokes still prevalent on Saturday night prime-time television in Britain.

It was a brilliant politically charged and indignant song covering a sensitive subject, and as such there was no way that it was ever going to breach the top forty due to lack of radio play, peaking at number sixty-eight early in January 1983. The Fun Boy Three went on to have another couple of top ten hits throughout the year and toured the world with their brilliant band, before Hall announced he was leaving due to internal tension. He went on to form other acts throughout the decade, such as The Colour Field and Vegas, but struggled to commit to the one project, something that could be explained by a later bi-polar diagnosis following a suicide attempt.

The three were later re-united when The Specials got together again in the new millennium, turning into the nostalgia act that Hall had been running from the entire time.

---

[643] Holland was a former keyboard player with early 1980's female trio The Ravishing Beauties and took responsibility for the arrangements of the songs on *Waiting*, crafting them into things of beauty. She later did the same thing for Tears for Fears, Lloyd Cole & Cyndi Lauper.

[644] Schroeder sang and played keyboards, later appearing with The Waterboys.

[645] Peters had been bass player in Yorkshire post-punks The Delta 5.

[646] Miles-Kingston had been the drummer in The Mod-ettes and would later play and sing with The Communards.

[647] Whitehead played trombone and later joined The Penguin Café Orchestra.

[648] Lavelle played cello and would later contribute to Radiohead's *The Bends*.

ʊ ʊ ʊ

When the February 1982 edition of *Time Magazine* ran a feature on young entrepreneurs, it claimed that *"At 26 [Steve] Jobs heads a company that six years ago was located in a bedroom and garage of his parents' house, but this year is expected to have sales of $600 million."* Just over a year before that, when his company Apple went public four days after the assassination of John Lennon, Jobs had been worth $256 million.

With such a successful year, Jobs was convinced he was going to be named *Time Magazine Man of the Year*, giving journalists full access to his staff. Instead, he was stunned to find the *Man of the Year* award being given on Sunday 26th December to a non-human: the computer. The multi-millionaire considered the feature to be a hatchet job, stating *"It was so awful that I actually cried"*, whilst an anonymous employee described him as *"an anti-materialistic hippy who capitalized on the inventions of a friend who wanted to give them away for free"*. Another staff member made the double-edged claim that Jobs *"would have made an excellent King of France"*.

The staff knew by now how difficult their boss could be, and Jobs was put on the Macintosh team to keep him away from everyone else at Apple, such was his reputation. Each year Apple gave a prize to the person who did the best job of standing up to him. However, his vision was important as the company moved away from the traditional dark colour for technological products towards a sleeker Japanese influenced simplicity, one which would create the look of the future.

ʊ ʊ ʊ

For some politicians Christmas was not a time for rest. Whilst Margaret Thatcher and her husband had spent the previous day entertaining Jimmy Savile, on Sunday 26th December Labour leader Michael Foot, along with his wife Jill and pet dog Dizzy, visited the Greenham Common peace camp in Berkshire, taking the women Christmas presents and wine.

Foot had been something of an odd choice for the leader of a major political party. He had spent the end of the 1970's as Leader of the House for Jim Callaghan's minority Labour government, where everyone found him a man of conviction, a perfect gentleman of the old school, and effusive company. At the defeat of Labour in the 1979 General Election, Callaghan clung on to the leadership for over a year, whilst the party almost tore itself in two with a hard left-wing which Foot was closer to, and a softer right wing, led by Dennis Healey. At one point, the battle even boiled over into a fistfight in a Brighton washroom, involving Neil Kinnock. When Foot was made leader at the end of 1980, the press had a field day discussing his image rather than his politics, and that he often appeared scruffy, and occasionally unhygienic, did him no favours. The criticism reached a peak when he turned up at the Cenotaph for the Remembrance Day ceremony wearing what was memorably described as a donkey jacket but was closer to a duffel coat. In the House of Commons, it was always felt that he should be able to destroy Margaret Thatcher given his superior intellect, knowledge, and debating skills, however his old-fashioned courtesy to women held him back.

A near-fatal car crash had left Foot permanently using a cane, whilst an attack of shingles had robbed him of sight in one eye. Not long after winning the Labour leadership contest he fell down a set of stairs, breaking his ankle and leaving him encased in plaster, leading to Bernard Levin in *The Times* rather cruelly describing him as *"half-blind and at least quarter crippled"*. In the days of increasing political judgement on looks, Foot was a limping public relations disaster.

Only his good charm and bonhomie initially kept the party together through a war between the two wings, however with the left becoming more dominant in policy making, and Thatcher's Conservatives moving towards the right, a large enough space had opened up in the middle. It was into this space that the soft right of Labour had split to form the Social Democratic Liberal Party (SDLP) back in January 1981.

The 1983 Labour manifesto would turn out to be a last-minute rambling rushed-job full of policies which alarmed people in the middle of a cold war, such as universal nuclear disarmament. It became known as *"the longest suicide note in history"* and was so damaging to Labour that the Conservatives bought 1,000 copies and distributed them for free.

When it came to nuclear weapons, the Government had long stuck by the line that the information provided in their *Protect and Survive* booklet would see everyone through a nuclear conflict, in which we painted our windows white and waited under the kitchen table for a few days, after which we could emerge and return to normal lives. The truth was very different, with procedures in place if a nuclear war was imminent for the Queen to sign a document suspending democracy, before being taken to an underground shelter in Essex, along with the government and key people. Six million Londoners would be dead within twelve weeks, and the only chance of survival was to head out of the city to rural areas, where food stocks would soon be exhausted, with the army instructed to shoot anyone trying to leave the capital.

It was against this unknown background that Foot's anti-nuclear policy was ridiculed by the press, and therefore the public too.

ʊ ʊ ʊ

The Stranglers had spent the last few months of the year signing a new record deal following a bidding war in the wake of their new-found pop success, steering away from the most likely label, Virgin, to do a deal with Epic Records instead. Complete artistic freedom was what clinched the deal, and for tax reasons they set about working on their next album in Belgium, which also allowed them to further explore European influences and utilise their recently bought acoustic guitars. The album *Feline* was an attempt to *"Marry the northern element of Europe – with the southern element of Spanish and acoustic guitars"*, and saw The Stranglers move indefinitely away from any punk influences and roots (disputed as they were) and allow them to break into the European market.

The first single from the album was released in the last week of 1982, hoping to cash in on the post-Christmas pre-New Year lull in the market. *European Female* had been

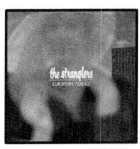

written by Jean Jacques Burnel, the London-born son of French parents, and saw the guitars and keyboards pushed back in the mix as his bass and vocals were emphasised. Burnel had long been over-aware of his European identity, having previously recorded a solo album about continental unity entitled *Euroman Commeth*, and *European Female* was his attempt to create a continental version of *California Girls* by The Beach Boys. It was based upon his Parisian ballerina girlfriend Anna, who had the French habit of pouting when forming words, which he translated as *"When she speaks, her lips are kissing"*, whilst also comparing the *"thousand years"* love to the idea of a thousand-year Reich[649]. Drummer Jet Black had turned his back on real drums in the studio in

---

[649] Burnel would also admit to delivering the song *"like Marlene Dietrich"*.

favour of a Simmons electronic kit, thus limiting any fills and providing a more pulsing beat throughout. The single climbed to number nine during January 1983, providing the band with three top ten hits in twelve months and establishing them as chart regulars[650].

The Stranglers continued to record and tour throughout the 1980's, enjoying occasional forays into the top forty with pop singles such as *Skin Deep* and *Always the Sun*, however they never regained the heights achieved in 1982. Whilst remaining a popular live act, increasingly on the punk nostalgia circuit especially after main vocalist Hugh Cornwell departed in 1990, The Stranglers would be fondly remembered for their six glorious years between 1977 and 1982.

℧ ℧ ℧

Launched in 1977, the most popular video games console of the previous five years had been the Atari 2600, the first to introduce games with a computer-controlled opponent, as well as *Adventure*, the first game with a virtual space larger than the screen, both of which would become hugely influential. By 1979 the console was the largest selling Christmas gift in the United States, and their market grew further when they licenced the arcade game *Space Invaders* from Taito in January 1980.

Atari seemed unstoppable in late 1982 when they paid $25 million for the rights to produce a game based upon the movie *E.T. The Extra-terrestrial*. This was to be a combination of the most successful movie in years by the hottest director in Hollywood and the in-demand games console, and everyone expected it to be lucrative on a previously unseen scale, not least Atari themselves. However, several basic mistakes were made by the company. Developer Howard Scott Warshaw was given just thirty days to finish the game, the company skipped audience-testing to get it released by Christmas, and then ignored all suggestions made by the movie's director Steven Spielberg. Anticipating record sales, Atari produced more copies of the game than there were consoles, leading to stacks of cartridges being left in shops and warehouses.

E.T. became the largest financial failure in gaming history, with a large amount of the cartridges ploughed into landfill sites in New Mexico, and Atari posting losses of $536 million in 1983. It is credited with being the primary cause of the video games crash of 1983, when home computers started to seriously challenge games consoles in sales. Developers began to leave companies such as Atari in droves, due to them refusing to allow credits on their games or fully share the profits from them, starting up their own companies such as Activision.

The bottom line, however, was that far too many games were being released, many of which were of extremely poor quality, and the small but growing market was over-saturated. Stores tried to return large numbers of unsold games to the publishers, many of whom did not have sufficient cash to offer refunds. When the publishers started to fold, the games were pulped or sold at a massive discount, which was then taken up in business as a sure-fire sign that the computer game "*fad*" was over.

There were two long term effects of the crash, with video games seeming to disappear as a growth area over the next three or four years. Firstly, companies stopped handing over games manufacture to third party developers, a major factor in the poor quality of

---

[650] Towards the end of 1982 Burnel and keyboard player Dave Greenfield also recorded the soundtrack for a film that was never released, *Ecoutez Vos Murs* (Fire & Water), directed by Vincent Coudanne, with Mike Oldfield collaborator Maggie Reilly, which was released by Epic Records the following year.

many of the initial games. Secondly, the focus of the industry moved from America to Japan, as companies such as Nintendo and Sega saw the gap in the market.

℧ ℧ ℧

In the United States, unemployment was sitting at 10.8%, a new high for recent years. Inflation, on the other hand, had dropped another point since mid-year, to around 6%. The Dow Jones Industrial Average, which had been moving sideways for more than a decade, had risen from 800 to 1046 in recent months. A new market rally was on the way as people begin to put their money back into stocks and shares. It was a trend which would become both desirable and consistent throughout the decade: people were less important than money.

℧ ℧ ℧

1983 was going to be an important year for nuclear weapons, with the proposed arrival of Cruise missiles at Greenham Common. To draw attention to this, the women protesters decided to go *over the fences* for the first time. Instead of cutting their way through the fence, which many considered to be a violent action, some of the women visited Newbury and bought twelve ladders, saying they were for use in a woman's theatre group.

At 4 a.m. on Saturday 1st January the women were waiting in bushes at the periphery of the base, along with the press and television crews, anxious after Michael Heseltine had admitted in parliament a few days previously that the American soldiers had the legal right to shoot intruders. Forty-four of the women made it successfully to the missile silos, where they linked hands and danced, the subsequent iconic photographs being beamed around the world. The women were then arrested and charged with Breach of the Peace rather than the more serious charges which came under the Official Secrets Act.

℧ ℧ ℧

At the same time Dexy's Midnight Runners' Kevin Rowland sat on his own in his flat in Birmingham, full of self-pity and misery. "*I had nobody to go out with. When I wasn't working I was lost. I saw Duran Duran walking through the Top of the Pops studio and they seemed to be enjoying themselves and I remember thinking 'I understand what this pop business is all about now. You get some success and you pretend you're enjoying it. That's what it is. They must be pretending.'*"

Rowland was dismayed by the new Dexy's audience on the last tour who just wanted to see the pop hits and were not interested in being taken on a journey of the soul. In 1983 things were to get worse, as *Come On, Eileen* climbed to the top of the American charts, providing a true worldwide smash and sealing this version of Dexy's in the collective memory.

Reflecting on his encounter with Duran Duran, the band who would best represent the zeal of the decade, Rowland wryly added "*Now I look back and think, actually they probably were enjoying themselves. It was me who wasn't enjoying myself.*"

At the dawn of a new year, the time for deep thinking and conscientious musicians was over. Instead, the future would be about ambition, aspiration, following trends, learned behaviour, and greed.

AFTERWORD

Dave Rimmer, in his 1980's dissection of the New Pop movement, *Like Punk Never Happened*, imagines himself in the hotbed of punk, The Roxy, in early 1977, hoping for *no future*, a cultural full-stop, when he finds himself *"suddenly drawn into a procession of nightmarish scenes: pop stars dripping with pearls and swilling champagne, pop stars counting their money in long black limousines, pop stars bowing humbly to Prince Charles and chatting amiably to Terry Wogan on prime time television, pop stars – many of them familiar faces from the very club in which* [I am] *standing, transfixed – flying on Concorde and buying mansions around the world"*. This, it turned out, was to be the unexpected reality and legacy of 1982.

The year began with songs in the charts about animal exploitation in silk production, heroin addiction, and graphic descriptions of rape, and ended with models drinking champagne on yachts and a completely non-ironic celebration of *"the best years of our lives"*. The concept of *new pop* as the thinking man's guilty pleasure, smuggling the political into the ears of the populace died a little bit more with every suit sleeve being rolled up. According to cultural author Simon Reynolds, after Thatcher's election win in 1983 *"new pop, whatever it had started out meaning to be, had very clearly turned into the soundtrack to affluent complacency"*.

From such high hopes at the start of the year, with a promised take-over by musicians who came through the punk era and applied its lessons to their music, 1982 ended in disappointment. In 1983 we saw the rise of Nik Kershaw and Howard Jones, artists who wrote their pop through the filter of Genesis and Steely Dan rather than the do-it-yourself approach of punk. The record companies did not care about the philosophical approach of the music, just how it sounded, and if it sounded a bit like what was already in the charts, then that was fine. Paul Morley blamed *"the record companies for sucking the energy out of things and making everything standardized"*. The most important thing for the new acts was dollars, and as Rimmer said, *"To make matters worse,* [they are not] *the least bit guilty about it"*. Orange Juice's Steven Daly claimed *"we* [went] *from a country of freethinkers to a country of semi-hip semi-ironic clones. During post-punk there was still a lot of people talking about a lot of ideas. They were literate and had frame of reference, and the music was mediated strongly through the music press. The result of that was that the bar had been set"*.

Sunday Times journalist, Ian Jack, whilst talking to youth around the country at the end of the year, came to the conclusion that *"the young now live in a kind of ghetto, marooned there because they lack the money or the will – for the adult world no longer seems such an attractive place – to scale the walls"*, however he was very wrong. Many young people in the 1980's wanted everything their parents had lacked: money, cars, houses, white goods, designer clothes, expensive meals, jewellery, and foreign holidays. And only Margaret Thatcher was offering that, but at a great cost to the concept of society. Being a musician became all about commercial success, for the artists and the record labels, and then even for the public, who became enthralled by the size of the act: the more records sold, the better they must be.

1982 was also the year the concept of *millennials* began, as defined by Neil Howe and William Strass in their *Howe-Strauss Generational Theory*. Children born this year would be the first to come of age in the next millennium and have since been described by the Pew Research Center as *"empowered by digital technology; coddled by parents; slow to adulthood;* [and] *at ease with radical, ethnic and sexual diversity"*.[651] They

---

[651] Millennials were also the product of over-protective parenting, and it may be no coincidence that *Baby on Board* stickers were first marketed and sold in 1982. Before long, playgrounds were fitted with

would be born into *late-Capitalism* or *Neo-Liberalism* and grow up in a world of de-regulation and reduced public spending on social services. For them, the idea of *monetising* everything was not alien, even if they reacted against the concept.

Simon Reynolds claimed *"the true sign that you're living through a golden age is the feeling that it's never going to end"* and that is what being twelve felt like to me. But of course, as always, the onward unrelenting march of the future ensured everything changed, ultimately and ostensibly for the better.

And yet there is a part of me that longs for a more innoxious time, for a more innocent me, for a time of eternal optimism.

For 1982.

---

soft ground, and kids encouraged to wear safety helmets whilst riding bikes. Not that those are necessarily bad things.

BIBLIOGRAPHY

BOOKS

Almond, Marc, *Tainted* Life, Pan Macmillan, London, 1999

Ant, Adam, *Stand & Deliver: The Autobiography*, Sidgwick & Jackson, London, 2006

Aston, Martin, *Breaking Down the Walls of Heartache: How Music Came Out*, Constable, London, 2016

Aston, Martin, *Facing the Other Way: The Story of 4AD*, The Friday Project, London, 2004

Ball, Dave, *Electronic Boy: My Life in and Out of Soft Cell*, Omnibus Press, London, 2020

Beckett, Andy, *Promised You a Miracle: Why 1980 – 1982 Made Modern Britain*, Penguin, London, 2016

Benn, Tony, *The End of an Era: Diaries 1980 – 90*, Hutchinson, London, 1992

Bennett, Samantha, *Modern Records, Maverick Methods*, Bloomsbury, London, 2018

Beviglia, Jim, *Pump It Up: Elvis Costello's 100 Best Songs*, Endeavor Press, 2018

Bicheno, Hugh, *Razor's Edge: The Unofficial History of the Falklands War*, Pheonix, London, 2006

Black, Ian, *Enemies and Neighbours: Arab and Jews in Palestine and Israel, 1917 – 2017*, Random House, London, 2017

Blake, Mark, *Is This the Real Life? The Untold Story of Queen*, Aurum, London, 2010

Blaney, John, *Paul McCartney: The Songs He Was Singing Volume 2: The Eighties*, Paper Jukebox, 2011

Boy George & Bright, Spencer, *Take it Like a Man: The Autobiography of Boy George*, Pan Books, London, 1995

Bradley, Lloyd, *Sounds Like London: 100 Years of Black Music in the Capital*, Serpents Tail, London, 2013

Bromberg, Craig, *The Wicked Ways of Malcolm McLaren*, Harper & Row, New York, 1989

Brown, Gordon, *My Life, Our Times*, Bodley Head, London, 2017

Buckler, Rick & Snowball, Ian, *The Dead Straight Guide to The Jam*, This Day in Music Publishing, London, 2018

Bullock, Daryl, *David Bowie made me Gay: 100 Years of LGBT Music*, Duckworth & Co, London, 2017

Cain, Jonathan, *Don't Stop Believin'*, Zondervan Books, Michigan, 2018

Campbell, Ali & Robin, *Blood & Fire: The Autobiography of the UB40 Brothers*, Century Press, London, 2005

Campbell, John, *Roy Jenkins: A Well-Rounded Life*, Jonathan Cape, London, 2014

Carlin, Peter Ames, *Bruce*, Simon & Schuster, London, 2012

Cavanagh, David, *Good Night and Good Riddance: How Thirty-Five Years of John Peel Helped to Shape Modern Life*, Faber & Faber, London, 2015

Charnas, Dan, *The Big Payback: The History of the Business of Hip-Hop*, Penguin, London, 2010

Che, Cathy, *Deborah Harry: The Biography*, Carlton, London, 1999

Clayton-Lea, Tony, *Elvis Costello: A Biography*, Andre Deutsch, 1998

Clinton, Bill, *My Life*, Hutchinson, London, 2004

Collins, Andrew, *Billy Bragg: Still Suitable for Miners*, Virgin Books, London, 2018

Cope, Julian, *Head On: Memories of the Liverpool Punk Scene and the Story of The Teardrop Explodes (1976 – 82)*, Harper Collins, London, 1994

Cope, Julian, *Repossessed: Shamanic Depressions in Tamworth and London (1983 – 1989)*, Harper Collins, London, 1999

Cornwell, Hugh, *A Multitude of Sins: The Autobiography*, Harper Collins, London, 2005

Cornwell, Rupert, *God's Banker: The Life & Death of Roberto Calvi*, Counterpoint Press, London, 1984

Costello, Elvis, *Unfaithful Music and Disappearing Ink*, Blue Rider Press, New York, 2015

Dallin, Sara & Woodward, Keren, *Really Saying Something: Sara & Keren – Our Bananarama Story*, Hutchinson, London, 2020

De Semlyen, Nick, *Wild and Crazy Guys: How the Comedy Mavericks of the 80's Changed Hollywood Forever*, Picador, London, 2019

Difford, Chris, *Some Fantastic Place: My Life in And Out of Squeeze*, W&N, London, 2017

Dillon, Martin, *The Shankill Butchers: A Case Study in Mass Murder*, Arrow Press, London, 1990

Dolby, Thomas, *Speed of Sound: Breaking the Barrier Between Music and Technology*, Flatiron Books, New York, 2008

Doyle Tom, *The Glamour Chase: The Maverick Life of Billy MacKenzie*, Polygon, Edinburgh, 2011

Ellen, Mark, *Rock Stars Stole My Life*, Hodder & Stoughton, London 2015

Elliot, Francis & Hanning, James, *Cameron: The Rise of the New Conservative*, Fourth Estate, London, 2007

Fisk, Robert, *The Great War for Civilisation: The Conquest of the Middle East*, Fourth Estate, London, 2005

Fisk, Robert, *Pity the Nation: Lebanon at War*, Oxford University Press, Oxford, 1990

Fletcher, Tony, *R.E.M. Perfect Circle*, Omnibus, London, 2013

Foster, Robert, *Grant & I: Inside and Outside The Go-Betweens*, Omnibus, London, 2016

Frantz, Chris, *Remain in Love: Talking Heads, Tom Tom Club, Tina*, Orion, London, 2020

Freestone, Dave, *Freddie Mercury*, Omnibus, London, 2001

Friedman, Lester D. (Ed), *Fires Were Started: British Cinema and Thatcherism*, Wallflower Press, London, 1993

Fry, Stephen, *The Fry Chronicles*, Penguin, London, 2010

Glen, Allan, *Stuart Adamson: In a Big Country*, Polygon, Edinburgh, 2010

Goddard, Simon, *Simply Thrilled: The Preposterous Story of Postcard Records*, Ebury, London, 2014

Goodwin, Paul, *Electric Pioneer: An Armchair Guide to Gary Numan*, JPG Productions, 2013

Gorman, Paul, *The Life & Times of Malcolm McLaren: The Biography*, Constable, London, 2020

Grandmaster Flash, *The Adventures of Grandmaster Flash: My Life, My Beats*, Broadway Books, New York, 2008

Grant, Michael, *Fergie Rises: How Britain's Greatest Football manager was Made at Aberdeen*, Aurum Press, London, 2014

Hanley, Paul, *Have a Bleedin' Guess: The Story of Hex Enduction Hour*, Route Publishing, London, 2020

Hanley, Steve & Piekarski, Olivia, *The Big Midweek: Life Inside The Fall*, Route, London, 2016

Harris, Robert, *Gotcha! The Media, the Government and the Falklands Crisis*, Faber & Faber, London, 1983

Harry, Debbie, *Face It*, Harper Collins, London, 2019

Harvie, Christopher, *Fool's Gold: The Story of North Sea Oil*, Penguin, London, 1994

Haslam, Dave, *Life After Dark: A History of British Nightclubs and Music Venues*, Simon & Schuster, London, 2015

Haslam, Dave, *Searching for Love: Courtney Love in Liverpool 1982*, Confingo Publishing, Manchester, 2020

Haslam, Dave, *Sonic Youth Slept on my Floor: Music, Manchester and More*, Constable, London, 2018

Heatley, Michael, *Shaky: The Biography of Shakin' Stevens*, Michael O'Mara Books, London, 2005

Hepworth, David, *A Fabulous Creation: How the LP Saved Our Lives*, Bantam, London, 2019

Hepworth, David, *1971: Never a Dull Moment*, Bantam, London, 2015

Hepworth, David, *Uncommon People: The Rise & Fall of the Rock Stars*, Bantam, London, 2017

Hodges, Chas, *Chas & Dave: All About Us*, John Blake, London, 2008

Holland, Jools, *Barefaced Lies & Boogie-Woogie Boasts*, Penguin Books, London, 2007

Holt, Nick, *The Mammoth Book of the World Cup: The Definitive Guide 1930 – 2018*, Robinson, London, 2018

Hook, Peter, *The Haçienda: How Not to Run a Club*, Simon & Schuster, London, 2009

Hook, Peter, *Substance: Inside New Order* Simon & Schuster, London, 2016

Hynde, Chrissie, *Reckless*, Penguin, London, 2016

Idol, Billy, *Dancing with Myself*, Simon & Schuster, London, 2014

Isaacs, Jeremy, *Storm Over 4: A Personal Account*, Weidenfeld & Nicolson, London, 1989

Isaacson, Walter, *Steve Jobs*, Simon & Schuster, New York, 2011

Jack, Ian, *Before the Oil Ran Out: Britain 1977 – 87*, Flamingo, London, 1987

Jackson, Michael, *Moonwalk*, Doubleday, New York, 1988

Jobbling, John, *U2: The Definitive Biography*, St Martin's Press, New York, 2014

Johnston, Ian, *Bad Seed: The Biography of Nick Cave*, Abacus, London, 1996

Jones, Allan, *Can't Stand Up for Falling Down: Rock 'n' Roll War Stories*, Bloomsbury Press, London, 2017

Jones, Dylan, *David Bowie: A Life*, Windmill, London, 2018

Jones, Dylan, *Sweet Dreams: The Story of the New Romantics*, Faber & Faber, London, 2020

Jones, Steve, *Lonely Boy: Tales from a Sex Pistol*, De Capo Press, London, 2017

Jordan, Gary, *Out of the Shadows: The Story of the 1982 England World Cup Team*, Pitch Publishing, Worthing, 2017

Jovanovic, Rob, *George Michael: The Biography*, Portrait, London, 2007

Julien, Isaac & McCabe, Colin, *Diary of a Young Soul Rebel*, BFI Publishing, London, 1991

Kemp, Gary, *I Know This Much: From Soho to Spandau*, Fourth Estate, London, 2009

Kemp, Martin, *True: The Autobiography*, Orion, London, 2000

Kiss, Charlie, *A New Man: Lesbian. Protest. Mania. Trans Man*, Matador, London, 2017

Kranesh, Michael & Fisher, Marc, *Trump Revealed*, Simon & Schuster, London, 2016

Laurie, David, *Dare: How Bowie & Kraftwerk Inspired the Death of Rock'n'Roll & Invented Modern Pop Music*, Something in Construction Book, London, 2015

Lawrence, Tim, *Life and Death on the New York Dance Floor 1980 – 1983*, Duke University Press, New York, 2008

Lefargue, Paul, *The Right to be Lazy*, Charles Kerr & Co, London, 1883

Leigh, Wendy, *Bowie: The Biography*, Gallery Books, London, 2014

Lemmy, *White Line Fever*, Simon & Schuster, London, 2016

Lester, Paul, *Gang of Four: Damaged Gods*, Omnibus Press, London, 2008

Liddington, Jill, *The Road to Greenham Common: Feminism and Anti-Militarism in Britain Since 1820*, Syracuse University Press, 1989

Light, Alan, *Let's Go Crazy: Prince and the Making of Purple Rain*, Atria Books, New York, 2014

Livingstone, Ken, *You Can't Say That: Memoirs*, Faber & Faber, London, 2011

Long, Pat, *The History of the NME: High Times and Low Lives at the World's Most Famous Music Magazine*, Portico, London, 2012

Lukather, Steve, *The Gospel According to Luke*, Constable, London, 2018

Lynskey, Dorian, *33 Revolutions per Minute: The History of Protest Songs*, Faber & Faber, London, 2012

Maconie, Stuart, *The People's Songs: The Story of Modern Britain in 50 Records*, Ebury Press, London, 2013

MacPherson, Archie, *Adventures in the Golden Age: Scotland in the World Cup Finals 1974 -1998*, Black & White, Edinburgh, 2018

MacPherson, Archie, *Jock Stein: The Definitive Biography*, Highdown Press, Newbury, 2004

Major, John, *The Autobiography*, Harper Collins, London, 1999

Maraniss, David, *Barack Obama: The Making of the Man*, Atlantic Books, London, 2012

Marr, Johnny, *Set the Boy Free: The Autobiography*, Century, London, 2016

Marshall, George, *The Two-Tone Story*, ST Publishing, 2011

McBride, Joseph, *Steven Spielberg: A Biography*, Faber & Faber, London, 2012

Meikle, Graham (ed.), *The Routledge Companion to Media and Activism*, Routledge, Abingdon, 2018

Middlebrook, Martin, *The Falklands War*, Pen & Sword, Barnsley, 2012

Morgan, Kenneth O., *Michael Foot: A Life*, Harper Collins, London, 2007

Muller, Jurgen (Ed.), *Movies of the 80's*, Taschen, London, 2018

Nash, Brian, *Nasher Says Relax: Inside the Band and Beyond the Pleasuredome*, Trinity Mirror Media, Liverpool, 2012

Needs, Kris, *George Clinton & the Cosmic Odyssey of the P-Funk Empire*, Omnibus Press, London, 2014

Oates, John, *Change of Seasons: A Memoir*, MacMillan, London, 2017

O'Brien, Lucy, *She-Bop: The Definitive History of Women in Popular Music*, Jawbone, London, 2012

O'Connor, Garry, *Universal Father: A Life of Pope John Paul II*, Bloomsbury, London, 2003

Osbourne, Ozzy, *I Am Ozzy*, Sphere, London, 2009

Osbourne, Sharon, *Extreme: My Autobiography*, Time Warner Books, London, 2005

O'Shea, Mick (2015), *Mick Jones: Stayin' in Tune, the Unofficial Biography*, Elusinian Press, London, 2015

Pitman, Jed, *The Invisible Man: The Story of Rod Temperman, the Thriller Songwriter*, History Press, Stroud, 2017

Porter, Dick & Needs, Kris *Blondie: Parallel Lives*, Omnibus Press, London, 2017

Power, Martin, *David Sylvian: The Last Romantic*, Omnibus Press, London, 2012

Preston, Paul, *The Triumph of Democracy in Spain*, Methuen, London, 1986

Prince, Rosa, *Theresa May: The Enigmatic Prime Minister*, Bierback, London, 2017

Purnell, Sonia, *Just Boris: The Irresistible Rise of a Political Celebrity*, Aurum, London, 2011

Rachel, Daniel, *Walls Come Tumbling Down: The Music & Politics of Rock Against Racism, 2 Tone & Red Wedge*, Picador, London, 2016

Rachel, Daniel & Ranking Roger, *I Just Can't Stop It: My Life in The Beat*, Omnibus Press, London, 2019

Reed, Jeremy, *Marc Almond: The Last Star*, Creation Books, London, 1995
Reed, John, *Paul Weller: My Ever-Changing Moods,* Omnibus Press, London, 2005
Reynolds, Simon, *Rip It Up and Start Again: Post-punk 1978 – 1984*, Faber & Faber, London, 2005
Reynolds, Simon, *Shock & Awe: Glam Rock & its Legacy*, Faber & Faber, London, 2016
Reynolds, Simon, *Totally Wired: Post-punk Interviews and Overviews*, Faber & Faber, London, 2009
Richard, David, *The Annotated ABC Discography*, Ninthwave Publishing, 2015
Richards, Matt & Langthorne, Mark, *Somebody to Love: The Life, Death and Legacy of Freddie Mercury*, Blink Publishing, London, 2016
Richter, Morgan, *Duranalysis: Essays on the Duran Duran Experience*, Luft Books, USA, 2017
Ridgeley, Andrew, *Wham! George and Me*, Michael Joseph, London, 2019
Rimmer, Dave, *Like Punk Never Happened: Culture Club and the New Pop*, Faber & Faber, London, 1985
Roberts, Chris, *The Complete Michael Jackson: The Man, the Music, the Moves, the Magic*, Carlton Books, London, 2018
Rogan, Johnny, *Morrissey & Marr: The Severed Alliance*, Omnibus Press, London, 2012
Sandbrook, Dominic, *Who Dares Wins: Britain 1979 – 1982*, Penguin Books, London, 2019
Sanders, Andrew, *Times of Troubles: Britain's War in Northern Ireland*, Edinburgh University Press, 2012
Sarzo, Rudy, *Off the Rails*, self-published, 2016
Sayle, Alexis, *Thatcher Stole My Trousers*, Bloomsbury, London, 2016
Salewicz, Chris, *Redemption Song: The Definitive Biography of Joe Strummer*, Harper Collin, London, 2006
Seaton, Jean, *Pinkoes and Traitors: The BBC and the Nation, 1974 – 1987*, Profile Books, London, 2015
Scott, Shaun, *Millennials and the Moments that Made Us: A Cultural History of the U.S. from 1982 – Present*, Zero Books, Winchester, 2018
Shilts, Randy, *And the Band Played On: Politics, People and the AIDS Epidemic*, Souvenir, London, 2011
Shooman, Joe, *Bruce Dickenson: Maiden Voyage*, Music Press, London, 2007
Simmons, Ian & Newman, James *A History of Videogames*, Carlton, London, 2018
Simper, Paul, *Pop Stars in my Pantry: A Memoir of Pop Mags and Clubbing in the 1980's*, Unbound, London, 2017
Smith, Sean, *George*, Harper Collins, London, 2017
Souness, Howard, *Fab: An Intimate Life of Paul McCartney*, Harper Collins, London, 2010
Spence, Simon, *Just Can't Get Enough: The Making of Depeche Mode*, Jawbone, London, 2011
Springsteen, Bruce, *Born to Run*, Simon & Schuster, London, 2016
Stalker, John, *Stalker: Ireland, 'Shoot to kill' and the 'Affair'* Penguin, London, 1988
Strachan, Gordon, *My Life in Football*, Time Warner, London, 2006
Stewart, Dave, *Sweet Dreams Are Made of This: A Life in Music*, New American Library, New York, 2016
Stewart, Graham, *Bang! A History of Britain in the 1980's*, Atlantic Books, London, 2013
Stewart, Rod, *Rod: The Autobiography*, Random House, London, 2012
Strange, Steve, *Blitzed! The Autobiography of Steve Strange*, Orion, London, 2002

Stratton, John & Zuberi, Nabeel, *Black Popular Music in Britain Since 1945*, Routledge, London, 2017

Suggs, *That Close*, Quercus, London, 2013

Summers, Andy, *One Train Later*, Thomas Dunne Books, New York, 2006

Summers, Jazz, *Big Life*, Quartet Books, London, 2013

Sumner, Bernard, *Chapter and Verse: Joy Division, New Order and Me*, Corgi, London, 2015

Taraborrelli, J. Randy, *Madonna: An Intimate Biography of an Icon at Sixty*, Sidgewick & Jackson, London, 2018

Tarpley, Webster G. & Chaitkin, Anton, *George Bush: The Unauthorised Biography*, Progressive Press, 2004

Taylor, Andy, *Wild Boy: My Life with Duran Duran*, Orion, London, 2008

Taylor, John, *In the Pleasure Groove: Love, Death & Duran Duran*, Sphere, London, 2012

Taylor, Neil, *Document and Witness: An Intimate History of Rough Trade*, Orion, London, 2010

Thatcher, Margaret, *The Downing Street Years*, Harper Collins, London, 1993

Thomas, Bruce, *Rough Notes*, Createspace Publishing, 2015

Thomson, Ben (Ed.), *Ban This Filth: Letters from the Mary Whitehouse Archive*, Faber & Faber, London, 2012

Thomson Graeme, *Complicated Shadows: The Life & Music of Elvis Costello*, Canongate, Edinburgh, 2005

Thomson, Graeme, *Under the Ivy: The Life & Music of Kate Bush*, Omnibus Press, London, 2010

Thorn, Tracey, *Bedsit Disco Queen*, Virago, London, 2013

Thornton, Chris, Kelters, Seamus, Feeney, Brian & McKittrick, David, *Lost Lives: The stories of the Men, Women and Children who Died as a Result of the Northern Ireland Troubles*, Mainstream Publishing, Edinburgh, 1999

Tolhurst, Lol, *Cured: The Tale of Two Imaginary Boys*, Quercus, London, 2016

Tyler, Kieron, *Smashing It Up: A Decade of Chaos with The Damned*, Omnibus Press, London, 2017

Ure, Midge, *If I Was… The Autobiography*, Virgin Books, London, 2005

Vinen, Richard, *Thatcher's Britain: The Politics and Social Upheaval of the 1980's*, Simon & Schuster, London, 2009

Walker, Tony & Gowers, Andrew, *Arafat: The Biography*, Virgin Books, London, 2003

Walls, Mick, *Iron Maiden: Run to the Hills*, Sanctuary Publishing, 2004

Warner, Timothy, *Pop Music – Technology and Creativity: Trevor Horn and the Digital Revolution*, Ashgate, Aldershot, 2003

Watkins, Tom, *Let's Make Lots of Money*, Virgin Books, London, 2016

Whelan, David, *Choose Wham! The Definitive Guide to Wham! & Their Music*, Whelanmedia, 2019

White, Richard, *Dexy's Midnight Runners: Young Soul Rebels*, Omnibus Press, London, 2006

Wilmut, Roger & Rosengard, Peter, *Didn't You Kill my Mother-in-law: The Story of Alternative Comedy in Britain from the Comedy Store to Saturday Live*, Methuen, London, 1989

Womack, Kenneth, *Sound Pictures: The Life of Beatles Producer George Martin: The Later Years 1966 – 2006*, Orphans Publishing, Chicago, 2018

Zepezauer, Mark, *The C.I.A.'s Greatest Hits*, Odonian Press, Tuscon, 1995

OTHER SOURCES

Anderson, Thomas, Petranker, Rotem, Christopher, Adam, Rosenbaum, Daniel, Weissman, Cory, Dinh-Williams, Le-Anh, Hui, Katrina & Hapke, Emma (December 2019) "Psychedelic microdosing benefits and challenges: an empirical codebook" in *Harm Reduction Journal*, 16 (1): 43

B, Marke (2018) "93 Ways to Hear Alison Moyet's Laugh" in *Red Bull Music Academy*, 7th August 2018

Ballon, Bruce & Leszcz, Molyn (2007) "Horror Films: Tales to Master Terror or Shapers of Trauma" in *American Journal of Psychotherapy*, Volume 61, pp. 211 - 230

Baumeister, Roy, Sara Wotman & Arlene Stillwell (1993) "Unrequited Love: On Heartbreak, Anger, Guilt, Scriptlessnes, and Humiliation" in *Journal of Personality and Social Psychology*, Volume 64, pp. 377 – 394

Burkus, David (2014) "The Creative Benefits of Boredom" in *The Harvard Business Review*, 9th September 2014

Buskin, Richard (2006) "Classic Tracks: Madness, Our House" in *Sound on Sound, June 2006*

Buskin, Richard (2008) "Classic Tracks: Afrika Bambaataa & The Soul Sonic Force, Planet Rock" in *Sound on Sound,* November 2008

Buskin, Richard (2010) "Classic Tracks: Joan Jett, I Love Rock & Roll" in *Sound on Sound,* February 2010

Buskin, Richard (2010), "Classic Tracks: The Human League, Don't You Want Me" in *Sound on Sound,* July 2010

Buskin, Richard (2011) "Classic Tracks: John Cougar, Jack & Diane" in *Sound on Sound,* September 2011

Campbell, Andrew (2017) "If You Didn't Get the Belt, You Can Thank My Mum" in *TES*, 24th March 2017

Coulter, Colin (2019), "Straight to Hell: The Clash and 'Left-Melancholia'" in *Rebel*, 14th November 2019

Doyle, Tom (2018) "Classic Tracks: The Eurythmics, Sweet Dreams (Are Made of This)" in *Sound on Sound, July 2018*

Gould, Mark (2007) "Sparing the Rod" in *The Guardian*, 9th January 2007

Gupta, Akhil (1983) "Attenborough's Truth: The Politics of Gandhi" in *The Threepenny Review*, No. 15 (Autumn 1983) pp. 22 – 23

Horn, Delton T., "The Shocking Truth About Cover Records: What 'Everybody Knows' isn't Always True" in self-published book on Amazon.

Hurd, Ian (2018), "Everything I Know About Human Rights I Learned from The Clash" at http://blog.press.princeton.edu/2018/02/07/ian-hurd-everything-i-know-about-international-human-rights-i-learned-from-the-clash/

Jack, Malcolm (2020), "Survivor: How We Made *Eye of the Tiger*" in *The Guardian*, 27th January 2020

Kirkham, Neil, "Polluting Young Minds? Smash Hits and High Thatcherism"

McKay, Alastair (2010), "Orange Juice: If Anything Became too Smooth Edwyn Collins Liked to Fuck it up", *Uncut Magazine*, April 2010.

Noble, Will (2017) "What's It Like Living in the Barbican?" in *Londonist*, 23rd February 2017

Nunns, Alex (2015) "1983: The Biggest Myth in Labour Party History" in *Red Pepper*, 6th September 2015

Shinn, Ken (2018) "He jests at Ska: An Appreciation of Bad Manners" in *We Are Cult*, 24th August 2018

Simpson, Dave (2013) "Tears For Fears: How We Made *Mad World*" in *The Guardian*, 10th December 2013

Simpson, Dave (2018) "How We Made Musical Youth's *Pass the Dutchie*" in *The Guardian*, 20th August 2018

Simpson, Dave (2018) "How We Made Eddy Grant's *Electric Avenue*" in *The Guardian*, 3rd September 2018

Simpson, Dave (2020) "The Stranglers: How We Made *European Female*" in *The Guardian*, 2nd March 2020

Simpson, Dave (2020) "Christmas Wrapping: The Waitresses on how they made a festive classic" in *The Guardian*, 13th December 2020

Sullivan, Caroline (2015) "Boy George and Jon Moss: How we made *Do You Really Want to Hurt Me*" in *The Guardian,* 20th January 2015

Wiles, Colin (2016) "A Tale of Two Brutalist Housing Estates: One Thriving, One Facing Demoilition" in *The Guardian*, 13th January 2016

Wilkins, Frank (2012) "The Death of John Belushi at the Château Marmont" in *ReelReviews, 2012*

Williams, Dana (2003) "Beyond Rap: Musical Misogyny" in *Tolerance.org*, 12th August 2003

Womack, Malcolm (2009) "Thank You for the Music: Catherine's Johnson's Feminist Rejoicing in Mamma Mia!" in *Studies in Musical Theatre*, Volume 3, Number 2, November 2009

Issues of *Smash Hits* magazine from 1982, accessed at "Like Punk Never Happened - Brian McCloskey's Smash Hits archive"